THE SACRAMENTARY

THE ROMAN MISSAL

Revised by Decree of the Second Vatican Ecumenical Council

and Published by Authority of Pope Paul VI

THE SACRAMENTARY

Approved for Use in the Dioceses of the United

States of America by the National Conference of

Catholic Bishops and Confirmed by the Apostolic See

English Translation Prepared by the International

Committee on English in the Liturgy

THE LITURGICAL PRESS

Collegeville   Minnesota

1985

Concordat cum Originali:

Reverend John A. Gurrieri, Executive Director
Bishops' Committee on the Liturgy, National Conference of Catholic Bishops

Approved by the National Conference of Catholic Bishops for use in the dioceses of the United States of America, November 13, 1973. Confirmed by decree of the Congregation for Divine Worship, February 4, 1973 (Prot. N. CD 1762/73).

Revised according to the second typical edition of the *Missale Romanum* (1975), March 1, 1985, for use in the dioceses of the United States of America.

Published by authority of the Bishops' Committee on the Liturgy, National Conference of Catholic Bishops.

ISBN 0-8146-1434-5

CONTENTS

6   Contents

COMMONS

RITUAL MASSES

MASSES AND PRAYERS FOR VARIOUS NEEDS AND OCCASIONS

VOTIVE MASSES

MASSES FOR THE DEAD

SACRED CONGREGATION FOR DIVINE WORSHIP

Prot. n. 166/70

DECREE

The Order of Mass has been established and the texts for the Roman Missal have been approved by Pope Paul VI in the Apostolic Constitution *Missale Romanum,* 3 April 1969. This Congregation for Divine Worship, at the mandate of the Pope, now promulgates and declares to be the *editio typica* this new edition of the Roman Missal prepared in accord with the decrees of Vatican Council II.

As to use of the new Missal, the Latin edition may be put into use as soon as it is published, with the necessary adjustments of saints' days until the revised calendar is put into definitive effect. As to vernacular editions, the conferences of bishops are given the responsibility for their preparation and for setting the effective date for their use, after due confirmation by the Apostolic See.

All things to the contrary notwithstanding.

Congregation for Divine Worship, Holy Thursday, 26 March 1970.

✠ Benno Cardinal Gut
Prefect

✠ Annibale Bugnini
Secretary

Prot. n. 1970/74

DECREE

Since the Roman Missal must be reprinted, variations and additions have been included in order that this new edition might be in accord with the documents published after the appearance of the first edition in 1970.

In the General Instruction, the marginal numbers are unchanged, but a description of the liturgical functions of acolyte and reader is inserted in place of the paragraphs that formerly dealt with the subdeacon (nos. 142–152).

There is another change of some importance in the section of the Roman Missal that contains the ritual Masses and the Masses for various needs and occasions. Certain formularies have been completed by supplying entrance and communion antiphons.

Texts not found in the first edition have also been added, namely, among the ritual Masses, texts for the Mass of Dedication of a Church and an Altar and for the Mass of Reconciliation; among votive Masses, texts for Masses of Mary, Mother of the Church and of the Most Holy Name of Mary.

Some other, less important changes have been introduced in headings and rubrics so that they may better correspond to the words or expressions occurring in the new liturgical books.

Pope Paul VI has approved this second edition of the Roman Missal by his authority and the Congregation for Divine Worship now issues it and declares it to be the *editio typica.*

It will be the responsibility of the conferences of bishops to introduce into the respective vernacular editions the changes contained in this second edition of the Roman Missal.

All things to the contrary notwithstanding.

Congregation for Divine Worship, Holy Thursday, 27 March 1975.

✠ James Robert Cardinal Knox
Prefect

✠ Annibale Bugnini
Titular Archbishop of Diocletiana
Secretary

APOSTOLIC CONSTITUTION

PROMULGATION OF THE ROMAN MISSAL REVISED BY DECREE OF THE SECOND VATICAN ECUMENICAL COUNCIL

PAUL, BISHOP

Servant of the Servants of God

For an Everlasting Memorial

The *Missale Romanum* was promulgated in 1570 by our predecessor St. Pius V, in execution of the decree of the Council of Trent.[1] It has been recognized by all as one of the many admirable results that the Council achieved for the benefit of the entire Church of Christ. For four centuries it provided Latin-rite priests with norms for the celebration of the eucharistic sacrifice; moreover messengers of the Gospel brought this Missal to almost the entire world. Innumerable holy men and women nurtured their spiritual life on its readings from Scripture and on its prayer texts. In large part these prayer texts owed their arrangement to St. Gregory the Great.

A deep interest in fostering the liturgy has become widespread and strong among the Christian people and our predecessor Pius XII has viewed this both as a sign of God's caring will regarding today's people and as a saving movement of the Holy Spirit through his Church.[2] Since the beginning of this liturgical renewal, it has also become clear that the formularies of the Roman Missal had to be revised and enriched. A beginning was made by Pius XII in the restoration of the Easter Vigil and Holy Week services;[3] he thus took the first step toward adapting the Roman Missal to the contemporary mentality.

The Second Vatican Ecumenical Council, in the Constitution *Sacrosanctum Concilium*, laid down the basis for the general revision of the Roman Missal: "Both texts and rites should be drawn up so that they express more clearly the holy things they signify";[4] therefore, "the Order of Mass is to be revised in such a way that the intrinsic nature and purpose of its several parts, as also the connection between them, may be more clearly brought out, and devout, active participation by the faithful more easily achieved."[5] The Council also decreed that "the treasures of the Bible are

to be opened up more lavishly, so that a richer share in God's word may be provided for the faithful";[6] and finally that "a new rite for concelebration is to be drawn up and incorporated into the Roman Pontifical and Roman Missal."[7]

No one should think, however, that this revision of the Roman Missal has come out of nowhere. The progress in liturgical studies during the last four centuries has certainly prepared the way. Just after the Council of Trent, the study "of ancient manuscripts in the Vatican library and elsewhere," as St. Pius V attests in the Apostolic Constitution *Quo primum*, helped greatly in the correction of the Roman Missal. Since then, however, other ancient sources have been discovered and published and liturgical formularies of the Eastern Church have been studied. Accordingly many have had the desire for these doctrinal and spiritual riches not to be stored away in the dark, but to be put into use for the enlightenment of the mind of Christians and for the nurture of their spirit.

Now, however, our purpose is to set out, at least in broad terms, the new plan of the Roman Missal. We therefore point out, first, that a General Instruction, for use as a preface to the book, gives the new regulations for the celebration of the eucharistic sacrifice. These regulations cover the rites to be carried out and the functions of each minister or participant as well as the furnishings and the places needed for divine worship.

It must be acknowledged that the chief innovation in the reform concerns the eucharistic prayer. Although the Roman Rite over the centuries allowed for a multiplicity of different texts in the first part of the prayer (the preface), the second part, called the *Canon actionis*, took on a fixed form during the period of the fourth and fifth centuries. The Eastern liturgies, on the other hand, allowed a degree of variety into the anaphoras themselves. On this point, first of all, the eucharistic prayer has been enriched with a great number of prefaces—drawn from the early tradition of the Roman Church or recently composed—in order that the different facets of the mystery of salvation will stand out more clearly and that there will be more and richer themes of thanksgiving. But besides this, we have decided to add three

---

1. See apostolic constitution *Quo primum*, 14 July 1570.

2. See Pius XII, Discourse to the participants in the First International Congress of Pastoral Liturgy at Assisi, 22 September 1956: *AAS* 48 (1956) 712.

3. See Congregation of Rites, decree *Dominicae Resurrectionis*, 9 February 1951: *AAS* 43 (1951) 128ff.; decree *Maxima redemptionis nostrae mysteria*, 16 November 1955: *AAS* 47 (1955) 838ff.

4. Second Vatican Council, Constitution on the Sacred Liturgy, *Sacrosanctum Concilium* [= SC], art. 21.

5. SC, art. 50.

6. SC, art. 51.

7. SC, art. 58.

new canons to the eucharistic prayer. Both for pastoral reasons, however, and for the facilitation of concelebration, we have ordered that the words of the Lord be identical in each form of the canon. Thus in each eucharistic prayer we wish those words to be as follows: over the bread: *Accipite et manducate ex hoc omnes: Hoc est enim Corpus meum, quod pro vobis tradetur;* over the chalice: *Accipite et bibite ex eo omnes: Hic est enim calix Sanguinis mei novi et aeterni testamenti, qui pro vobis et pro multis effundetur in remissionem peccatorum. Hoc facite in meam commemorationem.* The words *Mysterium fidei* have been removed from the context of Christ's own words and are spoken by the priest as an introduction to the faithful's acclamation.

In the Order of Mass the rites have been "simplified, due care being taken to preserve their substance."[8] "Elements that, with the passage of time, came to be duplicated or were added with but little advantage"[9] have been eliminated, especially in the rites for the presentation of the bread and wine, the breaking of the bread, and communion.

Also, "other elements that have suffered injury through accident of history" are restored "to the tradition of the Fathers,"[10] for example, the homily,[11] the general intercessions or prayer of the faithful,[12] and the penitential rite or act of reconciliation with God and the community at the beginning of the Mass, which thus, as is right, regains its proper importance.

According to the decree of the Second Vatican Council, that "a more representative portion of the holy Scriptures be read to the people over the course of a prescribed number of years,"[13] the Sunday readings are arranged in a cycle of three years. In addition, on Sundays and all the major feasts the epistle and gospel are preceded by an Old Testament reading or, at Easter, by readings from Acts. This is meant to provide a fuller exposition of the continuing process of the mystery of salvation, as shown in the words of divine revelation. These broadly selected biblical readings, which set before the faithful on Sundays and holydays the most important part of sacred Scripture, are complemented by other parts of the Bible read on other days.

All this has been planned to arouse among the faithful a greater hunger for the word of God.[14] Under the guidance of the Holy Spirit, this hunger will seem, so to speak, to impel the people of the New Covenant toward the perfect unity of the Church. We are fully confident that under this arrangement both priest and faithful will prepare their minds and hearts more devoutly for the Lord's Supper and that, meditating on the Scriptures, they will be nourished more each day by the words of the Lord. In accord with the teachings of the Second Vatican Council, all will thus regard sacred Scripture as the abiding source of spiritual life, the foundation for Christian instruction, and the core of all theological study.

This reform of the Roman Missal, in addition to the three changes already mentioned (the eucharistic prayer, the Order of Mass, and the readings), has also corrected and considerably modified other of its components: the Proper of Seasons, the Proper of Saints, the Common of Saints, ritual Masses, and votive Masses. In all of these changes, particular care has been taken with the prayers. Their number has been increased, so that the new forms might better correspond to new needs, and the text of older prayers has been restored on the basis of the ancient sources. As a result, each weekday of the principal liturgical seasons, Advent, Christmas, Lent, and Easter, now has its own, distinct prayer.

The text of the *Graduale Romanum* has not been changed as far as the music is concerned. In the interest of their being more readily understood, however, the responsorial psalm (which St. Augustine and St. Leo the Great often mention) as well as the entrance and communion antiphons have been revised for use in Masses that are not sung.

After what we have presented concerning the new Roman Missal, we wish in conclusion to insist on one point in particular and to make it have its effect. When he promulgated the *editio princeps* of the Roman Missal, our predecessor St. Pius V offered it to the people of Christ as the instrument of liturgical unity and the expression of a pure and reverent worship in the Church. Even though, in virtue of the decree of the Second Vatican Council, we have accepted into the new Roman Missal lawful variations and adaptations,[15] our own expectation in no way differs from that of our predecessor. It is that the faithful will receive the new Missal as a help toward witnessing and strengthening their unity with one another; that through the new Missal one and the same prayer in a great diversity of languages will ascend, more fragrant than any incense, to our heavenly Father, through our High Priest, Jesus Christ, in the Holy Spirit.

The effective date for what we have prescribed in this Constitution shall be the First Sunday of Advent of this year, 30 November. We decree that these laws and prescriptions be firm and effective now and in the future, notwithstanding, to the extent necessary, the apostolic constitutions and ordinances issued by our predecessors and other prescriptions, even those deserving particular mention and amendment.

Given at Rome, at Saint Peter's, on Holy Thursday, 3 April 1969, the sixth year of our pontificate.

PAUL PP. VI

---

8. SC, art. 50.
9. SC, art. 50.
10. SC, art. 50.
11. See SC, art. 52.
12. See SC, art. 53.
13. SC, art. 51.
14. See Amos 8:11.
15. See SC, art. 38–40.

FOREWORD

The purpose of this foreword is to draw attention to particular features of this Sacramentary and to make it clearer and easier to use for the priest who presides over the eucharistic celebration. The foreword has some few parts applicable only in the dioceses of the United States.

For the most part this volume is a translation, approved by the National Conference of Catholic Bishops and confirmed by the Apostolic See, of the *Missale Romanum* of 1969 with the variations introduced into the second edition of 1975. The Missal was revised by decree of the Second Vatican Council and promulgated by Pope Paul VI. In addition to the translation of liturgical texts and other material, however, this edition in English includes other texts, with the same approbation as the translations, and follows a somewhat different format.

It is important, first of all, to call attention to the General Instruction of the Roman Missal, which is translated below. The present foreword in no way replaces the General Instruction, which deserves careful study, in part for its doctrinal and liturgical explanation of the structure, elements, and ministries in the celebration. Without a thorough knowledge of the General Instruction, it is impossible for the priest to understand the conciliar reform or to take the principal role in planning the celebration with the other ministers and all who have special responsibilities for it.

NATURE OF THE SACRAMENTARY

A sacramentary is a collection of presidential prayers for the celebration of the eucharist. Such books have been in use from about the fifth century, but in the middle ages they were combined with other service books, lectionaries, and collections of chants. The complete missal of the modern period was thus much more than a sacramentary, and it reflected the development by which the priest ordinarily took not only his own part in the eucharistic celebration but also the parts of the assembly, singers, readers, and even the deacon.

The Second Vatican Council restored the basic rule that each member of the worshiping community, whether ordained minister or lay person, should perform all of those parts, but only those parts, which pertain to his or her office by the nature of the rite and the principles of liturgy. This conciliar decision is reflected in the distinct Sacramentary, a volume which is limited, with some slight exceptions, to the parts of the rite of Mass which pertain to the priest. The Sacramentary, as a volume of presidential prayers, thus reflects a basic element of the liturgical reform: the distinction between the part of the priest and the parts of other members of the assembly, just as in the past the complete missal was a symbol of the absorption of the roles of others by the celebrant.

The Sacramentary does not contain Scripture readings, responsorial psalms, or verses for the gospel acclamation. These are found in the Lectionary for Mass. Entrance and communion antiphons have been included for the conveni-

ence of the priest, who may use them on occasion. Their use is explained below.

When there are no readers for the first and second readings and when no deacon or other priest is present to proclaim the gospel, the priest uses the Lectionary for Mass and, where it is available, the Book of the Gospels at the pulpit or lectern. Otherwise, the Sacramentary is the single book of the priest who presides: he reads from it at the chair (for the opening prayer of Mass, for the prayer after communion, and for the solemn form of concluding blessing) as well as at the altar. The priest needs no other book, except when he joins the people in singing from a hymnal or booklet.

Partly because of its long tradition of use in the Church, the Sacramentary as a book has symbolic meanings similar to that of the Lectionary from which the word of God is proclaimed. It represents the office of presidency in the prayer of the liturgical assembly—both in the prayers of petition and in the central eucharistic prayer of praise, thanksgiving, and memorial. Since these prayers articulate the action of the Church in celebrating the sacrifice of the Lord, even the book of prayer is an important sign. For this reason it is expected to be of sufficiently worthy proportions and artistic design to create respect and reverence for its contents.

FORMAT FOR SUNDAY MASSES

A distinctive feature of this edition of the Sacramentary is the double-page spread given for each Sunday Mass and for some feasts of greater importance. This arrangement is intended to stress the importance of the Sunday celebration of the eucharist, the reform of which was the primary conciliar concern. The actual format is designed to make the relationship of structure and parts completely clear, so that the priest will see immediately the two parts of the eucharistic celebration: the liturgy of the word (only referred to, but with an indication of the section of the Lectionary for Mass, for convenience) and the liturgy of the eucharist. The introductory rites and the concluding rite have been placed in proper subordination.

TRANSLATION OF LATIN TEXTS

In accord with directions from the Apostolic See, the translations of Latin texts, prepared by the International Committee on English in the Liturgy, are faithful but not literal. They preserve the intent and substance of the original, but avoid the translation of words in favor of the translation of ideas. This principle is explained at length in the instruction on the subject issued by the Consilium for the Implementation of the Constitution on the Liturgy (January 25, 1969):

> A faithful translation cannot be judged on the basis of individual words: the total context of this specific act of communication must be kept in mind, as well as the literary form proper to the respective language (no. 6).

The translator must always keep in mind that the "unit of meaning" is not the individual word but the whole passage. The translator must therefore be careful that the translation is not so analytical that it exaggerates the importance of particular phrases while it obscures or weakens the meaning of the whole (no. 12).

The prayer of the Church is always the prayer of some actual community, assembled here and now. It is not sufficient that a formula handed down from some other time or region be translated verbatim, even if accurately, for liturgical use. The formula translated must become the genuine prayer of the assembly and in it each of its members should be able to find and express himself or herself (no. 20).

The prayers (opening prayer, prayer over the gifts, prayer after communion, and prayer over the people) from the ancient Roman tradition are succinct and abstract. In translation they may need to be rendered somewhat more freely while conserving the original ideas. This can be done by moderately amplifying them, or, if necessary, paraphrasing expressions in order to concretize them for the celebration and needs of today. In every case pompous and superfluous language should be avoided (no. 34).

LITURGIES WITH CHILDREN

Because the directory was prepared as a supplement to the General Instruction of the Roman Missal, this edition of the Sacramentary includes the Directory for Masses with Children, issued by the Congregation for Divine Worship on November 1, 1973. It appears below, after the General Instruction.

The directory offers guidelines for the eucharistic celebration with assemblies of pre-adolescents. It is for liturgies with those baptized children who "have yet to be fully initiated through the sacraments of confirmation and eucharist as well as for children who have only recently been admitted to holy communion" (no. 1). It may also be adapted for liturgies with assemblies of the physically or mentally retarded (no. 6). And it contains recommended adaptations not only for Masses at which the assembly consists principally of children (Chapter III) but also for Masses with adult congregations in which a number of children participate (Chapter II).

MUSIC

The following music for the ministerial chants has been included in this edition of the Sacramentary:

(a) the chants of the prefaces of the eucharistic prayer have been included for every text, in a setting based on the plain chant; in addition the settings already in use in the United States have been appended from *The Order of Mass* (1969);

(b) in the Order of Mass, both the chants of the priest and the chants of the priest and the people together (such as the *Sanctus* and the Lord's Prayer);

(c) in the appendix, alternate settings of the Lord's Prayer and additional chants proper to the priest, including the body of the four eucharistic prayers;

(d) seasonal ministerial chants, such as the Easter proclamation of the deacon.

The chant adaptation was prepared by the International Committee on English in the Liturgy. The various appended settings of the Lord's Prayer, prefaces of the eucharistic prayer, etc., are taken from earlier liturgical books approved by the National Conference of Catholic Bishops.

SUNDAY RENEWAL OF BAPTISM

As an alternative to the penitential rite at all Sunday Masses, the blessing and sprinkling of the people with holy water may be substituted. This revised rite of sprinkling is no longer restricted to the principal Mass or to parish churches but may be used "at all Sunday Masses, even those anticipated on Saturday evening, in all churches and oratories."

To make this point clear, the rite is printed in the Order of Mass as an alternative to the penitential rite. The latter is simply omitted when holy water is blessed and sprinkled. The prayer of blessing of the water, which follows the priest's initial greeting, and the selection of songs to accompany the sprinkling indicate the purpose of the rite: to express the paschal character of Sunday and to be a memorial of baptism.

The directions for this brief rite are given in the Order of Mass and in Appendix I of the Sacramentary. After the rite of sprinkling, the Order of Mass continues with the *Gloria* or the opening prayer.

OPENING PRAYER

The collect, sometimes called the prayer of the assembly, has now been given the name "opening prayer," because it is the first prayer of the eucharistic celebration and because it completes the opening or introductory rite. In the Roman Missal, this prayer is not directly related to the biblical readings which follow. Instead it is a general prayer, related to the occasion or celebration, which concludes the entrance rite and serves to introduce the whole eucharist.

The General Instruction of the Roman Missal says:

The priest invites the people to pray and together with him they observe a brief silence so that they may realize they are in God's presence and may call their petitions to mind. The priest then says the opening prayer, which custom has named the "collect." This expresses the theme of the celebration and the priest's words address a petition to God the Father through Christ in the Holy Spirit.

The people make the prayer their own and give their assent by the acclamation, *Amen*.

In the Mass only one opening prayer is said; this rule applies also to the prayer over the gifts and the prayer after communion (no. 32).

In this edition an optional invitatory (explained below) has been given for the opening prayers on Sundays and certain feasts. It is placed within square brackets to indicate that its use is at the discretion of the priest.

The text of the opening prayer—after the invitatory and the period of silence—has been arranged in sense lines to help the priest to pray it in an audible, deliberate, and intelligible manner. The texts of the other prayers have been similarly arranged. The use of sense lines also avoids the necessity of pointing the text of prayers for occasions when they are sung. Melodies for singing the opening prayer are given in Appendix III.

ALTERNATIVE OPENING PRAYERS

The prayers of the Roman Missal have been translated in a style which, for the most part, retains the succinct character of the original Latin. The translations do not ordinarily employ the development or expansion mentioned in the instruction on liturgical translations (above). In the case of the opening prayer on Sundays and some major feasts, however, an alternative text is printed for use at the discretion of the priest.

The alternative opening prayers are not direct or faithful translations of the corresponding Latin text. They follow its theme or are inspired by it, but they are generally more concrete and expansive. The addition of such texts was prompted by the practice in other Roman liturgical books of offering alternatives and by the following statement in the 1969 instruction on translation:

Texts translated from another language are clearly not sufficient for the celebration of a fully renewed liturgy. The creation of new texts will be necessary. But translation of texts transmitted through the tradition of the Church is the best school and discipline for the creation of new texts so "that any new forms adopted should in some way grow organically from forms already in existence" (SC art. 23)— (no. 43).

Thus, on those occasions when two opening prayers appear side by side, the one on the left is a faithful but not necessarily literal translation of the corresponding Latin prayer, the one on the right is an alternative prayer suggested by the Latin text and in harmony with its theme. Either text may be chosen by the priest.

CONCLUSIONS TO PRAYERS

Because the revised rite concludes the presidential prayers in different ways (a lengthy conclusion to the opening prayer or collect, a briefer conclusion to most other prayers), this edition gives the complete conclusion in every case. Very often the precise formulations of the conclusions are almost interchangeable. Their use is explained in no. 32 of the General Instruction, although in English it is sometimes possible to weave the formal conclusion into the last clause of the body of the prayer.

In most instances the distinct conclusion begins either "We ask this . . ." or "Grant this . . . ." The purpose of the variation is that the mediation and intercession of Jesus expressed simply in Latin by the preposition *per* bears at least two meanings: (1) that the prayer of petition is addressed to the Father through Jesus in the Holy Spirit and (2) that the action of the Father comes through Jesus in the Holy Spirit. In the lengthy conclusion the concept expressed in Latin by the words *in unitate Spiritus Sancti, Deus* is conveyed more directly in English, "with you [Father] and the Holy Spirit, one God . . . ."

In the light of several years of experience with provisional texts, a slight variation has been introduced into the very last words of the conclusions to prayers, namely, "in the name of Jesus the Lord" in addition to "through Christ our Lord" and "for ever and ever." Several variants to express the biblical concept of prayer in Jesus' name are in common use.

The one chosen ("in the name of Jesus the Lord") is very close to the already accepted text, "through Christ our Lord," so that it should be easy for the priest to elicit the response of the people, *Amen.*

INVITATORIES AND INTRODUCTIONS

For the opening prayer, the priest first invites the people to pray, either with the simple "Let us pray" or with the expanded alternative invitatory found in the Sacramentary, or in his own words.

This invitatory or invitation to pray is a kind of *monitio* which the priest or other minister may employ to introduce or conclude—in very few words—different parts of Mass (see General Instruction, no. 11). In this edition of the Sacramentary it is expanded so that in the period of silence which follows the people may form their petitions. The period of silence will be richer and demand sufficient time so that the people can actually pray. Silence then becomes a real and meaningful part of the celebration (see no. 23). The brief, optional expansion of the invitatory structures the silence and helps people to be aware of the petitionary character of the opening prayer. If the priest uses his own words, the invitatory can be more concrete and effective.

The use of adapted introductory comments or invitatories has been explained in the following statement of the Congregation for Divine Worship (circular letter, April 27, 1973):

Introductions are ways of leading the faithful to a more thorough grasp of the meaning of the sacred rites or certain of their parts and to an inner participation in them. Particularly important are the introductions that the General Instruction assigns to be prepared and spoken by the priest: the comments introducing the faithful to the day's Mass before the celebration, to the liturgy of the word before the readings, and to the eucharistic prayer before the preface; the comments concluding the whole rite before the dismissal. Prominence should also be given to those introductions that the Order of Mass provides for certain rites, for example, the introductions to the penitential rite and the Lord's Prayer. By their very nature such introductions do not require that they be given verbatim in the form they have in the Missal; consequently it may well be helpful, at least in certain cases, to adapt them to the actual situation of a community. But the way any of these introductions is presented must respect the character proper to each and not turn into a sermon or homily. There must be a concern for brevity and the avoidance of a wordiness that would bore the participants (no. 14).

OTHER RECOMMENDATIONS

The circular letter of the Congregation for Divine Worship from which the above quotation is taken also speaks of accommodating the homily, general intercessions, and other elements of the eucharistic celebration to the particular congregation:

The homily must also be mentioned. It is "a part of the liturgy" by which the word of God proclaimed in the liturgical assembly is explained to help the community present. It is given in a way that is suited to the community's capacity and way of life and that is relevant to the circumstances of the celebration.

Finally much is to be made of the general intercessions, which in a sense is the community's response to the word of God proclaimed and received. To ensure its effectiveness care must be taken that the intentions made on behalf of the whole world's needs are suited to the gathered assembly; this means that there be a certain flexibility proportioned to the nature of this prayer in the preparation of the intentions.

For the celebration to belong to the community and to be vital requires more than choosing texts. The one presiding and others with a special role in the celebration must have a precise sense of the different styles of verbal communication that are involved in the readings, homily, introductions, and the like (nos. 15–17).

SILENCE

Silence should be observed at the designated times as part of the celebration. Its function depends on the time it occurs in each part of the celebration. Thus at the penitential rite and again after the invitation to pray, all recollect themselves; at the conclusion of a reading or the homily, all meditate briefly on what has been heard; after communion, all praise God in silent prayer (General Instruction, no. 23).

In order to facilitate the use of silence, rubrical directions for silent prayer have been indicated in this edition. These silent periods for prayer ordinarily should not be too brief or too lengthy. A more lengthy pause for reflection may take place at the penitential rite and after the readings or homily.

The proper use of periods of silent prayer and reflection will help to render the celebration less mechanical and impersonal and lend a more prayerful spirit to the liturgical rite. Just as there should be no celebration without song, so too there should be no celebration without periods for silent prayer and reflection.

PRAYER OVER THE GIFTS

The prayer over the gifts in style is similar to the opening prayer but with a brief concluding formula. It completes the preparation of the gifts: the people's presentation of the bread and wine and their preparation on the altar.

The prayer over the gifts has its own invitatory ("Pray, brethren . . ."). For clarity this invitatory has been directly indicated in the Mass formularies. No optional expansion of the invitation to pray has been provided, as was done in the case of the opening prayer.

If song or other music has accompanied the preparation of the gifts, as the General Instruction (no. 50) and the Order of Mass (no. 17) prefer, it will be appropriate to pause for a period of silence after the invitation and response, before the text of the prayer over the gifts is said.

If, as is also appropriate, the preparation of the gifts has taken place in silence, there will be no need for an additional period of silence before the priest says the prayer over the gifts.

After the prayer over the gifts, the priest should pause briefly before beginning the eucharistic prayer with the greeting "The Lord be with you."

PRAYER AFTER COMMUNION

"After communion, the priest and people may spend some time in silent prayer. If desired, a hymn, psalm, or other song of praise may be sung by the entire assembly" (no. 56j; see no. 23). After this period of prayer in silence and/or song the priest prays for the effects of the mystery just celebrated (cf. no. 56k).

No expanded invitatory is printed for the prayer after communion; in most cases "Let us pray" will suffice.

If the assembly has joined in a song, hymn, or psalm of praise after communion, there should be the usual period of silence—sufficiently protracted for recollection and reflection—after the invitation "Let us pray" (no. 23; Order of Mass, no. 33).

CONCLUDING RITE

The Order of Mass has a simple concluding rite:
(a) From his chair or at the altar the priest or another minister may make brief announcements, if any.
(b) The priest gives the formal liturgical greeting, "The Lord be with you," and the people respond.
(c) The priest gives the blessing, and
(d) the deacon gives the liturgical dismissal—or, in the absence of a deacon, this is done by the priest.

A directive in the Order of Mass mentions a substitute for the usual style of blessing: "On certain days or occasions another more solemn form of blessing or prayer over the people may be used as the rubrics direct" (Order of Mass, no. 113).

The Sacramentary gives extensive texts for these substitutes for the usual blessing and thus makes it possible to enrich and somewhat enlarge the concluding rite. All these solemn blessings and prayers over the people are printed together, to allow complete freedom of choice. In addition, the individual Mass formularies for Sundays in the principal seasons and on other occasions give a suggested example so that the pattern may become clear.

Either the solemn blessing or the prayer over the people may be chosen. During Lent, in keeping with ancient tradition, the prayer over the people is principally used. Some of the texts of the blessings and prayers are very general; others are specified for particular seasons or occasions.

The textual differences are these: the solemn blessings are usually divided into three parts or verses to each of which the people answer "Amen"; the prayer over the people is in the style of a collect, to which the people also respond "Amen."

Since the prayer over the people has a conclusion like other presidential prayers (". . . through Christ our Lord" or "in the name of Jesus the Lord"), the people will respond readily. Special attention is needed in the case of the solemn blessings, since the people will be unfamiliar with the style and the text. The priest should try to invite and encourage response by the inflection of his voice. In the absence of a fixed formula for concluding each of the verses, the tone or stress of the priest's voice must indicate the moment for common response.

RITE OF BLESSING AND DISMISSAL

The rite for the conclusion of Mass, when the option of a special blessing or prayer over the people is chosen, is as follows:
(1) After the usual greeting by the priest ("The Lord be with you"), the deacon gives the invitation: "Bow your heads and pray for God's blessing." He may also use similar words. In the absence of a deacon, the priest gives the invitation.
(2) The priest then extends his hands over the people while he sings or says the solemn blessing or prayer over the people.

This gesture of stretching his hands over the people is a form of the imposition of hands over the whole community. It should be done carefully so that it truly signifies the priest's role as he invokes God's power and strength on the assembly. (The book should be held for the priest by a server or minister, unless he goes to the altar for the concluding rite.)

(3) In either case—solemn blessing or prayer over the people—the priest concludes with the trinitarian formula and the usual gesture of blessing with the sign of the cross.

Finally the deacon (or the priest, in the absence of a deacon) gives the dismissal "which sends each member (of the assembly) back to doing good works, while praising and blessing the Lord" (no. 57). The recession begins as soon as the assembly has received this formal dismissal. It may be accompanied by a recessional song or other music.

ENTRANCE ANTIPHON

Although the Sacramentary is a book of presidential prayers sung or spoken by the priest, for the sake of completeness this edition does contain the brief sung antiphons for the entrance and communion processions. These are printed in smaller type in order to indicate that they are not ordinarily said by the priest and indeed are not parts of a sacramentary.

The General Instruction takes for granted that there will be singing at the entrance of the priest and other ministers (and during the communion rite; see nos. 26, 56, 83, 119), certainly in the Sunday celebration of the eucharist. When the antiphons are set to music, they may be used for this purpose, i.e., as refrains to psalms. Ordinarily, however, it is expected that full use will be made of the decision to employ appropriate substitutes sung by the assembly with a cantor or choir. For the United States, the National Conference of Catholic Bishops has given the criteria for texts to be sung as entrance songs. (See Appendix to the General Instruction, no. 26, below.)

Only in the absence of song is the entrance antiphon used as a spoken or recited text. Since these antiphons are too abrupt for communal recitation, it is preferable when there is no singing that the priest, the deacon, or another minister adapt the antiphon and incorporate it in the introduction to the Mass of the day. After the initial greeting, "the priest, deacon, or other suitable minister may very briefly introduce the Mass of the day" (Order of Mass, no. 3). The adaptation of the text of the entrance antiphon for this purpose is suggested by the Congregation for Divine Worship (Instruction on Particular Calendars and Offices, June 24, 1970, no. 40a).

COMMUNION ANTIPHON

The communion antiphon, although it is not ordinarily to be said by the priest, has also been included for completeness. The Order of Mass (no. 108) and the General Instruction call for singing during the communion of the priest and people, to "express outwardly the communicants' union in spirit by means of the unity of their voices, to give evidence of joy of heart, and to make the procession to receive Christ's body more fully an act of community" (no. 56i). The National Conference of Catholic Bishops has provided criteria for texts to be used (see Appendix to the General Instruction, no. 56i, below). For use of the communion antiphon if there is no singing, the directives given in no. 56i of the General Instruction are to be followed.

NAME OF THE BISHOP

By decree of the Congregation for Divine Worship, October 8, 1972, not only the diocesan bishop but an Ordinary equivalent in law to a diocesan bishop must be named in the eucharistic prayer. This includes a diocesan bishop transferred to another diocese as long as he administers the former diocese; an apostolic administrator, *sede plena* or *sede vacante*, whether permanent or temporary, if he is a bishop and actually exercises the entire governance of the diocese, especially in spiritual matters; a vicar or prefect apostolic; and a prelate or abbot *nullius*. However, it does not include a diocesan administrator *sede vacante*.

In addition, coadjutor and auxiliary bishops who assist the diocesan bishop in the governance of the diocese and other bishops may be named after the Ordinary. If there are several bishops, they may be mentioned as a group ("and his assistant bishops") without adding their names.

In the case of a priest celebrating the eucharist outside his own diocese but with a congregation from his diocese, he names his own bishop and then the local bishop ("N., the bishop of this Church of N.").

The diocesan bishop may mention his coadjutor or auxiliary bishops and, when outside his own diocese, both the local bishop and himself.

COMMUNION MORE THAN ONCE A DAY

Canon 917 of the 1983 Code of Canon Law states that apart from the reception of Viaticum "a person who has received the Most Holy Eucharist may receive it again on the same day only during the celebration of the Eucharist in which the person participates." The Pontifical Commission for the Authoritative Interpretation of the Code of Canon Law decreed that this canon is to be interpreted as referring only to a *second* Mass, not *as often,* as a person participates in the Eucharist on a given day (*AAS* 76 [1984] 746–747).

MINISTERS OF COMMUNION

On June 21, 1973, the section of the Roman Ritual entitled, *De Sacra Communione et de Cultu Mysterii Eucharistici extra Missam* was published. It contains the following paragraphs about the minister of communion, which are applicable to the celebration of Mass:

It is, first of all, the office of the priest and the deacon to minister holy communion to the faithful who ask to receive it. It is most fitting, therefore, that they give a suitable part of their time to this ministry of their order, depending on the needs of the faithful.

It is the office of an acolyte who has been properly instituted to give communion as a special minister when the priest and deacon are absent or impeded by sickness, old age, or pastoral ministry or when the number of the faithful at the holy table is so great that the Mass or other service may be unreasonably protracted.

The local Ordinary may give other special ministers the faculty to give holy communion whenever it seems necessary for the pastoral benefit of the faithful and a priest, deacon, or acolyte is not available (no. 17).

In cases of necessity a priest may even designate a member of a particular worshiping assembly to assist in giving communion for a single occasion. The special form for this designation is given in Appendix V.

MANNER OF MINISTERING COMMUNION

The Roman Ritual (*De Sacra Communione et de Cultu Mysterii Eucharistici extra Missam*) gives the following norm concerning the manner of administration of holy communion:

In giving communion the custom of placing the particle of consecrated bread on the tongue of the communicant is to be maintained because it is based on a tradition of several centuries.

Conferences of bishops, however, may decree, their actions having been confirmed by the Apostolic See, that communion may also be given in their territories by placing the consecrated bread in the hands of the faithful, provided there is no danger of irreverence or false opinions about the eucharist entering the minds of the faithful.

The faithful should be instructed that Jesus Christ is Lord and Savior and that, present in the sacrament, he must be given the same worship and adoration which is to be given to God.

In either case, communion must be given by the competent minister, who shows the particle of consecrated bread to the communicant and gives it to him or her, saying, "The body of Christ," to which the communicant replies "Amen" (no. 21).

The faculty of distributing communion in the hand was conceded by the Sacred Congregation for the Sacraments and Divine Worship to the National Conference of Catholic Bishops on June 17, 1977. For norms pertaining to this practice, see Appendix to the General Instruction for Dioceses of the United States of America, no. 240, below.

EUCHARISTIC FAST

The Roman Ritual (*De Sacra Communione et de Cultu Mysterii Eucharistici extra Missam*, with the revisions decreed in 1983) gives the present discipline of the eucharistic fast:

Communicants are not to receive the sacrament unless they have fasted for at least one hour from foods and beverages, with the exception only of water and medicine.

The elderly and those suffering from any kind of infirmity, as well as those who take care of such persons, may receive the eucharist even if they have taken something within the hour before communion (no. 24).

EUCHARISTIC PRAYERS FOR MASSES WITH CHILDREN AND FOR MASSES OF RECONCILIATION

Appendix VI contains the Eucharistic Prayers for Masses with Children and the Eucharistic Prayers for Masses of Reconciliation. While these prayers have been approved by the Apostolic See for an indeterminate period of time, the Latin texts of the prayers are still designated as *ad experimentum*. Hence, they may not be included in the same place as the other four eucharistic prayers in the Sacramentary and have been included in this appendix.

BLESSING OF OILS

Appendix II to the Sacramentary contains, for convenience, the English text of the rites for the blessing of oils and consecration of the chrism, for use on Holy Thursday or on another day chosen by the bishop.

APPENDIX OF LATIN TEXTS

A special Latin appendix is included in this edition by direction of the Congregation for Divine Worship. It contains the *Ordo Missae* in Latin (including the four eucharistic prayers and a number of prefaces) and a selection of formularies for Mass in Latin.

This appendix is intended for the use of visiting priests who may not be familiar with the language of the country. For the ordinary celebration of Mass in Latin, in whole or in part, the *Missale Romanum* and *Lectionarium* should be used.

ADDITIONAL APPENDICES VII, VIII, IX, X

The 1985 reprinting of the Sacramentary includes appendices containing the additional presidential prayers approved since 1974. These prayers are from the 1975 *editio typica altera* of the Roman Missal, *Pastoral Care of the Sick: Rites of Anointing and Viaticum,* and *The Dedication of a Church and an Altar.* The *Blessing of a Chalice and Paten* Mass is also included in an appendix for use on those occasions when these vessels are blessed at Mass. The last appendix contains additional presidential prayers from the 1975 edition of the *Missale Romanum* in a provisional translation approved for interim use, as well as the "Bicentennial Mass" of 1976 with the new title "Independence Day and Other Civic Observances."

GENERAL INSTRUCTION OF THE ROMAN MISSAL

Fourth Edition, 27 March 1975

INTRODUCTION

1. When Christ the Lord was about to celebrate the passover meal with his disciples and institute the sacrifice of his body and blood, he directed them to prepare a large room, arranged for the supper (Lk 22:12). The Church has always regarded this command of Christ as applying to itself when it gives directions about the preparation of the sentiments of the worshipers, the place, rites, and texts for the celebration of the eucharist. The current norms, laid down on the basis of the intent of Vatican Council II, and the new Missal that will be used henceforth in the celebration of Mass by the Church of the Roman Rite, are fresh evidence of the great care, faith, and unchanged love that the Church shows toward the eucharist. They attest as well to its coherent tradition, continuing amid the introduction of some new elements.

A WITNESS TO UNCHANGED FAITH

2. The sacrificial nature of the Mass was solemnly proclaimed by the Council of Trent in agreement with the whole tradition of the Church.[1] Vatican Council II reaffirmed this teaching in these significant words: "At the Last Supper our Savior instituted the eucharistic sacrifice of his body and blood. He did this in order to perpetuate the sacrifice of the cross throughout the centuries until he should come again and in this way entrust to his beloved Bride, the Church, a memorial of his death and resurrection."[2]

The Council's teaching is expressed constantly in the formularies of the Mass. This teaching, in the concise words of the Leonine Sacramentary, is that "the work of our redemption is carried out whenever we celebrate the memory of this sacrifice";[3] it is aptly and accurately brought out in the eucharistic prayers. At the anamnesis or memorial, the priest, addressing God in the name of all the people, offers in thanksgiving the holy and living sacrifice: the Church's offering and the Victim whose death has reconciled us with God.[4] The priest also prays that the body and blood of Christ may be a sacrifice acceptable to the Father, bringing salvation to the whole world.[5]

In this new Missal, then, the Church's rule of prayer (lex orandi) corresponds to its constant rule of faith (lex credendi). This rule of faith instructs us that the sacrifice of the cross and its sacramental renewal in the Mass, which Christ instituted at the Last Supper and commanded his apostles to do in his memory, are one and the same, differing only in the manner of offering and that consequently the Mass is at once a sacrifice of praise and thanksgiving, of reconciliation and expiation.

3. The celebration of Mass also proclaims the sublime mystery of the Lord's real presence under the eucharistic elements, which Vatican Council II[6] and other documents of the Church's magisterium[7] have reaffirmed in the same sense and as the same teaching that the Council of Trent had proposed as a matter of faith.[8] The Mass does this not only by means of the very words of consecration, by which Christ becomes present through transubstantiation, but also by that spirit and expression of reverence and adoration in which the eucharistic liturgy is carried out. For the same reason the Christian people are invited in Holy Week on Holy Thursday and on the solemnity of Corpus Christi to honor this wonderful sacrament in a special way by their adoration.

4. Further, because of the priest's more prominent place and office in the rite, its form sheds light on the ministerial priesthood proper to the presbyter, who offers the sacrifice in the person of Christ and presides over the assembly of a holy people. The meaning of his office is declared and detailed in the preface for the chrism Mass on Thursday of Holy Week, the day celebrating the institution of the priesthood. The preface brings out the passing on of the sacerdotal power through the laying on of hands and, by listing its various offices, describes that power. It is the continuation of the power of Christ, High Priest of the New Testament.

5. In addition, the ministerial priesthood puts into its proper light another reality of which much should be made, namely, the royal priesthood of believers. Through the ministry of presbyters the people's spiritual sacrifice to God is brought to completeness in union with the sacrifice of Christ, our one and only Mediator.[9] For the celebration of the eucharist is the action of the whole Church; in it all should do only, but all of, those parts that belong to them in virtue of their place within the people of God. In this way greater attention will be given to some aspects of the eucharistic celebration that have sometimes been neglected in the course of time. For these people are the people of God, purchased by Christ's blood, gathered together by the Lord, nourished by his word. They are a people called to offer God the prayers of the entire human family, a people giving thanks in Christ for the mystery of salvation by offer-

---

1. See Council of Trent, Session 22, 17 September 1562: Denz-Schön 1738–1759.

2. Second Vatican Council, Constitution on the Sacred Liturgy, *Sacrosanctum Concilium* [= SC], art. 47; see Dogmatic Constitution on the Church, *Lumen gentium* [= LG], nos. 3, 28; Decree on the Ministry and Life of Priests, *Presbyterorum ordinis* [= PO], nos. 2, 4, 5.

3. *Sacramentarium Veronense*, ed. Mohlberg, no. 93.

4. See Roman Missal, Eucharistic Prayer III.

5. See Roman Missal, Eucharistic Prayer IV.

6. See SC, art. 7, 47; PO, nos. 5, 18.

7. See Pius XII, encyclical letter *Humani generis: AAS* 42 (1950) 570–571; Paul VI, encyclical letter *Mysterium fidei: AAS* 57 (1965) 762–769, nos. 33–55; Solemn Profession of Faith, 30 June 1968: *AAS* 60 (1968) 442–443, nos. 24–26; Congregation of Rites, instruction *Eucharisticum mysterium* [= EM], 25 May 1967, nos. 3f, 9: *AAS* 59 (1967) 543, 547.

8. See Council of Trent, Session 13, 11 October 1551: Denz-Schön 1635–1661.

9. See PO, no. 2.

ing his sacrifice. Finally, they are a people growing together into unity by sharing in Christ's body and blood. These people are holy by their origin, but becoming ever more holy by conscious, active, and fruitful participation in the mystery of the eucharist.[10]

A WITNESS TO UNBROKEN TRADITION

6. In setting forth its decrees for the revision of the Order of Mass, Vatican Council II directed, among other things, that some rites be restored "to the vigor they had in the tradition of the Fathers";[11] this is a quotation from the Apostolic Constitution *Quo primum* of 1570, by which St. Pius V promulgated the Tridentine Missal. The fact that the same words are used in reference to both Roman Missals indicates how both of them, although separated by four centuries, embrace one and the same tradition. And when the more profound elements of this tradition are considered, it becomes clear how remarkably and harmoniously this new Roman Missal improves on the older one.

7. The older Missal belongs to the difficult period of attacks against Catholic teaching on the sacrificial nature of the Mass, the ministerial priesthood, and the real and permanent presence of Christ under the eucharistic elements. St. Pius V was therefore especially concerned with preserving the relatively recent developments in the Church's tradition, then unjustly being assailed, and introduced only very slight changes into the sacred rites. In fact, the Roman Missal of 1570 differs very little from the first printed edition of 1474, which in turn faithfully follows the Missal used at the time of Pope Innocent III (1198–1216). Manuscripts in the Vatican Library provided some verbal emendations, but they seldom allowed research into "ancient and approved authors" to extend beyond the examination of a few liturgical commentaries of the Middle Ages.

8. Today, on the other hand, countless studies of scholars have enriched the "tradition of the Fathers" that the revisers of the Missal under St. Pius V followed. After the Gregorian Sacramentary was first published in 1571, many critical editions of other ancient Roman and Ambrosian sacramentaries appeared. Ancient Spanish and Gallican liturgical books also became available, bringing to light many prayers of profound spirituality that had hitherto been unknown.

Traditions dating back to the first centuries before the formation of the Eastern and Western rites are also better known today because so many liturgical documents have been discovered.

The continuing progress in patristic studies has also illumined eucharistic theology through the teachings of such illustrious saints of Christian antiquity as Irenaeus, Ambrose, Cyril of Jerusalem, and John Chrysostom.

9. The "tradition of the Fathers" does not require merely the preservation of what our immediate predecessors have passed on to us. There must also be profound study and understanding of the Church's entire past and of all the ways in which its single faith has been expressed in the quite diverse human and social forms prevailing in Semitic, Greek, and Latin cultures. This broader view shows us how the Holy Spirit endows the people of God with a marvelous fidelity in preserving the deposit of faith unchanged, even though prayers and rites differ so greatly.

10. See SC, art. 11.
11. SC, art. 50.

ADAPTATION TO MODERN CONDITIONS

10. As it bears witness to the Roman Church's rule of prayer *(lex orandi)* and guards the deposit of faith handed down by the later councils, the new Roman Missal in turn marks a major step forward in liturgical tradition.

The Fathers of Vatican Council II in reaffirming the dogmatic statements of the Council of Trent were speaking at a far different time in the world's history. They were able therefore to bring forward proposals and measures of a pastoral nature that could not have even been foreseen four centuries ago.

11. The Council of Trent recognized the great catechetical value of the celebration of Mass, but was unable to bring out all its consequences for the actual life of the Church. Many were pressing for permission to use the vernacular in celebrating the eucharistic sacrifice, but the Council, judging the conditions of that age, felt bound to answer such a request with a reaffirmation of the Church's traditional teaching. This teaching is that the eucharistic sacrifice is, first and foremost, the action of Christ himself and therefore the manner in which the faithful take part in the Mass does not affect the efficacy belonging to it. The Council thus stated in firm but measured words: "Although the Mass contains much instruction for the faithful, it did not seem expedient to the Fathers that as a general rule it be celebrated in the vernacular."[12] The Council accordingly anathematized anyone maintaining that "the rite of the Roman Church, in which part of the canon and the words of consecration are spoken in a low voice, should be condemned or that the Mass must be celebrated only in the vernacular."[13] Although the Council of Trent on the one hand prohibited the use of the vernacular in the Mass, nevertheless, on the other, it did direct pastors to substitute appropriate catechesis: "Lest Christ's flock go hungry . . . the Council commands pastors and others having the care of souls that either personally or through others they frequently give instructions during Mass, especially on Sundays and holydays, on what is read at Mass and that among their instructions they include some explanation of the mystery of this sacrifice."[14]

12. Convened in order to adapt the Church to the contemporary requirements of its apostolic task, Vatican Council II examined thoroughly, as had Trent, the pedagogic and pastoral character of the liturgy.[15] Since no Catholic would now deny the lawfulness and efficacy of a sacred rite celebrated in Latin, the Council was able to acknowledge that "the use of the mother tongue frequently may be of great advantage to the people" and gave permission for its use.[16] The enthusiasm in response to this decision was so great that, under the leadership of the bishops and the Apostolic See, it has resulted in the permission for all liturgical celebrations in which the faithful participate to be in the vernacular for the sake of a better comprehension of the mystery being celebrated.

13. The use of the vernacular in the liturgy may certainly be considered an important means for presenting more clearly the catechesis on the mystery that is part of the

12. Council of Trent, Session 22, *Doctrina de SS. Missae Sacrificio,* cap. 8: Denz-Schön 1749.
13. *Ibid.,* can. 9: Denz-Schön 1759.
14. *Ibid.,* cap. 8: Denz-Schön 1749.
15. See SC, art. 33.
16. See SC, art. 36.

celebration itself. Nevertheless, Vatican Council II also ordered the observance of certain directives, prescribed by the Council of Trent but not obeyed everywhere. Among these are the obligatory homily on Sundays and holydays[17] and the permission to interpose some commentary during the sacred rites themselves.[18]

Above all, Vatican Council II strongly endorsed ''that more complete form of participation in the Mass by which the faithful, after the priest's communion, receive the Lord's body from the same sacrifice.''[19] Thus the Council gave impetus to the fulfillment of the further desire of the Fathers of Trent that for fuller participation in the holy eucharist ''the faithful present at each Mass should communicate not only by spiritual desire but also by sacramental communion.''[20]

14. Moved by the same spirit and pastoral concern, Vatican Council II was able to reevaluate the Tridentine norm on communion under both kinds. No one today challenges the doctrinal principles on the completeness of eucharistic communion under the form of bread alone. The Council thus gave permission for the reception of communion under both kinds on some occasions, because this more explicit form of the sacramental sign offers a special means of deepening the understanding of the mystery in which the faithful are taking part.[21]

15. Thus the Church remains faithful in its responsibility as teacher of truth to guard ''things old,'' that is, the deposit of tradition; at the same time it fulfills another duty, that of examining and prudently bringing forth ''things new'' (see Mt 13:52).

Accordingly, a part of the new Roman Missal directs the prayer of the Church expressly to the needs of our times. This is above all true of the ritual Masses and the Masses for various needs and occasions, which happily combine the traditional and the contemporary. Thus many expressions, drawn from the Church's most ancient tradition and become familiar through the many editions of the Roman Missal, have remained unchanged. Other expressions, however, have been adapted to today's needs and circumstances and still others—for example, the prayers for the Church, the laity, the sanctification of human work, the community of all peoples, certain needs proper to our era— are completely new compositions, drawing on the thoughts and even the very language of the recent conciliar documents.

The same awareness of the present state of the world also influenced the use of texts from very ancient tradition. It seemed that this cherished treasure would not be harmed if some phrases were changed so that the style of language would be more in accord with the language of modern theology and would faithfully reflect the actual state of the Church's discipline. Thus there have been changes of some expressions bearing on the evaluation and use of the good things of the earth and of allusions to a particular form of outward penance belonging to another age in the history of the Church.

In short, the liturgical norms of the Council of Trent have been completed and improved in many respects by those of Vatican Council II. This Council has brought to realiza-

tion the efforts of the last four hundred years to move the faithful closer to the sacred liturgy, especially the efforts of recent times and above all the zeal for the liturgy promoted by St. Pius X and his successors.

CHAPTER I

IMPORTANCE AND DIGNITY OF THE EUCHARISTIC CELEBRATION

1. The celebration of Mass, the action of Christ and the people of God arrayed hierarchically, is for the universal and the local Church as well as for each person the center of the whole Christian life.[1] In the Mass we have the high point of the work that in Christ God accomplishes to sanctify us and the high point of the worship that in adoring God through Christ, his Son, we offer to the Father.[2] During the cycle of the year, moreover, the mysteries of redemption are recalled in the Mass in such a way that they are somehow made present.[3] All other liturgical rites and all the works of the Christian life are linked with the eucharistic celebration, flow from it, and have it as their end.[4]

2. Therefore, it is of the greatest importance that the celebration of the Mass, the Lord's Supper, be so arranged that the ministers and the faithful who take their own proper part in it may more fully receive its good effects.[5] This is the reason why Christ the Lord instituted the eucharistic sacrifice of his body and blood and entrusted it to the Church, his beloved Bride, as the memorial of his passion and resurrection.[6]

3. This purpose will best be accomplished if, after due regard for the nature and circumstances of each assembly, the celebration is planned in such a way that it brings about in the faithful a participation in body and spirit that is conscious, active, full, and motivated by faith, hope, and charity. The Church desires this kind of participation, the nature of the celebration demands it, and for the Christian people it is a right and duty they have by reason of their baptism.[7]

4. The presence and active participation of the people bring out more plainly the ecclesial nature of the celebration.[8] But even when their participation is not possible, the eucharistic celebration still retains its effectiveness and worth because it is the action of Christ and the Church[9], in which the priest always acts on behalf of the people's salvation.

---

17. See SC, art. 52.
18. See SC, art. 35:3.
19. SC, art. 55.
20. Council of Trent, Session 22, *Doctrina de SS. Missae Sacrificio*, cap. 6: Denz-Schön 1747.
21. See SC, art. 55.

1. See SC, art. 41; LG, no. 11; PO, nos. 2, 5, 6; Decree on the Pastoral Office of Bishops in the Church, *Christus Dominus*, no. 30; Decree on Ecumenism, *Unitatis redintegratio*, no. 15; EM, nos. 3e, 6.
2. See SC, art. 10.
3. See SC, art. 102.
4. See PO, no. 5; SC, art. 10.
5. See SC, art. 14, 19, 26, 28, 30.
6. See SC, art. 47.
7. See SC, art. 14.
8. See SC, art. 41.
9. See PO, no. 13.

5. The celebration of the eucharist, like the entire liturgy, involves the use of outward signs that foster, strengthen, and express faith.[10] There must be the utmost care therefore to choose and to make wise use of those forms and elements provided by the Church that, in view of the circumstances of the people and the place, will best foster active and full participation and serve the spiritual well-being of the faithful.

6. The purpose of this Instruction is to give the general guidelines for planning the eucharistic celebration properly and to set forth the rules for arranging the individual forms of celebration.[11] In accord with the Constitution on the Liturgy, each conference of bishops has the power to lay down norms for its own territory that are suited to the traditions and character of peoples, regions, and various communities.[12]

CHAPTER II

STRUCTURE, ELEMENTS, AND PARTS OF THE MASS

I. GENERAL STRUCTURE OF THE MASS

7. At Mass or the Lord's Supper, the people of God are called together, with a priest presiding and acting in the person of Christ, to celebrate the memorial of the Lord or eucharistic sacrifice.[13] For this reason Christ's promise applies supremely to such a local gathering together of the Church: "Where two or three come together in my name, there am I in their midst" (Mt 18:20). For at the celebration of Mass, which perpetuates the sacrifice of the cross,[14] Christ is really present to the assembly gathered in his name; he is present in the person of the minister, in his own word, and indeed substantially and permanently under the eucharistic elements.[15]

8. The Mass is made up as it were of the liturgy of the word and the liturgy of the eucharist, two parts so closely connected that they form but one single act of worship.[16] For in the Mass the table of God's word and of Christ's body is laid for the people of God to receive from it instruction and food.[17] There are also certain rites to open and conclude the celebration.

10. See SC, art. 59.

11. For Masses with special groups, see Congregation for Divine Worship, instruction *Actio pastoralis*, 15 May 1969; for Masses with children, Congregation for Divine Worship, Directory for Masses with Children, 1 November 1973; for the manner of joining the liturgy of the hours with the Mass, General Instruction on the Liturgy of the Hours, nos. 93–98.

12. See SC, art. 37–40.

13. See PO, no. 5; SC, art. 33.

14. See Council of Trent, Session 22, cap. 1: Denz-Schön 1740; Paul VI, Solemn Profession of Faith, 30 June 1968, no. 24: *AAS* 60 (1968) 442.

15. See SC, art. 7; Paul VI, encyclical letter *Mysterium fidei*, 3 September 1965; EM, no. 9.

16. See SC, art. 56; EM, no. 10.

17. See SC, art. 48, 51; Dogmatic Constitution on Divine Revelation, *Dei Verbum*, no. 21; PO, no. 4.

II. DIFFERENT ELEMENTS OF THE MASS

READING AND EXPLAINING THE WORD OF GOD

9. When the Scriptures are read in the Church, God himself is speaking to his people, and Christ, present in his own word, is proclaiming the Gospel.

The readings must therefore be listened to by all with reverence; they make up a principal element of the liturgy. In the biblical readings God's word addresses all people of every era and is understandable to them, but a living commentary on the word, that is, the homily, as an integral part of the liturgy, increases the word's effectiveness.[18]

PRAYERS AND OTHER PARTS ASSIGNED TO THE PRIEST

10. Among the parts assigned to the priest, the eucharistic prayer is preeminent; it is the high point of the entire celebration. Next are the prayers: the opening prayer or collect, the prayers over the gifts, and the prayer after communion. The priest, presiding over the assembly in the person of Christ, addresses these prayers to God in the name of the entire holy people and all present.[19] Thus there is good reason to call them "the presidential prayers."

11. It is also up to the priest in the exercise of his office of presiding over the assembly to pronounce the instructions and words of introduction and conclusion that are provided in the rites themselves. By their very nature these introductions do not need to be expressed verbatim in the form in which they are given in the Missal; at least in certain cases it will be advisable to adapt them somewhat to the concrete situation of the community.[20] It also belongs to the priest presiding to proclaim the word of God and to give the final blessing. He may give the faithful a very brief introduction to the Mass of the day (before the celebration begins), to the liturgy of the word (before the readings), and to the eucharistic prayer (before the preface); he may also make comments concluding the entire sacred service before the dismissal.

12. The nature of the presidential prayers demands that they be spoken in a loud and clear voice and that everyone present listen with attention.[21] While the priest is reciting them there should be no other prayer and the organ or other instruments should not be played.

13. But the priest does not only pray in the name of the whole community as its president; he also prays at times in his own name that he may exercise his ministry with attention and devotion. Such prayers are said inaudibly.

OTHER TEXTS IN THE CELEBRATION

14. Since by nature the celebration of Mass has the character of being the act of a community,[22] both the dialogues between celebrant and congregation and the acclamations take on special value;[23] they are not simply outward signs of the community's celebration, but the means of greater communion between priest and people.

18. See SC, art. 7, 33, 52.   19. See SC, art. 33.

20. See Congregation for Divine Worship, Circular letter on the eucharistic prayers, 27 April 1973, no. 14.

21. See Congregation of Rites, instruction *Musicam sacram* [= MS], 5 March 1967, no. 14.

22. See SC, art. 26, 27.   23. See SC, art. 30.

15. The acclamations and the responses to the priest's greeting and prayers create a degree of the active participation that the gathered faithful must contribute in every form of the Mass, in order to express clearly and to further the entire community's involvement.[24]

16. There are other parts, extremely useful for expressing and encouraging the people's active participation, that are assigned to the whole congregation: the penitential rite, the profession of faith, the general intercessions, and the Lord's Prayer.

17. Finally, of the other texts:

a. Some constitute an independent rite or act, such as the *Gloria,* the responsorial psalm, the *Alleluia* verse and the verse before the gospel, the *Sanctus,* the memorial acclamation, and the song after communion.

b. Others accompany another rite, such as the songs at the entrance, at the preparation of the gifts, at the breaking of the bread (*Agnus Dei*), and at communion.

VOCAL EXPRESSION OF THE DIFFERENT TEXTS

18. In texts that are to be delivered in a clear, loud voice, whether by the priest or by the ministers or by all, the tone of voice should correspond to the genre of the text, that is, accordingly as it is a reading, a prayer, an instruction, an acclamation, or a song; the tone should also be suited to the form of celebration and to the solemnity of the gathering. Other criteria are the idiom of different languages and the genius of peoples.

In the rubrics and in the norms that follow, the words *say (dicere)* or *proclaim (proferre)* are to be understood of both singing and speaking, and in accordance with the principles just stated.

IMPORTANCE OF SINGING

19. The faithful who gather together to await the Lord's coming are instructed by the Apostle Paul to sing psalms, hymns, and inspired songs (see Col 3:16). Song is the sign of the heart's joy (see Acts 2:46). Thus St. Augustine says rightly: "To sing belongs to lovers."[25] There is also the ancient proverb: "One who sings well prays twice."

With due consideration for the culture and ability of each congregation, great importance should be attached to the use of singing at Mass; but it is not always necessary to sing all the texts that are of themselves meant to be sung.

In choosing the parts actually to be sung, however, preference should be given to those that are more significant and especially to those to be sung by the priest or ministers with the congregation responding or by the priest and people together.[26]

Since the faithful from different countries come together ever more frequently, it is desirable that they know how to sing at least some parts of the Ordinary of the Mass in Latin, especially the profession of faith and the Lord's Prayer, set to simple melodies.[27]

MOVEMENTS AND POSTURES

20. The uniformity in standing, kneeling, or sitting to be observed by all taking part is a sign of the community and the unity of the assembly; it both expresses and fosters the spiritual attitude of those taking part.[28]

21. For the sake of uniformity in movement and posture, the people should follow the directions given during the celebration by the deacon, the priest, or another minister. Unless other provision is made, at every Mass the people should stand from the beginning of the entrance song or when the priest enters until the end of the opening prayer or collect; for the singing of the *Alleluia* before the gospel; while the gospel is proclaimed; during the profession of faith and the general intercessions; from the prayer over the gifts to the end of the Mass, except at the places indicated later in this paragraph. They should sit during the readings before the gospel and during the responsorial psalm, for the homily and the presentation of the gifts, and, if this seems helpful, during the period of silence after communion. They should kneel at the consecration unless prevented by the lack of space, the number of people present, or some other good reason.

But it is up to the conference of bishops to adapt the actions and postures described in the Order of the Roman Mass to the customs of the people.[29] But the conference must make sure that such adaptations correspond to the meaning and character of each part of the celebration.

22. Included among the external actions of the Mass are those of the priest going to the altar, of the faithful presenting the gifts, and their coming forward to receive communion. While the songs proper to these movements are being sung, they should be carried out becomingly in keeping with the norms prescribed for each.

SILENCE

23. Silence should be observed at the designated times as part of the celebration.[30] Its function depends on the time it occurs in each part of the celebration. Thus at the penitential rite and again after the invitation to pray, all recollect themselves; at the conclusion of a reading or the homily, all meditate briefly on what has been heard; after communion, all praise God in silent prayer.

III. INDIVIDUAL PARTS OF THE MASS

A. Introductory Rites

24. The parts preceding the liturgy of the word, namely, the entrance song, greeting, penitential rite, *Kyrie, Gloria,* and opening prayer or collect, have the character of a beginning, introduction, and preparation.

The purpose of these rites is that the faithful coming together take on the form of a community and prepare themselves to listen to God's word and celebrate the eucharist properly.

ENTRANCE

25. After the people have assembled, the entrance song begins as the priest and the ministers come in. The purpose of this song is to open the celebration, intensify the unity of the gathered people, lead their thoughts to the mystery of the season or feast, and accompany the procession of priest and ministers.

26. The entrance song is sung alternately either by the choir and the congregation or by the cantor and the congregation; or it is sung entirely by the congregation or by the choir alone. The antiphon and psalm of the *Graduale Romanum* or the Simple Gradual may be used, or another

24. See MS, no. 16a.   25. Augustine, *Sermo* 336, 1: PL 38, 1472.

26. See MS, nos. 7, 16; *Missale Romanum . . . Ordo cantus Missae,* ed. typica, 1972, Introduction.

27. See SC, art. 54; Congregation of Rites, instruction *Inter Oecumenici* [= IOe], 26 September 1964, no. 59: AAS 56 (1964) 891; MS, no. 47.

28. See SC, art. 30.

29. See SC, art. 39.   30. See SC, art. 30; MS, no. 17.

song that is suited to this part of the Mass, the day, or the seasons and that has a text approved by the conference of bishops.

If there is no singing for the entrance, the antiphon in the Missal is recited either by the faithful, by some of them, or by a reader; otherwise it is recited by the priest after the greeting.

VENERATION OF THE ALTAR
AND GREETING OF THE CONGREGATION

27. When the priest and the ministers enter the sanctuary, they reverence the altar. As a sign of veneration, the priest and deacon kiss the altar; when the occasion warrants, the priest may also incense the altar.

28. After the entrance song, the priest and the whole assembly make the sign of the cross. Then through his greeting the priest declares to the assembled community that the Lord is present. This greeting and the congregation's response express the mystery of the gathered Church.

PENITENTIAL RITE

29. After greeting the congregation, the priest or other qualified minister may very briefly introduce the faithful to the Mass of the day. Then the priest invites them to take part in the penitential rite, which the entire community carries out through a communal confession and which the priest's absolution brings to an end.

KYRIE ELEISON

30. Then the *Kyrie* begins, unless it has already been included as part of the penitential rite. Since it is a song by which the faithful praise the Lord and implore his mercy, it is ordinarily prayed by all, that is, alternately by the congregation and the choir or cantor.

As a rule each of the acclamations is said twice, but, because of the idiom of different languages, the music, or other circumstances, it may be said more than twice or a short verse (trope) may be interpolated. If the *Kyrie* is not sung, it is to be recited.

GLORIA

31. The *Gloria* is an ancient hymn in which the Church, assembled in the Holy Spirit, praises and entreats the Father and the Lamb. It is sung by the congregation, or by the congregation alternately with the choir, or by the choir alone. If not sung, it is to be recited either by all together or in alternation.

The *Gloria* is sung or said on Sundays outside Advent and Lent, on solemnities and feasts, and in special, more solemn celebrations.

OPENING PRAYER OR COLLECT

32. Next the priest invites the people to pray and together with him they observe a brief silence so that they may realize they are in God's presence and may call their petitions to mind. The priest then says the opening prayer, which custom has named the "collect." This expresses the theme of the celebration and the priest's words address a petition to God the Father through Christ in the Holy Spirit.

The people make the prayer their own and give their assent by the acclamation, Amen.

In the Mass only one opening prayer is said; this rule applies also to the prayer over the gifts and the prayer after communion.

The opening prayer ends with the longer conclusion, namely:

—if the prayer is directed to the Father:
We ask this (Grant this)
through our Lord Jesus Christ, your Son,
who lives and reigns with you and the Holy Spirit,
one God, for ever and ever;

—if it is directed to the Father, but the Son is mentioned at the end:
Who lives and reigns with you and the Holy Spirit,
one God, for ever and ever;

—if directed to the Son:
You live and reign with the Father and the Holy Spirit,
one God, for ever and ever.

The prayer over the gifts and the prayer after communion end with the shorter conclusion, namely:

—if the prayer is directed to the Father:
We ask this (Grant this) through Christ our Lord;

—if it is directed to the Father, but the Son is mentioned at the end:
Who lives and reigns with you for ever and ever;

—if it is directed to the Son:
You live and reign for ever and ever.

B. Liturgy of the Word

33. Readings from Scripture and the chants between the readings form the main part of the liturgy of the word. The homily, profession of faith, and general intercessions or prayer of the faithful expand and complete this part of the Mass. In the readings, explained by the homily, God is speaking to his people,[31] opening up to them the mystery of redemption and salvation, and nourishing their spirit; Christ is present to the faithful through his own word.[32] Through the chants the people make God's word their own and through the profession of faith affirm their adherence to it. Finally, having been fed by this word, they make their petitions in the general intercessions for the needs of the Church and for the salvation of the whole world.

SCRIPTURE READINGS

34. The readings lay the table of God's word for the faithful and open up the riches of the Bible to them.[33] Since by tradition the reading of the Scriptures is a ministerial, not a presidential function, it is proper that as a rule a deacon or, in his absence, a priest other than the one presiding read the gospel. A reader proclaims the other readings. In the absence of a deacon or another priest, the priest celebrant reads the gospel.[34]

35. The liturgy itself inculcates the great reverence to be shown toward the reading of the gospel, setting it off from

31. See SC, art. 33.   33. See SC, art. 51.
32. See SC, art. 7.   34. See IOe, no. 50.

the other readings by special marks of honor. A special minister is appointed to proclaim it and prepares himself by a blessing or prayer. The people, who by their acclamations acknowledge and confess Christ present and speaking to them, stand as they listen to it. Marks of reverence are given to the Book of the Gospels itself.

CHANTS BETWEEN THE READINGS

36. After the first reading comes the responsorial psalm or gradual, an integral part of the liturgy of the word. The psalm as a rule is drawn from the Lectionary because the individual psalm texts are directly connected with the individual readings: the choice of psalm depends therefore on the readings. Nevertheless, in order that the people may be able to join in the responsorial psalm more readily, some texts of responses and psalms have been chosen, according to the different seasons of the year and classes of saints, for optional use, whenever the psalm is sung, in place of the text corresponding to the reading.

The psalmist or cantor of the psalm sings the verses of the psalm at the lectern or other suitable place. The people remain seated and listen, but also as a rule take part by singing the response, except when the psalm is sung straight through without the response.

The psalm when sung may be either the psalm assigned in the Lectionary or the gradual from the *Graduale Romanum* or the responsorial psalm or the psalm with *Alleluia* as the response from the Simple Gradual in the form they have in those books.

37. As the season requires, the *Alleluia* or another chant follows the second reading.

a. The *Alleluia* is sung in every season outside Lent. It is begun either by all present or by the choir or cantor; it may then be repeated. The verses are taken from the Lectionary or the *Graduale*.

b. The other chant consists of the verse before the gospel or another psalm or tract, as found in the Lectionary or the *Graduale*.

38. When there is only one reading before the gospel:

a. during a season calling for the *Alleluia*, there is an option to use either the psalm with *Alleluia* as the response, or the responsorial psalm and the *Alleluia* with its verse, or just the psalm, or just the *Alleluia*;

b. during the season when the *Alleluia* is not allowed, either the responsorial psalm or the verse before the gospel may be used.

39. If the psalm after the reading is not sung, it is to be recited. If not sung, the *Alleluia* or the verse before the gospel may be omitted.

40. Sequences are optional, except on Easter Sunday and Pentecost.

HOMILY

41. The homily is an integral part of the liturgy and is strongly recommended:[35] it is necessary for the nurturing of the Christian life. It should develop some point of the readings or of another text from the Ordinary or from the Proper of the Mass of the day, and take into account the mystery being celebrated and the needs proper to the listeners.[36]

42. There must be a homily on Sundays and holydays of obligation at all Masses that are celebrated with a congregation; it may not be omitted without a serious reason. It is recommended on other days, especially on the weekdays of Advent, Lent and the Easter season, as well as on other feasts and occasions when the people come to church in large numbers.[37]

The homily should ordinarily be given by the priest celebrant.

PROFESSION OF FAITH

43. The symbol or profession of faith in the celebration of Mass serves as a way for the people to respond and to give their assent to the word of God heard in the readings and through the homily and for them to call to mind the truths of faith before they begin to celebrate the eucharist.

44. Recitation of the profession of faith by the priest together with the people is obligatory on Sundays and solemnities. It may be said also at special, more solemn celebrations.

If it is sung, as a rule all are to sing it together or in alternation.

GENERAL INTERCESSIONS

45. In the general intercessions or prayer of the faithful, the people, exercising their priestly function, intercede for all humanity. It is appropriate that this prayer be included in all Masses celebrated with a congregation, so that petitions will be offered for the Church, for civil authorities, for those oppressed by various needs, for all people, and for the salvation of the world.[38]

46. As a rule the sequence of intentions is to be:

a. for the needs of the Church;

b. for public authorities and the salvation of the world;

c. for those oppressed by any need;

d. for the local community.

In particular celebrations, such as confirmations, marriages, funerals, etc., the series of intercessions may refer more specifically to the occasion.

47. It belongs to the priest celebrant to direct the general intercessions, by means of a brief introduction to invite the congregation to pray, and after the intercessions to say the concluding prayer. It is desirable that a deacon, cantor, or other person announce the intentions.[39] The whole assembly gives expression to its supplication either by a response said together after each intention or by silent prayer.

C. Liturgy of the Eucharist

48. At the last supper Christ instituted the sacrifice and paschal meal that make the sacrifice of the cross to be continuously present in the Church, when the priest, representing Christ the Lord, carries out what the Lord did and handed over to his disciples to do in his memory.[40]

Christ took the bread and the cup and gave thanks; he broke the bread and gave it to his disciples, saying: "Take and eat, this is my body." Giving the cup, he said: "Take and drink, this is the cup of my blood. Do this in memory of me." Accordingly, the Church has planned the celebra-

35. See SC, art. 52.
36. See IOe, no. 54.

37. See IOe, no. 56.
38. See SC, art. 53.

39. See IOe, no. 56.
40. See SC, art. 47; EM, no. 3a, b.

tion of the eucharistic liturgy around the parts corresponding to these words and actions of Christ:

1. In the preparation of the gifts, the bread and the wine with water are brought to the altar, that is, the same elements that Christ used.

2. In the eucharistic prayer thanks is given to God for the whole work of salvation and the gifts of bread and wine become the body and blood of Christ.

3. Through the breaking of the one bread the unity of the faithful is expressed and through communion they receive the Lord's body and blood in the same way the apostles received them from Christ's own hands.

PREPARATION OF THE GIFTS

49. At the beginning of the liturgy of the eucharist the gifts, which will become Christ's body and blood, are brought to the altar.

First the altar, the Lord's table, which is the center of the whole eucharistic liturgy,[41] is prepared: the corporal, purificator, missal, and chalice are placed on it (unless the chalice is prepared at a side table).

The gifts are then brought forward. It is desirable for the faithful to present the bread and wine, which are accepted by the priest or deacon at a convenient place. The gifts are placed on the altar to the accompaniment of the prescribed texts. Even though the faithful no longer, as in the past, bring the bread and wine for the liturgy from their homes, the rite of carrying up the gifts retains the same spiritual value and meaning.

This is also the time to receive money or other gifts for the church or the poor brought by the faithful or collected at the Mass. These are to be put in a suitable place but not on the altar.

50. The procession bringing the gifts is accompanied by the presentation song, which continues at least until the gifts have been placed on the altar. The rules for this song are the same as those for the entrance song (no. 26). If it is not sung, the presentation antiphon is omitted.

51. The gifts on the altar and the altar itself may be incensed. This is a symbol of the Church's offering and prayer going up to God. Afterward the deacon or other minister may incense the priest and the people.

52. The priest then washes his hands as an expression of his desire to be cleansed within.

53. Once the gifts have been placed on the altar and the accompanying rites completed, the preparation of the gifts comes to an end through the invitation to pray with the priest and the prayer over the gifts, which are a preparation for the eucharistic prayer.

EUCHARISTIC PRAYER

54. Now the center and summit of the entire celebration begins: the eucharistic prayer, a prayer of thanksgiving and sanctification. The priest invites the people to lift up their hearts to the Lord in prayer and thanks; he unites them with himself in the prayer he addresses in their name to the Father through Jesus Christ. The meaning of the prayer is that the entire congregation joins itself to Christ in acknowledging the great things God has done and in offering the sacrifice.

55. The chief elements making up the eucharistic prayer are these:

a. Thanksgiving (expressed especially in the preface): in the name of the entire people of God, the priest praises the Father and gives thanks to him for the whole work of salvation or for some special aspect of it that corresponds to the day, feast, or season.

b. Acclamation: joining with the angels, the congregation sings or recites the *Sanctus.* This acclamation is an intrinsic part of the eucharistic prayer and all the people join with the priest in singing or reciting it.

c. Epiclesis: in special invocations the Church calls on God's power and asks that the gifts offered by human hands be consecrated, that is, become Christ's body and blood, and that the victim to be received in communion be the source of salvation for those who will partake.

d. Institution narrative and consecration: in the words and actions of Christ, that sacrifice is celebrated which he himself instituted at the Last Supper, when, under the appearances of bread and wine, he offered his body and blood, gave them to his apostles to eat and drink, then commanded that they carry on this mystery.

e. Anamnesis: in fulfillment of the command received from Christ through the apostles, the Church keeps his memorial by recalling especially his passion, resurrection, and ascension.

f. Offering: in this memorial, the Church—and in particular the Church here and now assembled—offers the spotless victim to the Father in the Holy Spirit. The Church's intention is that the faithful not only offer this victim but also learn to offer themselves and so to surrender themselves, through Christ the Mediator, to an ever more complete union with the Father and with each other, so that at last God may be all in all.[42]

g. Intercessions: the intercessions make it clear that the eucharist is celebrated in communion with the entire Church of heaven and earth and that the offering is made for the Church and all its members, living and dead, who are called to share in the salvation and redemption purchased by Christ's body and blood.

h. Final doxology: the praise of God is expressed in the doxology, to which the people's acclamation is an assent and a conclusion.

The eucharistic prayer calls for all to listen in silent reverence, but also to take part through the acclamations for which the rite makes provision.

COMMUNION RITE

56. Since the eucharistic celebration is the paschal meal, it is right that the faithful who are properly disposed receive the Lord's body and blood as spiritual food as he commanded.[43] This is the purpose of the breaking of bread and the other preparatory rites that lead directly to the communion of the people:

a. Lord's Prayer: this is a petition both for daily food, which for Christians means also the eucharistic bread, and for the forgiveness of sin, so that what is holy may be given to those who are holy. The priest offers the invitation to pray, but all the faithful say the prayer with him; he alone adds the embolism, Deliver us, which the people conclude with a doxology. The embolism, developing the last peti-

---

41. See IOe, no. 91.

42. See SC, art. 48; PO, no. 5; EM, no. 12.
43. See EM, nos. 12, 33a.

tion of the Lord's Prayer, begs on behalf of the entire community of the faithful deliverance from the power of evil. The invitation, the prayer itself, the embolism, and the people's doxology are sung or are recited aloud.

b. Rite of peace: before they share in the same bread, the faithful implore peace and unity for the Church and for the whole human family and offer some sign of their love for one another.

The form the sign of peace should take is left to the conference of bishops to determine, in accord with the culture and customs of the people.

c. Breaking of the bread: in apostolic times this gesture of Christ at the last supper gave the entire eucharistic action its name. This rite is not simply functional, but is a sign that in sharing in the one bread of life which is Christ we who are many are made one body (see 1 Cor 10:17).

d. Commingling: the celebrant drops a part of the host into the chalice.

e. *Agnus Dei:* during the breaking of the bread and the commingling, the *Agnus Dei* is as a rule sung by the choir or cantor with the congregation responding; otherwise it is recited aloud. This invocation may be repeated as often as necessary to accompany the breaking of the bread. The final reprise concludes with the words, grant us peace.

f. Personal preparation of the priest: the priest prepares himself by the prayer, said softly, that he may receive Christ's body and blood to good effect. The faithful do the same by silent prayer.

g. The priest then shows the eucharistic bread for communion to the faithful and with them recites the prayer of humility in words from the Gospels.

h. It is most desirable that the faithful receive the Lord's body from hosts consecrated at the same Mass and that, in the instances when it is permitted, they share in the chalice. Then even through the signs communion will stand out more clearly as a sharing in the sacrifice actually being celebrated.[44]

i. During the priest's and the faithful's reception of the sacrament the communion song is sung. Its function is to express outwardly the communicants' union in spirit by means of the unity of their voices, to give evidence of joy of heart, and to make the procession to receive Christ's body more fully an act of community. The song begins when the priest takes communion and continues for as long as seems appropriate while the faithful receive Christ's body. But the communion song should be ended in good time whenever there is to be a hymn after communion.

An antiphon from the *Graduale Romanum* may also be used, with or without the psalm, or an antiphon with psalm from the Simple Gradual or another suitable song approved by the conference of bishops. It is sung by the choir alone or by the choir or cantor with the congregation.

If there is no singing, the communion antiphon in the Missal is recited either by the people, by some of them, or by a reader. Otherwise the priest himself says it after he has received communion and before he gives communion to the faithful.

j. After communion, the priest and people may spend some time in silent prayer. If desired, a hymn, psalm, or other song of praise may be sung by the entire congregation.

k. In the prayer after communion, the priest petitions for the effects of the mystery just celebrated and by their acclamation, Amen, the people make the prayer their own.

D. Concluding Rite

57. The concluding rite consists of:

a. the priest's greeting and blessing, which on certain days and occasions is expanded and expressed in the prayer over the people or another more solemn formulary;

b. the dismissal of the assembly, which sends each member back to doing good works, while praising and blessing the Lord.

CHAPTER III

OFFICES AND MINISTRIES IN THE MASS

58. All in the assembly gathered for Mass have an individual right and duty to contribute their participation in ways differing according to the diversity of their order and liturgical function.[45] Thus in carrying out this function, all, whether ministers or laypersons, should do all and only those parts that belong to them,[46] so that the very arrangement of the celebration itself makes the Church stand out as being formed in a structure of different orders and ministries.

I. OFFICES AND MINISTRIES OF HOLY ORDERS

59. Every authentic celebration of the eucharist is directed by the bishop, either in person or through the presbyters, who are his helpers.[47]

Whenever he is present at a Mass with a congregation, it is fitting that the bishop himself preside over the assembly and associate the presbyters with himself in the celebration, if possible by concelebrating with them.

This is done not to add external solemnity, but to express in a clearer light the mystery of the Church, which is the sacrament of unity.[48]

Even if the bishop is not the celebrant of the eucharist but assigns someone else, he should preside over the liturgy of the word and give the blessing at the end of Mass.

60. Within the community of believers, the presbyter is another who possesses the power of orders to offer sacrifice in the person of Christ.[49] He therefore presides over the assembly and leads its prayer, proclaims the message of salvation, joins the people to himself in offering the sacrifice to the Father through Christ in the Spirit, gives them the bread of eternal life, and shares in it with them. At the eucharist he should, then, serve God and the people with dignity and humility; by his bearing and by the way he recites the words of the liturgy he should communicate to the faithful a sense of the living presence of Christ.

61. Among ministers, the deacon, whose order has been held in high honor since the early Church, has first place. At Mass he has his own functions: he proclaims the gospel, sometimes preaches God's word, leads the general intercessions, assists the priest, gives communion to the people (in

---

44. See EM, nos. 31, 32, on communion twice a day; see also *Codex Iuris Canonici* [= CIC], can. 917.

45. See SC, art. 14, 26.
46. See SC, art. 28.
47. See LG, nos. 26, 28; SC, art. 42.

48. See SC, art. 26.
49. See PO, no. 2; LG, no. 28.

particular, ministering the chalice), and sometimes gives directions regarding the assembly's moving, standing, kneeling, or sitting.

II. OFFICE AND FUNCTION OF THE PEOPLE OF GOD

62. In the celebration of Mass the faithful are a holy people, a people God has made his own, a royal priesthood: they give thanks to the Father and offer the victim not only through the hands of the priest but also together with him and learn to offer themselves.[50] They should endeavor to make this clear by their deep sense of reverence for God and their charity toward all who share with them in the celebration.

They therefore are to shun any appearance of individualism or division, keeping before their mind that they have the one Father in heaven and therefore are all brothers and sisters to each other.

They should become one body, whether by hearing the word of God, or joining in prayers and song, or above all by offering the sacrifice together and sharing together in the Lord's table. There is a beautiful expression of this unity when the faithful maintain uniformity in their actions and in standing, sitting, or kneeling.

The faithful should serve the people of God willingly when asked to perform some particular ministry in the celebration.

63. The *schola cantorum* or choir exercises its own liturgical function within the assembly. Its task is to ensure that the parts proper to it, in keeping with the different types of chants, are carried out becomingly and to encourage active participation of the people in the singing.[51] What is said about the choir applies in a similar way to other musicians, especially the organist.

64. There should be a cantor or a choir director to lead and sustain the people in the singing. When in fact there is no choir, it is up to the cantor to lead the various songs, and the people take part in the way proper to them.[52]

III. SPECIAL MINISTRIES

65. The acolyte is instituted to serve at the altar and to assist the priest and deacon. In particular it is for him to prepare the altar and the vessels and, as a special minister of the eucharist, to give communion to the faithful.

66. The reader is instituted to proclaim the readings from Scripture, with the exception of the gospel. He may also announce the intentions for the general intercessions and, in the absence of the psalmist, sing or read the psalm between the readings.

The reader has his own proper function in the eucharistic celebration and should exercise this even though ministers of a higher rank may be present.

Those who exercise the ministry of reader, even if they have not received institution, must be truly qualified and carefully prepared in order that the faithful will develop a warm and lively love for Scripture[53] from listening to the reading of the sacred texts.

67. The cantor of the psalm is to sing the psalm or other biblical song that comes between the readings. To fulfill their function correctly, these cantors should possess singing talent and an aptitude for correct pronunciation and diction.

68. As for other ministers, some perform different functions inside the sanctuary, others outside.

The first kind include those deputed as special ministers of communion[54] and those who carry the missal, the cross, candles, the bread, wine, water, and the thurible.

The second kind include:

a. The commentator. This minister provides explanations and commentaries with the purpose of introducing the faithful to the celebration and preparing them to understand it better. The commentator's remarks must be meticulously prepared and marked by a simple brevity.

In performing this function the commentator stands in a convenient place visible to the faithful, but it is preferable that this not be at the lectern where the Scriptures are read.

b. Those who, in some places, meet the people at the church entrance, seat them, and direct processions.

c. Those who take up the collection.

69. Especially in larger churches and communities, a person should be assigned responsibility for planning the services properly and for their being carried out by the ministers with decorum, order, and devotion.

70. Laymen, even if they have not received institution as ministers, may perform all the functions below those reserved to deacons. At the discretion of the rector of the church, women may be appointed to ministries that are performed outside the sanctuary.

The conference of bishops may permit qualified women to proclaim the readings before the gospel and to announce the intentions of the general intercessions. The conference may also more precisely designate a suitable place for a woman to proclaim the word of God in the liturgical assembly.[55]

71. If there are several persons present who are empowered to exercise the same ministry, there is no objection to their being assigned different parts to perform. For example, one deacon may take the sung parts, another assist at the altar; if there are several readings, it is better to distribute them among a number of readers. The same applies for the other ministries.

72. If only one minister is present at a Mass with a congregation, he may carry out several different functions.

73. All concerned should work together in the effective preparation of each liturgical celebration as to its rites, pastoral aspects, and music. They should work under the direction of the rector of the church and should consult the faithful.

---

50. See SC, art. 48; EM, no. 12.
51. See MS, no. 19.
52. See MS, no. 21.

53. See SC, art. 24.
54. See Congregation for the Discipline of the Sacraments, instruction *Immensae caritatis*, 29 January 1973, no. 1.
55. See Congregation for Divine Worship, instruction *Liturgicae instaurationes*, 5 September 1970, no. 7.

CHAPTER IV

THE DIFFERENT FORMS OF CELEBRATION

74. In the local Church, first place should be given, because of its meaning, to the Mass at which the bishop presides surrounded by the college of presbyters and the ministers[56] and in which the people take full and active part. For this Mass is the preeminent expression of the Church.

75. Great importance should be attached to a Mass celebrated by any community, but especially by the parish community, inasmuch as it represents the universal Church gathered at a given time and place. This is particularly true of the community's celebration of the Lord's Day.[57]

76. Of those Masses celebrated by some communities, the conventual Mass, which is a part of the daily office, or the "community" Mass have particular significance. Although such Masses do not have a special form of celebration, it is most proper that they be celebrated with singing, with the full participation of all community members, whether religious or canons. In these Masses, therefore, individuals should exercise the function proper to the order or ministry they have received. All the priests who are not bound to celebrate individually for the pastoral benefit of the faithful should thus concelebrate at the conventual or community Mass, if possible. Further, all priests belonging to the community who are obliged to celebrate individually for the pastoral benefit of the faithful may also on the same day concelebrate at the conventual or community Mass.[58]

I. MASS WITH A CONGREGATION

77. Mass with a congregation means a Mass celebrated with the people taking part. As far as possible, and especially on Sundays and holydays of obligation, this Mass should be celebrated with song and with a suitable number of ministers.[59] But it may be celebrated without music and with only one minister.

78. It is desirable that as a rule an acolyte, a reader, and a cantor assist the priest celebrant; this form of celebration will hereafter be referred to as the "basic" or "typical" form. But the rite to be described also allows for a greater number of ministers.

A deacon may exercise his office in any of the forms of celebration.

ARTICLES TO BE PREPARED

79. The altar is to be covered with at least one cloth. On or near the altar there are to be candlesticks with lighted candles, at least two but even four, six, or, if the bishop of the diocese celebrates, seven. There is also to be a cross on or near the altar. The candles and cross may be carried in the entrance procession. The Book of the Gospels, if distinct from the book of other readings, may be placed on the altar, unless it is carried in the entrance procession.

80. The following are also to be prepared:

a. next to the priest's chair: the Missal and, as may be useful, a book with the chants;

b. at the lectern: the lectionary

c. on a side table: the chalice, corporal, purificator, and, if useful, a pall; a paten and ciboria, if needed, with the bread for the communion of the ministers and the people, together with cruets containing wine and water, unless all of these are brought in by the faithful at the presentation of the gifts; a communion plate for the communion of the faithful; the requisites for the washing of hands. The chalice should be covered with a veil, which may always be white.

81. In the sacristy the vestments for the priest and ministers are to be prepared according to the various forms of celebration:

a. for the priest: alb, stole, and chasuble;

b. for the deacon: alb, stole, and dalmatic; the last may be omitted either out of necessity or for less solemnity;

c. for the other ministers: albs or other lawfully approved vestments.

All who wear an alb should use a cincture and an amice, unless other provision is made.

A. Basic Form of Celebration

INTRODUCTORY RITES

82. Once the congregation has gathered, the priest and the ministers, clad in their vestments, go to the altar in this order:

a. a server with a lighted censer, if incense is used;

b. the servers, who, according to the occasion, carry lighted candles, and between them the crossbearer, if the cross is to be carried;

c. acolytes and other ministers;

d. a reader, who may carry the Book of the Gospels;

e. the priest who is to celebrate the Mass.

If incense is used, the priest puts some in the censer before the procession begins.

83. During the procession to the altar the entrance song is sung (see nos. 25–26).

84. On reaching the altar the priest and ministers make the proper reverence, that is, a low bow or, if there is a tabernacle containing the blessed sacrament, a genuflection.

If the cross has been carried in the procession, it is placed near the altar or at some other convenient place; the candles carried by the servers are placed near the altar or on a side table; the Book of the Gospels is placed on the altar.

85. The priest goes up to the altar and kisses it. If incense is used, he incenses the altar while circling it.

86. The priest then goes to the chair. After the entrance song, and with all standing, the priest and the faithful make the sign of the cross. The priest says: In the name of the Father, and of the Son, and of the Holy Spirit; the people answer: Amen.

Then, facing the people and with hands outstretched, the priest greets all present, using one of the formularies indicated. He or some other qualified minister may give the faithful a very brief introduction to the Mass of the day.

87. After the penitential rite, the Kyrie and Gloria are said, in keeping with the rubrics (nos. 30–31). Either the priest or the cantors or even everyone together may begin the Gloria.

---

56. See SC, art. 41.

57. See SC, art. 42; EM, no. 26; LG, no. 28; PO, no. 5.

58. See EM, no. 47; Congregation for Divine Worship, Declaration on concelebration, 7 August 1972.

59. See EM, no. 26; MS, nos. 16, 27.

88. With his hands joined, the priest then invites the people to pray, saying: Let us pray. All pray silently with the priest for a while. Then the priest with hands outstretched says the opening prayer, at the end of which the people respond: Amen.

LITURGY OF THE WORD

89. After the opening prayer, the reader goes to the lectern for the first reading. All sit and listen and make the acclamation at the end.

90. After the reading, the psalmist or cantor of the psalm, or even the reader, sings or recites the psalm and the congregation sings or recites the response (see no. 36).

91. Then, if there is a second reading before the gospel, the reader reads it at the lectern as before. All sit and listen and make the acclamation at the end.

92. The *Alleluia* or other chant, according to the season, follows (see nos. 37–39).

93. During the singing of the *Alleluia* or other chant, if incense is being used, the priest puts some into the censer. Then with hands joined he bows before the altar and inaudibly says the prayer, Almighty God, cleanse my heart.

94. If the Book of the Gospels is on the altar, he takes it and goes to the lectern, the servers, who may carry the censer and candles, walking ahead of him.

95. At the lectern the priest opens the book and says: The Lord be with you. Then he says: A reading from . . ., making the sign of the cross with his thumb on the book and on his forehead, mouth, and breast. If incense is used, he then incenses the book. After the acclamation of the people, he proclaims the gospel and at the end kisses the book, saying inaudibly May the words of the gospel wipe away our sins. After the reading the people make the acclamation customary to the region.

96. If no reader is present, the priest himself proclaims all the readings at the lectern and there also, if necessary, the chants between the readings. If incense is used, he puts some into the censer at the lectern and then, bowing, says the prayer, Almighty God, cleanse my heart.

97. The homily is given at the chair or at the lectern.

98. The profession of faith is said by the priest together with the people (see no. 44). At the words, by the power of the Holy Spirit, etc., all bow; on the solemnities of the Annunciation and Christmas all kneel.

99. Next, with the people taking their proper part, follow the general intercessions (prayer of the faithful), which the priest directs from his chair or at the lectern (see nos. 45–47).

LITURGY OF THE EUCHARIST

100. After the general intercessions, the presentation song begins (see no. 50). The servers place the corporal, purificator, chalice, and missal on the altar.

101. It is fitting for the faithful's participation to be expressed by their presenting both the bread and wine for the celebration of the eucharist and other gifts to meet the needs of the church and of the poor.

The faithful's offerings are received by the priest, assisted by the ministers, and put in a suitable place; the bread and wine for the eucharist are taken to the altar.

102. At the altar the priest receives the paten with the bread from a minister. With both hands he holds it slightly raised above the altar and says the accompanying prayer. Then he places the paten with the bread on the corporal.

103. Next, as a minister presents the cruets, the priest stands at the side of the altar and pours wine and a little water into the chalice, saying the accompanying prayer softly. He returns to the middle of the altar, takes the chalice, raises it a little with both hands, and says the appointed prayer. Then he places the chalice on the corporal and may cover it with a pall.

104. The priest bows and inaudibly says the prayer, Lord God, we ask you to receive.

105. If incense is used, he incenses the gifts and the altar. A minister incenses the priest and the congregation.

106. After the prayer, Lord God, we ask you to receive, or after the incensation, the priest washes his hands at the side of the altar and inaudibly says the prescribed prayer as a minister pours the water.

107. The priest returns to the center and, facing the people and extending then joining his hands, pronounces the invitation: Pray, brothers and sisters. After the people's response, he says the prayer over the gifts with hands outstretched. At the end the people make the acclamation: Amen.

108. The priest then begins the eucharistic prayer. With hands outstretched, he says: The Lord be with you. As he says: Lift up your hearts, he raises his hands; with hands outstretched, he adds: Let us give thanks to the Lord our God. When the people have answered: It is right to give him thanks and praise, the priest continues the preface. At its conclusion, he joins his hands and sings or says aloud with the ministers and people the *Sanctus-Benedictus* (see no. 55 b).

109. The priest continues the eucharistic prayer according to the rubrics that are given for each of them. If the priest celebrant is a bishop, after the words N. our Pope or the equivalent, he adds: and for me your unworthy servant. The local Ordinary must be mentioned in this way: N. our Bishop or Vicar, Prelate, Prefect, Abbot). Coadjutor and auxiliary bishops may be mentioned in the eucharistic prayer. When several are named, this is done with the collective formula, N. our Bishop and his assistant bishops.[60] All these phrases should be modified grammatically to fit with each one of the eucharistic prayers.

A little before the consecration, the server may ring a bell as a signal to the faithful. Depending on local custom, he also rings the bell at the showing of both the host and the chalice.

110. After the doxology at the end of the eucharistic prayer, the priest, with hands joined, says the introduction to the Lord's Prayer. With hands outstretched he then sings or says this prayer with the people.

111. After the Lord's Prayer, the priest alone, with hands outstretched, says the embolism, Deliver us. At the end the congregation makes the acclamation, For the kingdom.

112. Then the priest says aloud the prayer, Lord Jesus Christ. After this prayer, extending then joining his hands, he gives the greeting of peace: The peace of the Lord be with you always. The people answer: And also with you. Then the priest may add: Let us offer each other the sign of peace. All exchange some sign of peace and love, according to local custom. The priest may give the sign of peace to the ministers.

---

60. See Congregation for Divine Worship, decree *Cum de nomine*, 9 October 1972: *AAS* 64 (1972) 692–694.

113. The priest then takes the eucharistic bread and breaks it over the paten. He places a small piece in the chalice, saying inaudibly: May this mingling. Meanwhile the *Agnus Dei* is sung or recited by the choir and congregation (see no. 56 e).

114. Then the priest inaudibly says the prayer, Lord Jesus Christ, Son of the living God, or Lord Jesus Christ, with faith in your love and mercy.

115. After the prayer the priest genuflects, takes the eucharistic bread, and, holding it slightly above the paten while facing the people, says: This is the Lamb of God. With the people he adds, once only: Lord, I am not worthy to receive you.

116. Next, facing the altar, the priest says inaudibly: May the body of Christ bring me to everlasting life and reverently consumes the body of Christ. Then he takes the chalice, saying: May the blood of Christ bring me to everlasting life, and reverently drinks the blood of Christ.

117. He then takes the paten or a ciborium and goes to the communicants. If communion is given only under the form of bread, he raises the eucharistic bread slightly and shows it to each one, saying: The body of Christ. The communicants reply: Amen and, holding the communion plate under their chin, receive the sacrament.

118. For communion under both kinds, the rite described in nos. 240–252 is followed.

119. The communion song is begun while the priest is receiving the sacrament (see no. 56 i).

120. After communion the priest returns to the altar and collects any remaining particles. Then, standing at the side of the altar or at a side table, he purifies the paten or ciborium over the chalice, then purifies the chalice, saying inaudibly: Lord, may I receive these gifts, etc., and dries it with a purificator. If this is done at the altar, the vessels are taken to a side table by a minister. It is also permitted, especially if there are several vessels to be purified, to leave them, properly covered and on a corporal, either at the altar or at a side table and to purify them after Mass when the people have left.

121. Afterward the priest may return to the chair. A period of silence may now be observed, or a hymn of praise or a psalm may be sung (see no. 56 j).

122. Then, standing at the altar or at the chair and facing the people, the priest says, with hands outstretched: Let us pray. There may be a brief period of silence, unless this has been already observed immediately after communion. He recites the prayer after communion, at the end of which the people make the response: Amen.

123. If there are any brief announcements, they may be made at this time.

124. Then the priest, with hands outstretched, greets the people: The Lord be with you. They answer: And also with you. The priest immediately adds: May almighty God bless you and, as he blesses with the sign of the cross, continues: the Father, and the Son, and the Holy Spirit. All answer: Amen. On certain days and occasions another, more solemn form of blessing or the prayer over the people precedes this form of blessing as the rubrics direct.

Immediately after the blessing, with hands joined, the priest adds: Go in the peace of Christ, or: Go in peace to love and serve the Lord, or: The Mass is ended, go in peace, and the people answer: Thanks be to God.

125. As a rule, the priest then kisses the altar, makes the proper reverence with the ministers, and leaves.

126. If another liturgical service follows the Mass, the concluding rites (greeting, blessing, and dismissal) are omitted.

B. Functions of the Deacon

127. When there is a deacon present to exercise his ministry, the norms in the preceding section apply, with the following exceptions.

In general the deacon: a. assists the priest and walks at his side; b. at the altar, assists with the chalice or the book; c. if there is no other minister present, carries out other ministerial functions as required.

INTRODUCTORY RITES

128. Vested and carrying the Book of the Gospels, the deacon precedes the priest on the way to the altar or else walks at the priest's side.

129. With the priest he makes the proper reverence and goes up to the altar. After placing the Book of the Gospels on it, along with the priest he kisses the altar. If incense is used, he assists the priest in putting some in the censer and in incensing the altar.

130. After the incensing, he goes to the chair with the priest, sits next to him, and assists him as required.

LITURGY OF THE WORD

131. If incense is used, the deacon assists the priest when he puts incense in the censer during the singing of the *Alleluia* or other chant. Then he bows before the priest and asks for the blessing, saying in a low voice: Father, give me your blessing. The priest blesses him: The Lord be in your heart. The deacon answers: Amen. If the Book of the Gospels is on the altar, he takes it and goes to the lectern; the servers, if there are any, precede, carrying candles and the censer when used. At the lectern the deacon greets the people, incenses the book, and proclaims the gospel. After the reading, he kisses the book, saying inaudibly: May the words of the gospel wipe away our sins, and returns to the priest. If there is no homily or profession of faith, he may remain at the lectern for the general intercessions, but the servers leave.

132. After the priest introduces the general intercessions, the deacon announces the intentions at the lectern or other suitable place.

LITURGY OF THE EUCHARIST

133. At the presentation of the gifts, while the priest remains at the chair, the deacon prepares the altar, assisted by other ministers, but the care of the sacred vessels belongs to the deacon. He assists the priest in receiving the people's gifts. Next, he hands the priest the paten with the bread to be consecrated, pours wine and a little water into the chalice, saying inaudibly the prayer, Through the mystery of this water and wine, then passes the chalice to the priest. (He may also prepare the chalice and pour the wine and water at a side table.) If incense is used, the deacon assists the priest with the incensing of the gifts and the altar; afterward he, or another minister, incenses the priest and the people.

134. During the eucharistic prayer, the deacon stands near but slightly behind the priest, so that when necessary

he may assist the priest with the chalice or the missal.

135. At the final doxology of the eucharistic prayer, the deacon stands next to the priest, holding up the chalice as the priest raises the paten with the eucharistic bread, until the people have said the acclamation: Amen.

136. After the priest has said the prayer for peace and the greeting: The peace of the Lord be with you always, and the people have made the response: And also with you, the deacon may invite all to exchange the sign of peace, saying: Let us offer each other the sign of peace. He himself receives the sign of peace from the priest and may offer it to other ministers near him.

137. After the priest's communion, the deacon receives under both kinds and then assists the priest in giving communion to the people. But if communion is given under both kinds, the deacon ministers the chalice to the communicants and is the last to drink from it.

138. After communion, the deacon returns to the altar with the priest and collects any remaining fragments. He then takes the chalice and other vessels to the side table, where he purifies them and arranges them in the usual way; the priest returns to the chair. But it is permissible to leave the vessels to be purified, properly covered and on a corporal, at a side table and to purify them after Mass, when the people have left.

CONCLUDING RITE

139. Following the prayer after communion, if there are any brief announcements, the deacon may make them, unless the priest prefers to do so himself.

140. After the priest's blessing, the deacon dismisses the people, saying: Go in the peace of Christ, or: Go in peace to love and serve the Lord, or: The Mass is ended, go in peace.

141. Along with the priest, the deacon kisses the altar, makes the proper reverence, and leaves in the manner followed for the entrance procession.

C. Functions of the Acolyte

142. The acolyte may have functions of various kinds and several may occur at the same time. It is therefore desirable that these functions be suitably distributed among several acolytes. But if there is only a single acolyte present, he should perform the more important functions and the rest are distributed among other ministers.

INTRODUCTORY RITES

143. In the procession to the altar the acolyte may carry the cross, walking between two servers with lighted candles. When he reaches the altar, he places the cross near it and takes his own place in the sanctuary.

144. Throughout the celebration it belongs to the acolyte to go to the priest or the deacon, whenever necessary, in order to present the book to them and to assist them in any other way required. Thus it is appropriate that, if possible, he have a place from which he can conveniently carry out his ministry both at the chair and at the altar.

LITURGY OF THE EUCHARIST

145. After the general intercessions, when no deacon is present, the acolyte places the corporal, purificator, chalice,

and missal on the altar, while the priest remains at the chair. Then, if necessary, the acolyte assists the priest in receiving the gifts of the people and he may bring the bread and wine to the altar and present them to the priest. If incense is used, the acolyte gives the censer to the priest and assists him in incensing the gifts and the altar.

146. The acolyte may assist the priest as a special minister in giving communion to the people.[61] If communion is given under both kinds, the acolyte ministers the chalice to the communicants or he holds the chalice when communion is given by intinction.

147. After communion, the acolyte helps the priest or deacon to purify and arrange the vessels. If no deacon is present, the acolyte takes the vessels to the side table, where he purifies and arranges them.

D. Functions of the Reader

INTRODUCTORY RITES

148. In the procession to the altar, when no deacon is present, the reader may carry the Book of the Gospels. In that case he walks in front of the priest; otherwise he walks with the other ministers.

149. Upon reaching the altar, the reader makes the proper reverence along with the priest, goes up to the altar, and places the Book of the Gospels on it. Then he takes his place in the sanctuary with the other ministers.

LITURGY OF THE WORD

150. At the lectern the reader proclaims the readings that precede the gospel. If there is no cantor of the psalm, he may also sing or recite the responsorial psalm after the first reading.

151. After the priest gives the introduction to the general intercessions, the reader may announce the intentions when no deacon is present.

152. If there is no entrance song or communion song and the antiphons in the Missal are not said by the faithful, the reader recites them at the proper time.

II. CONCELEBRATED MASSES

INTRODUCTION

153. Concelebration effectively brings out the unity of the priesthood, of the sacrifice, and of the whole people of God. The rite itself prescribes concelebration at the ordination of bishops and of priests and at the chrism Mass.

Unless the good of the faithful requires or suggests otherwise, concelebration is also recommended at:

a. the evening Mass on Holy Thursday;
b. the Mass for councils, meetings of bishops, and synods;
c. the Mass for the blessing of an abbot;
d. the conventual Mass and the principal Mass in churches and oratories;
e. the Mass for any kind of meeting of priests, either secular or religious.[62]

154. Where there is a large number of priests, the authorized superior may permit concelebration several times on the same day, but either at different times or in different places.[63]

61. See Paul VI, motu proprio Ministeria quaedam, 15 August 1972, no. VI: AAS 64 (1972) 532.
62. See SC, art. 57; CIC, can. 902.   63. See EM, no. 47.

155. The right to regulate, in accord with the law, the discipline for concelebration in his diocese, even in churches and oratories of exempt religious, belongs to the bishop.[64]

156. No one is ever to be admitted into a concelebration once Mass has already begun.[65]

157. A concelebration in which the priests of any diocese concelebrate with their own bishop, especially at the chrism Mass on Holy Thursday and on the occasion of a synod or pastoral visitation, is to be held in high regard. Concelebration is likewise recommended whenever priests gather together with their bishop during a retreat or at any other meeting. That sign of the unity of the priesthood and of the Church itself which marks every concelebration stands out even more clearly in the instances mentioned.[66]

158. For a particular reason, having to do either with the meaning of the rite or of the liturgical feast, to celebrate or concelebrate more than once on the same day is permitted as follows:

a. One who has celebrated or concelebrated the chrism Mass on Holy Thursday may also celebrate or concelebrate the evening Mass.

b. One who has celebrated or concelebrated the Mass of the Easter Vigil may celebrate or concelebrate the second Mass of Easter.

c. All priests may celebrate or concelebrate the three Masses of Christmas, provided the Masses are at their proper times of day.

d. One who concelebrates with the bishop or his delegate at a synod or pastoral visitation, or concelebrates on the occasion of a meeting of priests, may celebrate another Mass for the benefit of the people.[67] This holds also, in analogous circumstances, for gatherings of religious.

159. The structure of a concelebrated Mass, whatever its form, follows the norms for an individual celebration, except for the points prescribed or changed in the next section.

160. If neither a deacon nor other ministers assist in a concelebrated Mass, their functions are carried out by the concelebrants.

INTRODUCTORY RITES

161. In the sacristy or other suitable place, the concelebrants put on the vestments usual for individual celebrants. For a good reason, however, as when there are more concelebrants than vestments, the concelebrants may omit the chasuble and simply wear the stole over the alb; but the principal celebrant always wears the chasuble.

162. When everything is ready, there is the usual procession through the church to the altar. The concelebrating priests go ahead of the principal celebrant.

163. On reaching the altar, the concelebrants and the celebrant make the prescribed reverence, kiss the altar, then go to their chairs. When incense is used, the principal celebrant incenses the altar, then goes to the chair.

---

64. See *Rite of Concelebration*, Introduction, no. 3.

65. *Ibid.*, no. 8.

66. See Congregation of Rites, decree *Ecclesiae semper*, 7 March 1965: *AAS* 57 (1965) 410–412; EM, no. 47.

67. See *Rite of Concelebration*, Introduction, no. 9; Congregation for Divine Worship, Declaration on concelebration, 7 August 1972.

LITURGY OF THE WORD

164. During the liturgy of the word, the concelebrants remain at their places, sitting or standing as the principal celebrant does.

165. As a rule the principal celebrant or one of the concelebrants gives the homily.

LITURGY OF THE EUCHARIST

166. The rites for the preparation of the gifts are carried out by the principal celebrant; the other concelebrants remain at their places.

167. At the end of the preparation of the gifts, the concelebrants come near the altar and stand around it in such a way that they do not interfere with the actions of the rite and that the people have a clear view. They should not be in the deacon's way when he has to go to the altar in the performance of his ministry.

Manner of Reciting the Eucharistic Prayer

168. The preface is said by the principal celebrant alone; the *Sanctus* is sung or recited by all the concelebrants with the congregation and the choir.

169. After the *Sanctus*, the concelebrants continue the eucharistic prayer in the way to be described. Unless otherwise indicated, only the principal celebrant makes the gestures.

170. The parts said by all the concelebrants together are to be recited in such a way that the concelebrants say them in a softer voice and the principal celebrant's voice stands out clearly. In this way the congregation should be able to hear the text without difficulty.

A. Eucharistic Prayer I, the Roman Canon

171. The prayer, We come to you, Father, is said by the principal celebrant alone, with hands outstretched.

172. The intercessions, Remember, Lord, your people and In union with the whole Church, may be assigned to one of the concelebrants; he alone says these prayers, with hands outstretched and aloud.

173. The prayer, Father, accept this offering, is said by the principal celebrant alone, with hands outstretched.

174. From Bless and approve our offering to Almighty God, we pray inclusive, all the concelebrants recite everything together in this manner:

a. They say Bless and approve our offering with hands outstretched toward the offerings.

b. They say The day before he suffered and When supper was ended with hands joined.

c. While saying the words of the Lord, each extends his right hand toward the bread and toward the chalice, if this seems appropriate; they look at the eucharistic bread and chalice as these are shown and afterward bow low.

d. They say Father, we celebrate the memory of Christ and Look with favor with hands outstretched.

e. From Almighty God, we pray to the sacred body and blood of your Son inclusive, they bow with hands joined; then they stand upright and cross themselves at the words, let us be filled.

175. The intercessions, Remember, Lord, those who have died and For ourselves, too, may be assigned to one of the

concelebrants; he alone says these prayers, with hands outstretched and aloud.

176. At the words, Though we are sinners, all the concelebrants strike their breast.

177. The prayer, Through Christ our Lord you give us all these gifts, is said by the principal celebrant alone.

178. In this eucharistic prayer the parts from Bless and approve our offering to Almighty God, we pray inclusive and the concluding doxology may be sung.

B. Eucharistic Prayer II

179. The prayer, Lord, you are holy indeed, is said by the principal celebrant alone, with hands outstretched.

180. From Let your Spirit come to May all of us who share inclusive, all the concelebrants together say the prayer in this manner:

a. They say Let your Spirit come with hands outstretched toward the offerings.

b. They say Before he was given up to death and When supper was ended with hands joined.

c. While saying the words of the Lord, each extends his right hand toward the bread and toward the chalice, if this seems appropriate; they look at the eucharistic bread and the chalice as they are shown and afterward bow low.

d. They say In memory of his death and May all of us who share with hands outstretched.

181. The intercessions for the living, Lord, remember your Church, and for the dead, Remember our brothers and sisters, may be assigned to one of the concelebrants; he alone says the intercessions, with hands outstretched.

182. In this eucharistic prayer the parts from Before he was given up to death to In memory of his death inclusive and the concluding doxology may be sung.

C. Eucharistic Prayer III

183. The prayer, Father, you are holy indeed, is said by the principal celebrant alone, with hands outstretched.

184. From And so, Father, we bring you these gifts to Look with favor inclusive, all the concelebrants together say the prayer in this manner:

a. They say And so, Father, we bring you these gifts with hands outstretched toward the offerings.

b. They say On the night he was betrayed and When supper was ended with hands joined.

c. While saying the words of the Lord, each extends his right hand toward the bread and toward the chalice, if this seems appropriate; they look at the eucharistic bread and chalice as these are shown and afterward bow low.

d. They say Father, calling to mind and Look with favor with hands outstretched.

185. The intercessions, May he make us an everlasting gift and Lord, may this sacrifice, may be assigned to one of the concelebrants; he alone says these prayers, with hands outstretched.

186. In this eucharistic prayer the parts from On the night he was betrayed to Father, calling to mind inclusive and the concluding doxology may be sung.

D. Eucharistic Prayer IV

187. The prayer, Father, we acknowledge, is said by the principal celebrant alone, with hands outstretched.

188. From Father, may this Holy Spirit to Lord, look upon this sacrifice inclusive, all the concelebrants together say the prayer in this manner:

a. They say Father, may this Holy Spirit with hands outstretched toward the offerings.

b. They say He always loved those and In the same way with hands joined.

c. While saying the words of the Lord, each extends his right hand toward the bread and toward the chalice, if this seems appropriate; they look at the eucharistic bread and chalice as these are shown and afterward bow low.

d. They say Father, we now celebrate and Lord, look upon this sacrifice with hands outstretched.

189. The intercessions, Lord, remember those, may be assigned to one of the concelebrants; he alone says them, with hands outstretched.

190. In this eucharistic prayer the parts from He always loved those to Father, we now celebrate inclusive and the concluding doxology may be sung.

191. The concluding doxology of the eucharistic prayer may be sung or said either by the principal celebrant alone or together with all the concelebrants.

COMMUNION RITE

192. Next, with hands joined, the celebrant introduces the Lord's Prayer; with hands outstretched, he then says this prayer itself with the other concelebrants and the congregation.

193. The embolism, Deliver us, is said by the principal celebrant alone, with hands outstretched. All the concelebrants together with the congregation say the final acclamation, For the kingdom.

194. After the deacon (or one of the concelebrants) says: Let us offer each other the sign of peace, all exchange the sign of peace. The concelebrants who are nearer the principal celebrant receive the sign of peace from him ahead of the deacon.

195. During the *Agnus Dei*, some of the concelebrants may help the principal celebrant break the eucharistic bread for communion, both for the concelebrants and for the congregation.

196. After the commingling, the principal celebrant alone says inaudibly the prayer, Lord Jesus Christ, Son of the living God, or Lord Jesus Christ, with faith in your love and mercy.

197. After this prayer, the principal celebrant genuflects and steps back a little. One by one the concelebrants come to the middle of the altar, genuflect, and reverently take the body of Christ from the altar. Then holding the eucharistic bread in the right hand, with the left hand under it, they return to their places. The concelebrants may, however, remain in their places and take the body of Christ from the paten presented to them by the principal celebrant or by one or more of the concelebrants, or from the paten as it is passed from one to the other.

198. Then the principal celebrant takes the eucharistic bread, holds it slightly raised above the paten, and, facing the congregation, says: This is the Lamb of God. With the concelebrants and the congregation he continues: Lord, I am not worthy.

199. Then the principal celebrant, facing the altar, says inaudibly: May the body of Christ bring me to everlasting life and reverently consumes the body of Christ. The con-

celebrants do the same. After them the deacon receives the body of Christ from the principal celebrant.

200. The blood of the Lord may be taken by drinking from the chalice directly, through a tube, with a spoon, or even by intinction.

201. If communion is received directly from the chalice, either of two procedures may be followed.

a. The principal celebrant takes the chalice and says inaudibly: May the blood of Christ bring me to everlasting life. He drinks a little and hands the chalice to the deacon or a concelebrant. Then he gives communion to the faithful or returns to the chair. The concelebrants approach the altar one by one or, if two chalices are used, two by two. They drink the blood of Christ and return to their seats. The deacon or a concelebrant wipes the chalice with a purificator after each concelebrant communicates.

b. The principal celebrant stands at the middle of the altar and drinks the blood of Christ in the usual manner.

But the concelebrants may receive the blood of the Lord while remaining in their places. They drink from the chalice presented by the deacon or by one of their number, or else passed from one to the other. Either the one who drinks from the chalice or the one who presents it always wipes it off. After communicating, each one returns to his seat.

202. If communion is received through a tube, this is the procedure. The principal celebrant takes the tube and says inaudibly: May the blood of Christ bring me to everlasting life. He drinks a little and immediately cleans the tube by sipping some water from a container at hand on the altar, then places the tube on the paten. The deacon or one of the concelebrants puts the chalice at a convenient place in the middle of the altar or at the right side on another corporal. A container of water for purifying the tubes is placed near the chalice, with a paten to hold them afterward.

The concelebrants come forward one by one, take a tube, and drink a little from the chalice. They then purify the tube, by sipping a little water, and place it on the paten.

203. If communion is received by using a spoon, the same procedure is followed as for communion with a tube. But care is to be taken that after each communion the spoon is placed in a container of water. After communion has been completed, the acolyte carries this container to a side table to wash and dry the spoons.

204. The deacon receives communion last. He then drinks what remains in the chalice and takes it to the side table. There he or the acolyte washes and dries the chalice and arranges it in the usual way.

205. The concelebrants may also receive from the chalice at the altar immediately after receiving the body of the Lord.

In this case the principal celebrant receives under both kinds as he would when celebrating Mass alone, but for the communion from the chalice he follows the rite that in each instance has been decided on for the concelebrants.

After the principal celebrant's communion, the chalice is placed on another corporal at the right side of the altar. The concelebrants come forward one by one, genuflect, and receive the body of the Lord; then they go to the side of the altar and drink the blood of the Lord, following the rite decided upon, as has just been said.

The communion of the deacon and the purification of the chalice take place as already described.

206. If the concelebrants receive communion by intinction, the principal celebrant receives the body and blood of the Lord in the usual way, making sure that enough remains in the chalice for their communion. Then the deacon or one of the concelebrants arranges the paten with the eucharistic bread and the chalice conveniently in the center of the altar or at the right side on another corporal. The concelebrants approach the altar one by one, genuflect, and take a particle, dip part of it into the chalice, and, holding a paten under their chin, communicate. Afterward they return to their places as at the beginning of Mass.

The deacon receives communion also by intinction and to the concelebrant's words: The body and blood of Christ, makes the response: Amen. At the altar the deacon drinks all that remains in the chalice, takes it to the side table and there he or the acolyte purifies and dries it, then arranges it in the usual way.

CONCLUDING RITE

207. The principal celebrant does everything else until the end of Mass in the usual way; the other concelebrants remain at their seats.

208. Before leaving, the concelebrants make the proper reverence to the altar; as a rule, the principal celebrant kisses the altar.

III. MASS WITHOUT A CONGREGATION

INTRODUCTION

209. This section gives the norms for Mass celebrated by a priest with only one server to assist him and to make the responses.

210. In general this form of Mass follows the rite of Mass with a congregation. The server takes the people's part to the extent possible.

211. Mass should not be celebrated without a server or the participation of at least one of the faithful, except for some legitimate and reasonable cause. In this case the greetings and the blessing at the end of Mass are omitted.

212. The chalice is prepared before Mass, either on a side table near the altar or on the altar itself; the missal is placed on the left side of the altar.

INTRODUCTORY RITES

213. After he reverences the altar, the priest crosses himself, saying: In the name of the Father, etc. He turns to the server and gives one of the forms of greeting. For the penitential rite the priest stands at the foot of the altar.

214. The priest then goes up to the altar and kisses it, goes to the missal at the left side of the altar, and remains there until the end of the general intercessions.

215. He reads the entrance antiphon and says the Kyrie and the Gloria, in keeping with the rubrics.

216. Then, with hands joined, the priest says: Let us pray. After a suitable pause, he says the opening prayer, with hands outstretched. At the end the server responds: Amen.

LITURGY OF THE WORD

217. After the opening prayer, the server or the priest himself reads the first reading and psalm, the second reading, when it is to be said, and the Alleluia verse or other chant.

218. The priest remains in the same place, bows and says: Almighty God, cleanse my heart. He then reads the gospel and at the conclusion kisses the book, saying inaudibly: May

the words of the gospel wipe away our sins. The server says the acclamation.

219. The priest then says the profession of faith with the server, if the rubrics call for it.

220. The general intercessions may be said even in this form of Mass; the priest gives the intentions and the server makes the response.

LITURGY OF THE EUCHARIST

221. The antiphon for the preparation of the gifts is omitted. The minister places the corporal, purificator, and chalice on the altar, unless they have already been put there at the beginning of Mass.

222. Preparation of the bread and wine, including the pouring of the water, are carried out as at a Mass with a congregation, with the formularies given in the Order of Mass. After placing the bread and wine on the altar, the priest washes his hands at the side of the altar as the server pours the water.

223. The priest says the prayer over the gifts and the eucharistic prayer, following the rite described for Mass with a congregation.

224. The Lord's Prayer and the embolism, Deliver us, are said as at Mass with a congregation.

225. After the acclamation concluding the embolism, the priest says the prayer, Lord Jesus Christ, you said. He then adds: The peace of the Lord be with you always, and the server answers: And also with you. The priest may give the sign of peace to the server.

226. Then, while he says the Agnus Dei with the server, the priest breaks the eucharistic bread over the paten. After the Agnus Dei, he places a particle in the chalice, saying inaudibly: May this mingling.

227. After the commingling, the priest inaudibly says the prayer, Lord Jesus Christ, Son of the living God, or Lord Jesus Christ, with faith in your love and mercy. Then he genuflects and takes the eucharistic bread. If the server is to receive communion, the priest turns to him and, holding the eucharistic bread a little above the paten, says: This is the Lamb of God, adding once with the server: Lord, I am not worthy. Facing the altar, the priest then receives the body of Christ. If the server is not receiving communion, the priest, after making a genuflection, takes the host and, facing the altar, says once inaudibly: Lord, I am not worthy, and eats the body of Christ. The blood of Christ is received in the way described in the Order of Mass with a congregation.

228. Before giving communion to the server, the priest says the communion antiphon.

229. The chalice is washed at the side of the altar and then may be carried by the server to a side table or left on the altar, as at the beginning.

230. After the purification of the chalice, the priest may observe a period of silence. Then he says the prayer after communion.

CONCLUDING RITES

231. The concluding rites are carried out as at Mass with a congregation, but the dismissal formulary is omitted.

IV. SOME GENERAL RULES FOR ALL FORMS OF MASS

VENERATION OF THE ALTAR AND THE BOOK OF THE GOSPELS

232. According to traditional liturgical practice, the altar and the Book of the Gospels are kissed as a sign of veneration. But if this sign of reverence is not in harmony with the traditions or the culture of the region, the conference of bishops may substitute some other sign, after informing the Apostolic See.

GENUFLECTIONS AND BOWS

233. Three genuflections are made during Mass: after the showing of the eucharistic bread, after the showing of the chalice, and before communion.

If there is a tabernacle with the blessed sacrament in the sanctuary, a genuflection is made before and after Mass and whenever anyone passes in front of the blessed sacrament.

234. There are two kinds of bow, a bow of the head and a bow of the body:

a. A bow of the head is made when the three divine Persons are named together and at the name of Jesus, Mary, and the saint in whose honor Mass is celebrated.

b. A bow of the body, or profound bow, is made: toward the altar if there is no tabernacle with the blessed sacrament; during the prayers, Almighty God, cleanse and Lord God, we ask you to receive; within the profession of faith at the words, by the power of the Holy Spirit; in Eucharistic Prayer I (Roman Canon) at the words, Almighty God, we pray. The same kind of bow is made by the deacon when he asks the blessing before the gospel. In addition, the priest bends over slightly as he says the words of the Lord at the consecration.

INCENSATION

235. The use of incense is optional in any form of Mass:

a. during the entrance procession;

b. at the beginning of Mass, to incense the altar;

c. at the procession and proclamation of the gospel;

d. at the preparation of the gifts, to incense them, as well as the altar, priest, and people;

e. at the showing of the eucharistic bread and chalice after the consecration.

236. The priest puts the incense in the censer and blesses it with the sign of the cross, saying nothing.

This is the way to incense the altar:

a. If the altar is freestanding, the priest incenses it as he walks around it.

b. If the altar is not freestanding, he incenses it while walking first to the right side, then to the left.

If there is a cross on or beside the altar, he incenses it before he incenses the altar. If the cross is behind the altar, the priest incenses it when he passes in front of it.

PURIFICATIONS

237. Whenever a particle of the eucharistic bread adheres to his fingers, especially after the breaking of the bread or the communion of the people, the priest cleanses his fingers

over the paten or, if necessary, washes them. He also gathers any particles that may fall outside the paten.

238. The vessels are purified by the priest or else by the deacon or acolyte after the communion or after Mass, if possible at a side table. Wine and water or water alone are used for the purification of the chalice, then drunk by the one who purifies it. The paten is usually to be wiped with the purificator.

239. If the eucharistic bread or any particle of it should fall, it is to be picked up reverently. If any of the precious blood spills, the area should be washed and the water poured into the sacrarium.

COMMUNION UNDER BOTH KINDS

240. Holy communion has a more complete form as a sign when it is received under both kinds. For in this manner of reception a fuller light shines on the sign of the eucharistic banquet. Moreover there is a clearer expression of that will by which the new and everlasting covenant is ratified in the blood of the Lord and of the relationship of the eucharistic banquet to the eschatological banquet in the Father's kingdom.[68]

241. For the faithful who take part in the rite or are present at it, pastors should take care to call to mind as clearly as possible Catholic teaching according to the Council of Trent on the manner of communion. Above all they should instruct the people that according to Catholic faith Christ, whole and entire, as well as the true sacrament are received even under one kind only; that, therefore, as far as the effects are concerned, those who receive in this manner are not deprived of any grace necessary for salvation.[69]

Pastors are also to teach that the Church has power in its stewardship of the sacraments, provided their substance remains intact. The Church may make those rules and changes that, in view of the different conditions, times, and places, it decides to be in the interest of reverence for the sacraments or the well-being of the recipients.[70] At the same time the faithful should be guided toward a desire to take part more intensely in a sacred rite in which the sign of the eucharistic meal stands out more explicitly.

242. At the discretion of the Ordinary and after the prerequisite catechesis, communion from the chalice is permitted in the case of:[71]

1. newly baptized adults at the Mass following their baptism; adults at the Mass at which they receive confirmation; baptized persons who are being received into the full communion of the Church;

2. the bride and bridegroom at their wedding Mass;

3. deacons at the Mass of their ordination;

4. an abbess at the Mass in which she is blessed; those consecrated to a life of virginity at the Mass of their consecration; professed religious, their relatives, friends, and the other members of their community at the Mass of first or perpetual vows or renewal of vows;

5. those who receive institution for a certain ministry at the Mass of their institution; lay missionary helpers at the

Mass in which they publicly receive their mission; others at the Mass in which they receive an ecclesiastical mission;

6. the sick person and all present at the time viaticum is to be administered when Mass is celebrated in the sick person's home;

7. the deacon and ministers who exercise their office at Mass;

8. when there is a concelebration, in the case of:

a. all who exercise a liturgical function at this concelebration and also all seminarians present;

b. in their churches or oratories, all members of institutes professing the evangelical counsels and other societies whose members dedicate themselves to God by religious vows or by an offering or promise; also all those who reside in the houses of members of such institutes and societies;

9. priests who are present at major celebrations and are not able to celebrate or concelebrate;

10. all who make a retreat at a Mass in which they actively participate and which is specially celebrated for the group; also all who take part in the meeting of any pastoral body at a Mass they celebrate as a group;

11. those listed in nos. 2 and 4, at Masses celebrating their jubilees;

12. godparents, relatives, wife or husband, and lay catechists of newly baptized adults at the Mass of their initiation;

13. relatives, friends, and special benefactors who take part in the Mass of a newly ordained priest;

14. members of communities at the conventual or community Mass, in accord with the provisions of this Instruction no. 76.

Further, the conferences of bishops have the power to decide to what extent and under what considerations and conditions Ordinaries may allow communion under both kinds in other instances that are of special significance in the spiritual life of any community or group of the faithful.

Within such limits, Ordinaries may designate the particular instances, but on condition that they grant permission not indiscriminately but for clearly defined celebrations and that they point out matters for caution. They are also to exclude occasions when there will be a large number of communicants. The groups receiving this permission must also be specific, well-ordered, and homogeneous.

243. Preparations for giving communion under both kinds:

a. If communion is received from the chalice with a tube, silver tubes are needed for the celebrant and each communicant. There should also be a container of water for purifying the tubes and a paten on which to put them afterward.

b. If communion is given with a spoon, only one spoon is necessary.

c. If communion is given by intinction, care is to be taken that the eucharistic bread is not too thin or too small, but a little thicker than usual so that after being partly dipped into the precious blood it can still easily be given to the communicant.

1. Rite of Communion under Both Kinds Directly from the Chalice

244. If there is a deacon or another assisting priest or an acolyte:

a. The celebrant receives the Lord's body and blood as usual, making sure enough remains in the chalice for the

---

68. See EM, no. 32.

69. See Council of Trent, Session 21, *Decretum de Communione eucharistica*, cap. 1–3: Denz-Schön 1725–1729.

70. See *ibid.*, cap. 2: Denz-Schön 1728.

71. See Congregation for Divine Worship, instruction *Sacramentali communione*, 29 June 1970; the list that follows in the text here is an appendix to that instruction, but is emended.

other communicants. He wipes the outside of the chalice with a purificator.

b. The priest gives the chalice with purificator to the minister and himself takes the paten or ciborium with the hosts; then both station themselves conveniently for the communion of the people.

c. The communicants approach, making the proper reverence, and stand in front of the priest. Showing the host he says: The body of Christ. The communicant answers: Amen and receives the body of Christ from the priest.

d. The communicant then moves to the minister of the chalice and stands before him. The minister says: The blood of Christ, the communicant answers: Amen, and the minister holds out the chalice with purificator. For the sake of convenience, communicants may raise the chalice to their mouth themselves. Holding the purificator under the mouth with one hand, they drink a little from the chalice, taking care not to spill it, and then return to their place. The minister wipes the outside of the chalice with the purificator.

e. The minister places the chalice on the altar after all who are receiving under both kinds have drunk from it. If there are others who are not receiving communion under both kinds, the priest gives these communion, then returns to the altar. The priest or minister drinks whatever remains in the chalice and carries out the usual purifications.

245. If there is no deacon, other priest, or acolyte:

a. The priest receives the Lord's body and blood as usual, making sure enough remains in the chalice for the other communicants. He wipes the outside of the chalice with the purificator.

b. The priest then stations himself conveniently for communion and distributes the body of Christ in the usual way to all who are receiving under both kinds. The communicants approach, make the proper reverence, and stand in front of the priest. After receiving the body of Christ, they step back a little.

c. After all have received, the celebrant places the ciborium on the altar and takes the chalice with the purificator. All those receiving from the chalice come forward again and stand in front of the priest. He says: The blood of Christ, the communicant answers: Amen, and the priest presents the chalice with purificator. The communicants hold the purificator under their mouth with one hand, taking care that none of the precious blood is spilled, drink a little from the chalice, and then return to their place. The priest wipes the outside of the chalice with the purificator.

d. After the communion from the chalice, the priest places it on the altar and if there are others receiving under one kind only, he gives them communion in the usual way, then returns to the altar. He drinks whatever remains in the chalice and carries out the usual purifications.

2. Rite of Communion under Both Kinds by Intinction

246. If there is a deacon, another priest assisting, or an acolyte present:

a. The priest hands this minister the chalice with purificator and he himself takes the paten or ciborium with the hosts. The priest and the minister of the chalice station themselves conveniently for distributing communion.

b. The communicants approach, make the proper reverence, stand in front of the priest, and hold the communion plate below their chin. The celebrant dips a particle into the chalice and, showing it, says: The body and blood of Christ. The communicants respond: Amen, receive communion from the priest, and return to their place.

c. The communion of those who do not receive under both kinds and the rest of the rite take place as already described.

247. If there is no deacon, assisting priest, or acolyte present:

a. After drinking the blood of the Lord, the priest takes the ciborium, or paten with the hosts, between the index and middle fingers of one hand and holds the chalice between the thumb and index finger of the same hand. Then he stations himself conveniently for communion.

b. The communicants approach, make the proper reverence, stand in front of the priest, and hold a plate beneath their chin. The priest takes a particle, dips it into the chalice, and, showing it, says: The body and blood of Christ. The communicants respond: Amen, receive communion from the priest, and return to their place.

c. It is also permitted to place a small table covered with a cloth and corporal at a suitable place. The priest places the chalice or ciborium on the table in order to make the distribution of communion easier.

d. The communion of those who do not receive under both kinds, the consumption of the blood remaining in the chalice, and the purifications take place as already described.

3. Rite of Communion under Both Kinds Using a Tube

248. In this case the priest celebrant also uses a tube when receiving the blood of the Lord.

249. If there is a deacon, another assisting priest, or an acolyte present:

a. For the communion of the body of the Lord, everything is done as described in nos. 224 b and c.

b. The communicant goes to the minister of the chalice and stands in front of him. The minister says: The blood of Christ and the communicant responds: Amen. The communicant receives the tube from the minister, places it in the chalice, and drinks a little. The communicant then removes the tube, careful not to spill any drops, and places it in a container of water held by the minister. The communicant sips a little water to purify the tube, then puts it into another container presented by the minister.

250. If there is no deacon, other assisting priest, or acolyte present, the priest celebrant offers the chalice to each communicant in the way described already for communion from the chalice (no. 245). The minister standing next to him holds the container of water for purifying the tube.

4. Rite of Communion under Both Kinds Using a Spoon

251. If a deacon, another assisting priest, or an acolyte is pesent, he holds the chalice and, saying: The blood of Christ, ministers the blood of the Lord with a spoon to the individual communicants, who hold the plate beneath their chin. He is to take care that the spoon does not touch the lips or tongue of the communicants.

252. If there is no deacon, other assisting priest, or acolyte present, the priest celebrant himself gives them the Lord's

blood, after all receiving communion under both kinds have received the Lord's body.

CHAPTER V
ARRANGEMENT AND FURNISHING OF CHURCHES FOR THE EUCHARISTIC CELEBRATION

I. GENERAL PRINCIPLES

253. For the celebration of the eucharist, the people of God normally assemble in a church or, if there is none, in some other fitting place worthy of so great a mystery. Churches and other places of worship should therefore be suited to celebrating the liturgy and to ensuring the active participation of the faithful. Further, the places and requisites for worship should be truly worthy and beautiful, signs and symbols of heavenly realities.[72]

254. At all times, therefore, the Church seeks out the service of the arts and welcomes the artistic expressions of all peoples and regions.[73] The Church is intent on keeping the works of art and the treasures handed down from the past[74] and, when necessary, on adapting them to new needs. It strives as well to promote new works of art that appeal to the contemporary mentality.[75]

In commissioning artists and choosing works of art that are to become part of a church, the highest artistic standard is therefore to be set, in order that art may aid faith and devotion and be true to the reality it is to symbolize and the purpose it is to serve.[76]

255. All churches are to be solemnly dedicated or at least blessed. But cathedral and parish churches are always to be dedicated. The faithful should give due honor to the cathedral of their diocese and to their own church as symbols of the spiritual Church that their Christian vocation commits them to build up and extend.

256. All who are involved in the construction, restoration, and remodeling of churches are to consult the diocesan commission on liturgy and art. The local Ordinary is to use the counsel and help of this commission whenever it comes to laying down norms on this matter, approving plans for new buildings, and making decisions on the more important issues.[77]

II. ARRANGEMENT OF A CHURCH FOR THE LITURGICAL ASSEMBLY

257. The people of God assembled at Mass possess an organic and hierarchical structure, expressed by the various ministries and actions for each part of the celebration. The general plan of the sacred edifice should be such that in some way it conveys the image of the gathered assembly. It should also allow the participants to take the place most appropriate to them and assist all to carry out their individual functions properly.

The congregation and the choir should have a place that facilitates their active participation.[78]

The priest and his ministers have their place in the sanctuary, that is, in the part of the church that brings out their distinctive role, namely, to preside over the prayers, to proclaim the word of God, or to minister at the altar.

Even though these elements must express a hierarchical arrangement and the diversity of offices, they should at the same time form a complete and organic unity, clearly expressive of the unity of the entire holy people. The character and beauty of the place and all its appointments should foster devotion and show the holiness of the mysteries celebrated there.

III. SANCTUARY

258. The sanctuary should be clearly marked off from the body of the church either by being somewhat elevated or by its distinctive design and appointments. It should be large enough to accommodate all the rites.[79]

IV. ALTAR

259. At the altar the sacrifice of the cross is made present under sacramental signs. It is also the table of the Lord and the people of God are called together to share in it. The altar is, as well, the center of the thanksgiving that the eucharist accomplishes.[80]

260. In a place of worship, the celebration of the eucharist must be on an altar, either fixed or movable. Outside a place of worship, especially if the celebration is only for a single occasion, a suitable table may be used, but always with a cloth and corporal.

261. A fixed altar is one attached to the floor so that it cannot be moved; a movable altar is one that can be transferred from place to place.

262. In every church there should ordinarily be a fixed, dedicated altar, which should be freestanding to allow the ministers to walk around it easily and Mass to be celebrated facing the people. It should be so placed as to be a focal point on which the attention of the whole congregation centers naturally.[81]

263. According to the Church's traditional practice and the altar's symbolism, the table of a fixed altar should be of stone and indeed of natural stone. But at the discretion of the conference of bishops some other solid, becoming, and well-crafted material may be used.

The pedestal or base of the table may be of any sort of material, as long as it is becoming and solid.

264. A movable altar may be constructed of any becoming, solid material suited to liturgical use, according to the traditions and customs of different regions.

265. Altars both fixed and movable are dedicated according to the rite described in the liturgical books; but movable altars may simply be blessed.

266. The practice of placing under the altar to be dedicated relics of saints, even of nonmartyrs, is to be maintained. Care must be taken to have solid evidence of the authenticity of such relics.

---

72. See SC, art. 122–124; PO, no. 5; IOe, no. 90; EM, no. 24.

73. See SC, art. 123.   74. See EM, no. 24.

75. See SC, art. 123, 129; IOe, no. 13c.

76. See SC, art. 123.   77. See SC, art. 126.

78. See IOe, nos. 97–98.   79. See IOe, no. 91.

80. See EM, no. 24.   81. See IOe, no. 91.

267. Other altars should be fewer in number. In new churches they should be placed in chapels separated in some way from the body of the church.[82]

V. ALTAR FURNISHINGS

268. At least one cloth should be placed on the altar out of reverence for the celebration of the memorial of the Lord and the banquet that gives us his body and blood. The shape, size, and decoration of the altar cloth should be in keeping with the design of the altar.

269. Candles are to be used at every liturgical service as a sign of reverence and festiveness. The candlesticks are to be placed either on or around the altar in a way suited to the design of the altar and the sanctuary. Everything is to be well balanced and must not interfere with the faithful's clear view of what goes on at the altar or is placed on it.

270. There is also to be a cross, clearly visible to the congregation, either on the altar or near it.

VI. CHAIR FOR THE PRIEST CELEBRANT AND THE MINISTERS, THAT IS, THE PLACE WHERE THE PRIEST PRESIDES

271. The priest's chair ought to stand as a symbol of his office of presiding over the assembly and of directing prayer. Thus the best place for the chair is at the back of the sanctuary and turned toward the congregation, unless the structure or other circumstances are an obstacle (for example, if too great a distance would interfere with communication between the priest and people). Anything resembling a throne is to be avoided. The seats for the ministers should be so placed in the sanctuary that they can readily carry out their appointed functions.[83]

VII. LECTERN (AMBO) OR PLACE FROM WHICH THE WORD OF GOD IS PROCLAIMED

272. The dignity of the word of God requires the church to have a place that is suitable for proclamation of the word and is a natural focal point for the people during the liturgy of the word.[84]

As a rule the lectern or ambo should be stationary, not simply a movable stand. In keeping with the structure of each church, it must be so placed that the ministers may be easily seen and heard by the faithful.

The readings, responsorial psalm, and the Easter Proclamation (*Exsultet*) are proclaimed from the lectern; it may be used also for the homily and general intercessions (prayer of the faithful).

It is better for the commentator, cantor, or choir director not to use the lectern.

VIII. PLACES FOR THE FAITHFUL

273. The places for the faithful should be arranged with care so that the people are able to take their rightful part in the celebration visually and mentally. As a rule, there should be benches or chairs for their use. But the custom of reserving seats for private persons must be abolished.[85] Chairs or benches should be set up in such a way that the

people can easily take the positions required during various celebrations and have unimpeded access to receive communion.

The congregation must be enabled not only to see the priest and the other ministers but also, with the aid of modern sound equipment, to hear them without difficulty.

IX. CHOIR, ORGAN, AND OTHER MUSICAL INSTRUMENTS

274. In relation to the design of each church, the *schola cantorum* should be so placed that its character as a part of the assembly of the faithful that has a special function stands out clearly. The location should also assist the choir's liturgical ministry and readily allow each member complete, that is, sacramental participation in the Mass.[86]

275. The organ and other lawfully approved musical instruments are to be placed suitably in such a way that they can sustain the singing of the choir and congregation and be heard with ease when they are played alone.

X. RESERVATION OF THE EUCHARIST

276. Every encouragement should be given to the practice of eucharistic reservation in a chapel suited to the faithful's private adoration and prayer.[87] If this is impossible because of the structure of the church, the sacrament should be reserved at an altar or elsewhere, in keeping with local custom, and in a part of the church that is worthy and properly adorned.[88]

277. The eucharist is to be reserved in a single, solid, unmovable tabernacle that is opaque and is locked in such a way as to provide every possible security against the danger of desecration. Thus as a rule there should be only one tabernacle in each church.[89]

XI. IMAGES FOR VENERATION BY THE FAITHFUL

278. In keeping with the Church's very ancient tradition, it is lawful to set up in places of worship images of Christ, Mary, and the saints for veneration by the faithful. But there is need both to limit their number and to situate them in such a way that they do not distract the people's attention from the celebration.[90] There is to be only one image of any one saint. In general, the devotion of the entire community is to be the criterion regarding images in the adornment and arrangement of a church.

XII. GENERAL PLAN OF THE CHURCH

279. The style in which a church is decorated should be a means to achieve noble simplicity, not ostentation. The choice of materials for church appointments must be marked by concern for genuineness and by the intent to

82. See IOe, no. 93.
83. See IOe, no. 92.

84. See IOe, no. 96.
85. See SC, art. 32; IOe, no. 98.

86. See MS, no. 23.
87. See EM, no. 53; Roman Ritual, *Holy Communion and Worship of the Eucharist Outside Mass*, ed. typica, 1973, Introduction, no. 9.
88. See EM, no. 54; IOe, no. 95.
89. See EM, no. 52; IOe, no. 95; Congregation of the Sacraments, instruction *Nullo umquam tempore*, 28 May 1938, no. 4: *AAS* 30 (1938) 199–200; Roman Ritual, *Holy Communion and Worship of the Eucharist Outside Mass*, Introduction, nos. 10–11; CIC, can. 938.
90. See SC, art. 125.

foster instruction of the faithful and the dignity of the place of worship.

280. Proper planning of a church and its surroundings that meets contemporary needs requires attention not only to the elements belonging directly to liturgical services but also to those facilities for the comfort of the people that are usual in places of public gatherings.

CHAPTER VI
REQUISITES FOR CELEBRATING MASS

I. BREAD AND WINE

281. Following the example of Christ, the Church has always used bread and wine with water to celebrate the Lord's Supper.

282. The bread must be made only from wheat and must have been baked recently; according to the long-standing tradition of the Latin Church, it must be unleavened.

283. The nature of the sign demands that the material for the eucharistic celebration truly have the appearance of food. Accordingly, even though unleavened and baked in the traditional shape, the eucharistic bread should be made in such a way that in a Mass with a congregation the priest is able actually to break the host into parts and distribute them to at least some of the faithful. (When, however, the number of communicants is large or other pastoral needs require it, small hosts are in no way ruled out.) The action of the breaking of the bread, the simple term for the eucharist in apostolic times, will more clearly bring out the force and meaning of the sign of the unity of all in the one bread and of their charity, since the one bread is being distributed among the members of one family.

284. The wine for the eucharist must be from the fruit of the vine (see Lk 22:18), natural, and pure, that is not mixed with any foreign substance.

285. Care must be taken to ensure that the elements are kept in good condition: that the wine does not turn to vinegar or the bread spoil or become too hard to be broken easily.

286. If the priest notices after the consecration or as he receives communion that water instead of wine was poured into the chalice, he pours the water into another container, then pours wine with water into the chalice and consecrates it. He says only the part of the institution narrative related to the consecration of the chalice, without being obliged to consecrate the bread again.

II. SACRED FURNISHINGS IN GENERAL

287. As in the case of architecture, the Church welcomes the artistic style of every region for all sacred furnishings and accepts adaptations in keeping with the genius and traditions of each people, provided they fit the purpose for which the sacred furnishings are intended.[91]

In this matter as well the concern is to be for the noble simplicity that is the perfect companion of genuine art.

91. See SC, art. 128; EM, no. 24.

288. In the choice of materials for sacred furnishings, others besides the traditional are acceptable that by contemporary standards are considered to be of high quality, are durable, and well suited to sacred uses. The conference of bishops is to make the decisions for each region.

III. SACRED VESSELS

289. Among the requisites for the celebration of Mass, the sacred vessels hold a place of honor, especially the chalice and paten, which are used in presenting, consecrating, and receiving the bread and wine.

290. Vessels should be made from materials that are solid and that in the particular region are regarded as noble. The conference of bishops will be the judge in this matter. But preference is to be given to materials that do not break easily or become unusable.

291. Chalices and other vessels that serve as receptacles for the blood of the Lord are to have a cup of nonabsorbent material. The base may be of any other solid and worthy material.

292. Vessels that serve as receptacles for the eucharistic bread, such as a paten, ciborium, pyx, monstrance, etc., may be made of other materials that are prized in the region, for example, ebony or other hard woods, as long as they are suited to sacred use.

293. For the consecration of hosts one rather large paten may properly be used; on it is placed the bread for the priest as well as for the ministers and the faithful.

294. Vessels made from metal should ordinarily be gilded on the inside if the metal is one that rusts; gilding is not necessary if the metal is more precious than gold and does not rust.

295. The artist may fashion the sacred vessels in a shape that is in keeping with the culture of each region, provided each type of vessel is suited to the intended liturgical use.

296. For the blessing or consecration of vessels the rites prescribed in the liturgical books are to be followed.

IV. VESTMENTS

297. In the Church, the Body of Christ, not all members have the same function. This diversity of ministries is shown outwardly in worship by the diversity of vestments. These should therefore symbolize the function proper to each ministry. But at the same time the vestments should also contribute to the beauty of the rite.

298. The vestment common to ministers of every rank is the alb, tied at the waist with a cincture, unless it is made to fit without a cincture. An amice should be put on first if the alb does not completely cover the street clothing at the neck. A surplice may not be substituted for the alb when the chasuble or dalmatic is to be worn or when a stole is used instead of the chasuble or dalmatic.

299. Unless otherwise indicated, the chasuble, worn over the alb and stole, is the vestment proper to the priest celebrant at Mass and other rites immediately connected with Mass.

300. The dalmatic, worn over the alb and stole, is the vestment proper to the deacon.

301. Ministers below the order of deacon may wear the alb or other vestment that is lawfully approved in each region.

302. The priest wears the stole around his neck and hanging down in front. The deacon wears it over his left shoulder and drawn across the chest to the right side, where it is fastened.

303. The cope is worn by the priest in processions and other services, in keeping with the rubrics proper to each rite.

304. Regarding the design of vestments, the conferences of bishops may determine and propose to the Apostolic See adaptations that correspond to the needs and usages of their regions.[92]

305. In addition to the traditional materials, natural fabrics proper to the region may be used for making vestments; artificial fabrics that are in keeping with the dignity of the liturgy and the person wearing them may also be used. The conference of bishops will be the judge in this matter.[93]

306. The beauty of a vestment should derive from its material and design rather than from lavish ornamentation. Representations on vestments should consist only of symbols, images, or pictures portraying the sacred. Anything out of keeping with the sacred is to be avoided.

307. Variety in the color of the vestments is meant to give effective, outward expression to the specific character of the mysteries of the faith being celebrated and, in the course of the year, to a sense of progress in the Christian life.

308. Traditional usage should be retained for the vestment colors.

a. White is used in the offices and Masses of the Easter and Christmas seasons; on feasts and memorials of the Lord, other than of his passion; on feasts and memorials of Mary, the angels, saints who were not martyrs, All Saints (1 November), John the Baptist (24 June), John the Evangelist (27 December), the Chair of St. Peter (22 February), and the Conversion of St. Paul (25 January).

b. Red is used on Passion Sunday (Palm Sunday) and Good Friday, Pentecost, celebrations of the Lord's passion, birthday feasts of the apostles and evangelists, and celebrations of martyrs.

c. Green is used in the offices and Masses of Ordinary Time.

d. Violet is used in Lent and Advent. It may also be worn in offices and Masses for the dead.

e. Black may be used in Masses for the dead.

f. Rose may be used on *Gaudete* Sunday (Third Sunday of Advent) and *Laetare* Sunday (Fourth Sunday of Lent).

The conference of bishops may choose and propose to the Apostolic See adaptations suited to the needs and culture of peoples.

309. On solemn occasions more precious vestments may be used, even if not of the color of the day.

310. Ritual Masses are celebrated in their proper color, in white, or in a festive color; Masses for various needs and occasions are celebrated in the color proper to the day or the season or in violet if they bear a penitential character, for example, Masses nos. 23, 28, and 40; votive Masses are celebrated in the color suited to the Mass itself or in the color proper to the day or season.

V. OTHER REQUISITES FOR CHURCH USE

311. Besides vessels and vestments for which some special material is prescribed, any other furnishings that either have

a liturgical use or are in any other way introduced into a church should be worthy and suited to their particular purpose.

312. Even in minor matters, every effort should be made to respect the canons of art and to combine cleanliness and a noble simplicity.

CHAPTER VII
CHOICE OF THE MASS AND ITS PARTS

313. The pastoral effectiveness of a celebration will be heightened if the texts of readings, prayers, and songs correspond as closely as possible to the needs, religious dispositions, and aptitude of the participants. This will be achieved by an intelligent use of the broad options described in this chapter.

In planning the celebration, then, the priest should consider the general spiritual good of the assembly rather than his personal outlook. He should be mindful that the choice of texts is to be made in consultation with the ministers and others who have a function in the celebration, including the faithful in regard to the parts that more directly belong to them.

Since a variety of options is provided for the different parts of the Mass, it is necessary for the deacon, readers, psalmists, cantors, commentator, and choir to be completely sure beforehand of those texts for which they are responsible so that nothing is improvised. A harmonious planning and execution will help dispose the people spiritually to take part in the eucharist.

I. CHOICE OF MASS

314. On solemnities the priest is bound to follow the calendar of the church where he is celebrating.

315. On Sundays, on weekdays of Advent, the Christmas season, Lent, and the Easter season, on feasts, and on obligatory memorials:

a. if Mass is celebrated with a congregation, the priest should follow the calendar of the church where he is celebrating;

b. if Mass is celebrated without a congregation, the priest may choose either the calendar of the church or his own calendar.

316. On optional memorials:

a. On the weekdays of Advent from 17 December to 24 December, during the octave of Christmas, and on the weekdays of Lent, apart from Ash Wednesday and in Holy Week, the priest celebrates the Mass of the day; but he may take the opening prayer from a memorial listed in the General Roman Calendar for that day, except on Ash Wednesday and during Holy Week.

b. On the weekdays of Advent before 17 December, the weekdays of the Christmas season from 2 January on, and the weekdays of the Easter season, the priest may choose the weekday Mass, the Mass of the saint or of one of the saints whose memorial is observed, or the Mass of a saint inscribed in the martyrology for that day.

92. See SC, art. 128.
93. See SC, art. 128.

c. On the weekdays in Ordinary Time, the priest may choose the weekday Mass, the Mass of an optional memorial, the Mass of a saint inscribed in the martyrology for that day, a Mass for various needs and occasions, or a votive Mass.

If he celebrates with a congregation, the priest should first consider the spiritual good of the faithful and avoid imposing his own personal preferences. In particular, he should not omit the readings assigned for each day in the weekday lectionary too frequently or without sufficient reason, since the Church desires that a richer portion of God's word be provided for the people.[94]

For similar reasons he should use Masses for the dead sparingly. Every Mass is offered for both the living and the dead and there is a remembrance of the dead in each eucharistic prayer.

Where the faithful are attached to the optional memorials of Mary or the saints, at least one Mass of the memorial should be celebrated to satisfy their devotion.

When an option is given between a memorial in the General Roman Calendar and one in a diocesan or religious calendar, the preference should be given, all things being equal and depending on tradition, to the memorial in the particular calendar.

II. CHOICE OF INDIVIDUAL TEXTS

317. In the choice of texts for the several parts of the Mass, the following rules are to be observed. They apply to Masses of the season and of the saints.

READINGS

318. Sundays and holydays have three readings, that is, from the Old Testament, from the writings of an apostle, and from a Gospel. Thus God's own teaching brings the Christian people to a knowledge of the continuity of the work of salvation.

Accordingly, it is expected that there will be three readings, but for pastoral reasons and by decree of the conference of bishops the use of only two readings is allowed in some places. In such a case, the choice between the first two readings should be based on the norms in the Lectionary and on the intention to lead the people to a deeper knowledge of Scripture; there should never be any thought of choosing a text because it is shorter or easier.

319. In the weekday Lectionary, readings are provided for each day of every week throughout the year; therefore, unless a solemnity or feast occurs, these readings are for the most part to be used on the days to which they are assigned.

The continuous reading during the week, however, is sometimes interrupted by the occurrence of a feast or particular celebration. In this case the priest, taking into consideration the entire week's plan of readings, is allowed either to combine omitted parts with other readings or to give preference to certain readings.

In Masses with special groups, the priest may choose texts more suited to the particular celebration, provided they are taken from the texts of an approved lectionary.

320. The Lectionary has a special selection of texts from Scripture for Masses that incorporate certain sacraments or

94. See SC, art. 51.

sacramentals or that are celebrated by reason of special circumstances.

These selections of readings have been assigned so that by hearing a more pertinent message from God's word the faithful may be led to a better understanding of the mystery they are taking part in and may be led to a more ardent love for God's word.

Therefore the texts for proclamation in the liturgical assembly are to be chosen on the basis of their pastoral relevance and the options allowed in this matter.

PRAYERS

321. The many prefaces enriching the Roman Missal are intended to develop in different ways the theme of thanksgiving in the eucharistic prayer and bring out more clearly the different facets of the mystery of salvation.

322. The choice of the eucharistic prayer may be guided by the following norms.

a. Eucharistic Prayer I, the Roman Canon, which may be used on any day, is particularly apt on days when there is a special text for the prayer, In union with the whole Church or in Masses that have a special form of the prayer, Father, accept this offering; also on the feasts of the apostles and saints mentioned in it and on Sundays, unless for pastoral considerations another eucharistic prayer is preferred.

b. Eucharistic Prayer II has features that make it particularly suitable for weekdays and special circumstances.

Although it has its own preface, it may also be used with other prefaces, especially those that summarize the mystery of salvation, such as the Sunday prefaces or the common prefaces.

When Mass is celebrated for a dead person, the special formulary may be inserted in the place indicated, namely, before the intercession, Remember our brothers and sisters.

c. Eucharistic Prayer III may be said with any preface. Its use is particularly suited to Sundays and holydays.

The special formulary for a dead person may be used with this prayer in the place indicated, namely, at the prayer, In mercy and love unite all your children.

d. Eucharistic Prayer IV has a fixed preface and provides a fuller summary of the history of salvation. It may be used when a Mass has no preface of its own.

Because of the structure of this prayer no special formulary for the dead may be inserted.

e. A eucharistic prayer that has its own preface may be used with that preface, even when the Mass calls for the preface of the season.

323. In any Mass the prayers belonging to that Mass are used, unless otherwise noted.

In Masses on a memorial, however, the opening prayer or collect may be from the Mass itself or from the common; the prayer over the gifts and prayer after communion, unless they are proper, may be taken either from the common or from the weekdays of the current season.

On the weekdays in Ordinary Time, the prayers may be taken from the preceding Sunday, from another Sunday in Ordinary Time, or from the prayers for various needs and occasions listed in the Missal. It is always permissible even to use the opening prayer from these Masses.

This provides a rich collection of texts that create an opportunity continually to rephrase the themes of prayer for the liturgical assembly and also to adapt the prayer to the needs of the people, the Church, and the world. During the more important seasons of the year, however, the proper seasonal prayers appointed for each day in the Missal already make this adaptation.

SONG

324. The norms laid down in their proper places are to be observed for the choice of chants between the readings and the songs for the processions at the entrance, presentation of the gifts, and communion.

SPECIAL PERMISSIONS

325. In addition to the permissions just given to choose more suitable texts, the conferences of bishops have the right in some circumstances to make further adaptations of readings, but on condition that the texts are taken from an approved lectionary.

CHAPTER VIII

MASSES AND PRAYERS FOR VARIOUS NEEDS AND OCCASIONS AND MASSES FOR THE DEAD

I. MASSES AND PRAYERS FOR VARIOUS NEEDS AND OCCASIONS

326. For well-disposed Christians the liturgy of the sacraments and sacramentals causes almost every event in human life to be made holy by divine grace that flows from the paschal mystery.[95] The eucharist, in turn, is the sacrament of sacraments. Accordingly, the Missal provides formularies for Masses and prayers that may be used in the various circumstances of Christian life, for the needs of the whole world, and for the needs of the Church, both local and universal.

327. In view of the broad options for choosing the readings and prayers, the Masses for various needs and occasions should be used sparingly, that is, when the occasion requires.

328. In all the Masses for various needs and occasions, unless otherwise indicated, the weekday readings and the chants between them may be used, if they are suited to the celebration.

329. The Masses for various needs and occasions are of three types:

a. the ritual Masses, which are related to the celebration of certain sacraments or sacramentals;

b. the Masses for various needs and occasions, which are used either as circumstances arise or at fixed times;

c. the votive Masses of the mysteries of the Lord or in honor of Mary or a particular saint or of all the saints, which are options provided in favor of the faithful's devotion.

330. Ritual Masses are prohibited on the Sundays of Advent, Lent, and the Easter season, on solemnities, on days within the octave of Easter, on All Souls, on Ash Wednesday, and during Holy Week. In addition, the norms in the ritual books or in the Masses themselves also apply.

95. See SC, art. 61.

331. From the selection of Masses for various needs and occasions, the competent authority may choose Masses for those special days of prayer that the conferences of bishops may decree during the course of the year.

332. In cases of serious need or pastoral advantage, at the direction of the local Ordinary or with his permission, an appropriate Mass may be celebrated on any day except solemnities, the Sundays of Advent, Lent, and the Easter season, days within the octave of Easter, on All Souls, Ash Wednesday, and during Holy Week.

333. On obligatory memorials, on the weekdays of Advent until 16 December, of the Christmas season after 2 January, and of the Easter season after the octave of Easter, Masses for various needs and occasions are per se forbidden. But if some real need or pastoral advantage requires, at the discretion of the rector of the church or the priest celebrant, the Masses corresponding to such need or advantage may be used in a celebration with a congregation.

334. On weekdays in Ordinary Time when there is an optional memorial or the office is of that weekday, any Mass or prayer for various needs and occasions is permitted, but ritual Masses are excluded.

II. MASSES FOR THE DEAD

335. The Church offers Christ's paschal sacrifice for the dead so that on the basis of the communion existing between all Christ's members, the petition for spiritual help on behalf of some members may bring others comforting hope.

336. The funeral Mass has first place among the Masses for the dead and may be celebrated on any day except solemnities that are days of obligation, Holy Thursday, the Easter triduum, and the Sundays of Advent, Lent, and the Easter season.

337. On the occasions of news of a death, final burial, or the first anniversary, Mass for the dead may be celebrated even on days within the Christmas octave, on obligatory memorials, and on weekdays, except Ash Wednesday and during Holy Week.

Other Masses for the dead, that is, daily Masses, may be celebrated on weekdays in Ordinary Time when there is an optional memorial or the office is of the weekday, provided such Masses are actually offered for the dead.

338. At the funeral Mass there should as a rule be a short homily, but never a eulogy of any kind. The homily is also recommended at other Masses for the dead celebrated with a congregation.

339. All the faithful, and especially the family, should be urged to share in the eucharistic sacrifice offered for the deceased person by receiving communion.

340. If the funeral Mass is directly joined to the burial rite, once the prayer after communion has been said and omitting the rite of dismissal, the rite of final commendation or of farewell takes place, but only when the body is present.

341. In the planning and choosing of the variable parts of the Mass for the dead, especially the funeral Mass (for example, prayers, readings, general intercessions) pastoral considerations bearing upon the deceased, the family, and those attending should rightly be foremost.

Pastors should, moreover, take into special account those who are present at a liturgical celebration or hear the Gospel only because of the funeral. These may be non-Catholics or Catholics who never or rarely share in the eucharist or who have apparently lost the faith. Priests are, after all, ministers of Christ's Gospel for all people.

APPENDIX TO THE GENERAL INSTRUCTION

For the Dioceses of the United States of America

The following notes, related to the individual sections of the General Instruction of the Roman Missal, include adaptations made by the National Conference of Catholic Bishops for the dioceses of the United States, as well as supplementary references.

For further documentation concerning the eucharistic celebration, see Congregation of Rites, *Instruction on Eucharistic Worship* (May 25, 1967), especially "Some General Principles of Particular Importance in the Catechesis of the People on the Mystery of the Eucharist" (nos. 5–15) and "The Celebration of the Memorial of the Lord" (nos. 16–48); and Sacred Congregation for the Sacraments and Divine Worship, *On Certain Norms Concerning Worship of the Eucharistic Mystery* (April 17, 1980).

The number at the beginning of each section below refers to the respective section of the General Instruction. Unless otherwise indicated, decisions of the National Conference of Catholic Bishops were taken at the plenary session of November, 1969.

11. INTRODUCTIONS AND INVITATIONS

With regard to the adaptation of words of introduction, see the circular letter of the Congregation for Divine Worship, April 27, 1973. No. 14 reads:

Among the possibilities for further accommodating any individual celebration, it is important to consider the admonitions, the homily and the general intercessions. First of all are the admonitions. These enable the people to be drawn into a fuller understanding of the sacred action, or any of its parts, and lead them into a true spirit of participation. The General Instruction of the Roman Missal entrusts the more important admonitions to the priest for preparation and use. He may introduce the Mass to the people before the celebration begins, during the liturgy of the word prior to the actual readings, and in the Eucharistic prayer before the preface; he may also conclude the entire sacred action before the dismissal. The Order of Mass provides others as well, which are important to certain portions of the rite, such as during the penitential rite, or before the Lord's Prayer. By their very nature these brief admonitions do not require that everyone use them in the form in which they appear in the Missal. Provision can be made in certain cases that they be adapted to some degree to the varying circumstances of the community. In all cases it is well to remember the nature of an admonition, and not make them into a sermon or homily; care should be taken to keep them brief and not too wordy, for otherwise they become tedious.

19. SINGING

See the statements of the Bishops' Committee on the Liturgy, *The Place of Music in Eucharistic Celebrations* (1968), *Music in Catholic Worship* (revised edition, 1983), *Liturgical Music Today* (1982).

The settings for liturgical texts to be sung by the priest and ministers that are given in the Sacramentary are chant adaptations prepared by the International Commission on English in the Liturgy, rather than new melodies. Other settings for the ministerial chants are those approved by the National Conference of Catholic Bishops (November, 1965).

No official approbation is needed for new melodies for the Lord's Prayer at Mass or for the chants, acclamations and other song of the congregation.

In accord with no. 55 of the instruction of the Congregation of Rites on music in the liturgy (March 5, 1967), the Conference of Bishops has determined that vernacular texts set to music composed in earlier periods may be used in liturgical services even though they may not conform in all details with the legitimately approved versions of liturgical texts (November, 1967). This decision authorizes the use of choral and other music in English when the older text is not precisely the same as the official version.

21. ACTIONS AND POSTURES

At its meeting in November, 1969, the National Conference of Catholic Bishops voted that in general, the directives of the Roman Missal concerning the posture of the congregation at Mass should be left unchanged, but that no. 21 of the General Instruction should be adapted so that the people kneel beginning after the singing or recitation of the *Sanctus* until after the "Amen" of the eucharistic prayer, that is, before the Lord's Prayer.

26. ENTRANCE SONG

As a further alternative to the singing of the entrance antiphon and psalm of the Roman Gradual (Missal) or of the Simple Gradual, the Conference of Bishops has approved the use of other collections of psalms and antiphons in English, as supplements to the Simple Gradual, including psalms arranged in responsorial form, metrical and similar versions of psalms, provided they are used in accordance with the principles of the Simple Gradual and are selected in harmony with the liturgical season, feast or occasion (decree confirmed by the Consilium for the Implementation of the Constitution on the Liturgy, December 17, 1968).

With regard to texts of other sacred songs from the psalter that may be used as the entrance song, the following criterion was adopted by the Conference of Bishops in November, 1969:

The entrance rite should create an atmosphere of celebration. It serves the function of putting the assembly in the proper frame of mind for listening to the word of God. It helps people to become conscious of themselves as a worshiping community. The choice of texts for the entrance song should not conflict with these purposes.

In general, during the most important seasons of the Church year, Easter time, Lent, Christmas and Advent, it is preferable that most songs used at the entrance be seasonal in nature.

There are thus four options for the entrance song:

1. the entrance antiphon and psalm of the Roman Gradual;
2. the entrance antiphon and psalm of the Simple Gradual;
3. song from other collections of psalms and antiphons;
4. other sacred song chosen in accord with the above criterion.

The same options exist for the sacred song at the offertory and communion, but not for the chants between the readings (below).

Only if none of the above alternatives is employed and there is no entrance song, is the antiphon in the Missal recited.

36. CHANTS BETWEEN THE READINGS

As a further alternative to (1) the singing of the psalm with its response in the Lectionary, (2) the gradual in the Roman Gradual, or (3) the responsorial or alleluia psalm in the Simple Gradual, the Conference of Bishops has approved the use of other collections of psalms and antiphons in English, as supplements to the Simple Gradual, including psalms arranged in responsorial form, metrical and similar versions of psalms, provided they are used in accordance with the principles of the Simple Gradual and are selected in harmony with the liturgical season, feast or occasion (decree confirmed by the Consilium for the Implementation of the Constitution on the Liturgy, December 17, 1968).

The choice of texts that are *not* from the psalter (permitted at the entrance, offertory and communion) is not extended to the chants between the readings.

For further information concerning the use of the chants between the readings, see the Foreword and the Introduction (VIII) to the *Lectionary for Mass* (New York; Collegeville, Minn., 1970). In particular, see the common texts for sung responsorial psalms (nos. 174–175), which may be used in place of the text corresponding to the reading whenever the psalm is sung.

During Lent the alleluia is not sung with the verse before the gospel. Instead one of the following (or similar) acclamations may be sung before and after the verse before the gospel:

Praise and honor to you, Lord Jesus Christ,
    King of endless glory!
Praise and honor to you, Lord Jesus Christ!
Glory and praise to you, Lord Jesus Christ!
Glory to you, Word of God, Lord Jesus Christ!

If the psalm after the reading is not sung, it is recited. The alleluia or the verse before the gospel may be omitted if not sung (see no. 39 of the General Instruction). The people stand for the singing of the alleluia before the gospel (see no. 21 of the General Instruction).

45. GENERAL INTERCESSIONS

See the statement of the Bishops' Committee on the Liturgy, *General Prayer or Prayer of the Faithful* (1969) and *General Intercessions* (1979).

50. OFFERTORY SONG

The choice of texts for the offertory song is governed by the same rule as the entrance song, with the several options described above (no. 26). If there is no offertory song, the offertory antiphon is omitted.

With regard to texts not from the psalter that may be used as the offertory song, the following criterion was adopted by the National Conference of Bishops in November, 1969:

The offertory song need not speak of bread and wine or of offering. The proper function of the offertory song is rather to accompany and celebrate the communal aspects of the procession. The text, therefore, may be an appropriate song of praise or of rejoicing in keeping with the season. Those texts are not acceptable that speak of the offering completely apart from the action of Christ.

In general, during the most important seasons of the Church year, Easter time, Lent, Christmas and Advent, it is preferable that most songs used during the offertory be seasonal in character. During the remainder of the Church year, however, topical songs may be used during the offertory procession provided that these texts do not conflict with the paschal character of every Sunday (Constitution on the Liturgy, arts. 102, 106).

With regard to the offertory song, the statement of the Bishops' Committee on the Liturgy of 1968 (*The Place of Music in Eucharistic Celebrations*) gives additional comments:

The procession can be accompanied by song. Song is not always necessary or desirable. Organ or instrumental music is also fitting at this time. The song need not speak of bread or wine or offering. The proper function of this song is to accompany and celebrate the communal aspects of the procession. The text, therefore, can be any appropriate song of praise or of rejoicing in keeping with the season. (See approved criterion above.) The song need not accompany the entire preparation rite. (The song, if any, continues at least until the priest has placed the bread and wine on the altar, while saying the accompanying prayers quietly; see no. 50 of the General Instruction, nos. 19–21 of the Order of Mass.)

If there is no singing or organ or instrumental music, this may be a period of silence (see no. 23 of the General Instruction). In fact, it is good to give the assembly a period of quiet (that is, while the gifts are prepared and placed on the altar, until the introduction to the prayer over the gifts: Pray, brethren . . .) before demanding, at the preface, their full attention to the eucharistic prayer.

56b. SIGN OF PEACE

The Conference of Bishops has left the development of specific modes of exchanging the sign of peace to local usage. Neither a specific form nor specific words are determined (November, 1969). See the statement of the Bishops' Committee on the Liturgy, *The Sign of Peace* (1977).

56i. COMMUNION SONG

The choice of texts for the communion song is governed by the same rule as the entrance song, with the several options described above (no. 26).

With regard to the texts not from the psalter that may be used as the communion song, the following criterion was adopted by the National Conference of Catholic Bishops in November, 1969:

The communion song should foster a sense of unity. It should be simple and not demand great effort. It gives expression to the joy of unity in the body of Christ and the fulfillment of the mystery being celebrated. Most benediction hymns, by reason of their concentration on adoration rather than on communion, are not acceptable, as indicated in the instruction on music in the liturgy, no. 36.

In general, during the most important seasons of the Church year, Easter time, Lent, Christmas and Advent, it is preferable that most songs used at the communion be seasonal in nature. During the remainder of the Church year, however, topical songs may be used during the communion procession provided these texts do not conflict with the paschal character of every Sunday (Constitution on the Liturgy, arts. 102, 106).

Only if none of the above alternatives is employed and there is no communion song, is the antiphon in the Missal recited. Until the publication of the complete new Missal, the antiphon from the present Missal is said in such cases (Congregation for Divine Worship, instruction, October 20, 1969, no. 13).

59. CELEBRATION BY THE BISHOP

See Congregation of Rites, instruction on the simplification of pontifical rites and insignia, June 21, 1968.

For occasions when the bishop is present at a celebration of the eucharist but, for a just reason, does not elect to be the principal celebrant, he may assign another to celebrate the liturgy of the eucharist while he presides over the introductory rites, the liturgy of the word and the concluding rite of the Mass. For directives on the manner in which this is done, see *Newsletter* of the Bishops' Committee on the Liturgy, May-June, 1981.

66. WOMEN AS READERS

The Conference of Bishops has given permission for women to serve as readers in accord with no. 66 of the General Instruction (November, 1969).

In February, 1971, the Bishops' Committee on the Liturgy prepared a commentary on the liturgical ministry of women:

a. With the exception of service at the altar itself, women may be admitted to the exercise of other liturgical ministries. In particular the designation of women to serve in such ministries as reader, cantor, leader of singing, commentator, director of liturgical participation, etc., is left to the judgment of the pastor or the priest who presides over the celebration, in the light of the culture and mentality of the congregation.

b. Worthiness of life and character and other qualifications are required in women who exercise liturgical ministries in the same way as for men who exercise the same ministries.

c. Women who read one or other biblical reading during the liturgy of the word (other than the gospel, which is reserved to a deacon or priest) should do so from the lectern or ambo where the other readings are proclaimed: the reservation of a single place for all the biblical readings is more significant than the person of the reader, whether ordained or lay, whether woman or man (cf. General Instruction, no. 272).

d. Other ministries performed by women, such as leading the singing or otherwise directing the congregation, should be done either within or outside the sanctuary area, depending on circumstances or convenience.

127. OFFICE OF DEACON

The various ministries of the deacon at Mass may be distributed among several deacons, present and wearing their vestments. (See Congregation of Rites, instruction, June 21, 1968, nos. 4, 5). Other deacons who are present but not called upon to function in the celebration normally should not vest or occupy a specific place in the liturgy, unless they are participating as the *order of deacons,* e.g.,

at the liturgy of ordination of another deacon. (See Bishops' Committee on the Liturgy, *Newsletter,* October, 1981. See also the guidelines established by the Bishops' Committee on the Liturgy for the liturgical ministry of the deacon in *Study Text 6: The Deacon, Minister of Word and Sacrament* [1979].)

153. CONCELEBRATED MASS

See the statement of the Bishops' Committee on the Liturgy, ''Concelebration,'' *Newsletter,* June, 1966, and the guidelines of the Bishops' Committee on the Liturgy in *Study Text 5: Eucharistic Concelebration* (1978).

240. DISTRIBUTION OF COMMUNION

On June 17, 1977, the Congregation of Sacraments and Divine Worship approved the request of the National Conference of Catholic Bishops to permit the optional practice of communion in the hand. The Bishops' Committee on the Liturgy, in its catechesis about this optional practice, drew attention to these considerations:

a. Proper catechesis must be provided to assure the proper and reverent reception of communion without any suggestion of wavering on the part of the Church in its faith in the eucharistic presence.

b. The practice must remain the option of the communicant. The priest or minister of communion does not make the decision as to the manner of reception of communion. It is the communicant's personal choice.

c. When communion is distributed under both kinds by intinction, the host is not placed in the hands of the communicants, nor may the communicants receive the host and dip it into the chalice. Intinction should not be introduced as a means of circumventing the practice of communion in the hand.

d. Children have the option to receive communion in the hand or on the tongue. No limitations because of age have been established. Careful preparation for first reception of the eucharist will provide the necessary instruction. (See also the Roman Ritual, ''Holy Communion and Worship of the Eucharist Outside Mass,'' no. 21).

242. COMMUNION UNDER BOTH KINDS

See the statement of the Bishops' Committee on the Liturgy, ''Communion under Both Kinds,'' *Newsletter,* July, 1966.

In accord with the instruction of the Congregation for Divine Worship on communion under both kinds (June 29, 1970), the National Conference of Catholic Bishops in November, 1970, added the following cases:

15. other members of the faithful present on the special occasions enumerated in no. 242 of the General Instruction;

16. at funeral Masses and at Masses for a special family observance;

17. at Masses on days of special religious or civil significance for the people of the United States;

18. at Masses on Holy Thursday and at the Mass of the Easter Vigil, the norms of the instruction of June 29, 1970, being observed;

19. at weekday Masses.

At its meeting in November, 1978, the National Conference of Catholic Bishops further extended the occasions on which holy communion under both kinds might be given when it approved the motion that holy communion may be given under both kinds to the faithful at Masses on Sundays and holydays of obligation if, in the judgment of the Ordinary, communion may be given in an orderly and reverent manner. The Congregation for Divine Worship confirmed this decree of the National Conference of Catholic Bishops on October 13, 1984 (Prot. N. CD 1297/78). In all that pertains to communion under both kinds the norms of *This Holy and Living Sacrifice: Directory for the Celebration and Reception of Communion under Both Kinds* are to be followed.

253. ARRANGEMENTS AND FURNISHINGS OF CHURCHES FOR EUCHARISTIC CELEBRATIONS

In those things which pertain to the arrangement and furnishing of churches and other requisites of liturgical art and architecture, the principles and directives of the 1978 statement of the Bishops' Committee on the Liturgy, *Environment and Art in Catholic Worship,* should be consulted and applied.

263. MATERIALS FOR FIXED ALTARS

Materials other than natural stone may be used for fixed altars provided these are worthy, solid and properly constructed, subject to the further judgment of the local Ordinary in doubtful cases.

270. ALTAR CROSS

Only a single cross should be carried in a procession in order to give greater dignity and reverence to the cross. It is desirable to place the cross that has been carried in the procession near the altar so that it may serve as the cross of the altar. Otherwise it should be put away during the service. (See Congregation of Rites, instruction, June 21, 1968, no. 20.)

275. MUSICAL INSTRUMENTS

The Conference of Bishops has decreed that musical instruments other than the organ may be used in liturgical services provided they are played in a manner that is suitable to public worship (November, 1967; see Constitution on the Liturgy, art. 120). This decision deliberately refrains from singling out specific instruments. Their use depends on circumstances, the nature of the congregation, etc. In particular cases, if there should be doubt as to the suitability of the instruments, it is the responsibility of the diocesan bishop, in consultation with the diocesan liturgical and music commissions, to render a decision. See also the statements of the Bishops' Committee on the Liturgy, *Music in Catholic Worship* (revised edition, 1983) and *Liturgical Music Today* (1982).

288. MATERIALS FOR SACRED FURNISHINGS

Materials other than the traditional ones may be used for sacred furnishings provided they are suitable for liturgical use, subject to the further judgment of the local Ordinary in doubtful cases.

305. MATERIALS FOR VESTMENTS

Fabrics, both natural and artificial, other than the traditional ones may be used for sacred vesture provided they are suitable for liturgical use, subject to the further judgment of the local Ordinary in doubtful cases.

308. COLOR OF VESTMENTS

White, violet or black vestments may be worn at funeral services and at other offices and Masses for the dead (November, 1970).

318. READINGS ON SUNDAYS AND FEASTS

According to the decision of the National Conference of Catholic Bishops, the complete pattern of three readings for Sundays and feast days should be completely implemented.

331. DAYS OF PRAYER

The Conference of Bishops has decreed that there be observed in the dioceses of the United States, at times to be designated by the local Ordinary in consultation with the diocesan liturgical commission, days or periods of prayer for the fruits of the earth, prayer for human rights and equality, prayer for world justice and peace, and penitential observance outside Lent (November, 1971). This is in addition to observances customary on certain civic occasions such as Independence Day, Labor Day and Thanksgiving Day, for which either proper text or texts of the Sacramentary and Lectionary for Mass are provided.

The Bishops' Committee on the Liturgy presented the above decision in these terms: The expression of such days or periods of prayer should be left as general as possible, so that the time, length, occasion, and more specific intentions of prayer should be determined locally rather than nationally. In this way no arbitrary rule is imposed until it becomes evident that a pattern of such supplications is emerging from practice. See also General Norms for the Liturgical Year and the Calendar, nos. 45–47.

340. FUNERAL MASS

Although the rite of final commendation at the catafalque or pall is excluded, it is permitted to celebrate the funeral service, including the commendations, in those cases where it is physically or morally impossible for the body of the deceased person to be present (November, 1970).

For other adaptations in the funeral Mass and service, see the *Rite of Funerals* (1971); *Newsletter* of the Bishops' Committee on the Liturgy, April-May, 1971. The following refer directly to the eucharistic celebration:

It is appropriate that the paschal candle be carried in the entrance procession.

If the introductory rites have taken place at the church door, the priest venerates the altar and goes to his chair. The penitential rite is omitted, and the priest says or sings the opening prayer.

It is desirable that the first and second readings be read by relatives or friends of the deceased person.

The homily may properly include an expression of praise and gratitude to God for his gifts, particularly the gift of a Christian life, to the deceased person. The homily should relate Christian death to the paschal mystery of the Lord's victorious death and resurrection and to the hope of eternal life.

It is desirable that members of the family or friends of the deceased person participate in the usual offering of the bread and wine for the celebration of the eucharist, together with other gifts for the needs of the Church and of the poor.

If incense is used, the priest, after incensing the gifts and the altar, may incense the body. The deacon or another minister then incenses the priest and people.

DIRECTORY FOR MASSES WITH CHILDREN

INTRODUCTION

1. The Church must show special concern for baptized children who have yet to be fully initiated through the sacraments of confirmation and eucharist as well as for children who have only recently been admitted to holy communion. Today the circumstances in which children grow up are not favorable to their spiritual progress.[1] In addition parents sometimes scarcely fulfill the obligations they accepted at the baptism of their children to bring them up as Christians.

2. In the upbringing of children in the Church a special difficulty arises from the fact that liturgical celebrations, especially the eucharist, cannot fully exercise their inherent pedagogical force upon children.[2] Although the vernacular may now be used at Mass, still the words and signs have not been sufficiently adapted to the capacity of children.

In fact, even in daily life children do not always understand all their experiences with adults but rather may find them boring. It cannot therefore be expected of the liturgy that everything must always be intelligible to them. Nonetheless, we may fear spiritual harm if over the years children repeatedly experience in the Church things that are barely comprehensible: recent psychological study has established how profoundly children are formed by the religious experience of infancy and early childhood, because of the special religious receptivity proper to those years.[3]

3. The Church follows its Master, who "put his arms around the children . . . and blessed them" (Mk 10:16). It cannot leave children in the condition described. Vatican Council II had spoken in the Constitution on the Liturgy about the need of liturgical adaptation for various groups.[4] Soon afterwards, especially in the first Synod of Bishops held in Rome in 1967, the Church began to consider how participation by children could be made easier. On the occasion of the Synod, the President of the Consilium for the Implementation of the Constitution on the Liturgy said explicitly that it could not be a matter of "creating some entirely special rite but rather of retaining, shortening, or omitting some elements or of making a better selection of texts."[5]

4. All the details of eucharistic celebration with a congregation were determined in the General Instruction of the revised Roman Missal published in 1969. Then this Congregation began to prepare a special Directory for Masses with Children, as a supplement to the General Instruction. This was done in response to repeated petitions from the entire Catholic world and with the cooperation of men and women specialists from almost every nation.

5. Like the General Instruction of the Roman Missal, this Directory reserves some adaptations to the conferences of bishops or to individual bishops.[6]

Some adaptations of the Mass may be necessary for children in a given country but cannot be included in a general directory. In accord with the Constitution on the Liturgy art. 40, the conferences of bishops are to propose such adaptations to the Apostolic See for introduction into the liturgy with its consent.

6. The Directory is concerned with children who have not yet entered the period of preadolescence. It does not speak directly of children who are physically or mentally handicapped, because a broader adaptation is sometimes necessary for them.[7] Nevertheless, the following norms may also be applied to the handicapped, with the necessary changes.

7. The first chapter of the Directory (nos. 8–15) gives a kind of foundation by considering the different ways in which children are introduced to the eucharistic liturgy. The second chapter briefly treats Masses with adults in which children also take part (nos. 16–19). Finally, the third chapter (nos. 20–54) treats at greater length Masses with children in which only some adults take part.

Chapter I

THE INTRODUCTION OF CHILDREN TO THE EUCHARISTIC CELEBRATION

8. A fully Christian life is inconceivable without participation in the liturgical services in which the faithful, gathered into a single assembly, celebrate the paschal mystery. Therefore, the religious initiation of children must be in harmony with this purpose.[8] The Church baptizes children and therefore, relying on the gifts conferred by this sacrament, it must be concerned that once baptized they grow in communion with Christ and each other. The sign and pledge of that communion is participation in the eucharistic table, for which children are being prepared or led to a deeper realization of its meaning. This liturgical and eucharistic formation may not be separated from their general education, both human and Christian; indeed it would be harmful if their liturgical formation lacked such a basis.

9. For this reason all who have a part in the formation of children should consult and work together toward one objective: that even if children already have some feeling for God and the things of God, they may also experience in proportion to their age and personal development the human values that are present in the eucharistic celebration. These values include the community activity, exchange of greetings, capacity to listen and to seek and grant par-

---

1. See Sacred Congregation for the Clergy, *General Catechetical Directory* [= GCD], no. 5: *AAS* 64 (1972) 101–102.

2. See Second Vatican Council, Constitution on the Sacred Liturgy, *Sacrosanctum Concilium* [= SC], art. 33.

3. See GCD, no. 78.

4. See SC, art. 38. See also Congregation for Divine Worship, instruction *Actio pastoralis*, 15 May 1969.

5. "De Liturgia in prima Synodo Episcoporum": *Notitiae* 3 (1967) 368.

6. See nos. 19, 32, 33 of this Directory.

7. See the Order of Mass with deaf and mute children of German-speaking regions approved, that is, confirmed by this Congregation, 26 June 1970 (Prot. N. 1546/70).

8. See SC, art. 14, 19.

don, expression of gratitude, experience of symbolic actions, a meal of friendship, and festive celebration.[9]

Eucharistic catechesis, dealt with in no. 12, should develop such human values. Then, depending on their age and their psychological and social situation, children will gradually open their minds to the perception of Christian values and the celebration of the mystery of Christ.[10]

10. The Christian family has the greatest role in instilling these Christian and human values.[11] Thus Christian education, provided by parents and other educators, should be strongly encouraged in relation to the liturgical formation of children as well.

By reason of the duty in conscience freely accepted at the baptism of their children, parents are bound to teach them gradually how to pray. This they do by praying with them each day and by introducing them to prayers said privately.[12] If children, prepared in this way even from their early years, take part in the Mass with their family when they wish, they will easily begin to sing and to pray in the liturgical community and indeed will already have some initial idea of the eucharistic mystery.

If the parents are weak in faith but still wish their children to receive Christian formation, they should be urged at least to communicate to their children the human values mentioned already and, when the occasion arises, to participate in meetings of parents and in noneucharistic celebrations held with children.

11. The Christian communities to which the individual families belong or in which the children live also have a responsibility toward children baptized in the Church. By giving witness to the Gospel, living communal charity, and actively celebrating the mysteries of Christ, the Christian community is an excellent school of Christian and liturgical formation for the children who live in it.

Within the Christian community, godparents or other persons noted for their dedicated service can, out of apostolic zeal, contribute greatly to the necessary catechesis in the case of families that fail in their obligation toward the children's Christian upbringing.

Preschool programs, Catholic schools, and various kinds of associations for children serve these same ends in a special way.

12. Even in the case of children, the liturgy itself always exerts its own inherent power to instruct.[13] Yet within religious-education programs in the schools and parishes the necessary importance should be given to catechesis on the Mass.[14] This catechesis should be directed to the child's active, conscious, and authentic participation.[15] "Suited to children's age and capabilities, it should, by means of the main rites and prayers of the Mass, aim at conveying its meaning, including what relates to taking part in the Church's life."[16] This is especially true of the text of the

eucharistic prayer and of the acclamations by which the children take part in this prayer.

The catechesis preparing children for first communion calls for special mention. In it they should learn not only the truths of faith regarding the eucharist but also how from first communion on—after being prepared according to their capacity by penance—they can as full members of Christ's Body take part actively with the people of God in the eucharist, sharing in the Lord's table and the community of their brothers and sisters.

13. Various kinds of celebrations may also play a major role in the liturgical formation of children and in their preparation for the Church's liturgical life. By the very fact of such celebrations children easily come to appreciate some liturgical elements, for example, greetings, silence, and common praise (especially when this is sung together). But care must be taken that the instructive element does not become dominant in these celebrations.

14. Depending on the capacity of the children, the word of God should have a greater and greater place in these celebrations. In fact, as the children's spiritual capacity develops, celebrations of the word of God in the strict sense should be held frequently, especially during Advent and Lent.[17] These will help greatly to develop in the children an appreciation of the word of God.

15. While all that has been said remains true, the final purpose of all liturgical and eucharistic formation must be a greater and greater conformity to the Gospel in the daily life of the children.

Chapter II

MASSES WITH ADULTS IN WHICH CHILDREN ALSO PARTICIPATE

16. In many places parish Masses are celebrated, especially on Sundays and holydays, at which a good many children take part along with the large number of adults. On such occasions the witness of adult believers can have a great effect upon the children. Adults can in turn benefit spiritually from experiencing the part that the children have within the Christian community. The Christian spirit of the family is greatly fostered when children take part in these Masses together with their parents and other family members.

Infants who as yet are unable or unwilling to take part in the Mass may be brought in at the end of Mass to be blessed together with the rest of the community. This may be done, for example, if parish helpers have been taking care of them in a separate area.

17. Nevertheless, in Masses of this kind it is necessary to take great care that the children present do not feel neglected because of their inability to participate or to understand what happens and what is proclaimed in the celebration. Some account should be taken of their presence: for example, by speaking to them directly in the introductory comments (as at the beginning and the end of Mass) and at some point in the homily.

---

9. See GCD, no. 25.

10. Second Vatican Council, Declaration on Christian Education, *Gravissimum educationis*, 28 October 1965, no. 2: *AAS* 58 (1966) 728–739.

11. See *ibid.*, no. 3; *Sacrosanctum Oecumenicum Concilium Vaticanum II: Constitutiones, Decreta, Declarationes* (Vatican Polyglot Press, 1966) 392.

12. See GCD, no. 78.

13. See SC, art. 33.

14. See Congregation of Rites, instruction *Eucharisticum mysterium* [= EM], 25 May 1967, no. 14.

15. See GCD, no. 25.

16. See EM, no. 14; GCD, no. 57.

17. See SC, art. 35:4.

Sometimes, moreover, if the place itself and the nature of the community permit, it will be appropriate to celebrate the liturgy of the word, including a homily, with the children in a separate, but not too distant, room. Then, before the eucharistic liturgy begins, the children are led to the place where the adults have meanwhile celebrated their own liturgy of the word.

18. It may also be very helpful to give some tasks to the children. They may, for example, bring forward the gifts or perform one or other of the songs of the Mass.

19. If the number of children is large, it may at times be suitable to plan the Mass so that it corresponds more closely to the needs of the children. In this case the homily should be directed to them but in such a way that adults may also benefit from it. Wherever the bishop permits, in addition to the adaptations already provided in the Order of Mass, one or other of the particular adaptations described later in the Directory may be employed in a Mass celebrated with adults in which children also participate.

Chapter III

MASSES WITH CHILDREN IN WHICH ONLY A FEW ADULTS PARTICIPATE

20. In addition to the Masses in which children take part with their parents and other family members (which are not always possible everywhere), Masses with children in which only a few adults take part are recommended, especially during the week. From the beginning of the liturgical reform it has been clear to everyone that some adaptations are necessary in these Masses.[18]

Such adaptations, but only those of a more general kind, will be considered later (nos. 38–54).

21. It is always necessary to keep in mind that these eucharistic celebrations must lead children toward the celebration of Mass with adults, especially the Masses at which the Christian community must come together on Sundays.[19] Thus, apart from adaptations that are necessary because of the children's age, the result should not be entirely special rites, markedly different from the Order of Mass celebrated with a congregation.[20] The purpose of the various elements should always correspond with what is said in the General Instruction of the Roman Missal on individual points, even if at times for pastoral reasons an absolute *identity* cannot be insisted upon.

OFFICES AND MINISTRIES IN THE CELEBRATION

22. The principles of active and conscious participation are in a sense even more significant for Masses celebrated with children. Every effort should therefore be made to increase this participation and to make it more intense. For

this reason as many children as possible should have special parts in the celebration; for example: preparing the place and the altar (see no. 29), acting as cantor (see no. 24), singing in a choir, playing musical instruments (see no. 32), proclaiming the readings (see nos. 24 and 47), responding during the homily (see no. 48), reciting the intentions of the general intercessions, bringing the gifts to the altar, and performing similar activities in accord with the usage of various peoples (see no. 34).

To encourage participation, it will sometimes be helpful to have several additions, for example, the insertion of motives for giving thanks before the priest begins the dialogue of the preface.

In all this, it should be kept in mind that external activities will be fruitless and even harmful if they do not serve the internal participation of the children. Thus religious silence has its importance even in Masses with children (see no. 37). The children should not be allowed to forget that all the forms of participation reach their high point in eucharistic communion, when the body and blood of Christ are received as spiritual nourishment.[21]

23. It is the responsibility of the priest who celebrates with children to make the celebration festive, familial, and meditative.[22] Even more than in Masses with adults, the priest is the one to create this kind of attitude, which depends on his personal preparation and his manner of acting and speaking with others.

The priest should be concerned above all about the dignity, clarity, and simplicity of his actions and gestures. In speaking to the children he should express himself so that he will be easily understood, while avoiding any childish style of speech.

The free use of introductory comments[23] will lead children to a genuine liturgical participation, but these should be more than mere explanatory remarks.

It will help him to reach the hearts of the children if the priest sometimes expresses the invitations in his own words, for example, at the penitential rite, the prayer over the gifts, the Lord's Prayer, the sign of peace, and communion.

24. Since the eucharist is always the action of the entire ecclesial community, the participation of at least some adults is desirable. These should be present not as monitors but as participants, praying with the children and helping them to the extent necessary.

With the consent of the pastor or rector of the church, one of the adults may speak to the children after the gospel, especially if the priest finds it difficult to adapt himself to the mentality of children. In this matter the norms soon to be issued by the Congregation for the Clergy should be observed.

Even in Masses with children attention is to be paid to the diversity of ministries so that the Mass may stand out clearly as the celebration of a community.[24] For example, readers and cantors, whether children or adults, should be employed. In this way a variety of voices will keep the children from becoming bored.

PLACE AND TIME OF CELEBRATION

25. The primary place for the eucharistic celebration for children is the church. Within the church, however, a space

---

18. See no. 3 of this Directory.
19. See SC, art. 42 and 106.
20. See "De Liturgia in prima Synodo Episcoporum": *Notitiae* 3 (1967) 368.

21. See General Instruction of the Roman Missal [= GIRM], no. 56.
22. See no. 37 of this Directory.
23. See GIRM, no. 11.
24. See SC, art. 28.

should be carefully chosen, if available, that will be suited to the number of participants. It should be a place where the children can act with a feeling of ease according to the requirements of a living liturgy that is suited to their age.

If the church does not satisfy these demands, it will sometimes be suitable to celebrate the eucharist with children outside a place of worship. But in that case the place chosen should be appropriate and worthy of the celebration.[25]

26. The time of day chosen for Masses with children should correspond to the circumstances of their lives so that they may be most open to hearing the word of God and to celebrating the eucharist.

27. Weekday Mass in which children participate can certainly be celebrated with greater effect and less danger of boredom if it does not take place every day (for example, in boarding schools). Moreover, preparation can be more careful if there is a longer interval between diverse celebrations.

Sometimes it will be preferable to have common prayer, to which the children may contribute spontaneously, or else a common meditation, or a celebration of the word of God. These are ways of continuing the eucharistic celebrations already held and of leading to a deeper participation in subsequent celebrations.

28. When the number of children who celebrate the eucharist together is very great, attentive and conscious participation becomes more difficult. Therefore, if possible, several groups should be formed; these should not be set up rigidly according to age but with regard for the children's progress in religious formation and catechetical preparation.

During the week such groups may be invited to the sacrifice of the Mass on different days.

PREPARATION FOR THE CELEBRATION

29. Each eucharistic celebration with children should be carefully prepared beforehand, especially with regard to the prayers, songs, readings, and intentions of the general intercessions. This should be done in discussion with the adults and with the children who will have a special ministry in these Masses. If possible, some of the children should take part in preparing and ornamenting the place of celebration and preparing the chalice with the paten and the cruets. Presupposing the appropriate internal participation, such activity will help to develop the spirit of community celebration.

SINGING AND MUSIC

30. Singing must be given great importance in all celebrations, but it is to be especially encouraged in every way for Masses celebrated with children, in view of their special affinity for music.[26] The culture of various peoples and the capabilities of the children present should be taken into account.

If possible, the acclamations should be sung by the children rather than recited, especially the acclamations that form part of the eucharistic prayer.

31. To facilitate the children's participation in singing the *Gloria, Credo, Sanctus,* and *Agnus Dei,* it is permissible to use with the melodies appropriate vernacular texts, ac-

cepted by competent authority, even if these do not correspond exactly to the liturgical texts.[27]

32. The use of "musical instruments can add a great deal" in Masses with children, especially if they are played by the children themselves.[28] The playing of instruments will help to sustain the singing or to encourage the reflection of the children; sometimes in their own fashion instruments express festive joy and the praise of God.

Care should always be taken, however, that the musical accompaniment does not overpower the singing or become a distraction rather than a help to the children. Music should correspond to the purpose intended for the different periods at which it is played during the Mass.

With these precautions and with due and special discretion, recorded music may also be used in Masses with children, in accord with norms established by the conferences of bishops.

GESTURES

33. In view of the nature of the liturgy as an activity of the entire person and in view of the psychology of children, participation by means of gestures and posture should be strongly encouraged in Masses with children, with due regard for age and local customs. Much depends not only on the actions of the priest,[29] but also on the manner in which the children conduct themselves as a community.

If, in accord with the norm of the General Instruction of the Roman Missal,[30] a conference of bishops adapts the congregation's actions at Mass to the mentality of a people, it should take the special condition of children into account or should decide on adaptations that are for children only.

34. Among the actions that are considered under this heading, processions and other activities that involve physical participation deserve special mention.

The children's entering in procession with the priest can serve to help them to experience a sense of the communion that is thus being created.[31] The participation of at least some children in the procession with the Book of the Gospels makes clear the presence of Christ announcing the word to his people. The procession of children with the chalice and the gifts expresses more clearly the value and meaning of the preparation of the gifts. The communion procession, if properly arranged, helps greatly to develop the children's devotion.

VISUAL ELEMENTS

35. The liturgy of the Mass contains many visual elements and these should be given great prominence with children. This is especially true of the particular visual elements in the course of the liturgical year, for example, the veneration of the cross, the Easter candle, the lights on the feast of the Presentation of the Lord, and the variety of colors and liturgical appointments.

In addition to the visual elements that belong to the celebration and to the place of celebration, it is appropriate to introduce other elements that will permit children to

25. See GIRM, no. 253.
26. See GIRM, no. 19.

27. See Congregation of Rites, instruction *Musicam sacram* [= MS], 5 March 1967, no. 55.
28. *Ibid.,* no. 62.
29. See no. 23 of this Directory.
30. See GIRM, no. 21.
31. See GIRM, no. 24.

perceive visually the wonderful works of God in creation and redemption and thus support their prayer. The liturgy should never appear as something dry and merely intellectual.

36. For the same reason, the use of art work prepared by the children themselves may be useful, for example, as illustrations of a homily, as visual expressions of the intentions of the general intercessions, or as inspirations to reflection.

SILENCE

37. Even in Masses with children "silence should be observed at the designated times as part of the celebration"[32] lest too great a place be given to external action. In their own way children are genuinely capable of reflection. They need some guidance, however, so that they will learn how, in keeping with the different moments of the Mass (for example, after the homily or after communion[33]), to recollect themselves, meditate briefly, or praise God and pray to him in their hearts.[34]

Besides this, with even greater care than in Masses with adults, the liturgical texts should be proclaimed intelligibly and unhurriedly, with the necessary pauses.

PARTS OF THE MASS

38. The general structure of the Mass, which "is made up as it were of the liturgy of the word and the liturgy of the eucharist," should always be maintained, as should certain rites to open and conclude the celebration.[35] Within individual parts of the celebration, the adaptations that follow seem necessary if children are truly to experience, in their own way and according to the psychological patterns of childhood, "the mystery of faith . . . by means of rites and prayers."[36]

39. Some rites and texts should never be adapted for children lest the difference between Masses with children and the Masses with adults become too pronounced.[37] These are "the acclamations and the responses to the priest's greeting,"[38] the Lord's Prayer, and the Trinitarian formulary at the end of the blessing with which the priest concludes the Mass. It is urged, moreover, that children should become accustomed to the Nicene Creed little by little, the right to use the Apostles' Creed indicated in no. 49 remaining intact.

A. Introductory Rite

40. The introductory rite of Mass has as its purpose "that the faithful coming together take on the form of a community and prepare themselves to listen to God's word and celebrate the eucharist properly."[39] Therefore every effort should be made to create this disposition in the children and not to jeopardize it by any excess of rites in this part of Mass.

It is sometimes proper to omit one or other element of the introductory rite or perhaps to expand one of the elements. There should always be at least some introductory element, which is completed by the opening prayer.

In choosing individual elements, care should be taken that each one be used from time to time and that none be entirely neglected.

B. Reading and Explanation of the Word of God

41. Since readings taken from holy Scripture "form the main part of the liturgy of the word,"[40] even in Masses celebrated with children biblical reading should never be omitted.

42. With regard to the number of readings on Sundays and holydays, the decrees of the conferences of bishops are to be observed. If three or even two readings appointed on Sundays or weekdays can be understood by children only with difficulty, it is permissible to read two or only one of them, but the reading of the gospel should never be omitted.

43. If all the readings assigned to the day seem to be unsuited to the capacity of the children, it is permissible to choose readings or a reading either from the Lectionary of the Roman Missal or directly from the Bible, but taking into account the liturgical seasons. It is recommended, moreover, that the individual conferences of bishops see to the composition of lectionaries for Masses with children.

If, because of the limited capabilities of the children, it seems necessary to omit one or other verse of a biblical reading, this should be done cautiously and in such a way "that the meaning of the text or the intent and, as it were, style of the Scriptures are not distorted."[41]

44. In the choice of readings the criterion to be followed is the quality rather than the quantity of the texts from the Scriptures. A shorter reading is not as such always more suited to children than a lengthy reading. Everything depends on the spiritual advantage that the reading can bring to the children.

45. In the biblical texts "God is speaking to his people . . . and Christ is present to the faithful through his own word."[42] Paraphrases of Scripture should therefore be avoided. On the other hand, the use of translations that may already exist for the catechesis of children and that are accepted by the competent authority is recommended.

46. Verses of psalms, carefully selected in accord with the understanding of children, or singing in the form of psalmody or the *Alleluia* with a simple verse should be sung between the readings. The children should always have a part in this singing, but sometimes a reflective silence may be substituted for the singing.

If only a single reading is chosen, the singing may follow the homily.

47. All the elements that will help explain the readings should be given great consideration so that the children may make the biblical readings their own and may come more and more to appreciate the value of God's word.

Among such elements are the introductory comments that may precede the readings[43] and that by explaining the context or by introducing the text itself help the children to listen better and more fruitfully. The interpretation and explanation of the readings from the Scriptures in the Mass on a saint's day may include an account of the saint's life, not only in the homily but even before the readings in the form of an introduction.

32. GIRM, no. 23.
33. See EM, no. 38.
34. See GIRM, no. 23.
35. GIRM, no. 8.
36. SC, art. 48.
37. See no. 21 of this Directory.
38. GIRM, no. 15.
39. GIRM, no. 24.
40. GIRM, no. 33.
41. Roman Missal, *Lectionary for Mass*, Introduction, no. 7d.
42. GIRM, no. 33.
43. See GIRM, no. 11.

When the text of the readings lends itself to this, it may be helpful to have the children read it with parts distributed among them, as is provided for the reading of the Lord's passion during Holy Week.

48. The homily explaining the word of God should be given great prominence in all Masses with children. Sometimes the homily intended for children should become a dialogue with them, unless it is preferred that they should listen in silence.

49. If the profession of faith occurs at the end of the liturgy of the word, the Apostles' Creed may be used with children, especially because it is part of their catechetical formation.

C. Presidential Prayers

50. The priest is permitted to choose from the Roman Missal texts of presidential prayers more suited to children, so that he may truly associate the children with himself. But he is to take into account the liturgical season.

51. Since these prayers were composed for adult Christians, however, the principle simply of choosing from among them does not serve the purpose of having the children regard the prayers as an expression of their own life and religious experience.[44] If this is the case, the text of prayers of the Roman Missal may be adapted to the needs of children, but this should be done in such a way that, preserving the purpose of the prayer and to some extent its substance as well, the priest avoids anything that is foreign to the literary genre of a presidential prayer, such as moral exhortations or a childish manner of speech.

52. The eucharistic prayer is of the greatest importance in the eucharist celebrated with children because it is the high point of the entire celebration.[45] Much depends on the manner in which the priest proclaims this prayer[46] and on the way the children take part by listening and making their acclamations.

The disposition of mind required for this central part of the celebration and the calm and reverence with which everything is done must make the children as attentive as possible. Their attention should be on the real presence of Christ on the altar under the elements of bread and wine, on his offering, on the thanksgiving through him and with him and in him, and on the Church's offering, which is made during the prayer and by which the faithful offer themselves and their lives with Christ to the eternal Father in the Holy Spirit.

For the present, the four eucharistic prayers approved by the supreme authority for Masses with adults and introduced into liturgical use are to be employed until the Apostolic See makes other provision for Masses with children.

D. Rites Before Communion

53. When the eucharistic prayer has ended, the Lord's Prayer, the breaking of bread, and the invitation to communion should always follow,[47] that is, the elements that have the principal significance in the structure of this part of the Mass.

E. Communion and the Following Rites

54. Everything should be done so that the children who are properly disposed and who have already been admitted to the eucharist may go to the holy table calmly and with recollection and thus take part fully in the eucharistic mystery. If possible, there should be singing, suited to the children, during the communion procession.[48]

The comments that precede the final blessing[49] are important in Masses with children. Before they are dismissed they need some repetition and application of what they have heard, but this should be done in a very few words. In particular, this is the appropriate time to express the connection between the liturgy and life.

At least sometimes, depending on the liturgical seasons and different occasions in the children's life, the priest should use more expanded forms of blessing, but at the end should always retain the Trinitarian formulary with the sign of the cross.[50]

55. The contents of the Directory have as their purpose to help children readily and joyfully to encounter Christ together in the eucharistic celebration and to stand with him in the presence of the Father.[51] If they are formed by conscious and active participation in the eucharistic sacrifice and meal, they should learn day by day, at home and away from home, to proclaim Christ to others among their family and among their peers, by living the "faith, that works through love" (Gal 5:6).

This Directory was prepared by the Congregation for Divine Worship. On 22 October 1973, Pope Paul VI approved and confirmed it and ordered that it be published.

Congregation for Divine Worship, Solemnity of All Saints, 1 November 1973.

By special mandate of the Supreme Pontiff.

✠ Jean Cardinal Villot
Secretary of State

✠ Annibale Bugnini
Titular Archbishop of Diocletiana
Secretary of the Congregation for Divine Worship

---

44. See Consilium, Instruction on the translation of liturgical texts for celebrations with a congregation, 25 January 1969, no. 20.
45. See GIRM, no. 54.
46. See nos. 23 and 37 of this Directory.

47. See no. 23 of this Directory.
48. See MS, no. 32.
49. See GIRM, no. 11.
50. See no. 39 of this Directory.
51. See Roman Missal, Eucharistic Prayer II.

APOSTOLIC LETTER

MOTU PROPRIO

APPROVAL OF THE GENERAL NORMS FOR THE LITURGICAL YEAR AND THE NEW GENERAL ROMAN CALENDAR

POPE PAUL VI

Celebration of the paschal mystery is of supreme importance in Christian worship and the cycle of days, weeks, and the whole year unfold its meaning: this is the teaching so clearly given us by Vatican Council II. Consequently, as to both the plan of the Proper of Seasons and of Saints and the revision of the Roman Calendar it is essential that Christ's paschal mystery receive greater prominence in the reform of the liturgical year, for which the Council has given the norms.[1]

I

With the passage of centuries, it must be admitted, the faithful have become accustomed to so many special religious devotions that the principal mysteries of the redemption have lost their proper place. This was due partly to the increased number of vigils, holydays, and octaves, partly to the gradual overlapping of various seasons in the liturgical year.

But it is also clear that our predecessors St. Pius X and John XXIII laid down several rules aimed at restoring Sunday to its original rank and its place of esteem in the mind of all as the "first holyday of all."[2] They also restored the season of Lent to its rightful place.

It is true as well that our predecessor Pius XII decreed[3] for the Western Church restoration of the Easter Vigil, as the occasion for the people of God to reaffirm their spiritual covenant with the risen Lord during the celebration of the sacraments of Christian initiation.

Faithful to the teaching of the Fathers and of the tradition of the Catholic Church, these popes rightly perceived the true nature of the liturgical year's cycle. It is not simply the commemoration of the historical events by which Christ Jesus won our salvation through his death and a calling to mind of the past that instructs and nurtures the faithful, even the simplest, who meditate on it. They taught also that the cycle of the liturgical year "possesses a distinct sacramental power and efficacy to strengthen Christian life."[4] This is also our own mind and teaching.

Thus as we celebrate the "sacrament of the birth of Christ"[5] and his appearance in the world, it is right and proper for us to pray that "through him who is like us outwardly, we may be changed inwardly."[6] And that while we are celebrating his passage from death to life, we ask God that those who are reborn with Christ may "by their life hold fast to the sacrament they have received by faith."[7] In the words of Vatican Council II, "recalling the mysteries of redemption, the Church opens to the faithful the riches of the Lord's powers and merits, so that these are in some way made present in every age in order that the faithful may lay hold on them and be filled with saving grace."[8]

The purpose of the reordering of the liturgical year and of the norms accomplishing its reform, therefore, is that through faith, hope, and love the faithful may share more deeply in "the whole mystery of Christ as it unfolds throughout the year."[9]

II

We do not see as a conflict with this theme the splendor of feasts of the Blessed Virgin Mary, "who is joined by an inseparable bond to the saving work of her Son,"[10] and of memorials of the saints, which are rightly considered as the birthdays of "the martyrs and victors who lead us."[11] Indeed "the feasts of the saints proclaim the wonderful work of Christ in his servants, and display to the faithful fitting examples for their imitation."[12] Further, the Catholic Church has always firmly and securely held that the feasts of the saints proclaim and renew Christ's paschal mystery.[13]

Undeniably, however, over the course of the centuries more feasts of the saints were introduced than was necessary; therefore the Council pointed out: "Lest the feasts of the saints take precedence over the feasts commemorating the very mysteries of salvation, many of them should be left to be celebrated by a particular Church or nation or religious family; those only should be extended to the universal Church that commemorate saints of truly universal significance."[14]

To put these decrees of the Council into effect, the names of some saints have been deleted from the General Calendar and permission was granted to restore the memorials

---

1. Second Vatican Council, Constitution on the Sacred Liturgy, *Sacrosanctum Concilium* [= SC], art. 102–111.

2. SC, art. 106.

3. Congregation of Rites, decree *Dominicae Resurrectionis,* 9 February 1951: *AAS* 43 (1951) 128–129.

4. Congregation of Rites, decree *Maxima redemptionis nostrae mysteria,* 16 November 1955: *AAS* 47 (1955) 839.

5. Leo the Great, *Sermo XXVII in Nativitate Domini,* 7, 1: PL 54, 216.

6. See *Missale Romanum,* collect, Epiphany [Roman Missal, opening prayer, Baptism of the Lord].

7. *Missale Romanum,* collect, Tuesday of Easter Week [Roman Missal, opening prayer, Monday of the octave of Easter].

8. SC, art. 102.

9. SC, art. 102.

10. SC, art. 103.

11. See *Syriac Breviary* (5th century), B. Mariani, ed. (Rome, 1956) 27.

12. SC, art. 111.

13. See SC, art. 104.

14. SC, art. 111.

and veneration of other saints in those areas with which they have been traditionally associated. The removal of certain lesser-known saints from the Roman Calendar has allowed the addition of the names of martyrs from regions where the Gospel spread later in history. In consequence, the single catalogue displays in equal dignity as representatives of all peoples those who either shed their blood for Christ or were outstanding in their heroic virtues.

For these reasons we regard the new General Calendar drawn up for the Latin rite to be more in keeping with the spirituality and attitudes of the times and to be a clearer reflection of the Church's universality. In this last regard, the Calendar carries the names of the noblest of men and women who place before all the people of God striking examples of holiness and in a wide diversity of forms. The immense spiritual value of this to the whole Christian people hardly needs mention.

After carefully considering before the Lord all these matters, with our apostolic authority we approve the new Roman Calendar drawn up by the Consilium and also the general norms governing the arrangement of the liturgical year. The effective date for them is 1 January 1970. In accordance with the decrees that the Congregation of Rites has prepared in conjunction with the Consilium, they will remain in force until the publication of the duly reformed Roman Missal and Breviary.

We decree all we have established *motu proprio* in this Letter to be valid and confirmed, notwithstanding, to the extent necessary, the constitutions and apostolic ordinations issued by our predecessors, as well as other directives, even those worthy of explicit mention and amendment.

Given at Rome, at Saint Peter's, on 14 February 1969, the sixth year of our pontificate.

PAUL PP. VI

GENERAL NORMS FOR THE LITURGICAL YEAR
AND THE CALENDAR

CHAPTER I

THE LITURGICAL YEAR

1. Christ's saving work is celebrated in sacred memory by the Church on fixed days throughout the year. Each week on the day called the Lord's Day the Church commemorates the Lord's resurrection. Once a year at Easter the Church honors this resurrection and passion with the utmost solemnity. In fact through the yearly cycle the Church unfolds the entire mystery of Christ and keeps the anniversaries of the saints.

During the different seasons of the liturgical year, the Church, in accord with traditional discipline, carries out the formation of the faithful by means of devotional practices, both interior and exterior, instruction, and works of penance and mercy.[1]

2. The principles given here may and must be applied to both the Roman Rite and all others; but the practical rules are to be taken as pertaining solely to the Roman Rite, except in matters that of their nature also affect the other rites.[2]

Title I
Liturgical Days

I. THE LITURGICAL DAY IN GENERAL

3. Each day is made holy through the liturgical celebrations of the people of God, especially through the eucharistic sacrifice and the divine office.

The liturgical day runs from midnight to midnight, but the observance of Sunday and solemnities begins with the evening of the preceding day.

II. SUNDAY

4. The Church celebrates the paschal mystery on the first day of the week, known as the Lord's Day or Sunday. This follows a tradition handed down from the apostles and having its origin from the day of Christ's resurrection. Thus Sunday must be ranked as the first holyday of all.[3]

5. Because of its special importance, the Sunday celebration gives way only to solemnities or feasts of the Lord. The Sundays of the seasons of Advent, Lent, and Easter, however, take precedence over all solemnities and feasts of the Lord. Solemnities occurring on these Sundays are observed on the Saturday preceding.

6. By its nature, Sunday excludes any other celebration's being permanently assigned to that day, with these exceptions:

a. Sunday within the octave of Christmas is the feast of the Holy Family;

b. Sunday following 6 January is the feast of the Baptism of the Lord;

c. Sunday after Pentecost is the solemnity of the Holy Trinity;

d. the last Sunday in Ordinary Time is the solemnity of Christ the King.

7. In those places where the solemnities of Epiphany, Ascension, and Corpus Christi are not observed as holydays of obligation, they are assigned to a Sunday, which is then considered their proper day in the calendar. Thus:

a. Epiphany, to the Sunday falling between 2 January and 8 January;

b. Ascension, to the Seventh Sunday of Easter;

c. the solemnity of Corpus Christi, to the Sunday after Trinity Sunday.

III. SOLEMNITIES, FEASTS, AND MEMORIALS

8. As it celebrates the mystery of Christ in yearly cycle, the Church also venerates with a particular love Mary, the Mother of God, and sets before the devotion of the faithful the memory of the martyrs and other saints.[4]

9. The saints of universal significance have celebrations obligatory throughout the entire Church. Other saints either are listed in the General Calendar for optional celebration or are left to the veneration of some particular Church, region, or religious family.[5]

10. According to their importance, celebrations are distinguished from each other and named as follows: solemnities, feasts, memorials.

11. Solemnities are counted as the principal days in the calendar and their observance begins with evening prayer I of the preceding day. Some also have their own vigil Mass for use when Mass is celebrated in the evening of the preceding day.

12. The celebration of Easter and Christmas, the two greatest solemnities, continues for eight days, with each octave governed by its own rules.

13. Feasts are celebrated within the limits of the natural day and accordingly do not have evening prayer I. Exceptions are feasts of the Lord that fall on a Sunday in Ordinary Time and in the Christmas season and that replace the Sunday office.

14. Memorials are either obligatory or optional. Their observance is integrated into the celebration of the occurring weekday in accord with the norms set forth in the General Instructions of the Roman Missal and the Liturgy of the Hours.

Obligatory memorials occurring on Lenten weekdays may only be celebrated as optional memorials.

Should more than one optional memorial fall on the same day, only one may be celebrated; the others are omitted.

15. On Saturdays in Ordinary Time when there is no obligatory memorial, an optional memorial of the Blessed Virgin Mary is allowed.

---

1. See Second Vatican Council, Constitution on the Sacred Liturgy, *Sacrosanctum Concilium* [= SC], art. 102–105.

2. See SC, art. 5.

3. See SC, art. 106.

4. See SC, art. 103–104.

5. See SC, art. 111.

IV. WEEKDAYS

16. The days following Sunday are called weekdays. They are celebrated in different ways according to the importance each one has.

a. Ash Wednesday and the days of Holy Week, from Monday to Thursday inclusive, have precedence over all other celebrations.

b. The weekdays of Advent from 17 December to 24 December inclusive and all the weekdays of Lent have precedence over obligatory memorials.

c. All other weekdays give way to solemnities and feasts and are combined with memorials.

Title II
The Yearly Cycle

17. By means of the yearly cycle the Church celebrates the whole mystery of Christ, from his incarnation until the day of Pentecost and the expectation of his coming again.[6]

I. EASTER TRIDUUM

18. Christ redeemed us all and gave perfect glory to God principally through his paschal mystery: dying he destroyed our death and rising he restored our life. Therefore the Easter triduum of the passion and resurrection of Christ is the culmination of the entire liturgical year.[7] Thus the solemnity of Easter has the same kind of preeminence in the liturgical year that Sunday has in the week.[8]

19. The Easter triduum begins with the evening Mass of the Lord's Supper, reaches its high point in the Easter Vigil, and closes with evening prayer on Easter Sunday.

20. On Good Friday[9] and, if possible, also on Holy Saturday until the Easter Vigil,[10] the Easter fast is observed everywhere.

21. The Easter Vigil, during the holy night when Christ rose from the dead, ranks as the "mother of all vigils."[11] Keeping watch, the Church awaits Christ's resurrection and celebrates it in the sacraments. Accordingly, the entire celebration of this vigil should take place at night, that is, it should either begin after nightfall or end before the dawn of Sunday.

II. EASTER SEASON

22. The fifty days from Easter Sunday to Pentecost are celebrated in joyful exultation as one feast day, or better as one "great Sunday."[12]

These above all others are the days for the singing of the Alleluia.

23. The Sundays of this season rank as the paschal Sundays and, after Easter Sunday itself, are called the Second, Third, Fourth, Fifth, Sixth, and Seventh Sundays of Easter. The period of fifty sacred days ends on Pentecost Sunday.

24. The first eight days of the Easter season make up the octave of Easter and are celebrated as solemnities of the Lord.

25. On the fortieth day after Easter the Ascension is celebrated, except in places where, not being a holyday of obligation, it has been transferred to the Seventh Sunday of Easter (see no. 7).

26. The weekdays after the Ascension until the Saturday before Pentecost inclusive are a preparation for the coming of the Holy Spirit.

III. LENT

27. Lent is a preparation for the celebration of Easter. For the Lenten liturgy disposes both catechumens and the faithful to celebrate the paschal mystery: catechumens, through the several stages of Christian initiation; the faithful, through reminders of their own baptism and through penitential practices.[13]

28. Lent runs from Ash Wednesday until the Mass of the Lord's Supper exclusive.

The Alleluia is not used from the beginning of Lent until the Easter Vigil.

29. On Ash Wednesday, a universal day of fast,[14] ashes are distributed.

30. The Sundays of this season are called the First, Second, Third, Fourth, and Fifth Sundays of Lent. The Sixth Sunday, which marks the beginning of Holy Week, is called Passion Sunday (Palm Sunday).

31. Holy Week has as its purpose the remembrance of Christ's passion, beginning with his Messianic entrance into Jerusalem.

At the chrism Mass on Holy Thursday morning the bishop, concelebrating Mass with his body of priests, blesses the oils and consecrates the chrism.

IV. CHRISTMAS SEASON

32. Next to the yearly celebration of the paschal mystery, the Church holds most sacred the memorial of Christ's birth and early manifestations. This is the purpose of the Christmas season.

33. The Christmas season runs from evening prayer I of Christmas until the Sunday after Epiphany or after 6 January, inclusive.

34. The Mass of the vigil of Christmas is used in the evening of 24 December, either before or after evening prayer I.

On Christmas itself, following an ancient tradition of Rome, three Masses may be celebrated: namely, the Mass at Midnight, the Mass at Dawn, and the Mass during the Day.

35. Christmas has its own octave, arranged as follows:

a. Sunday within the octave is the feast of the Holy Family;

b. 26 December is the feast of Saint Stephen, First Martyr;

c. 27 December is the feast of Saint John, Apostle and Evangelist;

d. 28 December is the feast of the Holy Innocents;

e. 29, 30, and 31 December are days within the octave;

f. 1 January, the octave day of Christmas, is the solemnity of Mary, Mother of God. It also recalls the conferral of the holy Name of Jesus.

6. See SC, art. 102.

7. See SC, art. 5.

8. See SC, art. 106.

9. See Paul VI, apostolic constitution *Paenitemini,* 17 February 1966, II §3.

10. See SC, art. 110.

11. Augustine, *Sermo* 219: PL 38, 1088.

12. Athanasius, *Epist. fest.* 1: PG 26, 1366.

13. See SC, art. 109.

14. See Paul VI, apostolic constitution *Paenitemini,* 17 February 1966, II §3.

36. The Sunday falling between 2 January and 5 January is the Second Sunday after Christmas.

37. Epiphany is celebrated on 6 January, unless (where it is not observed as a holyday of obligation) it has been assigned to the Sunday occurring between 2 January and 8 January (see no. 7).

38. The Sunday falling after 6 January is the feast of the Baptism of the Lord.

V. ADVENT

39. Advent has a twofold character: as a season to prepare for Christmas when Christ's first coming to us is remembered; as a season when that remembrance directs the mind and heart to await Christ's Second Coming at the end of time. Advent is thus a period for devout and joyful expectation.

40. Advent begins with evening prayer I of the Sunday falling on or closest to 30 November and ends before evening prayer I of Christmas.

41. The Sundays of this season are named the First, Second, Third, and Fourth Sundays of Advent.

42. The weekdays from 17 December to 24 December inclusive serve to prepare more directly for the Lord's birth.

VI. ORDINARY TIME

43. Apart from those seasons having their own distinctive character, thirty-three or thirty-four weeks remain in the yearly cycle that do not celebrate a specific aspect of the mystery of Christ. Rather, especially on the Sundays, they are devoted to the mystery of Christ in all its aspects. This period is known as Ordinary Time.

44. Ordinary Time begins on Monday after the Sunday following 6 January and continues until Tuesday before Ash Wednesday inclusive. It begins again on Monday after Pentecost and ends before evening prayer I of the First Sunday of Advent.

This is also the reason for the series of liturgical texts found in both the Roman Missal and *The Liturgy of the Hours* (Vol. III–IV), for Sundays and weekdays in this season.

VII. ROGATION AND EMBER DAYS

45. On rogation and ember days the practice of the Church is to offer prayers to the Lord for the needs of all people, especially for the productivity of the earth and for human labor, and to give him public thanks.

46. In order to adapt the rogation and ember days to various regions and the different needs of the people, the conferences of bishops should arrange the time and plan of their celebration.

Consequently, the competent authority should lay down norms, in view of local conditions, on extending such celebrations over one or several days and on repeating them during the year.

47. On each day of these celebrations the Mass should be one of the votive Masses for various needs and occasions that is best suited to the intentions of the petitioners.

CHAPTER II

THE CALENDAR

Title I
Calendar and Celebrations to Be Entered

48. The arrangement for celebrating the liturgical year is governed by the calendar: the General Calendar, for use in the entire Roman Rite, or a particular calendar, for use in a particular Church or in families of religious.

49. In the General Calendar the entire cycle of celebrations is entered: celebrations of the mystery of salvation as found in the Proper of Seasons, of those saints having universal significance who must therefore be celebrated by everyone or of saints who show the universality and continuity of holiness within the people of God.

Particular calendars have more specialized celebrations, arranged to harmonize with the general cycle.[1] The individual Churches or families of religious should show a special honor to those saints who are properly their own.

Particular calendars, drawn up by the competent authority, must be approved by the Apostolic See.

50. The drawing up of a particular calendar is to be guided by the following considerations:

a. The Proper of Seasons (that is, the cycle of seasons, solemnities, and feasts that unfold and honor the mystery of redemption during the liturgical year) must be kept intact and retain its rightful preeminence over particular celebrations.

b. Particular celebrations must be coordinated harmoniously with universal celebrations, with care for the rank and precedence indicated for each in the Table of Liturgical Days. Lest particular calendars be enlarged disproportionately, individual saints may have only one feast in the liturgical year. For persuasive pastoral reasons there may be another celebration in the form of an optional memorial marking the transfer or discovery of the bodies of patrons or founders of Churches or of families of religious.

c. Feasts granted by indult may not duplicate other celebrations already contained in the cycle of the mystery of salvation, nor may they be multiplied out of proportion.

51. Although it is reasonable for each diocese to have its own calendar and propers for the Mass and office, there is no reason why entire provinces, regions, countries, or even larger areas may not have common calendars and propers, prepared with the cooperation of all the parties involved.

This principle may also be followed in the case of the calendars for several provinces of religious within the same civil territory.

52. A particular calendar is prepared by inserting in the General Calendar special solemnities, feasts, and memorials proper to that calendar:

a. in a diocesan calendar, in addition to celebrations of its patrons and the dedication of the cathedral, the saints and the blessed who bear some special connection with that diocese, for example, as their birthplace, residence over a long period, or place of death;

---

1. See Congregation for Divine Worship, *Calendaria particularia*, 24 June 1970.

b. in the calendar of religious, besides celebrations of their title, founder, or patron, those saints and blessed who were members of that religious family or had some special relationship with it;

c. in a calendar for individual churches, celebrations proper to a diocese or religious community, those celebrations that are proper to that church and are listed in the Table of Liturgical Days and also the saints who are buried in that church. Members of religious communities should join with the community of the local Church in celebrating the anniversary of the dedication of the cathedral and the principal patrons of the place and of the larger region where they live.

53. When a diocese or religious family has the distinction of having many saints and blessed, care must be taken not to overload the calendar of the entire diocese or institute. Consequently:

a. The first measure that can be taken is to have a common feast of all the saints and the blessed of a given diocese or religious family or of some category.

b. Only the saints and blessed of particular significance for an entire diocese or religious family may be entered in the calendar with an individual celebration.

c. The other saints or blessed are to be celebrated only in those places with which they have closer ties or where their bodies are buried.

54. Proper celebrations should be entered in the calendar as obligatory or optional memorials, unless other provisions have been made for them in the Table of Liturgical Days or there are special historical or pastoral reasons. But there is no reason why some celebrations may not be observed with greater solemnity in some places than in the rest of the diocese or religious community.

55. Celebrations entered in a particular calendar must be observed by all who are bound to follow that calendar. Only with the approval of the Apostolic See may celebrations be removed from a calendar or changed in rank.

Title II

The Proper Date for Celebrations

56. The Church's practice has been to celebrate the saints on the date of their death (''birthday''), a practice it would be well to follow when entering proper celebrations in particular calendars.

Even though proper celebrations have special importance for individual local Churches or religious families, it is of great advantage that there be as much unity as possible in the observance of solemnities, feasts, and obligatory memorials listed in the General Calendar.

In entering proper celebrations in a particular calendar, therefore, the following are to be observed.

a. Celebrations listed in the General Calendar are to be entered on the same date in a particular calendar, with a change in rank of celebration if necessary.

This also applies to diocesan or religious calendars when celebrations proper to an individual church alone are added.

b. Celebrations for saints not included in the General Calendar should be assigned to the date of their death. If the date of death is not known, the celebrations should be assigned to a date associated with the saint on some other grounds, such as the date of ordination or of the discovery or transfer of the saint's body; otherwise it is celebrated on a date unimpeded by other celebrations in that particular calendar.

c. If the date of death or other appropriate date is impeded in the General Calendar or in a particular calendar by another obligatory celebration, even of lower rank, the celebrations should be assigned to the closest date not so impeded.

d. If, however, it is a question of celebrations that cannot be transferred to another date because of pastoral reasons, the impeding celebration should itself be transferred.

e. Other celebrations, called feasts granted by indult, should be entered on a date more pastorally appropriate.

f. The cycle of the liturgical year should stand out with its full preeminence, but at the same time the celebration of the saints should not be permanently impeded. Therefore, dates that most of the time fall during Lent and the octave of Easter, as well as the weekdays between 17 December and 31 December, should remain free of any particular celebration, unless it is a question of optional memorials, feasts found in the Table of Liturgical Days under no. 8 a, b, c, d, or solemnities that cannot be transferred to another season.

The solemnity of Saint Joseph (19 March), except where it is observed as a holyday of obligation, may be transferred by the conferences of bishops to another day outside Lent.

57. If some saints or blessed are listed in the calendar on the same date, they are always celebrated together whenever they are of equal rank, even though one or more of them may be more proper to that calendar. If one or other of these saints or blessed is to be celebrated with a higher rank, that office alone is observed and the others are omitted, unless it is appropriate to assign them to another date in the form of an obligatory memorial.

58. For the pastoral advantage of the people, it is permissible to observe on the Sundays in Ordinary Time those celebrations that fall during the week and have special appeal to the devotion of the faithful, provided the celebrations take precedence over these Sundays in the Table of Liturgical Days. The Mass for such celebrations may be used at all the Masses at which a congregation is present.

59. Precedence among liturgical days relative to the celebration is governed solely by the following table.

TABLE OF LITURGICAL DAYS

according to their order of precedence

I

1. Easter triduum of the Lord's passion and resurrection.
2. Christmas, Epiphany, Ascension, and Pentecost.
Sundays of Advent, Lent, and the Easter season.
Ash Wednesday.
Weekdays of Holy Week from Monday to Thursday inclusive.
Days within the octave of Easter.
3. Solemnities of the Lord, the Blessed Virgin Mary, and saints listed in the General Calendar.
All Souls.

4. Proper solemnities, namely:

a. Solemnity of the principal patron of the place, that is, the city or state.

b. Solemnity of the dedication of a particular church and the anniversary.

c. Solemnity of the title of a particular church.

d. Solemnity of the title, or of the founder, or of the principal patron of a religious order or congregation.

II

5. Feasts of the Lord in the General Calendar.

6. Sundays of the Christmas season and Sundays in Ordinary Time.

7. Feasts of the Blessed Virgin Mary and of the saints in the General Calendar.

8. Proper feasts, namely:

a. Feast of the principal patron of the diocese.

b. Feast of the anniversary of the dedication of the cathedral.

c. Feast of the principal patron of a region or province, or a country, or of a wider territory.

d. Feast of the title, founder, or principal patron of an order or congregation and of a religious province, without prejudice to the directives in no. 4.

e. Other feasts proper to an individual church.

f. Other feasts listed in the calendar of a diocese or of a religious order or congregation.

9. Weekdays of Advent from 17 December to 24 December inclusive.

Days within the octave of Christmas.

Weekdays of Lent.

III

10. Obligatory memorials in the General Calendar.

11. Proper obligatory memorials, namely:

a. Memorial of a secondary patron of the place, diocese, region, or province, country or wider territory, or of an order or congregation and of a religious province.

b. Obligatory memorials listed in the calendar of a diocese, or of an order or congregation.

12. Optional memorials; but these may be celebrated even on the days listed in no. 9, in the special manner described by the General Instructions of the Roman Missal and of the Liturgy of the Hours.

In the same manner obligatory memorials may be celebrated as optional memorials if they happen to fall on the Lenten weekdays.

13. Weekdays of Advent up to 16 December inclusive.

Weekdays of the Christmas season from 2 January until the Saturday after Epiphany.

Weekdays of the Easter season from Monday after the octave of Easter until the Saturday before Pentecost inclusive.

Weekdays in Ordinary Time.

60. If several celebrations fall on the same day, the one that holds the highest rank according to the preceding Table of Liturgical Days is observed. But a solemnity impeded by a liturgical day that takes precedence over it should be transferred to the closest day not listed in nos. 1–8 in the table of precedence; the rule of no. 5 remains in effect. Other celebrations are omitted that year.

61. If the same day were to call for celebration of evening prayer of that day's office and evening prayer I of the following day, evening prayer of the day with the higher rank in the Table of Liturgical Days takes precedence; in cases of equal rank, evening prayer of the actual day takes precedence.

GENERAL ROMAN CALENDAR

(incorporating the Proper Calendar for the Dioceses of the United States of America)

JANUARY

1.	Octave of Christmas SOLEMNITY OF MARY, MOTHER OF GOD	Solemnity
2.	Basil the Great and Gregory Nazianzen, bishops and doctors	Memorial
3.		
4.	Elizabeth Ann Seton, religious (United States)	Memorial
5.	John Neumann, bishop (United States)	Memorial
6.	*Blessed André Bessette, religious* (United States)*	
7.	*Raymond of Penyafort, priest*	
8.		
9.		
10.		
11.		
12.		
13.	*Hilary, bishop and doctor*	
14.		
15.		
16.		
17.	Anthony, abbot	Memorial
18.		
19.		
20.	*Fabian, pope and martyr* *Sebastian, martyr*	
21.	Agnes, virgin and martyr	Memorial
22.	*Vincent, deacon and martyr*	
23.		
24.	Francis de Sales, bishop and doctor	Memorial
25.	Conversion of Paul, apostle	Feast
26.	Timothy and Titus, bishops	Memorial
27.	*Angela Merici, virgin*	
28.	Thomas Aquinas, priest and doctor	Memorial
29.		
30.		
31.	John Bosco, priest	Memorial
Sunday between January 2 and January 8: EPIPHANY		Solemnity
Sunday after Epiphany: Baptism of the Lord		Feast

*When no rank is given, it is an optional memorial.

FEBRUARY

1.		
2.	Presentation of the Lord	Feast
3.	*Blase, bishop and martyr*	
	Ansgar, bishop	
4.		
5.	Agatha, virgin and martyr	Memorial
6.	Paul Miki and companions, martyrs	Memorial
7.		
8.	*Jerome Emiliani*	
9.		
10.	Scholastica, virgin	Memorial
11.	*Our Lady of Lourdes*	
12.		
13.		
14.	Cyril, monk, and Methodius, bishop	Memorial
15.		
16.		
17.	*Seven Founders of the Order of Servites*	
18.		
19.		
20.		
21.	*Peter Damian, bishop and doctor*	
22.	Chair of Peter, apostle	Feast
23.	Polycarp, bishop and martyr	Memorial
24.		
25.		
26.		
27.		
28.		

MARCH

1.

2.

3.

4. *Casimir*

5.

6.

7. Perpetua and Felicity, martyrs   Memorial

8. *John of God, religious*

9. *Frances of Rome, religious*

10.

11.

12.

13.

14.

15.

16.

17. *Patrick, bishop*

18. *Cyril of Jerusalem, bishop and doctor*

19. JOSEPH, HUSBAND OF MARY   Solemnity

20.

21.

22.

23. *Turibius de Mogrovejo, bishop*

24.

25. ANNUNCIATION   Solemnity

26.

27.

28.

29.

30.

31.

APRIL

1.

2. *Francis of Paola, hermit*

3.

4. *Isidore, bishop and doctor*

5. *Vincent Ferrer, priest*

6.

7. John Baptist de la Salle, priest   Memorial

8.

9.

10.

11. Stanislaus, bishop and martyr   Memorial

12.

13. *Martin I, pope and martyr*

14.

15.

16.

17.

18.

19.

20.

21. *Anselm, bishop and doctor*

22.

23. *George, martyr*

24. *Fidelis of Sigmaringen, priest and martyr*

25. Mark, evangelist   Feast

26.

27.

28. *Peter Chanel, priest and martyr*

29. Catherine of Siena, virgin and doctor   Memorial

30. *Pius V, pope*

MAY

1.	*Joseph the Worker*	
2.	Athanasius, bishop and doctor	Memorial
3.	Philip and James, apostles	Feast
4.		
5.		
6.		
7.		
8.		
9.		
10.		
11.		
12.	*Nereus and Achilleus, martyrs*	
	Pancras, martyr	
13.		
14.	Matthias, apostle	Feast
15.	*Isidore* (United States)	
16.		
17.		
18.	*John I, pope and martyr*	
19.		
20.	*Bernardine of Siena, priest*	
21.		
22.		
23.		
24.		
25.	*Venerable Bede, priest and doctor*	
	Gregory VII, pope	
	Mary Magdalene de Pazzi, virgin	
26.	Philip Neri, priest	Memorial
27.	*Augustine of Canterbury, bishop*	
28.		
29.		
30.		
31.	Visitation	Feast

First Sunday after Pentecost: **HOLY TRINITY**	Solemnity
Thursday after Holy Trinity: **THE BODY AND BLOOD OF CHRIST**	Solemnity
Friday following Second Sunday after Pentecost: **SACRED HEART**	Solemnity
Saturday following Second Sunday after Pentecost: *Immaculate Heart of Mary*	

JUNE

1.	Justin, martyr	Memorial
2.	*Marcellinus and Peter, martyrs*	
3.	Charles Lwanga and companions, martyrs	Memorial
4.		
5.	Boniface, bishop and martyr	Memorial
6.	*Norbert, bishop*	
7.		
8.		
9.	*Ephrem, deacon and doctor*	
10.		
11.	Barnabas, apostle	Memorial
12.		
13.	Anthony of Padua, priest and doctor	Memorial
14.		
15.		
16.		
17.		
18.		
19.	*Romuald, abbot*	
20.		
21.	Aloysius Gonzaga, religious	Memorial
22.	*Paulinus of Nola, bishop* *John Fisher, bishop and martyr, and* *Thomas More, martyr*	
23.		
24.	BIRTH OF JOHN THE BAPTIST	Solemnity
25.		
26.		
27.	*Cyril of Alexandria, bishop and doctor*	
28.	Irenaeus, bishop and martyr	Memorial
29.	PETER AND PAUL, APOSTLES	Solemnity
30.	*First Martyrs of the Church of Rome*	

JULY

1.

2.

3. Thomas, apostle — Feast

4. *Elizabeth of Portugal*
   Independence Day (United States)

5. *Anthony Zaccaria, priest*

6. *Maria Goretti, virgin and martyr*

7.

8.

9.

10.

11. Benedict, abbot — Memorial

12.

13. *Henry*

14. Blessed Kateri Tekakwitha, virgin (United States) — Memorial
    Camillus de Lellis, priest

15. Bonaventure, bishop and doctor — Memorial

16. *Our Lady of Mount Carmel*

17.

18.

19.

20.

21. *Lawrence of Brindisi, priest and doctor*

22. Mary Magdalene — Memorial

23. *Bridget, religious*

24.

25. James, apostle — Feast

26. Joachim and Ann, parents of Mary — Memorial

27.

28.

29. Martha — Memorial

30. *Peter Chrysologus, bishop and doctor*

31. Ignatius of Loyola, priest — Memorial

AUGUST

1.	Alphonsus Liguori, bishop and doctor	Memorial
2.	*Eusebius of Vercelli, bishop*	
3.		
4.	John Vianney, priest	Memorial
5.	*Dedication of Saint Mary Major*	
6.	Transfiguration	Feast
7.	*Sixtus II, pope and martyr, and companions, martyrs* *Cajetan, priest*	
8.	Dominic, priest	Memorial
9.		
10.	Lawrence, deacon and martyr	Feast
11.	Clare, virgin	Memorial
12.		
13.	*Pontian, pope and martyr, and Hippolytus, priest and martyr*	
14.	Maximilian Mary Kolbe, priest and martyr	Memorial
15.	ASSUMPTION	Solemnity
16.	*Stephen of Hungary*	
17.		
18.		
19.	*John Eudes, priest*	
20.	Bernard, abbot and doctor	Memorial
21.	Pius X, pope	Memorial
22.	Queenship of Mary	Memorial
23.	*Rose of Lima, virgin*	
24.	Bartholomew, apostle	Feast
25.	*Louis* *Joseph Calasanz, priest*	
26.		
27.	Monica	Memorial
28.	Augustine, bishop and doctor	Memorial
29.	Beheading of John the Baptist, martyr	Memorial
30.		
31.		

SEPTEMBER

1.

2.

3. Gregory the Great, pope and doctor   Memorial

4.

5.

6.

7.

8. Birth of Mary   Feast

9. Peter Claver, priest (United States)   Memorial

10.

11.

12.

13. John Chrysostom, bishop and doctor   Memorial

14. Triumph of the Cross   Feast

15. Our Lady of Sorrows   Memorial

16. Cornelius, pope and martyr, and Cyprian,
    bishop and martyr   Memorial

17. *Robert Bellarmine, bishop and doctor*

18.

19. *Januarius, bishop and martyr*

20. Andrew Kim Taegon, priest and martyr, Paul Chong Hasang,
    and companions, martyrs   Memorial

21. Matthew, apostle and evangelist   Feast

22.

23.

24.

25.

26. *Cosmas and Damian, martyrs*

27. Vincent de Paul, priest   Memorial

28. *Wenceslaus, martyr*

29. Michael, Gabriel, and Raphael, archangels   Feast

30. Jerome, priest and doctor   Memorial

OCTOBER

1.	Theresa of the Child Jesus, virgin	Memorial
2.	Guardian Angels	Memorial
3.		
4.	Francis of Assisi	Memorial
5.		
6.	*Bruno, priest* *Blessed Marie Rose Durocher, virgin* (United States)	
7.	Our Lady of the Rosary	Memorial
8.		
9.	*Denis, bishop and martyr, and companions,* * martyrs* *John Leonardi, priest*	
10.		
11.		
12.		
13.		
14.	*Callistus I, pope and martyr*	
15.	Teresa of Jesus, virgin and doctor	Memorial
16.	*Hedwig, religious* *Margaret Mary Alacoque, virgin*	
17.	Ignatius of Antioch, bishop and martyr	Memorial
18.	Luke, evangelist	Feast
19.	Isaac Jogues and John de Brébeuf, priests and martyrs, and companions, martyrs (United States) *Paul of the Cross, priest*	Memorial
20.		
21.		
22.		
23.	*John of Capistrano, priest*	
24.	*Anthony Claret, bishop*	
25.		
26.		
27.		
28.	Simon and Jude, apostles	Feast
29.		
30.		
31.		

NOVEMBER

1.	ALL SAINTS	Solemnity
2.	ALL SOULS	
3.	*Martin de Porres, religious*	
4.	Charles Borromeo, bishop	Memorial
5.		
6.		
7.		
8.		
9.	Dedication of Saint John Lateran	Feast
10.	Leo the Great, pope and doctor	Memorial
11.	Martin of Tours, bishop	Memorial
12.	Josaphat, bishop and martyr	Memorial
13.	Frances Xavier Cabrini, virgin (United States)	Memorial
14.		
15.	*Albert the Great, bishop and doctor*	
16.	*Margaret of Scotland* *Gertrude, virgin*	
17.	Elizabeth of Hungary, religious	Memorial
18.	*Dedication of the churches of Peter and Paul,* *apostles*	
19.		
20.		
21.	Presentation of Mary	Memorial
22.	Cecilia, virgin and martyr	Memorial
23.	*Clement I, pope and martyr* *Columban, abbot*	
24.		
25.		
26.		
27.		
28.		
29.		
30.	Andrew, apostle	Feast

Fourth Thursday: *Thanksgiving Day* (United States)

Last Sunday in Ordinary Time: **CHRIST THE KING** Solemnity

DECEMBER

1.

2.

3.   Francis Xavier, priest   Memorial

4.   *John Damascene, priest and doctor*

5.

6.   *Nicholas, bishop*

7.   Ambrose, bishop and doctor   Memorial

8.   IMMACULATE CONCEPTION   Solemnity

9.

10.

11. *Damasus I, pope*

12. Our Lady of Guadalupe (United States)   Memorial
     Jane Frances de Chantal, religious

13. Lucy, virgin and martyr   Memorial

14. John of the Cross, priest and doctor   Memorial

15.

16.

17.

18.

19.

20.

21. *Peter Canisius, priest and doctor*

22.

23. *John of Kanty, priest*

24.

25. CHRISTMAS   Solemnity

26. Stephen, first martyr   Feast

27. John, apostle and evangelist   Feast

28. Holy Innocents, martyrs   Feast

29. *Thomas Becket, bishop and martyr*

30.

31. *Sylvester I, pope*

Sunday within the octave of Christmas or if there
is no Sunday within the octave, December 30: **Holy Family**   Feast

TABLE OF PRINCIPAL CELEBRATIONS OF THE LITURGICAL YEAR

Year	Lectionary Cycle – Sunday Cycle	Lectionary Cycle – Weekday Cycle	Epiphany	Baptism of the Lord	Ash Wednesday	Easter	Ascension	Pentecost	The Body and Blood of Christ	Weeks in Ordinary Time – before Lent – Number of weeks	before Lent – Ending	after Easter Season – Beginning	after Easter Season – In week number	First Sunday of Advent
1985	B	I	6 January	13 January	20 February	7 April	16 May	26 May	9 June	6	19 February	27 May	8	1 December
1986	C	II	5 January	12 January	12 February	30 March	8 May	18 May	1 June	5	11 February	19 May	7	30 November
1987	A	I	4 January	11 January	4 March	19 April	28 May	7 June	21 June	8	3 March	8 June	10	29 November
1988	B	II	3 January	10 January	17 February	3 April	12 May	22 May	5 June	6	16 February	23 May	8	27 November
1989	C	I	8 January	9 January	8 February	26 March	4 May	14 May	28 May	5	7 February	15 May	6	3 December
1990	A	II	7 January	8 January	28 February	15 April	24 May	3 June	17 June	8	27 February	4 June	9	2 December
1991	B	I	6 January	13 January	13 February	31 March	9 May	19 May	2 June	5	12 February	20 May	7	1 December
1992	C	II	5 January	12 January	4 March	19 April	28 May	7 June	21 June	8	3 March	8 June	10	29 November
1993	A	I	3 January	10 January	24 February	11 April	20 May	30 May	13 June	7	23 February	31 May	9	28 November
1994	B	II	2 January	9 January	16 February	3 April	12 May	22 May	5 June	6	15 February	23 May	8	27 November
1995	C	I	8 January	9 January	1 March	16 April	25 May	4 June	18 June	8	28 February	5 June	9	3 December
1996	A	II	7 January	8 January	21 February	7 April	16 May	26 May	9 June	7	20 February	27 May	8	1 December
1997	B	I	5 January	12 January	12 February	30 March	8 May	28 May	1 June	5	11 February	19 May	7	30 November
1998	C	II	4 January	11 January	25 February	12 April	21 May	31 May	14 June	7	24 February	1 June	9	29 November
1999	A	I	3 January	10 January	17 February	4 April	13 May	23 May	6 June	6	16 February	24 May	8	28 November
2000	B	II	2 January	9 January	8 March	23 April	1 June	11 June	25 June	9	7 March	12 June	10	3 December
2001	C	I	7 January	8 January	28 February	15 April	24 May	31 May	17 June	7	27 February	1 June	9	2 December
2002	A	II	6 January	13 January	13 February	31 March	9 May	19 May	2 June	5	12 February	20 May	7	1 December
2003	B	I	5 January	12 January	4 March	20 April	29 May	8 June	22 June	8	4 March	9 June	10	30 November
2004	C	II	4 January	11 January	25 February	11 April	20 May	30 May	13 June	7	24 February	31 May	9	28 November
2005	A	I	2 January	9 January	9 February	27 March	5 May	15 May	29 May	5	8 February	16 May	7	27 November
2006	B	II	8 January	9 January	1 March	16 April	25 May	4 June	18 June	8	28 February	5 June	9	3 December
2007	C	I	7 January	8 January	21 February	8 April	17 May	27 May	10 June	7	20 February	28 May	8	2 December
2008	A	II	6 January	13 January	6 February	23 March	1 May	11 May	25 May	4	5 February	12 May	6	30 November
2009	B	I	4 January	11 January	25 February	12 April	21 May	31 May	14 June	7	24 February	1 June	9	29 November
2010	C	II	3 January	10 January	17 February	4 April	13 May	23 May	6 June	6	16 February	24 May	8	28 November

PROPER OF SEASONS

ADVENT SEASON

FIRST SUNDAY OF ADVENT

Introductory Rites

> To you, my God, I lift my soul, I trust in you; let me never come to shame. Do not let my enemies laugh at me. No one who waits for you is ever put to shame. (Psalm 24:1-3)

The Gloria is omitted.

OPENING PRAYER

Let us pray
  **[that we may take Christ's
  coming seriously]**
Pause for silent prayer
**All-powerful God,
increase our strength of will for doing good
that Christ may find an eager welcome at his
  coming
and call us to his side in the kingdom of
  heaven,
where he lives and reigns with you and the
  Holy Spirit,
one God, for ever and ever.**

ALTERNATIVE OPENING PRAYER

Let us pray
  **[in Advent time with longing and
  waiting for the coming of the Lord]**
Pause for silent prayer
**Father in heaven,
our hearts desire the warmth of your love
and our minds are searching for the light of
  your Word.
Increase our longing for Christ our Savior
and give us the strength to grow in love,
that the dawn of his coming
may find us rejoicing in his presence
and welcoming the light of his truth.**

We ask this in the name of Jesus the Lord.

LITURGY OF THE WORD

See Lectionary for Mass, nos. 1-3.

LITURGY OF THE EUCHARIST

PRAYER OVER THE GIFTS

Pray, brethren . . .

**Father,
from all you give us
we present this bread and wine.
As we serve you now,
accept our offering
and sustain us with your promise of eternal life.**

Grant this through Christ our Lord.

Eucharistic Prayer:
Preface of Advent I, page 418.

Communion Rite

The Lord will shower his gifts, and our land will yield its
fruit. (Psalm 84:13)

A period of silence may be observed
after communion, or a psalm or song
of praise may be sung.

PRAYER AFTER COMMUNION

Let us pray.

Pause for silent prayer, if this has not preceded.
**Father,
may our communion
teach us to love heaven.
May its promise and hope
guide our way on earth.**

We ask this through Christ our Lord.

**SOLEMN BLESSING OR PRAYER
OVER THE PEOPLE**

The following may replace the simple
blessing.

After the greeting, the deacon (or in
his absence, the priest) gives the invitation in these or similar words:

Then the priest extends his hands
over the people while he sings or
says:

Bow your heads and pray for God's blessing.

**You believe that the Son of God once came to us;
you look for him to come again.
May his coming bring you the light of his holiness
and his blessing bring you freedom.**
℟. **Amen.**

**May God make you steadfast in faith,
joyful in hope, and untiring in love
all the days of your life.**
℟. **Amen.**

**You rejoice that our Redeemer came to live with us as man.
When he comes again in glory,
may he reward you with endless life.**
℟. **Amen.**

**May almighty God bless you,
the Father, and the Son, ✝ and the Holy Spirit.**
℟. **Amen.**

For other texts of solemn blessings and
prayers over the people, see pages
528–540.

MONDAY OF THE FIRST WEEK OF ADVENT

Introductory Rites

> Nations, hear the message of the Lord, and make it known
> to the ends of the earth: Our Savior is coming. Have no
> more fear. (See Jer. 31:10; Is. 35:4)

OPENING PRAYER

**Lord our God,
help us to prepare
for the coming of Christ your Son.
May he find us waiting,
eager in joyful prayer.**

**We ask this through our Lord Jesus Christ, your Son,
who lives and reigns with you and the Holy Spirit,
one God, for ever and ever.**

See Lectionary for Mass, no. 176.

PRAYER OVER THE GIFTS

Pray, brethren . . .

**Father,
from all you give us
we present this bread and wine.
As we serve you now,
accept our offering
and sustain us with your promise of eternal life.**

Grant this through Christ our Lord.

Preface of Advent I, page **418.**

Communion Rite

> Come to us, Lord, and bring us peace. We will rejoice in
> your presence and serve you with all our heart. (See Ps.
> 105:4-5; Is. 38:3)

PRAYER AFTER COMMUNION

Let us pray.
Pause for silent prayer, if this has not preceded.

**Father,
may our communion
teach us to love heaven.
May its promise and hope
guide our way on earth.**

We ask this through Christ our Lord.

TUESDAY OF THE FIRST WEEK OF ADVENT

Introductory Rites

See, the Lord is coming and with him all his saints. Then there will be endless day. (See Zech. 14:5, 7)

OPENING PRAYER

**God of mercy and consolation,
help us in our weakness and free us from sin.
Hear our prayers
that we may rejoice at the coming of your Son,
who lives and reigns with you and the Holy Spirit,
one God, for ever and ever.**

See Lectionary for Mass, no. 177.

PRAYER OVER THE GIFTS

Pray, brethren . . .

**Lord,
we are nothing without you.
As you sustain us with your mercy,
receive our prayers and offerings.**

We ask this through Christ our Lord.

Preface of Advent I, page 418.

Communion Rite

The Lord is just; he will award the crown of justice to all who have longed for his coming. (2 Tim. 4:8)

PRAYER AFTER COMMUNION

Let us pray.
Pause for silent prayer, if this has not preceded.

**Father,
you give us food from heaven.
By our sharing in this mystery,
teach us to judge wisely the things of earth
and to love the things of heaven.**

Grant this through Christ our Lord.

WEDNESDAY OF THE FIRST WEEK OF ADVENT

Introductory Rites

The Lord is coming and will not delay; he will bring every
hidden thing to light and reveal himself to every nation.
(See Hab. 2:3; 1 Cor. 4:5)

OPENING PRAYER

Lord our God,
grant that we may be ready
to receive Christ when he comes in glory
and to share in the banquet of heaven,
where he lives and reigns with you and the Holy Spirit,
one God, for ever and ever.

See Lectionary for Mass, no. 178.

PRAYER OVER THE GIFTS

Pray, brethren . . .

Lord,
may the gift we offer in faith and love
be a continual sacrifice in your honor
and truly become our eucharist and our salvation.

Grant this through Christ our Lord.

Preface of Advent I, page 418.

Communion Rite

The Lord our God comes in strength and will fill his servants with joy. (Is. 40:10; see 34:5)

PRAYER AFTER COMMUNION

Let us pray.
Pause for silent prayer, if this has not preceded.
God of mercy,
may this eucharist bring us your divine help,
free us from our sins,
and prepare us for the birthday of our Savior,
who is Lord for ever and ever.

THURSDAY OF THE FIRST WEEK OF ADVENT

Introductory Rites

Lord, you are near, and all your commandments are just;
long have I known that you decreed them for ever. (See Ps.
118:151-152)

OPENING PRAYER

**Father,
we need your help.
Free us from sin and bring us to life.
Support us by your power.**

**Grant this through our Lord Jesus Christ, your Son,
who lives and reigns with you and the Holy Spirit,
one God, for ever and ever.**

See Lectionary for Mass, no. 179.

PRAYER OVER THE GIFTS

Pray, brethren . . .

**Father,
from all you give us
we present this bread and wine.
As we serve you now,
accept our offering
and sustain us with your promise of eternal life.**

Grant this through Christ our Lord.

Preface of Advent I, page 418.

Communion Rite

Let our lives be honest and holy in this present age, as we
wait for the happiness to come when our great God reveals himself in glory. (Titus 2:12-13)

PRAYER AFTER COMMUNION

Let us pray.
Pause for silent prayer, if this has not preceded.

**Father,
may our communion
teach us to love heaven.
May its promise and hope
guide our way on earth.**

We ask this through Christ our Lord.

FRIDAY OF THE FIRST WEEK OF ADVENT

Introductory Rites

The Lord is coming from heaven in splendor to visit his people, and bring them peace and eternal life.

OPENING PRAYER

**Jesus, our Lord,
save us from our sins.
Come, protect us from all dangers
and lead us to salvation,
for you live and reign with the Father and the Holy Spirit,
one God, for ever and ever.**

See Lectionary for Mass, no. 180.

PRAYER OVER THE GIFTS

Pray, brethren . . .

**Lord,
we are nothing without you.
As you sustain us with your mercy,
receive our prayers and offerings.**

We ask this through Christ our Lord.

Preface of Advent I, page 418.

Communion Rite

We are waiting for our Savior, the Lord Jesus Christ; he will transfigure our lowly bodies into copies of his own glorious body. (Phil. 3:20-21)

PRAYER AFTER COMMUNION

Let us pray.
Pause for silent prayer, if this has not preceded.
**Father,
you give us food from heaven.
By our sharing in this mystery,
teach us to judge wisely the things of earth
and to love the things of heaven.**

Grant this through Christ our Lord.

SATURDAY OF THE FIRST WEEK OF ADVENT

Introductory Rites

Come, Lord, from your cherubim throne; let us see your
face, and we shall be saved. (Ps. 79:4, 2)

OPENING PRAYER

**God our Father,
you loved the world so much
you gave your only Son to free us
from the ancient power of sin and death.
Help us who wait for his coming,
and lead us to true liberty.**

**We ask this through our Lord Jesus Christ, your Son,
who lives and reigns with you and the Holy Spirit,
one God, for ever and ever.**

See Lectionary for Mass, no. 181.

PRAYER OVER THE GIFTS

Pray, brethren . . .

**Lord,
may the gift we offer in faith and love
be a continual sacrifice in your honor
and truly become our eucharist and our salvation.**

We ask this through Christ our Lord.

Preface of Advent I, page **418.**

Communion Rite

I am coming quickly, says the Lord, and will repay each
man according to his deeds. (Rev. 22:12)

PRAYER AFTER COMMUNION

Let us pray.
Pause for silent prayer, if this has not preceded.
**God of mercy,
may this eucharist bring us your divine help,
free us from our sins,
and prepare us for the birthday of our Savior,
who is Lord for ever and ever.**

SECOND SUNDAY OF ADVENT

Introductory Rites

People of Zion, the Lord will come to save all nations, and your hearts will exult to hear his majestic voice. (See Is. 30:19, 30)

The Gloria is omitted.

OPENING PRAYER

Let us pray
  [that nothing may hinder us
    from receiving Christ with joy]
Pause for silent prayer
God of power and mercy,
open our hearts in welcome.
Remove the things that hinder us from
  receiving Christ with joy,
so that we may share his wisdom
and become one with him
when he comes in glory,
for he lives and reigns with you and the Holy
  Spirit,
one God, for ever and ever.

ALTERNATIVE OPENING PRAYER

Let us pray
  [in Advent time for the coming Savior
    to teach us wisdom]
Pause for silent prayer
Father in heaven,
the day draws near when the glory of your Son
will make radiant the night of the waiting
  world.
May the lure of greed not impede us from the
  joy
which moves the hearts of those who seek
  him.
May the darkness not blind us
to the vision of wisdom
which fills the minds of those who find him.

We ask this in the name of Jesus the Lord.

LITURGY OF THE WORD

See Lectionary for Mass, nos. 4-6.

LITURGY OF THE EUCHARIST

PRAYER OVER THE GIFTS

Pray, brethren . . .

Lord,
we are nothing without you.
As you sustain us with your mercy,
receive our prayers and offerings.

We ask this through Christ our Lord.

Eucharistic Prayer:
Preface of Advent I, page 418.

Communion Rite
> Rise up, Jerusalem, stand on the heights, and see the joy
> that is coming to you from God. (Baruch 5:5; 4:36)

A period of silence may be observed
after communion, or a psalm or song
of praise may be sung.

PRAYER AFTER COMMUNION

Let us pray.
Pause for silent prayer, if this has not preceded.

**Father,
you give us food from heaven.
By our sharing in this mystery,
teach us to judge wisely the things of earth
and to love the things of heaven.**

Grant this through Christ our Lord.

**SOLEMN BLESSING OR PRAYER
OVER THE PEOPLE**

The following may replace the simple
blessing.

After the greeting, the deacon (or in
his absence, the priest) gives the
invitation in these or similar words:

Bow your heads and pray for God's blessing.

Then the priest extends his hands
over the people while he sings or
says:

**Lord,
have mercy on your people.
Grant us in this life the good things
that lead to the everlasting life you prepare for us.
We ask this through Christ our Lord.
℟. Amen.**

**May almighty God bless you,
the Father, and the Son, ☩ and the Holy Spirit.
℟. Amen.**

For other texts of solemn blessings and
prayers over the people, see pages
528–540.

MONDAY OF THE SECOND WEEK OF ADVENT

Introductory Rites

Nations, hear the message of the Lord, and make it known
to the ends of the earth: Our Savior is coming. Have no
more fear. (See Jer. 31:10; Is. 35:4)

OPENING PRAYER

**Lord,
free us from our sins and make us whole.
Hear our prayer,
and prepare us to celebrate the incarnation of your Son,
who lives and reigns with you and the Holy Spirit,
one God, for ever and ever.**

See Lectionary for Mass, no. 182.

PRAYER OVER THE GIFTS

Pray, brethren . . .

**Father,
from all you give us
we present this bread and wine.
As we serve you now,
accept our offering
and sustain us with your promise of eternal life.**

Grant this through Christ our Lord.

Preface of Advent I, page 418.

Communion Rite

Come to us, Lord, and bring us peace. We will rejoice in
your presence and serve you with all our heart. (See Ps.
105:4-5; Is. 38:3)

PRAYER AFTER COMMUNION

Let us pray.
Pause for silent prayer, if this has not preceded.
**Father,
may our communion
teach us to love heaven.
May its promise and hope
guide our way on earth.**

We ask this through Christ our Lord.

TUESDAY OF THE SECOND WEEK OF ADVENT

Introductory Rites

See, the Lord is coming and with him all his saints. Then
there will be endless day. (See Zech. 14:5, 7)

OPENING PRAYER

**Almighty God,
help us to look forward
to the glory of the birth of Christ our Savior:
his coming is proclaimed joyfully
to the ends of the earth,
for he lives and reigns with you and the Holy Spirit,
one God, for ever and ever.**

See Lectionary for Mass, no. 183.

PRAYER OVER THE GIFTS

Pray, brethren . . .

**Lord,
we are nothing without you.
As you sustain us with your mercy,
receive our prayers and offerings.**

We ask this through Christ our Lord.

Preface of Advent I, page 418.

Communion Rite

The Lord is just; he will award the crown of justice to all
who have longed for his coming. (2 Tim. 4:8)

PRAYER AFTER COMMUNION

Let us pray.

Pause for silent prayer, if this has not preceded.

**Father,
you give us food from heaven.
By our sharing in this mystery,
teach us to judge wisely the things of earth
and to love the things of heaven.**

Grant this through Christ our Lord.

WEDNESDAY OF THE SECOND WEEK OF ADVENT

Introductory Rites
> The Lord is coming and will not delay; he will bring every
> hidden thing to light and reveal himself to every nation.
> (See Hab. 2:3; 1 Cor. 4:5)

OPENING PRAYER

All-powerful Father,
we await the healing power of Christ your Son.
Let us not be discouraged by our weaknesses
as we prepare for his coming.
Keep us steadfast in your love.

We ask this through our Lord Jesus Christ, your Son,
who lives and reigns with you and the Holy Spirit,
one God, for ever and ever.

See Lectionary for Mass, no. 184.

PRAYER OVER THE GIFTS

Pray, brethren . . .

Lord,
may the gift we offer in faith and love
be a continual sacrifice in your honor
and truly become our eucharist and our salvation.

Grant this through Christ our Lord.

Preface of Advent I, page 418.

Communion Rite
> The Lord our God comes in strength and will fill his
> servants with joy. (Is. 40:10; see 34:5)

PRAYER AFTER COMMUNION

Let us pray.
Pause for silent prayer, if this has not preceded.
God of mercy,
may this eucharist bring us your divine help,
free us from our sins,
and prepare us for the birthday of our Savior,
who is Lord for ever and ever.

THURSDAY OF THE SECOND WEEK OF ADVENT

Introductory Rites

Lord, you are near, and all your commandments are just;
long have I known that you decreed them for ever. (See Ps.
118:151-152)

OPENING PRAYER

**Almighty Father,
give us the joy of your love
to prepare the way for Christ our Lord.
Help us to serve you and one another.**

**We ask this through our Lord Jesus Christ, your Son,
who lives and reigns with you and the Holy Spirit,
one God, for ever and ever.**

See Lectionary for Mass, no. 185.

PRAYER OVER THE GIFTS

Pray, brethren . . .

**Father,
from all you give us
we present this bread and wine.
As we serve you now,
accept our offering
and sustain us with your promise of eternal life.**

Grant this through Christ our Lord.

Preface of Advent I, page **418**.

Communion Rite

Let our lives be honest and holy in this present age, as we
wait for the happiness to come when our great God
reveals himself in glory. (Titus 2:12-13)

PRAYER AFTER COMMUNION

Let us pray.
Pause for silent prayer, if this has not preceded.
**Father,
may our communion
teach us to love heaven.
May its promise and hope
guide our way on earth.**

We ask this through Christ our Lord.

FRIDAY OF THE SECOND WEEK OF ADVENT

Introductory Rites

The Lord is coming from heaven in splendor to visit his
people, and bring them peace and eternal life.

OPENING PRAYER

**All-powerful God,
help us to look forward in hope
to the coming of our Savior.
May we live as he has taught,
ready to welcome him with burning love and faith.**

**We ask this through our Lord Jesus Christ, your Son,
who lives and reigns with you and the Holy Spirit,
one God, for ever and ever.**

See Lectionary for Mass, no. 186.

PRAYER OVER THE GIFTS

Pray, brethren . . .

**Lord,
we are nothing without you.
As you sustain us with your mercy,
receive our prayers and offerings.**

We ask this through Christ our Lord.

Preface of Advent I, page 418.

Communion Rite

We are waiting for our Savior, the Lord Jesus Christ; he
will transfigure our lowly bodies into copies of his own
glorious body. (Phil. 3:20-21)

PRAYER AFTER COMMUNION

Let us pray.

Pause for silent prayer, if this has not preceded.

**Father,
you give us food from heaven.
By our sharing in this mystery,
teach us to judge wisely the things of earth
and to love the things of heaven.**

Grant this through Christ our Lord.

SATURDAY OF THE SECOND WEEK OF ADVENT

Introductory Rites

Come, Lord, from your cherubim throne; let us see your
face, and we shall be saved. (Ps. 79:4, 2)

OPENING PRAYER

Lord,
let your glory dawn to take away our darkness.
May we be revealed as the children of light
at the coming of your Son,
who lives and reigns with you and the Holy Spirit,
one God, for ever and ever.

See Lectionary for Mass, no. 187.

PRAYER OVER THE GIFTS

Pray, brethren . . .

Lord,
may the gift we offer in faith and love
be a continual sacrifice in your honor
and truly become our eucharist and our salvation.

Grant this through Christ our Lord.

Preface of Advent I, page **418.**

Communion Rite

I am coming quickly, says the Lord, and will repay each
man according to his deeds. (Rev. 22:12)

PRAYER AFTER COMMUNION

Let us pray.
Pause for silent prayer, if this has not preceded.
God of mercy,
may this eucharist bring us your divine help,
free us from our sins,
and prepare us for the birthday of our Savior,
who is Lord for ever and ever.

THIRD SUNDAY OF ADVENT

Introductory Rites

Rejoice in the Lord always; again I say, rejoice! The Lord is near. (Phil. 4:4, 5)

The Gloria is omitted.

OPENING PRAYER

Let us pray
[that God will fill us with joy
at the coming of Christ]
Pause for silent prayer
Lord God,
may we, your people,
who look forward to the birthday of Christ
experience the joy of salvation
and celebrate that feast with love and
thanksgiving.

We ask this through our Lord Jesus Christ,
your Son,
who lives and reigns with you and the Holy
Spirit,
one God, for ever and ever.

ALTERNATIVE OPENING PRAYER

Let us pray
[this Advent for joy and hope
in the coming Lord]
Pause for silent prayer
Father of our Lord Jesus Christ,
ever faithful to your promises
and ever close to your Church:
the earth rejoices in hope of the Savior's
coming
and looks forward with longing
to his return at the end of time.
Prepare our hearts and remove the sadness
that hinders us from feeling the joy and hope
which his presence will bestow,
for he is Lord for ever and ever.

LITURGY OF THE WORD

See Lectionary for Mass, nos. 7-9.

LITURGY OF THE EUCHARIST

PRAYER OVER THE GIFTS

Pray, brethren . . .

Lord,
may the gift we offer in faith and love
be a continual sacrifice in your honor
and truly become our eucharist and our salvation.

Grant this through Christ our Lord.

Eucharistic Prayer:
Preface of Advent I or II, pages 418–
419.

Communion Rite

Say to the anxious: be strong and fear not, our God will
come to save us. (See Is. 35:4)

A period of silence may be observed
after communion, or a psalm or song
of praise may be sung.

PRAYER AFTER COMMUNION

Let us pray.
Pause for silent prayer, if this has not preceded.
**God of mercy,
may this eucharist bring us your divine help,
free us from our sins,
and prepare us for the birthday of our Savior,
who is Lord for ever and ever.**

**SOLEMN BLESSING OR PRAYER
OVER THE PEOPLE**

The following may replace the simple
blessing.

After the greeting, the deacon (or in
his absence, the priest) gives the
invitation in these or similar words:

Bow your heads and pray for God's blessing.

Then the priest extends his hands
over the people while he sings or
says:

**You believe that the Son of God once came to us;
you look for him to come again.
May his coming bring you the light of his holiness
and his blessing bring you freedom.
℟. Amen.**

**May God make you steadfast in faith,
joyful in hope, and untiring in love
all the days of your life.
℟. Amen.**

**You rejoice that our Redeemer came to live with us as man.
When he comes again in glory,
may he reward you with endless life.
℟. Amen.**

**May almighty God bless you,
the Father, and the Son, ✝ and the Holy Spirit.
℟. Amen.**

For other texts of solemn blessings and
prayers over the people, see pages
528–540.

MONDAY OF THE THIRD WEEK OF ADVENT

For the Advent weekday Masses from December 17 to December 24, see pages 101–107, 110.

Introductory Rites

Nations, hear the message of the Lord, and make it known to the ends of the earth: Our Savior is coming. Have no more fear. (See Jer. 31:10; Is. 35:4)

OPENING PRAYER

**Lord,
hear our voices raised in prayer.
Let the light of the coming of your Son
free us from the darkness of sin.**

**We ask this through our Lord Jesus Christ, your Son,
who lives and reigns with you and the Holy Spirit,
one God, for ever and ever.**

See Lectionary for Mass, no. 188.

PRAYER OVER THE GIFTS

Pray, brethren . . .

**Father,
from all you give us
we present this bread and wine.
As we serve you now,
accept our offering
and sustain us with your promise of eternal life.**

Grant this through Christ our Lord.

Preface of Advent I, page 418.

Communion Rite

Come to us, Lord, and bring us peace. We will rejoice in your presence and serve you with all our heart. (See Ps. 105:4-5; Is. 38:3)

PRAYER AFTER COMMUNION

Let us pray.

Pause for silent prayer, if this has not preceded.

**Father,
may our communion
teach us to love heaven.
May its promise and hope
guide our way on earth.**

We ask this through Christ our Lord.

TUESDAY OF THE THIRD WEEK OF ADVENT

For the Advent weekday Masses from
December 17 to December 24, see
pages 101–107, 110.

Introductory Rites

See, the Lord is coming and with him all his saints. Then
there will be endless day. (See Zech. 14:5, 7)

OPENING PRAYER

Father of love,
you made a new creation
through Jesus Christ your Son.
May his coming free us from sin
and renew his life within us,
for he lives and reigns with you and the Holy Spirit,
one God, for ever and ever.

See Lectionary for Mass, no. 189.

PRAYER OVER THE GIFTS

Pray, brethren . . .

Lord,
we are nothing without you.
As you sustain us with your mercy,
receive our prayers and offerings.

We ask this through Christ our Lord.

Preface of Advent I, page 418.

Communion Rite

The Lord is just; he will award the crown of justice to all
who have longed for his coming. (2 Tim. 4:8)

PRAYER AFTER COMMUNION

Let us pray.
Pause for silent prayer, if this has not preceded.
Father,
you give us food from heaven.
By our sharing in this mystery,
teach us to judge wisely the things of earth
and to love the things of heaven.

Grant this through Christ our Lord.

WEDNESDAY OF THE THIRD WEEK OF ADVENT

For the Advent weekday Masses from
December 17 to December 24, see
pages 101–107, 110.

Introductory Rites

The Lord is coming and will not delay; he will bring every
hidden thing to light and reveal himself to every nation.
(See Hab. 2:3; 1 Cor. 4:5)

OPENING PRAYER

Father,
may the coming celebration of the birth of your Son
bring us your saving help
and prepare us for eternal life.

Grant this through our Lord Jesus Christ, your Son,
who lives and reigns with you and the Holy Spirit,
one God, for ever and ever.

See Lectionary for Mass, no. 190.

PRAYER OVER THE GIFTS

Pray, brethren . . .

Lord,
may the gift we offer in faith and love
be a continual sacrifice in your honor
and truly become our eucharist and our salvation.

Grant this through Christ our Lord.

Preface of Advent I, page 418.

Communion Rite

The Lord our God comes in strength and will fill his
servants with joy. (Is. 40:10; see 34:5)

PRAYER AFTER COMMUNION

Let us pray.
Pause for silent prayer, if this has not preceded.
God of mercy,
may this eucharist bring us your divine help,
free us from our sins,
and prepare us for the birthday of our Savior,
who is Lord for ever and ever.

THURSDAY OF THE THIRD WEEK OF ADVENT

For the Advent weekday Masses from December 17 to December 24, see pages 101–107, 110.

Introductory Rites

Lord, you are near, and all your commandments are just; long have I known that you decreed them for ever. (See Ps. 118:151-152)

OPENING PRAYER

Lord,
our sins bring us unhappiness.
Hear our prayer for courage and strength.
May the coming of your Son
bring us the joy of salvation.

We ask this through our Lord Jesus Christ, your Son,
who lives and reigns with you and the Holy Spirit,
one God, for ever and ever.

See Lectionary for Mass, no. 191.

PRAYER OVER THE GIFTS

Pray, brethren . . .

Father,
from all you give us
we present this bread and wine.
As we serve you now,
accept our offering
and sustain us with your promise of eternal life.

Grant this through Christ our Lord.

Preface of Advent I, page 418.

Communion Rite

Let our lives be honest and holy in this present age, as we wait for the happiness to come when our great God reveals himself in glory. (Titus 2:12-13)

PRAYER AFTER COMMUNION

Let us pray.
Pause for silent prayer, if this has not preceded.

Father,
may our communion
teach us to love heaven.
May its promise and hope
guide our way on earth.

We ask this through Christ our Lord.

FRIDAY OF THE THIRD WEEK OF ADVENT

For the Advent weekday Masses from December 17 to December 24, see pages 101–107, 110.

Introductory Rites

The Lord is coming from heaven in splendor to visit his people, and bring them peace and eternal life.

OPENING PRAYER

**All-powerful Father,
guide us with your love
as we await the coming of your Son.
Keep us faithful
that we may be helped through life
and brought to salvation.**

**We ask this through our Lord Jesus Christ, your Son,
who lives and reigns with you and the Holy Spirit,
one God, for ever and ever.**

See Lectionary for Mass, no. 192.

PRAYER OVER THE GIFTS

Pray, brethren . . .

**Lord,
we are nothing without you.
As you sustain us with your mercy,
receive our prayers and offerings.**

We ask this through Christ our Lord.

Preface of Advent I, page 418.

Communion Rite

We are waiting for our Savior, the Lord Jesus Christ; he will transfigure our lowly bodies into copies of his own glorious body. (Phil. 3:20-21)

PRAYER AFTER COMMUNION

Let us pray.
Pause for silent prayer, if this has not preceded.

**Father,
you give us food from heaven.
By our sharing in this mystery,
teach us to judge wisely the things of earth
and to love the things of heaven.**

Grant this through Christ our Lord.

WEEKDAYS OF ADVENT

from December 17 to December 24

The following Masses are used on the days assigned, with the exception of Sunday.

DECEMBER 17

Introductory Rites

You heavens, sing for joy, and earth exult! Our Lord is coming; he will take pity on those in distress. (See Is. 49:13)

OPENING PRAYER

Father,
creator and redeemer of mankind,
you decreed, and your Word became man,
born of the Virgin Mary.
May we come to share the divinity of Christ,
who humbled himself to share our human nature,
for he lives and reigns with you and the Holy Spirit,
one God, for ever and ever.

See Lectionary for Mass, no. 194.

PRAYER OVER THE GIFTS

Pray, brethren . . .

Lord,
bless these gifts of your Church
and by this eucharist
renew us with the bread from heaven.

We ask this in the name of Jesus the Lord.

Preface of Advent II, page **419**.

Communion Rite

The Desired of all nations is coming, and the house of the Lord will be filled with his glory. (See Haggai 2:8)

PRAYER AFTER COMMUNION

Let us pray.

Pause for silent prayer, if this has not preceded.
God our Father,
as you nourish us with the food of life,
give us also your Spirit,
so that we may be radiant with his light
at the coming of Christ your Son,
who is Lord for ever and ever.

DECEMBER 18

Introductory Rites
> Christ our King is coming, the Lamb whom John pro-
> claimed.

OPENING PRAYER

**All-powerful God,
renew us by the coming feast of your Son
and free us from our slavery to sin.**

**Grant this through our Lord Jesus Christ, your Son,
who lives and reigns with you and the Holy Spirit,
one God, for ever and ever.**

See Lectionary for Mass, no. 195.

PRAYER OVER THE GIFTS

Pray, brethren . . .

**Lord,
may this sacrifice
bring us into the eternal life of your Son,
who died to save us from death,
for he is Lord for ever and ever.**

Preface of Advent II, page 419.

Communion Rite
> His name will be called Emmanuel, which means God is
> with us. (Matthew 1:23)

PRAYER AFTER COMMUNION

Let us pray.
Pause for silent prayer, if this has not preceded.
**Lord,
we receive mercy in your Church.
Prepare us to celebrate with fitting honor
the coming feast of our redemption.**

We ask this in the name of Jesus the Lord.

DECEMBER 19

Introductory Rites

He who is to come will not delay; and then there will be no fear in our lands, because he is our Savior. (See Heb. 10:37)

OPENING PRAYER

Father,
you show the world the splendor of your glory
in the coming of Christ, born of the Virgin.
Give to us true faith and love
to celebrate the mystery of God made man.

We ask this through our Lord Jesus Christ, your Son,
who lives and reigns with you and the Holy Spirit,
one God, for ever and ever.

See Lectionary for Mass, no. 196.

PRAYER OVER THE GIFTS

Pray, brethren . . .

Lord of mercy,
receive the gifts we bring to your altar.
Let your power take away our weakness
and make our offerings holy.

We ask this in the name of Jesus the Lord.

Preface of Advent II, page 419.

Communion Rite

The dawn from on high shall break upon us, to guide our feet on the road to peace. (Luke 1:78-79)

PRAYER AFTER COMMUNION

Let us pray.
Pause for silent prayer, if this has not preceded.
Father,
we give you thanks for the bread of life.
Open our hearts in welcome
to prepare for the coming of our Savior,
who is Lord for ever and ever.

DECEMBER 20

Introductory Rites

A shoot will spring from Jesse's stock, and all mankind will see the saving power of God. (See Is. 11:1; 40:5; Luke 3:6)

OPENING PRAYER

**God of love and mercy,
help us to follow the example of Mary,
always ready to do your will.
At the message of an angel
she welcomed your eternal Son
and, filled with the light of your Spirit,
she became the temple of your Word,
who lives and reigns with you and the Holy Spirit,
one God, for ever and ever.**

See Lectionary for Mass, no. 197.

PRAYER OVER THE GIFTS

Pray, brethren . . .

**Lord,
accept this sacrificial gift.
May the eucharist we share
bring us to the eternal life
we seek in faith and hope.**

Grant this through Christ our Lord.

Preface of Advent II, page 419.

Communion Rite

The angel said to Mary: you shall conceive and bear a son, and you shall call him Jesus. (Luke 1:31)

PRAYER AFTER COMMUNION

Let us pray.
Pause for silent prayer, if this has not preceded.
**Lord,
watch over the people you nourish with this eucharist.
Lead them to rejoice in true peace.**

We ask this in the name of Jesus the Lord.

DECEMBER 21

Soon the Lord God will come, and you will call him
Emmanuel, for God is with us. (See Is. 7:14; 8:10)

OPENING PRAYER

**Lord,
hear the prayers of your people.
May we who celebrate the birth of your Son as man
rejoice in the gift of eternal life when he comes in glory,
for he lives and reigns with you and the Holy Spirit,
one God, for ever and ever.**

See Lectionary for Mass, no. 198.

PRAYER OVER THE GIFTS

Pray, brethren . . .

**Lord of love,
receive these gifts which you have given to your Church.
Let them become for us
the means of our salvation.**

We ask this through Christ our Lord.

Preface of Advent II, page 419.

Communion Rite
Blessed are you for your firm believing, that the promises
of the Lord would be fulfilled. (Luke 1:45)

PRAYER AFTER COMMUNION

Let us pray.
Pause for silent prayer, if this has not preceded.
**Lord,
help us to serve you
that we may be brought to salvation.
May this eucharist be our constant protection.**

Grant this in the name of Jesus the Lord.

DECEMBER 22

Introductory Rites
> Gates, lift up your heads! Stand erect, ancient doors, and let in the King of glory. (Ps. 23:7)

OPENING PRAYER

**God our Father,
you sent your Son
to free mankind from the power of death.
May we who celebrate the coming of Christ as man
share more fully in his divine life,
for he lives and reigns with you and the Holy Spirit,
one God, for ever and ever.**

See Lectionary for Mass, no. 199.

PRAYER OVER THE GIFTS

Pray, brethren . . .

**Lord God,
with confidence in your love
we come with gifts to worship at your altar.
By the mystery of this eucharist
purify us and renew your life within us.**

We ask this through Christ our Lord. ·

Preface of Advent II, page 419.

Communion Rite
> My soul proclaims the greatness of the Lord, for the Almighty has done great things for me. (Luke 1:46, 49)

PRAYER AFTER COMMUNION

Let us pray.
Pause for silent prayer, if this has not preceded.
**Lord,
strengthen us by the sacrament we have received.
Help us to go out to meet our Savior
and to merit eternal life
with lives that witness to our faith.**

We ask this in the name of Jesus the Lord.

DECEMBER 23

Introductory Rites

A little child is born for us, and he shall be called the mighty God; every race on earth shall be blessed in him. (See Is. 9:6; Ps. 71:17)

OPENING PRAYER

**Father,
we contemplate the birth of your Son.
He was born of the Virgin Mary
and came to live among us.
May we receive forgiveness and mercy
through our Lord Jesus Christ, your Son,
who lives and reigns with you and the Holy Spirit,
one God, for ever and ever.**

See Lectionary for Mass, no. 200.

PRAYER OVER THE GIFTS

Pray, brethren . . .

**Lord,
you have given us this memorial
as the perfect form of worship.
Restore us to your peace
and prepare us to celebrate the coming of our Savior,
for he is Lord for ever and ever.**

Preface of Advent II, page 419.

Communion Rite

I stand at the door and knock, says the Lord. If anyone hears my voice and opens the door, I will come in and sit down to supper with him and he with me. (Rev. 3:20)

PRAYER AFTER COMMUNION

Let us pray.

Pause for silent prayer, if this has not preceded.

**Lord,
as you nourish us with the bread of life,
give peace to our spirits
and prepare us to welcome your Son with ardent faith.**

We ask this through Christ our Lord.

FOURTH SUNDAY OF ADVENT

Introductory Rites

> Let the clouds rain down the Just One, and the earth bring forth a Savior. (Is. 45:8)

The Gloria is omitted.

OPENING PRAYER

Let us pray

> **[as Advent draws to a close, that Christ will truly come into our hearts]**

Pause for silent prayer

**Lord,
fill our hearts with your love,
and as you revealed to us by an angel
the coming of your Son as man,
so lead us through his suffering and death
to the glory of his resurrection,
for he lives and reigns with you and the Holy Spirit,
one God, for ever and ever.**

ALTERNATIVE OPENING PRAYER

Let us pray

> **[as Advent draws to a close for the faith that opens our lives to the Spirit of God]**

Pause for silent prayer

**Father, all-powerful God,
your eternal Word took flesh on our earth
when the Virgin Mary placed her life
at the service of your plan.
Lift our minds in watchful hope
to hear the voice which announces his glory
and open our minds to receive the Spirit
who prepares us for his coming.**

We ask this through Christ our Lord.

LITURGY OF THE WORD

See Lectionary for Mass, nos. 10-12.

LITURGY OF THE EUCHARIST

PRAYER OVER THE GIFTS

Pray, brethren . . .

**Lord,
may the power of the Spirit,
which sanctified Mary the mother of your Son,
make holy the gifts we place upon this altar.**

Grant this through Christ our Lord.

Eucharistic Prayer:
Preface of Advent II, page 419.

Communion Rite

The Virgin is with child and shall bear a son, and she will
call him Emmanuel. (Is. 7:14)

A period of silence may be observed
after communion, or a psalm or song
of praise may be sung.

PRAYER AFTER COMMUNION

Let us pray.
Pause for silent prayer, if this has not preceded.
**Lord,
in this sacrament
we receive the promise of salvation;
as Christmas draws near
make us grow in faith and love
to celebrate the coming of Christ our Savior,
who is Lord for ever and ever.**

**SOLEMN BLESSING OR PRAYER
OVER THE PEOPLE**

The following may replace the
simple blessing.

After the greeting, the deacon (or in
his absence, the priest) gives the
invitation in these or similar words:

Bow your heads and pray for God's blessing.

Then the priest extends his hands
over the people while he sings or
says:

**Lord,
may all Christian people both know and cherish
the heavenly gifts they have received.
We ask this in the name of Jesus the Lord.
℟. Amen.**

**May almighty God bless you,
the Father, and the Son, ✠ and the Holy Spirit.
℟. Amen.**

For other texts of solemn blessings and
prayers over the people, see pages
528–540.

DECEMBER 24
Mass in the Morning

Introductory Rites

> The appointed time has come; God has sent his Son into
> the world. (See Gal. 4:4)

OPENING PRAYER

Come, Lord Jesus,
do not delay;
give new courage to your people who trust in your love.
By your coming, raise us to the joy of your kingdom,
where you live and reign with the Father and the Holy Spirit,
one God, for ever and ever.

See Lectionary for Mass, no. 201.

PRAYER OVER THE GIFTS

Pray, brethren . . .

Father,
accept the gifts we offer.
By our sharing in this eucharist
free us from sin
and help us to look forward in faith
to the glorious coming of your Son,
who is Lord for ever and ever.

Preface of Advent II, page 419.

Communion Rite

> Blessed be the Lord God of Israel, for he has visited and
> redeemed his people. (Luke 1:68)

PRAYER AFTER COMMUNION

Let us pray.
Pause for silent prayer, if this has not preceded.
Lord,
your gift of the eucharist has renewed our lives.
May we who look forward to the feast of Christ's birth
rejoice for ever in the wonder of his love,
for he is Lord for ever and ever.

CHRISTMAS SEASON

December 25

CHRISTMAS – VIGIL MASS

Solemnity

This Mass is celebrated during the afternoon of December 24, before or after Evening Prayer I of Christmas.

Introductory Rites

Today you will know that the Lord is coming to save us, and in the morning you will see his glory. (See Exod. 16:6-7)

OPENING PRAYER

Let us pray
  **[that Christmas morning
   will find us at peace]**

Pause for silent prayer
**God our Father,
every year we rejoice
as we look forward to this feast of our salvation.
May we welcome Christ as our Redeemer,
and meet him with confidence when he comes
   to be our judge,
who lives and reigns with you and the Holy
   Spirit,
one God, for ever and ever.**

ALTERNATIVE OPENING PRAYER

Let us pray
  **[and be ready to welcome
   the Lord]**

Pause for silent prayer
**God of endless ages, Father of all goodness,
we keep vigil for the dawn of salvation
and the birth of your Son.**

**With gratitude we recall his humanity,
the life he shared with the sons of men.
May the power of his divinity
help us answer his call to forgiveness and life.**

We ask this through Christ our Lord.

LITURGY OF THE WORD

See Lectionary for Mass, no. 13.

In the profession of faith, all genuflect at the words, **and became man.**

LITURGY OF THE EUCHARIST

PRAYER OVER THE GIFTS

Pray, brethren . . .

**Lord,
as we keep tonight the vigil of Christmas,
may we celebrate this eucharist
with greater joy than ever
since it marks the beginning of our redemption.**

We ask this in the name of Jesus the Lord.

Eucharistic Prayer:
Preface of Christmas I-III, pages **420–422**.

When Eucharistic Prayer I is used, the special Christmas form of **In union with the whole Church** is said.

Communion Rite

> The glory of the Lord will be revealed, and all mankind will see the saving power of God. (See Is. 40:5)

A period of silence may be observed after communion, or a psalm or song of praise may be sung.

PRAYER AFTER COMMUNION

Let us pray.
Pause for silent prayer, if this has not preceded.
Father,
we ask you to give us a new birth
as we celebrate the beginning
of your Son's life on earth.
Strengthen us in spirit
as we take your food and drink.

Grant this through Christ our Lord.

SOLEMN BLESSING OR PRAYER OVER THE PEOPLE

The following may replace the simple blessing.

After the greeting, the deacon (or in his absence, the priest) gives the invitation in these or similar words:

Bow your heads and pray for God's blessing.

Then the priest extends his hands over the people while he sings or says:

Lord,
bless and strengthen your people.
May they remain faithful to you
and always rejoice in your mercy.

We ask this in the name of Jesus the Lord.
℟. Amen.

May almighty God bless you,
the Father, and the Son, ✠ and the Holy Spirit.
℟. Amen.

For other texts of solemn blessings and prayers over the people, see pages **528–540**.

On Christmas, all priests may celebrate or concelebrate three Masses, provided that they are celebrated at their proper times.

CHRISTMAS—MASS AT MIDNIGHT

Introductory Rites

> The Lord said to me: You are my Son; this day have I
> begotten you. (Ps. 2:7)
>
> or:
>
> Let us all rejoice in the Lord, for our Savior is born to the
> world. True peace has descended from heaven.

OPENING PRAYER

Let us pray

**[in the peace of Christmas midnight that our
joy in the birth of Christ will last for ever]**

Pause for silent prayer

**Father,
you make this holy night radiant
with the splendor of Jesus Christ our light.
We welcome him as Lord, the true light of the
world.
Bring us to eternal joy in the kingdom of
heaven.
where he lives and reigns with you and the
Holy Spirit,
one God, for ever and ever.**

ALTERNATIVE OPENING PRAYER

Let us pray

**[with joy and hope as we await
the dawning of the Father's Word]**

Pause for silent prayer

**Lord our God,
with the birth of your Son,
your glory breaks on the world.**

**Through the night hours of the darkened earth
we your people watch for the coming of your
promised Son.
As we wait, give us a foretaste of the joy that
you will grant us
when the fullness of his glory has filled the
earth,
who lives and reigns with you for ever and
ever.**

LITURGY OF THE WORD

See Lectionary for Mass, no. 14.

In the profession of faith, all genuflect at the words, and became man.

LITURGY OF THE EUCHARIST

PRAYER OVER THE GIFTS

Pray, brethren . . .

**Lord,
accept our gifts on this joyful feast of our salvation.
By our communion with God made man,
may we become more like him
who joins our lives to yours,
for he is Lord for ever and ever.**

Eucharistic Prayer:
Preface of Christmas I–III, pages 420–
422.

When Eucharistic Prayer I is used, the
special Christmas form of **In union
with the whole Church** is said.

Communion Rite

The Word of God became man; we have seen his glory.
(John 1:14)

A period of silence may be observed after communion, or a psalm or song of praise may be sung.

PRAYER AFTER COMMUNION

Let us pray.
Pause for silent prayer, if this has not preceded.
**God our Father,
we rejoice in the birth of our Savior.
May we share his life completely
by living as he has taught.
We ask this in the name of Jesus the Lord.**

SOLEMN BLESSING OR PRAYER OVER THE PEOPLE

The following may replace the simple blessing.

After the greeting, the deacon (or in his absence, the priest) gives the invitation in these or similar words:

Bow your heads and pray for God's blessing.

Then the priest extends his hands over the people while he sings or says:

**When he came to us as man,
the Son of God scattered the darkness of this world,
and filled this holy night with his glory.
May the God of infinite goodness
scatter the darkness of sin
and brighten your hearts with holiness.**
℟. **Amen.**

**God sent his angels to shepherds
to herald the great joy of our Savior's birth.
May he fill you with joy
and make you heralds of his gospel.**
℟. **Amen.**

**When the Word became man,
earth was joined to heaven.
May he give you his peace and good will,
and fellowship with all the heavenly host.**
℟. **Amen.**

**May almighty God bless you,
the Father, and the Son, ☩ and the Holy Spirit.**
℟. **Amen.**

For other texts of solemn blessings and prayers over the people, see pages 528–540.

CHRISTMAS – MASS AT DAWN

Introductory Rites

> A light will shine on us this day, the Lord is born for us: he shall be called Wonderful God, Prince of peace, Father of the world to come; and his kingship will never end. (See Is. 9:2, 6; Luke 1:33)

OPENING PRAYER

Let us pray
  **[that the love of Christ will be
  a light to the world]**

Pause for silent prayer

**Father,
we are filled with the new light
by the coming of your Word among us.
May the light of faith
shine in our words and actions.**

**Grant this through our Lord Jesus Christ, your Son,
who lives and reigns with you and the Holy Spirit,
one God, for ever and ever.**

ALTERNATIVE OPENING PRAYER

Let us pray
  **[for the peace that comes
  from the Prince of Peace]**

Pause for silent prayer

**Almighty God and Father of light,
a child is born for us and a son is given to us.
Your eternal Word leaped down from heaven
in the silent watches of the night,
and now your Church is filled with wonder
at the nearness of her God.**

**Open our hearts to receive his life
and increase our vision with the rising of dawn,
that our lives may be filled with his glory and his peace,
who lives and reigns for ever and ever.**

LITURGY OF THE WORD

See Lectionary for Mass, no. 15.

In the profession of faith, all genuflect at the words, **and became man.**

LITURGY OF THE EUCHARIST

PRAYER OVER THE GIFTS

Pray, brethren . . .

**Father,
may we follow the example of your Son
who became man and lived among us.
May we receive the gift of divine life
through these offerings here on earth.**

We ask this in the name of Jesus the Lord.

Eucharistic Prayer:
Preface of Christmas I-III, pages 420–422.

When Eucharistic Prayer I is used, the special Christmas form of **In union with the whole Church** is said.

Communion Rite

Daughter of Zion, exult; shout aloud, daughter of Jerusalem! Your King is coming, the Holy One, the Savior of the world. (See Zech. 9:9)

A period of silence may be observed after communion, or a psalm or song of praise may be sung.

PRAYER AFTER COMMUNION

Let us pray.

Pause for silent prayer, if this has not preceded.

Lord,
with faith and joy
we celebrate the birthday of your Son.
Increase our understanding and our love
of the riches you have revealed in him,
who is Lord for ever and ever.

SOLEMN BLESSING OR PRAYER OVER THE PEOPLE

The following may replace the simple blessing.

After the greeting, the deacon (or in his absence, the priest) gives the invitation in these or similar words:

Bow your heads and pray for God's blessing.

Then the priest extends his hands over the people while he sings or says:

Lord,
grant your people your protection and grace.
Give them health of mind and body,
perfect love for one another,
and make them always faithful to you.

Grant this through Christ our Lord.
R̸. Amen.

May almighty God bless you,
the Father, and the Son, ✝ and the Holy Spirit.
R̸. Amen.

For other texts of solemn blessings and prayers over the people, see pages 528–540.

CHRISTMAS—MASS DURING THE DAY

Introductory Rites
A child is born for us, a son given to us; dominion is laid on his shoulder, and he shall be called Wonderful-Counsellor. (Is. 9:6)

OPENING PRAYER

Let us pray
  [for the glory promised
   by the birth of Christ]

Pause for silent prayer
Lord God,
we praise you for creating man,
and still more for restoring him in Christ.
Your Son shared our weakness:
may we share his glory,
for he lives and reigns with you and the Holy
  Spirit,
one God, for ever and ever.

ALTERNATIVE OPENING PRAYER

Let us pray
  [in the joy of Christmas because the
   Son of God lives among us]

Pause for silent prayer
God of love, Father of all,
the darkness that covered the earth
has given way to the bright dawn of your Word
  made flesh.
Make us a people of this light.
Make us faithful to your Word,
that we may bring your life to the waiting
  world.

Grant this through Christ our Lord.

LITURGY OF THE WORD

See Lectionary for Mass, no. 16.

In the profession of faith, all genuflect at the words, and became man.

LITURGY OF THE EUCHARIST

PRAYER OVER THE GIFTS

Pray, brethren . . .

Almighty God,
the saving work of Christ
made our peace with you.
May our offering today
renew that peace within us
and give you perfect praise.

We ask this in the name of Jesus the Lord.

Eucharistic Prayer:
Preface of Christmas I-III, pages 420–422

When Eucharistic Prayer I is used, the special Christmas form of In union with the whole Church is said.

Communion Rite
All the ends of the earth have seen the saving power of God. (Ps. 97:3)

A period of silence may be observed after communion, or a psalm or song of praise may be sung.

PRAYER AFTER COMMUNION

Let us pray.
Pause for silent prayer, if this has not preceded.
Father,
the child born today is the Savior of the world.
He made us your children.
May he welcome us into your kingdom
where he lives and reigns with you for ever and ever.

SOLEMN BLESSING OR PRAYER OVER THE PEOPLE

The following may replace the simple blessing.

After the greeting, the deacon (or in his absence, the priest) gives the invitation in these or similar words:

Then the priest extends his hands over the people while he sings or says:

Bow your heads and pray for God's blessing.

When he came to us as man,
the Son of God scattered the darkness of this world,
and filled this holy day with his glory.
May the God of infinite goodness
scatter the darkness of sin
and brighten your hearts with holiness.
℟. Amen.

God sent his angels to shepherds
to herald the great joy of our Savior's birth.
May he fill you with joy
and make you heralds of his gospel.
℟. Amen.

When the Word became man,
earth was joined to heaven.
May he give you his peace and good will,
and fellowship with all the heavenly host.
℟. Amen.

May almighty God bless you,
the Father, and the Son, ✝ and the Holy Spirit.
℟. Amen.

For other texts of solemn blessings and prayers over the people, see pages 528–540.

HOLY FAMILY

Feast

Introductory Rites

The shepherds hastened to Bethlehem, where they found
Mary and Joseph, and the baby lying in a manger. (Luke
2:16)

OPENING PRAYER

Let us pray
  [for peace in our families]

Pause for silent prayer

Father,
help us to live as the holy family,
united in respect and love.
**Bring us to the joy and peace of your eternal
  home.**
**Grant this through our Lord Jesus Christ, your
  Son,**
**who lives and reigns with you and the Holy
  Spirit,**
one God, for ever and ever.

ALTERNATIVE OPENING PRAYER

Let us pray
  [as the family of God,
   who share in his life]

Pause for silent prayer

Father in heaven, creator of all,
you ordered the earth to bring forth life
**and crowned its goodness by creating the
    family of man.**
In history's moment when all was ready,
you sent your Son to dwell in time,
obedient to the laws of life in our world.
Teach us the sanctity of human love,
show us the value of family life,
and help us to live in peace with all men
that we may share in your life for ever.

We ask this through Christ our Lord.

LITURGY OF THE WORD

See Lectionary for Mass, no. 17.

Profession of faith, when this feast is
celebrated on Sunday.

LITURGY OF THE EUCHARIST

PRAYER OVER THE GIFTS

Pray, brethren . . .

Lord,
accept this sacrifice
and through the prayers of Mary, the virgin Mother of God,
and of her husband, Joseph,
unite our families in peace and love.

We ask this in the name of Jesus the Lord.

Eucharistic Prayer:
Preface of Christmas I-III, pages 420–
422.

When Eucharistic Prayer I is used, the
special Christmas form of In union
with the whole Church is said.

Communion Rite

Our God has appeared on earth, and lived among men.
(Baruch 3:38)

A period of silence may be observed after communion, or a psalm or song of praise may be sung.

PRAYER AFTER COMMUNION

Let us pray.
Pause for silent prayer, if this has not preceded.

Eternal Father,
we want to live as Jesus, Mary, and Joseph,
in peace with you and one another.
May this communion strengthen us
to face the troubles of life.

Grant this through Christ our Lord.

SOLEMN BLESSING OR PRAYER OVER THE PEOPLE

The following may replace the simple blessing.

After the greeting, the deacon (or in his absence, the priest) gives the invitation in these or similar words:

Bow your heads and pray for God's blessing.

Then the priest extends his hands over the people while he sings or says:

Lord,
you care for your people even when they stray.
Grant us a complete change of heart,
so that we may follow you with greater fidelity.

Grant this through Christ our Lord.
℞. **Amen.**

May almighty God bless you,
the Father, and the Son, ✝ and the Holy Spirit.
℞. **Amen.**

For other texts of solemn blessings and prayers over the people, see pages 528–540.

When Christmas falls on a Sunday, the feast of the Holy Family is celebrated on December 30.

December 26
ST. STEPHEN, first martyr
Feast

Introductory Rites

The gates of heaven opened for Stephen, the first of the martyrs; in heaven he wears the crown of victory.

OPENING PRAYER

**Lord,
today we celebrate the entrance of St. Stephen
into eternal glory.
He died praying for those who killed him.
Help us to imitate his goodness
and to love our enemies.**

**We ask this through our Lord Jesus Christ, your Son,
who lives and reigns with you and the Holy Spirit,
one God, for ever and ever.**

See Lectionary for Mass, no. 696.

PRAYER OVER THE GIFTS

Pray, brethren . . .

**Father,
be pleased with the gifts we bring in your honor
as we celebrate the feast of St. Stephen.**

Grant this through Christ our Lord.

Preface of Christmas I-III, pages **420–422.**

Communion Rite

As they stoned him, Stephen prayed aloud: Lord Jesus, receive my spirit. (Acts 7:58)

PRAYER AFTER COMMUNION

Let us pray.
Pause for silent prayer, if this has not preceded.
**Lord,
we thank you for the many signs of your love for us.
Save us by the birth of your Son
and give us joy in honoring St. Stephen the martyr.**

We ask this through Christ our Lord.

December 27

ST. JOHN, apostle and evangelist

Feast

Introductory Rites

The Lord opened his mouth in the assembly, and filled him with the spirit of wisdom and understanding, and clothed him in a robe of glory. (Sir. 15:5)

or:

At the last supper, John reclined close to the Lord. Blessed apostle, to you were revealed the heavenly secrets! Your lifegiving words have spread over all the earth!

OPENING PRAYER

**God our Father,
you have revealed the mysteries of your Word
through St. John the apostle.
By prayer and reflection
may we come to understand the wisdom he taught.**

**Grant this through our Lord Jesus Christ, your Son,
who lives and reigns with you and the Holy Spirit,
one God, for ever and ever.**

See Lectionary for Mass, no. 697.

PRAYER OVER THE GIFTS

Pray, brethren . . .

**Lord,
bless these gifts we present to you.
With St. John may we share
in the hidden wisdom of your eternal Word
which you reveal at this eucharistic table.**

We ask this in the name of Jesus the Lord.

Preface of Christmas I-III, pages 420–422.

Communion Rite

The Word of God became man, and lived among us. Of his riches we have all received. (John 1:14, 16)

PRAYER AFTER COMMUNION

Let us pray.

Pause for silent prayer, if this has not preceded.

**Almighty Father,
St. John proclaimed that your Word became flesh
   for our salvation.
Through this eucharist may your Son always live in us,
for he is Lord for ever and ever.**

December 28

HOLY INNOCENTS, martyrs

Feast

Introductory Rites

These innocent children were slain for Christ. They follow the spotless Lamb, and proclaim for ever: Glory to you, Lord.

OPENING PRAYER

**Father,
the Holy Innocents offered you praise
by the death they suffered for Christ.
May our lives bear witness
to the faith we profess with our lips.**

**We ask this through our Lord Jesus Christ, your Son,
who lives and reigns with you and the Holy Spirit,
one God, for ever and ever.**

See Lectionary for Mass, no. 698.

PRAYER OVER THE GIFTS

Pray, brethren . . .

**Lord,
you give us your life even before we understand.
Receive the offerings we bring in love,
and free us from sin.**

We ask this in the name of Jesus the Lord.

Preface of Christmas I-III, pages **420–422.**

Communion Rite

These have been ransomed for God and the Lamb as the first-fruits of mankind; they follow the Lamb wherever he goes. (Rev. 14:4)

PRAYER AFTER COMMUNION

Let us pray.

Pause for silent prayer, if this has not preceded.

**Lord,
by a wordless profession of faith in your Son,
the innocents were crowned with life at his birth.
May all people who receive your holy gifts today
come to share in the fullness of salvation.**

We ask this through Christ our Lord.

December 29

FIFTH DAY IN THE OCTAVE OF CHRISTMAS

Introductory Rites

God loved the world so much, he gave his only Son, that
all who believe in him might not perish, but might have
eternal life. (John 3:16)

OPENING PRAYER

**All-powerful and unseen God,
the coming of your light into our world
has made the darkness vanish.
Teach us to proclaim the birth of your Son Jesus Christ,
who lives and reigns with you and the Holy Spirit,
one God, for ever and ever.**

See Lectionary for Mass, no. 203.

PRAYER OVER THE GIFTS

Pray, brethren . . .

**Lord,
receive our gifts in this wonderful exchange:
from all you have given us
we bring you these gifts,
and in return, you give us yourself.**

We ask this through Christ our Lord.

Preface of Christmas I-III, pages 420–
422.

When Eucharistic Prayer I is used, the
special Christmas form of **In union
with the whole Church** is said.

Communion Rite

Through the tender compassion of our God, the dawn
from on high shall break upon us. (Luke 1:78)

PRAYER AFTER COMMUNION

Let us pray.
Pause for silent prayer, if this has not preceded.

**Father of love and mercy,
grant that our lives may always be founded
on the power of this holy mystery.**

We ask this in the name of Jesus the Lord.

December 30

SIXTH DAY IN THE OCTAVE OF CHRISTMAS

When there is no Sunday within the octave of Christmas, the feast of the Holy Family is celebrated today (see page **120**).

Introductory Rites

When peaceful silence lay over all, and night had run half of her swift course, your all-powerful word, O Lord, leaped down from heaven, from the royal throne. (Wis. 18:14-15)

OPENING PRAYER

All-powerful God,
may the human birth of your Son
free us from our former slavery to sin
and bring us new life.

We ask this through our Lord Jesus Christ, your Son,
who lives and reigns with you and the Holy Spirit,
one God, for ever and ever.

See Lectionary for Mass, no. 204.

PRAYER OVER THE GIFTS

Pray, brethren . . .

Father,
in your mercy accept our gifts.
By sharing in this eucharist
may we come to live more fully the love we profess.

Grant this through Christ our Lord.

Preface of Christmas I-III, pages **420–422**.

When Eucharistic Prayer I is used, the special Christmas form of **In union with the whole Church** is said.

Communion Rite

From his riches we have all received, grace for grace. (John 1:16)

PRAYER AFTER COMMUNION

Let us pray.
Pause for silent prayer, if this has not preceded.
God our Father,
in this eucharist you touch our lives.
Keep your love alive in our hearts
that we may become worthy of you.

We ask this through Christ our Lord.

December 31

SEVENTH DAY IN THE OCTAVE OF CHRISTMAS

Introductory Rites

A child is born for us, a son given to us; dominion is laid on his shoulder, and he shall be called Wonderful-Counsellor. (Is. 9:6)

OPENING PRAYER

**Ever-living God,
in the birth of your Son
our religion has its origin and its perfect fulfillment.
Help us to share in the life of Christ
for he is the salvation of mankind,
who lives and reigns with you and the Holy Spirit,
one God, for ever and ever.**

See Lectionary for Mass, no. 205.

PRAYER OVER THE GIFTS

Pray, brethren . . .

**Father of peace,
accept our devotion and sincerity,
and by our sharing in this mystery
draw us closer to each other and to you.**

We ask this in the name of Jesus the Lord.

Preface of Christmas I-III, pages 420–422.

When Eucharistic Prayer I is used, the special Christmas form of **In union with the whole Church** is said.

Communion Rite

God's love for us was revealed when he sent his only Son into the world, so that we could have life through him. (1 John 4:9)

PRAYER AFTER COMMUNION

Let us pray.
Pause for silent prayer, if this has not preceded.
**Lord,
may this sacrament be our strength.
Teach us to value all the good you give us
and help us to strive for eternal life.**

Grant this through Christ our Lord.

January 1

Octave of Christmas

MARY, MOTHER OF GOD

Solemnity

Introductory Rites

A light will shine on us this day, the Lord is born for us: he shall be called Wonderful God, Prince of peace, Father of the world to come; and his kingship will never end. (See Is. 9:2, 6; Luke 1:33)

or:

Hail, holy Mother! The child to whom you gave birth is the King of heaven and earth for ever. (Sedulius)

OPENING PRAYER

Let us pray
[that Mary, the mother of the Lord,
will help us by her prayers]

Pause for silent prayer

God our Father,
may we always profit by the prayers
of the Virgin Mother Mary,
for you bring us life and salvation
through Jesus Christ her Son
who lives and reigns with you and the Holy
  Spirit,
one God, for ever and ever.

ALTERNATIVE OPENING PRAYER

Let us pray
[in the name of Jesus,
born of a virgin and Son of God]

Pause for silent prayer

Father,
source of light in every age,
the virgin conceived and bore your Son
who is called Wonderful God, Prince of Peace.
May her prayer, the gift of a mother's love,
be your people's joy through all ages.
May her response, born of a humble heart,
draw your Spirit to rest on your people.

Grant this through Christ our Lord.

LITURGY OF THE WORD

See Lectionary for Mass, no. 18.

LITURGY OF THE EUCHARIST

PRAYER OVER THE GIFTS

Pray, brethren . . .

God our Father,
we celebrate at this season
the beginning of our salvation.
On this feast of Mary, the Mother of God,
we ask that our salvation
will be brought to its fulfillment.

We ask this through Christ our Lord.

Eucharistic Prayer:
Preface of the Blessed Virgin Mary I (on the solemnity), page 473.

When Eucharistic Prayer I is used, the special Christmas form of **In union with the whole Church** is said.

Communion Rite

Jesus Christ is the same yesterday, today, and for ever.
(Heb. 13:8)

A period of silence may be observed after communion, or a psalm or song of praise may be sung.

PRAYER AFTER COMMUNION

Let us pray.
Pause for silent prayer, if this has not preceded.
Father,
as we proclaim the Virgin Mary
to be the mother of Christ and the mother of the Church,
may our communion with her Son
bring us to salvation.
We ask this through Christ our Lord.

SOLEMN BLESSING OR PRAYER OVER THE PEOPLE

The following may replace the simple blessing.

After the greeting, the deacon (or in his absence, the priest) gives the invitation in these or similar words:

Then the priest extends his hands over the people while he sings or says:

Bow your heads and pray for God's blessing.

Lord,
we pray for your people who believe in you.
May they enjoy the gift of your love.
We ask this in the name of Jesus the Lord.
℟. **Amen.**

May almighty God bless you,
the Father, and the Son, ☩ and the Holy Spirit.
℟. **Amen.**

For other texts of solemn blessings and prayers over the people, see pages **528–540.**

SECOND SUNDAY AFTER CHRISTMAS

Introductory Rites

When peaceful silence lay over all, and night had run half of her swift course, your all-powerful word, O Lord, leaped down from heaven, from the royal throne. (Wis. 18:14-15)

OPENING PRAYER

Let us pray
  [that all mankind may be enlightened
  by the gospel]
Pause for silent prayer
**God of power and life,
glory of all who believe in you,
fill the world with your splendor
and show the nations the light of your truth.**

**We ask this through our Lord Jesus Christ,
  your Son,
who lives and reigns with you and the Holy
  Spirit,
one God, for ever and ever.**

ALTERNATIVE OPENING PRAYER

Let us pray
  [aware of the dignity to which we are called
  by the love of Christ.]
Pause for silent prayer
**Father of our Lord Jesus Christ,
our glory is to stand before the world
as your own sons and daughters.
May the simple beauty of Jesus' birth
summon us always to love what is most deeply
  human,
and to see your Word made flesh
reflected in those whose lives we touch.**

We ask this through Christ our Lord.

LITURGY OF THE WORD

See Lectionary for Mass, no. 19.

LITURGY OF THE EUCHARIST

PRAYER OVER THE GIFTS

Pray, brethren . . .

**Lord,
make holy these gifts
through the coming of your Son,
who shows us the way of truth
and promises the life of your kingdom.**

We ask this through Christ our Lord.

Eucharistic Prayer:
Preface of Christmas I-III, pages 420–422.

Communion Rite

> He gave to all who accepted him the power to become children of God. (John 1:12)

A period of silence may be observed after communion, or a psalm or song of praise may be sung.

PRAYER AFTER COMMUNION

Let us pray.
Pause for silent prayer, if this has not preceded.
Lord,
hear our prayers.
By this eucharist free us from sin
and keep us faithful to your word.
Grant this through Christ our Lord.

SOLEMN BLESSING OR PRAYER OVER THE PEOPLE

The following may replace the simple blessing.

After the greeting, the deacon (or in his absence, the priest) gives the invitation in these or similar words:

Bow your heads and pray for God's blessing.

Then the priest extends his hands over the people while he sings or says:

Lord,
bless your people who hope for your mercy.
Grant that they may receive
the things they ask for at your prompting.
Grant this through Christ our Lord.
℟. Amen.

May almighty God bless you,
the Father, and the Son, ✠ and the Holy Spirit.
℟. Amen.

For other texts of solemn blessings and prayers over the people, see pages 528–540.

From January 2 to Epiphany

MONDAY

Introductory Rites

> A holy day has dawned upon us. Come, you nations, and adore the Lord. Today a great light has come upon the earth.

OPENING PRAYER

Lord,
keep us true in the faith,
proclaiming that Christ your Son,
who is one with you in eternal glory,
became man and was born of a virgin mother.
Free us from all evil
and lead us to the joy of eternal life.

We ask this through our Lord Jesus Christ, your Son,
who lives and reigns with you and the Holy Spirit,
one God, for ever and ever.

See Lectionary for Mass, nos. 206-211.

PRAYER OVER THE GIFTS

Pray, brethren . . .

Lord,
receive our gifts in this wonderful exchange:
from all you have given us
we bring you these gifts,
and in return, you give us yourself.

We ask this through Christ our Lord.

Preface of Christmas I-III, pages 420–422.

Communion Rite

> We have seen his glory, the glory of the Father's only Son, full of grace and truth. (John 1:14)

PRAYER AFTER COMMUNION

Let us pray.
Pause for silent prayer, if this has not preceded.

Father of love and mercy,
grant that our lives may always be founded
on the power of this holy mystery.

We ask this in the name of Jesus the Lord.

From January 2 to Epiphany
TUESDAY

Introductory Rites

Blessed is he who comes in the name of the Lord; the Lord God shines upon us. (Ps. 117:26-27)

OPENING PRAYER

**God our Father,
when your Son was born of the Virgin Mary
he became like us in all things but sin.
May we who have been reborn in him
be free from our sinful ways.**

**We ask this through our Lord Jesus Christ, your Son,
who lives and reigns with you and the Holy Spirit,
one God, for ever and ever.**

See Lectionary for Mass, nos. 206-211.

PRAYER OVER THE GIFTS

Pray, brethren . . .

**Father,
in your mercy accept our gifts.
By sharing in this eucharist
may we come to live more fully the love we profess.**

Grant this through Christ our Lord.

Preface of Christmas I-III, pages **420–422.**

Communion Rite

God loved us so much that he sent his own Son in the likeness of sinful flesh. (Eph. 2:4; Rom. 8:3)

PRAYER AFTER COMMUNION

Let us pray.

Pause for silent prayer, if this has not preceded.

**God our Father,
in this eucharist you touch our lives.
Keep your love alive in our hearts
that we may become worthy of you.**

We ask this through Christ our Lord.

From January 2 to Epiphany
WEDNESDAY

Introductory Rites
>The people who walked in darkness have seen a great light; on those who lived in the shadow of death, light has shone. (Is. 9:2)

OPENING PRAYER

**All-powerful Father,
you sent your Son Jesus Christ
to bring the new light of salvation to the world.
May he enlighten us with his radiance,
who lives and reigns with you and the Holy Spirit,
one God, for ever and ever.**

See Lectionary for Mass, nos. 206-211.

PRAYER OVER THE GIFTS

Pray, brethren . . .

**Father of peace,
accept our devotion and sincerity,
and by our sharing in this mystery
draw us closer to each other and to you.**

We ask this in the name of Jesus the Lord.

Preface of Christmas I-III, pages 420–422.

Communion Rite
>The eternal life which was with the Father has been revealed to us. (1 John 1:2)

PRAYER AFTER COMMUNION

Let us pray.
Pause for silent prayer, if this has not preceded.
**Lord,
may this sacrament be our strength.
Teach us to value all the good you give us
and help us to strive for eternal life.**

Grant this through Christ our Lord.

From January 2 to Epiphany
THURSDAY

Introductory Rites
In the beginning, before all ages, the Word was God; that
Word was born a man to save the world. (See John 1:1)

OPENING PRAYER

Father,
you make known the salvation of mankind
at the birth of your Son.
Make us strong in faith
and bring us to the glory you promise.

We ask this through our Lord Jesus Christ, your Son,
who lives and reigns with you and the Holy Spirit,
one God, for ever and ever.

See Lectionary for Mass, nos. 206-211.

PRAYER OVER THE GIFTS

Pray, brethren . . .

Lord,
receive our gifts in this wonderful exchange:
from all you have given us
we bring you these gifts,
and in return, you give us yourself.

We ask this through Christ our Lord.

Preface of Christmas I-III, pages 420–
422.

Communion Rite
God loved the world so much, he gave his only Son, that
all who believe in him might not perish, but might have
eternal life. (John 3:16)

PRAYER AFTER COMMUNION

Let us pray.
Pause for silent prayer, if this has not preceded.
Father of love and mercy,
grant that our lives may always be founded
on the power of this holy mystery.

We ask this in the name of Jesus the Lord.

From January 2 to Epiphany
FRIDAY

Introductory Rites

> The Lord is a light in darkness to the upright; he is gracious, merciful, and just. (Ps. 111:4)

OPENING PRAYER

Lord,
fill our hearts with your light.
May we always acknowledge Christ as our Savior
and be more faithful to his gospel,
for he lives and reigns with you and the Holy Spirit,
one God, for ever and ever.

See Lectionary for Mass, nos. 206-211.

PRAYER OVER THE GIFTS

Pray, brethren . . .

Father,
in your mercy accept our gifts.
By sharing in this eucharist
may we come to live more fully the love we profess.

Grant this through Christ our Lord.

Preface of Christmas I-III, pages 420–422.

Communion Rite

> God's love for us was revealed when he sent his only Son
> into the world, so that we could have life through him.
> (1 John 4:9)

PRAYER AFTER COMMUNION

Let us pray.
Pause for silent prayer, if this has not preceded.

God our Father,
in this eucharist you touch our lives.
Keep your love alive in our hearts
that we may become worthy of you.

We ask this through Christ our Lord.

From January 2 to Epiphany
SATURDAY

Introductory Rites

God sent his own Son, born of a woman, so that we could
be adopted as his sons. (Gal. 4:4-5)

OPENING PRAYER

**All-powerful and ever-living God,
you give us a new vision of your glory
in the coming of Christ your Son.
He was born of the Virgin Mary
and came to share our life.
May we come to share his eternal life
in the glory of your kingdom,
where he lives and reigns with you and the Holy Spirit,
one God, for ever and ever.**

See Lectionary for Mass, nos. 206-211.

PRAYER OVER THE GIFTS

Pray, brethren . . .

**Father of peace,
accept our devotion and sincerity,
and by our sharing in this mystery
draw us closer to each other and to you.**

We ask this in the name of Jesus the Lord.

Preface of Christmas I-III, pages 420–422.

Communion Rite

From his riches we have all received, grace for grace. (John
1:16)

PRAYER AFTER COMMUNION

Let us pray.
Pause for silent prayer, if this has not preceded.
**Lord,
may this sacrament be our strength.
Teach us to value all the good you give us
and help us to strive for eternal life.**

We ask this in the name of Jesus the Lord.

EPIPHANY

Solemnity

Epiphany is celebrated on January 6 where it is a holy day of obligation; elsewhere it is celebrated on the Sunday between January 2 and January 8.

Introductory Rites

> The Lord and ruler is coming; kingship is his, and government and power. (See Mal. 3:1; 1 Chr. 19:12)

OPENING PRAYER

Let us pray
  **[that we will be guided
  by the light of faith]**

Pause for silent prayer

**Father,
you revealed your Son to the nations
by the guidance of a star.
Lead us to your glory in heaven
by the light of faith.**

**We ask this through our Lord Jesus Christ,
  your Son,
who lives and reigns with you and the Holy
  Spirit,
one God, for ever and ever.**

ALTERNATIVE OPENING PRAYER

Let us pray
  **[grateful for the glory revealed today
  through God made man]**

Pause for silent prayer

**Father of light, unchanging God,
today you reveal to men of faith
the resplendent fact of the Word made flesh.
Your light is strong,
your love is near;
draw us beyond the limits which this world
  imposes,
to the life where your Spirit makes all life complete.**

We ask this through Christ our Lord.

LITURGY OF THE WORD

See Lectionary for Mass, no. 20.

LITURGY OF THE EUCHARIST

PRAYER OVER THE GIFTS

Pray, brethren . . .

**Lord,
accept the offerings of your Church,
not gold, frankincense and myrrh,
but the sacrifice and food they symbolize:
Jesus Christ, who is Lord for ever and ever.**

Eucharistic Prayer:
Preface of Epiphany, page 423.

When Eucharistic Prayer I is used, the special Epiphany form of In union with the whole Church is said.

138

Communion Rite
We have seen his star in the east, and have come with gifts
to adore the Lord. (See Matthew 2:2)

A period of silence may be observed
after communion, or a psalm or song
of praise may be sung.

PRAYER AFTER COMMUNION

Let us pray.
Pause for silent prayer, if this has not preceded.
Father,
guide us with your light.
Help us to recognize Christ in this eucharist
and welcome him with love,
for he is Lord for ever and ever.

**SOLEMN BLESSING OR PRAYER
OVER THE PEOPLE**

The following may replace the simple
blessing.

After the greeting, the deacon (or in
his absence, the priest) gives the invitation in these or similar words:

Bow your heads and pray for God's blessing.

Then the priest extends his hands
over the people while he sings or
says:

God has called you out of darkness,
into his wonderful light.
May you experience his kindness and blessings,
and be strong in faith, in hope, and in love.
℟. Amen.

Because you are followers of Christ,
who appeared on this day as a light shining in darkness,
may he make you a light to all your sisters and brothers.
℟. Amen.

The wise men followed the star,
and found Christ who is light from light.
May you too find the Lord
when your pilgrimage is ended.
℟. Amen.

May almighty God bless you,
the Father, and the Son, ✝ and the Holy Spirit.
℟. Amen.

For other texts of solemn blessings and
prayers over the people, see pages
528–540.

After Epiphany to the Baptism of the Lord
MONDAY

Introductory Rites

A holy day has dawned upon us. Come, you nations, and adore the Lord. Today a great light has come upon the earth.

OPENING PRAYER

**Lord,
let the light of your glory shine within us,
and lead us through the darkness of this world
to the radiant joy of our eternal home.**

**We ask this through our Lord Jesus Christ, your Son,
who lives and reigns with you and the Holy Spirit,
one God, for ever and ever.**

See Lectionary for Mass, no. 213.

PRAYER OVER THE GIFTS

Pray, brethren . . .

**Lord,
receive our gifts in this wonderful exchange:
from all you have given us
we bring you these gifts,
and in return, you give us yourself.**

We ask this through Christ our Lord.

Preface of Christmas I-III, pages 420–422, or of Epiphany, page 423.

Communion Rite

We have seen his glory, the glory of the Father's only Son, full of grace and truth. (John 1:14)

PRAYER AFTER COMMUNION

Let us pray.
Pause for silent prayer, if this has not preceded.
**Father of love and mercy,
grant that our lives may always be founded
on the power of this holy mystery.**

We ask this in the name of Jesus the Lord.

After Epiphany to the Baptism of the Lord
TUESDAY

Introductory Rites

Blessed is he who comes in the name of the Lord; the Lord
God shines upon us. (Ps. 117:26-27)

OPENING PRAYER

**Father,
your Son became like us
when he revealed himself in our nature:
help us to become more like him,
who lives and reigns with you and the Holy Spirit,
one God, for ever and ever.**

See Lectionary for Mass, no. 214.

PRAYER OVER THE GIFTS

Pray, brethren . . .

**Father,
in your mercy accept our gifts.
By sharing in this eucharist
may we come to live more fully the love we profess.**

Grant this through Christ our Lord.

Preface of Christmas I-III, pages 420–
422, or of Epiphany, page 423.

Communion Rite

God loved us so much that he sent his own Son in the
likeness of sinful flesh. (Eph. 2:4; Rom. 8:3)

PRAYER AFTER COMMUNION

Let us pray.
Pause for silent prayer, if this has not preceded.
**God our Father,
in this eucharist you touch our lives.
Keep your love alive in our hearts
that we may become worthy of you.**

We ask this through Christ our Lord.

After Epiphany to the Baptism of the Lord
WEDNESDAY

Introductory Rites

> The people who walked in darkness have seen a great light; on those who lived in the shadow of death, light has shone. (Is. 9:2)

OPENING PRAYER

God, light of all nations,
give us the joy of lasting peace,
and fill us with your radiance
as you filled the hearts of our fathers.

We ask this through our Lord Jesus Christ, your Son,
who lives and reigns with you and the Holy Spirit,
one God, for ever and ever.

See Lectionary for Mass, no. 215.

PRAYER OVER THE GIFTS

Pray, brethren . . .

Father of peace,
accept our devotion and sincerity,
and by our sharing in this mystery
draw us closer to each other and to you.

We ask this in the name of Jesus the Lord.

Preface of Christmas I-III, pages 420–422, or of Epiphany, page 423.

Communion Rite

> The eternal life which was with the Father has been revealed to us. (1 John 1:2)

PRAYER AFTER COMMUNION

Let us pray.
Pause for silent prayer, if this has not preceded.
Lord,
may this sacrament be our strength.
Teach us to value all the good you give us
and help us to strive for eternal life.

Grant this through Christ our Lord.

After Epiphany to the Baptism of the Lord
THURSDAY

Introductory Rites
In the beginning, before all ages, the Word was God: that
Word was born a man to save the world. (See John 1:1)

OPENING PRAYER

**God our Father,
through Christ your Son
the hope of eternal life dawned on our world.
Give to us the light of faith
that we may always acknowledge him as our Redeemer
and come to the glory of his kingdom,
where he lives and reigns with you and the Holy Spirit,
one God, for ever and ever.**

See Lectionary for Mass, no. 216.

PRAYER OVER THE GIFTS

Pray, brethren . . .

**Lord,
receive our gifts in this wonderful exchange:
from all you have given us
we bring you these gifts,
and in return, you give us yourself.**

We ask this through Christ our Lord.

Preface of Christmas I-III, pages 420–
422, or of Epiphany, page 423.

Communion Rite
God loved the world so much, he gave his only Son, that
all who believe in him might not perish, but might have
eternal life. (John 3:16)

PRAYER AFTER COMMUNION

Let us pray.
Pause for silent prayer, if this has not preceded.
**Father of love and mercy,
grant that our lives may always be founded
on the power of this holy mystery.**

We ask this in the name of Jesus the Lord.

After Epiphany to the Baptism of the Lord
FRIDAY

Introductory Rites

The Lord is a light in darkness to the upright; he is gracious, merciful, and just. (Ps. 111:4)

OPENING PRAYER

**All-powerful Father,
you have made known the birth of the Savior
by the light of a star.
May he continue to guide us with his light,
for he lives and reigns with you and the Holy Spirit,
one God, for ever and ever.**

See Lectionary for Mass, no. 217.

PRAYER OVER THE GIFTS

Pray, brethren . . .

**Father,
in your mercy accept our gifts.
By sharing in this eucharist
may we come to live more fully the love we profess.**

Grant this through Christ our Lord.

Preface of Christmas I-III, pages 420–
422, or of Epiphany, page 423

Communion Rite

God's love for us was revealed when he sent his only Son
into the world, so that we could have life through him.
(1 John 4:9)

PRAYER AFTER COMMUNION

Let us pray.
Pause for silent prayer, if this has not preceded.
**God our Father,
in this eucharist you touch our lives.
Keep your love alive in our hearts
that we may become worthy of you.**

We ask this through Christ our Lord.

After Epiphany to the Baptism of the Lord
SATURDAY

Introductory Rites

God sent his own Son, born of a woman, so that we could
be adopted as his sons. (Gal. 4:4-5)

OPENING PRAYER

**God our Father,
through your Son you made us a new creation.
He shared our nature and became one of us;
with his help, may we become more like him,
who lives and reigns with you and the Holy Spirit,
one God, for ever and ever.**

See Lectionary for Mass, no. 218.

PRAYER OVER THE GIFTS

Pray, brethren . . .

**Father of peace,
accept our devotion and sincerity,
and by our sharing in this mystery
draw us closer to each other and to you.**

We ask this in the name of Jesus the Lord.

Preface of Christmas I-III, pages 420–
422, or of Epiphany, page 423.

Communion Rite

From his riches we have all received, grace for grace. (John
1:16)

PRAYER AFTER COMMUNION

Let us pray.
Pause for silent prayer, if this has not preceded.
**Lord,
may this sacrament be our strength.
Teach us to value all the good you give us
and help us to strive for eternal life.**

Grant this through Christ our Lord.

BAPTISM OF THE LORD

Feast

Introductory Rites

When the Lord had been baptized, the heavens opened,
and the Spirit came down like a dove to rest on him. Then
the voice of the Father thundered: This is my beloved Son,
with him I am well pleased. (See Matthew 3:16-17)

OPENING PRAYER

Let us pray
[**that we will be faithful to our baptism**]

Pause for silent prayer

Almighty, eternal God,
when the Spirit descended upon Jesus
at his baptism in the Jordan,
you revealed him as your own beloved Son.
Keep us, your children born of water and the
  Spirit,
faithful to our calling.

We ask this through our Lord Jesus Christ,
  your Son,
who lives and reigns with you and the Holy
  Spirit,
one God, for ever and ever.

Or:

Father,
your only Son revealed himself to us
  by becoming man.
May we who share his humanity
come to share his divinity,
for he lives and reigns with you and
  the Holy Spirit,
one God, for ever and ever.

ALTERNATIVE OPENING PRAYER

Let us pray
[**as we listen to the voice of God's Spirit**]

Pause for silent prayer

Father in heaven,
you revealed Christ as your Son
by the voice that spoke over the waters of the
  Jordan.
May all who share in the sonship of Christ
follow in his path of service to man,
and reflect the glory of his kingdom
even to the ends of the earth,
for he is Lord for ever and ever.

LITURGY OF THE WORD

See Lectionary for Mass, no. 21.

LITURGY OF THE EUCHARIST

PRAYER OVER THE GIFTS

Pray, brethren . . .

Lord,
we celebrate the revelation of Christ your Son
who takes away the sins of the world.
Accept our gifts
and let them become one with his sacrifice,
for he is Lord for ever and ever.

Eucharistic Prayer:
Preface of the Baptism of the Lord, page 424.

Communion Rite

This is he of whom John said: I have seen and have given witness that this is the Son of God. (John 1:32, 34)

A period of silence may be observed after communion, or a psalm or song of praise may be sung.

PRAYER AFTER COMMUNION

Let us pray.
Pause for silent prayer, if this has not preceded.
Lord,
you feed us with bread from heaven.
May we hear your Son with faith
and become your children in name and in fact.

We ask this in the name of Jesus the Lord.

SOLEMN BLESSING OR PRAYER OVER THE PEOPLE

The following may replace the simple blessing.

After the greeting, the deacon (or in his absence, the priest) gives the invitation in these or similar words:

Bow your heads and pray for God's blessing.

Then the priest extends his hands over the people while he sings or says:

Lord,
send your light upon your family.
May they continue to enjoy your favor
and devote themselves to doing good.

We ask this through Christ our Lord.
℟. Amen.

For other texts of solemn blessings and prayers over the people, see pages 528–540.

May almighty God bless you,
the Father, and the Son, ✝ and the Holy Spirit.
℟. Amen.

Ordinary time begins on the Monday following this Sunday and continues until the Tuesday before Ash Wednesday. For Sunday and weekday Masses the texts given below, pages 325–390, are used.

LENTEN SEASON

It was the ancient custom of the Roman church for their bishop to visit various churches to celebrate the liturgy with his people, particularly during penitential seasons.

The Roman Missal strongly encourages the chief shepherd of the diocese to gather his people in this way.

Especially during Lent, he should meet with his people and celebrate the liturgy with them. This may be done on Sundays or weekdays, in parish churches or places of pilgrimage. The manner of celebration will vary according to local needs.

ASH WEDNESDAY

The ashes used today come from the branches blessed the preceding year for Passion Sunday.

Introductory Rites

Lord, you are merciful to all, and hate nothing you have created. You overlook the sins of men to bring them to repentance. You are the Lord our God. (See Wis. 11:24-25, 27)

The penitential rite and the Gloria are omitted.

OPENING PRAYER

Let us pray
  [for the grace to keep
  Lent faithfully]

Pause for silent prayer

Lord,
protect us in our struggle against evil.
As we begin the discipline of Lent,
make this season holy by our self-denial.

Grant this through our Lord Jesus Christ, your Son,
who lives and reigns with you and the Holy Spirit,
one God, for ever and ever.

ALTERNATIVE OPENING PRAYER

Let us pray
  [in quiet remembrance of our need
  for redemption]

Pause for silent prayer

Father in heaven,
the light of your truth bestows sight
to the darkness of sinful eyes.
May this season of repentance
bring us the blessing of your forgiveness
and the gift of your light.

Grant this through Christ our Lord.

LITURGY OF THE WORD

See Lectionary for Mass, no. 220.

BLESSING AND GIVING OF ASHES

After the homily the priest joins his hands and says:

Dear friends in Christ,
let us ask our Father
to bless these ashes
which we will use
as the mark of our repentance.

Pause for silent prayer

a   **Lord,
bless the sinner who asks for your forgiveness
and bless ✝ all those who receive these ashes.
May they keep this lenten season
in preparation for the joy of Easter.
We ask this through Christ our Lord.**

b   **Lord,
bless these ashes ✝
by which we show that we are dust.
Pardon our sins
and keep us faithful to the discipline of Lent,
for you do not want sinners to die
but to live with the risen Christ,
who reigns with you for ever and ever.**

He sprinkles the ashes with holy water in silence.

The priest then places ashes on those who come forward, saying to each:

a   **Turn away from sin and be faithful to the gospel.
(Mark 1:15)**

b   **Remember, man, you are dust
and to dust you will return.** (See Gen. 3:19)

Meanwhile some of the following antiphons or other appropriate songs are sung.

Antiphon 1

**Come back to the Lord with all your heart;
leave the past in ashes,
and turn to God with tears and fasting,
for he is slow to anger and ready to forgive.** (See Joel 2:13)

Antiphon 2

**Let the priests and ministers of the Lord
lament before his altar, and say:
Spare us, Lord; spare your people!
Do not let us die for we are crying out to you.** (See Joel 2:17;
  Est. 13:17)

Antiphon 3

Lord, take away our wickedness. (Ps. 50:3)

These may be repeated after each verse of Psalm 50, **Have mercy on me, O God.**

Responsory

Direct our hearts to better things, O Lord;
heal our sin and ignorance.
Lord, do not face us suddenly with death,
but give us time to repent. (See Baruch 3:5)

℞. Turn to us with mercy, Lord; we have sinned against
   you.
℣. Help us, God our Savior, rescue us for the honor of
   your name. (Ps. 78:9)
℞. Turn to us with mercy, Lord; we have sinned against
   you.

After the giving of ashes the priest
washes his hands; the rite concludes
with the general intercessions or
prayer of the faithful.

The profession of faith is not said.

LITURGY OF THE EUCHARIST

PRAYER OVER THE GIFTS

Pray, brethren . . .

Lord,
help us to resist temptation
by our lenten works of charity and penance.
By this sacrifice
may we be prepared to celebrate
the death and resurrection of Christ our Savior
and be cleansed from sin and renewed in spirit.

We ask this through Christ our Lord.

Preface of Lent IV, page 428.

Communion Rite

The man who meditates day and night on the law of the
Lord will yield fruit in due season. (Ps. 1:2-3)

PRAYER AFTER COMMUNION

Let us pray.

Pause for silent prayer, if this has not preceded.

Lord,
through this communion
may our lenten penance give you glory
and bring us your protection.

We ask this in the name of Jesus the Lord.

The blessing and giving of ashes may
be done outside Mass. In this case
the entire liturgy of the word should
be celebrated: entrance song, opening prayer, readings and chants,
homily, blessing and giving of ashes,
general intercessions.

THURSDAY AFTER ASH WEDNESDAY

Introductory Rites

When I cry to the Lord, he hears my voice and saves me
from the foes who threaten me. Unload your burden onto
the Lord, and he will support you. (See Ps. 54:17-20, 23)

OPENING PRAYER

**Lord,
may everything we do
begin with your inspiration,
continue with your help,
and reach perfection under your guidance.**

**We ask this through our Lord Jesus Christ, your Son,
who lives and reigns with you and the Holy Spirit,
one God, for ever and ever.**

See Lectionary for Mass, no. 221.

PRAYER OVER THE GIFTS

Pray, brethren . . .

**Lord,
accept these gifts.
May they bring us your mercy
and give you honor and praise.**

We ask this in the name of Jesus the Lord.

Preface of Lent I-IV, pages 425–428.

Communion Rite

Create a clean heart in me, O God; give me a new and
steadfast spirit. (Ps. 50:12)

PRAYER AFTER COMMUNION

Let us pray.
Pause for silent prayer, if this has not preceded.
**Merciful Father,
may the gifts and blessings we receive
bring us pardon and salvation.**

Grant this through Christ our Lord.

FRIDAY AFTER ASH WEDNESDAY

Introductory Rites
The Lord heard me and took pity on me. He came to my
help. (Ps. 29:11)

OPENING PRAYER

Lord,
with your loving care
guide the penance we have begun.
Help us to persevere with love and sincerity.

Grant this through our Lord Jesus Christ, your Son,
who lives and reigns with you and the Holy Spirit,
one God, for ever and ever.

See Lectionary for Mass, no. 222.

PRAYER OVER THE GIFTS

Pray, brethren . . .

Lord,
through this lenten eucharist
may we grow in your love and service
and become an acceptable offering to you.

We ask this through Christ our Lord.

Preface of Lent I-IV, pages 425–428.

Communion Rite
Teach us your ways, O Lord, and lead us in your paths.
(Ps. 24:4)

PRAYER AFTER COMMUNION

Let us pray.

Pause for silent prayer, if this has not preceded.
Lord,
may our sharing in this mystery
free us from our sins
and make us worthy of your healing.

We ask this in the name of Jesus the Lord.

SATURDAY AFTER ASH WEDNESDAY

Introductory Rites

Answer us, Lord, with your loving kindness, turn to us in
your great mercy. (Ps. 68:17)

OPENING PRAYER

Father,
look upon our weakness
and reach out to help us with your loving power.

We ask this through our Lord Jesus Christ, your Son,
who lives and reigns with you and the Holy Spirit,
one God, for ever and ever.

See Lectionary for Mass, no. 223.

PRAYER OVER THE GIFTS

Pray, brethren . . .

Lord,
receive our sacrifice of praise and reconciliation.
Let it free us from sin
and enable us to give you loving service.

We ask this in the name of Jesus the Lord.

Preface of Lent I-IV, pages 425–428.

Communion Rite

It is mercy that I want, and not sacrifice, says the Lord; I did
not come to call the virtuous, but sinners. (Matthew 9:13)

PRAYER AFTER COMMUNION

Let us pray.
Pause for silent prayer, if this has not preceded.

Lord,
we are nourished by the bread of life you give us.
May this mystery we now celebrate
help us to reach eternal life with you.

Grant this through Christ our Lord.

FIRST SUNDAY OF LENT

Introductory Rites

When he calls to me, I will answer; I will rescue him and
give him honor. Long life and contentment will be his. (Ps.
90:15-16)

The Gloria is omitted.

OPENING PRAYER

Let us pray
[that this Lent will help us reproduce
in our lives the self-sacrificing
love of Christ]

Pause for silent prayer

Father,
through our observance of Lent,
help us to understand the meaning
of your Son's death and resurrection,
and teach us to reflect it in our lives.

Grant this through our Lord Jesus Christ, your
Son,
who lives and reigns with you and the Holy
Spirit,
one God, for ever and ever.

ALTERNATIVE OPENING PRAYER

Let us pray
[at the beginning of Lent
for the spirit of repentance]

Pause for silent prayer

Lord our God,
you formed man from the clay of the earth
and breathed into him the spirit of life,
but he turned from your face and sinned.
In this time of repentance
we call out for your mercy.

Bring us back to you
and to the life your Son won for us
by his death on the cross,
for he lives and reigns for ever and ever.

LITURGY OF THE WORD

See Lectionary for Mass, nos. 22-24.

LITURGY OF THE EUCHARIST

PRAYER OVER THE GIFTS

Pray, brethren . . .

Lord,
make us worthy to bring you these gifts.
May this sacrifice
help to change our lives.

We ask this in the name of Jesus the Lord.

Eucharistic Prayer:

Preface of First Sunday of Lent, page
429, or Preface of Lent I or II, pages
425–426.

Communion Rite

Man does not live on bread alone, but on every word that comes from the mouth of God. (Matthew 4:4)

or:

The Lord will overshadow you, and you will find refuge under his wings. (Ps. 90:4)

A period of silence may be observed after communion, or a psalm or song of praise may be sung.

PRAYER AFTER COMMUNION

Let us pray.
Pause for silent prayer, if this has not preceded.
Father,
you increase our faith and hope,
you deepen our love in this communion.
Help us to live by your words
and to seek Christ, our bread of life,
who is Lord for ever and ever.

SOLEMN BLESSING OR PRAYER OVER THE PEOPLE

The following may replace the simple blessing.

After the greeting, the deacon (or in his absence, the priest) gives the invitation in these or similar words:

Bow your heads and pray for God's blessing.

Then the priest extends his hands over the people while he sings or says:

The Father of mercies has given us an example of unselfish love
in the sufferings of his only Son.
Through your service of God and neighbor
may you receive his countless blessings.
℟. Amen.

You believe that by his dying
Christ destroyed death for ever.
May he give you everlasting life.
℟. Amen.

He humbled himself for our sakes.
May you follow his example
and share in his resurrection.
℟. Amen.

May almighty God bless you,
the Father, and the Son, ✝ and the Holy Spirit.
℟. Amen.

For other texts of solemn blessings and prayers over the people, see pages 528–540.

MONDAY OF THE FIRST WEEK OF LENT

Introductory Rites

As the eyes of servants are on the hands of their master, so our eyes are fixed on the Lord our God, pleading for his mercy. Have mercy on us, Lord, have mercy. (Ps. 122:2-3)

OPENING PRAYER

God our savior,
bring us back to you
and fill our minds with your wisdom.
May we be enriched by our observance of Lent.

Grant this through our Lord Jesus Christ, your Son,
who lives and reigns with you and the Holy Spirit,
one God, for ever and ever.

See Lectionary for Mass, no. 225.

PRAYER OVER THE GIFTS

Pray, brethren . . .

Lord,
may this offering of our love
be acceptable to you.
Let it transform our lives
and bring us your mercy.

We ask this through Christ our Lord.

Preface of Lent I-IV, pages **425–428.**

Communion Rite

I tell you, anything you did for the least of my brothers, you did for me, says the Lord. Come, you whom my Father has blessed; inherit the kingdom prepared for you since the foundation of the world. (Matthew 25:40, 34)

PRAYER AFTER COMMUNION

Let us pray.
Pause for silent prayer, if this has not preceded.
Lord,
through this sacrament
may we rejoice in your healing power
and experience your saving love in mind and body.

We ask this in the name of Jesus the Lord.

TUESDAY OF THE FIRST WEEK OF LENT

Introductory Rites

> In every age, O Lord, you have been our refuge. From all
> eternity, you are God. (Ps. 89:1-2)

OPENING PRAYER

**Father,
look on us, your children.
Through the discipline of Lent
help us to grow in our desire for you.**

**We ask this through our Lord Jesus Christ, your Son,
who lives and reigns with you and the Holy Spirit,
one God, for ever and ever.**

See Lectionary for Mass, no. 226.

PRAYER OVER THE GIFTS

Pray, brethren . . .

**Father of creation,
from all you have given us
we bring you this bread and wine.
May it become for us the food of eternal life.**

We ask this in the name of Jesus the Lord.

Preface of Lent I-IV, pages 425–428.

Communion Rite

> My God of justice, you answer my cry; you come to my
> help when I am in trouble. Take pity on me, Lord, and hear
> my prayer. (Ps. 4:2)

PRAYER AFTER COMMUNION

Let us pray.
Pause for silent prayer, if this has not preceded.

**Lord,
may we who receive this sacrament
restrain our earthly desires
and grow in love for the things of heaven.**

Grant this through Christ our Lord.

WEDNESDAY OF THE FIRST WEEK OF LENT

Introductory Rites
> Remember your mercies, Lord, your tenderness from ages
> past. Do not let our enemies triumph over us; O God,
> deliver Israel from all her distress. (Ps. 24:6, 3, 22)

OPENING PRAYER

**Lord,
look upon us and hear our prayer.
By the good works you inspire,
help us to discipline our bodies
and to be renewed in spirit.**

**Grant this through our Lord Jesus Christ, your Son,
who lives and reigns with you and the Holy Spirit,
one God, for ever and ever.**

See Lectionary for Mass, no. 227.

PRAYER OVER THE GIFTS

Pray, brethren . . .

**Lord,
from all you have given us,
we bring you these gifts in your honor.
Make them the sacrament of our salvation.**

We ask this through Christ our Lord.

Preface of Lent I-IV, pages 425–428.

Communion Rite
> Lord, give joy to all who trust in you; be their defender and
> make them happy for ever. (Ps. 5:12)

PRAYER AFTER COMMUNION

Let us pray.
Pause for silent prayer, if this has not preceded.
**Father,
you never fail to give us the food of life.
May this eucharist renew our strength
and bring us to salvation.**

Grant this through Christ our Lord.

THURSDAY OF THE FIRST WEEK OF LENT

Introductory Rites

Let my words reach your ears, Lord; listen to my groaning,
and hear the cry of my prayer, O my King, my God. (Ps.
5:2-3)

OPENING PRAYER

**Father,
without you we can do nothing.
By your Spirit help us to know what is right
and to be eager in doing your will.**

**We ask this through our Lord Jesus Christ, your Son,
who lives and reigns with you and the Holy Spirit,
one God, for ever and ever.**

See Lectionary for Mass, no. 228.

PRAYER OVER THE GIFTS

Pray, brethren . . .

**Lord,
be close to your people,
accept our prayers and offerings,
and let us turn to you with all our hearts.**

We ask this in the name of Jesus the Lord.

Preface of Lent I-IV, pages 425–428.

Communion Rite

Everyone who asks will receive; whoever seeks shall find,
and to him who knocks it shall be opened. (Matthew 7:8)

PRAYER AFTER COMMUNION

Let us pray.
Pause for silent prayer, if this has not preceded.
**Lord our God,
renew us by these mysteries.
May they heal us now
and bring us eternal salvation.**

Grant this through Christ our Lord.

FRIDAY OF THE FIRST WEEK OF LENT

Introductory Rites
Lord, deliver me from my distress. See my hardship and
my poverty, and pardon all my sins. (Ps. 24:17-18)

OPENING PRAYER

**Lord,
may our observance of Lent
help to renew us and prepare us
to celebrate the death and resurrection of Christ,
who lives and reigns with you and the Holy Spirit,
one God, for ever and ever.**

See Lectionary for Mass, no. 229.

PRAYER OVER THE GIFTS

Pray, brethren . . .

**Lord of mercy,
in your love accept these gifts.
May they bring us your saving power.**

We ask this in the name of Jesus the Lord.

Preface of Lent I-IV, pages **425–428.**

Communion Rite
By my life, I do not wish the sinner to die, says the Lord,
but to turn to me and live. (Ezek. 33:11)

PRAYER AFTER COMMUNION

Let us pray.
Pause for silent prayer, if this has not preceded.
**Lord,
may the sacrament you give us
free us from our sinful ways and bring us new life.
May this eucharist lead us to salvation.**

Grant this through Christ our Lord.

SATURDAY OF THE FIRST WEEK OF LENT

Introductory Rites

The law of the Lord is perfect, reviving the soul; his commandments are the wisdom of the simple. (Ps. 18:8)

OPENING PRAYER

Eternal Father,
turn our hearts to you.
By seeking your kingdom
and loving one another,
may we become a people who worship you
in spirit and truth.

Grant this through our Lord Jesus Christ, your Son,
who lives and reigns with you and the Holy Spirit,
one God, for ever and ever.

See Lectionary for Mass, no. 230.

PRAYER OVER THE GIFTS

Pray, brethren . . .

Lord,
may we be renewed by this eucharist.
May we become more like Christ your Son,
who is Lord for ever and ever.

Preface of Lent I-IV, pages 425–428.

Communion Rite

Be perfect, as your heavenly Father is perfect, says the Lord. (Matthew 5:48)

PRAYER AFTER COMMUNION

Let us pray.
Pause for silent prayer, if this has not preceded.
Lord,
may the word we share
be our guide to peace in your kingdom.
May the food we receive
assure us of your constant love.

We ask this in the name of Jesus the Lord.

SECOND SUNDAY OF LENT

Introductory Rites

Remember your mercies, Lord, your tenderness from ages past. Do not let our enemies triumph over us; O God, deliver Israel from all her distress. (Ps. 24:6, 3, 22)

or:

My heart has prompted me to seek your face; I seek it, Lord; do not hide from me. (Ps. 26:8-9)

The Gloria is omitted.

OPENING PRAYER

Let us pray
[for the grace to respond
to the Word of God]
Pause for silent prayer
God our Father,
help us to hear your Son.
Enlighten us with your word,
that we may find the way to your glory.

We ask this through our Lord Jesus Christ,
your Son,
who lives and reigns with you and the Holy
Spirit,
one God, for ever and ever.

ALTERNATIVE OPENING PRAYER

Let us pray
[in this season of Lent
for the gift of integrity]
Pause for silent prayer
Father of light,
in you is found no shadow of change
but only the fullness of life and limitless truth.
Open our hearts to the voice of your Word
and free us from the original darkness that
shadows our vision.

Restore our sight that we may look upon your S
who calls us to repentance and a change of hea
for he lives and reigns with you for ever and
ever.

LITURGY OF THE WORD

See Lectionary for Mass, nos. 25-27.

LITURGY OF THE EUCHARIST

PRAYER OVER THE GIFTS

Pray, brethren . . .

Lord,
make us holy.
May this eucharist take away our sins
that we may be prepared
to celebrate the resurrection.

We ask this in the name of Jesus the Lord.

Eucharistic Prayer:
Preface of Second Sunday of Lent, page 430, or Preface of Lent I or II, pages 425–426.

Communion Rite

> This is my Son, my beloved, in whom is all my delight:
> listen to him. (Matthew 17:5)

A period of silence may be observed after communion, or a psalm or song of praise may be sung.

PRAYER AFTER COMMUNION

Let us pray.
Pause for silent prayer, if this has not preceded.
Lord,
we give thanks for these holy mysteries
which bring to us here on earth
a share in the life to come,
through Christ our Lord.

SOLEMN BLESSING OR PRAYER OVER THE PEOPLE

The following may replace the simple blessing.

After the greeting, the deacon (or in his absence, the priest) gives the invitation in these or similar words:

Bow your heads and pray for God's blessing.

Then the priest extends his hands over the people while he sings or says:

Lord,
we rejoice that you are our creator and ruler.
As we call upon your generosity,
renew and keep us in your love.

Grant this through Christ our Lord.
℟. Amen.

May almighty God bless you,
the Father, and the Son, ✛ and the Holy Spirit.
℟. Amen.

For other texts of solemn blessings and prayers over the people, see pages 528–540.

MONDAY OF THE SECOND WEEK OF LENT

Introductory Rites

Redeem me, Lord, and have mercy on me; my foot is set
on the right path, I worship you in the great assembly. (Ps.
25:11-12)

OPENING PRAYER

God our Father,
teach us to find new life through penance.
Keep us from sin,
and help us live by your commandment of love.

We ask this through our Lord Jesus Christ, your Son,
who lives and reigns with you and the Holy Spirit,
one God, for ever and ever.

See Lectionary for Mass, no. 231.

PRAYER OVER THE GIFTS

Pray, brethren . . .

Father of mercy,
hear our prayer.
May the grace of this mystery
prevent us from becoming absorbed in material things.

Grant this through Christ our Lord.

Preface of Lent I-IV, pages 425–428.

Communion Rite

Be merciful as your Father is merciful, says the Lord. (Luke
6:36)

PRAYER AFTER COMMUNION

Let us pray.
Pause for silent prayer, if this has not preceded.
Lord,
may this communion bring us pardon
and lead us to the joy of heaven.

We ask this in the name of Jesus the Lord.

TUESDAY OF THE SECOND WEEK OF LENT

Introductory Rites

Give light to my eyes, Lord, lest I sleep in death, and my
enemy say: I have overcome him. (Ps. 12:4-5)

OPENING PRAYER

**Lord,
watch over your Church,
and guide it with your unfailing love.
Protect us from what could harm us
and lead us to what will save us.
Help us always,
for without you we are bound to fail.**

**Grant this through our Lord Jesus Christ, your Son,
who lives and reigns with you and the Holy Spirit,
one God, for ever and ever.**

See Lectionary for Mass, no. 232.

PRAYER OVER THE GIFTS

Pray, brethren . . .

**Lord,
bring us closer to you by this celebration.
May it cleanse us from our faults
and lead us to the gifts of heaven.**

We ask this through Christ our Lord.

Preface of Lent I-IV, pages 425–428.

Communion Rite

I will tell all your marvelous works. I will rejoice and be
glad in you, and sing to your name, Most High. (Ps. 9:2-3)

PRAYER AFTER COMMUNION

Let us pray.
Pause for silent prayer, if this has not preceded.
**Lord,
may the food we receive
bring us your constant assistance
that we may live better lives.**

We ask this in the name of Jesus the Lord.

WEDNESDAY OF THE SECOND WEEK OF LENT

Introductory Rites

> Do not abandon me, Lord. My God, do not go away from
> me! Hurry to help me, Lord, my Savior. (Ps. 37:22-23)

OPENING PRAYER

**Father,
teach us to live good lives,
encourage us with your support
and bring us to eternal life.**

**We ask this through our Lord Jesus Christ, your Son,
who lives and reigns with you and the Holy Spirit,
one God, for ever and ever.**

See Lectionary for Mass, no. 233.

PRAYER OVER THE GIFTS

Pray, brethren . . .

**Lord,
accept this sacrifice,
and through this holy exchange of gifts
free us from the sins that enslave us.**

We ask this in the name of Jesus the Lord.

Preface of Lent I-IV, pages 425–428.

Communion Rite

> The Son of Man did not come to be served, but to serve,
> and to give his life as a ransom for many. (Matthew 20:28)

PRAYER AFTER COMMUNION

Let us pray.
Pause for silent prayer, if this has not preceded.
**Lord our God,
may the eucharist you give us
as a pledge of unending life
help us to salvation.**

Grant this through Christ our Lord.

THURSDAY OF THE SECOND WEEK OF LENT

Introductory Rites

Test me, O God, and know my thoughts; see whether I step in the wrong path, and guide me along the everlasting way. (Ps. 138:23-24)

OPENING PRAYER

**God of love,
bring us back to you.
Send your Spirit to make us strong in faith
and active in good works.**

**Grant this through our Lord Jesus Christ, your Son,
who lives and reigns with you and the Holy Spirit,
one God, for ever and ever.**

See Lectionary for Mass, no. 234.

PRAYER OVER THE GIFTS

Pray, brethren . . .

**Lord,
may this sacrifice bless our lenten observance.
May it lead us to sincere repentance.**

We ask this through Christ our Lord.

Preface of Lent I-IV, pages 425–428.

Communion Rite

Happy are those of blameless life, who follow the law of the Lord. (Ps. 118:1)

PRAYER AFTER COMMUNION

Let us pray.
Pause for silent prayer, if this has not preceded.
**Lord,
may the sacrifice we have offered strengthen our faith
and be seen in our love for one another.**

We ask this in the name of Jesus the Lord.

FRIDAY OF THE SECOND WEEK OF LENT

Introductory Rites

To you, Lord, I look for protection, never let me be disgraced. You are my refuge; save me from the trap they have laid for me. (Ps. 30:2, 5)

OPENING PRAYER

Merciful Father,
may our acts of penance bring us your forgiveness,
open our hearts to your love,
and prepare us for the coming feast of the resurrection.

We ask this through our Lord Jesus Christ, your Son,
who lives and reigns with you and the Holy Spirit,
one God, for ever and ever.

See Lectionary for Mass, no. 235.

PRAYER OVER THE GIFTS

Pray, brethren . . .

God of mercy,
prepare us to celebrate these mysteries.
Help us to live the love they proclaim.

We ask this in the name of Jesus the Lord.

Preface of Lent I-IV, pages 425–428.

Communion Rite

God loved us and sent his Son to take away our sins.
(1 John 4:10)

PRAYER AFTER COMMUNION

Let us pray.
Pause for silent prayer, if this has not preceded.
Lord,
may this communion so change our lives
that we may seek more faithfully
the salvation it promises.

Grant this through Christ our Lord.

SATURDAY OF THE SECOND WEEK OF LENT

Introductory Rites

The Lord is loving and merciful, to anger slow, and full of love; the Lord is kind to all, and compassionate to all his creatures. (Ps. 144:8-9)

OPENING PRAYER

**God our Father,
by your gifts to us on earth
we already share in your life.
In all we do,
guide us to the light of your kingdom.**

**Grant this through our Lord Jesus Christ, your Son,
who lives and reigns with you and the Holy Spirit,
one God, for ever and ever.**

See Lectionary for Mass, no. 236.

PRAYER OVER THE GIFTS

Pray, brethren . . .

**Lord,
may the grace of these sacraments
help us to reject all harmful things
and lead us to your spiritual gifts.**

We ask this through Christ our Lord.

Preface of Lent I-IV, pages 425–428.

Communion Rite

My son, you should rejoice, because your brother was dead and has come back to life; he was lost and is found. (Luke 15:32)

PRAYER AFTER COMMUNION

Let us pray.
Pause for silent prayer, if this has not preceded.
**Lord,
give us the spirit of love
and lead us to share in your life.**

We ask this in the name of Jesus the Lord.

THIRD SUNDAY OF LENT

If the first scrutiny in preparation for the baptism of adults takes place today, the proper ritual prayers and intercessions (page 751) may be used.

Introductory Rites

My eyes are ever fixed on the Lord, for he releases my feet from the snare. O look at me and be merciful, for I am wretched and alone. (Ps. 24:15-16)

or:

I will prove my holiness through you. I will gather you from the ends of the earth; I will pour clean water on you and wash away all your sins. I will give you a new spirit within you, says the Lord. (Ezek. 36:23-26)

The Gloria is omitted.

OPENING PRAYER

Let us pray
  [for confidence in the love of God and the
    strength to overcome all our weakness]
Pause for silent prayer
Father,
you have taught us to overcome our sins
by prayer, fasting and works of mercy.
When we are discouraged by our weakness,
give us confidence in your love.

We ask this through our Lord Jesus Christ,
  your Son,
who lives and reigns with you and the Holy
  Spirit,
one God, for ever and ever.

ALTERNATIVE OPENING PRAYER

Let us pray
  [to the Father and ask him to form
  a new heart within us]
Pause for silent prayer
God of all compassion, Father of all goodness,
to heal the wounds our sins and selfishness
  bring upon us
you bid us turn to fasting, prayer, and sharing
  with our brothers.
We acknowledge our sinfulness, our guilt is
  ever before us:
when our weakness causes discouragement,
let your compassion fill us with hope
and lead us through a Lent of repentance to the
  beauty of Easter joy.

Grant this through Christ our Lord.

LITURGY OF THE WORD

See Lectionary for Mass, nos. 28-30.

LITURGY OF THE EUCHARIST

PRAYER OVER THE GIFTS

Eucharistic Prayer:
Preface of Third Sunday of Lent, page 431, when the gospel of the Samaritan woman (Year A) is read. When this gospel is not read, Preface of Lent I or II, pages 425–426, is used.

Pray, brethren . . .

Lord,
by the grace of this sacrifice
may we who ask forgiveness
be ready to forgive one another.

We ask this in the name of Jesus the Lord.

170

Communion Rite

When the gospel of the Samaritan woman is read:
Whoever drinks the water that I shall give him, says the Lord, will have a spring inside him, welling up for eternal life. (John 4:13-14)

When other gospels are read:
The sparrow even finds a home, the swallow finds a nest wherein to place her young, near to your altars, Lord of hosts, my King, my God! How happy they who dwell in your house! For ever they are praising you. (Ps. 83:4-5)

A period of silence may be observed after communion, or a psalm or song of praise may be sung.

PRAYER AFTER COMMUNION

Let us pray.
Pause for silent prayer, if this has not preceded.
Lord,
in sharing this sacrament
may we receive your forgiveness
and be brought together in unity and peace.
We ask this through Christ our Lord.

SOLEMN BLESSING OR PRAYER OVER THE PEOPLE

The following may replace the simple blessing.

After the greeting, the deacon (or in his absence, the priest) gives the invitation in these or similar words:

Bow your heads and pray for God's blessing.

Then the priest extends his hands over the people while he sings or says:

The Father of mercies has given us an example
of unselfish love
in the sufferings of his only Son.
Through your service of God and neighbor
may you receive his countless blessings.
℞. Amen.

You believe that by his dying
Christ destroyed death for ever.
May he give you everlasting life.
℞. Amen.

He humbled himself for our sakes.
May you follow his example
and share in his resurrection.
℞. Amen.

For other texts of solemn blessings and prayers over the people, see pages 528–540.

May almighty God bless you,
the Father, and the Son,✛ and the Holy Spirit.
℞. Amen.

MONDAY OF THE THIRD WEEK OF LENT

Introductory Rites

My soul is longing and pining for the courts of the Lord;
my heart and my flesh sing for joy to the living God. (Ps.
83:3)

OPENING PRAYER

**God of mercy,
free your Church from sin
and protect it from evil.
Guide us, for we cannot be saved without you.**

**We ask this through our Lord Jesus Christ, your Son,
who lives and reigns with you and the Holy Spirit,
one God, for ever and ever.**

See Lectionary for Mass, no. 238.

PRAYER OVER THE GIFTS

Pray, brethren . . .

**Father,
bless these gifts
that they may become the sacrament of our salvation.**

We ask this in the name of Jesus the Lord.

Preface of Lent I-IV, pages 425–428.

Communion Rite

All you nations, praise the Lord, for steadfast is his kindly
mercy to us. (Ps. 116:1-2)

PRAYER AFTER COMMUNION

Let us pray.
Pause for silent prayer, if this has not preceded.
**Lord,
forgive the sins of those
who receive your sacrament,
and bring us together in unity and peace.**

Grant this through Christ our Lord.

TUESDAY OF THE THIRD WEEK OF LENT

Introductory Rites

I call upon you, God, for you will answer me; bend your
ear and hear my prayer. Guard me as the pupil of your eye;
hide me in the shade of your wings. (Ps. 16:6, 8)

OPENING PRAYER

Lord,
you call us to your service
and continue your saving work among us.
May your love never abandon us.

We ask this through our Lord Jesus Christ, your Son,
who lives and reigns with you and the Holy Spirit,
one God, for ever and ever.

See Lectionary for Mass, no. 239.

PRAYER OVER THE GIFTS

Pray, brethren . . .

Lord,
may the saving sacrifice we offer
bring us your forgiveness,
so that freed from sin, we may always please you.

Grant this through Christ our Lord.

Preface of Lent I-IV, pages 425–428.

Communion Rite

Lord, who may stay in your dwelling place? Who shall live
on your holy mountain? He who walks without blame and
does what is right. (Ps. 14:1-2)

PRAYER AFTER COMMUNION

Let us pray.

Pause for silent prayer, if this has not preceded.
Lord,
may our sharing in this holy mystery
bring us your protection, forgiveness and life.

We ask this in the name of Jesus the Lord.

WEDNESDAY OF THE THIRD WEEK OF LENT

Introductory Rites
>   Lord, direct my steps as you have promised, and let no evil
>   hold me in its power. (Ps. 118:133)

OPENING PRAYER

Lord,
during this lenten season
nourish us with your word of life
and make us one in love and prayer.

Grant this through our Lord Jesus Christ, your Son,
who lives and reigns with you and the Holy Spirit,
one God, for ever and ever.

See Lectionary for Mass, no. 240.

PRAYER OVER THE GIFTS

Pray, brethren . . .

Lord,
receive our prayers and offerings.
In time of danger,
protect all who celebrate this sacrament.

We ask this in the name of Jesus the Lord.

Preface of Lent I-IV, pages 425–428.

Communion Rite
>   Lord, you will show me the path of life and fill me with joy
>   in your presence. (Ps. 15:11)

PRAYER AFTER COMMUNION

Let us pray.
Pause for silent prayer, if this has not preceded.
Lord,
may this eucharist forgive our sins,
make us holy,
and prepare us for the eternal life you promise.

We ask this through Christ our Lord.

THURSDAY OF THE THIRD WEEK OF LENT

Introductory Rites

I am the Savior of all people, says the Lord. Whatever their troubles, I will answer their cry, and I will always be their Lord.

OPENING PRAYER

**Father,
help us to be ready to celebrate the great paschal mystery.
Make our love grow each day
as we approach the feast of our salvation.**

**We ask this through our Lord Jesus Christ, your Son,
who lives and reigns with you and the Holy Spirit,
one God, for ever and ever.**

See Lectionary for Mass, no. 241.

PRAYER OVER THE GIFTS

Pray, brethren . . .

**Lord,
take away our sinfulness and be pleased with our offerings.
Help us to pursue the true gifts you promise
and not become lost in false joys.**

Grant this through Christ our Lord.

Preface of Lent I-IV, pages 425–428.

Communion Rite

You have laid down your precepts to be faithfully kept.
May my footsteps be firm in keeping your commands. (Ps. 118:4-5)

PRAYER AFTER COMMUNION

Let us pray.
Pause for silent prayer, if this has not preceded.
**Lord,
may your sacrament of life
bring us the gift of salvation
and make our lives pleasing to you.**

We ask this in the name of Jesus the Lord.

FRIDAY OF THE THIRD WEEK OF LENT

Introductory Rites

Lord, there is no god to compare with you; you are great
and do wonderful things, you are the only God. (Ps. 85:8,
10)

OPENING PRAYER

**Merciful Father,
fill our hearts with your love
and keep us faithful to the gospel of Christ.
Give us the grace to rise above our human weakness.**

**Grant this through our Lord Jesus Christ, your Son,
who lives and reigns with you and the Holy Spirit,
one God, for ever and ever.**

See Lectionary for Mass, no. 242.

PRAYER OVER THE GIFTS

Pray, brethren . . .

**Lord,
bless the gifts we have prepared.
Make them acceptable to you
and a lasting source of salvation.**

We ask this in the name of Jesus the Lord.

Preface of Lent I-IV, pages 425–428.

Communion Rite

To love God with all your heart, and your neighbor as
yourself, is a greater thing than all the temple sacrifices.
(See Mark 12:33)

PRAYER AFTER COMMUNION

Let us pray.
Pause for silent prayer, if this has not preceded.
**Lord,
fill us with the power of your love.
As we share in this eucharist,
may we come to know fully the redemption we have received.**

We ask this through Christ our Lord.

SATURDAY OF THE THIRD WEEK OF LENT

Introductory Rites

Bless the Lord, my soul, and remember all his kindnesses, for he pardons all my faults. (Ps. 102:2-3)

OPENING PRAYER

**Lord,
may this lenten observance
of the suffering, death and resurrection of Christ
bring us to the full joy of Easter.**

**We ask this through our Lord Jesus Christ, your Son,
who lives and reigns with you and the Holy Spirit,
one God, for ever and ever.**

See Lectionary for Mass, no. 243.

PRAYER OVER THE GIFTS

Pray, brethren . . .

**Lord,
by your grace you enable us
to come to these mysteries with renewed lives.
May this eucharist give you worthy praise.**

Grant this through Christ our Lord.

Preface of Lent I-IV, pages 425–428.

Communion Rite

He stood at a distance and beat his breast, saying: O God, be merciful to me, a sinner. (Luke 18:13)

PRAYER AFTER COMMUNION

Let us pray.
Pause for silent prayer, if this has not preceded.
**God of mercy,
may the holy gifts we receive
help us to worship you in truth,
and to receive your sacraments with faith.**

We ask this in the name of Jesus the Lord.

FOURTH SUNDAY OF LENT

If the second scrutiny in preparation for the baptism of adults takes place today, the proper ritual prayers and intercessions (page 751) may be used.

Introductory Rites

Rejoice, Jerusalem! Be glad for her, you who love her; rejoice with her, you who mourned for her, and you will find contentment at her consoling breasts. (See Is. 66:10-11)

The Gloria is omitted.

OPENING PRAYER

Let us pray
  [for a greater faith and love]
Pause for silent prayer
**Father of peace,
we are joyful in your Word,
your Son Jesus Christ,
who reconciles us to you.
Let us hasten toward Easter
with the eagerness of faith and love.**

**We ask this through our Lord Jesus Christ,
    your Son,
who lives and reigns with you and the Holy
    Spirit,
one God, for ever and ever.**

ALTERNATIVE OPENING PRAYER

Let us pray
  **[that by growing in love this lenten season we
    may bring the peace of Christ to our world]**
Pause for silent prayer
**God our Father,
your Word, Jesus Christ, spoke peace to a sinful world
and brought mankind the gift of reconciliation
by the suffering and death he endured.
Teach us, the people who bear his name,
to follow the example he gave us:
may our faith, hope, and charity
turn hatred to love, conflict to peace, death to
    eternal life.**

We ask this through Christ our Lord.

LITURGY OF THE WORD

See Lectionary for Mass, nos. 31-33.

LITURGY OF THE EUCHARIST

PRAYER OVER THE GIFTS

Pray, brethren . . .

**Lord,
we offer you these gifts
which bring us peace and joy.
Increase our reverence by this eucharist,
and bring salvation to the world.**

We ask this in the name of Jesus the Lord.

Eucharistic Prayer:
Preface of Fourth Sunday of Lent, page 432, when the gospel of the man born blind (Year A) is read. When this gospel is not read, Preface of Lent I or II, pages 425–426, is used.

Communion Rite

When the gospel of the man born blind is read:

The Lord rubbed my eyes: I went away and washed; then I could see, and I believed in God. (See John 9:11)

Year B

To Jerusalem, that binds them together in unity, the tribes of the Lord go up to give him praise. (Ps. 121:3-4)

Year C

My son, you should rejoice, because your brother was dead and has come back to life; he was lost and is found. (Luke 15:32)

A period of silence may be observed after communion, or a psalm or song of praise may be sung.

PRAYER AFTER COMMUNION

Let us pray.
Pause for silent prayer, if this has not preceded.
Father,
you enlighten all who come into the world.
Fill our hearts with the light of your gospel,
that our thoughts may please you,
and our love be sincere.
Grant this through Christ our Lord.

SOLEMN BLESSING OR PRAYER OVER THE PEOPLE

The following may replace the simple blessing.

After the greeting, the deacon (or in his absence, the priest) gives the invitation in these or similar words:

Bow your heads and pray for God's blessing.

Then the priest extends his hands over the people while he sings or says:

Father,
look with love upon your people,
the love which our Lord Jesus Christ showed us
when he delivered himself to evil men
and suffered the agony of the cross.

Grant this through Christ our Lord.
℟. Amen.

May almighty God bless you,
the Father, and the Son, ✠ and the Holy Spirit.
℟. Amen.

For other texts of solemn blessings and prayers over the people, see pages 528–540.

MONDAY OF THE FOURTH WEEK OF LENT

Introductory Rites

Lord, I put my trust in you; I shall be glad and rejoice in your mercy, because you have seen my affliction. (Ps. 30:7-8)

OPENING PRAYER

**Father, creator,
you give the world new life by your sacraments.
May we, your Church, grow in your life
and continue to receive your help on earth.**

**Grant this through our Lord Jesus Christ, your Son,
who lives and reigns with you and the Holy Spirit,
one God, for ever and ever.**

See Lectionary for Mass, no. 245.

PRAYER OVER THE GIFTS

Pray, brethren . . .

**Lord,
through the gifts we present
may we receive the grace
to cast off the old ways of life
and to redirect our course toward the life of heaven.**

We ask this in the name of Jesus the Lord.

Preface of Lent I–IV, pages 425–428.

Communion Rite

I shall put my spirit within you, says the Lord; you will obey my laws and keep my decrees. (Ezek. 36:27)

PRAYER AFTER COMMUNION

Let us pray.
Pause for silent prayer, if this has not preceded.
**Lord,
may your gifts bring us life and holiness
and lead us to the happiness of eternal life.**

We ask this through Christ our Lord.

TUESDAY OF THE FOURTH WEEK OF LENT

Introductory Rites

Come to the waters, all who thirst; though you have no
money, come and drink with joy. (See Is. 55:1)

OPENING PRAYER

Father,
may our lenten observance
prepare us to embrace the paschal mystery
and to proclaim your salvation with joyful praise.

We ask this through our Lord Jesus Christ, your Son,
who lives and reigns with you and the Holy Spirit,
one God, for ever and ever.

See Lectionary for Mass, no. 246.

PRAYER OVER THE GIFTS

Pray, brethren . . .

Lord,
may your gifts of bread and wine
which nourish us here on earth
become the food of our eternal life.

Grant this through Christ our Lord.

Preface of Lent I-IV, pages 425–428.

Communion Rite

The Lord is my shepherd; there is nothing I shall want. In
green pastures he gives me rest, he leads me beside the
waters of peace. (Ps. 22:1-2)

PRAYER AFTER COMMUNION

Let us pray.
Pause for silent prayer, if this has not preceded.

Lord,
may your holy sacraments cleanse and renew us;
may they bring us your help
and lead us to salvation.

We ask this in the name of Jesus the Lord.

WEDNESDAY OF THE FOURTH WEEK OF LENT

Introductory Rites

I pray to you, O God, for the time of your favor. Lord, in
your great love, answer me. (Ps. 68:14)

OPENING PRAYER

Lord,
you reward virtue
and forgive the repentant sinner.
Grant us your forgiveness
as we come before you confessing our guilt.

We ask this through our Lord Jesus Christ, your Son,
who lives and reigns with you and the Holy Spirit,
one God, for ever and ever.

See Lectionary for Mass, no. 247.

PRAYER OVER THE GIFTS

Pray, brethren . . .

Lord God,
may the power of this sacrifice wash away our sins,
renew our lives and bring us to salvation.

We ask this in the name of Jesus the Lord.

Preface of Lent I-IV, pages 425–428.

Communion Rite

God sent his Son into the world, not to condemn it, but so
that the world might be saved through him. (John 3:17)

PRAYER AFTER COMMUNION

Let us pray.
Pause for silent prayer, if this has not preceded.
Lord,
may we never misuse your healing gifts,
but always find in them a source of life and salvation.

Grant this through Christ our Lord.

THURSDAY OF THE FOURTH WEEK OF LENT

Introductory Rites

Let hearts rejoice who search for the Lord. Seek the Lord
and his strength, seek always the face of the Lord. (Ps.
104:3-4)

OPENING PRAYER

**Merciful Father,
may the penance of our lenten observance
make us your obedient people.
May the love within us be seen in what we do
and lead us to the joy of Easter.**

**Grant this through our Lord Jesus Christ, your Son,
who lives and reigns with you and the Holy Spirit,
one God, for ever and ever.**

See Lectionary for Mass, no. 248.

PRAYER OVER THE GIFTS

Pray, brethren . . .

**All-powerful God,
look upon our weakness.
May the sacrifice we offer
bring us purity and strength.**

We ask this in the name of Jesus the Lord.

Preface of Lent I-IV, pages 425–428.

Communion Rite

I will put my law within them, I will write it on their hearts;
then I shall be their God, and they will be my people. (Jer.
31:33)

PRAYER AFTER COMMUNION

Let us pray.
Pause for silent prayer, if this has not preceded.
**Lord,
may the sacraments we receive
cleanse us of sin and free us from guilt,
for our sins bring us sorrow
but your promise of salvation brings us joy.**

We ask this through Christ our Lord.

FRIDAY OF THE FOURTH WEEK OF LENT

Introductory Rites
> Save me, O God, by your power, and grant me justice!
> God, hear my prayer; listen to my plea. (Ps. 53:3-4)

OPENING PRAYER

Father, our source of life,
you know our weakness.
May we reach out with joy to grasp your hand
and walk more readily in your ways.

We ask this through our Lord Jesus Christ, your Son,
who lives and reigns with you and the Holy Spirit,
one God, for ever and ever.

See Lectionary for Mass, no. 249.

PRAYER OVER THE GIFTS

Pray, brethren . . .

All-powerful God,
may the healing power of this sacrifice
free us from sin
and help us to approach you with pure hearts.

Grant this through Christ our Lord.

Preface of Lent I-IV, pages 425–428.

Communion Rite
> In Christ, through the shedding of his blood, we have
> redemption and forgiveness of our sins by the abundance
> of his grace. (Eph. 1:7)

PRAYER AFTER COMMUNION

Let us pray.
Pause for silent prayer, if this has not preceded.
Lord,
in this eucharist we pass from death to life.
Keep us from our old and sinful ways
and help us to continue in the new life.

We ask this in the name of Jesus the Lord.

SATURDAY OF THE FOURTH WEEK OF LENT

Introductory Rites

The snares of death overtook me, the ropes of hell tightened around me; in my distress I called upon the Lord,
and he heard my voice. (Ps. 17:5-7)

OPENING PRAYER

**Lord,
guide us in your gentle mercy,
for left to ourselves
we cannot do your will.**

**Grant this through our Lord Jesus Christ, your Son,
who lives and reigns with you and the Holy Spirit,
one God, for ever and ever.**

See Lectionary for Mass, no. 250.

PRAYER OVER THE GIFTS

Pray, brethren . . .

**Father,
accept our gifts
and make our hearts obedient to your will.**

We ask this in the name of Jesus the Lord.

Preface of Lent I-IV, pages 425–428.

Communion Rite

We have been ransomed with the precious blood of
Christ, as with the blood of a lamb without blemish or
spot. (1 Peter 1:19)

PRAYER AFTER COMMUNION

Let us pray.
Pause for silent prayer, if this has not preceded.
**Lord,
may the power of your holy gifts free us from sin
and help us to please you in our daily lives.**

We ask this through Christ our Lord.

The practice of covering crosses and
images in the church may be observed, if the episcopal conference
decides. The crosses are to be covered until the end of the celebration
of the Lord's passion on Good Friday.
Images are to remain covered until
the beginning of the Easter vigil.

FIFTH SUNDAY OF LENT

If the third scrutiny in preparation for the baptism of adults takes place today, the proper ritual prayers and intercessions (page 751) may be used.

Introductory Rites

Give me justice, O God, and defend my cause against the wicked; rescue me from deceitful and unjust men. You, O God, are my refuge. (Ps. 42:1-2)

The Gloria is omitted.

OPENING PRAYER

Let us pray
[for the courage to follow Christ]

Pause for silent prayer

Father,
help us to be like Christ your Son,
who loved the world and died for our salvation.
Inspire us by his love,
guide us by his example,
who lives and reigns with you and the Holy Spirit,
one God, for ever and ever.

ALTERNATIVE OPENING PRAYER

Let us pray
[for the courage to embrace the world in the name of Christ]

Pause for silent prayer

Father in heaven,
the love of your Son led him to accept the suffering of the cross
that his brothers might glory in new life.
Change our selfishness into self-giving.
Help us to embrace the world you have given us
that we may transform the darkness of its pain
into the life and joy of Easter.
Grant this through Christ our Lord.

LITURGY OF THE WORD

See Lectionary for Mass, nos. 34-36.

LITURGY OF THE EUCHARIST

PRAYER OVER THE GIFTS

Pray, brethren . . .

Almighty God,
may the sacrifice we offer
take away the sins of those
whom you enlighten with the Christian faith.

We ask this in the name of Jesus the Lord.

Eucharistic Prayer:
Preface of Fifth Sunday of Lent, page 433, when the gospel of Lazarus (Year A) is read. When this gospel is not read, Preface of Lent I or II, pages 425–426, is used.

Communion Rite

> When the gospel of Lazarus is read:
>
> He who lives and believes in me will not die for ever, says the Lord. (John 11:26)
>
> When the gospel of the adulteress is read (Year C)
>
> Has no one condemned you? The woman answered: No one, Lord. Neither do I condemn you: go and do not sin again. (John 8:10-11)
>
> When other gospels are read:
>
> I tell you solemnly: Unless a grain of wheat falls on the ground and dies, it remains a single grain; but if it dies, it yields a rich harvest. (John 12:24-25)

A period of silence may be observed after communion, or a psalm or song of praise may be sung.

PRAYER AFTER COMMUNION

Let us pray.

Pause for silent prayer, if this has not preceded.

Almighty Father,
by this sacrifice
may we always remain one with your Son, Jesus Christ,
whose body and blood we share,
for he is Lord for ever and ever.

SOLEMN BLESSING OR PRAYER OVER THE PEOPLE

The following may replace the simple blessing.

After the greeting, the deacon (or in his absence, the priest) gives the invitation in these or similar words:

Bow your heads and pray for God's blessing.

Then the priest extends his hands over the people while he sings or says:

Lord,
protect your people always,
that they may be free from every evil
and serve you with all their hearts.

We ask this through Christ our Lord.
℟. Amen.

May almighty God bless you,
the Father, and the Son, ✚ and the Holy Spirit.
℟. Amen.

For other texts of solemn blessings and prayers over the people, see pages 528–540.

MONDAY OF THE FIFTH WEEK OF LENT

Introductory Rites

God, take pity on me! My enemies are crushing me; all
day long they wage war on me. (Ps. 55:2)

OPENING PRAYER

**Father of love, source of all blessings,
help us to pass from our old life of sin
to the new life of grace.
Prepare us for the glory of your kingdom.**

**We ask this through our Lord Jesus Christ, your Son,
who lives and reigns with you and the Holy Spirit,
one God, for ever and ever.**

See Lectionary for Mass, no. 252.

PRAYER OVER THE GIFTS   **Pray, brethren . . .**

**Lord,
as we come with joy
to celebrate the mystery of the eucharist,
may we offer you hearts
purified by bodily penance.**

Grant this through Christ our Lord.

Preface of the Passion of the Lord I,
page 434.

Communion Rite

When the gospel of the adulteress is read (Year C):

Has no one condemned you? The woman answered: No
one, Lord. Neither do I condemn you: go and do not sin
again. (John 8:10-11)

When other gospels are read:

I am the light of the world, says the Lord; the man who
follows me will have the light of life. (John 8:12)

PRAYER AFTER COMMUNION   **Let us pray.**

Pause for silent prayer, if this has not preceded.

**Father,
through the grace of your sacraments
may we follow Christ more faithfully
and come to the joy of your kingdom,
where he is Lord for ever and ever.**

TUESDAY OF THE FIFTH WEEK OF LENT

Introductory Rites

> Put your hope in the Lord. Take courage and be strong.
> (Ps. 26:14)

OPENING PRAYER

Lord,
help us to do your will
that your Church may grow
and become more faithful in your service.

Grant this through our Lord Jesus Christ, your Son,
who lives and reigns with you and the Holy Spirit,
one God, for ever and ever.

See Lectionary for Mass, no. 253.

PRAYER OVER THE GIFTS

Pray, brethren . . .

Merciful Lord,
we offer this gift of reconciliation
so that you will forgive our sins
and guide our wayward hearts.

We ask this through Christ our Lord.

Preface of the Passion of the Lord I,
page 434.

Communion Rite

> When I am lifted up from the earth, I will draw all men to
> myself, says the Lord. (John 12:32)

PRAYER AFTER COMMUNION

Let us pray.
Pause for silent prayer, if this has not preceded.
All-powerful God,
may the holy mysteries we share in this eucharist
make us worthy to attain the gift of heaven.

We ask this in the name of Jesus the Lord.

WEDNESDAY OF THE FIFTH WEEK OF LENT

Introductory Rites

Lord, you rescue me from raging enemies, you lift me up
above my attackers, you deliver me from violent men. (Ps.
17:48-49)

OPENING PRAYER

**Father of mercy,
hear the prayers of your repentant children
who call on you in love.
Enlighten our minds and sanctify our hearts.**

**We ask this through our Lord Jesus Christ, your Son,
who lives and reigns with you and the Holy Spirit,
one God, for ever and ever.**

See Lectionary for Mass, no. 254.

PRAYER OVER THE GIFTS

Pray, brethren . . .

**Lord,
you have given us these gifts to honor your name.
Bless them,
and let them become a source of health and strength.**

We ask this through Christ our Lord.

Preface of the Passion of the Lord I,
page 434.

Communion Rite

God has transferred us into the kingdom of the Son he
loves; in him we are redeemed, and find forgiveness of
our sins. (Col. 1:13-14)

PRAYER AFTER COMMUNION

Let us pray.
Pause for silent prayer, if this has not preceded.
**Lord,
may the mysteries we receive heal us,
remove sin from our hearts,
and make us grow strong
under your constant protection.**

Grant this through Christ our Lord.

THURSDAY OF THE FIFTH WEEK OF LENT

Introductory Rites

Christ is the mediator of a new covenant so that since he has died, those who are called may receive the eternal inheritance promised to them. (Heb. 9:15)

OPENING PRAYER

**Lord,
come to us:
free us from the stain of our sins.
Help us to remain faithful to a holy way of life,
and guide us to the inheritance you have promised.**

**Grant this through our Lord Jesus Christ, your Son,
who lives and reigns with you and the Holy Spirit,
one God, for ever and ever.**

See Lectionary for Mass, no. 255.

PRAYER OVER THE GIFTS

Pray, brethren . . .

**Merciful Lord,
accept the sacrifice we offer you
that it may help us grow in holiness
and advance the salvation of the world.**

We ask this in the name of Jesus the Lord.

Preface of the Passion of the Lord I, page 434.

Communion Rite

God did not spare his own Son, but gave him up for us all: with Christ he will surely give us all things. (Rom. 8:32)

PRAYER AFTER COMMUNION

Let us pray.
Pause for silent prayer, if this has not preceded.
**Lord of mercy,
let the sacrament which renews us
bring us to eternal life.**

We ask this through Christ our Lord.

FRIDAY OF THE FIFTH WEEK OF LENT

Introductory Rites

Have mercy on me, Lord, for I am in distress; rescue me from the hands of my enemies. Lord, keep me from shame, for I have called to you. (Ps. 30:10, 16, 18)

OPENING PRAYER

**Lord,
grant us your forgiveness,
and set us free from our enslavement to sin.**

**We ask this through our Lord Jesus Christ, your Son,
who lives and reigns with you and the Holy Spirit,
one God, for ever and ever.**

See Lectionary for Mass, no. 256.

PRAYER OVER THE GIFTS

Pray, brethren . . .

**God of mercy,
may the gifts we present at your altar
help us to achieve eternal salvation.**

Grant this through Christ our Lord.

Preface of the Passion of the Lord I, page 434.

Communion Rite

Jesus carried our sins in his own body on the cross so that we could die to sin and live in holiness; by his wounds we have been healed. (1 Peter 2:24)

PRAYER AFTER COMMUNION

Let us pray.
Pause for silent prayer, if this has not preceded.
**Lord,
may we always receive the protection of this sacrifice.
May it keep us safe from all harm.**

We ask this in the name of Jesus the Lord.

SATURDAY OF THE FIFTH WEEK OF LENT

Introductory Rites

> Lord, do not stay away; come quickly to help me! I am a
> worm and no man: men scorn me, people despise me.
> (Ps. 21:20, 7)

OPENING PRAYER

God our Father,
you always work to save us,
and now we rejoice in the great love
you give to your chosen people.
Protect all who are about to become your children,
and continue to bless those who are already baptized.

Grant this through our Lord Jesus Christ, your Son,
who lives and reigns with you and the Holy Spirit,
one God, for ever and ever.

See Lectionary for Mass, no. 257.

PRAYER OVER THE GIFTS

Pray, brethren . . .

Ever-living God,
in baptism, the sacrament of our faith,
you restore us to life.
Accept the prayers and gifts of your people:
forgive our sins and fulfill our hopes and desires.

We ask this in the name of Jesus the Lord.

Preface of the Passion of the Lord I,
page 434.

Communion Rite

> Christ was sacrificed so that he could gather together the
> scattered children of God. (John 11:52)

PRAYER AFTER COMMUNION

Let us pray.
Pause for silent prayer, if this has not preceded.
Father of mercy and power,
we thank you for nourishing us
with the body and blood of Christ
and for calling us to share in his divine life,
for he is Lord for ever and ever.

HOLY WEEK

HOLY WEEK

PASSION SUNDAY (Palm Sunday)

On this day the Church celebrates Christ's entrance into Jerusalem to accomplish his paschal mystery. Accordingly, the memorial of this event is included in every Mass, with the procession or the solemn entrance before the principal Mass, with the simple entrance before the other Masses. The solemn entrance (but not the procession) may be repeated before other Masses that are usually well attended.

Commemoration of the Lord's Entrance into Jerusalem

FIRST FORM: THE PROCESSION

At the scheduled time, the congregation assembles in a secondary church or chapel or in some other suitable place distinct from the church to which the procession will move. The faithful carry palm branches.

The priest and ministers put on red vestments for Mass and go to the place where the people have assembled. The priest may wear a cope instead of a chasuble; in this case he removes the cope after the procession.

Meanwhile, the following antiphon or any other appropriate song is sung.

**Hosanna to the Son of David,
the King of Israel.
Blessed is he who comes in the name of the Lord.
Hosanna in the highest.** (Matthew 21:9)

The priest then greets the people in the usual way and gives a brief introduction, inviting them to take a full part in the celebration. He may use these or similar words:

Dear friends in Christ, for five weeks of Lent we have been preparing, by works of charity and self-sacrifice, for the celebration of our Lord's paschal mystery. Today we come together to begin this solemn celebration in union with the whole Church throughout the world. Christ entered in triumph into his own city, to complete his work as our Messiah: to suffer, to die, and to rise again. Let us remember with devotion this entry which began his saving work and follow him with a lively faith. United with him in his suffering on the cross, may we share his resurrection and new life.

Afterwards the priest, with hands joined, says one of the following prayers:

Or:

Let us pray.
Pause for silent prayer
**Almighty God,
we pray you
bless ✠ these branches
and make them holy.
Today we joyfully acclaim Jesus our Messiah
   and King.
May we reach one day the happiness of the
   new and everlasting Jerusalem
by faithfully following him
who lives and reigns for ever and ever.**

Let us pray.
Pause for silent prayer
**Lord,
increase the faith of your people
and listen to our prayers.
Today we honor Christ our triumphant King
by carrying these branches.
May we honor you every day
by living always in him,
for he is Lord for ever and ever.**

The priest sprinkles the branches with holy water in silence.

Then the account of the Lord's entrance is proclaimed from one of the four gospels. This is done in the usual way or, if there is no deacon, by the priest. See Lectionary for Mass, no. 37.

After the gospel, a brief homily may be given. Before the procession begins, the celebrant or other suitable minister may address the people in these or similar words:

The procession to the church where Mass will be celebrated then begins.

If incense is used, the thurifer goes first with a lighted censer, followed by the cross-bearer (with the cross suitably decorated) between two ministers with lighted candles, then the priest with the ministers, and finally the congregation carrying branches.

During the procession, the choir and people sing the following or other appropriate songs:

The above antiphon may be repeated between verses of Psalm 23.

The above antiphon may be repeated between the verses of Psalm 46.

A hymn in honor of Christ the King, such as **All Glory, Laud and Honor,** is sung during the procession.

As the procession enters the church, the following responsory or another song which refers to the Lord's entrance is sung.

When the priest comes to the altar he venerates it and may also incense it. Then he goes to his chair (removes the cope and puts on the chasuble) and begins immediately the opening prayer of Mass, which concludes the procession. Mass then continues in the usual way.

**Let us go forth in peace,
praising Jesus our Messiah,
as did the crowds who welcomed him to Jerusalem.**

**The children of Jerusalem
welcomed Christ the King.
They carried olive branches
and loudly praised the Lord:
Hosanna in the highest.**

**The children of Jerusalem
welcomed Christ the King.
They spread their cloaks before him
and loudly praised the Lord:
Hosanna to the Son of David!
Blessed is he who comes
in the name of the Lord!**

**℟. The children of Jerusalem
welcomed Christ the King.
They proclaimed the resurrection of life,
and, waving olive branches,
they loudly praised the Lord:
Hosanna in the highest.**

**℣. When the people heard that Jesus
was entering Jerusalem,
they went to meet him
and, waving olive branches,
they loudly praised the Lord:
Hosanna in the highest.**

SECOND FORM: THE SOLEMN ENTRANCE

If the procession cannot be held outside the church, the commemoration of the Lord's entrance may be celebrated before the principal Mass with the solemn entrance, which takes place within the church.

The faithful, holding the branches, assemble either in front of the church door or inside the church. The priest and ministers, with a representative group of the faithful, go to a suitable place in the church outside the sanctuary, so that most of the people will be able to see the rite.

While the priest goes to the appointed place, the antiphon **Hosanna** or other suitable song is sung. Then the blessing of branches and proclamation of the gospel about the Lord's entrance into Jerusalem take place, as above. After the gospel the priest, with the ministers and the group of the faithful, moves solemnly through the church to the sanctuary, while the responsory **The children of Jerusalem** or other appropriate song is sung.

When the priest comes to the altar he venerates it, goes to his chair, and immediately begins the opening prayer of Mass, which then continues in the usual way.

THIRD FORM: THE SIMPLE ENTRANCE

At all other Masses on this Sunday, if the solemn entrance is not held, the Lord's entrance is commemorated with the following simple entrance.

While the priest goes to the altar, the entrance antiphon with its psalm or another song with the same theme is sung. After the priest venerates the altar, he goes to his chair and greets the people. Mass continues in the usual way.

At Masses without a congregation and other Masses at which the entrance antiphon cannot be sung, the priest goes at once to the altar and venerates it. Then he greets the people and reads the entrance antiphon, and Mass continues in the usual way.

Entrance Antiphon

Six days before the solemn passover the Lord came to Jerusalem, and children waving palm branches ran out to welcome him. They loudly praised the Lord: Blessed are you who have come to us so rich in love and mercy.

Psalm 23:9-10:

Open wide the doors and gates.
Lift high the ancient portals.
The King of glory enters.

Who is this King of glory?
He is God the mighty Lord.

Hosanna in the highest.
Blessed are you who have come to us
so rich in love and mercy.
Hosanna in the highest.

Where neither the procession nor the solemn entrance can be celebrated, there should be a bible service on the theme of the Lord's messianic entrance and passion, either on Saturday evening or on Sunday at a convenient time.

MASS

After the procession or solemn entrance the priest begins the Mass with the opening prayer.

OPENING PRAYER

Let us pray
   [for a closer union with Christ during this holy season]

Pause for silent prayer

**Almighty, ever-living God,
you have given the human race Jesus Christ our Savior
as a model of humility.
He fulfilled your will by becoming man
and giving his life on the cross.
Help us to bear witness to you
by following his example of suffering
and make us worthy to share in his resurrection.**

**We ask this through our Lord Jesus Christ, your Son,
who lives and reigns with you and the Holy Spirit,
one God, for ever and ever.**

ALTERNATIVE OPENING PRAYER

Let us pray
   [as we accompany our King to Jerusalem]

Pause for silent prayer

**Almighty Father of our Lord Jesus Christ,
you sent your Son
to be born of woman and to die on a cross,
so that through the obedience of one man,
estrangement might be dissolved for all men.**

**Guide our minds by his truth
and strengthen our lives by the example of his death,
that we may live in union with you
in the kingdom of your promise.**

Grant this through Christ our Lord.

LITURGY OF THE WORD

See Lectionary for Mass, no. 38.

The passion is read by the deacon or, if there is no deacon, by the priest. It may also be read by lay readers, with the part of Christ, if possible, reserved to the priest. It is proclaimed without candles or incense. The greeting and signs of the cross are omitted. Only a deacon asks the blessing before the passion, as he does before the gospel.

After the passion, a brief homily may be given.

LITURGY OF THE EUCHARIST

PRAYER OVER THE GIFTS

Pray, brethren . . .

**Lord,
may the suffering and death of Jesus, your only Son,
make us pleasing to you.
Alone we can do nothing,
but may this perfect sacrifice
win us your mercy and love.**

We ask this in the name of Jesus the Lord.

Eucharistic Prayer:
Preface of Passion Sunday (Palm Sunday), page **436**.

Communion Rite

>Father, if this cup may not pass, but I must drink it, then your will be done. (Matthew 26:42)

A period of silence may be observed after communion, or a psalm or song of praise may be sung.

PRAYER AFTER COMMUNION

Let us pray.
Pause for silent prayer, if this has not preceded.
Lord,
you have satisfied our hunger with this eucharistic food.
The death of your Son gives us hope and strengthens our faith.
May his resurrection give us perseverance
and lead us to salvation.
We ask this through Christ our Lord.

SOLEMN BLESSING OR PRAYER OVER THE PEOPLE

The following may replace the simple blessing.

After the greeting, the deacon (or in his absence, the priest) gives the invitation in these or similar words:

Bow your heads and pray for God's blessing.

Then the priest extends his hands over the people while he sings or says:

The Father of mercies has given us an example
of unselfish love
in the sufferings of his only Son.
Through your service of God and neighbor
may you receive his countless blessings.
℟. Amen.

You believe that by his dying
Christ destroyed death for ever.
May he give you everlasting life.
℟. Amen.

He humbled himself for our sakes.
May you follow his example
and share in his resurrection.
℟. Amen.

May almighty God bless you,
the Father, and the Son, ✠ and the Holy Spirit.
℟. Amen.

For other texts of solemn blessings and prayers over the people, see pages 528–540.

MONDAY OF HOLY WEEK

Introductory Rites

Defend me, Lord, from all my foes: take up your arms and
come swiftly to my aid, for you have the power to save me.
(Pss. 34:1-2; 139:8)

OPENING PRAYER

**All-powerful God,
by the suffering and death of your Son,
strengthen and protect us in our weakness.**

**We ask this through our Lord Jesus Christ, your Son,
who lives and reigns with you and the Holy Spirit,
one God, for ever and ever.**

See Lectionary for Mass, no. 258.

PRAYER OVER THE GIFTS

Pray, brethren . . .

**Lord,
look with mercy on our offerings.
May the sacrifice of Christ, your Son,
bring us to eternal life,
for he is Lord for ever and ever.**

Preface of the Passion of the Lord II,
page **435**.

Communion Rite

When I am in trouble, Lord, do not hide your face from
me; hear me when I call, and answer me quickly. (Ps.
101:3)

PRAYER AFTER COMMUNION

Let us pray.
Pause for silent prayer, if this has not preceded.
**God of mercy,
be close to your people.
Watch over us who receive this sacrament of salvation,
and keep us in your love.**

We ask this in the name of Jesus the Lord.

TUESDAY OF HOLY WEEK

Introductory Rites
> False witnesses have stood up against me, and my enemies
> threaten violence; Lord, do not surrender me into their
> power! (Ps. 26:12)

OPENING PRAYER

Father,
may we receive your forgiveness and mercy
as we celebrate the passion and death of the Lord,
who lives and reigns with you and the Holy Spirit,
one God, for ever and ever.

See Lectionary for Mass, no. 259.

PRAYER OVER THE GIFTS

Pray, brethren . . .

Lord,
look with mercy on our offerings.
May we who share the holy gifts
receive the life they promise.

We ask this in the name of Jesus the Lord.

Preface of the Passion of the Lord II,
page 435.

Communion Rite
> God did not spare his own Son, but gave him up for us all.
> (Rom. 8:32)

PRAYER AFTER COMMUNION

Let us pray.
Pause for silent prayer, if this has not preceded.
God of mercy,
may the sacrament of salvation
which now renews our strength
bring us a share in your life for ever.

Grant this through Christ our Lord.

WEDNESDAY OF HOLY WEEK

Introductory Rites

At the name of Jesus every knee must bend, in heaven, on
earth, and under the earth; Christ became obedient for us
even to death, dying on the cross. Therefore, to the glory
of God the Father: Jesus Christ is Lord. (Phil. 2:10, 8, 11)

OPENING PRAYER

Father,
in your plan of salvation
your Son Jesus Christ accepted the cross
and freed us from the power of the enemy.
May we come to share the glory of his resurrection,
for he lives and reigns with you and the Holy Spirit,
one God, for ever and ever.

See Lectionary for Mass, no. 260.

PRAYER OVER THE GIFTS

Pray, brethren . . .

Lord,
accept the gifts we present
as we celebrate this mystery
of the suffering and death of your Son.
May we share in the eternal life he won for us,
for he is Lord for ever and ever.

Preface of the Passion of the Lord II,
page 435.

Communion Rite

The Son of Man did not come to be served, but to serve,
and to give his life as a ransom for many. (Matthew 20:28)

PRAYER AFTER COMMUNION

Let us pray.
Pause for silent prayer, if this has not preceded.
All-powerful God,
the eucharist proclaims the death of your Son.
Increase our faith in its saving power
and strengthen our hope in the life it promises.

We ask this in the name of Jesus the Lord.

HOLY THURSDAY

CHRISM MASS

This Mass, which the bishop concelebrates with his presbyterium and at which the oils are blessed, manifests the communion of the priests with their bishop. It is thus desirable that, if possible, all the priests take part in it and receive communion under both kinds. To show the unity of the presbyterium, the priests who con-celebrate with the bishop should come from different parts of the diocese.

In the United States, communion may be given under both kinds to those present, in accordance with the judgment of the Ordinary, at Masses on Holy Thursday.

For Rites of Blessing of Oils and Consecrating the Chrism, see page 918.

Introductory Rites

> Jesus Christ has made us a kingdom of priests to serve his God and Father: glory and kingship be his for ever and ever. Amen. (Rev. 1:6)

The Gloria is sung or said.

OPENING PRAYER

Let us pray.

Pause for silent prayer

Father,
by the power of the Holy Spirit
you anointed your only Son Messiah and Lord of creation;
you have given us a share in his consecration
to priestly service in your Church.
Help us to be faithful witnesses in the world
to the salvation Christ won for all mankind.

We ask this through our Lord Jesus Christ, your Son,
who lives and reigns with you and the Holy Spirit,
one God, for ever and ever.

LITURGY OF THE WORD

See Lectionary for Mass, no. 39.

In his homily the bishop should urge the priests to be faithful in fulfilling their office in the Church and should invite them to renew publicly their priestly promises.

RENEWAL OF COMMITMENT TO PRIESTLY SERVICE

After the homily the bishop speaks to the priests in these or similar words:

My brothers,
today we celebrate the memory of the first eucharist,
at which our Lord Jesus Christ
shared with his apostles and with us
his call to the priestly service of his Church.
Now, in the presence of your bishop and God's holy people,
are you ready to renew your own dedication to Christ
as priests of his new covenant?

Priests: **I am.**

Bishop:

**At your ordination
you accepted the responsibilities of the priesthood
out of love for the Lord Jesus and his Church.
Are you resolved to unite yourselves more closely to Christ
and to try to become more like him
by joyfully sacrificing your own pleasure and ambition
to bring his peace and love to your brothers and sisters?**

Priests:

I am.

Bishop:

**Are you resolved
to be faithful ministers of the mysteries of God,
to celebrate the eucharist and the other liturgical services
with sincere devotion?
Are you resolved to imitate Jesus Christ,
the head and shepherd of the Church,
by teaching the Christian faith
without thinking of your own profit,
solely for the well-being of the people
you were sent to serve?**

Priests:

I am.

Then the bishop addresses the people:

**My brothers and sisters,
pray for your priests.
Ask the Lord to bless them with the fullness of his love,
to help them be faithful ministers of Christ the High Priest,
so that they will be able to lead you to him,
the fountain of your salvation.**

People:

Lord Jesus Christ, hear us and answer our prayer.

Bishop:

**Pray also for me
that despite my own unworthiness
I may faithfully fulfill the office of apostle
which Jesus Christ has entrusted to me.
Pray that I may become more like
our High Priest and Good Shepherd,
the teacher and servant of all,
and so be a genuine sign
of Christ's loving presence among you.**

People:

Lord Jesus Christ, hear us and answer our prayer.

Bishop:

**May the Lord in his love
keep you close to him always,
and may he bring all of us,
his priests and people,
to eternal life.**

All:

Amen.

The profession of faith and general intercessions are omitted.

LITURGY OF THE EUCHARIST

PRAYER OVER THE GIFTS

Pray, brethren . . .

Lord God,
may the power of this sacrifice
cleanse the old weakness of our human nature.
Give us a newness of life
and bring us to salvation.

Grant this through Christ our Lord.

Eucharistic Prayer:
Preface of the Priesthood (Chrism Mass), page **437**.

Communion Rite

For ever I will sing the goodness of the Lord; I will proclaim your faithfulness to all generations. (Ps. 88:2)

A period of silence may be observed after communion, or a psalm or song of praise may be sung.

PRAYER AFTER COMMUNION

Let us pray.
Pause for silent prayer, if this has not preceded.
Lord God almighty,
you have given us fresh strength
in these sacramental gifts.
Renew in us the image of Christ's goodness.

We ask this in the name of Jesus the Lord.

SOLEMN BLESSING OR PRAYER OVER THE PEOPLE

The following may replace the simple blessing.

After the greeting, the deacon (or in his absence, the priest) gives the invitation in these or similar words:

Bow your heads and pray for God's blessing.

Then the priest extends his hands over the people while he sings or says:

Father,
look with love upon your people,
the love which our Lord Jesus Christ showed us
when he delivered himself to evil men
and suffered the agony of the cross.

Grant this through Christ our Lord.
℟. **Amen.**

For other texts of solemn blessings and prayers over the people, see pages 528–540.

May almighty God bless you,
the Father, and the Son, ✝ and the Holy Spirit.
℟. **Amen.**

EASTER TRIDUUM

EVENING MASS OF THE LORD'S SUPPER

According to the Church's ancient tradition, all Masses without a congregation are prohibited on this day.

The Mass of the Lord's Supper is celebrated in the evening, at a convenient hour, with the full participation of the whole local community and with all the priests and clergy exercising their ministry.

Priests who have already celebrated the chrism Mass or a Mass for the convenience of the faithful may concelebrate again at the evening Mass.

For pastoral reasons the local Ordinary may permit another Mass to be celebrated in churches and public or semipublic oratories in the evening or, in the case of genuine necessity, even in the morning, but exclusively for those who are in no way able to take part in the evening Mass. Such Masses must not be celebrated for the advantage of private persons or prejudice the principal evening Mass.

Holy Communion may be given to the faithful only during Mass, but may be brought to the sick at any hour of the day.

In the United States, communion may be given under both kinds, in accordance with the judgment of the Ordinary, at Masses on Holy Thursday.

If the local Ordinary permits one or more additional Masses of the Lord's Supper, in accord with the rubrics, the washing of feet may take place at such Masses.

The tabernacle should be entirely empty; a sufficient amount of bread should be consecrated at this Mass for the communion of clergy and laity today and tomorrow.

Introductory Rites

We should glory in the cross of our Lord Jesus Christ, for he is our salvation, our life and our resurrection; through him we are saved and made free. (See Gal. 6:14)

During the singing of the Gloria, the church bells are rung and then remain silent until the Easter Vigil, unless the conference of bishops or the Ordinary decrees otherwise.

OPENING PRAYER

Let us pray.
Pause for silent prayer
God our Father,
we are gathered here to share in the supper
which your only Son left to his Church to reveal his love.
He gave it to us when he was about to die
and commanded us to celebrate it as the new and eternal
 sacrifice.
We pray that in this eucharist
we may find the fullness of love and life.

Grant this through our Lord Jesus Christ, your Son,
who lives and reigns with you and the Holy Spirit,
one God, for ever and ever.

LITURGY OF THE WORD

See Lectionary for Mass, no. 40.

The homily should explain the principal mysteries which are commemorated in this Mass: the institution of the eucharist, the institution of the priesthood, and Christ's commandment of brotherly love.

WASHING OF FEET

Depending on pastoral circumstances, the washing of feet follows the homily.

The men who have been chosen are led by the ministers to chairs prepared in a suitable place. Then the priest (removing his chasuble if necessary) goes to each man. With the help of the ministers, he pours water over each one's feet and dries them.

Meanwhile some of the following antiphons or other appropriate songs are sung.

Antiphon 1

**The Lord Jesus,
when he had eaten with his disciples,
poured water into a basin
and began to wash their feet, saying:
This example I leave you. (See John 13:4, 5, 15)**

Antiphon 2

**Lord, do you wash my feet?
Jesus said to him:
If I do not wash your feet,
you can have no part with me.**

℣. **So he came to Simon Peter,
who said to him:
Lord, do you wash my feet?**

℣. **Now you do not know what I am doing,
but later you will understand.
Lord, do you wash my feet? (John 13:6, 7, 8)**

Antiphon 3

**If I, your Lord and Teacher, have washed your feet,
then surely you must wash one another's feet.
(See John 13:14)**

Antiphon 4

**If there is this love among you,
all will know that you are my disciples.**

℣. **Jesus said to his disciples:
If there is this love among you,
all will know that you are my disciples. (John 13:35)**

Antiphon 5

**I give you a new commandment:
love one another as I have loved you, says the Lord.
(John 13:34)**

Antiphon 6

**Faith, hope, and love,
let these endure among you;
and the greatest of these is love. (1 Cor. 13:13)**

The general intercessions follow the washing of feet, or, if this does not take place, they follow the homily. The profession of faith is not said in this Mass.

LITURGY OF THE EUCHARIST

At the beginning of the liturgy of the eucharist, there may be a procession of the faithful with gifts for the poor.

During the procession the following may be sung, or another appropriate song.

Antiphon

Where charity and love are found, there is God.

℣. **The love of Christ has gathered us together into one.**

℣. **Let us rejoice and be glad in him.**

℣. **Let us fear and love the living God,**

℣. **and love each other from the depths of our heart.**

Antiphon

Where charity and love are found, there is God.

℣. **Therefore when we are together,**

℣. **let us take heed not to be divided in mind.**

℣. **Let there be an end to bitterness and quarrels, an end to strife,**

℣. **and in our midst be Christ our God.**

Antiphon

Where charity and love are found, there is God.

℣. **And, in company with the blessed, may we see**

℣. **your face in glory, Christ our God,**

℣. **pure and unbounded joy**

℣. **for ever and ever.**

Antiphon

Where charity and love are found, there is God.

PRAYER OVER THE GIFTS

Pray, brethren . . .

Lord,
make us worthy to celebrate these mysteries.
Each time we offer this memorial sacrifice
the work of our redemption is accomplished.
We ask this in the name of Jesus the Lord.

Eucharistic Prayer:
Preface of Holy Eucharist I, page 464.

When Eucharistic Prayer I is used, the special Holy Thursday forms of In union with the whole Church, Father, accept this offering, and The day before he suffered are said.

Communion Rite

This body will be given for you. This is the cup of the new covenant in my blood; whenever you receive them, do so in remembrance of me. (1 Cor. 11:24-25)

After the distribution of communion, the ciborium with hosts for
Good Friday is left on the altar.

A period of silence may be observed
after communion, or a psalm or song
of praise may be sung.

PRAYER AFTER COMMUNION

Let us pray.
Pause for silent prayer, if this has not preceded.
Almighty God,
we receive new life
from the supper your Son gave us in this world.
May we find full contentment
in the meal we hope to share
in your eternal kingdom.
We ask this through Christ our Lord.

The Mass concludes with this prayer.

Transfer of the Holy Eucharist

After the prayer the priest stands before the altar and puts incense in the thurible. Kneeling, he incenses the Blessed Sacrament three times. Then he receives the humeral veil, takes the ciborium, and covers it with the ends of the veil.

The Blessed Sacrament is carried through the church in procession, led by a cross-bearer and accompanied by candles and incense, to the place of reposition prepared in a chapel suitably decorated for the occasion. During the procession the hymn **Pange, lingua** (exclusive of the last two stanzas) or some other eucharistic song is sung.

When the procession reaches the place of reposition, the priest sets the ciborium down. Then he puts incense in the thurible and, kneeling, incenses the Blessed Sacrament, while **Tantum ergo Sacramentum** is sung. The tabernacle of reposition is then closed.

After a period of silent adoration, the priest and ministers genuflect and return to the sacristy.

Then the altar is stripped and, if possible, the crosses are removed from the church. It is desirable to cover any crosses which remain in the church.

Evening Prayer is not said by those who participate in the evening Mass.

The faithful should be encouraged to continue adoration before the Blessed Sacrament for a suitable period of time during the night, according to local circumstances, but there should be no solemn adoration after midnight.

GOOD FRIDAY

Celebration of the Lord's Passion

1. According to the Church's ancient tradition, the sacraments are not celebrated today or tomorrow.

2. The altar should be completely bare, without cloths, candles, or cross.

3. The celebration of the Lord's passion takes place in the afternoon, about three o'clock, unless pastoral reasons suggest a later hour. The celebration consists of three parts: liturgy of the word, veneration of the cross, and holy communion.

In the United States, if the size or nature of a parish or other community indicates the pastoral need for an additional liturgical service, the local Ordinary may permit the service to be repeated later.

Holy communion may be given to the faithful only at the celebration of the Lord's passion, but may be brought at any hour of the day to the sick who cannot take part in this service.

4. The priest and deacon, wearing red Mass vestments, go to the altar. There they make a reverence and prostrate themselves, or they may kneel. All pray silently for a while.

5. Then the priest goes to the chair with the ministers. He faces the people and, with hands joined, sings or says one of the following prayers.

PRAYER

(Let us pray is not said.)

Lord,
by shedding his blood for us,
your Son, Jesus Christ,
established the paschal mystery.
In your goodness, make us holy
and watch over us always.

We ask this through Christ our Lord.
℟. **Amen.**

Or:

Lord,
by the suffering of Christ your Son
you have saved us all from the death
we inherited from sinful Adam.
By the law of nature
we have borne the likeness of his manhood.
May the sanctifying power of grace
help us to put on the likeness of our Lord in
  heaven,
who lives and reigns for ever and ever.

℟. **Amen.**

Part One: Liturgy of the Word

See Lectionary for Mass, no. 41.

6. All sit and the first reading, from the book of the prophet Isaiah (52:13–53:12), is read, with its responsorial psalm.

7. The second reading, from the letter to the Hebrews (4:14-16; 5:7-9), follows, and then the chant before the gospel is sung.

8. Finally the account of the passion according to John (18:1–19:42) is read, in the same way as on the preceding Sunday.

9. After the reading of the passion there may be a brief homily.

General Intercessions

10. The general intercessions conclude the liturgy of the word. The deacon, standing at the ambo, sings or says the introduction in which each intention is stated. All kneel and pray silently for some period of time, and then the priest, with hands outstretched, standing either at the chair or at the altar, sings or says the prayer. The people may either kneel or stand throughout the entire period of the general intercessions.

11. The conference of bishops may provide an acclamation for the people to sing before the priest's prayer or decree that the deacon's traditional invitation to kneel and pray be continued: **Let us kneel — let us stand.**

In the United States, if desired, an appropriate acclamation by the people may be introduced before each of the solemn prayers of intercession, or the traditional period of kneeling at each of the prayers (at the invitation of the deacon) may be continued.

12. In case of serious public need, the local Ordinary may permit or decree the addition of a special intention.

13. The priest may choose from the prayers in the missal those which are more appropriate to local circumstances, provided the series follows the rule for the general intercessions (see General Instruction of the Roman Missal, no. 46).

I. For the Church

Let us pray, dear friends, for the holy Church of God through-out the world, that God the almighty Father guide it and gath-er it to - geth - er so that we may worship him in peace and tran-quil-i-ty. [*Deacon* Let us kneel. Let us stand.]

Almighty and eternal God, you have shown your glory to all nations in Christ, your Son. Guide the work of your Church. Help it to persevere in faith, pro-claim your name, and bring your salvation to peo-ple eve-ry-where. We ask this through Christ our Lord. ℟. A - men.

II. For the pope

Let us pray for our Holy Fa-ther, Pope N., that God who chose him to be bish-op may give him health and strength to guide and gov - ern God's ho - ly peo-ple.

Let us kneel. Let us stand.

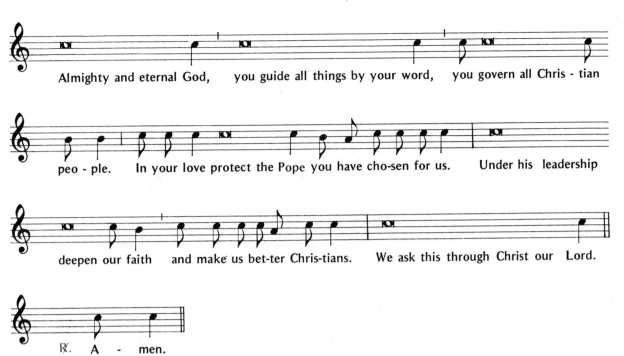

Almighty and eternal God, you guide all things by your word, you govern all Christian people. In your love protect the Pope you have chosen for us. Under his leadership deepen our faith and make us better Christians. We ask this through Christ our Lord.

℟. A - men.

III. For the clergy and laity of the Church

Let us pray for N., our bishop, for all bishops, priests, and deacons; for all who have a special minis - try in the Church and for all God's people. Let us kneel. Let us stand.

Almighty and eternal God, your Spirit guides the Church and makes it ho-ly. Listen to our prayers and help each of us in his own vocation to do your work more faith-ful-ly.

We ask this through Christ our Lord. ℟. A - men.

IV. For those preparing for baptism

Let us pray for those [among us] pre-par-ing for bap-tism, that God in his mercy make

them responsive to his love, forgive their sins through the wa-ters of new birth, and give

them life in Je-sus Christ our Lord. Let us kneel. Let us stand.

Almighty and eternal God, you continually bless your Church with new mem - bers.

Increase the faith and understanding of those [among us] pre-par-ing for bap - tism.

Give them a new birth in these liv-ing wa-ters and make them members of your cho-sen

fam - i - ly. We ask this through Christ our Lord. ℟. A - men.

V. For the unity of Christians

Let us pray for all our brothers and sisters who share our faith in Je-sus Christ, that

God may gather and keep to-geth-er in one Church all those who seek the truth with

sin - cer - i - ty. Let us kneel. Let us stand.

Almighty and eternal God, you keep together those you have u-nit-ed. Look kindly on all who follow Je-sus your Son. We are all consecrated to you by our com-mon bap-tism. Make us one in the fullness of faith, and keep us one in the fellow-ship of love. We ask this through Christ our Lord. ℟. A - men.

VI. For the Jewish people

Let us pray for the Jewish peo-ple, the first to hear the word of God, that they may con-tinue to grow in the love of his name and in faith-ful-ness to his cov-e-nant.

Let us kneel. Let us stand.

Almighty and eternal God, long ago you gave your promise to Abraham and his pos-ter-i-ty. Listen to your Church as we pray that the people you first made your own may arrive at the fullness of re-demp-tion. We ask this through Christ our Lord. ℟. A - men.

VII. For those who do not believe in Christ

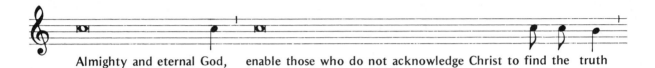

Let us pray for those who do not be - lieve in Christ,   that the light of the Ho-ly Spir-it

may show them the way to sal-va-tion.   Let us kneel.   Let us stand.

Almighty and eternal God,   enable those who do not acknowledge Christ to find the truth

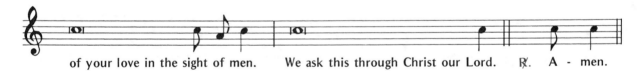

as they walk before you in sincer-i-ty of heart.   Help us to grow in love for one an-oth-er,

to grasp more fully the mystery of your god-head,   and to become more perfect witnesses

of your love in the sight of men.   We ask this through Christ our Lord.   ℟. A - men.

VIII. For those who do not believe in God

Let us pray for those who do not be-lieve in God,   that they may find him by sincerely

follow-ing all that is right.   Let us kneel.   Let us stand.

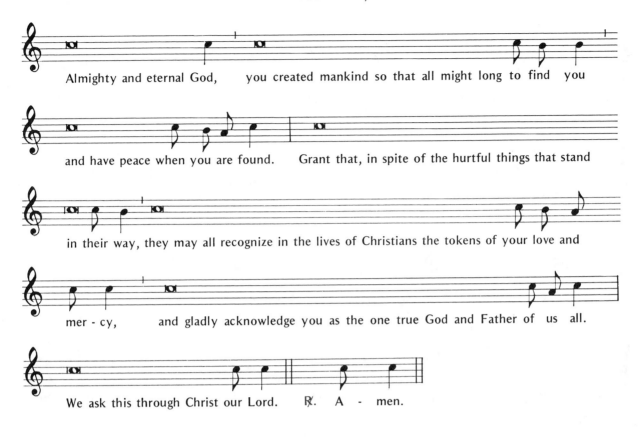

Almighty and eternal God, you created mankind so that all might long to find you and have peace when you are found. Grant that, in spite of the hurtful things that stand in their way, they may all recognize in the lives of Christians the tokens of your love and mer - cy, and gladly acknowledge you as the one true God and Father of us all.

We ask this through Christ our Lord. ℟. A - men.

IX. For all in public office

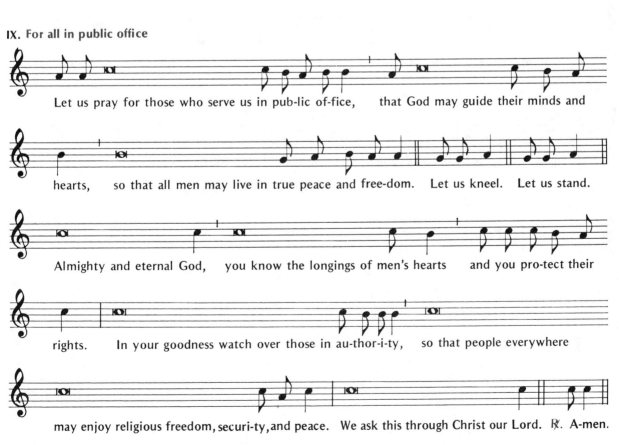

Let us pray for those who serve us in pub-lic of-fice, that God may guide their minds and hearts, so that all men may live in true peace and free-dom. Let us kneel. Let us stand.

Almighty and eternal God, you know the longings of men's hearts and you pro-tect their rights. In your goodness watch over those in au-thor-i-ty, so that people everywhere may enjoy religious freedom, securi-ty, and peace. We ask this through Christ our Lord. ℟. A-men.

X. **For those in special need**

Let us pray, dear friends, that God the almighty Father may heal the sick, com - fort the

dy-ing, give safety to travel-lers, free those unjustly de-prived of lib-er-ty, and rid the

world of false - hood, hun-ger, and dis - ease.   Let us kneel.   Let us stand.

Almighty, ever-living God, you give strength to the wea-ry and new courage to those who

have lost heart.   Hear the prayers of all who call on you in an-y trou-ble that they may

have the joy of receiving your help in their need.   We ask this through Christ our Lord.

℞. A - men.

I. For the Church

Let us pray, dear friends,
for the holy Church of God throughout the world,
that God the almighty Father
guide it and gather it together
so that we may worship him
in peace and tranquility.

Silent prayer. Then the priest sings
or says:

Almighty and eternal God,
you have shown your glory to all nations
in Christ, your Son.
Guide the work of your Church.
Help it to persevere in faith,
proclaim your name,
and bring your salvation to people everywhere.

We ask this through Christ our Lord.
℟. Amen.

II. For the pope

Let us pray
for our Holy Father, Pope N.,
that God who chose him to be bishop
may give him health and strength
to guide and govern God's holy people.

Silent prayer. Then the priest sings
or says:

Almighty and eternal God,
you guide all things by your word,
you govern all Christian people.
In your love protect the Pope you have chosen for us.
Under his leadership deepen our faith
and make us better Christians.

We ask this through Christ our Lord.
℟. Amen.

III. For the clergy and laity of the Church

Let us pray
for N., our bishop,
for all bishops, priests, and deacons;
for all who have a special ministry in the Church
and for all God's people.

Silent prayer. Then the priest sings
or says:

Almighty and eternal God,
your Spirit guides the Church
and makes it holy.
Listen to our prayers
and help each of us
in his own vocation
to do your work more faithfully.

We ask this through Christ our Lord.
℟. Amen.

IV. **For those preparing for baptism**

Let us pray
for those [among us] preparing for baptism,
that God in his mercy
make them responsive to his love,
forgive their sins through the waters of new birth,
and give them life in Jesus Christ our Lord.

Silent prayer. Then the priest sings
or says:

Almighty and eternal God,
you continually bless your Church with new members.
Increase the faith and understanding
of those [among us] preparing for baptism.
Give them a new birth in these living waters
and make them members of your chosen family.

We ask this through Christ our Lord.
R̴. Amen.

V. **For the unity of Christians**

Let us pray
for all our brothers and sisters
who share our faith in Jesus Christ,
that God may gather and keep together in one Church
all those who seek the truth with sincerity.

Silent prayer. Then the priest sings
or says:

Almighty and eternal God,
you keep together those you have united.
Look kindly on all who follow Jesus your Son.
We are all consecrated to you by our common baptism.
Make us one in the fullness of faith,
and keep us one in the fellowship of love.

We ask this through Christ our Lord.
R̴. Amen.

VI. **For the Jewish people**

Let us pray
for the Jewish people,
the first to hear the word of God,
that they may continue to grow in the love of his name
and in faithfulness to his covenant.

Silent prayer. Then the priest sings
or says:

Almighty and eternal God,
long ago you gave your promise to Abraham and his
   posterity.
Listen to your Church as we pray
that the people you first made your own
may arrive at the fullness of redemption.

We ask this through Christ our Lord.
R̴. Amen.

VII. For those who do not believe in Christ

Silent prayer. Then the priest sings or says:

Let us pray
for those who do not believe in Christ,
that the light of the Holy Spirit
may show them the way to salvation.

Almighty and eternal God,
enable those who do not acknowledge Christ
to find the truth
as they walk before you in sincerity of heart.
Help us to grow in love for one another,
to grasp more fully the mystery of your godhead,
and to become more perfect witnesses of your love
in the sight of men.
We ask this through Christ our Lord.
℟. Amen.

VIII. For those who do not believe in God

Silent prayer. Then the priest sings or says:

Let us pray
for those who do not believe in God,
that they may find him
by sincerely following all that is right.

Almighty and eternal God,
you created mankind
so that all might long to find you
and have peace when you are found.
Grant that, in spite of the hurtful things
that stand in their way,
they may all recognize in the lives of Christians
the tokens of your love and mercy,
and gladly acknowledge you
as the one true God and Father of us all.
We ask this through Christ our Lord.
℟. Amen.

IX. For all in public office

Silent prayer. Then the priest sings or says:

Let us pray
for those who serve us in public office,
that God may guide their minds and hearts,
so that all men may live in true peace and freedom.

Almighty and eternal God,
you know the longings of men's hearts
and you protect their rights.
In your goodness
watch over those in authority,
so that people everywhere may enjoy
religious freedom, security, and peace.
We ask this through Christ our Lord.
℟. Amen.

X. For those in special need

Let us pray, dear friends,
that God the almighty Father
may heal the sick,
comfort the dying,
give safety to travellers,
free those unjustly deprived of liberty,
and rid the world of falsehood,
hunger, and disease.

Silent prayer. Then the priest sings
or says:

Almighty, ever-living God,
you give strength to the weary
and new courage to those who have lost heart.
Hear the prayers of all who call on you in any trouble
that they may have the joy of receiving your help in their
**   need.**
We ask this through Christ our Lord.

℟. **Amen.**

Part Two: Veneration of the Cross

14. After the general intercessions, the veneration of the cross takes place. Pastoral demands will determine which of the two forms is more effective and should be chosen.

First Form of Showing the Cross

15. The veiled cross is carried to the altar, accompanied by two ministers with lighted candles. Standing at the altar, the priest takes the cross, uncovers the upper part of it, then elevates it and begins the invitation **This is the wood of the cross.** He is assisted in the singing by the deacon or, if convenient, by the choir. All respond: **Come, let us worship.** At the end of the singing all kneel and venerate the cross briefly in silence; the priest remains standing and holds the cross high.

Then the priest uncovers the right arm of the cross, lifts it up, and again begins the invitation **This is the wood of the cross,** and the rite is repeated as before.

Finally he uncovers the entire cross, lifts it up, and begins the invitation **This is the wood of the cross** a third time, and the rite is repeated as before.

16. Accompanied by two ministers with lighted candles, the priest then carries the cross to the entrance of the sanctuary or to another suitable place. There he lays the cross down or hands it to the ministers to hold. Candles are placed on either side of the cross, and the veneration follows as below, no. 18.

Second Form of Showing the Cross

17. The priest or deacon, accompanied by the ministers or by another suitable minister, goes to the church door. There he takes the (uncovered) cross, and the ministers take lighted candles. They go in procession through the church to the sanctuary. Near the entrance of the church, in the middle of the church, and at the entrance to the sanctuary, the one carrying the cross stops, lifts it up, and sings the invitation **This is the wood of the cross.** All respond: **Come, let us worship.** After each response all kneel and venerate the cross briefly in silence as above.

Then the cross and candles are placed at the entrance to the sanctuary.

Invitation

℣. **This is the wood of the cross, on which hung the Savior of the world.**
℟. **Come, let us worship.**

Veneration of the Cross

18. The priest, clergy, and faithful approach to venerate the cross in a kind of procession. They make a simple genuflection or perform some other appropriate sign of reverence according to local custom, for example, kissing the cross.

During the veneration the antiphon We worship you, Lord, the reproaches, or other suitable songs are sung. All who have venerated the cross return to their places and sit.

19. Only one cross should be used for the veneration. If the number of people makes it impossible for everyone to venerate the cross individually, the priest may take the cross, after some of the faithful have venerated it, and stand in the center in front of the altar. In a few words he invites the people to venerate the cross and then holds it up briefly for them to worship in silence. In the United States, if pastoral reasons suggest that there be individual veneration even though the number of people is very large, a second or third cross may be used.

20. After the veneration, the cross is carried to its place at the altar, and the lighted candles are placed around the altar or near the cross.

Songs at the Veneration of the Cross

Individual parts are indicated by
no. 1 (first choir) and no. 2 (second
choir); parts sung by both choirs together are indicated by nos. 1 and 2.

Ant. We wor - ship you, Lord,   we ven-er-ate your cross,   we praise your res - ur - rec - tion.

Through the cross you brought joy to the world.   *Ps.66:2* May God be gra-cious and bless

us;   and let his face shed its light up - on us.   *(Choirs 1 and 2 repeat antiphon.)*

Antiphon

1 and 2: Antiphon	**We worship you, Lord,** **we venerate your cross,** **we praise your resurrection.** **Through the cross you brought joy to the world.**
1: Psalm 66:2	**May God be gracious and bless us;** **and let his face shed its light upon us.**
1 and 2: Antiphon	**We worship you, Lord,** **we venerate your cross,** **we praise your resurrection.** **Through the cross you brought joy to the world.**

REPROACHES I

1 and 2 My peo - ple, what have I done to you? How have I of-fend-ed you? An - swer me!

1 I led you out of E - gypt, from slav-ery to free - dom, but you led your Sav - ior to the cross. *2* My peo - ple . . . An - swer me! *1* Ho - ly is God! *2* Ho - ly and strong! *1* Ho - ly im - mor - tal One, have mer - cy on us!

1 and 2 For for - ty years I led you safe - ly through the des - ert. I fed you with man-na from heav - en and brought you to a land of plen - ty; but you led your Sav - ior to the cross. *1* Ho - ly . . . have mer - cy on us! *1 and 2* What more could I have done for you? I plant - ed you as my fair-est vine, but you yield - ed on - ly bit - ter - ness: when I was thir - sty you gave me vin - e - gar to drink, and you pierced your Sav-ior's side with a lance. *1* Ho-ly . . . have mer-cy on us!

Good Friday

REPROACHES II

1 For your sake I scourged your cap - tors and their first - born sons, but you brought
your scourg-es down on me. 2 My peo - ple . . . An - swer me!

1 I led you from slav-ery to free - dom and drowned your cap-tors in the sea, but you
hand - ed me o - ver to your high priests. 2 My peo - ple . . . An - swer me! 1 I

o-pened the sea be - fore you, but you o - pened my side with a spear. 2 My
peo - ple . . . An - swer me! 1 I led you on your way in a pil-lar of cloud, but

you led me to Pi-late's court. 2 My peo- ple . . . An - swer me! 1 I bore you
up with man-na in the des - ert, but you struck me down and scourged me.

2 My peo - ple . . . An - swer me! 1 I gave you sav - ing wa - ter from the rock,

but you gave me gall and vin - e - gar to drink. 2 My peo - ple . . . An - swer me!

I

REPROACHES

1 and 2: **My people, what have I done to you?
How have I offended you? Answer me!**

1: **I led you out of Egypt, from slavery to freedom,
but you led your Savior to the cross.**

2: **My people, what have I done to you?
How have I offended you? Answer me!**

1: **Holy is God!**

2: **Holy and strong!**

1: **Holy immortal One,
have mercy on us!**

1 and 2: **For forty years I led you safely through the desert.
I fed you with manna from heaven
and brought you to a land of plenty;
but you led your Savior to the cross.**

1: **Holy is God!**

2: **Holy and strong!**

1: **Holy immortal One,
have mercy on us!**

1 and 2:   **What more could I have done for you?**
I planted you as my fairest vine,
but you yielded only bitterness:
when I was thirsty you gave me vinegar to drink,
and you pierced your Savior with a lance.

1:     **Holy is God!**

2:     **Holy and strong!**

1:     **Holy immortal One,**
have mercy on us!

II

1:     **For your sake I scourged your captors and their firstborn sons,**
but you brought your scourges down on me.

2:     **My people, what have I done to you?**
How have I offended you? Answer me!

1:     **I led you from slavery to freedom**
and drowned your captors in the sea,
but you handed me over to your high priests.

2:     **My people, what have I done to you?**
How have I offended you? Answer me!

1:     **I opened the sea before you,**
but you opened my side with a spear.

2:     **My people, what have I done to you?**
How have I offended you? Answer me!

1:     **I led you on your way in a pillar of cloud,**
but you led me to Pilate's court.

2:     **My people, what have I done to you?**
How have I offended you? Answer me!

1:     **I bore you up with manna in the desert,**
but you struck me down and scourged me.

2:     **My people, what have I done to you?**
How have I offended you? Answer me!

1:     **I gave you saving water from the rock,**
but you gave me gall and vinegar to drink.

2:     **My people, what have I done to you?**
How have I offended you? Answer me!

1:    **For you I struck down the kings of Canaan,**
      but you struck my head with a reed.

2:    **My people, what have I done to you?**
      How have I offended you? Answer me!

1:    **I gave you a royal scepter,**
      but you gave me a crown of thorns.

2:    **My people, what have I done to you?**
      How have I offended you? Answer me!

1:    **I raised you to the height of majesty,**
      but you have raised me high on a cross.

2:    **My people, what have I done to you?**
      How have I offended you? Answer me!

Hymn
(''Pange, lingua, gloriosi proelium
certaminis'')

Part Three: Holy Communion

21. The altar is covered with a cloth and the corporal and book are placed on it. Then the deacon or, if there is no deacon, the priest brings the ciborium with the Blessed Sacrament from the place of reposition to the altar without any procession, while all stand in silence.

Two ministers with lighted candles accompany him and they place their candles near the altar or on it.

22. The deacon places the ciborium on the altar and uncovers it. Meanwhile the priest comes from his chair, genuflects, and goes up to the altar.

With hands joined, he says aloud:

Let us pray with confidence to the Father
in the words our Savior gave us:

He extends his hands and continues, with all present:

Our Father, who art in heaven,
hallowed be thy name;
thy kingdom come;
thy will be done on earth as it is in heaven.
Give us this day our daily bread;
and forgive us our trespasses
as we forgive those who trespass against us;
and lead us not into temptation,
but deliver us from evil.

With hands extended, the priest continues alone:

Deliver us, Lord, from every evil,
and grant us peace in our day.
In your mercy keep us free from sin
and protect us from all anxiety
as we wait in joyful hope
for the coming of our Savior, Jesus Christ.

He joins his hands. The people end the prayer with the acclamation:

For the kingdom, the power, and the glory are yours,
**   now and for ever.**

23. Then the priest joins his hands and says inaudibly:

Lord Jesus Christ, with faith in your love and mercy I eat your
    body and drink your blood.
Let it not bring me condemnation, but health in mind and
    body.

24. The priest genuflects. Taking the host, he raises it slightly over the ciborium and, facing the people, says aloud:

This is the Lamb of God
who takes away the sins of the world.
Happy are those who are called to his supper.

He adds, once only, with the people:

Lord, I am not worthy to receive you,
but only say the word and I shall be healed.

Facing the altar, he reverently consumes the body of Christ.

25. Then communion is distributed to the faithful. Any appropriate song may be sung during communion.

26. When the communion has been completed, a suitable minister may take the ciborium to a place prepared outside the church or, if circumstances require, may place it in the tabernacle.

27. A period of silence may now be observed. The priest then says the following prayer:

Let us pray.
Pause for silent prayer, if this has not preceded.
Almighty and eternal God,
you have restored us to life
by the triumphant death and resurrection of Christ.
Continue this healing work within us.
May we who participate in this mystery
never cease to serve you.

We ask this through Christ our Lord.
℟. Amen.

28. For the dismissal the priest faces the people, extends his hands towards them, and says the following prayer:

PRAYER OVER THE PEOPLE

Lord,
send down your abundant blessing
upon your people who have devoutly recalled the death
  of your Son
in the sure hope of the resurrection.
Grant them pardon; bring them comfort.
May their faith grow stronger
and their eternal salvation be assured.

We ask this through Christ our Lord.

℟. **Amen.**

All depart in silence. The altar is stripped at a convenient time.
29. Evening Prayer is not said by those who participate in this afternoon liturgical service.

HOLY SATURDAY

On Holy Saturday the Church waits at the Lord's tomb, meditating on his suffering and death. The altar is left bare, and the sacrifice of the Mass is not celebrated. Only after the solemn vigil during the night, held in anticipation of the resurrection, does the Easter celebration begin, with a spirit of joy that overflows into the following period of fifty days.

On this day holy communion may be given only as viaticum.

EASTER SEASON

EASTER SUNDAY

THE EASTER VIGIL DURING THE NIGHT

1. In accord with ancient tradition, this night is one of vigil for the Lord (Exod. 12:42). The Gospel of Luke (12:35ff.) is a reminder to the faithful to have their lamps burning ready, to be like men awaiting their master's return so that when he arrives he will find them wide awake and will seat them at his table.

2. The night vigil is arranged in four parts:

a) a brief service of light;

b) the liturgy of the word, when the Church meditates on all the wonderful things God has done for his people from the beginning;

c) the liturgy of baptism, when new members of the Church are reborn as the day of resurrection approaches; and

d) the liturgy of the eucharist, when the whole Church is called to the table which the Lord has prepared for his people through his death and resurrection.

3. The entire celebration of the Easter Vigil takes place at night. It should not begin before nightfall; it should end before daybreak on Sunday.

In the United States, although it is never permitted to celebrate the entire Easter Vigil more than once in a given church or to anticipate the Mass of Easter before the vigil, in those places where the local Ordinary permits the anticipation of Sunday Masses on Saturday evening, for pastoral reasons an additional Mass may be celebrated after the Mass of the Easter Vigil. Such a Mass may follow the liturgy of the word of the Mass of the Easter Vigil (nos. 23-26) and other texts of that Mass and should include the renewal of baptismal promises (nos. 46-47).

4. Even if the vigil Mass takes place before midnight, the Easter Mass of the resurrection is celebrated.

In the United States, communion may be given under both kinds, in accordance with the judgment of the Ordinary, at the Mass of the Easter Vigil.

Those who participate in the Mass at night may receive communion again at the second Mass of Easter Sunday.

5. Those who celebrate or concelebrate the Mass at night may celebrate or concelebrate the second Mass of Easter Sunday.

6. The priest and deacon wear white Mass vestments.

Candles should be prepared for all who take part in the vigil.

Part One

Solemn Beginning of the Vigil: The Service of Light

Blessing of the Fire and Lighting of the Candle

7. All the lights in the church are put out.

A large fire is prepared in a suitable place outside the church. When the people have assembled, the priest goes there with the ministers, one of whom carries the Easter candle.

If it is not possible to light the fire outside the church, the rite is carried out as in no. 13 below.

8. The priest greets the congregation in the usual manner and briefly instructs them about the vigil in these or similar words:

Dear friends in Christ,
on this most holy night,
when our Lord Jesus Christ passed from death to life,
the Church invites her children throughout the world
to come together in vigil and prayer.
This is the passover of the Lord:
if we honor the memory of his death and resurrection
by hearing his word and celebrating his mysteries,
then we may be confident
that we shall share his victory over death
and live with him for ever in God.

9. Then the fire is blessed.

Let us pray.
Pause for silent prayer
Father,
we share in the light of your glory
through your Son, the light of the world.
Make this new fire ☩ holy, and inflame us with new hope.
Purify our minds by this Easter celebration
and bring us one day to the feast of eternal light.

We ask this through Christ our Lord.

℟. Amen.

The Easter candle is lighted from the new fire.

[Preparation of the Candle]

10. Depending on the nature of the congregation, it may seem appropriate to stress the dignity and significance of the Easter candle with other symbolic rites. This may be done as follows:
   After the blessing of the new fire, an acolyte or one of the ministers brings the Easter candle to the celebrant, who cuts a cross in the wax with a stylus. Then he traces the Greek letter alpha above the cross, the letter omega below, and the numerals of the current year between the arms of the cross. Meanwhile he says:

1. **Christ yesterday and today**   (as he traces the vertical arm of the cross),
2. **the beginning and the end**   (the horizontal arm),
3. **Alpha**   (alpha, above the cross),
4. **and Omega**   (omega, below the cross);
5. **all time belongs to him**   (the first numeral, in the upper left corner of the cross),
6. **and all the ages**   (the second numeral in the upper right corner);
7. **to him be glory and power**   (the third numeral in the lower left corner),
8. **through every age for ever. Amen.** (the last numeral in the lower right corner).

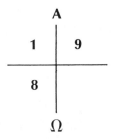

11. When the cross and other marks have been made, the priest may insert five grains of incense in the candle. He does this in the form of a cross, saying:

1. **By his holy**   1
2. **and glorious wounds**
3. **may Christ our Lord**   4 2 5
4. **guard us**
5. **and keep us. Amen.**   3

12. The priest lights the candle from the new fire, saying:

May the light of Christ, rising in glory,
dispel the darkness of our hearts and minds.

Any or all of the preceding rites may be used, depending on local pastoral circumstances. The conferences of bishops may also determine other rites better adapted to the culture of the people.

13. Where it may be difficult to have a large fire, the blessing of the fire is adapted to the circumstances. When the people have assembled in the church as on other occasions, the priest goes with the ministers (carrying the Easter candle) to the church door. If possible, the people turn to face the priest.

The greeting and brief instruction take place as above in no. 8. Then the fire is blessed (no. 9) and, if desired, the candle is prepared and lighted as above in nos. 10-12.

Procession

14. Then the deacon or, if there is no deacon, the priest takes the Easter candle, lifts it high, and sings alone:

All answer:

The conference of bishops may determine a richer acclamation.

15. Then all enter the church, led by the deacon with the Easter candle. If incense is used, the thurifer goes before the deacon.

At the church door the deacon lifts the candle high and sings a second time:

All answer:

All light their candles from the Easter candle and continue in the procession.

When the deacon arrives before the altar, he faces the people and sings a third time:

All answer:

Then the lights in the church are put on.

Easter Proclamation (Exsultet)

16. When he comes to the altar, the priest goes to his chair. The deacon places the Easter candle on a stand in the middle of the sanctuary or near the lectern. If incense is used, the priest puts some in the censer, as at the gospel of Mass. Then the deacon asks the blessing of the priest, who says in a low voice:

The Lord be in your heart and on your lips, that you may worthily proclaim his Easter praise.
In the name of the Father, and of the Son, ✟ and of the Holy Spirit.
℟. **Amen.**

This blessing is omitted if the Easter proclamation is sung by one who is not a deacon.

17. The book and candle may be incensed. Then the deacon or, if there is no deacon, the priest sings the Easter proclamation at the lectern or pulpit. All stand and hold lighted candles.

If necessary, the Easter proclamation may be sung by one who is not a deacon. In this case the bracketed words My dearest friends up to the end of the introduction are omitted, as is the greeting The Lord be with you.

The Easter proclamation may be sung either in the long or short form. The conferences of bishops may also adapt the text by inserting acclamations for the people.

EASTER PROCLAMATION

Parentheses around a text indicate that it is to be sung by a priest or deacon only.
For the short form, the parts within square brackets are omitted, and parts to be added are indicated above the music.

Re-joice, heav-en-ly pow-ers! Sing, choirs of an - gels! Ex-ult, all cre-a-

tion a-round God's throne! Je-sus Christ, our King, is ris-en! Sound the trum-pet

of sal-va - tion! Re-joice, O earth, in shin-ing splen - dor, ra-diant in the

bright-ness of your King! Christ has con-quered! Glo - ry fills you! Dark - ness

van-ish-es for ev - er! Re-joice, O Moth-er Church! Ex-ult in glo -

ry! The ris - en Sav-ior shines up - on you! Let this place re-sound with

joy, ech-o-ing the might-y song of all God's peo - ple!

(Deacon or Priest only)

([My dear-est friends, stand-ing with me in this ho - ly light, join me in

ask-ing God for mer - cy, that he may give his unwor-thy min - is - ter

grace to sing his Eas - ter prais - es.])

(Deacon or Priest only)

(℣. The Lord be with you. ℟. And al - so with you.) ℣. Lift up your

hearts. ℟. We lift them up to the Lord. ℣. Let us give thanks to the Lord

our God. ℟. It is right to give him thanks and praise. It is tru - ly right that

with full hearts and minds and voic - es we should praise the un-seen God, the all-power-

ful Fa - ther, and his on - ly Son, our Lord Je - sus Christ. For Christ has

ran - somed us with his blood, and paid for us the price of Ad - am's sin to

our e - ter - nal Fa - ther! This is our pass - o - ver feast, when Christ,

the true Lamb, is slain, whose blood con - se - crates the homes of all be -

liev - ers. This is the night. when first you saved our fa - thers:

you freed the people of Is - ra - el from their slav - er - y. and led them dry -

shod through the sea.   [This is the night when the pil-lar of fire de-stroyed the dark-

ness of sin!]   This is   the night when Chris-tians eve-ry-where,   washed clean of

sin and freed from all de-file-ment,   are re-stored to grace and grow to-geth - er

in ho - li - ness.   This   is the night when Je-sus Christ broke the chains

of death   and rose tri - um - phant from the grave.   [What good would life   have

been to us,   had Christ not come as our Re - deem - er?]   Fa - ther, how won-

der - ful your care for us!   How bound-less your mer - ci - ful love!   To ran-som a slave

you gave a - way   your Son.   O   hap - py fault,   O nec - es - sar - y sin   of

Ad - am,   which gained for us so great a Re - deem - er!   [Most blessed of

all nights,   cho - sen by God   to see Christ ris - ing from the dead!

Of this night scrip-ture says: "The night will be as clear as day: it will be-come my light, my joy." The power of this ho-ly night dis-pels all e-vil, wash-es guilt a-way, re-stores lost in-no-cence, brings mourn-ers joy; it casts out ha-tred, brings us peace, and hum-bles earth-ly pride.]

Short form only:

The power of this ho-ly night dis-pels all e-vil, wash-es guilt a-way, re-stores lost in-no-cence and brings mourn-ers joy.

Night tru-ly blessed when heav-en is wed-ded to earth and man is rec-on-ciled with God! There-fore, heav-en-ly Fa-ther, in the joy of this night, re-ceive our eve-ning sac-ri-fice of praise, your Chur-ch's sol-emn of-fer-ing. [Ac-cept this Eas-ter can-dle, a flame di-vid-ed but un-dimmed, a pil-lar of fire

that glows to the hon-or of God.   Let it min-gle with the lights of heav - en

and con-tin-ue brave-ly burn-ing to dis - pel the dark - ness of this night!]

Short form only:

Ac-cept this Eas - ter can - dle.   May it al - ways dis-pel the dark-ness of

this night!

May the Morn - ing Star which nev - er sets   find this flame still burn - ing: Christ,

that Morn - ing Star,   who came back from the dead, and shed his peace-ful light on

all man-kind,   your Son who lives and reigns for ev - er and ev - er.   ℞. A - men.

LONG FORM OF THE EASTER PROCLAMATION

18.

Rejoice, heavenly powers! Sing, choirs of angels!
    Exult, all creation around God's throne!
    Jesus Christ, our King, is risen!
    Sound the trumpet of salvation!

Rejoice, O earth, in shining splendor,
    radiant in the brightness of your King!
    Christ has conquered! Glory fills you!
    Darkness vanishes for ever!

Rejoice, O Mother Church! Exult in glory!
    The risen Savior shines upon you!
    Let this place resound with joy,
    echoing the mighty song of all God's people!

[My dearest friends, standing with me in this holy light,
    join me in asking God for mercy,
    that he may give his unworthy minister
    grace to sing his Easter praises.]

[℣. The Lord be with you.
℟. And also with you.]

℣. Lift up your hearts.
℟. We lift them up to the Lord.

℣. Let us give thanks to the Lord our God.
℟. It is right to give him thanks and praise.

It is truly right
that with full hearts and minds and voices
we should praise the unseen God, the all-powerful Father,
and his only Son, our Lord Jesus Christ.

For Christ has ransomed us with his blood,
    and paid for us the price of Adam's sin
        to our eternal Father!

This is our passover feast,
    when Christ, the true Lamb, is slain,
    whose blood consecrates the homes of all believers.

This is the night when first you saved our fathers:
    you freed the people of Israel from their slavery
    and led them dry-shod through the sea.

This is the night when the pillar of fire
    destroyed the darkness of sin!

This is the night when Christians everywhere,
    washed clean of sin
    and freed from all defilement,
    are restored to grace and grow together in holiness.

This is the night when Jesus Christ
    broke the chains of death
    and rose triumphant from the grave.

What good would life have been to us,
    had Christ not come as our Redeemer?

Father, how wonderful your care for us!
    How boundless your merciful love!
    To ransom a slave
    you gave away your Son.

O happy fault, O necessary sin of Adam,
    which gained for us so great a Redeemer!

Most blessed of all nights, chosen by God
    to see Christ rising from the dead!

Of this night scripture says:
    "The night will be as clear as day:
    it will become my light, my joy."

The power of this holy night
    dispels all evil, washes guilt away,
    restores lost innocence, brings mourners joy;
    it casts out hatred, brings us peace, and humbles earthly pride.

Night truly blessed when heaven is wedded to earth
    and man is reconciled with God!

Therefore, heavenly Father, in the joy of this night,
    receive our evening sacrifice of praise,
    your Church's solemn offering.

Accept this Easter candle,
    a flame divided but undimmed,
    a pillar of fire that glows to the honor of God.

Let it mingle with the lights of heaven
    and continue bravely burning
    to dispel the darkness of this night!

May the Morning Star which never sets find this flame still burning:
    Christ, that Morning Star, who came back from the dead,
    and shed his peaceful light on all mankind,
    your Son who lives and reigns for ever and ever.

    ℟.   Amen.

SHORT FORM OF THE EASTER PROCLAMATION

Rejoice, heavenly powers! Sing, choirs of angels!
    Exult, all creation around God's throne!
    Jesus Christ, our King, is risen!
    Sound the trumpet of salvation!

Rejoice, O earth, in shining splendor,
    radiant in the brightness of your King!
    Christ has conquered! Glory fills you!
    Darkness vanishes for ever!

Rejoice, O Mother Church! Exult in glory!
    The risen Savior shines upon you!
    Let this place resound with joy,
    echoing the mighty song of all God's people!

[℣. The Lord be with you.
℟. And also with you.]

℣. Lift up your hearts.
℟. We lift them up to the Lord.

℣. Let us give thanks to the Lord our God.
℟. It is right to give him thanks and praise.

It is truly right
that with full hearts and minds and voices
we should praise the unseen God, the all-powerful Father,
and his only Son, our Lord Jesus Christ.

For Christ has ransomed us with his blood,
    and paid for us the price of Adam's sin
    to our eternal Father!

This is our passover feast,
    when Christ, the true Lamb, is slain,
    whose blood consecrates the homes of all believers.

This is the night when first you saved our fathers:
    you freed the people of Israel from their slavery
    and led them dry-shod through the sea.

This is the night when Christians everywhere,
    washed clean of sin
    and freed from all defilement,
    are restored to grace and grow together in holiness.

This is the night when Jesus Christ
    broke the chains of death
    and rose triumphant from the grave.

Father, how wonderful your care for us!
How boundless your merciful love!
To ransom a slave
you gave away your Son.

O happy fault, O necessary sin of Adam,
which gained for us so great a Redeemer!

The power of this holy night
dispels all evil, washes guilt away,
restores lost innocence, brings mourners joy.

Night truly blessed when heaven is wedded to earth
and man is reconciled with God!

Therefore, heavenly Father, in the joy of this night,
receive our evening sacrifice of praise,
your Church's solemn offering.

Accept this Easter candle.
May it always dispel the darkness of this night!

May the Morning Star which never sets find this flame still burning:
Christ, that Morning Star, who came back from the dead,
and shed his peaceful light on all mankind,
your Son who lives and reigns for ever and ever.

℟.   Amen.

Part Two

Liturgy of the Word

See Lectionary for Mass, no. 42.

20. In this vigil, the mother of all vigils, nine readings are provided, seven from the Old Testament and two from the New Testament (the epistle and gospel).

21. The number of readings from the Old Testament may be reduced for pastoral reasons, but it must always be borne in mind that the reading of the word of God is the fundamental element of the Easter Vigil. At least three readings from the Old Testament should be read, although for more serious reasons the number may be reduced to two. The reading of Exodus 14, however, is never to be omitted.

22. After the Easter proclamation, the candles are put aside and all sit down. Before the readings begin, the priest speaks to the people in these or similar words:

Dear friends in Christ,
we have begun our solemn vigil.
Let us now listen attentively to the word of God,
recalling how he saved his people throughout history
and, in the fullness of time,
sent his own Son to be our Redeemer.

Through this Easter celebration,
may God bring to perfection
the saving work he has begun in us.

23. The readings follow. A reader goes to the lectern and proclaims the first reading. Then the cantor leads the psalm and the people respond. All rise and the priest sings or says **Let us pray.** When all have prayed silently for a while, he sings or says the prayer.

Instead of the responsorial psalm a period of silence may be observed. In this case the pause after **Let us pray** is omitted.

Prayers after the Readings

I

24. After the first reading (about creation: Genesis 1:1–2:2 or 1:1, 26-31a):

Let us pray.
Pause for silent prayer, if this has not preceded.
Almighty and eternal God,
you created all things in wonderful beauty and order.
Help us now to perceive
how still more wonderful is the new creation
by which in the fullness of time
you redeemed your people
through the sacrifice of our passover, Jesus Christ,
who lives and reigns for ever and ever.

℟. **Amen.**

Or (on the creation of man):
Let us pray.
Pause for silent prayer, if this has not preceded.
Lord God,
the creation of man was a wonderful work,
his redemption still more wonderful.
May we persevere in right reason
against all that entices to sin
and so attain to everlasting joy.
We ask this through Christ our Lord.

℟. **Amen.**

II

25. After the second reading (about Abraham's sacrifice: Genesis 22:1-18; or 22:1-2, 9a, 10-13, 15-18):

Let us pray.
Pause for silent prayer, if this has not preceded.
God and Father of all who believe in you,
you promised Abraham that he would become the father
  of all nations,
and through the death and resurrection of Christ
you fulfill that promise:
everywhere throughout the world you increase your chosen
  people.
May we respond to your call
by joyfully accepting your invitation to the new life of grace.
We ask this through Christ our Lord.

℟. **Amen.**

III

26. After the third reading (about the passage through the Red Sea: Exodus 14:15–15:1):

Let us pray.

Pause for silent prayer, if this has not preceded.

Father,
even today we see the wonders
of the miracles you worked long ago.
You once saved a single nation from slavery,
and now you offer that salvation to all through baptism.
May the peoples of the world become true sons of Abraham
and prove worthy of the heritage of Israel.

We ask this through Christ our Lord.

℟. Amen.

Or:

Let us pray.

Pause for silent prayer, if this has not preceded.

Lord God,
in the new covenant
you shed light on the miracles you worked in ancient times:
the Red Sea is a symbol of our baptism,
and the nation you freed from slavery
is a sign of your Christian people.
May every nation
share the faith and privilege of Israel
and come to new birth in the Holy Spirit.

We ask this through Christ our Lord.

℟. Amen.

IV

27. After the fourth reading (about the new Jerusalem: Isaiah 54:5-14):

Let us pray.

Pause for silent prayer, if this has not preceded.

Almighty and eternal God,
glorify your name by increasing your chosen people
as you promised long ago.
In reward for their trust,
may we see in the Church the fulfillment of your promise.

We ask this through Christ our Lord.

℟. Amen.

Prayers may also be chosen from those given after the following readings, if the readings are omitted.

V

28. After the fifth reading (about salvation freely offered to all: Isaiah 55:1-11):

Let us pray.

Pause for silent prayer, if this has not preceded.

Almighty, ever-living God,
only hope of the world,
by the preaching of the prophets
you proclaimed the mysteries we are celebrating tonight.
Help us to be your faithful people,
for it is by your inspiration alone
that we can grow in goodness.

We ask this through Christ our Lord.

℟. Amen.

VI

29. After the sixth reading (about the fountain of wisdom: Baruch 3:9-15, 32–4:4):

Let us pray.
Pause for silent prayer, if this has not preceded.
**Father,
you increase your Church
by continuing to call all people to salvation.
Listen to our prayers
and always watch over those you cleanse in baptism.**

We ask this through Christ our Lord.

℟. **Amen.**

VII

30. After the seventh reading (about a new heart and a new spirit: Ezekiel 36:16-17a, 18-28):

Let us pray.
Pause for silent prayer, if this has not preceded.
**God of unchanging power and light,
look with mercy and favor on your entire
    Church.
Bring lasting salvation to mankind,
so that the world may see
the fallen lifted up,
the old made new,
and all things brought to perfection,
through him who is their origin,
our Lord Jesus Christ,
who lives and reigns for ever and ever.**

℟. **Amen.**

Or:

Let us pray.
Pause for silent prayer, if this has not preceded.
**Father,
you teach us in both the Old and the New
    Testament
to celebrate this passover mystery.
Help us to understand your great love for us.
May the goodness you now show us
confirm our hope in your future mercy.**

We ask this through Christ our Lord.

℟. **Amen.**

Gloria

31. After the last reading from the Old Testament with its responsory and prayer, the altar candles are lighted, and the priest intones the Gloria, which is taken up by all present. The church bells are rung, according to local custom.

Prayer

32. At the end of the hymn, the priest sings or says the opening prayer in the usual way.

Let us pray.

Pause for silent prayer

**Lord God,
you have brightened this night
with the radiance of the risen Christ.
Quicken the spirit of sonship in your Church;
renew us in mind and body
to give you whole-hearted service.**

**Grant this through our Lord Jesus Christ, your Son,
who lives and reigns with you and the Holy Spirit,
one God, for ever and ever.**

℟. **Amen.**

Epistle

33. Then a reader proclaims the reading from the Apostle Paul.

Alleluia

34. After the epistle all rise, and the priest solemnly intones the alleluia, which is repeated by all present.

The cantor sings the psalm and the people answer Alleluia. If necessary, the cantor of the psalm may himself intone the alleluia.

Gospel

35. Incense may be used at the gospel, candles are not carried.

Homily

36. The homily follows the gospel, and then the liturgy of baptism begins.

Part Three

Liturgy of Baptism

37. The priest goes with the ministers to the baptismal font, if this can be seen by the congregation. Otherwise a vessel of water is placed in the sanctuary.

If there are candidates to be baptized, they are called forward and presented by their godparents. If they are children, the parents and godparents bring them forward in front of the congregation.

38. Then the priest speaks to the people in these or similar words:

If there are candidates to be baptized

Dear friends in Christ,
as our brothers and sisters approach the waters of rebirth,
let us help them by our prayers
and ask God, our almighty Father,
to support them with his mercy and love.

If the font is to be blessed, but there is no one to be baptized

Dear friends in Christ,
let us ask God, the almighty Father,
to bless this font,
that those reborn in it
may be made one with his adopted children in Christ.

Litany

39. The litany is sung by two cantors. All present stand (as is customary during the Easter season) and answer.

If there is to be a procession of some length to the baptistery, the litany is sung during the procession. In this case those who are to be baptized are first called forward. Then the procession begins: the Easter candle is carried first, followed by the candidates with their godparents, and the priest with the ministers. The above instruction is given before the blessing of the water.

40. If there is no one to be baptized and the font is not to be blessed the litany is omitted, and the blessing of water (no. 45) takes place at once.

41. In the litany some names of saints may be added, especially the titular of the church, the local patrons, or the saints of those to be baptized.

Lord, have mer - cy   Christ, have mer - cy   Lord, have mer - cy

℟. pray for us

Holy Mary, Mother of God
Saint Michael
Holy angels of God
Saint John the Baptist
Saint Joseph
Saint Peter and Saint Paul
Saint Andrew
Saint John
Saint Mary Magdalene
Saint Stephen
Saint Ig - natius
Saint Lawrence
Saint Perpetua and Saint Fe - licity
Saint Agnes
Saint Gregory
Saint Au - gustine
Saint Atha - nasius
Saint Basil
Saint Martin
Saint Benedict
Saint Francis and Saint Dominic
Saint Francis Xavier
Saint John Vi - anney
Saint Catherine
Saint Te - resa
All holy men and women

Lord, be merciful
From all evil
From eve - ry sin
From everlast - ing death
By your coming as man
By your death and rising to new life
By your gift of the Ho - ly Spirit

℟. Lord, save your peo - ple

Be merciful to us sinners.   ℟. Lord, hear our prayer

If there are candidates to be baptized
[Give new life to these
    chosen ones by the grace of baptism.]

If there is no one to be baptized

[By your grace bless this
    font where your children will be re - born.]
Jesus, Son of the liv - ing God.

Christ, hear us

Lord Je - sus, hear our prayer

Christ, hear us

Lord Je - sus, hear our prayer

Lord, have mercy	Lord, have mercy
Christ, have mercy	Christ, have mercy
Lord, have mercy	Lord, have mercy
Holy Mary, Mother of God	pray for us
Saint Michael	pray for us
Holy angels of God	pray for us
Saint John the Baptist	pray for us
Saint Joseph	pray for us
Saint Peter and Saint Paul	pray for us
Saint Andrew	pray for us
Saint John	pray for us
Saint Mary Magdalene	pray for us
Saint Stephen	pray for us
Saint Ignatius	pray for us
Saint Lawrence	pray for us
Saint Perpetua and Saint Felicity	pray for us
Saint Agnes	pray for us
Saint Gregory	pray for us
Saint Augustine	pray for us
Saint Athanasius	pray for us
Saint Basil	pray for us
Saint Martin	pray for us
Saint Benedict	pray for us
Saint Francis and Saint Dominic	pray for us
Saint Francis Xavier	pray for us
Saint John Vianney	pray for us
Saint Catherine	pray for us
Saint Teresa	pray for us
All holy men and women	pray for us
Lord, be merciful	Lord, save your people
From all evil	Lord, save your people
From every sin	Lord, save your people
From everlasting death	Lord, save your people
By your coming as man	Lord, save your people
By your death and rising to new life	Lord, save your people
By your gift of the Holy Spirit	Lord, save your people
Be merciful to us sinners	Lord, hear our prayer

If there are candidates to be baptized

**Give new life to these chosen ones
by the grace of baptism**

Lord, hear our prayer

If there is no one to be baptized

**By your grace bless this font
where your children will be reborn**

Lord, hear our prayer

**Jesus, Son of the living God
Christ, hear us
Lord Jesus, hear our prayer**

**Lord, hear our prayer
Christ, hear us
Lord Jesus, hear our prayer**

If there are candidates to be baptized,
the priest, with hands joined, says the
following prayer:

Let us pray.
Pause for silent prayer, if this has not preceded.
**Almighty and eternal God,
be present in this sacrament of your love.
Send your Spirit of adoption
on those to be born again in baptism.
And may the work of our humble ministry
be brought to perfection by your mighty power.**

We ask this through Christ our Lord.

℟. **Amen.**

BLESSING OF WATER

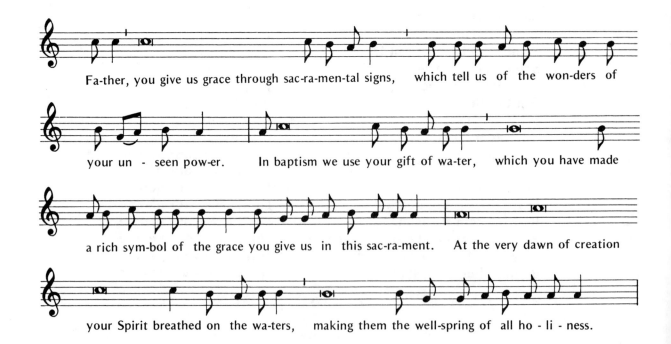

Fa-ther, you give us grace through sac-ra-men-tal signs, which tell us of the won-ders of your un - seen pow-er. In baptism we use your gift of wa-ter, which you have made a rich sym-bol of the grace you give us in this sac-ra-ment. At the very dawn of creation your Spirit breathed on the wa-ters, making them the well-spring of all ho - li - ness.

The waters of the great flood you made a sign of the wa-ters of bap-tism, that make an end of sin and a new be-gin-ning of good-ness. Through the waters of the Red Sea you led Is-ra-el out of slav-ery, to be an image of God's ho-ly peo-ple, set free from sin by bap-tism. In the waters of the Jordan your Son was bap-tized by John and a-noint-ed with the Spir-it. Your Son willed that water and blood should flow from his side as he hung up-on the cross. After his resurrection he told his dis-ci-ples: "Go out and teach all na-tions, baptizing them in the name of the Father and of the Son and of the Ho-ly Spir-it." Fa-ther, look now with love up-on your Church, and un-seal for her the foun-tain of bap-tism. By the power of the Ho-ly Spir-it give to the wa-ter of this font the grace of your Son. You cre-ated man in your own like-ness: cleanse him from sin in a new birth of in-no-cence by wa-ter and the Spir-it.

(The priest may lower the Easter candle into the water once or three times.)

We ask you, Fa-ther, with your Son to send the Ho - ly Spir-it up-on the wa-ters of this font.

May all who are buried with Christ in the death of bap-tism   rise al - so with him to

new-ness of life.   We ask this through Christ our Lord.   ℟.   A - men.

Acclamation:

Springs of wa-ter, bless the Lord.   Give him glo-ry and praise for ev - er.

BLESSING OF WATER

42. The priest then blesses the baptismal water. With hands joined, he sings or says the following prayer:

Father, you give us grace through sacramental signs,
**   which tell us of the wonders of your unseen power.**

In baptism we use your gift of water,
**   which you have made a rich symbol**
**   of the grace you give us in this sacrament.**

At the very dawn of creation
**   your Spirit breathed on the waters,**
**   making them the wellspring of all holiness.**

The waters of the great flood
**   you made a sign of the waters of baptism,**
**   that make an end of sin and a new beginning of goodnes**

Through the waters of the Red Sea
**   you led Israel out of slavery,**
**   to be an image of God's holy people,**
**   set free from sin by baptism.**

In the waters of the Jordan
**   your Son was baptized by John**
**   and anointed with the Spirit.**

Your Son willed that water and blood
**   should flow from his side**
**   as he hung upon the cross.**

After his resurrection he told his disciples:
"Go out and teach all nations,
baptizing them in the name of the Father
and of the Son and of the Holy Spirit."

Father, look now with love upon your Church,
and unseal for her the fountain of baptism.

By the power of the Holy Spirit
give to the water of this font
the grace of your Son.

You created man in your own likeness:
cleanse him from sin in a new birth of innocence
by water and the Spirit.

The priest may lower the Easter candle into the water either once or three times, as he continues:

He holds the candle in the water:

We ask you, Father, with your Son
to send the Holy Spirit upon the waters of this font.

May all who are buried with Christ
in the death of baptism
rise also with him to newness of life.

We ask this through Christ our Lord.

℟. Amen.

43. Then the candle is taken out of the water as the people sing the acclamation:

Any other appropriate acclamation may be sung.

Springs of water, bless the Lord.
Give him glory and praise for ever.

44. Those who are to be baptized renounce the devil individually. Then they are questioned about their faith and are baptized.

Adults are confirmed immediately after baptism if a bishop or a priest with the faculty to confirm is present.

45. If no one is to be baptized and the font is not to be blessed, the priest blesses the water with the following prayer:

My brothers and sisters,
let us ask the Lord our God
to bless this water he has created,
which we shall use to recall our baptism.
May he renew us
and keep us faithful to the Spirit
we have all received.

All pray silently for a short while. With hands joined, the priest continues:

Lord our God,
this night your people keep prayerful vigil.
Be with us as we recall the wonder of our creation
and the greater wonder of our redemption.
Bless this water: it makes the seed to grow,
it refreshes us and makes us clean.
You have made of it a servant of your loving kindness:
through water you set your people free,
and quenched their thirst in the desert.
With water the prophets announced a new covenant
that you would make with man.
By water, made holy by Christ in the Jordan,
you made our sinful nature new
in the bath that gives rebirth.
Let this water remind us of our baptism;
let us share the joys of our brothers
who are baptized this Easter.
We ask this through Christ our Lord.

℟.   Amen.

Renewal of Baptismal Promises

46. When the rite of baptism (and confirmation) has been completed, or if there is no baptism, immediately after the blessing of the water, all present stand with lighted candles and renew their baptismal profession of faith.

The priest speaks to the people in these or similar words:

Dear friends,
through the paschal mystery
we have been buried with Christ in baptism,
so that we may rise with him to a new life.
Now that we have completed our lenten observance,
let us renew the promises we made in baptism
when we rejected Satan and his works,
and promised to serve God faithfully
in his holy Catholic Church.

And so:

a

Priest: Do you reject Satan?

All: I do.

Priest: And all his works?

All: I do.

Priest: And all his empty promises?

All: I do.

b

Priest: **Do you reject sin,
so as to live in the freedom of God's children?**

All: **I do.**

Priest: **Do you reject the glamor of evil,
and refuse to be mastered by sin?**

All: **I do.**

Priest: **Do you reject Satan, father of sin and prince of darkness?**

All: **I do.**

According to circumstances, this second form may be adapted to local needs by the conference of bishops.

Then the priest continues: **Do you believe in God, the Father almighty,
creator of heaven and earth?**

All: **I do.**

Priest: **Do you believe in Jesus Christ, his only Son, our Lord,
who was born of the Virgin Mary,
was crucified, died, and was buried,
rose from the dead,
and is now seated at the right hand of the Father?**

All: **I do.**

Priest: **Do you believe in the Holy Spirit,
the holy Catholic Church, the communion of saints,
the forgiveness of sins, the resurrection of the body,
and life everlasting?**

All: **I do.**

The priest concludes: **God, the all-powerful Father of our Lord Jesus Christ,
has given us a new birth by water and the Holy Spirit,
and forgiven all our sins.**

**May he also keep us faithful to our Lord Jesus Christ
for ever and ever.**

All: **Amen.**

47. The priest sprinkles the people with the blessed water, while all sing: I saw water; or any other song which is baptismal in character may be sung.

**I saw water flowing
from the right side of the temple, alleluia.
It brought God's life and his salvation,
and the people sang in joyful praise:
alleluia, alleluia. (See Ezek. 47:1-2, 9)**

48. Meanwhile the newly baptized are led to their place among the faithful.

If the blessing of the baptismal water does not take place in the baptistery, the ministers reverently carry the vessel of water to the font.

If the blessing of the font does not take place, the blessed water is put in a convenient place.

49. After the people have been sprinkled, the priest returns to the chair. The profession of faith is omitted, and the priest directs the general intercessions, in which the newly baptized take part for the first time.

Part Four

Liturgy of the Eucharist

50. The priest goes to the altar and begins the liturgy of the eucharist in the usual way.

51. It is fitting that the bread and wine be brought forward by the newly baptized.

52. **PRAYER OVER THE GIFTS**

Pray, brethren . . .

**Lord,
accept the prayers and offerings of your people.
With your help
may this Easter mystery of our redemption
bring to perfection the saving work you have begun in us.**

We ask this through Christ our Lord.

53. **Eucharistic Prayer:**
Preface of Easter I, page 438 (on this Easter night).

When Eucharistic Prayer I is used, the special Easter forms of In union with the whole Church, and Father, accept this offering are said.

54. **Communion Antiphon**

Christ has become our paschal sacrifice; let us feast with the unleavened bread of sincerity and truth, alleluia.
(1 Cor. 5:7-8)

55. **PRAYER AFTER COMMUNION**

Let us pray.
Pause for silent prayer, if this has not preceded.
**Lord,
you have nourished us with your Easter sacraments.
Fill us with your Spirit,
and make us one in peace and love.**

We ask this through Christ our Lord.

56. The deacon (or the priest) sings
or says the dismissal as follows:

Or:

Or:

a ℣. **Go in the peace of Christ, alleluia, alleluia.**

b ℣. **The Mass is ended, go in peace, alleluia, alleluia.**

c ℣. **Go in peace to love and serve the Lord, alleluia, alleluia.**

℟. **Thanks be to God, alleluia, alleluia.**

EASTER SUNDAY

I have risen: I am with you once more; you placed your
hand on me to keep me safe. How great is the depth of your
wisdom, alleluia. (Ps. 138:18, 5-6)

or:

The Lord has indeed risen, alleluia. Glory and kingship be
his for ever and ever. (Luke 24:34; see Rev. 1:6)

OPENING PRAYER

Let us pray
[**that the risen Christ will raise us up
and renew our lives**]
Pause for silent prayer
**God our Father,
by raising Christ your Son
you conquered the power of death
and opened for us the way to eternal life.
Let our celebration today
raise us up and renew our lives
by the Spirit that is within us.**

**Grant this through our Lord Jesus Christ, your
Son,
who lives and reigns with you and the Holy
Spirit,
one God, for ever and ever.**

ALTERNATIVE OPENING PRAYER

Let us pray
[**on this Easter morning for the life
that never again shall see darkness**]
Pause for silent prayer
**God our Father, creator of all,
today is the day of Easter joy.
This is the morning on which the Lord appeared to men
who had begun to lose hope
and opened their eyes to what the scriptures
foretold:
that first he must die, and then he would rise
and ascend into his Father's glorious presence.
May the risen Lord
breathe on our minds and open our eyes
that we may know him in the breaking of
bread,
and follow him in his risen life.**

Grant this through Christ our Lord.

LITURGY OF THE WORD

See Lectionary for Mass, no. 43.

RENEWAL OF BAPTISMAL PROMISES

In Easter Sunday Masses which are
celebrated with a congregation, the
rite of the renewal of baptismal
promises is repeated after the homily. The profession of faith is omitted.

The priest speaks to the people in
these or similar words:

**Dear friends,
through the paschal mystery
we have been buried with Christ in baptism,
so that we may rise with him to a new life.
Now that we have completed our lenten observance,
let us renew the promises we made in baptism
when we rejected Satan and his works,
and promised to serve God faithfully
in his holy Catholic Church.**

And so:

260

a

Priest:	**Do you reject Satan?**
All:	**I do.**
Priest:	**And all his works?**
All:	**I do.**
Priest:	**And all his empty promises?**
All:	**I do.**

b

Priest:	**Do you reject sin, so as to live in the freedom of God's children?**
All:	**I do.**
Priest:	**Do you reject the glamor of evil, and refuse to be mastered by sin?**
All:	**I do.**
Priest:	**Do you reject Satan, father of sin and prince of darkness?**
All:	**I do.**

Then the priest continues:	**Do you believe in God, the Father almighty, creator of heaven and earth?**
All:	**I do.**
Priest:	**Do you believe in Jesus Christ, his only Son, our Lord, who was born of the Virgin Mary, was crucified, died, and was buried, rose from the dead, and is now seated at the right hand of the Father?**
All:	**I do.**
Priest:	**Do you believe in the Holy Spirit, the holy Catholic Church, the communion of saints, the forgiveness of sins, the resurrection of the body, and life everlasting?**
All:	**I do.**
The priest concludes:	**God, the all-powerful Father of our Lord Jesus Christ, has given us a new birth by water and the Holy Spirit, and forgiven all our sins. May he also keep us faithful to our Lord Jesus Christ for ever and ever.**
All:	**Amen.**

The priest sprinkles the people with the blessed water, while all sing: **I saw water;** or any other song which is baptismal in character may be sung.

LITURGY OF THE EUCHARIST

PRAYER OVER THE GIFTS

Pray, brethren . . .

Lord,
with Easter joy we offer you the sacrifice
by which your Church is reborn and nourished,
through Christ our Lord.

Eucharistic Prayer:

Preface of Easter I, page 438 (on this Easter day).

When Eucharistic Prayer I is used, the special Easter forms of In union with the whole Church and Father, accept this offering are said.

Communion Rite

Christ has become our paschal sacrifice; let us feast with the unleavened bread of sincerity and truth, alleluia.

(1 Cor. 5:7-8)

A period of silence may be observed after communion, or a psalm or song of praise may be sung.

PRAYER AFTER COMMUNION

Let us pray.
Pause for silent prayer, if this has not preceded.
Father of love,
watch over your Church
and bring us to the glory of the resurrection
promised by this Easter sacrament.

We ask this in the name of Jesus the Lord.

SOLEMN BLESSING OR PRAYER OVER THE PEOPLE

The following may replace the simple blessing.

After the greeting, the deacon (or in his absence, the priest) gives the invitation in these or similar words:

Bow your heads and pray for God's blessing.

Then the priest extends his hands over the people while he sings or says:

May almighty God bless you on this solemn feast of Easter,
and may he protect you against all sin.
℟. Amen.

Through the resurrection of his Son
God has granted us healing.
May he fulfill his promises,
and bless you with eternal life.
℟. Amen.

**You have mourned for Christ's sufferings;
now you celebrate the joy of his resurrection.
May you come with joy to the feast which lasts for ever.**
℞. **Amen.**

**May almighty God bless you,
the Father, and the Son, ✠ and the Holy Spirit.**
℞. **Amen.**

For other texts of solemn blessings and prayers over the people, see pages 528–540.

The following dismissal is used during the entire octave:

a   ℣. **Go in the peace of Christ, alleluia, alleluia.**

b   ℣. **The Mass is ended, go in peace, alleluia, alleluia.**

c   ℣. **Go in peace to love and serve the Lord, alleluia, alleluia.**

℞. **Thanks be to God, alleluia, alleluia.**

MONDAY WITHIN THE OCTAVE OF EASTER

Introductory Rites

> The Lord brought you to a land flowing with milk and honey, so that his law would always be given honor among you, alleluia. (See Exod. 13:5, 9)
>
> or:
>
> The Lord has risen from the dead, as he foretold. Let there be happiness and rejoicing for he is our King for ever, alleluia.

The Gloria is said or sung.

OPENING PRAYER

**Father,
you give your Church constant growth
by adding new members to your family.
Help us put into action in our lives
the baptism we have received with faith.**

**We ask this through our Lord Jesus Christ, your Son,
who lives and reigns with you and the Holy Spirit,
one God, for ever and ever.**

See Lectionary for Mass, no. 261.

The profession of faith is not said.

PRAYER OVER THE GIFTS

Pray, brethren . . .

**Father,
you have given us new light by baptism
and the profession of your name.
Accept the gifts of your children
and bring us to eternal joy in your presence.**

We ask this in the name of Jesus the Lord.

Preface of Easter I, page 438.

When Eucharistic Prayer I is used, the special Easter forms of In union with the whole Church and Father, accept this offering are said.

Communion Rite

> Christ now raised from the dead will never die again;
> death no longer has power over him, alleluia. (Rom. 6:9)

PRAYER AFTER COMMUNION

Let us pray.

Pause for silent prayer, if this has not preceded.

**Lord,
may the life we receive in these Easter sacraments
continue to grow in our hearts.
As you lead us along the way of eternal salvation,
make us worthy of your many gifts.**

Grant this through Christ our Lord.

TUESDAY WITHIN THE OCTAVE OF EASTER

Introductory Rites

    If men desire wisdom, she will give them the water of
knowledge to drink. They will never waver from the truth;
they will stand firm for ever, alleluia. (Sir. 15:3-4)

The Gloria is said or sung.

OPENING PRAYER

**Father,
by this Easter mystery you touch our lives
with the healing power of your love.
You have given us the freedom of the sons of God.
May we who now celebrate your gift
find joy in it for ever in heaven.**

**Grant this through our Lord Jesus Christ, your Son,
who lives and reigns with you and the Holy Spirit,
one God, for ever and ever.**

See Lectionary for Mass, no. 262.

The profession of faith is not said.

PRAYER OVER THE GIFTS

Pray, brethren . . .

**Lord,
accept these gifts from your family.
May we hold fast to the life you have given us
and come to the eternal gifts you promise.**

We ask this in the name of Jesus the Lord.

Preface of Easter I, page 438.

When Eucharistic Prayer I is used, the
special Easter forms of **In union with
the whole Church** and **Father, accept
this offering** are said.

Communion Rite

    If you have been raised with Christ, seek the things that
are above, where Christ is seated at the right hand of God,
alleluia. (Col. 3:1-2)

PRAYER AFTER COMMUNION

Let us pray.
Pause for silent prayer, if this has not preceded.
**All-powerful Father,
hear our prayers.
Prepare for eternal joy
the people you have renewed in baptism.**

We ask this through Christ our Lord.

WEDNESDAY WITHIN THE OCTAVE OF EASTER

Introductory Rites

> Come, you whom my Father has blessed; inherit the kingdom prepared for you since the foundation of the world, alleluia. (Matthew 25:34)

The Gloria is said or sung.

OPENING PRAYER

**God our Father,
on this solemn feast you give us the joy of recalling
the rising of Christ to new life.
May the joy of our annual celebration
bring us to the joy of eternal life.**

**We ask this through our Lord Jesus Christ, your Son,
who lives and reigns with you and the Holy Spirit,
one God, for ever and ever.**

See Lectionary for Mass, no. 263.

The profession of faith is not said.

PRAYER OVER THE GIFTS

Pray, brethren . . .

**Lord,
accept this sacrifice of our redemption
and accomplish in us salvation of mind and body.**

Grant this through Christ our Lord.

Preface of Easter I, page 438.

When Eucharistic Prayer I is used, the special Easter forms of **In union with the whole Church** and **Father, accept this offering** are said.

Communion Rite

> The disciples recognized the Lord Jesus in the breaking of bread, alleluia. (Luke 24:35)

PRAYER AFTER COMMUNION

Let us pray.

Pause for silent prayer, if this has not preceded.

**Lord,
may this sharing in the sacrament of your Son
free us from our old life of sin
and make us your new creation.**

We ask this in the name of Jesus the Lord.

THURSDAY WITHIN THE OCTAVE OF EASTER

Introductory Rites

Your people praised your great victory, O Lord. Wisdom opened the mouth that was dumb, and made the tongues of babies speak, alleluia. (Wis. 10:20-21)

The Gloria is said or sung.

OPENING PRAYER

Father,
you gather the nations to praise your name.
May all who are reborn in baptism
be one in faith and love.

Grant this through our Lord Jesus Christ, your Son,
who lives and reigns with you and the Holy Spirit,
one God, for ever and ever.

See Lectionary for Mass, no. 264.

The profession of faith is not said.

PRAYER OVER THE GIFTS

Pray, brethren . . .

Lord,
accept our gifts
and grant your continuing protection
to all who have received new life in baptism.

We ask this in the name of Jesus the Lord.

Preface of Easter I, page 438.

When Eucharistic Prayer I is used, the special Easter forms of In union with the whole Church and Father, accept this offering are said.

Communion Rite

You are a people God claims as his own, to praise him who called you out of darkness into his marvelous light, alleluia. (1 Peter 2:9)

PRAYER AFTER COMMUNION

Let us pray.
Pause for silent prayer, if this has not preceded.
Lord,
may this celebration of our redemption
help us in this life
and lead us to eternal happiness.

We ask this through Christ our Lord.

FRIDAY WITHIN THE OCTAVE OF EASTER

Introductory Rites

> The Lord led his people out of slavery. He drowned their
> enemies in the sea, alleluia. (Ps. 77:53)

The Gloria is said or sung.

OPENING PRAYER

**Eternal Father,
you gave us the Easter mystery
as our covenant of reconciliation.
May the new birth we celebrate
show its effects in the way we live.**

**We ask this through our Lord Jesus Christ, your Son,
who lives and reigns with you and the Holy Spirit,
one God, for ever and ever.**

See Lectionary for Mass, no. 265.

The profession of faith is not said.

PRAYER OVER THE GIFTS

Pray, brethren . . .

**Lord,
bring to perfection the spirit of life
we receive from these Easter gifts.
Free us from seeking after the passing things in life
and help us set our hearts on the kingdom of heaven.**

Grant this through Christ our Lord.

Preface of Easter I, page **438**.

When Eucharistic Prayer I is used, the
special Easter forms of **In union with
the whole Church** and **Father, accept
this offering** are said.

Communion Rite

> Jesus said to his disciples: Come and eat. And he took the
> bread, and gave it to them, alleluia. (See John 21:12-13)

PRAYER AFTER COMMUNION

Let us pray.
Pause for silent prayer, if this has not preceded.
**Lord,
watch over those you have saved in Christ.
May we who are redeemed by his suffering and death
always rejoice in his resurrection,
for he is Lord for ever and ever.**

SATURDAY WITHIN THE OCTAVE OF EASTER

Introductory Rites

The Lord led his people to freedom and they shouted with
joy and gladness, alleluia. (Ps. 104:43)

The Gloria is said or sung.

OPENING PRAYER

**Father of love,
by the outpouring of your grace
you increase the number of those who believe in you.
Watch over your chosen family.
Give undying life to all
who have been born again in baptism.**

**Grant this through our Lord Jesus Christ, your Son,
who lives and reigns with you and the Holy Spirit,
one God, for ever and ever.**

See Lectionary for Mass, no. 266.

The profession of faith is not said.

PRAYER OVER THE GIFTS

Pray, brethren . . .

**Lord,
give us joy by these Easter mysteries.
Let the continuous offering of this sacrifice
by which we are renewed
bring us to eternal happiness.**

We ask this in the name of Jesus the Lord.

Preface of Easter I, page 438.

When Eucharistic Prayer I is used, the
special Easter forms of In union with
the whole Church and Father, accept
this offering are said.

Communion Rite

All you who have been baptized have been clothed in
Christ, alleluia. (Gal. 3:27)

PRAYER AFTER COMMUNION

Let us pray.
Pause for silent prayer, if this has not preceded.
**Lord,
look on your people with kindness
and by these Easter mysteries
bring us to the glory of the resurrection.**

We ask this in the name of Jesus the Lord.

SECOND SUNDAY OF EASTER

Introductory Rites

Like newborn children you should thirst for milk, on which your spirit can grow to strength, alleluia. (1 Peter 2:2)

or:

Rejoice to the full in the glory that is yours, and give thanks to God who called you to his kingdom, alleluia. (4 Esdras 2:36-37)

OPENING PRAYER

Let us pray
  [for a deeper awareness of our Christian baptism]
Pause for silent prayer
God of mercy,
you wash away our sins in water,
you give us new birth in the Spirit,
and redeem us in the blood of Christ.
As we celebrate Christ's resurrection
increase our awareness of these blessings,
and renew your gift of life within us.

We ask this through our Lord Jesus Christ,
  your Son,
who lives and reigns with you and the Holy
  Spirit,
one God, for ever and ever.

ALTERNATIVE OPENING PRAYER

Let us pray
  [as Christians thirsting for the risen life]
Pause for silent prayer
Heavenly Father and God of mercy,
we no longer look for Jesus among the dead,
for he is alive and has become the Lord of life.
From the waters of death you raise us with him
and renew your gift of life within us.
Increase in our minds and hearts
the risen life we share with Christ
and help us to grow as your people
toward the fullness of eternal life with you.

We ask this through Christ our Lord.

LITURGY OF THE WORD

See Lectionary for Mass, nos. 44-46.

LITURGY OF THE EUCHARIST

PRAYER OVER THE GIFTS

Pray, brethren . . .

Lord,
through faith and baptism
we have become a new creation.
Accept the offerings of your people
(and of those born again in baptism)
and bring us to eternal happiness.

Grant this through Christ our Lord.

Eucharistic Prayer:
Preface of Easter I, page 438.

When Eucharistic Prayer I is used, the special Easter forms of In union with the whole Church and Father, accept this offering are said.

Communion Rite

Jesus spoke to Thomas: Put your hand here, and see the place of the nails. Doubt no longer, but believe, alleluia.
(See John 20:27)

A period of silence may be observed after communion, or a psalm or song of praise may be sung.

PRAYER AFTER COMMUNION

Let us pray.
Pause for silent prayer, if this has not preceded.
**Almighty God,
may the Easter sacraments we have received
live for ever in our minds and hearts.**

We ask this through Christ our Lord.

SOLEMN BLESSING OR PRAYER OVER THE PEOPLE

The following may replace the simple blessing.

After the greeting, the deacon (or in his absence, the priest) gives the invitation in these or similar words:

Bow your heads and pray for God's blessing.

Then the priest extends his hands over the people while he sings or says:

**Through the resurrection of his Son
God has redeemed you and made you his children.
May he bless you with joy.
℟. Amen.**

**The Redeemer has given you lasting freedom.
May you inherit his everlasting life.
℟. Amen.**

**By faith you rose with him in baptism.
May your lives be holy,
so that you will be united with him for ever.
℟. Amen.**

**May almighty God bless you,
the Father, and the Son, ✠ and the Holy Spirit.
℟. Amen.**

For other texts of solemn blessings and prayers over the people, see pages 528–540.

MONDAY OF THE SECOND WEEK OF EASTER

Introductory Rites

Christ now raised from the dead will never die again;
death no longer has power over him, alleluia. (Rom. 6:9)

OPENING PRAYER

**Almighty and ever-living God,
your Spirit made us your children,
confident to call you Father.
Increase your Spirit of love within us
and bring us to our promised inheritance.**

**Grant this through our Lord Jesus Christ, your Son,
who lives and reigns with you and the Holy Spirit,
one God, for ever and ever.**

See Lectionary for Mass, no. 267.

PRAYER OVER THE GIFTS

Pray, brethren . . .

**Lord,
receive these gifts from your Church.
May the great joy you give us
come to perfection in heaven.**

Grant this through Christ our Lord.

Preface of Easter I-V, pages **438–442.**

Communion Rite

Jesus came and stood among his disciples and said to
them: Peace be with you, alleluia. (John 20:19)

PRAYER AFTER COMMUNION

Let us pray.

Pause for silent prayer, if this has not preceded.

**Lord,
look on your people with kindness
and by these Easter mysteries
bring us to the glory of the resurrection.**

We ask this in the name of Jesus the Lord.

TUESDAY OF THE SECOND WEEK OF EASTER

Introductory Rites

Let us shout out our joy and happiness, and give glory to
God, the Lord of all, because he is our King, alleluia. (Rev.
19:7, 6)

OPENING PRAYER

**All-powerful God,
help us to proclaim the power of the Lord's resurrection.
May we who accept this sign of the love of Christ
come to share the eternal life he reveals,
for he lives and reigns with you and the Holy Spirit,
one God, for ever and ever.**

See Lectionary for Mass, no. 268.

PRAYER OVER THE GIFTS

Pray, brethren . . .

**Lord,
give us joy by these Easter mysteries.
Let the continuous offering of this sacrifice
by which we are renewed
bring us to eternal happiness.**

We ask this in the name of Jesus the Lord.

Preface of Easter I-V, pages **438–442**.

Communion Rite

Christ had to suffer and to rise from the dead, and so enter
into his glory, alleluia. (See Luke 24:46, 26)

PRAYER AFTER COMMUNION

Let us pray.
Pause for silent prayer, if this has not preceded.
**Lord,
may this celebration of our redemption
help us in this life
and lead us to eternal happiness.**

We ask this through Christ our Lord.

WEDNESDAY OF THE SECOND WEEK OF EASTER

Introductory Rites

I will be a witness to you in the world, O Lord. I will spread
the knowledge of your name among my brothers, alleluia.
(Ps. 17:50; 21:23)

OPENING PRAYER

**God of mercy,
you have filled us with the hope of resurrection
by restoring man to his original dignity.
May we who relive this mystery each year
come to share it in perpetual love.**

**Grant this through our Lord Jesus Christ, your Son,
who lives and reigns with you and the Holy Spirit,
one God, for ever and ever.**

See Lectionary for Mass, no. 269.

PRAYER OVER THE GIFTS

Pray, brethren . . .

**Lord God,
by this holy exchange of gifts
you share with us your divine life.
Grant that everything we do
may be directed by the knowledge of your truth.**

We ask this in the name of Jesus the Lord.

Preface of Easter I-V, pages 438–442.

Communion Rite

The Lord says, I have chosen you from the world to go and
bear fruit that will last, alleluia. (See John 15:16, 19)

PRAYER AFTER COMMUNION

Let us pray.
Pause for silent prayer, if this has not preceded.
**Merciful Father,
may these mysteries give us new purpose
and bring us to a new life in you.**

Grant this through Christ our Lord.

THURSDAY OF THE SECOND WEEK OF EASTER

Introductory Rites

When you walked at the head of your people, O God, and lived with them on their journey, the earth shook at your presence, and the skies poured forth their rain, alleluia. (See Ps. 67:8-9, 20)

OPENING PRAYER

**God of mercy,
may the Easter mystery we celebrate
be effective throughout our lives.**

**Grant this through our Lord Jesus Christ, your Son,
who lives and reigns with you and the Holy Spirit,
one God, for ever and ever.**

See Lectionary for Mass, no. 270.

PRAYER OVER THE GIFTS

Pray, brethren . . .

**Lord,
accept our prayers and offerings.
Make us worthy of your sacraments of love
by granting us your forgiveness.**

We ask this in the name of Jesus the Lord.

Preface of Easter I-V, pages **438–442.**

Communion Rite

I, the Lord, am with you always, until the end of the world, alleluia. (Matthew 28:20)

PRAYER AFTER COMMUNION

Let us pray.
Pause for silent prayer, if this has not preceded.
**Almighty and ever-living Lord,
you restored us to life
by raising Christ from death.
Strengthen us by this Easter sacrament;
may we feel its saving power in our daily life.**

We ask this through Christ our Lord.

FRIDAY OF THE SECOND WEEK OF EASTER

Introductory Rites

By your blood, O Lord, you have redeemed us from every
tribe and tongue, from every nation and people: you have
made us into the kingdom of God, alleluia. (Rev. 5:9-10)

OPENING PRAYER

Father,
in your plan of salvation
your Son Jesus Christ accepted the cross
and freed us from the power of the enemy.
May we come to share the glory of his resurrection,
for he lives and reigns with you and the Holy Spirit,
one God, for ever and ever.

See Lectionary for Mass, no. 271.

PRAYER OVER THE GIFTS

Pray, brethren . . .

Lord,
accept these gifts from your family.
May we hold fast to the life you have given us
and come to the eternal gifts you promise.

We ask this in the name of Jesus the Lord.

Preface of Easter I-V, pages 438–442.

Communion Rite

Christ our Lord was put to death for our sins; and he rose
again to make us worthy of life, alleluia. (Rom. 4:25)

PRAYER AFTER COMMUNION

Let us pray.
Pause for silent prayer, if this has not preceded.
Lord,
watch over those you have saved in Christ.
May we who are redeemed by his suffering and death
always rejoice in his resurrection,
for he is Lord for ever and ever.

SATURDAY OF THE SECOND WEEK OF EASTER

Introductory Rites

You are a people God claims as his own, to praise him who called you out of darkness into his marvelous light, alleluia. (1 Peter 2:9)

OPENING PRAYER

**God our Father,
look upon us with love.
You redeem us and make us your children in Christ.
Give us true freedom
and bring us to the inheritance you promised.**

**We ask this through our Lord Jesus Christ, your Son,
who lives and reigns with you and the Holy Spirit,
one God, for ever and ever.**

See Lectionary for Mass, no. 272.

PRAYER OVER THE GIFTS

Pray, brethren . . .

**Merciful Lord,
make holy these gifts
and let our spiritual sacrifice
make us an everlasting gift to you.**

We ask this in the name of Jesus the Lord.

Preface of Easter I-V, pages **438–442.**

Communion Rite

Father, I want the men you have given me to be with me where I am, so that they may see the glory you have given me, alleluia. (John 17:24)

PRAYER AFTER COMMUNION

Let us pray.
Pause for silent prayer, if this has not preceded.
**Lord,
may this eucharist,
which we have celebrated in memory of your Son,
help us to grow in love.**

We ask this in the name of Jesus the Lord.

THIRD SUNDAY OF EASTER

Introductory Rites

Let all the earth cry out to God with joy; praise the glory of his name; proclaim his glorious praise, alleluia. (Ps. 65:1-2)

OPENING PRAYER

Let us pray
  [that Christ will give us a share in the glory of his unending life]
Pause for silent prayer
God our Father,
may we look forward with hope to our resurrection,
for you have made us your sons and daughters,
and restored the joy of our youth.

We ask this through our Lord Jesus Christ, your Son,
who lives and reigns with you and the Holy Spirit,
one God, for ever and ever.

ALTERNATIVE OPENING PRAYER

Let us pray
  [in confident peace and Easter hope]
Pause for silent prayer
Father in heaven, author of all truth,
a people once in darkness has listened to your Word
and followed your Son as he rose from the tomb.
Hear the prayer of this newborn people
and strengthen your Church to answer your call.
May we rise and come forth into the light of day
to stand in your presence until eternity dawns.

We ask this through Christ our Lord.

LITURGY OF THE WORD

See Lectionary for Mass, nos. 47-49.

LITURGY OF THE EUCHARIST

PRAYER OVER THE GIFTS

Pray, brethren . . .

Lord,
receive these gifts from your Church.
May the great joy you give us
come to perfection in heaven.

Grant this through Christ our Lord.

Eucharistic Prayer:
Preface of Easter I-V, pages 438–442.

Communion Rite

Year A

The disciples recognized the Lord Jesus in the breaking of bread, alleluia. (Luke 24:35)

Year B

Christ had to suffer and to rise from the dead on the third day. In his name penance for the remission of sins is to be preached to all nations, alleluia. (Luke 24:46-47)

Year C

Jesus said to his disciples: Come and eat. And he took the bread, and gave it to them, alleluia. (See John 21:12-13)

A period of silence may be observed after communion, or a psalm or song of praise may be sung.

PRAYER AFTER COMMUNION

Let us pray.
Pause for silent prayer, if this has not preceded.
Lord,
look on your people with kindness
and by these Easter mysteries
bring us to the glory of the resurrection.
We ask this in the name of Jesus the Lord.

SOLEMN BLESSING OR PRAYER OVER THE PEOPLE

The following may replace the simple blessing.

After the greeting, the deacon (or in his absence, the priest) gives the invitation in these or similar words:

Bow your heads and pray for God's blessing.

Then the priest extends his hands over the people while he sings or says:

Lord,
bless us with your heavenly gifts,
and in your mercy make us your obedient servants.
We ask this through Christ our Lord.
℟. **Amen.**

May almighty God bless you,
the Father, and the Son, ✝ and the Holy Spirit.
℟. **Amen.**

For other texts of solemn blessings and prayers over the people, see pages 528–540.

MONDAY OF THE THIRD WEEK OF EASTER

Introductory Rites

The Good Shepherd is risen! He who laid down his life for
his sheep, who died for his flock, he is risen, alleluia.

OPENING PRAYER

**God our Father,
your light of truth
guides us to the way of Christ.
May all who follow him
reject what is contrary to the gospel.**

**We ask this through our Lord Jesus Christ, your Son,
who lives and reigns with you and the Holy Spirit,
one God, for ever and ever.**

See Lectionary for Mass, no. 273.

PRAYER OVER THE GIFTS

Pray, brethren . . .

**Lord,
accept our prayers and offerings.
Make us worthy of your sacraments of love
by granting us your forgiveness.**

We ask this in the name of Jesus the Lord.

Preface of Easter I-V, pages 438–442.

Communion Rite

The Lord says, peace I leave with you, my own peace I give
you; not as the world gives, do I give, alleluia. (John 14:27)

PRAYER AFTER COMMUNION

Let us pray.
Pause for silent prayer, if this has not preceded.
**Almighty and ever-living Lord,
you restored us to life
by raising Christ from death.
Strengthen us by this Easter sacrament;
may we feel its saving power in our daily life.**

We ask this through Christ our Lord.

TUESDAY OF THE THIRD WEEK OF EASTER

Introductory Rites

All you who fear God, both the great and the small, give
praise to him! For his salvation and strength have come,
the power of Christ, alleluia. (Rev. 19:5; 12:10)

OPENING PRAYER

**Father,
you open the kingdom of heaven
to those born again by water and the Spirit.
Increase your gift of love in us.
May all who have been freed from sins in baptism
receive all that you have promised.**

**We ask this through our Lord Jesus Christ, your Son,
who lives and reigns with you and the Holy Spirit,
one God, for ever and ever.**

See Lectionary for Mass, no. 274.

PRAYER OVER THE GIFTS

Pray, brethren . . .

**Lord,
receive these gifts from your Church.
May the great joy you give us
come to perfection in heaven.**

Grant this through Christ our Lord.

Preface of Easter I-V, pages 438–442.

Communion Rite

Because we have died with Christ, we believe that we shall
also come to life with him, alleluia. (Rom. 6:8)

PRAYER AFTER COMMUNION

Let us pray.

Pause for silent prayer, if this has not preceded.

**Lord,
look on your people with kindness
and by these Easter mysteries
bring us to the glory of the resurrection.**

We ask this in the name of Jesus the Lord.

WEDNESDAY OF THE THIRD WEEK OF EASTER

Introductory Rites
> Fill me with your praise and I will sing your glory; songs of
> joy will be on my lips, alleluia. (Ps. 70:8, 23)

OPENING PRAYER

Merciful Lord,
hear the prayers of your people.
May we who have received your gift of faith
share for ever in the new life of Christ.

Grant this through our Lord Jesus Christ, your Son,
who lives and reigns with you and the Holy Spirit,
one God, for ever and ever.

See Lectionary for Mass, no. 275.

PRAYER OVER THE GIFTS

Pray, brethren . . .

Lord,
restore us by these Easter mysteries.
May the continuing work of our Redeemer
bring us eternal joy.

We ask this through Christ our Lord.

Preface of Easter I-V, pages **438–442**.

Communion Rite
> Christ has risen and shines upon us, whom he has re-
> deemed by his blood, alleluia.

PRAYER AFTER COMMUNION

Let us pray.
Pause for silent prayer, if this has not preceded.
Lord,
may this celebration of our redemption
help us in this life
and lead us to eternal happiness.

We ask this through Christ our Lord.

THURSDAY OF THE THIRD WEEK OF EASTER

Introductory Rites

Let us sing to the Lord, he has covered himself in glory!
The Lord is my strength, and I praise him: he is the Savior
of my life, alleluia. (Exod. 15:1-2)

OPENING PRAYER

**Father,
in this holy season
we come to know the full depth of your love.
You have freed us from the darkness of error and sin.
Help us to cling to your truths with fidelity.**

**We ask this through our Lord Jesus Christ, your Son,
who lives and reigns with you and the Holy Spirit,
one God, for ever and ever.**

See Lectionary for Mass, no. 276.

PRAYER OVER THE GIFTS

Pray, brethren . . .

**Lord God,
by this holy exchange of gifts
you share with us your divine life.
Grant that everything we do
may be directed by the knowledge of your truth.**

We ask this in the name of Jesus the Lord.

Preface of Easter I-V, pages 438–442.

Communion Rite

Christ died for all, so that living men should not live for
themselves, but for Christ who died and was raised to life
for them, alleluia. (2 Cor. 5:15)

PRAYER AFTER COMMUNION

Let us pray.

Pause for silent prayer, if this has not preceded.

**Merciful Father,
may these mysteries give us new purpose
and bring us to a new life in you.**

Grant this through Christ our Lord.

FRIDAY OF THE THIRD WEEK OF EASTER

Introductory Rites

The Lamb who was slain is worthy to receive strength and divinity, wisdom and power and honor, alleluia. (Rev. 5:12)

OPENING PRAYER

Father,
by the love of your Spirit,
may we who have experienced
the grace of the Lord's resurrection
rise to the newness of life in joy.

Grant this through our Lord Jesus Christ, your Son,
who lives and reigns with you and the Holy Spirit,
one God, for ever and ever.

See Lectionary for Mass, no. 277.

PRAYER OVER THE GIFTS

Pray, brethren . . .

Merciful Lord,
make holy these gifts
and let our spiritual sacrifice
make us an everlasting gift to you.

We ask this in the name of Jesus the Lord.

Preface of Easter I-V, pages **438–442.**

Communion Rite

The man who died on the cross has risen from the dead, and has won back our lives from death, alleluia.

PRAYER AFTER COMMUNION

Let us pray.

Pause for silent prayer, if this has not preceded.

Lord,
may this eucharist,
which we have celebrated in memory of your Son,
help us to grow in love.

We ask this in the name of Jesus the Lord.

SATURDAY OF THE THIRD WEEK OF EASTER

Introductory Rites

In baptism we have died with Christ, and we have risen to new life in him, because we believed in the power of God who raised him from the dead, alleluia. (Col. 2:12)

OPENING PRAYER

**God our Father,
by the waters of baptism
you give new life to the faithful.
May we not succumb to the influence of evil
but remain true to your gift of life.**

**We ask this through our Lord Jesus Christ, your Son,
who lives and reigns with you and the Holy Spirit,
one God, for ever and ever.**

See Lectionary for Mass, no. 278.

PRAYER OVER THE GIFTS

Pray, brethren . . .

**Lord,
accept these gifts from your family.
May we hold fast to the life you have given us
and come to the eternal gifts you promise.**

We ask this in the name of Jesus the Lord.

Preface of Easter I–V, pages 438–442.

Communion Rite

Father, I pray for them: may they be one in us, so that the world may believe it was you who sent me, alleluia. (John 17:20-21)

PRAYER AFTER COMMUNION

Let us pray.
Pause for silent prayer, if this has not preceded.
**Lord,
watch over those you have saved in Christ.
May we who are redeemed by his suffering and death
always rejoice in his resurrection,
for he is Lord for ever and ever.**

FOURTH SUNDAY OF EASTER

Introductory Rites

The earth is full of the goodness of the Lord; by the word
of the Lord the heavens were made, alleluia. (Ps. 32:5-6)

OPENING PRAYER

Let us pray
  **[that Christ our shepherd will lead us
    through the difficulties of this life]**
Pause for silent prayer
**Almighty and ever-living God,
give us new strength
from the courage of Christ our shepherd,
and lead us to join the saints in heaven,
where he lives and reigns with you and the
  Holy Spirit,
one God, for ever and ever.**

ALTERNATIVE OPENING PRAYER

Let us pray
  [to God our helper in time of distress]
Pause for silent prayer
**God and Father of our Lord Jesus Christ,
though your people walk in the valley of darkness,
no evil should they fear;
for they follow in faith the call of the shepherd
whom you have sent for their hope and
  strength.
Attune our minds to the sound of his voice,
lead our steps in the path he has shown,
that we may know the strength of his outstretched arm
and enjoy the light of your presence for ever.**

We ask this in the name of Jesus the Lord.

LITURGY OF THE WORD

See Lectionary for Mass, nos. 50-52.

LITURGY OF THE EUCHARIST

PRAYER OVER THE GIFTS

Pray, brethren . . .

**Lord,
restore us by these Easter mysteries.
May the continuing work of our Redeemer
bring us eternal joy.**

We ask this through Christ our Lord.

Eucharistic Prayer:
Preface of Easter I-V, pages **438–442**.

Communion Rite

The Good Shepherd is risen! He who laid down his life for
his sheep, who died for his flock, he is risen, alleluia.

A period of silence may be observed
after communion, or a psalm or song
of praise may be sung.

PRAYER AFTER COMMUNION

Let us pray.

Pause for silent prayer, if this has not preceded.

**Father, eternal shepherd,
watch over the flock redeemed by the blood of Christ
and lead us to the promised land.**

Grant this through Christ our Lord.

**SOLEMN BLESSING OR PRAYER
OVER THE PEOPLE**

The following may replace the simple
blessing.

After the greeting, the deacon (or in
his absence, the priest) gives the invitation in these or similar words:

Bow your heads and pray for God's blessing.

Then the priest extends his hands
over the people while he sings or
says:

**Through the resurrection of his Son
God has redeemed you and made you his children.
May he bless you with joy.**
℟. **Amen.**

**The Redeemer has given you lasting freedom.
May you inherit his everlasting life.**
℟. **Amen.**

**By faith you rose with him in baptism.
May your lives be holy,
so that you will be united with him for ever.**
℟. **Amen.**

**May almighty God bless you,
the Father, and the Son, ✚ and the Holy Spirit.**
℟. **Amen.**

For other texts of solemn blessings and
prayers over the people, see pages
528–540.

MONDAY OF THE FOURTH WEEK OF EASTER

Introductory Rites
Christ now raised from the dead will never die again;
death no longer has power over him, alleluia. (Rom. 6:9)

OPENING PRAYER

**Father,
through the obedience of Jesus,
your servant and your Son,
you raised a fallen world.
Free us from sin
and bring us the joy that lasts for ever.**

**We ask this through our Lord Jesus Christ, your Son,
who lives and reigns with you and the Holy Spirit,
one God, for ever and ever.**

See Lectionary for Mass, no. 279.

PRAYER OVER THE GIFTS

Pray, brethren . . .

**Lord,
receive these gifts from your Church.
May the great joy you give us
come to perfection in heaven.**

Grant this through Christ our Lord.

Preface of Easter I-V, pages **438–442.**

Communion Rite
Jesus came and stood among his disciples and said to
them: Peace be with you, alleluia. (John 20:19)

PRAYER AFTER COMMUNION

Let us pray.
Pause for silent prayer, if this has not preceded.
**Lord,
look on your people with kindness
and by these Easter mysteries
bring us to the glory of the resurrection.**

We ask this in the name of Jesus the Lord.

TUESDAY OF THE FOURTH WEEK OF EASTER

Introductory Rites

Let us shout out our joy and happiness, and give glory to God, the Lord of all, because he is our King, alleluia. (Rev. 19:7, 6)

OPENING PRAYER

**Almighty God,
as we celebrate the resurrection,
may we share with each other
the joy the risen Christ has won for us.**

**We ask this through our Lord Jesus Christ, your Son,
who lives and reigns with you and the Holy Spirit,
one God, for ever and ever.**

See Lectionary for Mass, no. 280.

PRAYER OVER THE GIFTS

Pray, brethren . . .

**Lord,
give us joy by these Easter mysteries;
let the continuous offering of this sacrifice
by which we are renewed
bring us to eternal happiness.**

We ask this in the name of Jesus the Lord.

Preface of Easter I–V, pages **438–442.**

Communion Rite

Christ had to suffer and to rise from the dead, and so enter into his glory, alleluia. (See Luke 24:46, 26)

PRAYER AFTER COMMUNION

Let us pray.

Pause for silent prayer, if this has not preceded.
**Lord,
may this celebration of our redemption
help us in this life
and lead us to eternal happiness.**

We ask this through Christ our Lord.

WEDNESDAY OF THE FOURTH WEEK OF EASTER

Introductory Rites

I will be a witness to you in the world, O Lord. I will spread
the knowledge of your name among my brothers, alleluia.
(Pss. 17:50; 21:23)

OPENING PRAYER

**God our Father,
life of the faithful,
glory of the humble,
happiness of the just,
hear our prayer.
Fill our emptiness
with the blessing of this eucharist,
the foretaste of eternal joy.**

**We ask this through our Lord Jesus Christ, your Son,
who lives and reigns with you and the Holy Spirit,
one God, for ever and ever.**

See Lectionary for Mass, no. 281.

PRAYER OVER THE GIFTS

Pray, brethren . . .

**Lord God,
by this holy exchange of gifts
you share with us your divine life.
Grant that everything we do
may be directed by the knowledge of your truth.**

We ask this in the name of Jesus the Lord.

Preface of Easter I-V, pages 438–442.

Communion Rite

The Lord says, I have chosen you from the world to go and
bear fruit that will last, alleluia. (See John 15:16, 19)

PRAYER AFTER COMMUNION

Let us pray.

Pause for silent prayer, if this has not preceded.

**Merciful Father,
may these mysteries give us new purpose
and bring us to a new life in you.**

Grant this through Christ our Lord.

THURSDAY OF THE FOURTH WEEK OF EASTER

Introductory Rites

When you walked at the head of your people, O God, and lived with them on their journey, the earth shook at your presence and the skies poured forth their rain, alleluia.
(See Ps. 67:8-9, 20)

OPENING PRAYER

Father,
in restoring human nature
you have given us a greater dignity
than we had in the beginning.
Keep us in your love
and continue to sustain those
who have received new life in baptism.

We ask this through our Lord Jesus Christ, your Son,
who lives and reigns with you and the Holy Spirit,
one God, for ever and ever.

See Lectionary for Mass, no. 282.

PRAYER OVER THE GIFTS

Pray, brethren . . .

Lord,
accept our prayers and offerings.
Make us worthy of your sacraments of love
by granting us your forgiveness.

We ask this in the name of Jesus the Lord.

Preface of Easter I-V, pages **438–442.**

Communion Rite

I, the Lord, am with you always, until the end of the world, alleluia. (Matthew 28:20)

PRAYER AFTER COMMUNION

Let us pray.
Pause for silent prayer, if this has not preceded.
Almighty and ever-living Lord,
you restored us to life
by raising Christ from death.
Strengthen us by this Easter sacrament;
may we feel its saving power in our daily life.

We ask this through Christ our Lord.

FRIDAY OF THE FOURTH WEEK OF EASTER

Introductory Rites

>By your blood, O Lord, you have redeemed us from every
>tribe and tongue, from every nation and people: you have
>made us into the kingdom of God, alleluia. (Rev. 5:9-10)

OPENING PRAYER

**Father of our freedom and salvation,
hear the prayers of those redeemed by your Son's suffering.
Through you may we have life;
with you may we have eternal joy.**

**We ask this through our Lord Jesus Christ, your Son,
who lives and reigns with you and the Holy Spirit,
one God, for ever and ever.**

See Lectionary for Mass, no. 283.

PRAYER OVER THE GIFTS   **Pray, brethren . . .**

**Lord,
accept these gifts from your family.
May we hold fast to the life you have given us
and come to the eternal gifts you promise.**

We ask this in the name of Jesus the Lord.

Preface of Easter I-V, pages 438–442.

Communion Rite

>Christ our Lord was put to death for our sins; and he rose
>again to make us worthy of life, alleluia. (Rom. 4:25)

PRAYER AFTER COMMUNION **Let us pray.**

Pause for silent prayer, if this has not preceded.

**Lord,
watch over those you have saved in Christ.
May we who are redeemed by his suffering and death
always rejoice in his resurrection,
for he is Lord for ever and ever.**

SATURDAY OF THE FOURTH WEEK OF EASTER

Introductory Rites
You are a people God claims as his own, to praise him who called you out of darkness into his marvelous light, alleluia. (1 Peter 2:9)

OPENING PRAYER

**Father,
may we whom you renew in baptism
bear witness to our faith by the way we live.
By the suffering, death, and resurrection of your Son
may we come to eternal joy.**

**We ask this through our Lord Jesus Christ, your Son,
who lives and reigns with you and the Holy Spirit,
one God, for ever and ever.**

See Lectionary for Mass, no. 284.

PRAYER OVER THE GIFTS

Pray, brethren . . .

**Merciful Lord,
make holy these gifts
and let our spiritual sacrifice
make us an everlasting gift to you.**

We ask this in the name of Jesus the Lord.

Preface of Easter I–V, pages **438–442.**

Communion Rite
Father, I want the men you have given me to be with me where I am, so that they may see the glory you have given me, alleluia. (John 17:24)

PRAYER AFTER COMMUNION

Let us pray.
Pause for silent prayer, if this has not preceded.
**Lord,
may this eucharist,
which we have celebrated in memory of your Son,
help us to grow in love.**

We ask this in the name of Jesus the Lord.

FIFTH SUNDAY OF EASTER

Introductory Rites

Sing to the Lord a new song, for he has done marvelous deeds; he has revealed to the nations his saving power, alleluia. (Ps. 97:1-2)

OPENING PRAYER

Let us pray
  [that we may enjoy true freedom]

Pause for silent prayer

God our Father,
look upon us with love.
You redeem us and make us your children in Christ.
Give us true freedom
and bring us to the inheritance you promised.

We ask this through our Lord Jesus Christ, your Son,
who lives and reigns with you and the Holy Spirit,
one God, for ever and ever.

ALTERNATIVE OPENING PRAYER

Let us pray
  [in the freedom of the sons of God]

Pause for silent prayer

Father of our Lord Jesus Christ,
you have revealed to the nations your saving power
and filled all ages with the words of a new song.
Hear the echo of this hymn.
Give us voice to sing your praise
throughout this season of joy.

We ask this through Christ our Lord.

LITURGY OF THE WORD

See Lectionary for Mass, nos. 53-55.

LITURGY OF THE EUCHARIST

PRAYER OVER THE GIFTS

Pray, brethren . . .

Lord God,
by this holy exchange of gifts
you share with us your divine life.
Grant that everything we do
may be directed by the knowledge of your truth.

We ask this in the name of Jesus the Lord.

Eucharistic Prayer:
Preface of Easter I-V, pages 438–442.

Communion Rite

> I am the vine and you are the branches, says the Lord; he who lives in me, and I in him, will bear much fruit, alleluia.
>
> (John 15:5)

A period of silence may be observed after communion, or a psalm or song of praise may be sung.

PRAYER AFTER COMMUNION

Let us pray.

Pause for silent prayer, if this has not preceded.

Merciful Father,
may these mysteries give us new purpose
and bring us to a new life in you.

Grant this through Christ our Lord.

SOLEMN BLESSING OR PRAYER OVER THE PEOPLE

The following may replace the simple blessing.

After the greeting, the deacon (or in his absence, the priest) gives the invitation in these or similar words:

Bow your heads and pray for God's blessing.

Then the priest extends his hands over the people while he sings or says:

Lord,
help your people to seek you with all their hearts
and to deserve what you promise.

Grant this through Christ our Lord.
℞. **Amen.**

May almighty God bless you,
the Father, and the Son, ✠ and the Holy Spirit.
℞. **Amen.**

For other texts of solemn blessings and prayers over the people, see pages **528–540.**

MONDAY OF THE FIFTH WEEK OF EASTER

Introductory Rites

> The Good Shepherd is risen! He who laid down his life for his sheep, who died for his flock, he is risen, alleluia.

OPENING PRAYER

**Father,
help us to seek the values
that will bring us eternal joy in this changing world.
In our desire for what you promise
make us one in mind and heart.**

**Grant this through our Lord Jesus Christ, your Son,
who lives and reigns with you and the Holy Spirit,
one God, for ever and ever.**

See Lectionary for Mass, no. 285.

PRAYER OVER THE GIFTS

Pray, brethren . . .

**Lord,
accept our prayers and offerings.
Make us worthy of your sacraments of love
by granting us your forgiveness.**

We ask this in the name of Jesus the Lord.

Preface of Easter I-V, pages 438–442.

Communion Rite

> The Lord says, peace I leave with you, my own peace I give you; not as the world gives, do I give, alleluia. (John 14:27)

PRAYER AFTER COMMUNION

Let us pray.
Pause for silent prayer, if this has not preceded.
**Almighty and ever-living Lord,
you restored us to life
by raising Christ from death.
Strengthen us by this Easter sacrament;
may we feel its saving power in our daily life.**

We ask this through Christ our Lord.

TUESDAY OF THE FIFTH WEEK OF EASTER

Introductory Rites

All you who fear God, both the great and the small, give
praise to him! For his salvation and strength have come,
the power of Christ, alleluia. (Rev. 19:5; 12:10)

OPENING PRAYER

**Father,
you restored your people to eternal life
by raising Christ your Son from death.
Make our faith strong and our hope sure.
May we never doubt that you will fulfill
the promises you have made.**

**Grant this through our Lord Jesus Christ, your Son,
who lives and reigns with you and the Holy Spirit,
one God, for ever and ever.**

See Lectionary for Mass, no. 286.

PRAYER OVER THE GIFTS

Pray, brethren . . .

**Lord,
receive these gifts from your Church.
May the great joy you give us
come to perfection in heaven.**

Grant this through Christ our Lord.

Preface of Easter I-V, pages 438–442.

Communion Rite

Because we have died with Christ, we believe that we shall
also come to life with him, alleluia. (Rom. 6:8)

PRAYER AFTER COMMUNION

Let us pray.
Pause for silent prayer, if this has not preceded.

**Lord,
look on your people with kindness
and by these Easter mysteries
bring us to the glory of the resurrection.**

We ask this in the name of Jesus the Lord.

WEDNESDAY OF THE FIFTH WEEK OF EASTER

Introductory Rites

Fill me with your praise and I will sing your glory; songs
of joy will be on my lips, alleluia. (Ps. 70:8, 23)

OPENING PRAYER

**Father of all holiness,
guide our hearts to you.
Keep in the light of your truth
all those you have freed from the darkness of unbelief.**

**We ask this through our Lord Jesus Christ, your Son,
who lives and reigns with you and the Holy Spirit,
one God, for ever and ever.**

See Lectionary for Mass, no. 287.

PRAYER OVER THE GIFTS

Pray, brethren . . .

**Lord,
restore us by these Easter mysteries.
May the continuing work of our Redeemer
bring us eternal joy.**

We ask this through Christ our Lord.

Preface of Easter I-V, pages **438–442.**

Communion Rite

Christ has risen and shines upon us, whom he has redeemed by his blood, alleluia.

PRAYER AFTER COMMUNION

Let us pray.

Pause for silent prayer, if this has not preceded.

**Lord,
may this celebration of our redemption
help us in this life
and lead us to eternal happiness.**

We ask this through Christ our Lord.

THURSDAY OF THE FIFTH WEEK OF EASTER

Introductory Rites

Let us sing to the Lord, he has covered himself in glory!
The Lord is my strength, and I praise him: he is the Savior
of my life, alleluia. (Exod. 15:1-2)

OPENING PRAYER

**Father,
in your love you have brought us
from evil to good and from misery to happiness.
Through your blessings
give the courage of perseverance
to those you have called and justified by faith.**

**Grant this through our Lord Jesus Christ, your Son,
who lives and reigns with you and the Holy Spirit,
one God, for ever and ever.**

See Lectionary for Mass, no. 288.

PRAYER OVER THE GIFTS

Pray, brethren . . .

**Lord God,
by this holy exchange of gifts
you share with us your divine life.
Grant that everything we do
may be directed by the knowledge of your truth.**

We ask this in the name of Jesus the Lord.

Preface of Easter I-V, pages **438–442.**

Communion Rite

Christ died for all, so that living men should not live for
themselves, but for Christ who died and was raised to life
for them, alleluia. (2 Cor. 5:15)

PRAYER AFTER COMMUNION

Let us pray.

Pause for silent prayer, if this has not preceded.

**Merciful Father,
may these mysteries give us new purpose
and bring us to a new life in you.**

Grant this through Christ our Lord.

FRIDAY OF THE FIFTH WEEK OF EASTER

Introductory Rites

> The Lamb who was slain is worthy to receive strength and divinity, wisdom and power and honor, alleluia. (Rev. 5:12)

OPENING PRAYER

**Lord,
by this Easter mystery
prepare us for eternal life.
May our celebration of Christ's death and resurrection
guide us to salvation.**

**We ask this through our Lord Jesus Christ, your Son,
who lives and reigns with you and the Holy Spirit,
one God, for ever and ever.**

See Lectionary for Mass, no. 289.

PRAYER OVER THE GIFTS

Pray, brethren . . .

**Merciful Lord,
make holy these gifts
and let our spiritual sacrifice
make us an everlasting gift to you.**

We ask this in the name of Jesus the Lord.

Preface of Easter I-V, pages **438–442.**

Communion Rite

> The man who died on the cross has risen from the dead,
> and has won back our lives from death, alleluia.

PRAYER AFTER COMMUNION

Let us pray.
Pause for silent prayer, if this has not preceded.
**Lord,
may this eucharist,
which we have celebrated in memory of your Son,
help us to grow in love.**

We ask this in the name of Jesus the Lord.

SATURDAY OF THE FIFTH WEEK OF EASTER

Introductory Rites

In baptism we have died with Christ, and we have risen to new life in him, because we believed in the power of God who raised him from the dead, alleluia. (Col. 2:12)

OPENING PRAYER

Loving Father,
through our rebirth in baptism
you give us your life and promise immortality.
By your unceasing care,
guide our steps toward the life of glory.

Grant this through our Lord Jesus Christ, your Son,
who lives and reigns with you and the Holy Spirit,
one God, for ever and ever.

See Lectionary for Mass, no. 290.

PRAYER OVER THE GIFTS

Pray, brethren . . .

Lord,
accept these gifts from your family.
May we hold fast to the life you have given us
and come to the eternal gifts you promise.

We ask this in the name of Jesus the Lord.

Preface of Easter I–V, pages 438–442.

Communion Rite

Father, I pray for them: may they be one in us, so that the world may believe it was you who sent me, alleluia. (John 17:20-21)

PRAYER AFTER COMMUNION

Let us pray.
Pause for silent prayer, if this has not preceded.

Lord,
watch over those you have saved in Christ.
May we who are redeemed by his suffering and death
always rejoice in his resurrection,
for he is Lord for ever and ever.

SIXTH SUNDAY OF EASTER

Introductory Rites

> Speak out with a voice of joy; let it be heard to the ends of the earth: The Lord has set his people free, alleluia. (See Is. 48:20)

OPENING PRAYER

Let us pray
   **[that we may practice in our lives
   the faith we profess]**
Pause for silent prayer

**Ever-living God,
help us to celebrate our joy
in the resurrection of the Lord
and to express in our lives
the love we celebrate.**

**Grant this through our Lord Jesus Christ, your Son,
who lives and reigns with you and the Holy Spirit,
one God, for ever and ever.**

ALTERNATIVE OPENING PRAYER

Let us pray
   [in silence, reflecting on the joy of Easter]
Pause for silent prayer

**God our Father, maker of all,
the crown of your creation was the Son of Man,
born of a woman, but without beginning;
he suffered for us but lives for ever.**

**May our mortal lives be crowned with the
   ultimate joy
of rising with him,
who is Lord for ever and ever.**

LITURGY OF THE WORD

See Lectionary for Mass, nos. 56-58.

LITURGY OF THE EUCHARIST

PRAYER OVER THE GIFTS

Pray, brethren . . .

**Lord,
accept our prayers and offerings.
Make us worthy of your sacraments of love
by granting us your forgiveness.**

We ask this in the name of Jesus the Lord.

Eucharistic Prayer:
Preface of Easter I-V, pages **438–442**.

Communion Rite

> If you love me, keep my commandments, says the Lord.
> The Father will send you the Holy Spirit, to be with you for
> ever, alleluia. (John 14:15-16)

A period of silence may be observed
after communion, or a psalm or song
of praise may be sung.

PRAYER AFTER COMMUNION

Let us pray.
Pause for silent prayer, if this has not preceded.
Almighty and ever-living Lord,
you restored us to life
by raising Christ from death.
Strengthen us by this Easter sacrament;
may we feel its saving power in our daily life.

We ask this through Christ our Lord.

**SOLEMN BLESSING OR PRAYER
OVER THE PEOPLE**

The following may replace the simple
blessing.

After the greeting, the deacon (or in
his absence, the priest) gives the invitation in these or similar words:

Bow your heads and pray for God's blessing.

Then the priest extends his hands
over the people while he sings or
says:

**Through the resurrection of his Son
God has redeemed you and made you his children.
May he bless you with joy.
℟. Amen.**

**The Redeemer has given you lasting freedom.
May you inherit his everlasting life.
℟. Amen.**

**By faith you rose with him in baptism.
May your lives be holy,
so that you will be united with him for ever.
℟. Amen.**

**May almighty God bless you,
the Father, and the Son, ✝ and the Holy Spirit.
℟. Amen.**

For other texts of solemn blessings and
prayers over the people, see pages
528–540.

MONDAY OF THE SIXTH WEEK OF EASTER

Introductory Rites

Christ now raised from the dead will never die again;
death no longer has power over him, alleluia. (Rom. 6:9)

OPENING PRAYER

**God of mercy,
may our celebration of your Son's resurrection
help us to experience its effect in our lives.**

**We ask this through our Lord Jesus Christ, your Son,
who lives and reigns with you and the Holy Spirit,
one God, for ever and ever.**

See Lectionary for Mass, no. 291.

PRAYER OVER THE GIFTS

Pray, brethren . . .

**Lord,
receive these gifts from your Church.
May the great joy you give us
come to perfection in heaven.**

Grant this through Christ our Lord.

Preface of Easter I-V, pages 438–442.

Communion Rite

Jesus came and stood among his disciples and said to
them: Peace be with you, alleluia. (John 20:19)

PRAYER AFTER COMMUNION

Let us pray.
Pause for silent prayer, if this has not preceded.
**Lord,
look on your people with kindness
and by these Easter mysteries
bring us to the glory of the resurrection.**

We ask this in the name of Jesus the Lord.

TUESDAY OF THE SIXTH WEEK OF EASTER

Introductory Rites

Let us shout out our joy and happiness, and give glory to
God, the Lord of all, because he is our King, alleluia.
(Rev. 19:7, 6)

OPENING PRAYER

God our Father,
may we look forward with hope to our resurrection,
for you have made us your sons and daughters,
and restored the joy of our youth.

We ask this through our Lord Jesus Christ, your Son,
who lives and reigns with you and the Holy Spirit,
one God, for ever and ever.

See Lectionary for Mass, no. 292.

PRAYER OVER THE GIFTS

Pray, brethren . . .

Lord,
give us joy by these Easter mysteries;
let the continuous offering of this sacrifice
by which we are renewed
bring us to eternal happiness.

We ask this in the name of Jesus the Lord.

Preface of Easter I-V, pages 438–442.

Communion Rite

Christ had to suffer and to rise from the dead, and so enter
into his glory, alleluia. (See Luke 24:46, 26)

PRAYER AFTER COMMUNION

Let us pray.
Pause for silent prayer, if this has not preceded.
Lord,
may this celebration of our redemption
help us in this life
and lead us to eternal happiness.

We ask this through Christ our Lord.

WEDNESDAY OF THE SIXTH WEEK OF EASTER

Introductory Rites

I will be a witness to you in the world, O Lord. I will spread
the knowledge of your name among my brothers, alleluia.
(Ps. 17:50; 21:23)

OPENING PRAYER

**Lord,
as we celebrate your Son's resurrection,
so may we rejoice with all the saints
when he returns in glory,
who lives and reigns with you and the Holy Spirit,
one God, for ever and ever.**

See Lectionary for Mass, no. 293.

PRAYER OVER THE GIFTS

Pray, brethren . . .

**Lord God,
by this holy exchange of gifts
you share with us your divine life.
Grant that everything we do
may be directed by the knowledge of your truth.**

We ask this in the name of Jesus the Lord.

Preface of Easter I–V, pages 438–442.

Communion Rite

The Lord says, I have chosen you from the world to go and
bear fruit that will last, alleluia. (See John 15:16, 19)

PRAYER AFTER COMMUNION

Let us pray.
Pause for silent prayer, if this has not preceded.
**Merciful Father,
may these mysteries give us new purpose
and bring us to a new life in you.**

Grant this through Christ our Lord.

THURSDAY OF THE SIXTH WEEK OF EASTER

Mass for the feast of the Ascension,
page 310.

This Mass is celebrated in countries
where the celebration of the Ascension is transferred to the Seventh
Sunday of Easter.

Introductory Rites

> When you walked at the head of your people, O God, and
> lived with them on their journey, the earth shook at your
> presence, and the skies poured forth their rain, alleluia.
> (See Ps. 67:8-9, 20)

OPENING PRAYER

**Father,
may we always give you thanks
for raising Christ our Lord to glory,
because we are his people
and share the salvation he won,
for he lives and reigns with you and the Holy Spirit,
one God, for ever and ever.**

See Lectionary for Mass, no. 294.

PRAYER OVER THE GIFTS

Pray, brethren . . .

**Lord,
accept our prayers and offerings.
Make us worthy of your sacraments of love
by granting us your forgiveness.**

We ask this in the name of Jesus the Lord.

Preface of Easter I-V, pages **438–442**.

Communion Rite

> I, the Lord, am with you always, until the end of the world,
> alleluia. (Matthew 28:20)

PRAYER AFTER COMMUNION

Let us pray.
Pause for silent prayer, if this has not preceded.
**Almighty and ever-living Lord,
you restored us to life
by raising Christ from death.
Strengthen us by this Easter sacrament;
may we feel its saving power in our daily life.**

We ask this through Christ our Lord.

FRIDAY OF THE SIXTH WEEK OF EASTER

Introductory Rites

By your blood, O Lord, you have redeemed us from every tribe and tongue, from every nation and people: you have made us into the kingdom of God, alleluia. (See Rev. 5:9-10)

OPENING PRAYER

Father,
you have given us eternal life
through Christ your Son who rose from the dead
and now sits at your right hand.
When he comes again in glory,
may he clothe with immortality
all who have been born again in baptism.
We ask this through our Lord Jesus Christ, your Son,
who lives and reigns with you and the Holy Spirit,
one God, for ever and ever.

See Lectionary for Mass, no. 295.

In countries where the Ascension is celebrated on the Seventh Sunday of Easter, the following opening prayer is said:

Lord,
hear our prayer
that your gospel may reach all men
and that we who receive salvation through your Word
may be your children in deed as well as in name.

We ask this through our Lord Jesus Christ, your Son,
who lives and reigns with you and the Holy Spirit,
one God, for ever and ever.

PRAYER OVER THE GIFTS

Pray, brethren . . .

Lord,
accept these gifts from your family.
May we hold fast to the life you have given us
and come to the eternal gifts you promise.

We ask this in the name of Jesus the Lord.

Preface of Easter I-V or Preface of Ascension I-II, pages **438–444.**

Communion Rite

Christ our Lord was put to death for our sins; and he rose again to make us worthy of life, alleluia. (Rom. 4:25)

PRAYER AFTER COMMUNION

Let us pray.
Pause for silent prayer, if this has not preceded.
Lord,
watch over those you have saved in Christ.
May we who are redeemed by his suffering and death
always rejoice in his resurrection,
for he is Lord for ever and ever.

SATURDAY OF THE SIXTH WEEK OF EASTER

Introductory Rites

> You are a people God claims as his own, to praise him who called you out of darkness into his marvelous light, alleluia. (1 Peter 2:9)

OPENING PRAYER

Father,
at your Son's ascension into heaven
you promised to send the Holy Spirit on your
**   apostles.**
You filled them with heavenly wisdom:
fill us also with the gift of your Spirit.

Grant this through our Lord Jesus Christ, your
**   Son,**
who lives and reigns with you and the Holy
**   Spirit,**
one God, for ever and ever.

In countries where the Ascension is celebrated on the Seventh Sunday of Easter, the following opening prayer is said:

Lord,
teach us to know you better
by doing good to others.
Help us to grow in your love
and come to understand the eternal mystery
of Christ's death and resurrection.

We ask this through our Lord Jesus Christ,
**   your Son,**
who lives and reigns with you and the Holy
**   Spirit,**
one God, for ever and ever.

See Lectionary for Mass, no. 296.

PRAYER OVER THE GIFTS   **Pray, brethren . . .**

Merciful Lord,
make holy these gifts,
and let our spiritual sacrifice
make us an everlasting gift to you.

We ask this in the name of Jesus the Lord.

Preface of Easter I-V or Preface of Ascension I-II, pages **438–444.**

Communion Rite

> Father, I want the men you have given me to be with me where I am, so that they may see the glory you have given me, alleluia. (John 17:24)

PRAYER AFTER COMMUNION   **Let us pray.**

Pause for silent prayer, if this has not preceded.

Lord,
may this eucharist,
which we have celebrated in memory of your Son,
help us to grow in love.

We ask this in the name of Jesus the Lord.

ASCENSION

Introductory Rites

> Men of Galilee, why do you stand looking in the sky? The
> Lord will return, just as you have seen him ascend, alleluia.
> (Acts 1:11)

OPENING PRAYER

Let us pray
  [that the risen Christ
    will lead us to eternal life]

Pause for silent prayer

God our Father,
make us joyful in the ascension of your Son
  Jesus Christ.
May we follow him into the new creation,
for his ascension is our glory and our hope.

We ask this through our Lord Jesus Christ,
  your Son,
who lives and reigns with you and the Holy
  Spirit,
one God, for ever and ever.

ALTERNATIVE OPENING PRAYER

Let us pray
  [on this day of Ascension as we watch and
    wait for Jesus' return]

Pause for silent prayer

Father in heaven,
our minds were prepared for the coming of
  your kingdom
when you took Christ beyond our sight
so that we might seek him in his glory.

May we follow where he has led
and find our hope in his glory,
for he is Lord for ever.

LITURGY OF THE WORD

See Lectionary for Mass, no. 59.

LITURGY OF THE EUCHARIST

PRAYER OVER THE GIFTS

Pray, brethren . . .

Lord,
receive our offering
as we celebrate the ascension of Christ your Son.
May his gifts help us rise with him
to the joys of heaven,
where he lives and reigns for ever and ever.

Eucharistic Prayer:

Preface of Ascension I-II, pages
443–444.

When Eucharistic Prayer I is used, the
special Ascension form of In union
with the whole Church is said.

Communion Rite

I, the Lord, am with you always, until the end of the world, alleluia. (Matthew 28:20)

A period of silence may be observed after communion, or a psalm or song of praise may be sung.

PRAYER AFTER COMMUNION

Let us pray.
Pause for silent prayer, if this has not preceded.
Father,
in this eucharist
we touch the divine life you give to the world.
Help us to follow Christ with love
to eternal life where he is Lord for ever and ever.

SOLEMN BLESSING OR PRAYER OVER THE PEOPLE

The following may replace the simple blessing.

After the greeting, the deacon (or in his absence, the priest) gives the invitation in these or similar words:

Then the priest extends his hands over the people while he sings or says:

Bow your heads and pray for God's blessing.

May almighty God bless you on this day
when his only Son ascended into heaven
to prepare a place for you.
℞. Amen.

After his resurrection, Christ was seen by his disciples.
When he appears as judge
may you be pleasing for ever in his sight.
℞. Amen.

You believe that Jesus has taken his seat in majesty
at the right hand of the Father.
May you have the joy of experiencing
that he is also with you to the end of time,
according to his promise.
℞. Amen.

May almighty God bless you,
the Father, and the Son, ✝ and the Holy Spirit.
℞. Amen.

For other texts of solemn blessings and prayers over the people, see pages 528–540.

Where the solemnity of the Ascension is not observed as a holyday of obligation, it is assigned to the Seventh Sunday of Easter, which is then considered its proper day in the calendar.

SEVENTH SUNDAY OF EASTER

Introductory Rites

> Lord, hear my voice when I call to you. My heart has prompted me to seek your face; I seek it, Lord; do not hide from me, alleluia. (Ps. 26:7-9)

OPENING PRAYER

Let us pray
  [that we may recognize the presence of
  Christ in our midst]
Pause for silent prayer
**Father,
help us keep in mind that Christ our Savior
lives with you in glory
and promised to remain with us until the end
  of time.
We ask this through our Lord Jesus Christ,
  your Son,
who lives and reigns with you and the Holy
  Spirit,
one God, for ever and ever.**

ALTERNATIVE OPENING PRAYER

Let us pray
  [to our Father who has raised
  us to life in Christ]
Pause for silent prayer
**Eternal Father,
reaching from end to end of the universe,
and ordering all things with your mighty arm:
for you, time is the unfolding of truth that
  already is,
the unveiling of beauty that is yet to be.
Your Son has saved us in history
by rising from the dead,
so that transcending time he might free us
  from death.
May his presence among us
lead to the vision of unlimited truth
and unfold the beauty of your love.**

We ask this in the name of Jesus the Lord.

LITURGY OF THE WORD

See Lectionary for Mass, nos. 60-62.

LITURGY OF THE EUCHARIST

PRAYER OVER THE GIFTS

Pray, brethren . . .

**Lord,
accept the prayers and gifts
we offer in faith and love.
May this eucharist
bring us to your glory.
Grant this through Christ our Lord.**

Eucharistic Prayer:
Preface of Easter I-V or Preface of Ascension I-II, pages 438–444.

Communion Rite
> This is the prayer of Jesus: that his believers may become
> one as he is one with the Father, alleluia. (John 17:22)

A period of silence may be observed after communion, or a psalm or song of praise may be sung.

PRAYER AFTER COMMUNION

Let us pray.
Pause for silent prayer, if this has not preceded.
**God our Savior,
hear us,
and through this holy mystery give us hope
that the glory you have given Christ
will be given to the Church, his body,
for he is Lord for ever and ever.**

SOLEMN BLESSING OR PRAYER OVER THE PEOPLE

The following may replace the simple blessing.

After the greeting, the deacon (or in his absence, the priest) gives the invitation in these or similar words:

Then the priest extends his hands over the people while he sings or says:

Bow your heads and pray for God's blessing.

**Father,
help your people to rejoice in the mystery of redemption
and to win its reward.**

We ask this in the name of Jesus the Lord.
℟. **Amen.**

**May almighty God bless you,
the Father, and the Son, ✛ and the Holy Spirit.**
℟. **Amen.**

For other texts of solemn blessings and prayers over the people, see pages 528–540.

MONDAY OF THE SEVENTH WEEK OF EASTER

Introductory Rites

You will receive power when the Holy Spirit comes upon you. You will be my witnesses to all the world, alleluia. (Acts 1:8)

OPENING PRAYER

**Lord,
send the power of your Holy Spirit upon us
that we may remain faithful
and do your will in our daily lives.**

**We ask this through our Lord Jesus Christ, your Son,
who lives and reigns with you and the Holy Spirit,
one God, for ever and ever.**

See Lectionary for Mass, no. 297.

PRAYER OVER THE GIFTS

Pray, brethren . . .

**Lord,
may these gifts cleanse us from sin
and make our hearts live with your gift of grace.**

Grant this through Christ our Lord.

Preface of Easter I-V or Preface of Ascension I-II, pages **438–444.**

Communion Rite

The Lord said: I will not leave you orphans. I will come back to you, and your hearts will rejoice, alleluia. (John 14:18; 16:22)

PRAYER AFTER COMMUNION

Let us pray.
Pause for silent prayer, if this has not preceded.
**Merciful Father,
may these mysteries give us new purpose
and bring us to a new life in you.**

Grant this through Christ our Lord.

TUESDAY OF THE SEVENTH WEEK OF EASTER

Introductory Rites
I am the beginning and the end of all things. I have met
death, but I am alive, and I shall live for eternity, alleluia.
(Rev. 1:17-18)

OPENING PRAYER

**God of power and mercy,
send your Holy Spirit
to live in our hearts
and make us temples of his glory.**

**We ask this through our Lord Jesus Christ, your Son,
who lives and reigns with you and the Holy Spirit,
one God, for ever and ever.**

See Lectionary for Mass, no. 298.

PRAYER OVER THE GIFTS

Pray, brethren . . .

**Father,
accept the prayers and offerings of your people
and bring us to the glory of heaven,
where Jesus is Lord for ever and ever.**

Preface of Easter I-V or Preface of Ascension I-II, pages 438–444.

Communion Rite
The Lord says, the Holy Spirit whom the Father will send in
my name will teach you all things, and remind you of all
I have said to you, alleluia. (John 14:26)

PRAYER AFTER COMMUNION

Let us pray.
Pause for silent prayer, if this has not preceded.
**Lord,
may this eucharist,
which we have celebrated in memory of your Son,
help us to grow in love.**

We ask this in the name of Jesus the Lord.

WEDNESDAY OF THE SEVENTH WEEK OF EASTER

Introductory Rites
All nations, clap your hands. Shout with a voice of joy to God, alleluia. (Ps. 46:2)

OPENING PRAYER

**God of mercy,
unite your Church in the Holy Spirit
that we may serve you with all our hearts
and work together with unselfish love.**

**Grant this through our Lord Jesus Christ, your Son,
who lives and reigns with you and the Holy Spirit,
one God, for ever and ever.**

See Lectionary for Mass, no. 299.

PRAYER OVER THE GIFTS

Pray, brethren . . .

**Lord,
accept this offering we make at your command.
May these sacred mysteries by which we worship you
bring your salvation to perfection within us.**

We ask this in the name of Jesus the Lord.

Preface of Easter I-V or Preface of Ascension I-II, pages **438–444.**

Communion Rite
The Lord says: When the Holy Spirit comes to you, the Spirit whom I shall send, the Spirit of truth who proceeds from the Father, he will bear witness to me, and you also will be my witnesses, alleluia. (John 15:26-27)

PRAYER AFTER COMMUNION

Let us pray.

Pause for silent prayer, if this has not preceded.
**Lord,
may our participation in the eucharist
increase your life in us,
cleanse us from sin,
and make us increasingly worthy of this holy sacrament.**

We ask this through Christ our Lord.

THURSDAY OF THE SEVENTH WEEK OF EASTER

Introductory Rites

Let us come to God's presence with confidence, because
we will find mercy, and strength when we need it, alleluia.
(Heb. 4:16)

OPENING PRAYER

**Father,
let your Spirit come upon us with power
to fill us with his gifts.
May he make our hearts pleasing to you,
and ready to do your will.**

**We ask this through our Lord Jesus Christ, your Son,
who lives and reigns with you and the Holy Spirit,
one God, for ever and ever.**

See Lectionary for Mass, no. 300.

PRAYER OVER THE GIFTS

Pray, brethren . . .

**Merciful Lord,
make holy these gifts,
and let our spiritual sacrifice
make us an everlasting gift to you.**

We ask this in the name of Jesus the Lord.

Preface of Easter I-V or Preface of Ascension I-II, pages 438–444.

Communion Rite

This is the word of Jesus: It is best for me to leave you;
because if I do not go, the Spirit will not come to you,
alleluia. (John 16:7)

PRAYER AFTER COMMUNION

Let us pray.
Pause for silent prayer, if this has not preceded.
**Lord,
renew us by the mysteries we have shared.
Help us to know you
and prepare us for the gifts of the Spirit.**

We ask this through Christ our Lord.

FRIDAY OF THE SEVENTH WEEK OF EASTER

Introductory Rites
> Christ loved us and has washed away our sins with his
> blood, and has made us a kingdom of priests to serve his
> God and Father, alleluia. (Rev. 1:5-6)

OPENING PRAYER

Father,
in glorifying Christ and sending us your Spirit,
you open the way to eternal life.
May our sharing in this gift increase our love
and make our faith grow stronger.

Grant this through our Lord Jesus Christ, your Son,
who lives and reigns with you and the Holy Spirit,
one God, for ever and ever.

See Lectionary for Mass, no. 301.

PRAYER OVER THE GIFTS

Pray, brethren . . .

Father of love and mercy,
we place our offering before you.
Send your Holy Spirit to cleanse our lives
so that our gifts may be acceptable.

We ask this through Christ our Lord.

Preface of Easter I-V or Preface of Ascension I-II, pages **438–444.**

Communion Rite
> When the Spirit of truth comes, says the Lord, he will lead
> you to the whole truth, alleluia. (John 16:13)

PRAYER AFTER COMMUNION

Let us pray.
Pause for silent prayer, if this has not preceded.
God our Father,
the eucharist is our bread of life
and the sacrament of our forgiveness.
May our sharing in this mystery
bring us to eternal life,
where Jesus is Lord for ever and ever.

SATURDAY OF THE SEVENTH WEEK OF EASTER

Morning Mass

Introductory Rites

The disciples were constantly at prayer together, with Mary the mother of Jesus, the other women, and the brothers of Jesus, alleluia. (Acts 1:14)

OPENING PRAYER

**Almighty Father,
let the love we have celebrated in this Easter season
be put into practice in our daily lives.**

**We ask this through our Lord Jesus Christ, your Son,
who lives and reigns with you and the Holy Spirit,
one God, for ever and ever.**

See Lectionary for Mass, no. 302.

PRAYER OVER THE GIFTS

Pray, brethren . . .

**Lord,
may the coming of the Holy Spirit
prepare us to receive these holy sacraments,
for he is our forgiveness.**

We ask this in the name of Jesus the Lord.

Preface of Easter I-V or Preface of Ascension I-II, pages 438–444.

Communion Rite

The Lord says: The Holy Spirit will give glory to me, because he takes my words from me and will hand them on to you, alleluia. (John 16:14)

PRAYER AFTER COMMUNION

Let us pray.

Pause for silent prayer, if this has not preceded.

**Father of mercy,
hear our prayers
that we may leave our former selves behind
and serve you with holy and renewed hearts.**

Grant this through Christ our Lord.

PENTECOST

Vigil Mass

This Mass is celebrated on Saturday
evening before or after Evening
Prayer I of Pentecost.

Introductory Rites

The love of God has been poured into our hearts by his Spirit
living in us, alleluia. (See Rom. 5:5; 8:11)

OPENING PRAYER

Let us pray
  [**that the Holy Spirit may bring peace and**
     unity to all mankind]

Pause for silent prayer

Almighty and ever-living God,
you fulfilled the Easter promise
by sending us your Holy Spirit.
May that Spirit unite the races and nations
   on earth
to proclaim your glory.

Grant this through our Lord Jesus Christ,
   your Son,
who lives and reigns with you and the Holy
   Spirit,
one God, for ever and ever.

Or:

God our Father,
you have given us new birth.
Strengthen us with your Holy Spirit
and fill us with your light.

Grant this through our Lord Jesus Christ, your Son,
who lives and reigns with you and the Holy Spirit,
one God, for ever and ever.

ALTERNATIVE OPENING PRAYER

Let us pray
  [**that the flame of the Spirit will**
     descend upon us]

Pause for silent prayer

Father in heaven,
fifty days have celebrated the fullness
of the mystery of your revealed love.
See your people gathered in prayer,
open to receive the Spirit's flame.
May it come to rest in our hearts
and disperse the divisions of word and tongue.
With one voice and one song
may we praise your name in joy and thanksgiving.

Grant this through Christ our Lord.

LITURGY OF THE WORD

See Lectionary for Mass, no. 63.

LITURGY OF THE EUCHARIST

PRAYER OVER THE GIFTS

Pray, brethren . . .

Lord,
send your Spirit on these gifts
and through them help the Church you love
to show your salvation to all the world.

We ask this in the name of Jesus the Lord.

Eucharistic Prayer:

Preface of Pentecost, page **445**.

When Eucharistic Prayer I is used, the special Pentecost form of **In union with the whole Church** is said.

Communion Rite

> On the last day of the festival, Jesus stood and cried aloud:
> If anyone is thirsty, let him come to me and drink, alleluia.
> (John 7:37)

A period of silence may be observed after communion, or a psalm or song of praise may be sung.

PRAYER AFTER COMMUNION

Let us pray.

Pause for silent prayer, if this has not preceded.

**Lord,
through this eucharist,
send the Holy Spirit of Pentecost into our hearts
to keep us always in your love.**

We ask this through Christ our Lord.

SOLEMN BLESSING OR PRAYER OVER THE PEOPLE

The following may replace the simple blessing.

After the greeting, the deacon (or in his absence, the priest) gives the invitation in these or similar words:

Bow your heads and pray for God's blessing.

Then the priest extends his hands over the people while he sings or says:

**Lord God,
in your great mercy,
enrich your people with your grace
and strengthen them by your blessing
so that they may praise you always.**

Grant this through Christ our Lord.
℟. **Amen.**

**May almighty God bless you,
the Father, and the Son, ✛ and the Holy Spirit.**
℟. **Amen.**

For other texts of solemn blessings and prayers over the people, see pages **528–540**.

PENTECOST

Mass during the Day

Introductory Rites

The Spirit of the Lord fills the whole world. It holds all things together and knows every word spoken by man, alleluia. (Wis. 1:7)

or:

The love of God has been poured into our hearts by his Spirit living in us, alleluia. (See Rom. 5:5; 8:11)

OPENING PRAYER

Let us pray
[that the Spirit will work through our lives
to bring Christ to the world]
Pause for silent prayer
God our Father,
let the Spirit you sent on your Church
to begin the teaching of the gospel
continue to work in the world
through the hearts of all who believe.

We ask this through our Lord Jesus Christ,
your Son,
who lives and reigns with you and the Holy
Spirit,
one God, for ever and ever.

ALTERNATIVE OPENING PRAYER

Let us pray
[in the Spirit who dwells within us]
Pause for silent prayer
Father of light, from whom every good gift
comes,
send your Spirit into our lives
with the power of a mighty wind,
and by the flame of your wisdom
open the horizons of our minds.
Loosen our tongues to sing your praise
in words beyond the power of speech,
for without your Spirit
man could never raise his voice in words of
peace
or announce the truth that Jesus is Lord,
who lives and reigns with you and the Holy
Spirit,
one God, for ever and ever.

LITURGY OF THE WORD

See Lectionary for Mass, no. 64.

LITURGY OF THE EUCHARIST

PRAYER OVER THE GIFTS

Pray, brethren . . .

Lord,
may the Spirit you promised
lead us into all truth
and reveal to us the full meaning of this sacrifice.

Grant this through Christ our Lord.

Eucharistic Prayer:
Preface of Pentecost, page 445.

When Eucharistic Prayer I is used, the special Pentecost form of In union with the whole Church is said.

Communion Rite

They were all filled with the Holy Spirit, and they spoke of the great things God had done, alleluia. (Acts 2:4, 11)

A period of silence may be observed after communion, or a psalm or song of praise may be sung.

PRAYER AFTER COMMUNION

Let us pray.
Pause for silent prayer, if this has not preceded.
**Father,
may the food we receive in the eucharist
help our eternal redemption.
Keep within us the vigor of your Spirit
and protect the gifts you have given to your Church.**

We ask this in the name of Jesus the Lord.

SOLEMN BLESSING OR PRAYER OVER THE PEOPLE

The following may replace the simple blessing.

After the greeting, the deacon (or in his absence, the priest) gives the invitation in these or similar words:

Then the priest extends his hands over the people while he sings or says:

Bow your heads and pray for God's blessing.

**This day the Father of light
has enlightened the minds of the disciples
by the outpouring of the Holy Spirit.
May he bless you
and give you the gifts of the Spirit for ever.**
℟. **Amen.**

**May that fire which hovered over the disciples
as tongues of flame
burn out all evil from your hearts
and make them glow with pure light.**
℟. **Amen.**

**God inspired speech in different tongues
to proclaim one faith.
May he strengthen your faith
and fulfill your hope to see him face to face.**
℟. **Amen.**

For other texts of solemn blessings and prayers over the people, see pages 528–540.

At the end of the Easter season, the Easter candle should be kept in the baptistery with due honor. During the celebration of baptism, the candles of the newly baptized are lighted from it. The Easter candle may also be used in funeral Masses in place of the lighted candles near the casket.

**May almighty God bless you,
the Father, and the Son, ✠ and the Holy Spirit.**
℟. **Amen.**

The deacon (or the priest), with hands joined, sings or says:

a   ℣. **Go in the peace of Christ, alleluia, alleluia.**

b   ℣. **The Mass is ended, go in peace, alleluia, alleluia.**

c   ℣. **Go in peace to love and serve the Lord, alleluia, alleluia.**

℟. **Thanks be to God, alleluia, alleluia.**

ORDINARY TIME

Ordinary time includes thirty-three or thirty-four weeks. It begins on Monday after the Sunday which follows January 6 and continues until the beginning of Lent; it begins again on Monday after Pentecost Sunday and ends on Saturday before the first Sunday of Advent.

The missal thus has thirty-four Masses for the Sundays and weekdays of this time. They are used as follows:

a) On Sundays the Mass corresponding to the number of that ordinary Sunday is used, unless there is a solemnity or a feast which replaces the Sunday.

b) On weekdays any of the thirty-four Masses may be celebrated, according to the pastoral needs of the people.

The ordinary Sundays and weekdays are computed in this way:

a) The Sunday when the feast of the Baptism of the Lord is celebrated replaces the first ordinary Sunday, but the week that follows is counted as the first ordinary week. The other Sundays and weeks are numbered in order until the beginning of Lent.

b) If the number of ordinary weeks is thirty-four, after Pentecost the series is resumed with the week which follows immediately the last week celebrated before Lent. The Masses of Pentecost, Trinity, [and in countries where the solemnity of the Body and Blood of Christ is not observed as a holyday of obligation and is therefore celebrated on the following Sunday] the Solemnity of the Body and Blood of Christ replace the Sunday Masses in these weeks. If the number of ordinary weeks is thirty-three, the first week which would otherwise follow Pentecost is omitted.

The *Gloria* and the profession of faith are sung or said on Sundays; they are omitted on weekdays.

On Sundays one of the prefaces for Sundays in ordinary time is sung or said; on weekdays, a weekday preface.

Two antiphons are given for communion, the first from the psalms, the second for the most part from the gospel. Either one may be selected, but preference should be given to the antiphon which may happen to come from the gospel of the Mass.

ORDINARY TIME

FIRST WEEK IN ORDINARY TIME

The feast of the Baptism of the Lord
takes the place of the First Sunday in
Ordinary Time.

Introductory Rites

I saw a man sitting on a high throne, being worshiped by
a great number of angels who were singing together: This
is he whose kingdom will last for ever.

OPENING PRAYER

Let us pray
[that we will know and do what God wills]

Pause for silent prayer

Father of love,
hear our prayers.
Help us to know your will
and to do it with courage and faith.

Grant this through our Lord Jesus Christ, your Son,
who lives and reigns with you and the Holy Spirit,
one God, for ever and ever.

PRAYER OVER THE GIFTS

Pray, brethren . . .

Lord,
accept our offering
Make us grow in holiness
and grant what we ask you in faith.

We ask this in the name of Jesus the Lord.

Communion Rite

Lord, you are the source of life, and in the light of your
glory we find happiness. (Ps. 35:10)

or:

I came that men may have life, and have it to the full, says
the Lord. (John 10:10)

PRAYER AFTER COMMUNION

Let us pray.

Pause for silent prayer, if this has not preceded.

All-powerful God,
you renew us with your sacraments.
Help us to thank you by lives of faithful service.

We ask this through Christ our Lord.

325

SECOND SUNDAY IN ORDINARY TIME

Introductory Rites

> May all the earth give you worship and praise, and break
> into song to your name, O God, Most High. (Ps. 65:4)

OPENING PRAYER

Let us pray
  [to our Father for the gift of peace]
Pause for silent prayer
**Father of heaven and earth,
hear our prayers,
and show us the way to peace in the world.**

**Grant this through our Lord Jesus Christ, your
  Son,
who lives and reigns with you and the Holy
  Spirit,
one God, for ever and ever.**

ALTERNATIVE OPENING PRAYER

Let us pray
  [for the gift of peace]
Pause for silent prayer
**Almighty and ever-present Father,
your watchful care reaches from end to end
and orders all things in such power
that even the tensions and the tragedies of sin
cannot frustrate your loving plans.
Help us to embrace your will,
give us the strength to follow your call,
so that your truth may live in our hearts
and reflect peace to those who believe in your
  love.**

We ask this in the name of Jesus the Lord.

LITURGY OF THE WORD

See Lectionary for Mass, nos. 65-67.

LITURGY OF THE EUCHARIST

PRAYER OVER THE GIFTS

Pray, brethren . . .

**Father,
may we celebrate the eucharist
with reverence and love,
for when we proclaim the death of the Lord
you continue the work of his redemption,
who is Lord for ever and ever.**

Eucharistic Prayer:
Preface of Sundays in Ordinary Time
I-VIII, pages 446–453.

Communion Rite

The Lord has prepared a feast for me: given wine in plenty for me to drink. (Ps. 22:5)

or:

We know and believe in God's love for us. (1 John 4:16)

A period of silence may be observed after communion, or a psalm or song of praise may be sung.

PRAYER AFTER COMMUNION

Let us pray.

Pause for silent prayer, if this has not preceded.

Lord,
you have nourished us with bread from heaven.
Fill us with your Spirit,
and make us one in peace and love.

We ask this through Christ our Lord.

On Sundays in ordinary time, the priest may choose the solemn blessing (pages **528–536)** or prayer over the people (pages **537–540)** to replace the simple blessing.

THIRD SUNDAY IN ORDINARY TIME

Introductory Rites

Sing a new song to the Lord! Sing to the Lord, all the earth.
Truth and beauty surround him, he lives in holiness and
glory. (Ps. 95:1, 6)

OPENING PRAYER

**Let us pray
[for unity and peace]**
Pause for silent prayer
**All-powerful and ever-living God,
direct your love that is within us,
that our efforts in the name of your Son
may bring mankind to unity and peace.**

**We ask this through our Lord Jesus Christ,
your Son,
who lives and reigns with you and the Holy
Spirit,
one God, for ever and ever.**

ALTERNATIVE OPENING PRAYER

**Let us pray
[pleading that our vision may overcome
our weakness]**
Pause for silent prayer
**Almighty Father,
the love you offer
always exceeds the furthest expression of our
human longing,
for you are greater than the human heart.
Direct each thought, each effort of our life,
so that the limits of our faults and weaknesses
may not obscure the vision of your glory
or keep us from the peace you have promised.**

We ask this through Christ our Lord.

LITURGY OF THE WORD

See Lectionary for Mass, nos. 68-70.

LITURGY OF THE EUCHARIST

PRAYER OVER THE GIFTS

Pray, brethren . . .

**Lord,
receive our gifts.
Let our offerings make us holy
and bring us salvation.**

Grant this through Christ our Lord.

Eucharistic Prayer:
Preface of Sundays in Ordinary Time
I-VIII, pages **446–453.**

Communion Rite

Look up at the Lord with gladness and smile; your face will never be ashamed. (Ps. 33:6)

or:

I am the light of the world, says the Lord; the man who follows me will have the light of life. (John 8:12)

A period of silence may be observed after communion, or a psalm or song of praise may be sung.

PRAYER AFTER COMMUNION

Let us pray.

Pause for silent prayer, if this has not preceded.

**God, all-powerful Father,
may the new life you give us increase our love
and keep us in the joy of your kingdom.**

We ask this in the name of Jesus the Lord.

FOURTH SUNDAY IN ORDINARY TIME

Introductory Rites

> Save us, Lord our God, and gather us together from the nations, that we may proclaim your holy name and glory in your praise. (Ps. 105:47)

OPENING PRAYER

Let us pray
  **[for a greater love of God
  and of our fellow men]**

Pause for silent prayer

**Lord our God,
help us to love you with all our hearts
and to love all men as you love them.**

**Grant this through our Lord Jesus Christ, your Son,
who lives and reigns with you and the Holy Spirit,
one God, for ever and ever.**

ALTERNATIVE OPENING PRAYER

Let us pray
  **[joining in the praise of the living God
  for we are his people]**

Pause for silent prayer

**Father in heaven,
from the days of Abraham and Moses
until this gathering of your Church in prayer,
you have formed a people in the image of your Son.**

Bless this people with the gift of your kingdom.

**May we serve you with our every desire
and show love for one another
even as you have loved us.**

Grant this through Christ our Lord.

LITURGY OF THE WORD

See Lectionary for Mass, nos. 71-73.

LITURGY OF THE EUCHARIST

PRAYER OVER THE GIFTS

Pray, brethren . . .

**Lord,
be pleased with the gifts we bring to your altar,
and make them the sacrament of our salvation.**

We ask this through Christ our Lord.

Eucharistic Prayer:
Preface of Sundays in Ordinary Time
I-VIII, pages **446–453**.

Communion Rite

> Let your face shine on your servant, and save me by your love. Lord, keep me from shame, for I have called to you.
> (Ps. 30:17-18)
>
> or:
>
> Happy are the poor in spirit; the kingdom of heaven is theirs! Happy are the lowly; they shall inherit the land.
> (Matthew 5:3-4)

A period of silence may be observed after communion, or a psalm or song of praise may be sung.

PRAYER AFTER COMMUNION

Let us pray.
Pause for silent prayer, if this has not preceded.
Lord,
you invigorate us with this help to our salvation.
By this eucharist give the true faith continued growth throughout the world.

We ask this in the name of Jesus the Lord.

FIFTH SUNDAY IN ORDINARY TIME

Introductory Rites

Come, let us worship the Lord. Let us bow down in the presence of our maker, for he is the Lord our God. (Ps. 94:6-7)

OPENING PRAYER

Let us pray
   **[that God will watch over us
   and protect us]**
Pause for silent prayer
Father,
watch over your family
and keep us safe in your care,
for all our hope is in you.

Grant this through our Lord Jesus Christ, your Son,
who lives and reigns with you and the Holy Spirit,
one God, for ever and ever.

ALTERNATIVE OPENING PRAYER

Let us pray
   **[with reverence in the presence
   of the living God]**
Pause for silent prayer
In faith and love we ask you, Father,
to watch over your family gathered here.
In your mercy and loving kindness
no thought of ours is left unguarded,
no tear unheeded, no joy unnoticed.
Through the prayer of Jesus
may the blessings promised to the poor in spirit
lead us to the treasures of your heavenly kingdom.

We ask this in the name of Jesus the Lord.

LITURGY OF THE WORD

See Lectionary for Mass, nos. 74-76.

LITURGY OF THE EUCHARIST

PRAYER OVER THE GIFTS

Pray, brethren . . .

Lord our God,
may the bread and wine
you give us for our nourishment on earth
become the sacrament of our eternal life.

We ask this through Christ our Lord.

Eucharistic Prayer:
Preface of Sundays in Ordinary Time
I-VIII, pages **446–453**.

Communion Rite

Give praise to the Lord for his kindness, for his wonderful deeds toward men. He has filled the hungry with good things, he has satisfied the thirsty. (Ps. 106:8-9)

or:

Happy are the sorrowing; they shall be consoled. Happy those who hunger and thirst for what is right; they shall be satisfied. (Matthew 5:5-6)

A period of silence may be observed after communion, or a psalm or song of praise may be sung.

PRAYER AFTER COMMUNION

Let us pray.
Pause for silent prayer, if this has not preceded.
**God our Father,
you give us a share in the one bread and the one cup
and make us one in Christ.
Help us to bring your salvation and joy
to all the world.**

We ask this through Christ our Lord.

SIXTH SUNDAY IN ORDINARY TIME

Introductory Rites

Lord, be my rock of safety, the stronghold that saves me.
For the honor of your name, lead me and guide me. (Ps. 30:3-4)

OPENING PRAYER

Let us pray
  [that everything we do will be guided
   by God's law of love]
Pause for silent prayer

God our Father,
you have promised to remain for ever
with those who do what is just and right.
Help us to live in your presence.

We ask this through our Lord Jesus Christ,
   your Son,
who lives and reigns with you and the Holy
   Spirit,
one God, for ever and ever.

ALTERNATIVE OPENING PRAYER

Let us pray
  [for the wisdom that is greater than
   human words]
Pause for silent prayer

Father in heaven,
the loving plan of your wisdom took flesh
   in Jesus Christ,
and changed mankind's history
by his command of perfect love.
May our fulfillment of his command reflect
   your wisdom
and bring your salvation to the ends of the
   earth.

We ask this through Christ our Lord.

LITURGY OF THE WORD

See Lectionary for Mass, nos. 77-79.

LITURGY OF THE EUCHARIST

PRAYER OVER THE GIFTS

Pray, brethren . . .

Lord,
we make this offering in obedience to your word.
May it cleanse and renew us,
and lead us to our eternal reward.

We ask this in the name of Jesus the Lord.

Eucharistic Prayer:
Preface of Sundays in Ordinary Time
I-VIII, pages **446–453.**

Communion Rite

They ate and were filled; the Lord gave them what they wanted: they were not deprived of their desire. (Ps. 77:29-30)

or:

God loved the world so much, he gave his only Son, that all who believe in him might not perish, but might have eternal life. (John 3:16)

A period of silence may be observed after communion, or a psalm or song of praise may be sung.

PRAYER AFTER COMMUNION

Let us pray.
Pause for silent prayer, if this has not preceded.
Lord,
you give us food from heaven.
May we always hunger
for the bread of life.

Grant this through Christ our Lord.

SEVENTH SUNDAY IN ORDINARY TIME

Introductory Rites

Lord, your mercy is my hope, my heart rejoices in your saving power. I will sing to the Lord for his goodness to me. (Ps. 12:6)

OPENING PRAYER

Let us pray
 [that God will make us more
  like Christ, his Son]
Pause for silent prayer
Father,
keep before us the wisdom and love
you have revealed in your Son.
Help us to be like him
in word and deed,
for he lives and reigns with you and the Holy
  Spirit,
one God, for ever and ever.

ALTERNATIVE OPENING PRAYER

Let us pray
 [to the God of power and might,
  for his mercy is our hope]
Pause for silent prayer
Almighty God,
Father of our Lord Jesus Christ,
faith in your word is the way to wisdom,
and to ponder your divine plan is to grow in
  the truth.
Open our eyes to your deeds,
our ears to the sound of your call,
so that our every act may increase our sharing
in the life you have offered us.

Grant this through Christ our Lord.

LITURGY OF THE WORD

See Lectionary for Mass, nos. 80-82.

LITURGY OF THE EUCHARIST

PRAYER OVER THE GIFTS

Pray, brethren . . .

Lord,
as we make this offering,
may our worship in Spirit and truth
bring us salvation.

We ask this in the name of Jesus the Lord.

Eucharistic Prayer:
Preface of Sundays in Ordinary Time
I-VIII, pages **446–453**.

Communion Rite

I will tell all your marvelous works. I will rejoice and be glad in you, and sing to your name, Most High. (Ps. 9:2-3)

or:

Lord, I believe that you are the Christ, the Son of God, who was to come into this world. (John 11:27)

A period of silence may be observed after communion, or a psalm or song of praise may be sung.

PRAYER AFTER COMMUNION

Let us pray.
Pause for silent prayer, if this has not preceded.
Almighty God,
help us to live the example of love
we celebrate in this eucharist,
that we may come to its fulfillment in your presence.

We ask this through Christ our Lord.

EIGHTH SUNDAY IN ORDINARY TIME

Introductory Rites

> The Lord has been my strength; he has led me into freedom. He saved me because he loves me. (Ps. 17:19-20)

OPENING PRAYER

Let us pray
  **[that God will bring peace to the world
    and freedom to his Church]**

Pause for silent prayer

**Lord,
guide the course of world events
and give your Church the joy and peace
of serving you in freedom.**

**We ask this through our Lord Jesus Christ,
  your Son,
who lives and reigns with you and the Holy
  Spirit,
one God, for ever and ever.**

ALTERNATIVE OPENING PRAYER

Let us pray
  **[that the peace of Christ
    may find welcome in the world]**

Pause for silent prayer

**Father in heaven,
form in us the likeness of your Son
and deepen his life within us.
Send us as witnesses of gospel joy
into a world of fragile peace and broken
  promises.
Touch the hearts of all men with your love
that they in turn may love one another.**

We ask this through Christ our Lord.

LITURGY OF THE WORD

See Lectionary for Mass, nos. 83-85.

LITURGY OF THE EUCHARIST

PRAYER OVER THE GIFTS

Pray, brethren . . .

**God our Creator,
may this bread and wine we offer
as a sign of our love and worship
lead us to salvation.**

Grant this through Christ our Lord.

Eucharistic Prayer:
Preface of Sundays in Ordinary Time
I-VIII, pages 446–453.

Communion Rite

I will sing to the Lord for his goodness to me, I will sing the name of the Lord, Most High. (Ps. 12:6)

or:

I, the Lord, am with you always, until the end of the world. (Matthew 28:20)

A period of silence may be observed after communion, or a psalm or song of praise may be sung.

PRAYER AFTER COMMUNION

Let us pray.

Pause for silent prayer, if this has not preceded.

**God of salvation,
may this sacrament which strengthens us here on earth
bring us to eternal life.**

We ask this in the name of Jesus the Lord.

NINTH SUNDAY IN ORDINARY TIME

Introductory Rites

O look at me and be merciful, for I am wretched and
alone. See my hardship and my poverty, and pardon all my
sins. (Ps. 24:16, 18)

OPENING PRAYER

Let us pray
  [for God's care and protection]

Pause for silent prayer

Father,
your love never fails.
Hear our call.
Keep us from danger
and provide for all our needs.

Grant this through our Lord Jesus Christ, your
  Son,
who lives and reigns with you and the Holy
  Spirit,
one God, for ever and ever.

ALTERNATIVE OPENING PRAYER

Let us pray
  [for the confidence born of faith]

Pause for silent prayer

God our Father,
teach us to cherish the gifts that surround us.
Increase our faith in you
and bring our trust to its promised fulfillment
in the joy of your kingdom.

Grant this through Christ our Lord.

LITURGY OF THE WORD

See Lectionary for Mass, nos. 86-88.

LITURGY OF THE EUCHARIST

PRAYER OVER THE GIFTS

Pray, brethren . . .

Lord,
as we gather to offer our gifts
confident in your love,
make us holy by sharing your life with us
and by this eucharist forgive our sins.

We ask this through Christ our Lord.

Eucharistic Prayer:
Preface of Sundays in Ordinary Time
I-VIII, pages 446–453.

Communion Rite

I call upon you, God, for you will answer me; bend your ear and hear my prayer. (Ps. 16:6)

or:

I tell you solemnly, whatever you ask for in prayer, believe that you have received it, and it will be yours, says the Lord. (Mark 11:23-24)

A period of silence may be observed after communion, or a psalm or song of praise may be sung.

PRAYER AFTER COMMUNION

Let us pray.

Pause for silent prayer, if this has not preceded.

Lord,
as you give us the body and blood of your Son,
guide us with your Spirit
that we may honor you
not only with our lips,
but also with the lives we lead,
and so enter your kingdom.

We ask this in the name of Jesus the Lord.

TENTH SUNDAY IN ORDINARY TIME

Introductory Rites

> The Lord is my light and my salvation. Who shall frighten
> me? The Lord is the defender of my life. Who shall make
> me tremble? (Ps. 26:1-2)

OPENING PRAYER

Let us pray
  [for the guidance of the Holy Spirit]

Pause for silent prayer

God of wisdom and love,
source of all good,
send your Spirit to teach us your truth
and guide our actions
in your way of peace.

We ask this through our Lord Jesus Christ,
  your Son,
who lives and reigns with you and the Holy
  Spirit,
one God, for ever and ever.

ALTERNATIVE OPENING PRAYER

Let us pray
  [to our Father who calls us to
    freedom in Jesus his Son]

Pause for silent prayer

Father in heaven,
words cannot measure the boundaries of love
for those born to new life in Christ Jesus.
Raise us beyond the limits this world imposes,
so that we may be free to love as Christ teaches
and find our joy in your glory.

We ask this through Christ our Lord.

LITURGY OF THE WORD

See Lectionary for Mass, nos. 89-91.

LITURGY OF THE EUCHARIST

PRAYER OVER THE GIFTS

Pray, brethren . . .

Lord,
look with love on our service.
Accept the gifts we bring
and help us grow in Christian love.

Grant this through Christ our Lord.

Eucharistic Prayer:
Preface of Sundays in Ordinary Time
I-VIII, pages 446–453.

Communion Rite

> I can rely on the Lord; I can always turn to him for shelter. It was he who gave me my freedom. My God, you are always there to help me! (Ps. 17:3)
>
> or:
>
> God is love, and he who lives in love, lives in God, and God in him. (1 John 4:16)

A period of silence may be observed after communion, or a psalm or song of praise may be sung.

PRAYER AFTER COMMUNION

Let us pray.

Pause for silent prayer, if this has not preceded.

Lord,
may your healing love
turn us from sin
and keep us on the way that leads to you.

We ask this in the name of Jesus the Lord.

ELEVENTH SUNDAY IN ORDINARY TIME

Introductory Rites
> Lord, hear my voice when I call to you. You are my help;
> do not cast me off, do not desert me, my Savior God. (Ps.
> 26:7, 9)

OPENING PRAYER

Let us pray
  **[for the grace to follow
  Christ more closely]**

Pause for silent prayer
Almighty God,
our hope and our strength,
without you we falter.
Help us to follow Christ
and to live according to your will.

**We ask this through our Lord Jesus Christ,
  your Son,**
**who lives and reigns with you and the Holy
  Spirit,**
one God, for ever and ever.

ALTERNATIVE OPENING PRAYER

Let us pray
  **[to the Father whose love gives us
  strength to follow his Son]**

Pause for silent prayer
God our Father,
we rejoice in the faith that draws us together,
aware that selfishness can drive us apart.
**Let your encouragement be our constant
  strength.**
**Keep us one in the love that has sealed our
  lives,**
help us to live as one family
the gospel we profess.

We ask this through Christ our Lord.

LITURGY OF THE WORD

See Lectionary for Mass, nos. 92-94.

LITURGY OF THE EUCHARIST

PRAYER OVER THE GIFTS

Pray, brethren . . .

Lord God,
in this bread and wine
you give us food for body and spirit.
May the eucharist renew our strength
and bring us health of mind and body.

We ask this in the name of Jesus the Lord.

Eucharistic Prayer:
Preface of Sundays in Ordinary Time
I-VIII, pages 446–453.

Communion Rite

One thing I seek: to dwell in the house of the Lord all the days of my life. (Ps. 26:4)

or:

Father, keep in your name those you have given me, that they may be one as we are one, says the Lord. (John 17:11)

A period of silence may be observed after communion, or a psalm or song of praise may be sung.

PRAYER AFTER COMMUNION

Let us pray.
Pause for silent prayer, if this has not preceded.
Lord,
may this eucharist
accomplish in your Church
the unity and peace it signifies.

Grant this through Christ our Lord.

TWELFTH SUNDAY IN ORDINARY TIME

Introductory Rites

God is the strength of his people. In him, we his chosen live in safety. Save us, Lord, who share in your life, and give us your blessing; be our shepherd for ever. (Ps. 27:8-9)

OPENING PRAYER

Let us pray
   **[that we may grow in the
   love of God]**

Pause for silent prayer

**Father,
guide and protector of your people,
grant us an unfailing respect for your name,
and keep us always in your love.**

**Grant this through our Lord Jesus Christ, your
   Son,
who lives and reigns with you and the Holy
   Spirit,
one God, for ever and ever.**

ALTERNATIVE OPENING PRAYER

Let us pray
   **[to God whose fatherly love
   keeps us safe]**

Pause for silent prayer

**God of the universe,
we worship you as Lord.
God, ever close to us,
we rejoice to call you Father.
From this world's uncertainty we look to your
   covenant.
Keep us one in your peace, secure in your
   love.**

We ask this through Christ our Lord.

LITURGY OF THE WORD

See Lectionary for Mass, nos. 95-97.

LITURGY OF THE EUCHARIST

PRAYER OVER THE GIFTS

Pray, brethren . . .

**Lord,
receive our offering,
and may this sacrifice of praise
purify us in mind and heart
and make us always eager to serve you.**

We ask this in the name of Jesus the Lord.

Eucharistic Prayer:

Preface of Sundays in Ordinary Time
I-VIII, pages **446–453.**

Communion Rite

The eyes of all look to you, O Lord, and you give them food
in due season. (Ps. 144:15)

or:

I am the Good Shepherd; I give my life for my sheep, says
the Lord. (John 10:11, 15)

A period of silence may be observed
after communion, or a psalm or song
of praise may be sung.

PRAYER AFTER COMMUNION

Let us pray.
Pause for silent prayer, if this has not preceded.
Lord,
you give us the body and blood of your Son
to renew your life within us.
In your mercy, assure our redemption
and bring us to the eternal life
we celebrate in this eucharist.

We ask this through Christ our Lord.

THIRTEENTH SUNDAY IN ORDINARY TIME

Introductory Rites

All nations, clap your hands. Shout with a voice of joy to
God. (Ps. 46:2)

OPENING PRAYER

Let us pray
[that Christ may be our light]

Pause for silent prayer

Father,
you call your children
to walk in the light of Christ.
Free us from darkness
and keep us in the radiance of your truth.

We ask this through our Lord Jesus Christ,
your Son,
who lives and reigns with you and the Holy
Spirit,
one God, for ever and ever.

ALTERNATIVE OPENING PRAYER

Let us pray
[for the strength to reject the darkness
of sin]

Pause for silent prayer

Father in heaven,
the light of Jesus
has scattered the darkness of hatred and sin.
Called to that light
we ask for your guidance.
Form our lives in your truth, our hearts in your
love.

We ask this through Christ our Lord.

LITURGY OF THE WORD

See Lectionary for Mass, nos. 98-100.

LITURGY OF THE EUCHARIST

PRAYER OVER THE GIFTS

Pray, brethren . . .

Lord God,
through your sacraments
you give us the power of your grace.
May this eucharist
help us to serve you faithfully.

We ask this in the name of Jesus the Lord.

Eucharistic Prayer:
Preface of Sundays in Ordinary Time
I-VIII, pages **446–453.**

Communion Rite

> O bless the Lord, my soul, and all that is within me bless his holy name. (Ps. 102:1)

> or:

> Father, I pray for them: may they be one in us, so that the world may believe it was you who sent me. (John 17:20-21)

A period of silence may be observed after communion, or a psalm or song of praise may be sung.

PRAYER AFTER COMMUNION

Let us pray.
Pause for silent prayer, if this has not preceded.
Lord,
may this sacrifice and communion
give us a share in your life
and help us bring your love to the world.

Grant this through Christ our Lord.

FOURTEENTH SUNDAY IN ORDINARY TIME

Introductory Rites
Within your temple, we ponder your loving kindness, O God. As your name, so also your praise reaches to the ends of the earth; your right hand is filled with justice. (Ps. 47:10-11)

OPENING PRAYER	ALTERNATIVE OPENING PRAYER

Let us pray
  [for forgiveness through the grace of
  Jesus Christ]
Pause for silent prayer
Father,
through the obedience of Jesus,
your servant and your Son,
you raised a fallen world.
Free us from sin
and bring us the joy that lasts for ever.
We ask this through our Lord Jesus Christ,
  your Son,
who lives and reigns with you and the Holy
  Spirit,
one God, for ever and ever.
	Let us pray
	  [for greater willingness to serve
	  God and our fellow man]
	Pause for silent prayer
	Father,
	in the rising of your Son
	death gives birth to new life.
	The sufferings he endured restored hope to a
	  fallen world.
	Let sin never ensnare us
	with empty promises of passing joy.
	Make us one with you always,
	so that our joy may be holy,
	and our love may give life.
	We ask this through Christ our Lord.

LITURGY OF THE WORD

See Lectionary for Mass, nos. 101-103.

LITURGY OF THE EUCHARIST

PRAYER OVER THE GIFTS   **Pray, brethren . . .**

Lord,
let this offering to the glory of your name
purify us and bring us closer to eternal life.
We ask this in the name of Jesus the Lord.

Eucharistic Prayer:
Preface of Sundays in Ordinary Time
I-VIII, pages **446-453.**

Communion Rite

Taste and see the goodness of the Lord; blessed is he who hopes in God. (Ps. 33:9)

or:

Come to me, all you that labor and are burdened, and I will give you rest, says the Lord. (Matthew 11:28)

A period of silence may be observed after communion, or a psalm or song of praise may be sung.

PRAYER AFTER COMMUNION   **Let us pray.**

Pause for silent prayer, if this has not preceded.

Lord,
may we never fail to praise you
for the fullness of life and salvation
you give us in this eucharist.

We ask this through Christ our Lord.

FIFTEENTH SUNDAY IN ORDINARY TIME

Introductory Rites
In my justice I shall see your face, O Lord; when your
glory appears, my joy will be full. (Ps. 16:15)

OPENING PRAYER

Let us pray
[that the gospel may be our rule of life]
Pause for silent prayer
God our Father,
your light of truth
guides us to the way of Christ.
May all who follow him
reject what is contrary to the gospel.

We ask this through our Lord Jesus Christ,
your Son,
who lives and reigns with you and the Holy
Spirit,
one God, for ever and ever.

ALTERNATIVE OPENING PRAYER

Let us pray
[to be faithful to the light we have received,
to the name we bear]
Pause for silent prayer
Father,
let the light of your truth
guide us to your kingdom
through a world filled with lights contrary to
your own.
Christian is the name and the gospel we glory
in.
May your love make us what you have called
us to be.

We ask this through Christ our Lord.

LITURGY OF THE WORD

See Lectionary for Mass, nos. 104-106.

LITURGY OF THE EUCHARIST

PRAYER OVER THE GIFTS

Pray, brethren . . .

Lord,
accept the gifts of your Church.
May this eucharist
help us grow in holiness and faith.

We ask this in the name of Jesus the Lord.

Eucharistic Prayer:
Preface of Sundays in Ordinary Time
I-VIII, pages **446–453.**

Communion Rite

The sparrow even finds a home, the swallow finds a nest wherein to place her young, near to your altars, Lord of hosts, my King, my God! How happy they who dwell in your house! For ever they are praising you. (Ps. 83:4-5)

or:

Whoever eats my flesh and drinks my blood will live in me and I in him, says the Lord. (John 6:57)

A period of silence may be observed after communion, or a psalm or song of praise may be sung.

PRAYER AFTER COMMUNION

Let us pray.

Pause for silent prayer, if this has not preceded.

Lord,
by our sharing in the mystery of this eucharist,
let your saving love grow within us.

Grant this through Christ our Lord.

SIXTEENTH SUNDAY IN ORDINARY TIME

Introductory Rites

God himself is my help. The Lord upholds my life. I will offer you a willing sacrifice; I will praise your name, O Lord, for its goodness. (Ps. 53:6, 8)

OPENING PRAYER

Let us pray
   **[to be kept faithful in the
   service of God]**
Pause for silent prayer
**Lord,
be merciful to your people.
Fill us with your gifts
and make us always eager to serve you
in faith, hope, and love.**

**Grant this through our Lord Jesus Christ, your
   Son,
who lives and reigns with you and the Holy
   Spirit,
one God, for ever and ever.**

ALTERNATIVE OPENING PRAYER

Let us pray
   **[that God will continue to bless us
   with his compassion and love]**
Pause for silent prayer
**Father,
let the gift of your life
continue to grow in us,
drawing us from death to faith, hope, and love.
Keep us alive in Christ Jesus.
Keep us watchful in prayer
and true to his teaching
till your glory is revealed in us.**

Grant this through Christ our Lord.

LITURGY OF THE WORD

See Lectionary for Mass, nos. 107-109.

LITURGY OF THE EUCHARIST

PRAYER OVER THE GIFTS

Pray, brethren . . .

**Lord,
bring us closer to salvation
through these gifts which we bring in your honor.
Accept the perfect sacrifice you have given us,
bless it as you blessed the gifts of Abel.**

We ask this through Christ our Lord.

Eucharistic Prayer:
Preface of Sundays in Ordinary Time
I-VIII, pages 446–453.

Communion Rite

The Lord keeps in our minds the wonderful things he has done. He is compassion and love; he always provides for his faithful. (Ps. 110:4-5)

or:

I stand at the door and knock, says the Lord. If anyone hears my voice and opens the door, I will come in and sit down to supper with him, and he with me. (Rev. 3:20)

A period of silence may be observed after communion, or a psalm or song of praise may be sung.

PRAYER AFTER COMMUNION

Let us pray.

Pause for silent prayer, if this has not preceded.

**Merciful Father,
may these mysteries
give us new purpose
and bring us to a new life in you.**

We ask this in the name of Jesus the Lord.

SEVENTEENTH SUNDAY IN ORDINARY TIME

Introductory Rites

God is in his holy dwelling; he will give a home to the lonely, he gives power and strength to his people. (Ps. 67:6-7, 36)

OPENING PRAYER

Let us pray
  [that we will make good use of the gifts that God has given us]
Pause for silent prayer
God our Father and protector,
without you nothing is holy,
nothing has value.
Guide us to everlasting life
by helping us to use wisely
the blessings you have given to the world.

We ask this through our Lord Jesus Christ, your Son,
who lives and reigns with you and the Holy Spirit,
one God, for ever and ever.

ALTERNATIVE OPENING PRAYER

Let us pray
  [for the faith to recognize God's presence in our world]
Pause for silent prayer
God our Father,
open our eyes to see your hand at work
in the splendor of creation,
in the beauty of human life.
Touched by your hand our world is holy.
Help us to cherish the gifts that surround us,
to share your blessings with our brothers and sisters,
and to experience the joy of life in your presence.

We ask this through Christ our Lord.

LITURGY OF THE WORD

See Lectionary for Mass, nos. 110-112.

LITURGY OF THE EUCHARIST

PRAYER OVER THE GIFTS

Pray, brethren . . .

Lord,
receive these offerings
chosen from your many gifts.
May these mysteries make us holy
and lead us to eternal joy.

Grant this through Christ our Lord.

Eucharistic Prayer:
Preface of Sundays in Ordinary Time I-VIII, pages 446–453.

Communion Rite
> O bless the Lord, my soul, and remember all his kindness.
>
> (Ps. 102:2)
>
> or:
>
> Happy are those who show mercy; mercy shall be theirs.
> Happy are the pure of heart, for they shall see God.
>
> (Matthew 5:7-8)

A period of silence may be observed
after communion, or a psalm or song
of praise may be sung.

PRAYER AFTER COMMUNION

Let us pray.
Pause for silent prayer, if this has not preceded.
Lord,
we receive the sacrament
which celebrates the memory
of the death and resurrection of Christ your Son.
May this gift bring us closer to our eternal salvation.

We ask this through Christ our Lord.

EIGHTEENTH SUNDAY IN ORDINARY TIME

Introductory Rites

> God, come to my help. Lord, quickly give me assistance.
> You are the one who helps me and sets me free: Lord, do
> not be long in coming. (Ps. 69:2, 6)

OPENING PRAYER

Let us pray
   **[for the gift of God's forgiveness
   and love]**
Pause for silent prayer
**Father of everlasting goodness,
our origin and guide,
be close to us
and hear the prayers of all who praise you.
Forgive our sins and restore us to life.
Keep us safe in your love.**

**Grant this through our Lord Jesus Christ, your
   Son,
who lives and reigns with you and the Holy
   Spirit,
one God, for ever and ever.**

ALTERNATIVE OPENING PRAYER

Let us pray
   **[to the Father whose kindness
   never fails]**
Pause for silent prayer
**God our Father,
gifts without measure flow from your goodness
to bring us your peace.
Our life is your gift.
Guide our life's journey,
for only your love makes us whole.
Keep us strong in your love.**

We ask this through Christ our Lord.

LITURGY OF THE WORD

See Lectionary for Mass, nos. 113-115.

LITURGY OF THE EUCHARIST

PRAYER OVER THE GIFTS

Pray, brethren . . .

**Merciful Lord,
make holy these gifts,
and let our spiritual sacrifice
make us an everlasting gift to you.**

We ask this in the name of Jesus the Lord.

Eucharistic Prayer:
Preface of Sundays in Ordinary Time
I-VIII, pages 446–453.

Communion Rite

You gave us bread from heaven, Lord: a sweet-tasting bread that was very good to eat. (Wis. 16:20)

or:

The Lord says: I am the bread of life. A man who comes to me will not go away hungry, and no one who believes in me will thirst. (John 6:35)

A period of silence may be observed after communion, or a psalm or song of praise may be sung.

PRAYER AFTER COMMUNION

Let us pray.
Pause for silent prayer, if this has not preceded.
Lord,
you give us the strength of new life
by the gift of the eucharist.
Protect us with your love
and prepare us for eternal redemption.

We ask this through Christ our Lord.

NINETEENTH SUNDAY IN ORDINARY TIME

Introductory Rites

Lord, be true to your covenant, forget not the life of your poor ones for ever. Rise up, O God, and defend your cause; do not ignore the shouts of your enemies. (Ps. 73:20, 19, 22, 23)

OPENING PRAYER

Let us pray
  [in the Spirit that we may grow
  in the love of God]

Pause for silent prayer

Almighty and ever-living God,
your Spirit made us your children,
confident to call you Father.
Increase your Spirit within us
and bring us to our promised inheritance.

Grant this through our Lord Jesus Christ, your Son,
who lives and reigns with you and the Holy Spirit,
one God, for ever and ever.

ALTERNATIVE OPENING PRAYER

Let us pray
  [that through us others may find
  the way to life in Christ]

Pause for silent prayer

Father,
we come, reborn in the Spirit,
to celebrate our sonship in the Lord Jesus Christ.
Touch our hearts,
help them grow toward the life you have promised.
Touch our lives,
make them signs of your love for all men.
Grant this through Christ our Lord.

LITURGY OF THE WORD

See Lectionary for Mass, nos. 116-118.

LITURGY OF THE EUCHARIST

PRAYER OVER THE GIFTS

Pray, brethren . . .

God of power,
giver of the gifts we bring,
accept the offering of your Church
and make it the sacrament of our salvation.

We ask this through Christ our Lord.

Eucharistic Prayer:

Preface of Sundays in Ordinary Time
I-VIII, pages 446–453.

Communion Rite

Praise the Lord, Jerusalem; he feeds you with the finest wheat. (Ps. 147:12, 14)

or:

The bread I shall give is my flesh for the life of the world, says the Lord. (John 6:52)

A period of silence may be observed after communion, or a psalm or song of praise may be sung.

PRAYER AFTER COMMUNION

Let us pray.

Pause for silent prayer, if this has not preceded.

**Lord,
may the eucharist you give us
bring us to salvation
and keep us faithful to the light of your truth.**

We ask this in the name of Jesus the Lord.

TWENTIETH SUNDAY IN ORDINARY TIME

God, our protector, keep us in mind; always give strength to your people. For if we can be with you even one day, it is better than a thousand without you. (Ps. 83:10-11)

OPENING PRAYER

Let us pray
[that the love of God
may raise us beyond what we see
to the unseen glory of his kingdom]

Pause for silent prayer

God our Father,
may we love you in all things and above all things
and reach the joy you have prepared for us
beyond all our imagining.

We ask this through our Lord Jesus Christ, your Son,
who lives and reigns with you and the Holy Spirit,
one God, for ever and ever.

ALTERNATIVE OPENING PRAYER

Let us pray
[with humility and persistence]

Pause for silent prayer

Almighty God, ever-loving Father,
your care extends beyond the boundaries of race and nation
to the hearts of all who live.
May the walls, which prejudice raises between us,
crumble beneath the shadow of your outstretched arm.

We ask this through Christ our Lord.

LITURGY OF THE WORD

See Lectionary for Mass, nos. 119-121.

LITURGY OF THE EUCHARIST

PRAYER OVER THE GIFTS

Pray, brethren . . .

Lord,
accept our sacrifice
as a holy exchange of gifts.
By offering what you have given us
may we receive the gift of yourself.

We ask this in the name of Jesus the Lord.

Eucharistic Prayer:
Preface of Sundays in Ordinary Time
I-VIII, pages **446-453**.

Communion Rite

With the Lord there is mercy, and fullness of redemption. (Ps. 129:7)

or:

I am the living bread from heaven, says the Lord; if any-one eats this bread he will live for ever. (John 6:51-52)

A period of silence may be observed after communion, or a psalm or song of praise may be sung.

PRAYER AFTER COMMUNION **Let us pray.**
Pause for silent prayer, if this has not preceded.
God of mercy,
by this sacrament you make us one with Christ.
By becoming more like him on earth,
may we come to share his glory in heaven,
where he lives and reigns for ever and ever.

TWENTY-FIRST SUNDAY IN ORDINARY TIME

Introductory Rites

> Listen, Lord, and answer me. Save your servant who trusts in you. I call to you all day long, have mercy on me, O Lord. (Ps. 85:1-3)

OPENING PRAYER

Let us pray
  [that God will make us one in mind and heart]

Pause for silent prayer

Father,
help us to seek the values
that will bring us lasting joy in this changing world.
In our desire for what you promise
make us one in mind and heart.

Grant this through our Lord Jesus Christ, your Son,
who lives and reigns with you and the Holy Spirit,
one God, for ever and ever.

ALTERNATIVE OPENING PRAYER

Let us pray
  [with minds fixed on eternal truth]

Pause for silent prayer

Lord our God,
all truth is from you,
and you alone bring oneness of heart.
Give your people the joy
of hearing your word in every sound
and of longing for your presence more than for life itself.
May all the attractions of a changing world
serve only to bring us
the peace of your kingdom which this world does not give.

Grant this through Christ our Lord.

LITURGY OF THE WORD

See Lectionary for Mass, nos. 122-124.

LITURGY OF THE EUCHARIST

PRAYER OVER THE GIFTS

Pray, brethren . . .

Merciful God,
the perfect sacrifice of Jesus Christ
made us your people.
In your love,
grant peace and unity to your Church.

We ask this through Christ our Lord.

Eucharistic Prayer:
Preface of Sundays in Ordinary Time
I-VIII, pages 446–453.

Communion Rite

Lord, the earth is filled with your gift from heaven; man grows bread from earth, and wine to cheer his heart. (Ps. 103:13-15)

or:

The Lord says: The man who eats my flesh and drinks my blood will live for ever; I shall raise him to life on the last day. (John 6:55)

A period of silence may be observed after communion, or a psalm or song of praise may be sung.

PRAYER AFTER COMMUNION

Let us pray.

Pause for silent prayer, if this has not preceded.

**Lord,
may this eucharist increase within us
the healing power of your love.
May it guide and direct our efforts
to please you in all things.**

We ask this in the name of Jesus the Lord.

TWENTY-SECOND SUNDAY IN ORDINARY TIME

Introductory Rites

I call to you all day long, have mercy on me, O Lord. You are good and forgiving, full of love for all who call to you.
(Ps. 85:3, 5)

OPENING PRAYER

Let us pray
[that God will increase our faith and
bring to perfection the gifts
he has given us]
Pause for silent prayer

Almighty God,
every good thing comes from you.
Fill our hearts with love for you,
increase our faith,
and by your constant care
protect the good you have given us.

We ask this through our Lord Jesus Christ,
your Son,
who lives and reigns with you and the Holy
Spirit,
one God, for ever and ever.

ALTERNATIVE OPENING PRAYER

Let us pray
[to God who forgives all
who call upon him]
Pause for silent prayer

Lord God of power and might,
nothing is good which is against your will,
and all is of value which comes from your
hand.
Place in our hearts a desire to please you
and fill our minds with insight into love,
so that every thought may grow in wisdom
and all our efforts may be filled with your
peace.

We ask this through Christ our Lord.

LITURGY OF THE WORD

See Lectionary for Mass, nos. 125-127.

LITURGY OF THE EUCHARIST

PRAYER OVER THE GIFTS

Pray, brethren . . .

Lord,
may this holy offering
bring us your blessing
and accomplish within us
its promise of salvation.

Grant this through Christ our Lord.

Eucharistic Prayer:
Preface of Sundays in Ordinary Time
I-VIII, pages **446–453**.

Communion Rite

> O Lord, how great is the depth of the kindness which you have shown to those who love you. (Ps. 30:20)
>
> or:
>
> Happy are the peacemakers; they shall be called sons of God. Happy are they who suffer persecution for justice' sake; the kingdom of heaven is theirs. (Matthew 5:9-10)

A period of silence may be observed after communion, or a psalm or song of praise may be sung.

PRAYER AFTER COMMUNION

Let us pray.
Pause for silent prayer, if this has not preceded.
Lord,
you renew us at your table with the bread of life.
May this food strengthen us in love
and help us to serve you in each other.

We ask this in the name of Jesus the Lord.

TWENTY-THIRD SUNDAY IN ORDINARY TIME

Introductory Rites

Lord, you are just, and the judgments you make are right.
Show mercy when you judge me, your servant. (Ps. 118:137, 124)

OPENING PRAYER

Let us pray
  **[that we may realize the freedom God
  has given us in making us
  his sons and daughters]**
Pause for silent prayer
**God our Father,
you redeem us
and make us your children in Christ.
Look upon us,
give us true freedom
and bring us to the inheritance you promised.**

**Grant this through our Lord Jesus Christ, your Son,
who lives and reigns with you and the Holy Spirit,
one God, for ever and ever.**

ALTERNATIVE OPENING PRAYER

Let us pray
  [to our just and merciful God]
Pause for silent prayer
**Lord our God,
in you justice and mercy meet.
With unparalleled love you have saved us from death
and drawn us into the circle of your life.
Open our eyes to the wonders this life sets before us,
that we may serve you free from fear
and address you as God our Father.**

We ask this in the name of Jesus the Lord.

LITURGY OF THE WORD

See Lectionary for Mass, nos. 128-130.

LITURGY OF THE EUCHARIST

PRAYER OVER THE GIFTS

Pray, brethren . . .

**God of peace and love,
may our offering bring you true worship
and make us one with you.**

Grant this through Christ our Lord.

Eucharistic Prayer:

Preface of Sundays in Ordinary Time
I-VIII, pages **446–453**.

Communion Rite

Like a deer that longs for running streams, my soul longs for you, my God. My soul is thirsting for the living God. (Ps. 41:2-3)

or:

I am the light of the world, says the Lord; the man who follows me will have the light of life. (John 8:12)

A period of silence may be observed after communion, or a psalm or song of praise may be sung.

PRAYER AFTER COMMUNION

Let us pray.
Pause for silent prayer, if this has not preceded.

**Lord,
your word and your sacrament
give us food and life.
May this gift of your Son
lead us to share his life for ever.**

We ask this through Christ our Lord.

TWENTY-FOURTH SUNDAY IN ORDINARY TIME

Introductory Rites

Give peace, Lord, to those who wait for you and your prophets will proclaim you as you deserve. Hear the prayers of your servant and of your people Israel. (See Sir. 36:18)

OPENING PRAYER

Let us pray
  **[that God will keep us
  faithful in his service]**
Pause for silent prayer
**Almighty God,
our creator and guide,
may we serve you with all our heart
and know your forgiveness in our lives.**

**We ask this through our Lord Jesus Christ,
  your Son,
who lives and reigns with you and the Holy
  Spirit,
one God, for ever and ever.**

ALTERNATIVE OPENING PRAYER

Let us pray
  **[for the peace which is born
  of faith and hope]**
Pause for silent prayer
**Father in heaven, Creator of all,
look down upon your people in their moments of need,
for you alone are the source of our peace.
Bring us to the dignity which distinguishes the
  poor in spirit
and show us how great is the call to serve,
that we may share in the peace of Christ
who offered his life in the service of all.**

We ask this through Christ our Lord.

LITURGY OF THE WORD

See Lectionary for Mass, nos. 131-133.

LITURGY OF THE EUCHARIST

PRAYER OVER THE GIFTS

Pray, brethren . . .

**Lord,
hear the prayers of your people
and receive our gifts.
May the worship of each one here
bring salvation to all.**

Grant this through Christ our Lord.

Eucharistic Prayer:
Preface of Sundays in Ordinary Time
I-VIII, pages 446–453.

Communion Rite

> O God, how much we value your mercy! All mankind can gather under your protection. (Ps. 35:8)

or:

> The cup that we bless is a communion with the blood of Christ; and the bread that we break is a communion with the body of the Lord. (See 1 Cor. 10:16)

A period of silence may be observed after communion, or a psalm or song of praise may be sung.

PRAYER AFTER COMMUNION

Let us pray.

Pause for silent prayer, if this has not preceded.

**Lord,
may the eucharist you have given us
influence our thoughts and actions.
May your Spirit guide and direct us in your way.**

We ask this in the name of Jesus the Lord.

TWENTY-FIFTH SUNDAY IN ORDINARY TIME

Introductory Rites

I am the Savior of all people, says the Lord. Whatever their troubles, I will answer their cry, and I will always be their Lord.

OPENING PRAYER

Let us pray

**[that we will grow in the love of God
and of one another]**

Pause for silent prayer

**Father,
guide us, as you guide creation
according to your law of love.
May we love one another
and come to perfection
in the eternal life prepared for us.**

**Grant this through our Lord Jesus Christ, your Son,
who lives and reigns with you and the Holy Spirit,
one God, for ever and ever.**

ALTERNATIVE OPENING PRAYER

Let us pray

**[to the Lord who is a God of love
to all peoples]**

Pause for silent prayer

**Father in heaven,
the perfection of justice is found in your love
and all mankind is in need of your law.
Help us to find this love in each other
that justice may be attained
through obedience to your law.**

We ask this through Christ our Lord.

LITURGY OF THE WORD

See Lectionary for Mass, nos. 134-136.

LITURGY OF THE EUCHARIST

PRAYER OVER THE GIFTS

Pray, brethren . . .

**Lord,
may these gifts which we now offer
to show our belief and our love
be pleasing to you.
May they become for us
the eucharist of Jesus Christ your Son,
who is Lord for ever and ever.**

Eucharistic Prayer:
Preface of Sundays in Ordinary Time
I-VIII, pages 446–453.

Communion Rite

You have laid down your precepts to be faithfully kept.
May my footsteps be firm in keeping your commands.
(Ps. 118:4-5)

or:

I am the Good Shepherd, says the Lord; I know my
sheep, and mine know me. (John 10:14)

A period of silence may be observed
after communion, or a psalm or song
of praise may be sung.

PRAYER AFTER COMMUNION

Let us pray.
Pause for silent prayer, if this has not preceded.
Lord,
help us with your kindness.
Make us strong through the eucharist.
May we put into action
the saving mystery we celebrate.

We ask this in the name of Jesus the Lord.

TWENTY-SIXTH SUNDAY IN ORDINARY TIME

Introductory Rites

O Lord, you had just cause to judge men as you did:
because we sinned against you and disobeyed your will.
But now show us your greatness of heart, and treat us
with your unbounded kindness. (Dan. 3:31, 29, 30, 43, 42)

OPENING PRAYER

Let us pray
 [for God's forgiveness and
 for the happiness it brings]

Pause for silent prayer

Father,
you show your almighty power
in your mercy and forgiveness.
Continue to fill us with your gifts of love.
Help us to hurry toward the eternal life you
** promise**
and come to share in the joys of your king-
** dom.**
Grant this through our Lord Jesus Christ, your
** Son,**
who lives and reigns with you and the Holy
** Spirit,**
one God, for ever and ever.

ALTERNATIVE OPENING PRAYER

Let us pray
 [for the peace of the kingdom
 which we have been promised]

Pause for silent prayer

Father of our Lord Jesus Christ,
in your unbounded mercy
you have revealed the beauty of your power
through your constant forgiveness of our sins.
May the power of this love be in our hearts
to bring your pardon and your kingdom to all
** we meet.**

We ask this through Christ our Lord.

LITURGY OF THE WORD

See Lectionary for Mass, nos. 137-139.

LITURGY OF THE EUCHARIST

PRAYER OVER THE GIFTS

Pray, brethren . . .

God of mercy,
accept our offering
and make it a source of blessing for us.
We ask this in the name of Jesus the Lord.

Eucharistic Prayer:
Preface of Sundays in Ordinary Time
I-VIII, pages 446–453.

Communion Rite

> O Lord, remember the words you spoke to me, your servant, which made me live in hope and consoled me when I was downcast. (Ps. 118:49-50)

> or:

> This is how we know what love is: Christ gave up his life for us; and we too must give up our lives for our brothers. (1 John 3:16)

A period of silence may be observed after communion, or a psalm or song of praise may be sung.

PRAYER AFTER COMMUNION

Let us pray.
Pause for silent prayer, if this has not preceded.
Lord,
may this eucharist
in which we proclaim the death of Christ
bring us salvation
and make us one with him in glory,
for he is Lord for ever and ever.

TWENTY-SEVENTH SUNDAY IN ORDINARY TIME

Introductory Rites

> O Lord, you have given everything its place in the world,
> and no one can make it otherwise. For it is your creation,
> the heavens and the earth and the stars: you are the Lord
> of all. (Esther 13:9, 10-11)

OPENING PRAYER

Let us pray
  **[that God will forgive our failings
    and bring us peace]**

Pause for silent prayer

**Father,
your love for us
surpasses all our hopes and desires.
Forgive our failings,
keep us in your peace
and lead us in the way of salvation.**

**We ask this through our Lord Jesus Christ,
  your Son,
who lives and reigns with you and the Holy
  Spirit,
one God, for ever and ever.**

ALTERNATIVE OPENING PRAYER

Let us pray
  **[before the face of God,
    in trusting faith]**

Pause for silent prayer

**Almighty and eternal God,
Father of the world to come,
your goodness is beyond what our spirit can
  touch
and your strength is more than the mind can
  bear.
Lead us to seek beyond our reach
and give us the courage to stand before your
  truth.**

We ask this through Christ our Lord.

LITURGY OF THE WORD

See Lectionary for Mass, nos. 140-142.

LITURGY OF THE EUCHARIST

PRAYER OVER THE GIFTS

Pray, brethren . . .

**Father,
receive these gifts
which our Lord Jesus Christ
has asked us to offer in his memory.
May our obedient service
bring us to the fullness of your redemption.**

We ask this in the name of Jesus the Lord.

Eucharistic Prayer:
Preface of Sundays in Ordinary Time
I-VIII, pages 446–453.

Communion Rite

The Lord is good to those who hope in him, to those who are searching for his love. (Lam. 3:25)

or:

Because there is one bread, we, though many, are one body, for we all share in the one loaf and in the one cup. (See 1 Cor. 10:17)

A period of silence may be observed after communion, or a psalm or song of praise may be sung.

PRAYER AFTER COMMUNION

Let us pray.

Pause for silent prayer, if this has not preceded.

Almighty God,
let the eucharist we share
fill us with your life.
May the love of Christ
which we celebrate here
touch our lives and lead us to you.

We ask this in the name of Jesus the Lord.

TWENTY-EIGHTH SUNDAY IN ORDINARY TIME

Introductory Rites

If you, O Lord, laid bare our guilt, who could endure it?
But you are forgiving, God of Israel. (Ps. 129:3-4)

OPENING PRAYER

Let us pray
  **[that God will help us to love
    one another]**
Pause for silent prayer
Lord,
our help and guide,
make your love the foundation of our lives.
May our love for you express itself
in our eagerness to do good for others.

**Grant this through our Lord Jesus Christ, your
  Son,**
**who lives and reigns with you and the Holy
  Spirit,**
one God, for ever and ever.

ALTERNATIVE OPENING PRAYER

Let us pray
  [in quiet for the grace of sincerity]
Pause for silent prayer
Father in heaven,
the hand of your loving kindness
powerfully yet gently guides all the moments
  of our day.
Go before us in our pilgrimage of life,
anticipate our needs and prevent our falling.
Send your Spirit to unite us in faith,
that sharing in your service,
we may rejoice in your presence.

We ask this through Christ our Lord.

LITURGY OF THE WORD

See Lectionary for Mass, nos. 143-145.

LITURGY OF THE EUCHARIST

PRAYER OVER THE GIFTS

Pray, brethren . . .

Lord,
accept the prayers and gifts
we offer in faith and love.
May this eucharist bring us to your glory.

We ask this in the name of Jesus the Lord.

Eucharistic Prayer:
Preface of Sundays in Ordinary Time
I-VIII, pages **446–453.**

Communion Rite

The rich suffer want and go hungry, but nothing shall be lacking to those who fear the Lord. (Ps. 33:11)

or:

When the Lord is revealed we shall be like him, for we shall see him as he is. (1 John 3:2)

A period of silence may be observed after communion, or a psalm or song of praise may be sung.

PRAYER AFTER COMMUNION   **Let us pray.**

Pause for silent prayer, if this has not preceded.

Almighty Father,
may the body and blood of your Son
give us a share in his life,
for he is Lord for ever and ever.

TWENTY-NINTH SUNDAY IN ORDINARY TIME

Introductory Rites

I call upon you, God, for you will answer me; bend your ear and hear my prayer. Guard me as the pupil of your eye; hide me in the shade of your wings. (Ps. 16:6, 8)

OPENING PRAYER

Let us pray
  [for the gift of simplicity and joy
   in our service of God and man]

Pause for silent prayer

Almighty and ever-living God,
our source of power and inspiration,
give us strength and joy
in serving you as followers of Christ,
who lives and reigns with you and the Holy
  Spirit,
one God, for ever and ever.

ALTERNATIVE OPENING PRAYER

Let us pray
  [to the Lord who bends close
   to hear our prayer]

Pause for silent prayer

Lord our God, Father of all,
you guard us under the shadow of your wings
and search into the depths of our hearts.
Remove the blindness that cannot know you
and relieve the fear that would hide us from
  your sight.

We ask this through Christ our Lord.

LITURGY OF THE WORD

See Lectionary for Mass, nos. 146-148.

LITURGY OF THE EUCHARIST

PRAYER OVER THE GIFTS

Pray, brethren . . .

Lord God,
may the gifts we offer
bring us your love and forgiveness
and give us freedom to serve you with our lives.

We ask this in the name of Jesus the Lord.

Eucharistic Prayer:
Preface of Sundays in Ordinary Time
I-VIII, pages **446–453**.

Communion Rite

See how the eyes of the Lord are on those who fear him, on those who hope in his love, that he may rescue them from death and feed them in time of famine. (Ps. 32:18-19)

or:

The Son of Man came to give his life as a ransom for many. (Mark 10:45)

A period of silence may be observed after communion, or a psalm or song of praise may be sung.

PRAYER AFTER COMMUNION   **Let us pray.**

Pause for silent prayer, if this has not preceded.

**Lord,
may this eucharist help us to remain faithful.
May it teach us the way to eternal life.**

Grant this through Christ our Lord.

THIRTIETH SUNDAY IN ORDINARY TIME

Introductory Rites

> Let hearts rejoice who search for the Lord. Seek the Lord
> and his strength, seek always the face of the Lord. (Ps.
> 104:3-4)

OPENING PRAYER

Let us pray
   [for the strength to do God's will]

Pause for silent prayer

**Almighty and ever-living God,
strengthen our faith, hope, and love.
May we do with loving hearts
what you ask of us
and come to share the life you promise.**

**We ask this through our Lord Jesus Christ,
   your Son,
who lives and reigns with you and the Holy
   Spirit,
one God, for ever and ever.**

ALTERNATIVE OPENING PRAYER

Let us pray
   [in humble hope for salvation]

Pause for silent prayer

**Praised be you, God and Father of our Lord
   Jesus Christ.
There is no power for good
which does not come from your covenant,
and no promise to hope in
that your love has not offered.
Strengthen our faith to accept your covenant
and give us the love to carry out your command.**

We ask this through Christ our Lord.

LITURGY OF THE WORD

See Lectionary for Mass, nos. 149-151.

LITURGY OF THE EUCHARIST

PRAYER OVER THE GIFTS

Pray, brethren . . .

**Lord God of power and might,
receive the gifts we offer
and let our service give you glory.**

Grant this through Christ our Lord.

Eucharistic Prayer:
Preface of Sundays in Ordinary Time
I-VIII, pages **446–453**.

Communion Rite

We will rejoice at the victory of God and make our boast in his great name. (Ps. 19:6)

or:

Christ loved us and gave himself up for us as a fragrant offering to God. (Eph. 5:2)

A period of silence may be observed after communion, or a psalm or song of praise may be sung.

PRAYER AFTER COMMUNION

Let us pray.
Pause for silent prayer, if this has not preceded.
Lord,
bring to perfection within us
the communion we share in this sacrament.
May our celebration have an effect in our lives.

We ask this in the name of Jesus the Lord.

THIRTY-FIRST SUNDAY IN ORDINARY TIME

Introductory Rites

> Do not abandon me, Lord. My God, do not go away from me! Hurry to help me, Lord, my Savior. (Ps. 37:22-23)

OPENING PRAYER

Let us pray
  [that our lives will reflect our faith]
Pause for silent prayer
God of power and mercy,
only with your help
can we offer you fitting service and praise.
May we live the faith we profess
and trust your promise of eternal life.

Grant this through our Lord Jesus Christ, your Son,
who lives and reigns with you and the Holy Spirit,
one God, for ever and ever.

ALTERNATIVE OPENING PRAYER

Let us pray
  [in the presence of God,
    the source of every good]
Pause for silent prayer
Father in heaven, God of power and Lord of mercy,
from whose fullness we have received,
direct our steps in our everyday efforts.
May the changing moods of the human heart
and the limits which our failings impose on hope
never blind us to you, source of every good.
Faith gives us the promise of peace
and makes known the demands of love.
Remove the selfishness that blurs the vision of faith.

Grant this through Christ our Lord.

LITURGY OF THE WORD

See Lectionary for Mass, nos. 152-154.

LITURGY OF THE EUCHARIST

PRAYER OVER THE GIFTS

Pray, brethren . . .

God of mercy,
may we offer a pure sacrifice
for the forgiveness of our sins.

We ask this through Christ our Lord.

Eucharistic Prayer:
Preface of Sundays in Ordinary Time
I-VIII, pages **446–453**.

Communion Rite

Lord, you will show me the path of life and fill me with joy in your presence. (Ps. 15:11)

or:

As the living Father sent me, and I live because of the Father, so he who eats my flesh and drinks my blood will live because of me. (John 6:58)

A period of silence may be observed after communion, or a psalm or song of praise may be sung.

PRAYER AFTER COMMUNION

Let us pray.

Pause for silent prayer, if this has not preceded.

Lord,
you give us new hope in this eucharist.
May the power of your love
continue its saving work among us
and bring us to the joy you promise.

We ask this in the name of Jesus the Lord.

THIRTY-SECOND SUNDAY IN ORDINARY TIME

Introductory Rites

Let my prayer come before you, Lord; listen, and answer
me. (Ps. 87:3)

OPENING PRAYER

Let us pray
  [for health of mind and body]

Pause for silent prayer

God of power and mercy,
protect us from all harm.
Give us freedom of spirit
and health in mind and body
to do your work on earth.

We ask this through our Lord Jesus Christ,
  your Son,
who lives and reigns with you and the Holy
  Spirit,
one God, for ever and ever.

ALTERNATIVE OPENING PRAYER

Let us pray
  [that our prayer rise like incense in the
  presence of the Lord]

Pause for silent prayer

Almighty Father,
strong is your justice and great is your mercy.
Protect us in the burdens and challenges of
  life.
Shield our minds from the distortion of pride
and enfold our desire with the beauty of
  truth.
Help us to become more aware of your loving
  design
so that we may more willingly give our lives in
  service to all.

We ask this through Christ our Lord.

LITURGY OF THE WORD

See Lectionary for Mass, nos. 155-157.

LITURGY OF THE EUCHARIST

PRAYER OVER THE GIFTS

Pray, brethren . . .

God of mercy,
in this eucharist we proclaim the death of the Lord.
Accept the gifts we present
and help us follow him with love,
for he is Lord for ever and ever.

Eucharistic Prayer:
Preface of Sundays in Ordinary Time
I-VIII, pages 446–453.

Communion Rite

> The Lord is my shepherd; there is nothing I shall want. In green pastures he gives me rest, he leads me beside the waters of peace. (Ps. 22:1-2)

> or:

> The disciples recognized the Lord Jesus in the breaking of bread. (Luke 24:35)

A period of silence may be observed after communion, or a psalm or song of praise may be sung.

PRAYER AFTER COMMUNION

Let us pray.

Pause for silent prayer, if this has not preceded.

**Lord,
we thank you for the nourishment you give us
through your holy gift.
Pour out your Spirit upon us
and in the strength of this food from heaven
keep us single-minded in your service.**

We ask this in the name of Jesus the Lord.

THIRTY-THIRD SUNDAY IN ORDINARY TIME

Introductory Rites

The Lord says: my plans for you are peace and not disaster; when you call to me, I will listen to you, and I will bring you back to the place from which I exiled you. (Jer. 29:11, 12, 14)

OPENING PRAYER

Let us pray
   [that God will help us to be faithful]

Pause for silent prayer

Father of all that is good,
keep us faithful in serving you,
for to serve you is our lasting joy.

We ask this through our Lord Jesus Christ,
   your Son,
who lives and reigns with you and the Holy
   Spirit,
one God, for ever and ever.

ALTERNATIVE OPENING PRAYER

Let us pray
   [with hearts that long for peace]

Pause for silent prayer

Father in heaven,
ever-living source of all that is good,
from the beginning of time you promised
   man salvation
through the future coming of your Son, our
   Lord Jesus Christ.
Help us to drink of his truth
and expand our hearts with the joy of his
   promises,
so that we may serve you in faith and in love
and know for ever the joy of your presence.

We ask this through Christ our Lord.

LITURGY OF THE WORD

See Lectionary for Mass, nos. 158-160.

LITURGY OF THE EUCHARIST

PRAYER OVER THE GIFTS

Pray, brethren . . .

Lord God,
may the gifts we offer
increase our love for you
and bring us to eternal life.

We ask this in the name of Jesus the Lord.

Eucharistic Prayer:
Preface of Sundays in Ordinary Time
I-VIII, pages **446–453.**

Communion Rite

It is good for me to be with the Lord and to put my hope in him. (Ps. 72:28)

or:

I tell you solemnly, whatever you ask for in prayer, believe that you have received it, and it will be yours, says the Lord. (Mark 11:23, 24)

A period of silence may be observed after communion, or a psalm or song of praise may be sung.

PRAYER AFTER COMMUNION

Let us pray.

Pause for silent prayer, if this has not preceded.

Father,
may we grow in love
by the eucharist we have celebrated
in memory of the Lord Jesus,
who is Lord for ever and ever.

THIRTY-FOURTH WEEK IN ORDINARY TIME

Introductory Rites

The Lord speaks of peace to his holy people, to those
who turn to him with all their heart. (Ps. 84:9)

OPENING PRAYER

Let us pray
   [that the Spirit of God will renew our lives]

Pause for silent prayer

Lord,
increase our eagerness to do your will
and help us to know the saving power of your love.

Grant this through our Lord Jesus Christ, your Son,
who lives and reigns with you and the Holy Spirit,
one God, for ever and ever.

PRAYER OVER THE GIFTS

Pray, brethren . . .

God of love,
may the sacrifice we offer
in obedience to your command
renew our resolution to be faithful to your word.

We ask this through Christ our Lord.

Communion Rite

All you nations, praise the Lord, for steadfast is his kindly
mercy to us. (Ps. 116:1-2)

or:

I, the Lord, am with you always, until the end of the world.
(Matthew 28:20)

PRAYER AFTER COMMUNION

Let us pray.

Pause for silent prayer, if this has not preceded.

Almighty God,
in this eucharist
you give us the joy of sharing your life.
Keep us in your presence.
Let us never be separated from you.

We ask this in the name of Jesus the Lord.

SOLEMNITIES OF THE LORD
DURING ORDINARY TIME

Sunday after Pentecost

TRINITY SUNDAY

Solemnity

Introductory Rites
  Blessed be God the Father and his only-begotten Son and
  the Holy Spirit: for he has shown that he loves us.

OPENING PRAYER

Let us pray
  [to the one God, Father, Son and Spirit,
  that our lives may bear witness to
  our faith]

Pause for silent prayer

**Father,
you sent your Word to bring us truth
and your Spirit to make us holy.
Through them we come to know the mystery
  of your life.
Help us to worship you, one God in three
  Persons,
by proclaiming and living our faith in you.**

**Grant this through our Lord Jesus Christ, your
  Son,
who lives and reigns with you and the Holy
  Spirit,
one God, for ever and ever.**

ALTERNATIVE OPENING PRAYER

Let us pray
  [to our God who is Father, Son, and Holy
  Spirit]

Pause for silent prayer

**God, we praise you:
Father all-powerful, Christ Lord and Savior,
  Spirit of love.
You reveal yourself in the depths of our
  being,
drawing us to share in your life and your love.
One God, three Persons,
be near to the people formed in your image,
close to the world your love brings to life.**

**We ask you this, Father, Son, and Holy Spirit,
one God, true and living, for ever and ever.**

LITURGY OF THE WORD

See Lectionary for Mass, nos. 165-167.

LITURGY OF THE EUCHARIST

PRAYER OVER THE GIFTS   **Pray, brethren . . .**

**Lord our God,
make these gifts holy,
and through them
make us a perfect offering to you.**

We ask this in the name of Jesus the Lord.

Eucharistic Prayer:
Preface of the Holy Trinity, page 460.

Communion Rite

>   You are the sons of God, so God has given you the Spirit
>   of his Son to form your hearts and make you cry out:
>   Abba, Father. (Gal. 4:6)

A period of silence may be observed
after communion, or a psalm or song
of praise may be sung.

PRAYER AFTER COMMUNION

Let us pray.

Pause for silent prayer, if this has not preceded.

**Lord God,
we worship you, a Trinity of Persons, one eternal God.
May our faith and the sacrament we receive
bring us health of mind and body.**

We ask this through Christ our Lord.

THE BODY AND BLOOD OF CHRIST

Solemnity

Where the solemnity of the Body and Blood of Christ is not observed as a holy day, it is assigned to the Sunday after Trinity Sunday, which is then considered its proper day in the calendar.

Introductory Rites

The Lord fed his people with the finest wheat and honey; their hunger was satisfied. (Ps. 80:17)

OPENING PRAYER

Let us pray

[to the Lord who gives himself in the eucharist, that this sacrament may bring us salvation and peace]

Pause for silent prayer

Lord Jesus Christ,
you gave us the eucharist
as the memorial of your suffering and death.
May our worship of this sacrament of your body and blood
help us to experience the salvation you won for us and the peace of the kingdom
where you live with the Father and the Holy Spirit,
one God, for ever and ever.

ALTERNATIVE OPENING PRAYER

Let us pray

[for the willingness to make present in our world the love of Christ shown to us in the eucharist]

Pause for silent prayer

Lord Jesus Christ,
we worship you living among us
in the sacrament of your body and blood.
May we offer to our Father in heaven
a solemn pledge of undivided love.
May we offer to our brothers and sisters
a life poured out in loving service of that kingdom
where you live with the Father and the Holy Spirit,
one God, for ever and ever.

LITURGY OF THE WORD

See Lectionary for Mass, nos. 168-170.

LITURGY OF THE EUCHARIST

PRAYER OVER THE GIFTS

Pray, brethren . . .

Lord,
may the bread and cup we offer
bring your Church the unity and peace they signify.

We ask this in the name of Jesus the Lord.

Eucharistic Prayer:
Preface of the Holy Eucharist I-II, pages 464–465.

Communion Rite

> Whoever eats my flesh and drinks my blood will live in
> me and I in him, says the Lord. (John 6:57)

A period of silence may be observed
after communion, or a psalm or song
of praise may be sung.

PRAYER AFTER COMMUNION

Let us pray.

Pause for silent prayer, if this has not preceded.

Lord Jesus Christ,
you give us your body and blood in the eucharist
as a sign that even now we share your life.
May we come to possess it completely in the kingdom
where you live for ever and ever.

SACRED HEART

Solemnity

Introductory Rites

The thoughts of his heart last through every generation, that he will rescue them from death and feed them in time of famine. (Ps. 32:11, 19)

OPENING PRAYER

Let us pray
[that we will respond to the love of Christ]
Pause for silent prayer
Father,
we rejoice in the gifts of love
we have received from the heart of Jesus your
Son.
Open our hearts to share his life
and continue to bless us with his love.

We ask this through our Lord Jesus Christ,
your Son,
who lives and reigns with you and the Holy
Spirit,
one God, for ever and ever.

or:

Father,
we have wounded the heart of Jesus your
Son,
but he brings us forgiveness and grace.
Help us to prove our grateful love
and make amends for our sins.

We ask this through our Lord Jesus Christ,
your Son,
who lives and reigns with you and the Holy
Spirit,
one God, for ever and ever.

ALTERNATIVE OPENING PRAYER

Let us pray
[that the love of Christ's heart may touch
the world with healing and peace]
Pause for silent prayer
Father,
we honor the heart of your Son
broken by man's cruelty,
yet symbol of love's triumph,
pledge of all that man is called to be.

Teach us to see Christ in the lives we touch,
to offer him living worship
by love-filled service to our brothers and sis-
ters.

We ask this through Christ our Lord.

LITURGY OF THE WORD

See Lectionary for Mass, nos. 171-173.

Profession of Faith

LITURGY OF THE EUCHARIST

PRAYER OVER THE GIFTS   **Pray, brethren . . .**

Lord,
look on the heart of Christ your Son
filled with love for us.
Because of his love
accept our eucharist and forgive our sins.

Grant this through Christ our Lord.

Eucharistic Prayer:

Preface of the Sacred Heart, page 462.

Communion Rite

The Lord says: If anyone is thirsty, let him come to me; whoever believes in me, let him drink. Streams of living water shall flow out from within him. (John 7:37-38)

or:

One of the soldiers pierced Jesus' side with a lance, and at once there flowed out blood and water. (John 19:34)

A period of silence may be observed after communion, or a psalm or song of praise may be sung.

PRAYER AFTER COMMUNION   **Let us pray.**
Pause for silent prayer, if this has not preceded.
Father,
may this sacrament fill us with love.
Draw us closer to Christ your Son
and help us to recognize him in others.

We ask this in the name of Jesus the Lord.

Last Sunday in Ordinary Time

CHRIST THE KING

Solemnity

The solemnity of Christ the King takes the place of the Thirty-fourth Sunday in Ordinary Time.

Introductory Rites

The Lamb who was slain is worthy to receive strength and divinity, wisdom and power and honor: to him be glory and power for ever. (Rev. 5:12; 1:6)

OPENING PRAYER

Let us pray
   [that all men will acclaim Jesus as Lord]
Pause for silent prayer

Almighty and merciful God,
you break the power of evil
and make all things new
in your Son Jesus Christ, the King of the universe.
May all in heaven and earth acclaim your glory
and never cease to praise you.

We ask this through our Lord Jesus Christ, your Son,
who lives and reigns with you and the Holy Spirit,
one God, for ever and ever.

ALTERNATIVE OPENING PRAYER

Let us pray
   [that the kingdom of Christ may live in our hearts and come to our world]
Pause for silent prayer

Father all-powerful, God of love,
you have raised our Lord Jesus Christ from death to life,
resplendent in glory as King of creation.
Open our hearts,
free all the world to rejoice in his peace,
to glory in his justice, to live in his love.
Bring all mankind together in Jesus Christ your Son,
whose kingdom is with you and the Holy Spirit,
one God, for ever and ever.

LITURGY OF THE WORD

See Lectionary for Mass, nos. 161-163.

LITURGY OF THE EUCHARIST

PRAYER OVER THE GIFTS

Pray, brethren . . .

Lord,
we offer you the sacrifice
by which your Son reconciles mankind.
May it bring unity and peace to the world.

We ask this through Christ our Lord.

Eucharistic Prayer:
Preface of Christ the King, page 468.

Communion Rite

The Lord will reign for ever and will give his people the
gift of peace. (Ps. 28:10-11)

A period of silence may be observed
after communion, or a psalm or song
of praise may be sung.

PRAYER AFTER COMMUNION

Let us pray.
Pause for silent prayer, if this has not preceded.
Lord,
you give us Christ, the King of all creation,
as food for everlasting life.
Help us to live by his gospel
and bring us to the joy of his kingdom,
where he lives and reigns for ever and ever.

ORDER OF MASS

THE ORDER OF MASS

INTRODUCTORY RITES

The purpose of these rites is to help the assembled people to become a worshiping community and to prepare them for listening to God's word and celebrating the eucharist. (See General Instruction, no. 24.) For Musical Setting A, see pages 919–1048.

ENTRANCE SONG
After the people have assembled, the priest and the ministers go to the altar while the entrance song is being sung.

When the priest comes to the altar, he makes the customary reverence with the ministers, kisses the altar and (if incense is used) incenses it. Then, with the ministers, he goes to the chair.

GREETING
After the entrance song, the priest and the faithful remain standing and make the sign of the cross, as the priest says:

In the name of the Father, and of the Son, and of the Holy Spirit.

The people answer:

Amen.

Then the priest, facing the people, extends his hands and greets all present with one of the following greetings:

a

The grace of our Lord Jesus Christ and the love of God and the fellowship of the Holy Spirit be with you all.

The people answer:

And also with you.

b   Or the priest says:

The grace and peace of God our Father and the Lord Jesus Christ be with you.

The people answer:

Blessed be God, the Father of our Lord Jesus Christ.

or:

And also with you.

c   Or the priest says:

The Lord be with you.

(Instead of the greeting, The Lord be with you, a bishop says, Peace be with you.)

The people answer:

And also with you.

403

The priest, deacon, or other suitable minister may very briefly introduce the Mass of the day.

A. The rite of blessing and sprinkling holy water may be celebrated in all churches and chapels at all Sunday Masses celebrated on Sunday or on Saturday evening.

Or:

B. The penitential rite follows.

Or:

C. If the Mass is preceded by some part of the liturgy of the hours, the penitential rite is omitted, and the *Kyrie* may be omitted. (See General Instruction on the Liturgy of the Hours, nos. 94-96.)

A. RITE OF BLESSING AND SPRINKLING HOLY WATER

When this rite is celebrated it takes the place of the penitential rite at the beginning of Mass. The *Kyrie* is also omitted.

After greeting the people the priest remains standing at his chair. A vessel containing the water to be blessed is placed before him. Facing the people, he invites them to pray, using these or similar words:

Dear friends,
this water will be used
to remind us of our baptism.
Let us ask God to bless it
and to keep us faithful
to the Spirit he has given us.

After a brief silence, he joins his hands and continues:

a **God our Father,**
your gift of water
brings life and freshness to the earth;
it washes away our sins
and brings us eternal life.

We ask you now
to bless ✠ this water,
and to give us your protection on this day
which you have made your own.
Renew the living spring of your life within us
and protect us in spirit and body,
that we may be free from sin
and come into your presence
to receive your gift of salvation.

We ask this through Christ our Lord.

b **Lord God almighty,**
creator of all life,
of body and soul,
we ask you to bless ✝ this water:
as we use it in faith
forgive our sins
and save us from all illness
and the power of evil.

Lord,
in your mercy
give us living water,
always springing up as a fountain of salvation:
free us, body and soul, from every danger,
and admit us to your presence
in purity of heart.
Grant this through Christ our Lord.

During the Easter season:

c **Lord God almighty,**
hear the prayers of your people:
we celebrate our creation and redemption.
Hear our prayers and bless ✝ this water
which gives fruitfulness to the fields,
and refreshment and cleansing to man.
You chose water to show your goodness
when you led your people to freedom
through the Red Sea
and satisfied their thirst in the desert
with water from the rock.
Water was the symbol used by the prophets
to foretell your new covenant with man.
You made the water of baptism holy
by Christ's baptism in the Jordan:
by it you give us a new birth
and renew us in holiness.
May this water remind us of our baptism,
and let us share the joy
of all who have been baptized at Easter.
We ask this through Christ our Lord.

Where it is customary, salt may be mixed with the holy water. The priest blesses the salt, saying:

**Almighty God,
we ask you to bless ✛ this salt
as once you blessed the salt scattered over the water
by the prophet Elisha.
Wherever this salt and water are sprinkled,
drive away the power of evil,
and protect us always
by the presence of your Holy Spirit.
Grant this through Christ our Lord.**

Then he pours the salt into the water in silence.

Taking the sprinkler, the priest sprinkles himself and his ministers, then the rest of the clergy and people. He may move through the church for the sprinkling of the people. Meanwhile, an antiphon or another appropriate song is sung.

When he returns to his place and the song is finished, the priest faces the people and, with joined hands, says:

**May almighty God cleanse us of our sins,
and through the eucharist we celebrate
make us worthy to sit at his table
in his heavenly kingdom.
Amen.**

The people answer:

When it is prescribed, the *Gloria* is then sung or said.

B. PENITENTIAL RITE

After the introduction to the day's Mass, the priest invites the people to recall their sins and to repent of them in silence. He may use these or similar words:

a   **As we prepare to celebrate the mystery of Christ's love,
    let us acknowledge our failures
    and ask the Lord for pardon and strength.**

b   **Coming together as God's family,
    with confidence let us ask the Father's forgiveness,
    for he is full of gentleness and compassion.**

¹At the discretion of the priest, other words which seem more suitable under the circumstances, such as friends, dearly beloved, brethren, may be used. This also applies to parallel instances in the liturgy.

c   **My brothers and sisters,¹
    to prepare ourselves to celebrate the sacred mysteries,
    let us call to mind our sins.**

A pause for silent reflection follows. After the silence, one of the following three forms is chosen:

a   All say:

**I confess to almighty God,
and to you, my brothers and sisters,
that I have sinned through my own fault**

They strike their breast:

**in my thoughts and in my words,
in what I have done,
and in what I have failed to do;
and I ask blessed Mary, ever virgin,
all the angels and saints,
and you, my brothers and sisters,
to pray for me to the Lord our God.**

The priest says the absolution:

**May almighty God have mercy on us,
forgive us our sins,
and bring us to everlasting life.**

The people answer:

Amen.

b   The priest says:

**Lord, we have sinned against you:
Lord, have mercy.**

The people answer:

Lord, have mercy.

Priest:

Lord, show us your mercy and love.

People:

And grant us your salvation.

The priest says the absolution:

**May almighty God have mercy on us,
forgive us our sins,
and bring us to everlasting life.**

The people answer:

Amen.

The priest (or other suitable minister) may make any one of the following or other invocations, in place of those given above:

C1   Priest:

**You were sent to heal the contrite:
Lord, have mercy.**

The people answer:

Lord, have mercy.

Priest:

**You came to call sinners:
Christ, have mercy.**

People:

Christ, have mercy.

Priest:

**You plead for us at the right hand of the Father:
Lord, have mercy.**

People:

Lord, have mercy.

The priest says the absolution:

**May almighty God have mercy on us,
forgive us our sins, and bring us to everlasting life.**

The people answer:

Amen.

C2

Priest: **Lord Jesus, you came to gather the nations into the peace of God's kingdom: Lord, have mercy.**

The people answer: **Lord, have mercy.**

Priest: **You come in word and sacrament to strengthen us in holiness: Christ, have mercy.**

People: **Christ, have mercy.**

Priest: **You will come in glory with salvation for your people: Lord, have mercy.**

People: **Lord, have mercy.**

The priest says the absolution: **May almighty God have mercy on us, forgive us our sins, and bring us to everlasting life.**

The people answer: **Amen.**

C3

Priest: **Lord Jesus, you are mighty God and Prince of Peace: Lord, have mercy.**

The people answer: **Lord, have mercy.**

Priest: **Lord Jesus, you are Son of God and Son of Mary: Christ, have mercy.**

People: **Christ, have mercy.**

Priest: **Lord Jesus, you are Word made flesh and splendor of the Father: Lord, have mercy.**

People: **Lord, have mercy.**

The priest says the absolution: **May almighty God have mercy on us, forgive us our sins, and bring us to everlasting life.**

The people answer: **Amen.**

C4

Priest: **Lord Jesus, you came to reconcile us to one another and to the Father: Lord, have mercy.**

The people answer: **Lord, have mercy.**

C4

Priest: **Lord Jesus, you heal the wounds of sin and division:**
Christ, have mercy.

People: **Christ, have mercy.**

Priest: **Lord Jesus, you intercede for us with your Father:**
Lord, have mercy.

People: **Lord, have mercy.**

The priest says the absolution: **May almighty God have mercy on us,**
forgive us our sins,
and bring us to everlasting life.

The people answer: **Amen.**

C5

Priest: **You raise the dead to life in the Spirit:**
Lord, have mercy.

The people answer: **Lord, have mercy.**

Priest: **You bring pardon and peace to the sinner:**
Christ, have mercy.

People: **Christ, have mercy.**

Priest: **You bring light to those in darkness:**
Lord, have mercy.

People: **Lord, have mercy.**

The priest says the absolution: **May almighty God have mercy on us,**
forgive us our sins,
and bring us to everlasting life.

The people answer: **Amen.**

C6

Priest: **Lord Jesus, you raise us to new life:**
Lord, have mercy.

The people answer: **Lord, have mercy.**

Priest: **Lord Jesus, you forgive us our sins:**
Christ, have mercy.

People: **Christ, have mercy.**

Priest: **Lord Jesus, you feed us with your body and blood:**
Lord, have mercy.

People: **Lord, have mercy.**

C6 The priest says the absolution: **May almighty God have mercy on us,**
forgive us our sins,
and bring us to everlasting life.

    The people answer: **Amen.**

C7

    Priest: **Lord Jesus, you have shown us the way to the Father:**
Lord, have mercy.

    The people answer: **Lord, have mercy.**

    Priest: **Lord Jesus, you have given us the consolation of the**
  truth:
Christ, have mercy.

    People: **Christ, have mercy.**

    Priest: **Lord Jesus, you are the Good Shepherd,**
leading us into everlasting life:
Lord, have mercy.

    People: **Lord, have mercy.**

    The priest says the absolution: **May almighty God have mercy on us,**
forgive us our sins,
and bring us to everlasting life.

    The people answer: **Amen.**

C8

    Priest: **Lord Jesus, you healed the sick:**
Lord, have mercy.

    The people answer: **Lord, have mercy.**

    Priest: **Lord Jesus, you forgave sinners:**
Christ, have mercy.

    People: **Christ, have mercy.**

    Priest: **Lord Jesus, you give us yourself to heal us and bring**
  us strength:
Lord, have mercy.

    People: **Lord, have mercy.**

    The priest says the absolution: **May almighty God have mercy on us,**
forgive us our sins,
and bring us to everlasting life.

    The people answer: **Amen.**

KYRIE
The invocations Lord, have mercy orKýrie, eléison, follow, unless they have already been used in one of the forms of the act of penance.

℣. **Lord, have mercy.**
℟. **Lord, have mercy.**

℣. **Kýrie, eléison.**
℟. **Kýrie, eléison.**

℣. **Christ, have mercy.**
℟. **Christ, have mercy.**

℣. **Christe, eléison.**
℟. **Christe, eléison.**

℣. **Lord, have mercy.**
℟. **Lord, have mercy.**

℣. **Kýrie, eléison.**
℟. **Kýrie, eléison.**

GLORIA
This hymn is said or sung on Sundays outside Advent and Lent, on solemnities and feasts, and in solemn local celebrations. (See General Instruction, no. 31.)

Glory to God in the highest,
   and peace to his people on earth.
Lord God, heavenly King,
almighty God and Father,
   we worship you, we give you thanks,
   we praise you for your glory.
Lord Jesus Christ, only Son of the Father,
Lord God, Lamb of God,
you take away the sin of the world:
   have mercy on us;
you are seated at the right hand of the Father:
   receive our prayer.
For you alone are the Holy One,
you alone are the Lord,
you alone are the Most High,
   Jesus Christ,
   with the Holy Spirit,
   in the glory of God the Father. Amen.

OPENING PRAYER
Afterwards the priest, with hands joined, sings or says:

Priest and people pray silently for a while.

Then the priest extends his hands and sings or says the opening prayer, at the end of which the people respond:

Let us pray.

Amen.

LITURGY OF THE WORD

FIRST READING

The reader goes to the lectern for the first reading. All sit and listen. To indicate the end, the reader adds:

All respond:

This is the Word of the Lord.
Thanks be to God.

RESPONSORIAL PSALM

The cantor sings or recites the psalm, and the people respond.

SECOND READING

When there is a second reading, it is read at the lectern as before. To indicate the end, the reader adds:

All respond:

This is the Word of the Lord.
Thanks be to God.

ALLELUIA OR GOSPEL ACCLAMATION

The alleluia or other chant follows. It is to be omitted if not sung. (General Instruction, no. 39; Introduction to the Lectionary [1981], no. 23)

GOSPEL

Meanwhile, if incense is used, the priest puts some in the censer. Then the deacon who is to proclaim the gospel bows to the priest and in a low voice asks his blessing:

Father, give me your blessing.

The priest says in a low voice:

The Lord be in your heart and on your lips that you may worthily proclaim his gospel. In the name of the Father, and of the Son, ✠ and of the Holy Spirit.

The deacon answers:

Amen.

If there is no deacon, the priest bows before the altar and says inaudibly:

Almighty God, cleanse my heart and my lips that I may worthily proclaim your gospel.

Then the deacon (or the priest) goes to the lectern. He may be accompanied by ministers with incense and candles. He sings or says:

The Lord be with you.

The people answer:

And also with you.

The deacon (or priest) sings or says:

A reading from the holy gospel according to N.

He makes the sign of the cross on the book, and then on his forehead, lips and breast. The people respond:

Glory to you, Lord.

Then, if incense is used, the deacon (or priest) incenses the book, and proclaims the gospel.

At the end of the gospel, the deacon (or priest) adds:

All respond:

Then he kisses the book, saying inaudibly:

This is the Gospel of the Lord.
Praise to you, Lord Jesus Christ.

May the words of the Gospel wipe away our sins.

HOMILY

A homily shall be given on all Sundays and holy days of obligation; it is recommended for other days.

412

PROFESSION OF FAITH
After the homily, the profession of faith is said on Sundays and solemnities; it may also be said in solemn local celebrations. (See General Instruction, no. 44.)

We believe in one God,
the Father, the Almighty,
maker of heaven and earth,
of all that is seen and unseen.

We believe in one Lord, Jesus Christ,
the only Son of God,
eternally begotten of the Father,
God from God, Light from Light,
true God from true God,
begotten, not made, one in Being with the Father.
Through him all things were made.
For us men and for our salvation
he came down from heaven:

All bow during these two lines:

by the power of the Holy Spirit
he was born of the Virgin Mary, and became man.
For our sake he was crucified under Pontius Pilate;
he suffered, died, and was buried.
On the third day he rose again
in fulfilment of the Scriptures;
he ascended into heaven
and is seated at the right hand of the Father.
He will come again in glory to judge the living and
the dead,
and his kingdom will have no end.

We believe in the Holy Spirit, the Lord, the giver of
life,
who proceeds from the Father and the Son.
With the Father and the Son he is worshiped and
glorified.
He has spoken through the Prophets.
We believe in one holy catholic and apostolic
Church.
We acknowledge one baptism for the forgiveness
of sins.
We look for the resurrection of the dead,
and the life of the world to come. Amen.

In celebrations of Masses with children, the Apostles' Creed may be said after the homily.[1]

I believe in God, the Father almighty,
   creator of heaven and earth.

I believe in Jesus Christ, his only Son, our Lord.
   He was conceived by the power of
         the Holy Spirit
      and born of the Virgin Mary.
   He suffered under Pontius Pilate,
      was crucified, died, and was buried.
   He descended to the dead.
   On the third day he rose again.
   He ascended into heaven,
      and is seated at the right hand of the Father.
   He will come again to judge the living
      and the dead.

I believe in the Holy Spirit,
   the holy catholic Church,
   the communion of saints,
   the forgiveness of sins,
   the resurrection of the body,
   and the life everlasting. Amen.

GENERAL INTERCESSIONS

Then follow the general intercessions (prayer of the faithful). The priest presides at the prayer. With a brief introduction, he invites the people to pray; after the intentions he says the concluding prayer.

It is desirable that the intentions be announced by the deacon, cantor, or other person. (See General Instruction, no. 47.)

[1]Directory for Masses with Children, no. 49.

LITURGY OF THE EUCHARIST

PREPARATION OF THE ALTAR AND THE GIFTS

After the liturgy of the word, the offertory song is begun. Meanwhile the ministers place the corporal, the purificator, the chalice, and the missal on the altar.

Sufficient hosts (and wine) for the communion of the faithful are to be prepared. It is most important that the faithful should receive the body of the Lord in hosts consecrated at the same Mass and should share the cup when it is permitted. Communion is thus a clearer sign of sharing in the sacrifice which is actually taking place (General Instruction, no. 56h).

It is desirable that the participation of the faithful be expressed by members of the congregation bringing up the bread and wine for the celebration of the eucharist or other gifts for the needs of the Church and the poor.

The priest, standing at the altar, takes the paten with the bread and, holding it slightly raised above the altar, says inaudibly:

Blessed are you, Lord, God of all creation. Through your goodness we have this bread to offer, which earth has given and human hands have made. It will become for us the bread of life.

Then he places the paten with the bread on the corporal.

If no offertory song is sung, the priest may say the preceding words in an audible voice; then the people may respond:

Blessed be God for ever.

The deacon (or the priest) pours wine and a little water into the chalice, saying inaudibly:

By the mystery of this water and wine may we come to share in the divinity of Christ, who humbled himself to share in our humanity.

Then the priest takes the chalice and, holding it slightly raised above the altar, says inaudibly:

Blessed are you, Lord, God of all creation. Through your goodness we have this wine to offer, fruit of the vine and work of human hands. It will become our spiritual drink.

Then he places the chalice on the corporal.

If no offertory song is sung, the priest may say the preceding words in an audible voice; then the people may respond:

Blessed be God for ever.

The priest bows and says inaudibly:

He may now incense the offerings and the altar. Afterwards the deacon or a minister incenses the priest and people.

Lord God, we ask you to receive us and be pleased with the sacrifice we offer you with humble and contrite hearts.

Next the priest stands at the side of the altar and washes his hands, saying inaudibly:

Lord, wash away my iniquity;
cleanse me from my sin.

Standing at the center of the altar, facing the people, he extends and then joins his hands, saying:

**Pray, brethren,¹ that our sacrifice
may be acceptable to God, the almighty Father.**

The people respond:

**May the Lord accept the sacrifice at your hands
for the praise and glory of his name,
for our good, and the good of all his Church.**

PRAYER OVER THE GIFTS

With hands extended, the priest sings or says the prayer over the gifts, at the end of which the people respond:

Amen.

EUCHARISTIC PRAYER

The priest begins the eucharistic prayer. With hands extended he sings or says:

℣. The Lord be with you.

The people answer:

℟. And al-so with you.

He lifts up his hands and continues:

℣. Lift up your hearts.

The people:

℟. We lift them up to the Lord.

With hands extended, he continues:

℣. Let us give thanks to the Lord our God.

The people:

℟. It is right to give him thanks and praise.

The priest continues the preface with hands extended.

¹At the discretion of the priest, other words which seem more suitable under the circumstances, such as friends, dearly beloved, my brothers and sisters, may be used.

ACCLAMATION

At the end of the preface, he joins his hands and, together with the people, concludes it by singing or saying aloud:

Holy, holy, holy Lord, God of power and might, heaven and earth are full of your glory.
  Hosanna in the highest.
  Blessed is he who comes in the name of the Lord.
  Hosanna in the highest.

Ho - ly, ho - ly, ho - ly Lord, God of power and might, heav-en and earth

are full of your glo - ry. Ho - san - na in the high-est. Bless-ed is he who

comes in the name of the Lord. Ho - san - na in the high - est.

In all Masses the priest may say the eucharistic prayer in an audible voice. In sung Masses he may sing those parts of the eucharistic prayer which may be sung in a concelebrated Mass; for musical notation, see pages 1024–1039.

In the first eucharistic prayer (the Roman canon) the words in brackets may be omitted.

ADVENT I

The two comings of Christ

This preface is said in the Masses of the season from the first Sunday of Advent to December 16 and in other Masses celebrated during this period which have no preface of their own.

Priest:	**The Lord be with you.**
People:	**And also with you.**
Priest:	**Lift up your hearts.**
People:	**We lift them up to the Lord.**
Priest:	**Let us give thanks to the Lord our God.**
People:	**It is right to give him thanks and praise.**

Father, all-powerful and ever-living God,
we do well always and everywhere to give you thanks
through Jesus Christ our Lord.

When he humbled himself to come among us as a
    man,
he fulfilled the plan you formed long ago
and opened for us the way to salvation.

Now we watch for the day,
hoping that the salvation promised us will be ours
when Christ our Lord will come again in his glory.

And so, with all the choirs of angels in heaven
we proclaim your glory
and join in their unending hymn of praise:

Holy, holy, holy Lord, God of power and might,
heaven and earth are full of your glory.
    Hosanna in the highest.
Blessed is he who comes in the name of the Lord.
    Hosanna in the highest.

ADVENT II

Waiting for the two comings of Christ

This preface is said in the Masses of the season from December 17 to December 24 inclusive and in other Masses celebrated during this period which have no preface of their own.

Priest: **The Lord be with you.**
People: **And also with you.**

Priest: **Lift up your hearts.**
People: **We lift them up to the Lord.**

Priest: **Let us give thanks to the Lord our God.**
People: **It is right to give him thanks and praise.**

**Father, all-powerful and ever-living God,
we do well always and everywhere to give you thanks
through Jesus Christ our Lord.**

**His future coming was proclaimed by all the
prophets.
The virgin mother bore him in her womb
with love beyond all telling.
John the Baptist was his herald
and made him known when at last he came.**

**In his love Christ has filled us with joy
as we prepare to celebrate his birth,
so that when he comes he may find us watching in
prayer,
our hearts filled with wonder and praise.**

**And so, with all the choirs of angels in heaven
we proclaim your glory
and join in their unending hymn of praise:**

**Holy, holy, holy Lord, God of power and might,
heaven and earth are full of your glory.
Hosanna in the highest.
Blessed is he who comes in the name of the Lord.
Hosanna in the highest.**

CHRISTMAS I
Christ the light

This preface is said in Masses of
Christmas and its octave; in Masses
within the Christmas octave even if
they have their own preface, with the
exception of Masses with a proper
preface of the divine mysteries or
Persons; and on weekdays of the
Christmas season.

Priest: **The Lord be with you.**
People: **And also with you.**

Priest: **Lift up your hearts.**
People: **We lift them up to the Lord.**

Priest: **Let us give thanks to the Lord our God.**
People: **It is right to give him thanks and praise.**

**Father, all-powerful and ever-living God,
we do well always and everywhere to give you thanks
through Jesus Christ our Lord.**

**In the wonder of the incarnation
your eternal Word has brought to the eyes of faith
a new and radiant vision of your glory.
In him we see our God made visible
and so are caught up in love of the God we cannot
 see.**

**And so, with all the choirs of angels in heaven
we proclaim your glory
and join in their unending hymn of praise:**

When Eucharistic Prayer I is used, the
special form of In union with the
whole Church is said.

Vigil Mass and Mass at midnight: we
 celebrate that night. . ...In other
Masses up to the octave of Christmas inclusive: we celebrate that
 day. . . .

**Holy, holy, holy Lord, God of power and might,
heaven and earth are full of your glory.
 Hosanna in the highest.
Blessed is he who comes in the name of the Lord.
 Hosanna in the highest.**

CHRISTMAS II

Christ restores unity to all creation

This preface is said in Masses of Christmas and its octave; in Masses within the Christmas octave even if they have their own preface, with the exception of Masses with a proper preface of the divine mysteries or Persons; and on weekdays of the Christmas season.

Priest: **The Lord be with you.**
People: **And also with you.**

Priest: **Lift up your hearts.**
People: **We lift them up to the Lord.**

Priest: **Let us give thanks to the Lord our God.**
People: **It is right to give him thanks and praise.**

**Father, all-powerful and ever-living God,
we do well always and everywhere to give you thanks
through Jesus Christ our Lord.**

**Today you fill our hearts with joy
as we recognize in Christ the revelation of your love.
No eye can see his glory as our God,
yet now he is seen as one like us.**

**Christ is your Son before all ages,
yet now he is born in time.
He has come to lift up all things to himself,
to restore unity to creation,
and to lead mankind from exile into your heavenly
　　kingdom.**

**With all the angels of heaven
we sing our joyful hymn of praise:**

When Eucharistic Prayer I is used, the special form of In union with the whole Church is said.

Vigil Mass and Mass at midnight: we celebrate that night. . . . In other Masses up to the octave of Christmas inclusive: we celebrate that day. . . .

**Holy, holy, holy Lord, God of power and might,
heaven and earth are full of your glory.
　　Hosanna in the highest.
Blessed is he who comes in the name of the Lord.
　　Hosanna in the highest.**

CHRISTMAS III

Divine and human exchange in the Incarnation of the Word

This preface is said in Masses of Christmas and its octave; in Masses within the Christmas octave even if they have their own preface, with the exception of Masses with a proper preface of the divine mysteries or Persons; and on weekdays of the Christmas season.

Priest: **The Lord be with you.**
People: **And also with you.**

Priest: **Lift up your hearts.**
People: **We lift them up to the Lord.**

Priest: **Let us give thanks to the Lord our God.**
People: **It is right to give him thanks and praise.**

**Father, all-powerful and ever-living God,
we do well always and everywhere to give you thanks
through Jesus Christ our Lord.**

**Today in him a new light has dawned upon the world:
God has become one with man,
and man has become one again with God.**

**Your eternal Word has taken upon himself our
human weakness,
giving our mortal nature immortal value.
So marvelous is this oneness between God and man
that in Christ man restores to man the gift of
everlasting life.**

**In our joy we sing to your glory
with all the choirs of angels:**

When Eucharistic Prayer I is used, the special form of In union with the whole Church is said.

Vigil Mass and Mass at midnight: we celebrate that night. . . .In other Masses up to the octave of Christmas inclusive: we celebrate that day. . . .

**Holy, holy, holy Lord, God of power and might,
heaven and earth are full of your glory.
     Hosanna in the highest.
Blessed is he who comes in the name of the Lord.
     Hosanna in the highest.**

EPIPHANY

Christ the light of the nations

This preface is said in Masses on Epiphany. It may be said, as may the Christmas prefaces, on the days between Epiphany and the Baptism of the Lord.

Priest: **The Lord be with you.**
People: **And also with you.**

Priest: **Lift up your hearts.**
People: **We lift them up to the Lord.**

Priest: **Let us give thanks to the Lord our God.**
People: **It is right to give him thanks and praise.**

**Father, all-powerful and ever-living God,
we do well always and everywhere to give you thanks.**

**Today you revealed in Christ your eternal plan of
 salvation
and showed him as the light of all peoples.
Now that his glory has shone among us
you have renewed humanity in his immortal image.**

**Now, with angels and archangels,
and the whole company of heaven,
we sing the unending hymn of your praise:**

**Holy, holy, holy Lord, God of power and might,
heaven and earth are full of your glory.
 Hosanna in the highest.
Blessed is he who comes in the name of the Lord.
 Hosanna in the highest.**

When Eucharistic Prayer I is used, the special form of In union with the whole Church is said.

BAPTISM OF THE LORD
Consecration and mission of Christ

Priest: **The Lord be with you.**
People: **And also with you.**

Priest: **Lift up your hearts.**
People: **We lift them up to the Lord.**

Priest: **Let us give thanks to the Lord our God.**
People: **It is right to give him thanks and praise.**

**Father, all-powerful and ever-living God,
we do well always and everywhere to give you thanks.**

**You celebrated your new gift of baptism
by signs and wonders at the Jordan.
Your voice was heard from heaven
to awaken faith in the presence among us
of the Word made man.**

**Your Spirit was seen as a dove,
revealing Jesus as your servant,
and anointing him with joy as the Christ,
sent to bring to the poor
the good news of salvation.**

**In our unending joy we echo on earth
the song of the angels in heaven
as they praise your glory for ever:**

**Holy, holy, holy Lord, God of power and might,
heaven and earth are full of your glory.
    Hosanna in the highest.
Blessed is he who comes in the name of the Lord.
    Hosanna in the highest.**

LENT I

The spiritual meaning of Lent

This preface is said in the Masses of Lent, especially on Sundays which have no preface of their own.

Priest:	**The Lord be with you.**
People:	**And also with you.**
Priest:	**Lift up your hearts.**
People:	**We lift them up to the Lord.**
Priest:	**Let us give thanks to the Lord our God.**
People:	**It is right to give him thanks and praise.**

**Father, all-powerful and ever-living God,
we do well always and everywhere to give you thanks
through Jesus Christ our Lord.**

**Each year you give us this joyful season
when we prepare to celebrate the paschal mystery
with mind and heart renewed.
You give us a spirit of loving reverence for you, our
    Father,
and of willing service to our neighbor.**

**As we recall the great events that gave us new life in
    Christ,
you bring the image of your Son to perfection within
    us.**

**Now, with angels and archangels,
and the whole company of heaven,
we sing the unending hymn of your praise:**

**Holy, holy, holy Lord, God of power and might,
heaven and earth are full of your glory.
    Hosanna in the highest.
Blessed is he who comes in the name of the Lord.
    Hosanna in the highest.**

LENT II

The spirit of penance

This preface is said in the Masses of Lent, especially on Sundays which have no preface of their own.

Priest:	**The Lord be with you.**
People:	**And also with you.**
Priest:	**Lift up your hearts.**
People:	**We lift them up to the Lord.**
Priest:	**Let us give thanks to the Lord our God.**
People:	**It is right to give him thanks and praise.**

Father, all-powerful and ever-living God,
we do well always and everywhere to give you thanks.

This great season of grace is your gift to your family
to renew us in spirit.
You give us strength to purify our hearts,
to control our desires,
and so to serve you in freedom.
You teach us how to live in this passing world
with our heart set on the world that will never end.

Now, with all the saints and angels,
we praise you for ever:

Holy, holy, holy Lord, God of power and might,
heaven and earth are full of your glory.
   Hosanna in the highest.
Blessed is he who comes in the name of the Lord.
   Hosanna in the highest.

LENT III

The fruits of self-denial

This preface is said in the Masses of the weekdays of Lent and on fast days.

Priest: **The Lord be with you.**
People: **And also with you.**

Priest: **Lift up your hearts.**
People: **We lift them up to the Lord.**

Priest: **Let us give thanks to the Lord our God.**
People: **It is right to give him thanks and praise.**

Father, all-powerful and ever-living God,
we do well always and everywhere to give you thanks.

You ask us to express our thanks by self-denial.
We are to master our sinfulness and conquer our
   pride.
We are to show to those in need your goodness to
   ourselves.

Now, with all the saints and angels,
we praise you for ever:

Holy, holy, holy Lord, God of power and might,
heaven and earth are full of your glory.
   Hosanna in the highest.
Blessed is he who comes in the name of the Lord.
   Hosanna in the highest.

LENT IV

The reward of fasting

This preface is said in the Masses of the weekdays of Lent and on fast days.

Priest: **The Lord be with you.**
People: **And also with you.**

Priest: **Lift up your hearts.**
People: **We lift them up to the Lord.**

Priest: **Let us give thanks to the Lord our God.**
People: **It is right to give him thanks and praise.**

Father, all-powerful and ever-living God,
we do well always and everywhere to give you thanks.

Through our observance of Lent
you correct our faults and raise our minds to you,
you help us grow in holiness,
and offer us the reward of everlasting life
through Jesus Christ our Lord.

Through him the angels and all the choirs of heaven
worship in awe before your presence.
May our voices be one with theirs
as they sing with joy the hymn of your glory:

Holy, holy, holy Lord, God of power and might,
heaven and earth are full of your glory.
    Hosanna in the highest.
Blessed is he who comes in the name of the Lord.
    Hosanna in the highest.

FIRST SUNDAY OF LENT
The temptation of the Lord

Priest: **The Lord be with you.**
People: **And also with you.**

Priest: **Lift up your hearts.**
People: **We lift them up to the Lord.**

Priest: **Let us give thanks to the Lord our God.**
People: **It is right to give him thanks and praise.**

**Father, all-powerful and ever-living God,
we do well always and everywhere to give you thanks
through Jesus Christ our Lord.**

**His fast of forty days
makes this a holy season of self-denial.
By rejecting the devil's temptations
he has taught us
to rid ourselves of the hidden corruption of evil,
and so to share his paschal meal in purity of heart,
until we come to its fulfillment
in the promised land of heaven.**

**Now we join the angels and the saints
as they sing their unending hymn of praise:**

**Holy, holy, holy Lord, God of power and might,
heaven and earth are full of your glory.
    Hosanna in the highest.
Blessed is he who comes in the name of the Lord.
    Hosanna in the highest.**

SECOND SUNDAY OF LENT
Transfiguration

Priest:	**The Lord be with you.**
People:	**And also with you.**
Priest:	**Lift up your hearts.**
People:	**We lift them up to the Lord.**
Priest:	**Let us give thanks to the Lord our God.**
People:	**It is right to give him thanks and praise.**

**Father, all-powerful and ever-living God,
we do well always and everywhere to give you thanks
through Jesus Christ our Lord.**

**On your holy mountain he revealed himself in glory
in the presence of his disciples.
He had already prepared them for his approaching
death.
He wanted to teach them through the Law and the
Prophets
that the promised Christ had first to suffer
and so come to the glory of his resurrection.**

**In our unending joy we echo on earth
the song of the angels in heaven
as they praise your glory for ever:**

**Holy, holy, holy Lord, God of power and might,
heaven and earth are full of your glory.
Hosanna in the highest.
Blessed is he who comes in the name of the Lord.
Hosanna in the highest.**

THIRD SUNDAY OF LENT
The woman of Samaria

This preface is said when the gospel about the Samaritan woman is read; otherwise one of the prefaces of Lent is said.

Priest: **The Lord be with you.**
People: **And also with you.**

Priest: **Lift up your hearts.**
People: **We lift them up to the Lord.**

Priest: **Let us give thanks to the Lord our God.**
People: **It is right to give him thanks and praise.**

Father, all-powerful and ever-living God,
we do well always and everywhere to give you thanks
through Jesus Christ our Lord.

When he asked the woman of Samaria for water to
drink,
Christ had already prepared for her the gift of faith.
In his thirst to receive her faith
he awakened in her heart the fire of your love.

With thankful praise,
in company with the angels,
we glorify the wonders of your power:

Holy, holy, holy Lord, God of power and might,
heaven and earth are full of your glory.
Hosanna in the highest.
Blessed is he who comes in the name of the Lord.
Hosanna in the highest.

FOURTH SUNDAY OF LENT

The man born blind

This preface is said when the gospel about the man born blind is read; otherwise one of the prefaces of Lent is said.

Priest: **The Lord be with you.**
People: **And also with you.**

Priest: **Lift up your hearts.**
People: **We lift them up to the Lord.**

Priest: **Let us give thanks to the Lord our God.**
People: **It is right to give him thanks and praise.**

Father, all-powerful and ever-living God,
we do well always and everywhere to give you thanks
through Jesus Christ our Lord.

He came among us as a man,
to lead mankind from darkness
into the light of faith.

Through Adam's fall we were born as slaves of sin,
but now through baptism in Christ
we are reborn as your adopted children.

Earth unites with heaven
to sing the new song of creation,
as we adore and praise you for ever:

Holy, holy, holy Lord, God of power and might,
heaven and earth are full of your glory.
   Hosanna in the highest.
Blessed is he who comes in the name of the Lord.
   Hosanna in the highest.

FIFTH SUNDAY OF LENT

Lazarus

This preface is said when the gospel
about Lazarus is read; otherwise one
of the prefaces of Lent is said.

Priest:	**The Lord be with you.**
People:	**And also with you.**
Priest:	**Lift up your hearts.**
People:	**We lift them up to the Lord.**
Priest:	**Let us give thanks to the Lord our God.**
People:	**It is right to give him thanks and praise.**

**Father, all-powerful and ever-living God,
we do well always and everywhere to give you thanks
through Jesus Christ our Lord.**

**As a man like us, Jesus wept for Lazarus his friend.
As the eternal God, he raised Lazarus from the dead.
In his love for us all,
Christ gives us the sacraments
to lift us up to everlasting life.**

**Through him the angels of heaven offer their prayer
        of adoration
as they rejoice in your presence for ever.
May our voices be one with theirs
in their triumphant hymn of praise:**

**Holy, holy, holy Lord, God of power and might,
heaven and earth are full of your glory.
        Hosanna in the highest.
Blessed is he who comes in the name of the Lord.
        Hosanna in the highest.**

PASSION OF THE LORD I
The power of the cross

This preface is said during the fifth week of Lent and in Masses of the mysteries of the cross and the passion of the Lord.

Priest: **The Lord be with you.**
People: **And also with you.**

Priest: **Lift up your hearts.**
People: **We lift them up to the Lord.**

Priest: **Let us give thanks to the Lord our God.**
People: **It is right to give him thanks and praise.**

Father, all-powerful and ever-living God,
we do well always and everywhere to give you thanks.

The suffering and death of your Son
brought life to the whole world,
moving our hearts to praise your glory.
The power of the cross reveals your judgment on this
       world
and the kingship of Christ crucified.

We praise you, Lord,
with all the angels and saints in their song of joy:

Holy, holy, holy Lord, God of power and might,
heaven and earth are full of your glory.
       Hosanna in the highest.
Blessed is he who comes in the name of the Lord.
       Hosanna in the highest.

PASSION OF THE LORD II
The victory of the passion

This preface is said on Monday, Tuesday, and Wednesday of Holy Week.

Priest:	**The Lord be with you.**
People:	**And also with you.**
Priest:	**Lift up your hearts.**
People:	**We lift them up to the Lord.**
Priest:	**Let us give thanks to the Lord our God.**
People:	**It is right to give him thanks and praise.**

**Father, all-powerful and ever-living God,
we do well always and everywhere to give you thanks
through Jesus Christ our Lord.**

**The days of his life-giving death and glorious
    resurrection are approaching.
This is the hour when he triumphed over Satan's
    pride,
the time when we celebrate the great event of our
    redemption.**

**Through Christ
the angels of heaven offer their prayer of adoration
as they rejoice in your presence for ever.
May our voices be one with theirs
in their triumphant hymn of praise:**

**Holy, holy, holy Lord, God of power and might,
heaven and earth are full of your glory.
    Hosanna in the highest.
Blessed is he who comes in the name of the Lord.
    Hosanna in the highest.**

PASSION SUNDAY (PALM SUNDAY)

The redeeming work of Christ

Priest: **The Lord be with you.**
People: **And also with you.**

Priest: **Lift up your hearts.**
People: **We lift them up to the Lord.**

Priest: **Let us give thanks to the Lord our God.**
People: **It is right to give him thanks and praise.**

**Father, all-powerful and ever-living God,
we do well always and everywhere to give you thanks
through Jesus Christ our Lord.**

**Though he was sinless, he suffered willingly for
 sinners.
Though innocent, he accepted death to save the
 guilty.
By his dying he has destroyed our sins.
By his rising he has raised us up to holiness of life.**

**We praise you, Lord, with all the angels
in their song of joy:**

**Holy, holy, holy Lord, God of power and might,
heaven and earth are full of your glory.
 Hosanna in the highest.
Blessed is he who comes in the name of the Lord.
 Hosanna in the highest.**

PRIESTHOOD (CHRISM MASS)

The priesthood of Christ and the ministry of priests

This preface is said in the Chrism Mass on Holy Thursday.

Priest:	**The Lord be with you.**
People:	**And also with you.**
Priest:	**Lift up your hearts.**
People:	**We lift them up to the Lord.**
Priest:	**Let us give thanks to the Lord our God.**
People:	**It is right to give him thanks and praise.**

**Father, all-powerful and ever-living God,
we do well always and everywhere to give you thanks.**

**By your Holy Spirit you anointed your only Son
High Priest of the new and eternal covenant.
With wisdom and love you have planned
that this one priesthood should continue in the
  Church.**

**Christ gives the dignity of a royal priesthood
to the people he has made his own.
From these, with a brother's love,
he chooses men to share his sacred ministry
by the laying on of hands.**

**He appoints them to renew in his name
the sacrifice of our redemption
as they set before your family his paschal meal.
He calls them to lead your holy people in love,
nourish them by your word,
and strengthen them through the sacraments.**

**Father, they are to give their lives in your service
and for the salvation of your people
as they strive to grow in the likeness of Christ
and honor you by their courageous witness of faith
  and love.**

**We praise you, Lord, with all the angels and saints
in their song of joy:**

**Holy, holy, holy Lord, God of power and might,
heaven and earth are full of your glory.
  Hosanna in the highest.
Blessed is he who comes in the name of the Lord.
  Hosanna in the highest.**

EASTER I

The paschal mystery

This preface is said during the Easter season. In the Mass of the Easter Vigil: on this Easter night; on Easter Sunday and during the octave: on this Easter day; on other days of the Easter season: in this Easter season.

Priest:	**The Lord be with you.**
People:	**And also with you.**
Priest:	**Lift up your hearts.**
People:	**We lift them up to the Lord.**
Priest:	**Let us give thanks to the Lord our God.**
People:	**It is right to give him thanks and praise.**

**Father, all-powerful and ever-living God,
we do well always and everywhere
    to give you thanks
through Jesus Christ our Lord.**

**We praise you with greater joy than ever
on this Easter night (day) (in this Easter season),
when Christ became our paschal sacrifice.**

**He is the true Lamb who took away the sins of the
    world.
By dying he destroyed our death;
by rising he restored our life.**

**And so, with all the choirs of angels in heaven
we proclaim your glory
and join in their unending hymn of praise:**

**Holy, holy, holy Lord, God of power and might,
heaven and earth are full of your glory.
    Hosanna in the highest.
Blessed is he who comes in the name of the Lord.
    Hosanna in the highest.**

When Eucharistic Prayer I is used, the special forms of In union with the whole Church and Father, accept this offering are said.

EASTER II

New life in Christ

This preface is said during the Easter
season.

Priest:　**The Lord be with you.**
People:　**And also with you.**

Priest:　**Lift up your hearts.**
People:　**We lift them up to the Lord.**

Priest:　**Let us give thanks to the Lord our God.**
People:　**It is right to give him thanks and praise.**

Father, all-powerful and ever-living God,
we do well always and everywhere to give you thanks
through Jesus Christ our Lord.

We praise you with greater joy than ever in this Easter
　　　season,
when Christ became our paschal sacrifice.

He has made us children of the light,
rising to new and everlasting life.
He has opened the gates of heaven
to receive his faithful people.
His death is our ransom from death;
his resurrection is our rising to life.

The joy of the resurrection renews the whole world,
while the choirs of heaven sing for ever to your glory:

Holy, holy, holy Lord, God of power and might,
heaven and earth are full of your glory.
　　　Hosanna in the highest.
Blessed is he who comes in the name of the Lord.
　　　Hosanna in the highest.

EASTER III

Christ lives and intercedes for us for ever

This preface is said during the Easter season.

Priest:	**The Lord be with you.**
People:	**And also with you.**
Priest:	**Lift up your hearts.**
People:	**We lift them up to the Lord.**
Priest:	**Let us give thanks to the Lord our God.**
People:	**It is right to give him thanks and praise.**

**Father, all-powerful and ever-living God,
we do well always and everywhere to give you thanks
through Jesus Christ our Lord.**

**We praise you with greater joy than ever in this Easter
    season,
when Christ became our paschal sacrifice.**

**He is still our priest,
our advocate who always pleads our cause.
Christ is the victim who dies no more,
the Lamb, once slain, who lives for ever.**

**The joy of the resurrection renews the whole world,
while the choirs of heaven sing for ever to your glory:**

**Holy, holy, holy Lord, God of power and might,
heaven and earth are full of your glory.
    Hosanna in the highest.
Blessed is he who comes in the name of the Lord.
    Hosanna in the highest.**

EASTER IV

The restoration of the universe through the paschal mystery

This preface is said during the Easter season.

Priest: **The Lord be with you.**
People: **And also with you.**

Priest: **Lift up your hearts.**
People: **We lift them up to the Lord.**

Priest: **Let us give thanks to the Lord our God.**
People: **It is right to give him thanks and praise.**

**Father, all-powerful and ever-living God,
we do well always and everywhere to give you thanks
through Jesus Christ our Lord.**

**We praise you with greater joy than ever in this Easter
season,
when Christ became our paschal sacrifice.**

**In him a new age has dawned,
the long reign of sin is ended,
a broken world has been renewed,
and man is once again made whole.**

**The joy of the resurrection renews the whole world,
while the choirs of heaven sing for ever to your glory:**

**Holy, holy, holy Lord, God of power and might,
heaven and earth are full of your glory.
Hosanna in the highest.
Blessed is he who comes in the name of the Lord.
Hosanna in the highest.**

EASTER V

Christ is priest and victim

This preface is said during the Easter
season.

Priest: **The Lord be with you.**
People: **And also with you.**

Priest: **Lift up your hearts.**
People: **We lift them up to the Lord.**

Priest: **Let us give thanks to the Lord our God.**
People: **It is right to give him thanks and praise.**

Father, all-powerful and ever-living God,
we do well always and everywhere to give you thanks
through Jesus Christ our Lord.

We praise you with greater joy than ever in this
         Easter season,
when Christ became our paschal sacrifice.

As he offered his body on the cross,
his perfect sacrifice fulfilled all others.
As he gave himself into your hands for our salvation,
he showed himself to be the priest, the altar,
         and the lamb of sacrifice.

The joy of the resurrection renews the whole world,
while the choirs of heaven sing for ever to your glory:

Holy, holy, holy Lord, God of power and might,
heaven and earth are full of your glory.
     Hosanna in the highest.
Blessed is he who comes in the name of the Lord.
     Hosanna in the highest.

ASCENSION I

The mystery of the ascension

This preface is said on the Ascension, and it may also be said (or an Easter preface) in all Masses which have no preface of their own, from the Ascension to the Saturday before Pentecost inclusive.

Priest: **The Lord be with you.**
People: **And also with you.**

Priest: **Lift up your hearts.**
People: **We lift them up to the Lord.**

Priest: **Let us give thanks to the Lord our God.**
People: **It is right to give him thanks and praise.**

Father, all-powerful and ever-living God,
we do well always and everywhere to give you thanks.

(Today) the Lord Jesus, the king of glory,
the conqueror of sin and death,
ascended to heaven while the angels sang his praises.

Christ, the mediator between God and man,
judge of the world and Lord of all,
has passed beyond our sight,
not to abandon us but to be our hope.
Christ is the beginning, the head of the Church;
where he has gone, we hope to follow.

The joy of the resurrection and ascension
renews the whole world,
while the choirs of heaven sing for ever to your glory:

Holy, holy, holy Lord, God of power and might,
heaven and earth are full of your glory.
Hosanna in the highest.
Blessed is he who comes in the name of the Lord.
Hosanna in the highest.

When Eucharistic Prayer I is used, the special form of In union with the whole Church is said.

ASCENSION II

The mystery of the ascension

This preface is said on the Ascension, and it may also be said (or an Easter preface) in all Masses which have no preface of their own, from the Ascension to the Saturday before Pentecost inclusive.

Priest: **The Lord be with you.**
People: **And also with you.**

Priest: **Lift up your hearts.**
People: **We lift them up to the Lord.**

Priest: **Let us give thanks to the Lord our God.**
People: **It is right to give him thanks and praise.**

**Father, all-powerful and ever-living God,
we do well always and everywhere to give you thanks
through Jesus Christ our Lord.**

**In his risen body he plainly showed himself
    to his disciples
and was taken up to heaven in their sight
to claim for us a share in his divine life.**

**And so, with all the choirs of angels in heaven
we proclaim your glory
and join in their unending hymn of praise:**

**Holy, holy, holy Lord, God of power and might,
heaven and earth are full of your glory.
    Hosanna in the highest.
Blessed is he who comes in the name of the Lord.
    Hosanna in the highest.**

When Eucharistic Prayer I is used, the special form of In union with the whole Church is said.

PENTECOST

The mystery of Pentecost

Priest: **The Lord be with you.**
People: **And also with you.**

Priest: **Lift up your hearts.**
People: **We lift them up to the Lord.**

Priest: **Let us give thanks to the Lord our God.**
People: **It is right to give him thanks and praise.**

**Father, all-powerful and ever-living God,
we do well always and everywhere to give you thanks.**

**Today you sent the Holy Spirit
on those marked out to be your children
by sharing the life of your only Son,
and so you brought the paschal mystery to its
        completion.**

**Today we celebrate the great beginning of your
        Church
when the Holy Spirit made known to all peoples
        the one true God,
and created from the many languages of man
one voice to profess one faith.**

**The joy of the resurrection renews the whole world,
while the choirs of heaven sing for ever to your glory:**

**Holy, holy, holy Lord, God of power and might,
heaven and earth are full of your glory.
        Hosanna in the highest.
Blessed is he who comes in the name of the Lord.
        Hosanna in the highest.**

When Eucharistic Prayer I is used, the
special Pentecost form of *In union
with the whole Church* is said.

SUNDAYS IN ORDINARY TIME I

The paschal mystery and the people of God

This preface is said on Sundays in
ordinary time.

Priest: **The Lord be with you.**
People: **And also with you.**

Priest: **Lift up your hearts.**
People: **We lift them up to the Lord.**

Priest: **Let us give thanks to the Lord our God.**
People: **It is right to give him thanks and praise.**

Father, all-powerful and ever-living God,
we do well always and everywhere to give you thanks
through Jesus Christ our Lord.

Through his cross and resurrection
he freed us from sin and death
and called us to the glory that has made us
a chosen race, a royal priesthood,
a holy nation, a people set apart.

Everywhere we proclaim your mighty works
for you have called us out of darkness
into your own wonderful light.

And so, with all the choirs of angels in heaven
we proclaim your glory
and join in their unending hymn of praise:

Holy, holy, holy Lord, God of power and might,
heaven and earth are full of your glory.
    Hosanna in the highest.
Blessed is he who comes in the name of the Lord.
    Hosanna in the highest.

SUNDAYS IN ORDINARY TIME II

The mystery of salvation

This preface is said on Sundays in
ordinary time.

Priest: **The Lord be with you.**
People: **And also with you.**

Priest: **Lift up your hearts.**
People: **We lift them up to the Lord.**

Priest: **Let us give thanks to the Lord our God.**
People: **It is right to give him thanks and praise.**

**Father, all-powerful and ever-living God,
we do well always and everywhere to give you thanks
through Jesus Christ our Lord.**

**Out of love for sinful man,
he humbled himself to be born of the Virgin.**

**By suffering on the cross
he freed us from unending death,
and by rising from the dead
he gave us eternal life.**

**And so, with all the choirs of angels in heaven
we proclaim your glory
and join in their unending hymn of praise:**

**Holy, holy, holy Lord, God of power and might,
heaven and earth are full of your glory.
Hosanna in the highest.
Blessed is he who comes in the name of the Lord.
Hosanna in the highest.**

SUNDAYS IN ORDINARY TIME III

The salvation of man by a man

This preface is said on Sundays in ordinary time.

Priest:	**The Lord be with you.**
People:	**And also with you.**
Priest:	**Lift up your hearts.**
People:	**We lift them up to the Lord.**
Priest:	**Let us give thanks to the Lord our God.**
People:	**It is right to give him thanks and praise.**

**Father, all-powerful and ever-living God,
we do well always and everywhere to give you thanks.**

**We see your infinite power
in your loving plan of salvation.
You came to our rescue by your power as God,
but you wanted us to be saved by one like us.
Man refused your friendship,
but man himself was to restore it
through Jesus Christ our Lord.**

**Through him the angels of heaven offer their prayer
of adoration
as they rejoice in your presence for ever.
May our voices be one with theirs
in their triumphant hymn of praise:**

**Holy, holy, holy Lord, God of power and might,
heaven and earth are full of your glory.
Hosanna in the highest.
Blessed is he who comes in the name of the Lord.
Hosanna in the highest.**

SUNDAYS IN ORDINARY TIME IV

The history of salvation

This preface is said on Sundays in ordinary time.

Priest: **The Lord be with you.**
People: **And also with you.**

Priest: **Lift up your hearts.**
People: **We lift them up to the Lord.**

Priest: **Let us give thanks to the Lord our God.**
People: **It is right to give him thanks and praise.**

**Father, all-powerful and ever-living God,
we do well always and everywhere to give you thanks
through Jesus Christ our Lord.**

**By his birth we are reborn.
In his suffering we are freed from sin.
By his rising from the dead we rise to everlasting life.
In his return to you in glory
we enter into your heavenly kingdom.**

**And so, we join the angels and the saints
as they sing their unending hymn of praise:**

**Holy, holy, holy Lord, God of power and might,
heaven and earth are full of your glory.
    Hosanna in the highest.
Blessed is he who comes in the name of the Lord.
    Hosanna in the highest.**

SUNDAYS IN ORDINARY TIME V

Creation

This preface is said on Sundays in
ordinary time.

Priest: **The Lord be with you.**
People: **And also with you.**

Priest: **Lift up your hearts.**
People: **We lift them up to the Lord.**

Priest: **Let us give thanks to the Lord our God.**
People: **It is right to give him thanks and praise.**

Father, all-powerful and ever-living God,
we do well always and everywhere to give you thanks.

All things are of your making,
all times and seasons obey your laws,
but you chose to create man in your own image,
setting him over the whole world in all its wonder.
You made man the steward of creation,
to praise you day by day for the marvels
   of your wisdom and power,
through Jesus Christ our Lord.

We praise you, Lord, with all the angels
in their song of joy:

Holy, holy, holy Lord, God of power and might,
heaven and earth are full of your glory.
   Hosanna in the highest.
Blessed is he who comes in the name of the Lord.
   Hosanna in the highest.

SUNDAYS IN ORDINARY TIME VI

The pledge of an eternal Easter

This preface is said on Sundays in ordinary time.

Priest:	**The Lord be with you.**
People:	**And also with you.**
Priest:	**Lift up your hearts.**
People:	**We lift them up to the Lord.**
Priest:	**Let us give thanks to the Lord our God.**
People:	**It is right to give him thanks and praise.**

**Father, all-powerful and ever-living God,
we do well always and everywhere to give you thanks.**

**In you we live and move and have our being.
Each day you show us a Father's love;
your Holy Spirit, dwelling within us,
gives us on earth the hope of unending joy.**

**Your gift of the Spirit,
who raised Jesus from the dead,
is the foretaste and promise
of the paschal feast of heaven.**

**With thankful praise,
in company with the angels,
we glorify the wonders of your power:**

**Holy, holy, holy Lord, God of power and might,
heaven and earth are full of your glory.
    Hosanna in the highest.
Blessed is he who comes in the name of the Lord.
    Hosanna in the highest.**

SUNDAYS IN ORDINARY TIME VII

Salvation through the obedience of Christ

This preface is said on Sundays in ordinary time.

Priest: **The Lord be with you.**
People: **And also with you.**

Priest: **Lift up your hearts.**
People: **We lift them up to the Lord.**

Priest: **Let us give thanks to the Lord our God.**
People: **It is right to give him thanks and praise.**

Father, all-powerful and ever-living God,
we do well always and everywhere to give you thanks.

So great was your love
that you gave us your Son as our redeemer.
You sent him as one like ourselves,
though free from sin,
that you might see and love in us
what you see and love in Christ.
Your gifts of grace, lost by disobedience,
are now restored by the obedience of your Son.

We praise you, Lord, with all the angels and saints
in their song of joy:

Holy, holy, holy Lord, God of power and might,
heaven and earth are full of your glory.
    Hosanna in the highest.
Blessed is he who comes in the name of the Lord.
    Hosanna in the highest.

SUNDAYS IN ORDINARY TIME VIII

The Church united in the mystery of the Trinity

This preface is said on Sundays in ordinary time.

Priest:	**The Lord be with you.**
People:	**And also with you.**
Priest:	**Lift up your hearts.**
People:	**We lift them up to the Lord.**
Priest:	**Let us give thanks to the Lord our God.**
People:	**It is right to give him thanks and praise.**

**Father, all-powerful and ever-living God,
we do well always and everywhere to give you thanks.**

**When your children sinned
and wandered far from your friendship,
you reunited them with yourself
through the blood of your Son
and the power of the Holy Spirit.**

**You gather them into your Church,
to be one as you, Father, are one
with your Son and the Holy Spirit.
You call them to be your people,
to praise your wisdom in all your works.
You make them the body of Christ
and the dwelling-place of the Holy Spirit.**

**In our joy we sing to your glory
with all the choirs of angels:**

**Holy, holy, holy Lord, God of power and might,
heaven and earth are full of your glory.
Hosanna in the highest.
Blessed is he who comes in the name of the Lord.
Hosanna in the highest.**

WEEKDAYS I

All things made one in Christ

This preface is said in Masses which have no preface of their own, unless they call for a seasonal preface.

Priest: **The Lord be with you.**
People: **And also with you.**

Priest: **Lift up your hearts.**
People: **We lift them up to the Lord.**

Priest: **Let us give thanks to the Lord our God.**
People: **It is right to give him thanks and praise.**

**Father, all-powerful and ever-living God,
we do well always and everywhere to give you thanks
through Jesus Christ our Lord.**

**In him you have renewed all things
and you have given us all a share in his riches.**

**Though his nature was divine,
he stripped himself of glory
and by shedding his blood on the cross
he brought his peace to the world.**

**Therefore he was exalted above all creation
and became the source of eternal life
to all who serve him.**

**And so, with all the choirs of angels in heaven
we proclaim your glory
and join in their unending hymn of praise:**

**Holy, holy, holy Lord, God of power and might,
heaven and earth are full of your glory.
    Hosanna in the highest.
Blessed is he who comes in the name of the Lord.
    Hosanna in the highest.**

WEEKDAYS II

Salvation through Christ

This preface is said in Masses which have no preface of their own, unless they call for a seasonal preface.

Priest:	**The Lord be with you.**
People:	**And also with you.**
Priest:	**Lift up your hearts.**
People:	**We lift them up to the Lord.**
Priest:	**Let us give thanks to the Lord our God.**
People:	**It is right to give him thanks and praise.**

**Father, all-powerful and ever-living God,
we do well always and everywhere to give you thanks.**

**In love you created man,
in justice you condemned him,
but in mercy you redeemed him,
through Jesus Christ our Lord.**

**Through him the angels and all the choirs of heaven
worship in awe before your presence.
May our voices be one with theirs
as they sing with joy
the hymn of your glory:**

**Holy, holy, holy Lord, God of power and might,
heaven and earth are full of your glory.
    Hosanna in the highest.
Blessed is he who comes in the name of the Lord.
    Hosanna in the highest.**

WEEKDAYS III

The praise of God in creation and through the conversion of man

This preface is said in Masses which
have no preface of their own, unless
they call for a seasonal preface.

Priest:	**The Lord be with you.**
People:	**And also with you.**
Priest:	**Lift up your hearts.**
People:	**We lift them up to the Lord.**
Priest:	**Let us give thanks to the Lord our God.**
People:	**It is right to give him thanks and praise.**

**Father, all-powerful and ever-living God,
we do well always and everywhere to give you thanks.**

**Through your beloved Son
you created our human family.
Through him you restored us to your likeness.**

**Therefore it is your right
to receive the obedience of all creation,
the praise of the Church on earth,
the thanksgiving of your saints in heaven.**

**We too rejoice with the angels
as we proclaim your glory for ever:**

**Holy, holy, holy Lord, God of power and might,
heaven and earth are full of your glory.
    Hosanna in the highest.
Blessed is he who comes in the name of the Lord.
    Hosanna in the highest.**

WEEKDAYS IV

Praise of God is his gift

This preface is said in Masses which
have no preface of their own, unless
they call for a seasonal preface.

Priest: **The Lord be with you.**
People: **And also with you.**

Priest: **Lift up your hearts.**
People: **We lift them up to the Lord.**

Priest: **Let us give thanks to the Lord our God.**
People: **It is right to give him thanks and praise.**

**Father, all-powerful and ever-living God,
we do well always and everywhere to give you thanks.**

**You have no need of our praise,
yet our desire to thank you is itself your gift.
Our prayer of thanksgiving adds nothing to your
        greatness,
but makes us grow in your grace,
through Jesus Christ our Lord.**

**In our joy we sing to your glory
with all the choirs of angels:**

**Holy, holy, holy Lord, God of power and might,
heaven and earth are full of your glory.
        Hosanna in the highest.
Blessed is he who comes in the name of the Lord.
        Hosanna in the highest.**

WEEKDAYS V

The mystery of Christ is proclaimed

This preface is said in Masses which
have no preface of their own, unless
they call for a seasonal preface.

Priest:	**The Lord be with you.**
People:	**And also with you.**
Priest:	**Lift up your hearts.**
People:	**We lift them up to the Lord.**
Priest:	**Let us give thanks to the Lord our God.**
People:	**It is right to give him thanks and praise.**

**Father, all-powerful and ever-living God,
we do well always and everywhere to give you thanks
through Jesus Christ our Lord.**

**With love we celebrate his death.
With living faith we proclaim his resurrection.
With unwavering hope we await his return in glory.**

**Now, with the saints and all the angels
we praise you for ever:**

**Holy, holy, holy Lord, God of power and might,
heaven and earth are full of your glory.
Hosanna in the highest.
Blessed is he who comes in the name of the Lord.
Hosanna in the highest.**

WEEKDAYS VI

Salvation in Christ

This preface, taken from Eucharistic Prayer II, is said in Masses which have no preface of their own, unless they call for a seasonal preface.

Priest: **The Lord be with you.**
People: **And also with you.**

Priest: **Lift up your hearts.**
People: **We lift them up to the Lord.**

Priest: **Let us give thanks to the Lord our God.**
People: **It is right to give him thanks and praise.**

**Father, it is our duty and our salvation,
always and everywhere to give you thanks
through your beloved Son, Jesus Christ.**

**He is the Word through whom you made the
  universe,
the Savior you sent to redeem us.
By the power of the Holy Spirit
he took flesh and was born of the Virgin Mary.**

**For our sake he opened his arms on the cross;
he put an end to death
and revealed the resurrection.
In this he fulfilled your will
and won for you a holy people.**

**And so we join the angels and the saints
in proclaiming your glory:**

**Holy, holy, holy Lord, God of power and might,
heaven and earth are full of your glory.
    Hosanna in the highest.
Blessed is he who comes in the name of the Lord.
    Hosanna in the highest.**

HOLY TRINITY

The mystery of the Holy Trinity

This preface is said in Masses of the
Holy Trinity.

Priest: **The Lord be with you.**
People: **And also with you.**

Priest: **Lift up your hearts.**
People: **We lift them up to the Lord.**

Priest: **Let us give thanks to the Lord our God.**
People: **It is right to give him thanks and praise.**

Father, all-powerful and ever-living God,
we do well always and everywhere to give you thanks.

We joyfully proclaim our faith
in the mystery of your Godhead.
You have revealed your glory
as the glory also of your Son
and of the Holy Spirit:
three Persons equal in majesty,
undivided in splendor,
yet one Lord, one God,
ever to be adored in your everlasting glory.

And so, with all the choirs of angels in heaven
we proclaim your glory
and join in their unending hymn of praise:

Holy, holy, holy Lord, God of power and might,
heaven and earth are full of your glory.
Hosanna in the highest.
Blessed is he who comes in the name of the Lord.
Hosanna in the highest.

ANNUNCIATION

March 25

The mystery of the Incarnation

Priest: **The Lord be with you.**
People: **And also with you.**

Priest: **Lift up your hearts.**
People: **We lift them up to the Lord.**

Priest: **Let us give thanks to the Lord our God.**
People: **It is right to give him thanks and praise.**

Father, all-powerful and ever-living God,
we do well always and everywhere to give you thanks
through Jesus Christ our Lord.

He came to save mankind by becoming a man
     himself.
The Virgin Mary, receiving the angel's message in
     faith,
conceived by the power of the Spirit
and bore your Son in purest love.

In Christ, the eternal truth,
your promise to Israel came true.
In Christ, the hope of all peoples,
man's hope was realized beyond all expectation.

Through Christ the angels of heaven
offer their prayer of adoration
as they rejoice in your presence for ever.
May our voices be one with theirs
in their triumphant hymn of praise:

Holy, holy, holy Lord, God of power and might,
heaven and earth are full of your glory.
     Hosanna in the highest.
Blessed is he who comes in the name of the Lord.
     Hosanna in the highest.

SACRED HEART

The boundless love of Christ

This preface is said in Masses of the Sacred Heart.

Priest: **The Lord be with you.**
People: **And also with you.**

Priest: **Lift up your hearts.**
People: **We lift them up to the Lord.**

Priest: **Let us give thanks to the Lord our God.**
People: **It is right to give him thanks and praise.**

Father, all-powerful and ever-living God,
we do well always and everywhere to give you thanks
through Jesus Christ our Lord.

Lifted high on the cross,
Christ gave his life for us,
so much did he love us.
From his wounded side flowed blood and water,
the fountain of sacramental life in the Church.
To his open heart the Savior invites all men,
to draw water in joy from the springs of salvation.

Now, with all the saints and angels,
we praise you for ever:

Holy, holy, holy Lord, God of power and might,
heaven and earth are full of your glory.
  Hosanna in the highest.
Blessed is he who comes in the name of the Lord.
  Hosanna in the highest.

TRIUMPH OF THE CROSS

The triumph of the glorious cross

This preface is said in Masses of the
Holy Cross.

Priest:	**The Lord be with you.**
People:	**And also with you.**
Priest:	**Lift up your hearts.**
People:	**We lift them up to the Lord.**
Priest:	**Let us give thanks to the Lord our God.**
People:	**It is right to give him thanks and praise.**

**Father, all-powerful and ever-living God,
we do well always and everywhere to give you thanks.**

**You decreed that man should be saved through the
      wood of the cross.
The tree of man's defeat became his tree of victory;
where life was lost, there life has been restored
through Christ our Lord.**

**Through him the choirs of angels
and all the powers of heaven
praise and worship your glory.
May our voices blend with theirs
as we join in their unending hymn:**

**Holy, holy, holy Lord, God of power and might,
heaven and earth are full of your glory.
      Hosanna in the highest.
Blessed is he who comes in the name of the Lord.
      Hosanna in the highest.**

HOLY EUCHARIST I

The sacrifice and sacrament of Christ

This preface is said in the Mass of the Lord's Supper on Holy Thursday. It may be said on the solemnity of the Body and Blood of Christ and in votive Masses of the Holy Eucharist.

Priest: **The Lord be with you.**
People: **And also with you.**

Priest: **Lift up your hearts.**
People: **We lift them up to the Lord.**

Priest: **Let us give thanks to the Lord our God.**
People: **It is right to give him thanks and praise.**

Father, all-powerful and ever-living God,
we do well always and everywhere to give you thanks
through Jesus Christ our Lord.

He is the true and eternal priest
who established this unending sacrifice.
He offered himself as a victim for our deliverance
and taught us to make this offering in his memory.
As we eat his body which he gave for us,
we grow in strength.
As we drink his blood which he poured out for us,
we are washed clean.

Now, with angels and archangels,
and the whole company of heaven,
we sing the unending hymn of your praise:

Holy, holy, holy Lord, God of power and might,
heaven and earth are full of your glory.
    Hosanna in the highest.
Blessed is he who comes in the name of the Lord.
    Hosanna in the highest.

When the Roman canon is used in the Mass of the Lord's Supper on Holy Thursday, the special In union with the whole Church, Father, accept this offering, and The day before he suffered are said.

HOLY EUCHARIST II

The effects of the holy eucharist

This preface is said on the solemnity of the Body and Blood of Christ and in votive Masses of the Holy Eucharist.

Priest:	**The Lord be with you.**
People:	**And also with you.**
Priest:	**Lift up your hearts.**
People:	**We lift them up to the Lord.**
Priest:	**Let us give thanks to the Lord our God.**
People:	**It is right to give him thanks and praise.**

**Father, all-powerful and ever-living God,
we do well always and everywhere to give you thanks
through Jesus Christ our Lord.**

**At the last supper,
as he sat at table with his apostles,
he offered himself to you as the spotless lamb,
the acceptable gift that gives you perfect praise.
Christ has given us this memorial of his passion
to bring us its saving power until the end of time.**

**In this great sacrament you feed your people
and strengthen them in holiness,
so that the family of mankind
may come to walk in the light of one faith,
in one communion of love.
We come then to this wonderful sacrament
to be fed at your table
and grow into the likeness of the risen Christ.**

**Earth unites with heaven
to sing the new song of creation
as we adore and praise you for ever:**

**Holy, holy, holy Lord, God of power and might,
heaven and earth are full of your glory.
Hosanna in the highest.
Blessed is he who comes in the name of the Lord.
Hosanna in the highest.**

PRESENTATION OF THE LORD

February 2

The mystery of the Presentation of the Lord

Priest: **The Lord be with you.**
People: **And also with you.**

Priest: **Lift up your hearts.**
People: **We lift them up to the Lord.**

Priest: **Let us give thanks to the Lord our God.**
People: **It is right to give him thanks and praise.**

Father, all-powerful and ever-living God,
we do well always and everywhere to give you thanks
through Jesus Christ our Lord.

Today your Son,
who shares your eternal splendor,
was presented in the temple,
and revealed by the Spirit
as the glory of Israel
and the light of all peoples.

Our hearts are joyful,
for we have seen your salvation,
and now with the angels and saints
we praise you for ever:

Holy, holy, holy Lord, God of power and might,
heaven and earth are full of your glory.
   Hosanna in the highest.
Blessed is he who comes in the name of the Lord.
   Hosanna in the highest.

TRANSFIGURATION

August 6

The mystery of the transfiguration

Priest: **The Lord be with you.**
People: **And also with you.**

Priest: **Lift up your hearts.**
People: **We lift them up to the Lord.**

Priest: **Let us give thanks to the Lord our God.**
People: **It is right to give him thanks and praise.**

**Father, all-powerful and ever-living God,
we do well always and everywhere to give you thanks
through Jesus Christ our Lord.**

**He revealed his glory to the disciples
to strengthen them for the scandal of the cross.
His glory shone from a body like our own,
to show that the Church,
which is the body of Christ,
would one day share his glory.**

**In our unending joy we echo on earth
the song of the angels in heaven
as they praise your glory for ever:**

**Holy, holy, holy Lord, God of power and might,
heaven and earth are full of your glory.**
   Hosanna in the highest.
Blessed is he who comes in the name of the Lord.
   Hosanna in the highest.

CHRIST THE KING

Christ, the King of the universe

Priest: **The Lord be with you.**
People: **And also with you.**

Priest: **Lift up your hearts.**
People: **We lift them up to the Lord.**

Priest: **Let us give thanks to the Lord our God.**
People: **It is right to give him thanks and praise.**

Father, all-powerful and ever-living God,
we do well always and everywhere to give you thanks.

You anointed Jesus Christ, your only Son, with the oil
**   of gladness,**
as the eternal priest and universal king.

As priest he offered his life on the altar of the cross
and redeemed the human race
by this one perfect sacrifice of peace.

As king he claims dominion over all creation,
that he may present to you, his almighty Father,
an eternal and universal kingdom:
a kingdom of truth and life,
a kingdom of holiness and grace,
a kingdom of justice, love, and peace.

And so, with all the choirs of angels in heaven
we proclaim your glory
and join in their unending hymn of praise:

Holy, holy, holy Lord, God of power and might,
heaven and earth are full of your glory.
**   Hosanna in the highest.**
Blessed is he who comes in the name of the Lord.
**   Hosanna in the highest.**

DEDICATION OF A CHURCH I

Anniversary of the Dedication

A. Celebration in the Dedicated Church

The mystery of God's temple, which is the Church

Priest: **The Lord be with you.**
People: **And also with you.**

Priest: **Lift up your hearts.**
People: **We lift them up to the Lord.**

Priest: **Let us give thanks to the Lord our God.**
People: **It is right to give him thanks and praise.**

**Father, all-powerful and ever-living God,
we do well always and everywhere to give you thanks.**

**We thank you now for this house of prayer
in which you bless your family
as we come to you on pilgrimage.**

**Here you reveal your presence
by sacramental signs,
and make us one with you
through the unseen bond of grace.
Here you build your temple of living stones,
and bring the Church to its full stature
as the body of Christ throughout the world,
to reach its perfection at last
in the heavenly city of Jerusalem,
which is the vision of your peace.**

**In communion with all the angels and saints
we bless and praise your greatness
in the temple of your glory:**

**Holy, holy, holy Lord, God of power and might,
heaven and earth are full of your glory.
Hosanna in the highest.
Blessed is he who comes in the name of the Lord.
Hosanna in the highest.**

DEDICATION OF A CHURCH II

Anniversary of the Dedication

B. Celebration in Other Churches

The mystery of the Church, the bride of Christ and the
temple of the Spirit

Priest: **The Lord be with you.**
People: **And also with you.**

Priest: **Lift up your hearts.**
People: **We lift them up to the Lord.**

Priest: **Let us give thanks to the Lord our God.**
People: **It is right to give him thanks and praise.**

**Father, all-powerful and ever-living God,
we do well always and everywhere to give you thanks.**

**Your house is a house of prayer,
and your presence makes it a place of blessing.
You give us grace upon grace
to build the temple of your Spirit,
creating its beauty from the holiness of our lives.**

**Your house of prayer
is also the promise of the Church in heaven.
Here your love is always at work,
preparing the Church on earth
for its heavenly glory
as the sinless bride of Christ,
the joyful mother of a great company of saints.**

**Now, with the saints and all the angels
we praise you for ever:**

**Holy, holy, holy Lord, God of power and might,
heaven and earth are full of your glory.
    Hosanna in the highest.
Blessed is he who comes in the name of the Lord.
    Hosanna in the highest.**

HOLY SPIRIT I

The Spirit sent by the Lord upon his Church

This preface is said in votive Masses
of the Holy Spirit.

Priest:	**The Lord be with you.**
People:	**And also with you.**
Priest:	**Lift up your hearts.**
People:	**We lift them up to the Lord.**
Priest:	**Let us give thanks to the Lord our God.**
People:	**It is right to give him thanks and praise.**

**Father, all-powerful and ever-living God,
we do well always and everywhere to give you thanks
through Jesus Christ our Lord.**

**He ascended above all the heavens,
and from his throne at your right hand
poured into the hearts of your adopted children
the Holy Spirit of your promise.**

**With steadfast love
we sing your unending praise;
we join with the hosts of heaven
in their triumphant song:**

**Holy, holy, holy Lord, God of power and might,
heaven and earth are full of your glory.**
Hosanna in the highest.
Blessed is he who comes in the name of the Lord.
Hosanna in the highest.

HOLY SPIRIT II

The working of the Spirit in the Church

This preface is said in votive Masses
of the Holy Spirit.

Priest:	**The Lord be with you.**
People:	**And also with you.**
Priest:	**Lift up your hearts.**
People:	**We lift them up to the Lord.**
Priest:	**Let us give thanks to the Lord our God.**
People:	**It is right to give him thanks and praise.**

**Father, all-powerful and ever-living God,
we do well always and everywhere to give you thanks.**

**You give your gifts of grace
for every time and season
as you guide the Church
in the marvelous ways of your providence.**

**You give us your Holy Spirit
to help us always by his power,
so that with loving trust
we may turn to you in all our troubles,
and give you thanks in all our joys,
through Jesus Christ our Lord.**

**In our joy we sing to your glory
with all the choirs of angels:**

**Holy, holy, holy Lord, God of power and might,
heaven and earth are full of your glory.
    Hosanna in the highest.
Blessed is he who comes in the name of the Lord.
    Hosanna in the highest.**

BLESSED VIRGIN MARY I

Motherhood of Mary

This preface is said in Masses of the Blessed Virgin Mary, with the mention of the particular celebration, as indicated in the individual Masses.

Priest: **The Lord be with you.**
People: **And also with you.**

Priest: **Lift up your hearts.**
People: **We lift them up to the Lord.**

Priest: **Let us give thanks to the Lord our God.**
People: **It is right to give him thanks and praise.**

**Father, all-powerful and ever-living God,
we do well always and everywhere to give you thanks
(as we celebrate . . . of the Blessed Virgin Mary).
(as we honor the Blessed Virgin Mary).**

**Through the power of the Holy Spirit,
she became the virgin mother of your only Son,
our Lord Jesus Christ,
who is for ever the light of the world.**

**Through him the choirs of angels
and all the powers of heaven
praise and worship your glory.
May our voices blend with theirs
as we join in their unending hymn:**

**Holy, holy, holy Lord, God of power and might,
heaven and earth are full of your glory.
Hosanna in the highest.
Blessed is he who comes in the name of the Lord.
Hosanna in the highest.**

BLESSED VIRGIN MARY II

The Church echoes Mary's song of praise

This preface is said in Masses of
the Blessed Virgin Mary.

Priest:	**The Lord be with you.**
People:	**And also with you.**
Priest:	**Lift up your hearts.**
People:	**We lift them up to the Lord.**
Priest:	**Let us give thanks to the Lord our God.**
People:	**It is right to give him thanks and praise.**

**Father, all-powerful and ever-living God,
we do well always and everywhere to give you thanks,
and to praise you for your gifts
as we contemplate your saints in glory.**

**In celebrating the memory of the Blessed Virgin
    Mary,
it is our special joy to echo her song of thanksgiving.
What wonders you have worked throughout the
    world.
All generations have shared the greatness of your
    love.
When you looked on Mary your lowly servant,
you raised her to be the mother of Jesus Christ,
    your Son, our Lord,
the Savior of all mankind.**

**Through him the angels of heaven
offer their prayer of adoration
as they rejoice in your presence for ever.
May our voices be one with theirs
in their triumphant hymn of praise:**

**Holy, holy, holy Lord, God of power and might,
heaven and earth are full of your glory.
    Hosanna in the highest.
Blessed is he who comes in the name of the Lord.
    Hosanna in the highest.**

IMMACULATE CONCEPTION

December 8

The mystery of Mary and the Church

Priest: **The Lord be with you.**
People: **And also with you.**

Priest: **Lift up your hearts.**
People: **We lift them up to the Lord.**

Priest: **Let us give thanks to the Lord our God.**
People: **It is right to give him thanks and praise.**

**Father, all-powerful and ever-living God,
we do well always and everywhere to give you thanks.**

**You allowed no stain of Adam's sin
to touch the Virgin Mary.
Full of grace, she was to be a worthy mother of your
     Son,
your sign of favor to the Church at its beginning,
and the promise of its perfection as the bride of
     Christ, radiant in beauty.**

**Purest of virgins, she was to bring forth your Son,
the innocent lamb who takes away our sins.
You chose her from all women to be our advocate
     with you
and our pattern of holiness.**

**In our joy we sing to your glory
with all the choirs of angels:**

**Holy, holy, holy Lord, God of power and might,
heaven and earth are full of your glory.
     Hosanna in the highest.
Blessed is he who comes in the name of the Lord.
     Hosanna in the highest.**

ASSUMPTION

August 15

Mary assumed into glory

Priest: **The Lord be with you.**
People: **And also with you.**

Priest: **Lift up your hearts.**
People: **We lift them up to the Lord.**

Priest: **Let us give thanks to the Lord our God.**
People: **It is right to give him thanks and praise.**

**Father, all-powerful and ever-living God,
we do well always and everywhere to give you thanks
through Jesus Christ our Lord.**

**Today the virgin Mother of God was taken up into
      heaven
to be the beginning and the pattern of the Church
      in its perfection,
and a sign of hope and comfort for your people
      on their pilgrim way.
You would not allow decay to touch her body,
for she had given birth to your Son, the Lord of all life,
in the glory of the incarnation.**

**In our joy we sing to your glory
with all the choirs of angels:**

**Holy, holy, holy Lord, God of power and might,
heaven and earth are full of your glory.
      Hosanna in the highest.
Blessed is he who comes in the name of the Lord.
      Hosanna in the highest.**

ANGELS

The glory of God in the angels

This preface is said in Masses of the angels.

Priest:	**The Lord be with you.**
People:	**And also with you.**
Priest:	**Lift up your hearts.**
People:	**We lift them up to the Lord.**
Priest:	**Let us give thanks to the Lord our God.**
People:	**It is right to give him thanks and praise.**

**Father, all-powerful and ever-living God,
we do well always and everywhere to give you thanks.**

**In praising your faithful angels and archangels,
we also praise your glory,
for in honoring them, we honor you, their creator.
Their splendor shows us your greatness,
which surpasses in goodness the whole of creation.**

**Through Christ our Lord
the great army of angels rejoices in your glory.
In adoration and joy
we make their hymn of praise our own:**

**Holy, holy, holy Lord, God of power and might,
heaven and earth are full of your glory.
    Hosanna in the highest.
Blessed is he who comes in the name of the Lord.
    Hosanna in the highest.**

ST. JOHN THE BAPTIST

The mission of John the Baptist

This preface is said in Masses of Saint John the Baptist.

Priest: **The Lord be with you.**
People: **And also with you.**

Priest: **Lift up your hearts.**
People: **We lift them up to the Lord.**

Priest: **Let us give thanks to the Lord our God.**
People: **It is right to give him thanks and praise.**

**Father, all-powerful and ever-living God,
we do well always and everywhere to give you thanks
through Jesus Christ our Lord.**

**We praise your greatness
as we honor the prophet
who prepared the way before your Son.
You set John the Baptist apart from other men,
marking him out with special favor.
His birth brought great rejoicing:
even in the womb he leapt for joy,
so near was man's salvation.**

**You chose John the Baptist from all the prophets
to show the world its redeemer,
the lamb of sacrifice.
He baptized Christ, the giver of baptism,
in waters made holy by the one who was baptized.
You found John worthy of a martyr's death,
his last and greatest act of witness to your Son.**

**In our unending joy we echo on earth
the song of the angels in heaven
as they praise your glory for ever:**

**Holy, holy, holy Lord, God of power and might,
heaven and earth are full of your glory.
    Hosanna in the highest.
Blessed is he who comes in the name of the Lord.
    Hosanna in the highest.**

ST. JOSEPH, HUSBAND OF MARY

The mission of Saint Joseph

This preface is said in Masses of Saint
Joseph.

Priest: **The Lord be with you.**
People: **And also with you.**

Priest: **Lift up your hearts.**
People: **We lift them up to the Lord.**

Priest: **Let us give thanks to the Lord our God.**
People: **It is right to give him thanks and praise.**

Father, all-powerful and ever-living God,
we do well always and everywhere to give you thanks
as we honor Saint Joseph.

He is that just man,
that wise and loyal servant,
whom you placed at the head of your family.
With a husband's love he cherished Mary,
the virgin Mother of God.
With fatherly care he watched over Jesus Christ your
        Son,
conceived by the power of the Holy Spirit.

Through Christ the choirs of angels
and all the powers of heaven
praise and worship your glory.
May our voices blend with theirs
as we join in their unending hymn:

Holy, holy, holy Lord, God of power and might,
heaven and earth are full of your glory.
    Hosanna in the highest.
Blessed is he who comes in the name of the Lord.
    Hosanna in the highest.

ST. PETER AND ST. PAUL, APOSTLES

The twofold mission of Peter and Paul in the Church

This preface is said in Masses of Saint
Peter and Saint Paul.

Priest: **The Lord be with you.**
People: **And also with you.**

Priest: **Lift up your hearts.**
People: **We lift them up to the Lord.**

Priest: **Let us give thanks to the Lord our God.**
People: **It is right to give him thanks and praise.**

Father, all-powerful and ever-living God,
we do well always and everywhere to give you thanks.

You fill our hearts with joy
as we honor your great apostles:
Peter, our leader in the faith,
and Paul, its fearless preacher.

Peter raised up the Church
from the faithful flock of Israel.
Paul brought your call to the nations,
and became the teacher of the world.
Each in his chosen way gathered into unity
the one family of Christ.
Both shared a martyr's death
and are praised throughout the world.

Now, with the apostles and all the angels and saints,
we praise you for ever:

Holy, holy, holy Lord, God of power and might,
heaven and earth are full of your glory.
    Hosanna in the highest.
Blessed is he who comes in the name of the Lord.
    Hosanna in the highest.

APOSTLES I

The apostles are shepherds of God's people

This preface is said in Masses of the
Apostles, especially of Saint Peter and
Saint Paul.

Priest:　　**The Lord be with you.**
People:　　**And also with you.**

Priest:　　**Lift up your hearts.**
People:　　**We lift them up to the Lord.**

Priest:　　**Let us give thanks to the Lord our God.**
People:　　**It is right to give him thanks and praise.**

**Father, all-powerful and ever-living God,
we do well always and everywhere to give you thanks.**

**You are the eternal Shepherd
who never leaves his flock untended.
Through the apostles
you watch over us and protect us always.
You made them shepherds of the flock
to share in the work of your Son,
and from their place in heaven they guide us still.**

**And so, with all the choirs of angels in heaven
we proclaim your glory
and join in their unending hymn of praise:**

**Holy, holy, holy Lord, God of power and might,
heaven and earth are full of your glory.
　　Hosanna in the highest.
Blessed is he who comes in the name of the Lord.
　　Hosanna in the highest.**

APOSTLES II

Apostolic foundation and witness

This preface is said in Masses of the apostles and evangelists.

Priest: **The Lord be with you.**
People: **And also with you.**

Priest: **Lift up your hearts.**
People: **We lift them up to the Lord.**

Priest: **Let us give thanks to the Lord our God.**
People: **It is right to give him thanks and praise.**

Father, all-powerful and ever-living God,
we do well always and everywhere to give you thanks.

You founded your Church on the apostles
to stand firm for ever
as the sign on earth of your infinite holiness
and as the living gospel for all men to hear.

With steadfast love
we sing your unending praise:
we join with the hosts of heaven
in their triumphant song:

Holy, holy, holy Lord, God of power and might,
heaven and earth are full of your glory.
    Hosanna in the highest.
Blessed is he who comes in the name of the Lord.
    Hosanna in the highest.

MARTYRS

The sign and example of martyrdom

This preface is said on the solemnities
and feasts of martyrs. It may also be said
on the memorials of martyrs.

Priest: **The Lord be with you.**
People: **And also with you.**

Priest: **Lift up your hearts.**
People: **We lift them up to the Lord.**

Priest: **Let us give thanks to the Lord our God.**
People: **It is right to give him thanks and praise.**

**Father, all-powerful and ever-living God,
we do well always and everywhere to give you thanks.**

**Your holy martyr N. followed the example of Christ,
and gave his (her) life for the glory of your name.
His (her) death reveals your power
shining through our human weakness.
You choose the weak and make them strong
in bearing witness to you,
through Jesus Christ our Lord.**

**In our unending joy we echo on earth
the song of the angels in heaven
as they praise your glory for ever:**

**Holy, holy, holy Lord, God of power and might,
heaven and earth are full of your glory.
  Hosanna in the highest.
Blessed is he who comes in the name of the Lord.
  Hosanna in the highest.**

PASTORS

The presence of shepherds in the Church

This preface is said on the solemnities and feasts of pastors. It may also be said on the memorials of pastors.

Priest: **The Lord be with you.**
People: **And also with you.**

Priest: **Lift up your hearts.**
People: **We lift them up to the Lord.**

Priest: **Let us give thanks to the Lord our God.**
People: **It is right to give him thanks and praise.**

**Father, all-powerful and ever-living God,
we do well always and everywhere to give you thanks.**

**You give the Church this feast in honor of Saint N.;
you inspire us by his holy life,
instruct us by his preaching,
and give us your protection in answer to his prayers.**

**We join the angels and the saints
as they sing their unending hymn of praise:**

**Holy, holy, holy Lord, God of power and might,
heaven and earth are full of your glory.
    Hosanna in the highest.
Blessed is he who comes in the name of the Lord.
    Hosanna in the highest.**

VIRGINS AND RELIGIOUS

The sign of a life consecrated to God

This preface is said on the solemnities and feasts of virgins and religious. It may also be said on the memorials of virgins and religious.

Priest: **The Lord be with you.**
People: **And also with you.**

Priest: **Lift up your hearts.**
People: **We lift them up to the Lord.**

Priest: **Let us give thanks to the Lord our God.**
People: **It is right to give him thanks and praise.**

**Father, all-powerful and ever-living God,
we do well always and everywhere to give you thanks.**

**Today we honor your saints
who consecrated their lives to Christ
for the sake of the kingdom of heaven.
What love you show us
as you recall mankind to its first innocence,
and invite us to taste on earth
the gifts of the world to come!**

**Now, with the saints and all the angels
we praise you for ever:**

**Holy, holy, holy Lord, God of power and might,
heaven and earth are full of your glory.**
    Hosanna in the highest.
Blessed is he who comes in the name of the Lord.
    Hosanna in the highest.

HOLY MEN AND WOMEN I
The glory of the saints

This preface is said in Masses of all saints, patrons, and titulars of churches, and on the solemnities and feasts of saints which have no preface of their own. It may also be said on the memorials of saints.

Priest: **The Lord be with you.**
People: **And also with you.**

Priest: **Lift up your hearts.**
People: **We lift them up to the Lord.**

Priest: **Let us give thanks to the Lord our God.**
People: **It is right to give him thanks and praise.**

Father, all-powerful and ever-living God,
we do well always and everywhere to give you thanks.

You are glorified in your saints,
for their glory is the crowning of your gifts.
In their lives on earth
you give us an example.
In our communion with them
you give us their friendship.
In their prayer for the Church
you give us strength and protection.
This great company of witnesses spurs us on to
**   victory,**
to share their prize of everlasting glory,
through Jesus Christ our Lord.

With angels and archangels
and the whole company of saints
we sing our unending hymn of praise:

Holy, holy, holy Lord, God of power and might,
heaven and earth are full of your glory.
**   Hosanna in the highest.**
Blessed is he who comes in the name of the Lord.
**   Hosanna in the highest.**

HOLY MEN AND WOMEN II
The activity of the saints

This preface is said in Masses of all saints, patrons, and titulars of churches, and on the solemnities and feasts of saints which have no preface of their own. It may also be said on the memorials of saints.

Priest: **The Lord be with you.**
People: **And also with you.**

Priest: **Lift up your hearts.**
People: **We lift them up to the Lord.**

Priest: **Let us give thanks to the Lord our God.**
People: **It is right to give him thanks and praise.**

**Father, all-powerful and ever-living God,
we do well always and everywhere to give you thanks.**

**You renew the Church in every age
by raising up men and women outstanding in
    holiness,
living witnesses of your unchanging love.
They inspire us by their heroic lives,
and help us by their constant prayers
to be the living sign of your saving power.**

**We praise you, Lord, with all the angels and saints
in their song of joy:**

**Holy, holy, holy Lord, God of power and might,
heaven and earth are full of your glory.
    Hosanna in the highest.
Blessed is he who comes in the name of the Lord.
    Hosanna in the highest.**

ALL SAINTS

November 1

Jerusalem, our mother

Priest: **The Lord be with you.**
People: **And also with you.**

Priest: **Lift up your hearts.**
People: **We lift them up to the Lord.**

Priest: **Let us give thanks to the Lord our God.**
People: **It is right to give him thanks and praise.**

**Father, all-powerful and ever-living God,
we do well always and everywhere to give you thanks.**

**Today we keep the festival of your holy city,
the heavenly Jerusalem, our mother.
Around your throne
the saints, our brothers and sisters,
sing your praise for ever.
Their glory fills us with joy,
and their communion with us in your Church
gives us inspiration and strength
as we hasten on our pilgrimage of faith,
eager to meet them.**

**With their great company and all the angels
we praise your glory
as we cry out with one voice:**

**Holy, holy, holy Lord, God of power and might,
heaven and earth are full of your glory.
　　Hosanna in the highest.
Blessed is he who comes in the name of the Lord.
　　Hosanna in the highest.**

MARRIAGE I

The dignity of the marriage bond

Priest: **The Lord be with you.**
People: **And also with you.**

Priest: **Lift up your hearts.**
People: **We lift them up to the Lord.**

Priest: **Let us give thanks to the Lord our God.**
People: **It is right to give him thanks and praise.**

Father, all-powerful and ever-living God,
we do well always and everywhere to give you thanks.

By this sacrament your grace unites man and woman
in an unbreakable bond of love and peace.

You have designed the chaste love of husband and
    wife
for the increase both of the human family
and of your own family born in baptism.

You are the loving Father of the world of nature;
you are the loving Father of the new creation of grace.
In Christian marriage you bring together the two
    orders of creation:
nature's gift of children enriches the world
and your grace enriches also your Church.

Through Christ the choirs of angels
and all the saints
praise and worship your glory.
May our voices blend with theirs
as we join in their unending hymn:

Holy, holy, holy Lord, God of power and might,
heaven and earth are full of your glory.
    Hosanna in the highest.
Blessed is he who comes in the name of the Lord.
    Hosanna in the highest.

MARRIAGE II

The great sacrament of marriage

Priest: **The Lord be with you.**
People: **And also with you.**

Priest: **Lift up your hearts.**
People: **We lift them up to the Lord.**

Priest: **Let us give thanks to the Lord our God.**
People: **It is right to give him thanks and praise.**

Father, all-powerful and ever-living God,
we do well always and everywhere to give you thanks
through Jesus Christ our Lord.

Through him you entered into a new covenant with
      your people.
You restored man to grace in the saving mystery of
      redemption.
You gave him a share in the divine life
through his union with Christ.
You made him an heir of Christ's eternal glory.

This outpouring of love in the new covenant of grace
is symbolized in the marriage covenant
that seals the love of husband and wife
and reflects your divine plan of love.

And so, with the angels and all the saints in heaven
we proclaim your glory
and join in their unending hymn of praise:

Holy, holy, holy Lord, God of power and might,
heaven and earth are full of your glory.
      Hosanna in the highest.
Blessed is he who comes in the name of the Lord.
      Hosanna in the highest.

MARRIAGE III

Marriage, a sign of God's love

Priest: **The Lord be with you.**
People: **And also with you.**

Priest: **Lift up your hearts.**
People: **We lift them up to the Lord.**

Priest: **Let us give thanks to the Lord our God.**
People: **It is right to give him thanks and praise.**

Father, all-powerful and ever-living God,
we do well always and everywhere to give you thanks.

You created man in love to share your divine life.
We see his high destiny in the love of husband and
     wife,
which bears the imprint of your own divine love.

Love is man's origin,
love is his constant calling,
love is his fulfillment in heaven.

The love of man and woman
is made holy in the sacrament of marriage,
and becomes the mirror of your everlasting love.

Through Christ the choirs of angels
and all the saints
praise and worship your glory.
May our voices blend with theirs
as we join in their unending hymn:

Holy, holy, holy Lord, God of power and might,
heaven and earth are full of your glory.
    Hosanna in the highest.
Blessed is he who comes in the name of the Lord.
    Hosanna in the highest.

RELIGIOUS PROFESSION

The religious life, serving God by imitating Christ

Priest: **The Lord be with you.**
People: **And also with you.**

Priest: **Lift up your hearts.**
People: **We lift them up to the Lord.**

Priest: **Let us give thanks to the Lord our God.**
People: **It is right to give him thanks and praise.**

**Father, all-powerful and ever-living God,
we do well always and everywhere to give you thanks
through Jesus Christ our Lord.**

**He came, the son of a virgin mother,
named those blessed who were pure of heart,
and taught by his whole life the perfection of chastity.**

**He chose always to fulfill your holy will,
and became obedient even to dying for us,
offering himself to you as a perfect oblation.**

**He consecrated more closely to your service
those who leave all things for your sake,
and promised that they would find a heavenly
treasure.**

**And so, we join the angels and the saints
as they sing their unending hymn of praise:**

**Holy, holy, holy Lord, God of power and might,
heaven and earth are full of your glory.
Hosanna in the highest.
Blessed is he who comes in the name of the Lord.
Hosanna in the highest.**

CHRISTIAN UNITY

The unity of Christ's body, which is the Church

Priest: **The Lord be with you.**
People: **And also with you.**

Priest: **Lift up your hearts.**
People: **We lift them up to the Lord.**

Priest: **Let us give thanks to the Lord our God.**
People: **It is right to give him thanks and praise.**

Father, all-powerful and ever-living God,
we do well always and everywhere to give you thanks
through Jesus Christ our Lord.

Through Christ you bring us to the knowledge of your
**   truth,**
that we may be united by one faith and one baptism
to become his body.
Through Christ you have given the Holy Spirit to all
**   peoples.**

How wonderful are the works of the Spirit,
revealed in so many gifts!
Yet how marvelous is the unity
the Spirit creates from their diversity,
as he dwells in the hearts of your children,
filling the whole Church with his presence
and guiding it with his wisdom!

In our joy we sing to your glory
with all the choirs of angels:

Holy, holy, holy Lord, God of power and might,
heaven and earth are full of your glory.
**   Hosanna in the highest.**
Blessed is he who comes in the name of the Lord.
**   Hosanna in the highest.**

CHRISTIAN DEATH I

The hope of rising in Christ

This preface is said in Masses for the dead.

Priest: **The Lord be with you.**
People: **And also with you.**

Priest: **Lift up your hearts.**
People: **We lift them up to the Lord.**

Priest: **Let us give thanks to the Lord our God.**
People: **It is right to give him thanks and praise.**

Father, all-powerful and ever-living God,
we do well always and everywhere to give you thanks
through Jesus Christ our Lord.

In him, who rose from the dead,
our hope of resurrection dawned.
The sadness of death gives way
to the bright promise of immortality.

Lord, for your faithful people life is changed, not
**   ended.**
When the body of our earthly dwelling lies in death
we gain an everlasting dwelling place in heaven.

And so, with all the choirs of angels in heaven
we proclaim your glory
and join in their unending hymn of praise:

Holy, holy, holy Lord, God of power and might,
heaven and earth are full of your glory.
**   Hosanna in the highest.**
Blessed is he who comes in the name of the Lord.
**   Hosanna in the highest.**

CHRISTIAN DEATH II

Christ's death, our life

This preface is said in Masses for the dead.

Priest:	**The Lord be with you.**
People:	**And also with you.**
Priest:	**Lift up your hearts.**
People:	**We lift them up to the Lord.**
Priest:	**Let us give thanks to the Lord our God.**
People:	**It is right to give him thanks and praise.**

**Father, all-powerful and ever-living God,
we do well always and everywhere to give you thanks
through Jesus Christ our Lord.**

**He chose to die
that he might free all men from dying.
He gave his life
that we might live to you alone for ever.**

**In our joy we sing to your glory
with all the choirs of angels:**

**Holy, holy, holy Lord, God of power and might,
heaven and earth are full of your glory.**
  Hosanna in the highest.
Blessed is he who comes in the name of the Lord.
  Hosanna in the highest.

CHRISTIAN DEATH III

Christ, salvation and life

This preface is said in Masses for the dead.

Priest: **The Lord be with you.**
People: **And also with you.**

Priest: **Lift up your hearts.**
People: **We lift them up to the Lord.**

Priest: **Let us give thanks to the Lord our God.**
People: **It is right to give him thanks and praise.**

**Father, all-powerful and ever-living God,
we do well always and everywhere to give you thanks
through Jesus Christ our Lord.**

**In him the world is saved,
man is reborn,
and the dead rise again to life.**

**Through Christ the angels of heaven
offer their prayer of adoration
as they rejoice in your presence for ever.
May our voices be one with theirs
in their triumphant hymn of praise:**

**Holy, holy, holy Lord, God of power and might,
heaven and earth are full of your glory.
     Hosanna in the highest.
Blessed is he who comes in the name of the Lord.
     Hosanna in the highest.**

CHRISTIAN DEATH IV

From earthly life to heaven's glory

This preface is said in Masses for the dead.

Priest:	**The Lord be with you.**
People:	**And also with you.**
Priest:	**Lift up your hearts.**
People:	**We lift them up to the Lord.**
Priest:	**Let us give thanks to the Lord our God.**
People:	**It is right to give him thanks and praise.**

Father, all-powerful and ever-living God,
we do well always and everywhere to give you thanks.

By your power you bring us to birth.
By your providence you rule our lives.
By your command you free us at last from sin
as we return to the dust from which we came.
Through the saving death of your Son
we rise at your word to the glory of the resurrection.

Now we join the angels and the saints
as they sing their unending hymn of praise:

Holy, holy, holy Lord, God of power and might,
heaven and earth are full of your glory.
    Hosanna in the highest.
Blessed is he who comes in the name of the Lord.
    Hosanna in the highest.

CHRISTIAN DEATH V

Our resurrection through Christ's victory

This preface is said in Masses for the dead.

Priest:	**The Lord be with you.**
People:	**And also with you.**
Priest:	**Lift up your hearts.**
People:	**We lift them up to the Lord.**
Priest:	**Let us give thanks to the Lord our God.**
People:	**It is right to give him thanks and praise.**

Father, all-powerful and ever-living God,
we do well always and everywhere to give you thanks
through Jesus Christ our Lord.

Death is the just reward for our sins,
yet, when at last we die,
your loving kindness calls us back to life
in company with Christ,
whose victory is our redemption.

Our hearts are joyful,
for we have seen your salvation,
and now with the angels and saints
we praise you for ever:

Holy, holy, holy Lord, God of power and might,
heaven and earth are full of your glory.
    Hosanna in the highest.
Blessed is he who comes in the name of the Lord.
    Hosanna in the highest.

In the dioceses of the United States

INDEPENDENCE DAY AND OTHER CIVIC OBSERVANCES I

Priest: **The Lord be with you.**
People: **And also with you.**

Priest: **Lift up your hearts.**
People: **We lift them up to the Lord.**

Priest: **Let us give thanks to the Lord our God.**
People: **It is right to give him thanks and praise.**

**Father,
all-powerful and ever-living God,
we do well to sing your praise for ever,
and to give you thanks in all we do
through Jesus Christ our Lord.**

**He spoke to men a message of peace
and taught us to live as brothers.
His message took form in the vision of our fathers
as they fashioned a nation
where men might live as one.
This message lives on in our midst
as a task for men today
and a promise for tomorrow.**

**We thank you, Father, for your blessings in the past
and for all that, with your help, we must yet achieve.
And so, with hearts full of love,
we join the angels, today and every day of our lives,
to sing your glory in a hymn of endless praise:**

**Holy, holy, holy Lord, God of power and might,
heaven and earth are full of your glory.
   Hosanna in the highest.
Blessed is he who comes in the name of the Lord.
   Hosanna in the highest.**

INDEPENDENCE DAY AND OTHER CIVIC OBSERVANCES II

Priest: **The Lord be with you.**
People: **And also with you.**

Priest: **Lift up your hearts.**
People: **We lift them up to the Lord.**

Priest: **Let us give thanks to the Lord our God.**
People: **It is right to give him thanks and praise.**

**Father, all-powerful and ever-living God,
we praise your oneness and truth.**

**We praise you as the God of creation,
as the Father of Jesus, the Savior of mankind,
in whose image we seek to live.
He loved the children of the lands he walked
and enriched them with his witness of justice and
      truth.
He lived and died that we might be reborn in the
      Spirit
and filled with love of all men.**

**And so, with hearts full of love,
we join the angels, today and every day of our lives,
to sing your glory in a hymn of endless praise:**

**Holy, holy, holy Lord, God of power and might,
heaven and earth are full of your glory.
      Hosanna in the highest.
Blessed is he who comes in the name of the Lord.
      Hosanna in the highest.**

In the dioceses of the United States

THANKSGIVING DAY

Priest: **The Lord be with you.**
People: **And also with you.**

Priest: **Lift up your hearts.**
People: **We lift them up to the Lord.**

Priest: **Let us give thanks to the Lord our God.**
People: **It is right to give him thanks and praise.**

Father,
we do well to join all creation,
in heaven and on earth, in praising you,
our mighty God through Jesus Christ our Lord.

You made man to your own image
and set him over all creation.
Once you chose a people and gave them a destiny
and, when you brought them out of bondage to
**　　　freedom they carried with them the promise**
that all men would be blessed
and all men could be free.

What the prophets pledged was fulfilled
in Jesus Christ, your Son and our saving Lord.
It has come to pass in every generation
for all men who have believed that Jesus,
by his death and resurrection
gave them a new freedom in his Spirit.

It happened to our fathers,
who came to this land as if out of the desert
into a place of promise and hope.
It happens to us still, in our time, as you lead all men
through your Church to the blessed vision of peace.

And so, with hearts full of love,
we join the angels, today and every day of our lives,
to sing your glory in a hymn of endless praise:

Holy, holy, holy Lord, God of power and might,
heaven and earth are full of your glory.
**　　　Hosanna in the highest.**
Blessed is he who comes in the name of the Lord.
**　　　Hosanna in the highest.**

EUCHARISTIC PRAYER I
ROMAN CANON

In the first eucharistic prayer the words in brackets may be omitted.
Celebrant alone
The priest, with hands extended, says:

**We come to you, Father,
with praise and thanksgiving,
through Jesus Christ your Son.**

He joins his hands and, making the sign of the cross once over both bread and chalice, says:

**Through him we ask you to accept and bless ✠
these gifts we offer you in sacrifice.**

With hands extended, he continues:

**We offer them for your holy catholic Church,
watch over it, Lord, and guide it;
grant it peace and unity throughout the world.
We offer them for N. our Pope,
for N. our bishop,**

When several are to be named, a general form is used: for N. our bishop and his assistant bishops (General Instruction, no. 172).

**and for all who hold and teach the catholic faith
that comes to us from the apostles.**

Commemoration of the living.
Celebrant alone or one of the concelebrants

**Remember, Lord, your people,
especially those for whom we now pray, N. and N.**

He prays for them briefly with hands joined. Then, with hands extended, he continues:

**Remember all of us gathered here before you.
You know how firmly we believe in you
and dedicate ourselves to you.
We offer you this sacrifice of praise
for ourselves and those who are dear to us.
We pray to you, our living and true God,
for our well-being and redemption.**

Special forms on page 503.

**In union with the whole Church
we honor Mary,
the ever-virgin mother of Jesus Christ our Lord and Go
✠We honor Joseph, her husband,
the apostles and martyrs
Peter and Paul, Andrew,**

> [James, John, Thomas, James, Philip,
> Bartholomew, Matthew, Simon and Jude;
> we honor Linus, Cletus, Clement, Sixtus,
> Cornelius, Cyprian, Lawrence, Chrysogonus,
> John and Paul, Cosmas and Damian]

**and all the saints.
May their merits and prayers
gain us your constant help and protection.**

> [Through Christ our Lord. Amen.]

SPECIAL FORM of
In union with the whole Church (*Communicantes*)

Christmas and during the octave

**In union with the whole Church
we celebrate that day (night)
when Mary without loss of her virginity
gave the world its Savior.
We honor Mary,
the ever-virgin mother of Jesus Christ our Lord and God. †**

Epiphany

**In union with the whole Church
we celebrate that day
when your only Son,
sharing your eternal glory,
showed himself in a human body.
We honor Mary,
the ever-virgin mother of Jesus Christ our Lord and God. †**

Holy Thursday

**In union with the whole Church
we celebrate that day
when Jesus Christ, our Lord,
was betrayed for us.
We honor Mary,
the ever-virgin mother of Jesus Christ our Lord and God.†**

From the Easter Vigil to the Second
Sunday of Easter inclusive

**In union with the whole Church
we celebrate that day (night)
when Jesus Christ, our Lord,
rose from the dead in his human body.
We honor Mary,
the ever-virgin mother of Jesus Christ our Lord and God.†**

Ascension

**In union with the whole Church
we celebrate that day
when your only Son, our Lord,
took his place with you
and raised our frail human nature to glory.
We honor Mary,
the ever-virgin mother of Jesus Christ our Lord and God.†**

Pentecost

**In union with the whole Church
we celebrate the day of Pentecost
when the Holy Spirit appeared to the apostles
in the form of countless tongues.
We honor Mary,
the ever-virgin mother of Jesus Christ our Lord and God.†**

SPECIAL FORM of
Father, accept this offering (*Hanc igitur*)

Holy Thursday

**Father, accept this offering
from your whole family
in memory of the day when Jesus Christ, our Lord,
gave the mysteries of his body and blood
for his disciples to celebrate.
Grant us your peace in this life,
save us from final damnation,
and count us among those you have chosen.**

    [Through Christ our Lord. Amen.]

**Bless and approve our offering;
make it acceptable to you,
an offering in spirit and in truth.
Let it become for us
the body and blood of Jesus Christ,
your only Son, our Lord.**

**The day before he suffered
to save us and all men,
that is today,
he took bread in his sacred hands . . .**

From the Easter Vigil to the Second
Sunday of Easter inclusive

**Father, accept this offering
from your whole family
and from those born into the new life
of water and the Holy Spirit,
with all their sins forgiven.
Grant us your peace in this life,
save us from final damnation,
and count us among those you have chosen.**

He joins his hands.

    [Through Christ our Lord. Amen.]

Celebrant alone

With hands extended, he continues:

Father, accept this offering
from your whole family.
Grant us your peace in this life,
save us from final damnation,
and count us among those you have chosen.

He joins his hands.

[**Through Christ our Lord. Amen.**]

Celebrant and concelebrants

With hands outstretched over the offerings, he says:

Bless and approve our offering;
make it acceptable to you,
an offering in spirit and in truth.
Let it become for us
the body and blood of Jesus Christ,
your only Son, our Lord.

He joins his hands.

[**Through Christ our Lord. Amen.**]

The words of the Lord in the following formulas should be spoken clearly and distinctly, as their meaning demands.

He takes the bread and, raising it a little above the altar, continues:

He looks upward.

The day before he suffered

he took bread in his sacred hands

and looking up to heaven,
to you, his almighty Father,
he gave you thanks and praise.
He broke the bread,
gave it to his disciples, and said:

He bows slightly.

He shows the consecrated host to the people, places it on the paten, and genuflects in adoration.

Then he continues:

He takes the chalice, and, raising it a little above the altar, continues:

Take this, all of you, and eat it:
this is my body which will be given up for you.

When supper was ended,

he took the cup.
Again he gave you thanks and praise,
gave the cup to his disciples, and said:

He bows slightly.

Take this, all of you, and drink from it:
this is the cup of my blood,
the blood of the new and everlasting covenant.
It will be shed for you and for all
so that sins may be forgiven.
Do this in memory of me.

He shows the chalice to the people, places it on the corporal, and genuflects in adoration.

Celebrant alone

Then he sings or says:

Let us proclaim the mystery of faith:

*People with celebrant
and concelebrants*

a   **Christ has died,
      Christ is risen,
      Christ will come again.**

Sung acclamations, page 1028.

b   **Dying you destroyed our death,
      rising you restored our life.
      Lord Jesus, come in glory.**

c   **When we eat this bread and drink this cup,
      we proclaim your death, Lord Jesus,
      until you come in glory.**

d   **Lord, by your cross and resurrection
      you have set us free.
      You are the Savior of the world.**

Celebrant and concelebrants

Then, with hands extended, the
priest says:

**Father, we celebrate the memory of Christ, your Son.
We, your people and your ministers,
recall his passion,
his resurrection from the dead,
and his ascension into glory;
and from the many gifts you have given us
we offer to you, God of glory and majesty,
this holy and perfect sacrifice:
the bread of life
and the cup of eternal salvation.**

**Look with favor on these offerings
and accept them as once you accepted
the gifts of your servant Abel,
the sacrifice of Abraham, our father in faith,
and the bread and wine offered by your priest
  Melchisedech.**

Bowing, with hands joined, he continues:

Almighty God,
we pray that your angel may take this sacrifice
to your altar in heaven.
Then, as we receive from this altar
the sacred body and blood of your Son,
let us be filled with every grace and blessing.

   [Through Christ our Lord. Amen.]

He stands up straight and makes the sign of the cross, saying:

He joins his hands.

Commemoration of the dead.

Celebrant alone or one of the concelebrants
With hands extended, he says:

Remember, Lord, those who have died
and have gone before us marked with the sign of
   faith,
especially those for whom we now pray, N. and N.

The priest prays for them briefly with joined hands. Then, with hands extended, he continues:

May these, and all who sleep in Christ,
find in your presence
light, happiness, and peace.

   [Through Christ our Lord. Amen.]

He joins his hands.

With hands extended, he continues:

For ourselves, too, we ask
some share in the fellowship of your apostles and
   martyrs,
with John the Baptist, Stephen, Matthias, Barnabas,
   [Ignatius, Alexander, Marcellinus, Peter,
   Felicity, Perpetua, Agatha, Lucy,
   Agnes, Cecilia, Anastasia]
and all the saints.

The priest strikes his breast with the right hand, saying:

Though we are sinners,
we trust in your mercy and love.

With hands extended as before, he continues:

Do not consider what we truly deserve,
but grant us your forgiveness.
Through Christ our Lord.

He joins his hands.

Celebrant alone
He continues:

Through him you give us all these gifts.
You fill them with life and goodness,
you bless them and make them holy.

*Celebrant alone or with the con-
celebrants*
He takes the chalice and the paten
with the host and, lifting them up,
sings or says:

**Through him,
with him,
in him,
in the unity of the Holy Spirit,
all glory and honor is yours,
almighty Father,
for ever and ever.**

The people respond: **Amen.**

Through him, with him, in him, in the u - ni - ty of the Ho - ly Spir - it, all glo - ry

and hon - or is yours, al - might - y Fa - ther,   for ev - er and ev - er. ℟. A - men.

EUCHARISTIC PRAYER II

Priest: **The Lord be with you.**
People: **And also with you.**

Priest: **Lift up your hearts.**
People: **We lift them up to the Lord.**

Priest: **Let us give thanks to the Lord our God.**
People: **It is right to give him thanks and praise.**

Celebrant alone

**Father, it is our duty and our salvation,
always and everywhere
to give you thanks
through your beloved Son, Jesus Christ.**

**He is the Word through whom you made the
    universe,
the Savior you sent to redeem us.
By the power of the Holy Spirit
he took flesh and was born of the Virgin Mary.**

**For our sake he opened his arms on the cross;
he put an end to death
and revealed the resurrection.
In this he fulfilled your will
and won for you a holy people.**

**And so we join the angels and the saints
in proclaiming your glory
as we say:**

**Holy, holy, holy Lord, God of power and might,
heaven and earth are full of your glory.
    Hosanna in the highest.
Blessed is he who comes in the name of the Lord.
    Hosanna in the highest.**

**Lord, you are holy indeed,
the fountain of all holiness.**

**Let your Spirit come upon these gifts to make them
    holy,
so that they may become for us
the body ✠ and blood of our Lord, Jesus Christ.**

**Before he was given up to death,
a death he freely accepted,**

**he took bread and gave you thanks.
He broke the bread,
gave it to his disciples, and said:**

**Take this, all of you, and eat it:
this is my body which will be given up for you.**

When supper was ended, he took the cup.

**Again he gave you thanks and praise,
gave the cup to his disciples, and said:**

**Take this, all of you, and drink from it:
this is the cup of my blood,
the blood of the new and everlasting covenant.
It will be shed for you and for all
so that sins may be forgiven.
Do this in memory of me.**

Celebrant alone
Then he sings or says:

Let us proclaim the mystery of faith:

Let us pro - claim   the mys - ter - y of faith:

*People with celebrant
and concelebrants*

Christ has died, Christ is ris - en, Christ will come a - gain.

a   **Christ has died,**
    Christ is risen,
    Christ will come again.

Sung acclamations, page 1028.

b   **Dying you destroyed our death,**
    rising you restored our life.
    Lord Jesus, come in glory.

c   **When we eat this bread and drink this cup,**
    we proclaim your death, Lord Jesus,
    until you come in glory.

d   **Lord, by your cross and resurrection**
    you have set us free.
    You are the Savior of the world.

Celebrant and concelebrants

Then, with hands extended, the priest says:

In memory of his death and resurrection,
we offer you, Father, this life-giving bread,
this saving cup.
We thank you for counting us worthy
to stand in your presence and serve you.
May all of us who share in the body and blood of
    Christ
be brought together in unity by the Holy Spirit.

Celebrant alone or one of the concelebrants

Lord, remember your Church throughout the world;
make us grow in love,
together with N. our Pope,
N. our bishop, and all the clergy.

When several are to be named, a general form is used: for N. our bishop and his assistant bishops (General Instruction, no. 172).

In Masses for the dead the following
may be added:

> Remember N., whom you have called from this life.
> In baptism he (she) died with Christ:
> may he (she) also share his resurrection.

Remember our brothers and sisters
who have gone to their rest
in the hope of rising again;
bring them and all the departed
into the light of your presence.
Have mercy on us all;
make us worthy to share eternal life
with Mary, the virgin Mother of God,
with the apostles, and with all the saints
who have done your will throughout the ages.
May we praise you in union with them,
and give you glory

He joins his hands.

through your Son, Jesus Christ.

*Celebrant alone or with the con-
celebrants*

He takes the chalice and the paten
with the host and, lifting them up,
sings or says:

Through him,
with him,
in him,
in the unity of the Holy Spirit,
all glory and honor is yours,
almighty Father,
for ever and ever.

The people respond: Amen.

Through him, with him, in him, in the u - ni - ty of the Ho - ly Spir - it, all glo - ry

and hon - or is yours, al - might - y Fa - ther, for ev - er and ev - er. ℟. A - men.

EUCHARISTIC PRAYER III

Celebrant alone

The priest, with hands extended, says:

Father, you are holy indeed,
and all creation rightly gives you praise.
All life, all holiness comes from you
through your Son, Jesus Christ our Lord,
by the working of the Holy Spirit.
From age to age you gather a people to yourself,
so that from east to west
a perfect offering may be made
to the glory of your name.

Celebrant and concelebrants

He joins his hands and, holding them outstretched over the offerings, says:

And so, Father, we bring you these gifts.
We ask you to make them holy by the power of your
  Spirit,

He joins his hands and, making the sign of the cross once over both bread and chalice, says:

that they may become the body ✝ and blood
of your Son, our Lord Jesus Christ,
at whose command we celebrate this eucharist.

He joins his hands.

The words of the Lord in the following formulas should be spoken clearly and distinctly, as their meaning demands.

He takes the bread and, raising it a little above the altar, continues:

On the night he was betrayed,

he took bread and gave you thanks and praise.
He broke the bread, gave it to his disciples, and said:

He bows slightly.

Take this, all of you, and eat it:
this is my body which will be given up for you.

He shows the consecrated host to the people, places it on the paten, and genuflects in adoration.
Then he continues:
He takes the chalice and, raising it a little above the altar, continues:

When supper was ended, he took the cup.

Again he gave you thanks and praise,
gave the cup to his disciples, and said:

He bows slightly.

Take this, all of you, and drink from it:
this is the cup of my blood,
the blood of the new and everlasting covenant.
It will be shed for you and for all
so that sins may be forgiven.
Do this in memory of me.

He shows the chalice to the people, places it on the corporal, and genuflects in adoration.

513

Celebrant alone
Then he sings or says:

Let us proclaim the mystery of faith:

Let us pro - claim   the mys - ter - y of faith:

*People with celebrant
and concelebrants*

Christ has died, Christ is ris - en, Christ will come a - gain.

a   **Christ has died,
Christ is risen,
Christ will come again.**

Sung acclamations, page 1028.

b   **Dying you destroyed our death,
rising you restored our life.
Lord Jesus, come in glory.**

c   **When we eat this bread and drink this cup,
we proclaim your death, Lord Jesus,
until you come in glory.**

d   **Lord, by your cross and resurrection
you have set us free.
You are the Savior of the world.**

Celebrant and concelebrants
With hands extended, the priest
says:

**Father, calling to mind the death your Son endured
for our salvation,
his glorious resurrection and ascension into heaven,
and ready to greet him when he comes again,
we offer you in thanksgiving this holy and living
sacrifice.**

**Look with favor on your Church's offering,
and see the Victim whose death has reconciled us to
yourself.
Grant that we, who are nourished by his body and
blood,
may be filled with his Holy Spirit,
and become one body, one spirit in Christ.**

Celebrant alone or one of the con-celebrants

**May he make us an everlasting gift to you
and enable us to share in the inheritance of your
saints,
with Mary, the virgin Mother of God;
with the apostles, the martyrs,
(Saint N. —** the saint of the day or the patron saint)
**and all your saints,
on whose constant intercession we rely for help.**

**Lord, may this sacrifice,
which has made our peace with you,
advance the peace and salvation of all the world.
Strengthen in faith and love your pilgrim Church on
earth;
your servant, Pope N., our bishop N.,
and all the bishops,
with the clergy and the entire people your Son has
gained for you.
Father, hear the prayers of the family you have
gathered here before you.
In mercy and love unite all your children wherever
they may be.*** In Masses for the dead, see page 516.

When several are to be named, a general form is used: for N. our bishop and his assistant bishops (General Instruction, no. 172).

**Welcome into your kingdom our departed brothers
and sisters,
and all who have left this world in your friendship.**

He joins his hands.

**We hope to enjoy for ever the vision of your glory,
through Christ our Lord, from whom all good things
come.**

Celebrant alone or with the con-celebrants

He takes the chalice and the paten with the host and, lifting them up, sings or says:

**Through him,
with him,
in him,
in the unity of the Holy Spirit,
all glory and honor is yours,
almighty Father,
for ever and ever.**

The people respond: **Amen.**

Through him, with him, in him, in the u - ni - ty of the Ho - ly Spir - it, all glo - ry

and hon - or is yours, al - might - y Fa - ther, for ev - er and ev - er. ℟. A - men.

*When this eucharistic prayer is used in Masses for the dead, the following may be said:

Remember N.
In baptism he (she) died with Christ:
may he (she) also share his resurrection,
when Christ will raise our mortal bodies
and make them like his own in glory.

Welcome into your kingdom our departed brothers and sisters,
and all who have left this world in your friendship.
There we hope to share in your glory
when every tear will be wiped away.
On that day we shall see you, our God, as you are.

He joins his hands.

We shall become like you
and praise you for ever through Christ our Lord,
from whom all good things come.

He takes the chalice and the paten with the host and, lifting them up, says:

Through him,
with him,
in him,
in the unity of the Holy Spirit,
all glory and honor is yours,
almighty Father,
for ever and ever.

The people respond: **Amen.**

EUCHARISTIC PRAYER IV

Priest: **The Lord be with you.**
People: **And also with you.**

Priest: **Lift up your hearts.**
People: **We lift them up to the Lord.**

Priest: **Let us give thanks to the Lord our God.**
People: **It is right to give him thanks and praise.**

Celebrant alone

**Father in heaven,
it is right that we should give you thanks and glory:
you are the one God, living and true.
Through all eternity you live in unapproachable
   light.
Source of life and goodness, you have created all
   things,
to fill your creatures with every blessing
and lead all men to the joyful vision of your light.
Countless hosts of angels stand before you
   to do your will;
they look upon your splendor
and praise you, night and day.
United with them,
and in the name of every creature under heaven,
we too praise your glory as we say:**

**Holy, holy, holy Lord, God of power and might,
heaven and earth are full of your glory.
   Hosanna in the highest.
Blessed is he who comes in the name of the Lord.
   Hosanna in the highest.**

Celebrant alone
The priest, with hands extended, says:

Father, we acknowledge your greatness:
all your actions show your wisdom and love.
You formed man in your own likeness
and set him over the whole world
to serve you, his creator,
and to rule over all creatures.
Even when he disobeyed you and lost your friendship
you did not abandon him to the power of death,
but helped all men to seek and find you.
Again and again you offered a covenant to man,
and through the prophets taught him to hope for
    salvation.
Father, you so loved the world
that in the fullness of time you sent your only Son to
    be our Savior.
He was conceived through the power of the Holy Spirit,
and born of the Virgin Mary,
a man like us in all things but sin.
To the poor he proclaimed the good news
    of salvation,
to prisoners, freedom,
and to those in sorrow, joy.
In fulfillment of your will
he gave himself up to death;
but by rising from the dead,
he destroyed death and restored life.
And that we might live no longer for ourselves but for
    him,
he sent the Holy Spirit from you, Father,
as his first gift to those who believe,
to complete his work on earth
and bring us the fullness of grace.

Celebrant and concelebrants

He joins his hands and, holding them outstretched over the offerings, says:

Father, may this Holy Spirit sanctify these offerings.

He joins his hands and, making the sign of the cross once over both bread and chalice, says:

Let them become the body ✛ and blood of Jesus
    Christ our Lord
as we celebrate the great mystery
which he left us as an everlasting covenant.

He joins his hands.

The words of the Lord in the following formulas should be spoken clearly and distinctly, as their meaning demands.

He always loved those who were his own in the world.
When the time came for him to be glorified by you, his heavenly Father,
he showed the depth of his love.

He takes the bread and, raising it a little above the altar, continues:

While they were at supper,
he took bread, said the blessing, broke the bread and gave it to his disciples, saying:

He bows slightly.

Take this, all of you, and eat it:
this is my body which will be given up for you.

He shows the consecrated host to the people, places it on the paten, and genuflects in adoration.

Then he continues:

In the same way, he took the cup, filled with wine.

He takes the chalice and, raising it a little above the altar, continues:

He gave you thanks, and giving the cup to his disciples, said:

He bows slightly.

Take this, all of you, and drink from it:
this is the cup of my blood,
the blood of the new and everlasting covenant.
It will be shed for you and for all
so that sins may be forgiven.
Do this in memory of me.

He shows the chalice to the people, places it on the corporal, and genuflects in adoration.

Celebrant alone
Then he sings or says:

Let us proclaim the mystery of faith:

People with celebrant and concelebrants

Let us pro - claim   the mys - ter - y of faith:
Christ has died, Christ is ris - en, Christ will come a - gain.

a   **Christ has died,**
     Christ is risen,
     Christ will come again.

Sung acclamations, page 1028.

b   **Dying you destroyed our death,**
     rising you restored our life.
     Lord Jesus, come in glory.

c   **When we eat this bread and drink this cup,**
     we proclaim your death, Lord Jesus,
     until you come in glory.

d   **Lord, by your cross and resurrection**
     you have set us free.
     You are the Savior of the world.

Celebrant and concelebrants

With hands extended, the priest says:

Father, we now celebrate this memorial of our
**   redemption.**
We recall Christ's death, his descent among
**   the dead,**
his resurrection, and his ascension to your
**   right hand;**
and, looking forward to his coming in glory,
we offer you his body and blood,
the acceptable sacrifice
which brings salvation to the whole world.

Lord, look upon this sacrifice which you have
**   given to your Church;**
and by your Holy Spirit, gather all who share this
**   one bread and one cup**
into the one body of Christ, a living sacrifice of
**   praise.**

Celebrant alone or one of the concelebrants

When several are to be named, a general form is used: for N. our bishop and his assistant bishops (General Instruction, no. 172).

Lord, remember those for whom we offer this
**   sacrifice,**
especially N. our Pope,
N. our bishop, and bishops and clergy everywhere.
Remember those who take part in this offering,
those here present and all your people,
and all who seek you with a sincere heart.
Remember those who have died in the peace of
**   Christ**
and all the dead whose faith is known to you alone.

Father, in your mercy grant also to us, your children,
to enter into our heavenly inheritance
in the company of the Virgin Mary, the Mother of
    God,
and your apostles and saints.
Then, in your kingdom, freed from the corruption of
    sin and death,
we shall sing your glory with every creature through
    Christ our Lord,

He joins his hands.

through whom you give us everything that is good.

Celebrant alone or with the con-celebrants

He takes the chalice and the paten with the host and, lifting them up, sings or says:

Through him,
with him,
in him,
in the unity of the Holy Spirit,
all glory and honor is yours,
almighty Father,
for ever and ever.

The people respond: Amen.

Through him, with him, in him, in the u-ni-ty of the Ho-ly Spir-it, all glo-ry

and hon-or is yours, al-might-y Fa-ther, for ev-er and ev-er. R̠. A-men.

COMMUNION RITE

LORD'S PRAYER

The priest sets down the chalice and paten and with hands joined, sings or says one of the following:

a **Let us pray with confidence to the Father in the words our Savior gave us.**

b **Jesus taught us to call God our Father, and so we have the courage to say:**

c **Let us ask our Father to forgive our sins and to bring us to forgive those who sin against us.**

d **Let us pray for the coming of the kingdom as Jesus taught us.**

He extends his hands and he continues, with the people:

**Our Father, who art in heaven,
hallowed be thy name;
thy kingdom come;
thy will be done on earth as it is in heaven.
Give us this day our daily bread;
and forgive us our trespasses
as we forgive those who trespass against us;
and lead us not into temptation,
but deliver us from evil.**

Let us pray with confidence to the Fa - ther in the words our Sav - ior gave us:

Our Fa - ther, who art in heav - en, hal - lowed be thy name; thy king - dom come;

thy will be done on earth as it is in heav - en. Give us this day our dai - ly bread;

and for - give us our tres - pass - es as we for - give those who tres - pass a - gainst us;

and lead us not in - to temp - ta - tion, but de - liv - er us from e - vil.

With hands extended, the priest continues alone:

**Deliver us, Lord, from every evil,
and grant us peace in our day.
In your mercy keep us free from sin
and protect us from all anxiety
as we wait in joyful hope
for the coming of our Savior, Jesus Christ.**

He joins his hands.
DOXOLOGY
The people end the prayer with the acclamation:

**For the kingdom, the power, and the glory are yours,
now and for ever.**

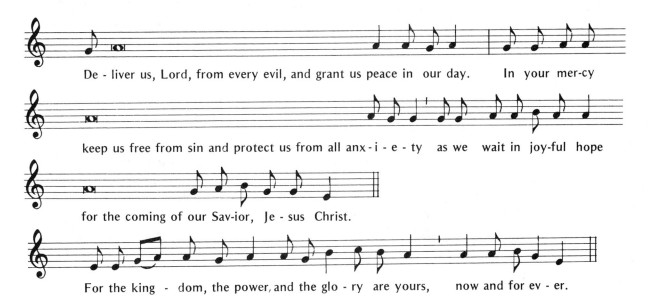

De - liver us, Lord, from every evil, and grant us peace in our day. In your mer-cy keep us free from sin and protect us from all anx-i-e-ty as we wait in joy-ful hope for the coming of our Sav-ior, Je-sus Christ. For the king - dom, the power, and the glo-ry are yours, now and for ev - er.

SIGN OF PEACE

Then the priest, with hands extended, says aloud:

**Lord Jesus Christ, you said to your apostles:
I leave you peace, my peace I give you.
Look not on our sins, but on the faith of your Church,
and grant us the peace and unity of your kingdom
where you live for ever and ever.**

He joins his hands.

The people answer:

Amen.

The priest, extending and joining his hands, adds:

The people answer:

**The peace of the Lord be with you always.
And also with you.**

Then the deacon (or the priest) may add:

Let us offer each other the sign of peace.

All make an appropriate sign of peace, according to local custom. The priest gives the sign of peace to the deacon or minister.

BREAKING OF THE BREAD

Then the following is sung or said:

Lamb of God, you take away the sins of the world: have mercy on us.
Lamb of God, you take away the sins of the world: have mercy on us.
Lamb of God, you take away the sins of the world: grant us peace.

This may be repeated until the breaking of the bread is finished, but the last phrase is always Grant us peace.

Meanwhile, he takes the host and breaks it over the paten. He places a small piece in the chalice, saying inaudibly:

May this mingling of the body and blood of our Lord Jesus Christ bring eternal life to us who receive it.

Private Preparation of the Priest
(General Instruction, no. 56f)

Then the priest joins his hands and says inaudibly:

a

Lord Jesus Christ, Son of the living God, by the will of the Father and the work of the Holy Spirit your death brought life to the world. By your holy body and blood free me from all my sins and from every evil. Keep me faithful to your teaching, and never let me be parted from you.

b

Lord Jesus Christ, with faith in your love and mercy I eat your body and drink your blood. Let it not bring me condemnation, but health in mind and body.

COMMUNION
The priest genuflects. Taking the host, he raises it slightly over the paten and, facing the people, says aloud:

This is the Lamb of God
who takes away the sins of the world.
Happy are those who are called to his supper.

He adds, once only, with the people:

Lord, I am not worthy to receive you,
but only say the word and I shall be healed.

Facing the altar, the priest says inaudibly:

May the body of Christ bring me to everlasting life.

He reverently consumes the body of Christ. Then he takes the chalice and says inaudibly:

May the blood of Christ bring me to everlasting life.

He reverently drinks the blood of Christ.

After this he takes the paten or other vessel and goes to the communicants. He takes a host for each one, raises it a little, and shows it, saying:

The body of Christ.

The communicant answers:

Amen.

and receives communion.

When a deacon gives communion, he does the same.

The sign of communion is more complete when given under both kinds, since the sign of the eucharistic meal appears more clearly. The intention of Christ that the new and eternal covenant be ratified in his blood is better expressed, as is the relation of the eucharistic banquet to the heavenly banquet (General Instruction, no. 240).

If any are receiving in both kinds, the rite described elsewhere is followed. When he presents the chalice, the priest or deacon says:

The blood of Christ.

The communicant answers:

Amen.

and drinks it.

The deacon and other ministers may receive communion from the chalice (General Instruction, no. 242).

COMMUNION SONG
While the priest receives the body of Christ, the communion song is begun.

The vessels are cleansed by the priest or deacon or acolyte after the communion or after Mass, if possible at the side table (General Instruction, no. 238).

Meanwhile he says inaudibly:

Lord, may I receive these gifts in purity of heart. May they bring me healing and strength, now and for ever.

**PERIOD OF SILENCE
OR SONG OF PRAISE**
Then the priest may return to the chair. A period of silence may now be observed, or a psalm or song of praise may be sung.

PRAYER AFTER COMMUNION
Then, standing at the chair or at the
altar, the priest sings or says:

Priest and people pray in silence for a
while, unless a period of silence has
already been observed. Then the
priest extends his hands and sings or
says the prayer after communion, at
the end of which the people respond:

Let us pray.

Amen.

CONCLUDING RITE

If there are any brief announcements, they are made at this time.

GREETING
The rite of dismissal takes place.
Facing the people, the priest extends
his hands and sings or says:

The Lord be with you.

The people answer:

And also with you.

BLESSING

A. Simple form

The priest blesses the people with
these words:

**May almighty God bless you,
the Father, and the Son, ✝ and the Holy Spirit.**

The people answer:

Amen.

On certain days or occasions another
more solemn form of blessing or
prayer over the people may be used
as the rubrics direct.

B. Solemn blessing

Texts of all the solemn blessings are
given on pages 528–536.

Deacon:

Bow your heads and pray for God's blessing.

The priest always concludes the solemn blessing by adding:

**May almighty God bless you,
the Father, and the Son, ✝ and the Holy Spirit.**

The people answer:

Amen.

C. Prayer over the people

Texts of all the prayers over the people are given on pages 537–540.

Deacon: **Bow your heads and pray for God's blessing.**

After the prayer over the people, the priest always adds:

**May almighty God bless you,
the Father, and the Son, ✠ and the Holy Spirit.**

The people answer: **Amen.**

DISMISSAL

The dismissal sends each member of the congregation to do good works, praising and blessing the Lord. (See General Instruction, no. 57.)

The deacon (or the priest), with hands joined, sings or says:

a **Go in the peace of Christ.**

b **The Mass is ended, go in peace.**

c **Go in peace to love and serve the Lord.**

The people answer: **Thanks be to God.**

The priest kisses the altar as at the beginning. Then he makes the customary reverence with the ministers and leaves.

If any liturgical service follows immediately, the rite of dismissal is omitted.

SOLEMN BLESSINGS

The following blessings may be used, at the discretion of the priest, at the end of Mass, or after the liturgy of the word, the office, and the celebration of the sacraments.

The deacon gives the invitation, or in his absence the priest himself may also give it: **Bow your heads and pray for God's blessing.** Another form of invitation may be used. Then the priest extends his hands over the people while he says or sings the blessings. All respond: **Amen.**

I. CELEBRATIONS DURING THE PROPER OF SEASONS

1. ADVENT

**You believe that the Son of God once came to us;
you look for him to come again.
May his coming bring you the light of his holiness
and free you with his blessing.**
℟. **Amen.**

**May God make you steadfast in faith,
joyful in hope, and untiring in love
all the days of your life.**
℟. **Amen.**

**You rejoice that our Redeemer came to live with us as man.
When he comes again in glory,
may he reward you with endless life.**
℟. **Amen.**

**May almighty God bless you,
the Father, and the Son, ☩ and the Holy Spirit.**
℟. **Amen.**

2. CHRISTMAS

**When he came to us as man,
the Son of God scattered the darkness of this world,
and filled this holy night (day) with his glory.
May the God of infinite goodness
scatter the darkness of sin
and brighten your hearts with holiness.**
℟. **Amen.**

**God sent his angels to shepherds
to herald the great joy of our Savior's birth.
May he fill you with joy
and make you heralds of his gospel.**
℟. **Amen.**

**When the Word became man,
earth was joined to heaven.
May he give you his peace and good will,
and fellowship with all the heavenly host.**
℟. **Amen.**

**May almighty God bless you,
the Father, and the Son, ☩ and the Holy Spirit.**
℟. **Amen.**

3. BEGINNING OF THE NEW YEAR

Every good gift comes from the Father of light.
May he grant you his grace and every blessing,
and keep you safe throughout the coming year.
℟. **Amen.**

May he grant you unwavering faith,
constant hope, and love that endures to the end.
℟. **Amen.**

May he order your days and work in his peace,
hear your every prayer,
and lead you to everlasting life and joy.
℟. **Amen.**

May almighty God bless you,
the Father, and the Son, ☩ and the Holy Spirit.
℟. **Amen.**

4. EPIPHANY

God has called you out of darkness
into his wonderful light.
May you experience his kindness and blessings,
and be strong in faith, in hope, and in love.
℟. **Amen.**

Because you are followers of Christ,
who appeared on this day as a light shining in darkness,
may he make you a light to all your sisters and brothers.
℟. **Amen.**

The wise men followed the star,
and found Christ who is light from light.
May you too find the Lord
when your pilgrimage is ended.
℟. **Amen.**

May almighty God bless you,
the Father, and the Son, ☩ and the Holy Spirit.
℟. **Amen.**

5. PASSION OF THE LORD

The Father of mercies has given us an example of unselfish love
in the sufferings of his only Son.
Through your service of God and neighbor
may you receive his countless blessings.
℟. Amen.

You believe that by his dying
Christ destroyed death for ever.
May he give you everlasting life.
℟. Amen.

He humbled himself for our sakes.
May you follow his example
and share in his resurrection.
℟. Amen.

May almighty God bless you,
the Father, and the Son, ✝ and the Holy Spirit.
℟. Amen.

6. EASTER VIGIL
AND EASTER SUNDAY

May almighty God bless you on this solemn feast of Easter,
and may he protect you against all sin.
℟. Amen.

Through the resurrection of his Son
God has granted us healing.
May he fulfill his promises,
and bless you with eternal life.
℟. Amen.

You have mourned for Christ's sufferings;
now you celebrate the joy of his resurrection.
May you come with joy to the feast which lasts for ever.
℟. Amen.

May almighty God bless you,
the Father, and the Son, ✝ and the Holy Spirit.
℟. Amen.

7. EASTER SEASON

Through the resurrection of his Son
God has redeemed you and made you his children.
May he bless you with joy.
℟. Amen.

The Redeemer has given you lasting freedom.
May you inherit his everlasting life.
℟. Amen.

By faith you rose with him in baptism.
May your lives be holy,
so that you will be united with him for ever.
℟. Amen.

May almighty God bless you,
the Father, and the Son, ✠ and the Holy Spirit.
℟. Amen.

8. ASCENSION

May almighty God bless you on this day
when his only Son ascended into heaven
to prepare a place for you.
℟. Amen.

After his resurrection, Christ was seen by his disciples.
When he appears as judge
may you be pleasing for ever in his sight.
℟. Amen.

You believe that Jesus has taken his seat in majesty
at the right hand of the Father.
May you have the joy of experiencing
that he is also with you to the end of time,
according to his promise.
℟. Amen.

May almighty God bless you,
the Father, and the Son, ✠ and the Holy Spirit.
℟. Amen.

9. HOLY SPIRIT

(This day) the Father of light
has enlightened the minds of the disciples
by the outpouring of the Holy Spirit.
May he bless you
and give you the gifts of the Spirit for ever.
℟. Amen.

May that fire which hovered over the disciples
as tongues of flame
burn out all evil from your hearts
and make them glow with pure light.
℟. Amen.

God inspired speech in different tongues
to proclaim one faith.
May he strengthen your faith
and fulfill your hope of seeing him face to face.
℟. Amen.

May almighty God bless you,
the Father, and the Son, ✝and the Holy Spirit.
℟. Amen.

10. ORDINARY TIME I
Blessing of Aaron (Num. 6:24-26)

May the Lord bless you and keep you.
℟. Amen.

May his face shine upon you,
and be gracious to you.
℟. Amen.

May he look upon you with kindness,
and give you his peace.
℟. Amen.

May almighty God bless you,
the Father, and the Son, ✝and the Holy Spirit.
℟. Amen.

11. ORDINARY TIME II
(Phil. 4:7)

May the peace of God
which is beyond all understanding
keep your hearts and minds
in the knowledge and love of God
and of his Son, our Lord Jesus Christ.
℟. Amen.

May almighty God bless you,
the Father, and the Son, ✝and the Holy Spirit.
℟. Amen.

12. ORDINARY TIME III

May almighty God bless you in his mercy,
and make you always aware of his saving wisdom.
℟. Amen.

May he strengthen your faith with proofs of his love,
so that you will persevere in good works.
℟. Amen.

May he direct your steps to himself,
and show you how to walk in charity and peace.
℟. Amen.

May almighty God bless you,
the Father, and the Son, ✢ and the Holy Spirit.
℟. Amen.

13. ORDINARY TIME IV

May the God of all consolation
bless you in every way
and grant you peace all the days of your life.
℟. Amen.

May he free you from all anxiety
and strengthen your hearts in his love.
℟. Amen.

May he enrich you with his gifts of faith, hope, and love,
so that what you do in this life
will bring you to the happiness of everlasting life.
℟. Amen.

May almighty God bless you,
the Father, and the Son, ✢ and the Holy Spirit.
℟. Amen.

14. ORDINARY TIME V

May almighty God keep you from all harm
and bless you with every good gift.
℟. Amen.

May he set his Word in your heart
and fill you with lasting joy.
℟. Amen.

May you walk in his ways,
always knowing what is right and good,
until you enter your heavenly inheritance.
℟. Amen.

May almighty God bless you,
the Father, and the Son, ✢ and the Holy Spirit.
℟. Amen.

II. CELEBRATIONS OF SAINTS

15. BLESSED VIRGIN MARY

Born of the Blessed Virgin Mary,
the Son of God redeemed mankind.
May he enrich you with his blessings.
℟. Amen.

You received the author of life through Mary.
May you always rejoice in her loving care.
℟. Amen.

You have come to rejoice at Mary's feast.
May you be filled with the joys of the Spirit
and the gifts of your eternal home.
℟. Amen.

May almighty God bless you,
the Father, and the Son, ✛ and the Holy Spirit.
℟. Amen.

16. PETER AND PAUL

The Lord has set you firm within his Church,
which he built upon the rock of Peter's faith.
May he bless you with a faith that never falters.
℟. Amen.

The Lord has given you knowledge of the faith
through the labors and preaching of St. Paul.
May his example inspire you to lead others to Christ
by the manner of your life.
℟. Amen.

May the keys of Peter, and the words of Paul,
their undying witness and their prayers,
lead you to the joy of that eternal home
which Peter gained by his cross, and Paul by the sword.
℟. Amen.

May almighty God bless you,
the Father, and the Son, ✛ and the Holy Spirit.
℟. Amen.

17. APOSTLES

May God who founded his Church upon the apostles
bless you through the prayers of St. N. (and St. N.).
℟. Amen.

May God inspire you to follow the example of the apostles,
and give witness to the truth before all men.
℟. Amen.

The teaching of the apostles has strengthened your faith.
May their prayers lead you
to your true and eternal home.
℟. Amen.

May almighty God bless you,
the Father, and the Son, ✙ and the Holy Spirit.
℟. Amen.

18. ALL SAINTS

God is the glory and joy of all his saints,
whose memory we celebrate today.
May his blessing be with you always.
℟. Amen.

May the prayers of the saints deliver you from present evil.
May their example of holy living
turn your thoughts to service of God and neighbor.
℟. Amen.

God's holy Church rejoices that her saints
have reached their heavenly goal,
and are in lasting peace.
May you come to share all the joys of our Father's house.
℟. Amen.

May almighty God bless you,
the Father, and the Son, ✙ and the Holy Spirit.
℟. Amen.

III. OTHER BLESSINGS

19. DEDICATION OF A CHURCH

The Lord of earth and heaven
has assembled you before him this day
to dedicate this house of prayer
(to recall the dedication of this church).
May he fill you with the blessings of heaven.
℟. Amen.

God the Father wills that all his children
scattered throughout the world
become one family in his Son.
May he make you his temple,
the dwelling-place of his Holy Spirit.
℟. Amen.

May God free you from every bond of sin,
dwell within you and give you joy.
May you live with him for ever
in the company of all his saints.
℟. Amen.

May almighty God bless you,
the Father, and the Son, ✠and the Holy Spirit.
℟. Amen.

20. THE DEAD

In his great love,
the God of all consolation gave man the gift of life.
May he bless you with faith
in the resurrection of his Son,
and with the hope of rising to new life.
℟. Amen.

To us who are alive
may he grant forgiveness,
and to all who have died
a place of light and peace.
℟. Amen.

As you believe that Jesus rose from the dead,
so may you live with him for ever in joy.
℟. Amen.

May almighty God bless you,
the Father, and the Son, ✠and the Holy Spirit.
℟. Amen.

PRAYERS OVER THE PEOPLE

The following prayers may be used, at the discretion of the priest, at the end of Mass, or after the liturgy of the word, the office, and the celebration of the sacraments.

The deacon gives the invitation, or in his absence the priest himself may also give it: Bow your heads and pray for God's blessing. Another form of invitation may be used. Then the priest extends his hands over the people while he says or sings the prayer. All respond: Amen.

After the prayer, the priest always adds:

**May almighty God bless you,
the Father, and the Son, ☩ and the Holy Spirit.
℟. Amen.**

1. **Lord,
   have mercy on your people.
   Grant us in this life the good things
   that lead to the everlasting life you prepare for us.
   We ask this through Christ our Lord.**

2. **Lord,
   grant your people your protection and grace.
   Give them health of mind and body,
   perfect love for one another,
   and make them always faithful to you.
   Grant this through Christ our Lord.**

3. **Lord,
   may all Christian people both know and cherish
   the heavenly gifts they have received.
   We ask this in the name of Jesus the Lord.**

4. **Lord,
   bless your people and make them holy
   so that avoiding evil,
   they may find in you the fulfillment of their longing.
   We ask this through Christ our Lord.**

5. **Lord,
   bless and strengthen your people.
   May they remain faithful to you
   and always rejoice in your mercy.
   We ask this in the name of Jesus the Lord.**

6.   **Lord,**
you care for your people even when they stray.
Grant us a complete change of heart,
so that we may follow you with greater fidelity.

      Grant this through Christ our Lord.

7.   **Lord,**
send your light upon your family.
May they continue to enjoy your favor
and devote themselves to doing good.

      We ask this through Christ our Lord.

8.   **Lord,**
we rejoice that you are our creator and ruler.
As we call upon your generosity,
renew and keep us in your love.

      Grant this through Christ our Lord.

9.   **Lord,**
we pray for your people who believe in you.
May they enjoy the gift of your love,
share it with others,
and spread it everywhere.

      We ask this in the name of Jesus the Lord.

10.   **Lord,**
bless your people who hope for your mercy.
Grant that they may receive
the things they ask for at your prompting.

      Grant this through Christ our Lord.

11.   **Lord,**
bless us with your heavenly gifts,
and in your mercy make us ready to do your will.

      We ask this through Christ our Lord.

12.   **Lord,**
protect your people always,
that they may be free from every evil
and serve you with all their hearts.

      We ask this through Christ our Lord.

13.   **Lord,**
help your people to seek you with all their hearts
and to deserve what you promise.

      Grant this through Christ our Lord.

14.   Father,
help your people to rejoice in the mystery of redemption
and to win its reward.

We ask this in the name of Jesus the Lord.

15.   Lord,
have pity on your people;
help them each day to avoid what displeases you
and grant that they may serve you with joy.

We ask this through Christ our Lord.

16.   Lord,
care for your people and purify them.
Console them in this life
and bring them to the life to come.

We ask this in the name of Jesus the Lord.

17.   Father,
look with love upon your people,
the love which our Lord Jesus Christ showed us
when he delivered himself to evil men
and suffered the agony of the cross,
for he is Lord for ever.

18.   Lord,
grant that your faithful people
may continually desire to relive the mystery of the eucharist
and so be reborn to lead a new life.

We ask this through Christ our Lord.

19.   Lord God,
in your great mercy,
enrich your people with your grace
and strengthen them by your blessing
so that they may praise you always.

Grant this through Christ our Lord.

20.   May God bless you with every good gift from on high.
May he keep you pure and holy in his sight at all times.
May he bestow the riches of his grace upon you,
bring you the good news of salvation,
and always fill you with love for all men.

We ask this through Christ our Lord.

21.   Lord,
make us pure in mind and body,
that we will avoid all evil pleasures
and always delight in you.

We ask this in the name of Jesus the Lord.

22.   **Lord,**
        bless your people and fill them with zeal.
        Strengthen them by your love to do your will.

        We ask this through Christ our Lord.

23.   **Lord,**
        come, live in your people
        and strengthen them by your grace.
        Help them to remain close to you in prayer
        and give them a true love for one another.

        Grant this through Christ our Lord.

24.   **Father,**
        look kindly on your children who put their trust in you;
        bless them and keep them from all harm,
        strengthen them against the attacks of the devil.
        May they never offend you
        but seek to love you in all they do.

        We ask this through Christ our Lord.

FEASTS OF SAINTS

25.   **God our Father,**
        may all Christian people rejoice in the glory of your saints.
        Give us fellowship with them
        and unending joy in your kingdom.

        We ask this in the name of Jesus the Lord.

26.   **Lord,**
        you have given us many friends in heaven.
        Through their prayers we are confident
        that you will watch over us always
        and fill our hearts with your love.

        Grant this through Christ our Lord.

THE ORDER OF MASS WITHOUT A CONGREGATION

THE ORDER OF MASS WITHOUT A CONGREGATION

INTRODUCTORY RITES

1. The priest and the minister make the customary reverence. Then the priest makes the sign of the cross and says:

In the name of the Father, and of the Son, and of the Holy Spirit.

The minister answers:

Amen.

2. The priest faces the minister, extends his hands, and greets him with one of the following greetings:

a

The grace of our Lord Jesus Christ and the love of God and the fellowship of the Holy Spirit be with you.

The minister answers:

And also with you.

b   The priest says:

The grace and peace of God our Father and the Lord Jesus Christ be with you.

The minister answers:

Blessed be God, the Father of our Lord Jesus Christ.

or:

And also with you.

c   The priest says:

The Lord be with you.

The minister answers:

And also with you.

3. Afterwards the priest and minister make their confession together:

I confess to almighty God,
and to you, my brother,
that I have sinned through my own fault

They strike their breast:

in my thoughts and in my words,
in what I have done
and in what I have failed to do;
and I ask blessed Mary, ever virgin,
all the angels and saints,
and you, my brother,
to pray for me to the Lord our God.

The priest says the absolution:

May almighty God have mercy on us,
forgive us our sins,
and bring us to everlasting life.

The minister answers:

Amen.

4. The priest goes up to the altar and kisses it. Then he goes to the missal placed on the left side of the altar and reads the entrance antiphon.

5. The invocations Lord, have mercy, are said by the priest alternately with the minister.

Priest:	**Lord, have mercy.**	**Kýrie, eléison.**
Minister:	**Lord, have mercy.**	**Kýrie, eléison.**
Priest:	**Christ, have mercy.**	**Christe, eléison.**
Minister:	**Christ, have mercy.**	**Christe, eléison.**
Priest:	**Lord, have mercy.**	**Kýrie, eléison.**
Minister:	**Lord, have mercy.**	**Kýrie, eléison.**

6. Then (when it is prescribed) the priest and minister say the hymn together:

Glory to God in the highest . . .

7. Afterwards the priest, with hands joined, says:

Let us pray.

Having prayed silently for a while, the priest extends his hands and says the opening prayer, at the end of which the minister responds:

Amen.

LITURGY OF THE WORD

8. Then the minister (or the priest himself) reads the first reading, the psalm and, if there is one, the second reading, with the second chant.

9. Then the priest bows and says inaudibly:

Almighty God, cleanse my heart and my lips that I may worthily proclaim your gospel.

10. With hands joined, he says:

The Lord be with you.

The minister answers:

And also with you.

The priest:

A reading from the holy gospel according to N.

He makes the sign of the cross on the book, and then on his forehead, lips and breast. The minister responds:

Glory to you, Lord.

Then the priest reads the gospel. At the end of the gospel he kisses the book, saying inaudibly:

May the words of the gospel wipe away our sins.

The minister answers:

Praise to you, Lord Jesus Christ.

11. If prescribed, the priest and minister make the profession of faith together.

12. The general intercessions (prayer of the faithful) may follow. The priest gives the intentions and the minister answers.

LITURGY OF THE EUCHARIST

13. The minister places the corporal, purificator, and chalice on the altar, unless they were already placed there at the beginning of Mass. The priest goes to the center of the altar.

14. Then the minister presents the paten with the bread. The priest holds it slightly raised above the altar and says:

**Blessed are you, Lord, God of all creation.
Through your goodness we have this bread to offer,
which earth has given and human hands have made.
It will become for us the bread of life.**

Then he places the paten with the bread on the corporal.

15. The priest pours wine and a little water into the chalice, saying inaudibly:

**By the mystery of this water and wine
may we come to share in the divinity of Christ
who humbled himself to share in our humanity.**

16. Then the priest takes the chalice and, holding it slightly raised above the altar, says:

**Blessed are you, Lord, God of all creation.
Through your goodness we have this wine to offer,
fruit of the vine and work of human hands.
It will become our spiritual drink.**

Then he places the chalice on the corporal.

17. The priest bows and says inaudibly:

**Lord God, we ask you to receive us
and be pleased with the sacrifice we offer you
with humble and contrite hearts.**

18. Next the priest stands at the side of the altar and washes his hands, saying inaudibly:

**Lord, wash away my iniquity;
cleanse me from my sin.**

19. Standing at the center of the altar, facing the minister, he extends and then joins his hands, saying:

**Pray, brother, that our sacrifice
may be acceptable to God, the almighty Father.**

The minister answers:

**May the Lord accept the sacrifice at your hands
for the praise and glory of his name,
for our good, and the good of all his Church.**

With hands extended, the priest says the prayer over the gifts, at the end of which the minister responds:

Amen.

20. Then the priest says the eucharistic prayer, according to the norms given in each form of the prayer

21. After the doxology at the end of the eucharistic prayer, standing up straight and with hands joined, the priest says:

He extends his hands and continues with the minister:

Let us pray with confidence to the Father in the words our Savior gave us:

**Our Father, who art in heaven,
hallowed be thy name;
thy kingdom come;
thy will be done on earth as it is in heaven.
Give us this day our daily bread;
and forgive us our trespasses
as we forgive those who trespass against us;
and lead us not into temptation,
but deliver us from evil.**

22. With hands extended, the priest continues alone:

**Deliver us, Lord, from every evil,
and grant us peace in our day.
In your mercy keep us free from sin
and protect us from all anxiety
as we wait in joyful hope
for the coming of our Savior, Jesus Christ.**

He joins his hands. The minister ends the prayer with the acclamation:

For the kingdom, the power, and the glory are yours, now and for ever.

23. Then the priest, with hands extended, says aloud:

**Lord Jesus Christ, you said to your apostles:
I leave you peace, my peace I give you.
Look not on our sins, but on the faith of your Church,
and grant us the peace and unity of your kingdom
where you live for ever and ever.**

He joins his hands.

The minister answers:

Amen.

24. The priest, extending and joining his hands, adds:

The peace of the Lord be with you always.

The minister answers:

And also with you.

The priest may give the minister the sign of peace.

25. He then takes the host and breaks it over the paten, saying with the minister:

Lamb of God, you take away the sins of the world: have mercy on us.
Lamb of God, you take away the sins of the world: have mercy on us.
Lamb of God, you take away the sins of the world: grant us peace.

When this is finished, he places a small piece in the chalice, saying inaudibly:

May this mingling of the body and blood of our Lord Jesus Christ
bring eternal life to us who receive it.

26. Then the priest joins his hands and says inaudibly:

a

Lord Jesus Christ, Son of the living God, by the will of the Father and the work of the Holy Spirit your death brought life to the world. By your holy body and blood free me from all my sins and from every evil. Keep me faithful to your teaching, and never let me be parted from you.

b

Lord Jesus Christ, with faith in your love and mercy I eat your body and drink your blood. Let it not bring me condemnation, but health in mind and body.

27. The priest genuflects. Taking the host, he raises it slightly over the paten and, facing the minister, says aloud:

This is the Lamb of God
who takes away the sins of the world.
Happy are those who are called to his supper.

He adds, once only, with the minister:

Lord, I am not worthy to receive you,
but only say the word and I shall be healed.

If the minister is not to receive communion, the priest takes the host and, facing the altar, says alone:

Lord, I am not worthy, etc.

28. Facing the altar, the priest says inaudibly:

He reverently consumes the body of Christ. Then he takes the chalice and says inaudibly:

May the body of Christ bring me to everlasting life.

He reverently drinks the blood of Christ.

May the blood of Christ bring me to everlasting life.

29. After this the priest says the communion antiphon.

30. Then he takes the paten and goes to the minister, if he is to receive communion. He raises the host a little and shows it to him, saying:

The body of Christ.

Amen.

The minister answers:

and receives the host.

31. Then the priest cleans the paten over the chalice and then the chalice itself. The minister places the chalice, paten, corporal, and purificator on the side table, or they may be left on the altar.

Meanwhile he says inaudibly:

Lord, may I receive these gifts in purity of heart.
May they bring me healing and strength, now and
for ever.

32. A period of silence may now be observed.

33. Then, with hands joined, the priest says:

Let us pray.

Priest and minister pray in silence for a while, unless a period of silence has already been observed; then the priest extends his hands and says the prayer after communion, at the end of which the minister responds:

Amen.

CONCLUDING RITE

34. Facing the minister, the priest extends his hands and says:

The Lord be with you.

The minister answers:

And also with you.

The priest blesses the minister with these words:

May almighty God bless you,
the Father, and the Son, ✠ and the Holy Spirit.

The minister answers:

Amen.

35. The priest kisses the altar, makes the customary reverence with the minister, and leaves.

PROPER OF SAINTS

PROPER OF SAINTS

1. The rank of the celebrations (solemnity, feast, or memorial) is indicated for each day. If there is no indication, it is an optional memorial.

2. For each solemnity and feast a proper Mass is provided in its entirety. This is therefore used as given.

3. For memorials:

a) Proper texts, given on some days, should always be used.

b) When there is a reference to a particular common, appropriate texts should be chosen according to the principles at the beginning of the commons. The page reference in each case indicates only the beginning of the common to which reference is made.

c) If the reference is to more than one common, one or the other may be used, according to pastoral need. It is always permissible to interchange texts from several Masses within the same common.

For example, if a saint is both a martyr and a bishop, either the common of martyrs or the common of pastors (for bishops) may be used.

d) In addition to the commons which express a special characteristic holiness (e.g., of martyrs, virgins, or pastors), the texts from the common of saints, referring to holiness in general, may always be used.

For example, in the case of a saint who is both a virgin and a martyr, texts from the common of saints in general may be used, in addition to texts from the common of martyrs or the common of virgins.

e) The prayers over the gifts and after communion, unless there are proper prayers, may be taken either from the common or from the current liturgical season.

4. The Masses in the proper may also be celebrated as votive Masses, with the exception of Masses of the mysteries of the life of the Lord and of the Blessed Virgin Mary and Masses of certain saints for whom a special votive Mass is provided. When Masses from the proper are used as votive Masses, words in the prayers referring to the day of death or to the solemnity or feast are omitted and "memorial" or "commemoration" is substituted. If the entrance antiphon, "Let us rejoice," occurs, it is to be replaced by another antiphon from the respective common.

JANUARY

January 2

ST. BASIL THE GREAT AND ST. GREGORY NAZIANZEN,

bishops and doctors

Memorial

Common of pastors: for bishops (p. **719**); or Common of doctors of the Church (p. **729**).

OPENING PRAYER

**God our Father,
you inspired the Church
with the example and teaching of your saints Basil and
  Gregory.
In humility may we come to know your truth
and put it into action with faith and love.**

**Grant this through our Lord Jesus Christ, your Son,
who lives and reigns with you and the Holy Spirit,
one God, for ever and ever.**

January 4

In the dioceses of the United States

ST. ELIZABETH ANN SETON, religious

Memorial

Introductory Rites

Praise to the holy woman whose home is built on faithful love
and whose pathway leads to God. (See Prov. 14:1-2)

or

This is the generation which seeks the face of the God of Jacob.
(Ps. 23)

OPENING PRAYER

**Lord God,
you blessed Elizabeth Seton with gifts of grace
as wife and mother, educator and foundress,
so that she might spend her life in service to your people.
Through her example and prayers
may we learn to express our love for you
in love for others.**

**We ask this through our Lord Jesus Christ, your Son,
who lives and reigns with you and the Holy Spirit,
one God, for ever and ever.**

First Reading: Sirach 26:1-4, 16-21
[Lectionary no. 737.14]
Responsorial Psalm: Psalm 128:1-5
[Lectionary no. 739.7]
Second Reading: 1 Corinthians 13:4-13
[Lectionary no. 740.3]
Gospel: Luke 10:38-42 [Lectionary no. 736.3]

or any readings from the Common of Saints, Lectionary nos. 737-742.

PRAYER OVER THE GIFTS

Pray, brethren . . .

**Lord,
give to us who offer these gifts at your altar
the same spirit of love that filled St. Elizabeth Seton.
By celebrating this sacred eucharist with pure minds
        and loving hearts
may we offer a sacrifice that pleases you,
and brings salvation to us.**

Grant this through Christ our Lord.

Communion Rite

I am the living bread from heaven, says the Lord. Whoever
eats this bread will live forever; the bread I shall give is my
flesh for the life of the world. (John 6:51)

PRAYER AFTER COMMUNION

**Lord,
we have shared
in the mystery of your love.
May we be strengthened in faith and love for the eucharist
as we recall the example of St. Elizabeth Seton.**

We ask this through Christ our Lord.

January 5

In the dioceses of the United States

ST. JOHN NEUMANN, bishop

Memorial

Introductory Rites

O Lord, my allotted portion and my cup, you it is who hold
fast my lot. For me the measuring lines have fallen on pleas-
ant sites; fair to me indeed is my inheritance. (Ps. 16:5-6)

OPENING PRAYER

**Almighty God,
you called St. John Neumann
to a life of service, zeal, and compassion
for the guidance of your people in the new world.**

**By his prayers
help us to build up the community of the Church
through our dedication to the Christian education of youth
and through the witness of our brotherly love.**

**Grant this through our Lord Jesus Christ, your Son,
who lives and reigns with you and the Holy Spirit,
one God, for ever and ever.**

First Reading: 1 Corinthians 9:16-19,
22-23 [Lectionary no. 75]
Responsorial Psalm: Psalm 96:1-2, 2-3,
7-8, 10 [Lectionary no. 67]
Gospel verse: John 10:14 [Lectionary
no. 723.4]
Gospel: John 10:11-16 [Lectionary no.
724.9]

PRAYER OVER THE GIFTS

Pray, brethren . . .

**Father of mercies,
look upon the gifts
that we present in memory of Christ your Son.**

**Form us in his likeness
as you formed St. John,
who imitated what he handled
in these holy mysteries.**

We ask this in the name of Jesus the Lord.

Communion Rite

Everyone who has given up home, brothers or sisters, father
or mother, wife or children or property for my sake will receive
many times as much and inherit everlasting life. (Matthew
19:29)

PRAYER AFTER COMMUNION

**Father of our Lord Jesus Christ,
you have united us with our Redeemer
in this memorial of his death and resurrection.**

**By the power of this sacrament,
help us to live,
one in spirit and in truth,
in the communion of Christ's body.**

Grant this through Christ our Lord.

January 6

In the dioceses of the United States

BLESSED ANDRÉ BESSETTE, religious

Common of holy men and women: for religious (p. 741).

OPENING PRAYER

Lord our God, friend of the lowly,
you gave your servant, Brother André,
a great devotion to St. Joseph
and a special commitment to the poor and afflicted.
Through his intercession
help us to follow his example of prayer and love
and so come to share with him in your glory.

We ask this through our Lord Jesus Christ, your Son,
who lives and reigns with you and the Holy Spirit,
one God, for ever and ever.

January 7

ST. RAYMOND OF PENYAFORT, priest

Common of pastors (p. 721).

OPENING PRAYER

Lord,
you gave St. Raymond the gift of compassion
in his ministry to sinners.
May his prayers free us from the slavery of sin
and help us to love and serve you in liberty.

We ask this through our Lord Jesus Christ, your Son,
who lives and reigns with you and the Holy Spirit,
one God, for ever and ever.

January 13

ST. HILARY, bishop and doctor

Common of pastors: for bishops (p. 719); or Common of doctors of the Church (p. 729).

OPENING PRAYER

All-powerful God,
as St. Hilary defended the divinity of Christ your Son,
give us a deeper understanding of this mystery
and help us to profess it in all truth.

Grant this through our Lord Jesus Christ, your Son,
who lives and reigns with you and the Holy Spirit,
one God, for ever and ever.

January 17

ST. ANTHONY, abbot

Memorial

Introductory Rites

The just man will flourish like the palm tree. Planted in the courts of God's house, he will grow great like the cedars of Lebanon. (Ps. 91:13-14)

OPENING PRAYER

**Father,
you called St. Anthony
to renounce the world
and serve you in the solitude of the desert.
By his prayers and example,
may we learn to deny ourselves
and to love you above all things.**

**We ask this through our Lord Jesus Christ, your Son,
who lives and reigns with you and the Holy Spirit,
one God, for ever and ever.**

See Lectionary for Mass, no. 513.

PRAYER OVER THE GIFTS

Pray, brethren . . .

**Lord,
accept the sacrifice we offer at your altar
in commemoration of St. Anthony.
May no earthly attractions keep us from loving you.**

Grant this through Christ our Lord.

Communion Rite

If you wish to be perfect, go, sell what you own, give it all to the poor, then come, follow me. (Matthew 19:21)

PRAYER AFTER COMMUNION

Let us pray.

Pause for silent prayer, if this has not preceded.

**Lord,
you helped St. Anthony conquer the powers of darkness.
May your sacrament strengthen us
in our struggle with evil.**

We ask this in the name of Jesus the Lord.

January 20

ST. FABIAN, pope and martyr

Common of martyrs (p. 709); or
Common of pastors: for popes (p. 717).

OPENING PRAYER

God our Father, glory of your priests,
may the prayers of your martyr Fabian
help us to share his faith
and offer you loving service.

Grant this through our Lord Jesus Christ, your Son,
who lives and reigns with you and the Holy Spirit,
one God, for ever and ever.

ST. SEBASTIAN, martyr

Common of martyrs (p. 709).

OPENING PRAYER

Lord,
fill us with that spirit of courage
which gave your martyr Sebastian
strength to offer his life in faithful witness.
Help us to learn from him to cherish your law
and to obey you rather than men.

We ask this through our Lord Jesus Christ, your Son,
who lives and reigns with you and the Holy Spirit,
one God, for ever and ever.

January 21

ST. AGNES, virgin and martyr
Memorial

Common of martyrs (p. 709); or
Common of virgins (p. 731).

OPENING PRAYER

Almighty, eternal God,
you choose what the world considers weak
to put the worldly power to shame.
May we who celebrate the birth of St. Agnes into eternal joy
be loyal to the faith she professed.

Grant this through our Lord Jesus Christ, your Son,
who lives and reigns with you and the Holy Spirit,
one God, for ever and ever.

January 22

ST. VINCENT, deacon and martyr

Common of martyrs (p. 709).

OPENING PRAYER

**Eternal Father,
you gave St. Vincent
the courage to endure torture and death for the gospel:
fill us with your Spirit
and strengthen us in your love.**

**We ask this through our Lord Jesus Christ, your Son,
who lives and reigns with you and the Holy Spirit,
one God, for ever and ever.**

January 24

ST. FRANCIS DE SALES, bishop and doctor

Memorial

Common of pastors: for bishops (p. 719); or Common of doctors of the Church (p. 729).

OPENING PRAYER

**Father,
you gave St. Francis de Sales the spirit of compassion
to befriend all men on the way to salvation.
By his example, lead us to show your gentle love
in the service of our fellow men.**

**Grant this through our Lord Jesus Christ, your Son,
who lives and reigns with you and the Holy Spirit,
one God, for ever and ever.**

PRAYER OVER THE GIFTS

Pray, brethren . . .

**Lord,
by this offering
may the divine fire of your Holy Spirit,
which burned in the gentle heart of St. Francis de Sales,
inspire us with compassion and love.**

We ask this through Christ our Lord.

PRAYER AFTER COMMUNION

Let us pray.
Pause for silent prayer, if this has not preceded.
**Merciful Father,
may the sacrament we have received
help us to imitate St. Francis de Sales in love and service;
bring us to share with him the glory of heaven.**

We ask this in the name of Jesus the Lord.

January 25

CONVERSION OF ST. PAUL, apostle

Feast

Introductory Rites

> I know whom I have believed. I am sure that he, the just
> judge, will guard my pledge until the day of judgment.
> (2 Tim. 1:12; 4:8)

OPENING PRAYER

God our Father,
you taught the gospel to all the world
through the preaching of Paul your apostle.
May we who celebrate his conversion to the faith
follow him in bearing witness to your truth.

We ask this through our Lord Jesus Christ, your Son,
who lives and reigns with you and the Holy Spirit,
one God, for ever and ever.

See Lectionary for Mass, no. 519.

PRAYER OVER THE GIFTS

Pray, brethren . . .

Lord, may your Spirit who helped Paul the apostle
to preach your power and glory
fill us with the light of faith
as we celebrate this holy eucharist.

Preface of the Apostles I or II, pages
481–482.

We ask this in the name of Jesus the Lord.

Communion Rite

> I live by faith in the Son of God, who loved me and
> sacrificed himself for me. (Gal. 2:20)

PRAYER AFTER COMMUNION

Let us pray.
Pause for silent prayer, if this has not preceded.
Lord God,
you filled Paul the apostle with love for all the churches:
may the sacrament we have received
foster in us this love for your people.
Grant this through Christ our Lord.

January 26

ST. TIMOTHY AND ST. TITUS, bishops

Memorial

Common of pastors: for bishops (p.
719).

OPENING PRAYER

God our Father,
you gave your saints Timothy and Titus
the courage and wisdom of the apostles:
may their prayers help us to live holy lives
and lead us to heaven, our true home.

Grant this through our Lord Jesus Christ, your Son,
who lives and reigns with you and the Holy Spirit,
one God, for ever and ever.

January 27

ST. ANGELA MERICI, virgin

Common of virgins (p. 731); or
Common of holy men and women: for
teachers (p. 744).

OPENING PRAYER

**Lord,
may St. Angela commend us to your mercy;
may her charity and wisdom help us
to be faithful to your teaching
and to follow it in our lives.**

**We ask this through our Lord Jesus Christ, your Son,
who lives and reigns with you and the Holy Spirit,
one God, for ever and ever.**

January 28

ST. THOMAS AQUINAS, priest and doctor
Memorial

Common of doctors of the Church (p.
729); or Common of pastors (p. 721).

OPENING PRAYER

**God our Father,
you made St. Thomas Aquinas known for his holiness and
learning.
Help us to grow in wisdom by his teaching,
and in holiness by imitating his faith.**

**Grant this through our Lord Jesus Christ, your Son,
who lives and reigns with you and the Holy Spirit,
one God, for ever and ever.**

January 31

ST. JOHN BOSCO, priest
Memorial

Common of pastors (p. 721); or
Common of holy men and women: for
teachers (p. 744).

OPENING PRAYER

**Lord,
you called St. John Bosco
to be a teacher and father to the young.
Fill us with love like his:
may we give ourselves completely to your service
and to the salvation of mankind.**

**We ask this through our Lord Jesus Christ, your Son,
who lives and reigns with you and the Holy Spirit,
one God, for ever and ever.**

FEBRUARY

February 2

PRESENTATION OF THE LORD
Feast

Blessing of Candles and Procession

FIRST FORM: PROCESSION

The people gather in a chapel or other suitable place outside the church where the Mass will be celebrated. They carry unlighted candles. The priest and his ministers wear white vestments. The priest may wear the cope instead of the chasuble during the procession.

While the candles are being lighted, this canticle or another hymn is sung:

**The Lord will come with mighty power,
and give light to the eyes of all who serve him, alleluia.**

The priest greets the people as usual, and briefly invites the people to take an active part in this celebration. He may use these or similar words:

Forty days ago we celebrated the joyful feast of the birth of our Lord Jesus Christ. Today we recall the holy day on which he was presented in the temple, fulfilling the law of Moses and at the same time going to meet his faithful people. Led by the Spirit, Simeon and Anna came to the temple, recognized Christ as their Lord, and proclaimed him with joy.

United by the Spirit, may we now go to the house of God to welcome Christ the Lord. There we shall recognize him in the breaking of bread until he comes again in glory.

Then the priest joins his hands and blesses the candles:

Let us pray.

**God our Father, source of all light,
today you revealed to Simeon
your Light of revelation to the nations.
Bless ✠ these candles and make them holy.
May we who carry them to praise your glory
walk in the path of goodness
and come to the light that shines for ever.**

Grant this through Christ our Lord.

He sprinkles the candles in silence.

or:

**God our Father, source of eternal light,
fill the hearts of all believers
with the light of faith.
May we who carry these candles in your church
come with joy to the light of glory.**

We ask this through Christ our Lord.

The priest then takes the candle prepared for him, and the procession begins with the acclamation:

Let us go in peace to meet the Lord.

During the procession, the following canticle or another hymn is sung:

Antiphon

**Christ is the light of the nations
and the glory of Israel his people.**

**Now, Lord, you have kept your word:
let your servant go in peace.**

Antiphon

**Christ is the light of the nations
and the glory of Israel his people.**

**With my own eyes I have seen the salvation
which you have prepared in the sight of every people.**

Antiphon

**Christ is the light of the nations
and the glory of Israel his people.**

**A light to reveal you to the nations
and the glory of your people Israel.**

Antiphon

**Christ is the light of the nations
and the glory of Israel his people.**

As the procession enters the church, the entrance chant of the Mass is sung. When the priest reaches the altar, he venerates it, and may incense it. Then he goes to the chair (and replaces the cope with the chasuble). After the Gloria, he sings or says the opening prayer. The Mass continues as usual.

SECOND FORM: SOLEMN ENTRANCE

The people, carrying unlighted candles, assemble in the church. The priest, vested in white, is accompanied by his ministers and by a representative group of the faithful. They go to a suitable place (either in front of the door or in the church itself) where most of the congregation can easily take part.

Then the candles are lighted while the antiphon, **The Lord will come,** or another hymn is sung.

After the greeting and introduction, he blesses the candles, as above, and goes in procession to the altar, while all are singing. The Mass is as described above.

MASS

Introductory Rites

> Within your temple, we ponder your loving kindness, O God. As your name, so also your praise reaches to the ends of the earth; your right hand is filled with justice. (Ps. 47:10-11)

OPENING PRAYER

**All-powerful Father,
Christ your Son became man for us
and was presented in the temple.
May he free our hearts from sin
and bring us into your presence.**

**We ask this through our Lord Jesus Christ, your Son,
who lives and reigns with you and the Holy Spirit,
one God, for ever and ever.**

LITURGY OF THE WORD

See Lectionary for Mass, no. 524.

LITURGY OF THE EUCHARIST

PRAYER OVER THE GIFTS

Pray, brethren . . .

**Lord,
accept the gifts your Church offers you with joy,
since in fulfillment of your will
your Son offered himself as a lamb without blemish
for the life of the world.**

We ask this through Christ our Lord.

Eucharistic Prayer:

Preface of the Presentation of the Lord, page 466.

Communion Rite

> With my own eyes I have seen the salvation which you have prepared in the sight of all the nations. (Luke 2:30-31)

PRAYER AFTER COMMUNION

Let us pray.

Pause for silent prayer, if this has not preceded.

**Lord,
you fulfilled the hope of Simeon,
who did not die
until he had been privileged to welcome the Messiah.
May this communion perfect your grace in us
and prepare us to meet Christ
when he comes to bring us into everlasting life,
for he is Lord for ever and ever.**

February 3

ST. BLASE, bishop and martyr

Common of martyrs (p. 709); or
Common of pastors: for bishops (p.
719).

OPENING PRAYER

**Lord,
hear the prayers of your martyr Blase.
Give us the joy of your peace in this life
and help us to gain the happiness that will never end.**

**Grant this through our Lord Jesus Christ, your Son,
who lives and reigns with you and the Holy Spirit,
one God, for ever and ever.**

ST. ANSGAR, bishop

Common of pastors: for missionaries (p.
726), or for bishops (p. 719).

OPENING PRAYER

**Father,
you sent St. Ansgar
to bring the light of Christ to many nations.
May his prayers help us
to walk in the light of your truth.**

**We ask this through our Lord Jesus Christ, your Son,
who lives and reigns with you and the Holy Spirit,
one God, for ever and ever.**

February 5

ST. AGATHA, virgin and martyr
Memorial

Common of martyrs (p. 709); or
Common of virgins (p. 731).

OPENING PRAYER

**Lord,
let your forgiveness be won for us
by the pleading of St. Agatha,
who found favor with you by her chastity
and by her courage in suffering death for the gospel.**

**Grant this through our Lord Jesus Christ, your Son,
who lives and reigns with you and the Holy Spirit,
one God, for ever and ever.**

February 6

ST. PAUL MIKI AND COMPANIONS, martyrs

Memorial

Common of martyrs (p. 704).

OPENING PRAYER

**God our Father,
source of strength for all your saints,
you led St. Paul Miki and his companions
through the suffering of the cross
to the joy of eternal life.
May their prayers give us the courage
to be loyal until death in professing our faith.**

**We ask this through our Lord Jesus Christ, your Son,
who lives and reigns with you and the Holy Spirit,
one God, for ever and ever.**

February 8

ST. JEROME EMILIANI

Common of holy men and women: for
teachers (p. 744).

OPENING PRAYER

**God of mercy,
you chose St. Jerome Emiliani
to be a father and friend of orphans:
May his prayers keep us faithful
to the Spirit we have received,
who makes us your children.**

**Grant this through our Lord Jesus Christ, your Son,
who lives and reigns with you and the Holy Spirit,
one God, for ever and ever.**

February 10

ST. SCHOLASTICA, virgin

Memorial

Common of virgins (p. 731); or
Common of holy men and women: for
religious (p. 741).

OPENING PRAYER

**Lord,
as we recall the memory of St. Scholastica,
we ask that by her example
we may serve you with love and obtain perfect joy.**

**Grant this through our Lord Jesus Christ, your Son,
who lives and reigns with you and the Holy Spirit,
one God, for ever and ever.**

February 11

OUR LADY OF LOURDES

Common of the Blessed Virgin Mary (p. 696).

OPENING PRAYER

**God of mercy,
we celebrate the feast of Mary,
the sinless mother of God.
May her prayers help us
to rise above our human weakness.**

**We ask this through our Lord Jesus Christ, your Son,
who lives and reigns with you and the Holy Spirit,
one God, for ever and ever.**

February 14

ST. CYRIL, monk, AND ST. METHODIUS, bishop
Memorial

Common of pastors: for founders of churches (p. 724), or for missionaries (p. 726).

OPENING PRAYER

**Father,
you brought the light of the gospel to the Slavic nations
through St. Cyril and his brother St. Methodius.
Open our hearts to understand your teaching
and help us to become one in faith and praise.**

**Grant this through our Lord Jesus Christ, your Son,
who lives and reigns with you and the Holy Spirit,
one God, for ever and ever.**

February 17

SEVEN FOUNDERS OF THE ORDER OF SERVITES

Common of holy men and women: for religious (p. 741).

OPENING PRAYER

**Lord,
fill us with the love
which inspired the seven holy brothers
to honor the mother of God with special devotion
and to lead your people to you.**

**We ask this through our Lord Jesus Christ, your Son,
who lives and reigns with you and the Holy Spirit,
one God, for ever and ever.**

February 21

ST. PETER DAMIAN, bishop and doctor

Common of doctors of the Church (p.
729); or Common of pastors: for bishops
(p. 719).

OPENING PRAYER

All-powerful God,
help us to follow the teachings and example of St. Peter Damian.
By making Christ and the service of his Church
the first love of our lives,
may we come to the joys of eternal light,
where he lives and reigns with you and the Holy Spirit,
one God, for ever and ever.

February 22

CHAIR OF ST. PETER, apostle

Feast

Introductory Rites

The Lord said to Simon Peter: I have prayed that your faith
may not fail; and you in your turn must strengthen your
brothers. (Luke 22:32)

OPENING PRAYER

All-powerful Father,
you have built your Church
on the rock of St. Peter's confession of faith.
May nothing divide or weaken
our unity in faith and love.

Grant this through our Lord Jesus Christ, your Son,
who lives and reigns with you and the Holy Spirit,
one God, for ever and ever.

See Lectionary for Mass, no. 535.

PRAYER OVER THE GIFTS

Pray, brethren . . .

Lord,
accept the prayers and gifts of your Church.
With St. Peter as our shepherd,
keep us true to the faith he taught
and bring us to your eternal kingdom.

We ask this through Christ our Lord.

Preface of the Apostles I or II, pages
481–482.

Communion Rite

>Peter said: You are the Christ, the Son of the living God.
>Jesus answered: You are Peter, the rock on which I will
>build my Church. (Matthew 16:16, 18)

PRAYER AFTER COMMUNION

Let us pray.

Pause for silent prayer, if this has not preceded.

God our Father,
you have given us the body and blood of Christ
as the food of life.
On this feast of Peter the apostle,
may this communion bring us redemption
and be the sign and source of our unity and peace.

We ask this in the name of Jesus the Lord.

February 23

ST. POLYCARP, bishop and martyr

Memorial

Common of martyrs (p. **709**); or
Common of pastors: for bishops (p.
719).

OPENING PRAYER

God of all creation,
you gave your bishop Polycarp
the privilege of being counted among the saints
who gave their lives in faithful witness to the gospel.
May his prayers give us the courage
to share with him the cup of suffering
and to rise to eternal glory.

We ask this through our Lord Jesus Christ, your Son,
who lives and reigns with you and the Holy Spirit,
one God, for ever and ever.

MARCH

March 4

ST. CASIMIR

Common of holy men and women (p. 735).

OPENING PRAYER

**All-powerful God,
to serve you is to reign:
by the prayers of St. Casimir,
help us to serve you in holiness and justice.**

**Grant this through our Lord Jesus Christ, your Son,
who lives and reigns with you and the Holy Spirit,
one God, for ever and ever.**

March 7

ST. PERPETUA AND ST. FELICITY, martyrs
Memorial

Common of martyrs (p. 704); or Common of holy men and women (p. 745).

OPENING PRAYER

**Father,
your love gave the saints Perpetua and Felicity
courage to suffer a cruel martyrdom.
By their prayers, help us to grow in love of you.**

**We ask this through our Lord Jesus Christ, your Son,
who lives and reigns with you and the Holy Spirit,
one God, for ever and ever.**

March 8

ST. JOHN OF GOD, religious

Common of holy men and women: for religious (p. 741), or for those who worked for the underprivileged (p.743).

OPENING PRAYER

**Father,
you gave St. John of God
love and compassion for others.
Grant that by doing good for others
we may be counted among the saints in your kingdom.**

**We ask this through our Lord Jesus Christ, your Son,
who lives and reigns with you and the Holy Spirit,
one God, for ever and ever.**

March 9

ST. FRANCES OF ROME, religious

Common of holy men and women: for
religious (p. 741).

OPENING PRAYER

Merciful Father,
in St. Frances of Rome
you have given us a unique example of love in marriage
as well as in religious life.
Keep us faithful in your service,
and help us to see and follow you
in all the aspects of life.

We ask this through our Lord Jesus Christ, your Son,
who lives and reigns with you and the Holy Spirit,
one God, for ever and ever.

March 17

ST. PATRICK, bishop

Common of pastors: for missionaries (p.
726), or for bishops (p. 719).

OPENING PRAYER

Let us pray
[that like St. Patrick the missionary
we will be fearless witnesses
to the gospel of Jesus Christ]
Pause for silent prayer
God our Father,
you sent St. Patrick
to preach your glory to the people of Ireland.
By the help of his prayers,
may all Christians proclaim your love to
all men.

Grant this through our Lord Jesus Christ, your
Son,
who lives and reigns with you and the Holy
Spirit,
one God, for ever and ever.

ALTERNATIVE OPENING PRAYER

Let us pray
[that, like St. Patrick,
we may be loyal to our faith in Christ]
Pause for silent prayer
Father in heaven,
you sent the great bishop Patrick
to the people of Ireland to share his faith
and to spend his life in loving service.
May our lives bear witness
to the faith we profess,
and our love bring others
to the peace and joy of your gospel.

We ask this through Christ our Lord.

March 18

ST. CYRIL OF JERUSALEM, bishop and doctor

Common of pastors: for bishops (p. 719); or Common of doctors of the Church (p. 729).

OPENING PRAYER

Father,
through St. Cyril of Jerusalem
you led your Church to a deeper understanding
of the mysteries of salvation.
Let his prayers help us to know your Son better
and to have eternal life in all its fullness.

We ask this through our Lord Jesus Christ, your Son,
who lives and reigns with you and the Holy Spirit,
one God, for ever and ever.

March 19

ST. JOSEPH, HUSBAND OF MARY

Solemnity

Introductory Rites

The Lord has put his faithful servant in charge of his household. (Luke 12:42)

OPENING PRAYER

Let us pray
 [that the Church will continue
  the saving work of Christ]

Pause for silent prayer

Father,
you entrusted our Savior to the care of St. Joseph.
By the help of his prayers
may your Church continue to serve its Lord, Jesus Christ,
who lives and reigns with you and the Holy Spirit,
one God, for ever and ever.

LITURGY OF THE WORD

See Lectionary for Mass, no. 543.

Profession of Faith

LITURGY OF THE EUCHARIST

PRAYER OVER THE GIFTS   **Pray, brethren . . .**

Father,
with unselfish love St. Joseph cared for your Son,
born of the Virgin Mary.
May we also serve you at your altar with pure hearts.

We ask this in the name of Jesus the Lord.

Eucharistic Prayer:

Preface of Joseph, husband of Mary,
page 479.

Communion Rite

Come, good and faithful servant! Share the joy of your
Lord! (Matthew 25:21)

PRAYER AFTER COMMUNION   **Let us pray.**

Pause for silent prayer, if this has not preceded.

Lord,
today you nourish us at this altar
as we celebrate the feast of St. Joseph.
Protect your Church always,
and in your love watch over the gifts you have given us.

Grant this through Christ our Lord.

March 23

ST. TURIBIUS DE MOGROVEJO, bishop

Common of pastors: for bishops (p.
719).

OPENING PRAYER   **Lord,**
through the apostolic work of St. Turibius
and his unwavering love of truth,
you helped your Church to grow.
May your chosen people continue to grow
in faith and holiness.

Grant this through our Lord Jesus Christ, your Son,
who lives and reigns with you and the Holy Spirit,
one God, for ever and ever.

March 25

ANNUNCIATION

Solemnity

Introductory Rites

As Christ came into the world, he said: Behold! I have come to do your will, O God. (Heb. 10:5, 7)

OPENING PRAYER	ALTERNATIVE OPENING PRAYER

Let us pray

[that Christ, the Word made flesh, will make us more like him]

Pause for silent prayer
**God our Father,
your Word became man and was born
of the Virgin Mary.
May we become more like Jesus Christ,
whom we acknowledge as our Redeemer,
God and man.
We ask this through our Lord Jesus Christ,
your Son,
who lives and reigns with you and the Holy
Spirit,
one God, for ever and ever.**

Let us pray

[that we may become more like Christ
who chose to become one of us]

Pause for silent prayer
**Almighty Father of our Lord Jesus Christ,
you have revealed the beauty of your power
by exalting the lowly virgin of Nazareth
and making her the mother of our Savior.
May the prayers of this woman
bring Jesus to the waiting world
and fill the void of incompletion
with the presence of her child,
who lives and reigns with you and the Holy
Spirit,
one God, for ever and ever.**

LITURGY OF THE WORD

See Lectionary for Mass, no. 545.

In the profession of faith, all genuflect at the words, and became man.

LITURGY OF THE EUCHARIST

PRAYER OVER THE GIFTS

Pray, brethren . . .

**Almighty Father,
as we recall the beginning of the Church
when your Son became man,
may we celebrate with joy today
this sacrament of your love.**

We ask this through Christ our Lord.

Eucharistic Prayer:
Preface of the Annunciation, page 461.

Communion Rite

> The Virgin is with child and shall bear a son, and she will
> call him Emmanuel. (Is. 7:14)

PRAYER AFTER COMMUNION

Let us pray.
Pause for silent prayer, if this has not preceded.

**Lord,
may the sacrament we share
strengthen our faith and hope in Jesus, born of a virgin
and truly God and man.
By the power of his resurrection
may we come to eternal joy.**

We ask this in the name of Jesus the Lord.

APRIL

April 2

ST. FRANCIS OF PAOLA, hermit

Common of holy men and women: for religious (p. 741).

OPENING PRAYER

Father of the lowly,
you raised St. Francis of Paola
to the glory of your saints.
By his example and prayers,
may we come to the rewards
you have promised the humble.

We ask this through our Lord Jesus Christ, your Son,
who lives and reigns with you and the Holy Spirit,
one God, for ever and ever.

April 4

ST. ISIDORE, bishop and doctor

Common of pastors: for bishops (p. 719); or Common of doctors of the Church (p. 729).

OPENING PRAYER

Lord,
hear the prayers we offer in commemoration of St. Isidore.
May your Church learn from his teaching
and benefit from his intercession.

Grant this through our Lord Jesus Christ, your Son,
who lives and reigns with you and the Holy Spirit,
one God, for ever and ever.

April 5

ST. VINCENT FERRER, priest

Common of pastors: for missionaries (p. 726).

OPENING PRAYER

Father,
you called St. Vincent Ferrer
to preach the gospel of the last judgment.
Through his prayers may we come with joy
to meet your Son in the kingdom of heaven,
where he lives and reigns with you and the Holy Spirit,
one God, for ever and ever.

April 7

ST. JOHN BAPTIST DE LA SALLE, priest
Memorial

Common of pastors (p. 721); or
Common of holy men and women: for
teachers (p. 744).

OPENING PRAYER

**Father,
you chose St. John Baptist de la Salle
to give young people a Christian education.
Give your Church teachers who will devote themselves
to helping your children grow
as Christian men and women.**

**We ask this through our Lord Jesus Christ, your Son,
who lives and reigns with you and the Holy Spirit,
one God, for ever and ever.**

April 11

ST. STANISLAUS, bishop and martyr
Memorial

Common of martyrs (p. 713); or
Common of pastors: for bishops (p.
719).

OPENING PRAYER

**Father,
to honor you, St. Stanislaus faced martyrdom with courage.
Keep us strong and loyal in our faith until death.**

**Grant this through our Lord Jesus Christ, your Son,
who lives and reigns with you and the Holy Spirit,
one God, for ever and ever.**

April 13

ST. MARTIN I, pope and martyr

Common of martyrs (p. 713); or
Common of pastors: for popes (p. 717).

OPENING PRAYER

**Merciful God, our Father,
neither hardship, pain, nor the threat of death
could weaken the faith of St. Martin.
Through our faith, give us courage
to endure whatever sufferings the world may inflict upon us.**

**We ask this through our Lord Jesus Christ, your Son,
who lives and reigns with you and the Holy Spirit,
one God, for ever and ever.**

April 21

ST. ANSELM, bishop and doctor

Common of pastors: for bishops (p. 719); or Common of doctors of the Church (p. 729).

OPENING PRAYER

**Father,
you called St. Anselm
to study and teach the sublime truths you have revealed.
Let your gift of faith come to the aid of our understanding
and open our hearts to your truth.**

**Grant this through our Lord Jesus Christ, your Son,
who lives and reigns with you and the Holy Spirit,
one God, for ever and ever.**

April 23

ST. GEORGE, martyr

Common of martyrs (p. 713).

OPENING PRAYER

**Lord,
hear the prayers of those who praise your mighty power.
As St. George was ready to follow Christ in suffering and
death,
so may he be ready to help us in our weakness.**

**We ask this through our Lord Jesus Christ, your Son,
who lives and reigns with you and the Holy Spirit,
one God, for ever and ever.**

April 24

ST. FIDELIS OF SIGMARINGEN, priest and martyr

Common of martyrs (p. 713); or Common of pastors (p. 721).

OPENING PRAYER

**Father,
you filled St. Fidelis with the fire of your love
and gave him the privilege of dying
that the faith might live.
Let his prayers keep us firmly grounded in your love,
and help us to come to know the power of Christ's resurrection.**

**We ask this through our Lord Jesus Christ, your Son,
who lives and reigns with you and the Holy Spirit,
one God, for ever and ever.**

April 25

ST. MARK, evangelist
Feast

Introductory Rites

Go out to the whole world, and preach the gospel to all creation, alleluia. (Mark 16:15)

OPENING PRAYER

**Father,
you gave St. Mark
the privilege of proclaiming your gospel.
May we profit by his wisdom
and follow Christ more faithfully.**

**Grant this through our Lord Jesus Christ, your Son,
who lives and reigns with you and the Holy Spirit,
one God, for ever and ever.**

See Lectionary for Mass, no. 555.

PRAYER OVER THE GIFTS

Pray, brethren . . .

**Lord,
as we offer the sacrifice of praise
on the feast of St. Mark,
we pray that your Church may always be faithful
to the preaching of the gospel.**

We ask this through Christ our Lord.

Preface of the Apostles II, page **482**.

Communion Rite

I, the Lord, am with you always, until the end of the world, alleluia. (Matthew 28:20)

PRAYER AFTER COMMUNION

Let us pray.
Pause for silent prayer, if this has not preceded.
**All-powerful God,
may the gifts we have received at this altar
make us holy, and strengthen us
in the faith of the gospel preached by St. Mark.**

We ask this in the name of Jesus the Lord.

April 28

ST. PETER CHANEL, priest and martyr

Common of martyrs (p. 713); or
Common of pastors: for missionaries (p. 726).

OPENING PRAYER

**Father,
you called St. Peter Chanel to work for your Church
and gave him the crown of martyrdom.
May our celebration of Christ's death and resurrection
make us faithful witnesses to the new life he brings,
for he lives and reigns with you and the Holy Spirit,
one God, for ever and ever.**

April 29

ST. CATHERINE OF SIENA, virgin and doctor
Memorial

Introductory Rites

Here is a wise and faithful virgin who went with lighted
lamp to meet her Lord, alleluia.

OPENING PRAYER

**Father,
in meditating on the sufferings of your Son
and in serving your Church,
St. Catherine was filled with the fervor of your love.
By her prayers,
may we share in the mystery of Christ's death
and rejoice in the revelation of his glory,
for he lives and reigns with you and the Holy Spirit,
one God, for ever and ever.**

See Lectionary for Mass, no. 557.

PRAYER OVER THE GIFTS

Pray, brethren . . .

**Lord,
accept this saving sacrifice
we offer on the feast of St. Catherine.
By following her teaching and example,
may we offer more perfect praise to you.**

Grant this through Christ our Lord.

Communion Rite
> If we walk in the light, as God is in light, there is fellowship
> among us, and the blood of his Son, Jesus Christ, will
> cleanse us from all sin, alleluia. (1 John 1:7)

PRAYER AFTER COMMUNION   **Let us pray.**
Pause for silent prayer, if this has not preceded.
Lord,
may the eucharist,
which nourished St. Catherine in this life,
bring us eternal life.

We ask this in the name of Jesus the Lord.

April 30

ST. PIUS V, pope

Common of pastors: for popes (p. 717).

OPENING PRAYER   **Father,**
you chose St. Pius V as pope of your Church
to protect the faith and give you more fitting worship.
By his prayers,
help us to celebrate your holy mysteries
with a living faith and an effective love.

We ask this through our Lord Jesus Christ, your Son,
who lives and reigns with you and the Holy Spirit,
one God, for ever and ever.

MAY

May 1

ST. JOSEPH THE WORKER

Introductory Rites

Happy are all who fear the Lord and walk in his ways. You shall enjoy the fruits of your labor, you will prosper and be happy, alleluia. (Ps. 127:1-2)

OPENING PRAYER

God our Father,
creator and ruler of the universe,
in every age you call man
to develop and use his gifts for the good of others.
With St. Joseph as our example and guide,
help us to do the work you have asked
and come to the rewards you have promised.

We ask this through our Lord Jesus Christ, your Son,
who lives and reigns with you and the Holy Spirit,
one God, for ever and ever.

See Lectionary for Mass, no. 559.

PRAYER OVER THE GIFTS

Pray, brethren . . .

Lord God,
fountain of all mercy,
look upon our gifts on this feast of St. Joseph.
Let our sacrifice
become the protection of all who call on you.

We ask this in the name of Jesus the Lord.

Preface of St. Joseph, husband of Mary, page 479.

Communion Rite

Let everything you do or say be in the name of the Lord with thanksgiving to God, alleluia. (Col. 3:17)

PRAYER AFTER COMMUNION

Let us pray.
Pause for silent prayer, if this has not preceded.
Lord,
hear the prayers of those you nourish in this eucharist.
Inspired by the example of St. Joseph,
may our lives manifest your love;
may we rejoice for ever in your peace.

Grant this through Christ our Lord.

May 2

ST. ATHANASIUS, bishop and doctor
Memorial

Common of pastors: for bishops (p. **719**); or Common of doctors of the Church (p. **729**).

OPENING PRAYER

Father,
you raised up St. Athanasius
to be an outstanding defender
of the truth of Christ's divinity.
By his teaching and protection
may we grow in your knowledge and love.

Grant this through our Lord Jesus Christ, your Son,
who lives and reigns with you and the Holy Spirit,
one God, for ever and ever.

See Lectionary for Mass, no. 560.

PRAYER OVER THE GIFTS

Pray, brethren . . .

Lord,
look upon the gifts we offer
on the feast of St. Athanasius.
Keep us true to the faith he professed
and let our own witness to your truth
bring us closer to salvation.

We ask this through Christ our Lord.

PRAYER AFTER COMMUNION

Let us pray.
Pause for silent prayer, if this has not preceded.
All-powerful God,
we join St. Athanasius in professing our belief
in the true divinity of Christ your Son.
Through this sacrament
may our faith always give us life and protection.

We ask this through Christ our Lord.

May 3

ST. PHILIP AND ST. JAMES, apostles
Feast

Introductory Rites

The Lord chose these holy men for their unfeigned love,
and gave them eternal glory, alleluia.

OPENING PRAYER

**God our Father,
every year you give us joy
on the festival of the apostles Philip and James.
By the help of their prayers
may we share in the suffering, death, and resurrection
of your only Son
and come to the eternal vision of your glory.**

**We ask this through our Lord Jesus Christ, your Son,
who lives and reigns with you and the Holy Spirit,
one God, for ever and ever.**

See Lectionary for Mass, no. 561.

PRAYER OVER THE GIFTS

Pray, brethren . . .

**Lord,
accept our gifts
at this celebration in honor of the apostles Philip and James.
Make our religion pure and undefiled.**

We ask this through Christ our Lord.

Preface of the Apostles I or II, pages
481–482.

Communion Rite

Lord, let us see the Father, and we shall be content. And
Jesus said: Philip, he who sees me, sees the Father, alleluia. (John 14:8-9)

PRAYER AFTER COMMUNION

Let us pray.
Pause for silent prayer, if this has not preceded.
**Father,
by the holy gifts we have received
free our minds and hearts from sin.
With the apostles Philip and James
may we see you in your Son
and be found worthy to have eternal life.**

We ask this through Christ our Lord.

May 12

ST. NEREUS AND ST. ACHILLEUS, martyrs

Common of martyrs (p. 704 or 711).

OPENING PRAYER

Father,
we honor Saints Nereus and Achilleus for their courage
in dying to profess their faith in Christ.
May we experience the help of their prayers
at the throne of your mercy.

Grant this through our Lord Jesus Christ, your Son,
who lives and reigns with you and the Holy Spirit,
one God, for ever and ever.

ST. PANCRAS, martyr

Common of martyrs (p. 709 or 713).

OPENING PRAYER

God of mercy,
give your Church joy and confidence
through the prayers of St. Pancras.
Keep us faithful to you
and steadfast in your service.

We ask this through our Lord Jesus Christ, your Son,
who lives and reigns with you and the Holy Spirit,
one God, for ever and ever.

May 14

ST. MATTHIAS, apostle

Feast

Introductory Rites

You have not chosen me; I have chosen you. Go and bear
fruit that will last, alleluia. (John 15:16)

OPENING PRAYER

Father,
you called St. Matthias to share in the mission of the apostles.
By the help of his prayers
may we receive with joy the love you share with us
and be counted among those you have chosen.

We ask this through our Lord Jesus Christ, your Son,
who lives and reigns with you and the Holy Spirit,
one God, for ever and ever.

See Lectionary for Mass, no. 564.

PRAYER OVER THE GIFTS

Pray, brethren . . .

Lord,
accept the gifts your Church offers
on the feast of the apostle, Matthias,
and by this eucharist
strengthen your grace within us.

We ask this through Christ our Lord.

Preface of the Apostles I or II, pages
481–482.

Communion Rite

This is my commandment: love one another as I have
loved you. (John 15:12)

PRAYER AFTER COMMUNION

Let us pray.
Pause for silent prayer, if this has not preceded.
Lord,
you constantly give life to your people
in this holy eucharist.
By the prayers of the apostle Matthias
prepare us to take our place
among your saints in eternal life.

We ask this through Christ our Lord.

May 15

In the dioceses of the United States

ST. ISIDORE

Common of holy men and women (p.
735).

OPENING PRAYER

Lord God,
all creation is yours, and you call us to serve you
by caring for the gifts that surround us.
May the example of St. Isidore urge us
to share our food with the hungry
and to work for the salvation of mankind.

We ask this through our Lord Jesus Christ, your Son,
who lives and reigns with you and the Holy Spirit,
one God, for ever and ever.

May 18

ST. JOHN I, pope and martyr

Common of martyrs (p. 709 or 713); or
Common of pastors: for popes (p. 717).

OPENING PRAYER

**God our Father,
rewarder of all who believe,
hear our prayers
as we celebrate the martyrdom of Pope John.
Help us to follow him in loyalty to the faith.**

**Grant this through our Lord Jesus Christ, your Son,
who lives and reigns with you and the Holy Spirit,
one God, for ever and ever.**

May 20

ST. BERNARDINE OF SIENA, priest

Common of pastors: for missionaries (p. 726).

OPENING PRAYER

**Father,
you gave St. Bernardine a special love
for the holy name of Jesus.
By the help of his prayers,
may we always be alive with the spirit of your love.**

**We ask this through our Lord Jesus Christ, your Son,
who lives and reigns with you and the Holy Spirit,
one God, for ever and ever.**

May 25

VENERABLE BEDE, priest and doctor

Common of doctors of the Church (p. 729); or Common of holy men and women: for religious (p. 741).

OPENING PRAYER

**Lord,
you have enlightened your Church
with the learning of St. Bede.
In your love
may your people learn from his wisdom
and benefit from his prayers.**

**Grant this through our Lord Jesus Christ, your Son,
who lives and reigns with you and the Holy Spirit,
one God, for ever and ever.**

May 25

ST. GREGORY VII, pope

Common of pastors: for popes (p. 717).

OPENING PRAYER

**Lord,
give your Church
the spirit of courage and love for justice
which distinguished Pope Gregory.
Make us courageous in condemning evil
and free us to pursue justice with love.**

**We ask this through our Lord Jesus Christ, your Son,
who lives and reigns with you and the Holy Spirit,
one God, for ever and ever.**

ST. MARY MAGDALENE DE PAZZI, virgin

Common of virgins (p. 731); or
Common of holy men and women: for
religious (p. 741).

OPENING PRAYER

**Father,
you love those who give themselves completely to your
　service,
and you filled St. Mary Magdalene de Pazzi
with heavenly gifts and the fire of your love.
As we honor her today
may we follow her example of purity and charity.**

**Grant this through our Lord Jesus Christ, your Son,
who lives and reigns with you and the Holy Spirit,
one God, for ever and ever.**

May 26

ST. PHILIP NERI, priest
Memorial

Common of pastors (p. 721); or Common of holy men and women: for religious (p. 741).

OPENING PRAYER

Father,
you continually raise up your faithful
to the glory of holiness.
In your love
kindle in us the fire of the Holy Spirit
who so filled the heart of St. Philip Neri.

We ask this through our Lord Jesus Christ, your Son,
who lives and reigns with you and the Holy Spirit,
one God, for ever and ever.

PRAYER OVER THE GIFTS

Pray, brethren . . .

Lord,
help us who offer you this sacrifice of praise
to follow the example of St. Philip.
Keep us always cheerful in our work
for the glory of your name and the good of our neighbor.

Grant this through Christ our Lord.

PRAYER AFTER COMMUNION

Let us pray.
Pause for silent prayer, if this has not preceded.
Lord,
strengthen us with the bread of life.
May we always imitate St. Philip
by hungering after this sacrament
in which we find true life.

We ask this in the name of Jesus the Lord.

May 27

ST. AUGUSTINE OF CANTERBURY, bishop

Common of pastors: for missionaries (p. 726); or for bishops (p. 719).

OPENING PRAYER

Father,
by the preaching of St. Augustine of Canterbury,
you led the people of England to the gospel.
May the fruits of his work continue in your Church.

Grant this through our Lord Jesus Christ, your Son,
who lives and reigns with you and the Holy Spirit,
one God, for ever and ever.

May 31

VISITATION
Feast

Introductory Rites

Come, all you who fear God, and hear the great things the
Lord has done for me. (Ps. 65:16)

OPENING PRAYER

Eternal Father,
you inspired the Virgin Mary, mother of your Son,
to visit Elizabeth and assist her in her need.
Keep us open to the working of your Spirit,
and with Mary may we praise you for ever.

We ask this through our Lord Jesus Christ, your Son,
who lives and reigns with you and the Holy Spirit,
one God, for ever and ever.

See Lectionary for Mass, no. 572.

PRAYER OVER THE GIFTS

Pray, brethren . . .

Father,
make our sacrifice acceptable and holy
as you accepted the love of Mary,
the mother of your Son, Jesus Christ,
who is Lord for ever and ever.

Preface of the Blessed Virgin Mary I or
II, pages **473–474.**

Communion Rite

All generations will call me blessed, for the Almighty has
done great things for me. Holy is his name. (Luke 1:48-49)

PRAYER AFTER COMMUNION

Let us pray.
Pause for silent prayer, if this has not preceded.
Lord,
let the Church praise you
for the great things you have done for your people.
May we always recognize with joy
the presence of Christ in the eucharist we celebrate,
as John the Baptist hailed the presence
of our Savior in the womb of Mary.

We ask this through Christ our Lord.

Saturday following the Second Sunday after Pentecost

IMMACULATE HEART OF MARY

Introductory Rites

My heart rejoices in your saving power. I will sing to the
Lord for his goodness to me. (Ps. 12:6)

OPENING PRAYER

**Father,
you prepared the heart of the Virgin Mary
to be a fitting home for your Holy Spirit.
By her prayers
may we become a more worthy temple of your glory.**

**Grant this through our Lord Jesus Christ, your Son,
who lives and reigns with you and the Holy Spirit,
one God, for ever and ever.**

See Lectionary for Mass, no. 573.

PRAYER OVER THE GIFTS

Pray, brethren . . .

**Lord,
accept the prayers and gifts we offer
in honor of Mary, the Mother of God.
May they please you
and bring us your help and forgiveness.**

We ask this in the name of Jesus the Lord.

Preface of the Blessed Virgin Mary I or
II, pages 473–474.

Communion Rite

Mary treasured all these words and pondered them in her
heart. (Luke 2:19)

PRAYER AFTER COMMUNION

Let us pray.

Pause for silent prayer, if this has not preceded.

**Lord,
you have given us the sacrament of eternal redemption.
May we who honor the mother of your Son
rejoice in the abundance of your blessings
and experience the deepening of your life within us.**

We ask this through Christ our Lord.

JUNE

June 1

ST. JUSTIN, martyr
Memorial

Introductory Rites
The wicked tempted me with their fables against your law, but I proclaimed your decrees before kings without fear or shame. (See Ps. 118:85, 46)

OPENING PRAYER

Father,
through the folly of the cross
you taught St. Justin the sublime wisdom of Jesus Christ.
May we too reject falsehood
and remain loyal to the faith.

We ask this through our Lord Jesus Christ, your Son,
who lives and reigns with you and the Holy Spirit,
one God, for ever and ever.

See Lectionary for Mass, no. 574.

PRAYER OVER THE GIFTS

Pray, brethren . . .

Lord,
help us to worship you as we should
when we celebrate these mysteries
which St. Justin vigorously defended.

We ask this in the name of Jesus the Lord.

Communion Rite

I resolved that while I was with you I would think of nothing but Jesus Christ and him crucified. (1 Cor. 2:2)

PRAYER AFTER COMMUNION

Let us pray.
Pause for silent prayer, if this has not preceded.
Lord,
hear the prayer of those you renew with spiritual food.
By following the teaching of St. Justin
may we offer constant thanks for the gifts we receive.

Grant this through Christ our Lord.

June 2

ST. MARCELLINUS AND ST. PETER, martyrs

Common of martyrs (p. 704 or 711).

OPENING PRAYER

**Father,
may we benefit from the example
of your martyrs Marcellinus and Peter,
and be supported by their prayers.**

**Grant this through our Lord Jesus Christ, your Son,
who lives and reigns with you and the Holy Spirit,
one God, for ever and ever.**

June 3

ST. CHARLES LWANGA AND COMPANIONS, martyrs
Memorial

Common of martyrs (p. 704 or 711).

OPENING PRAYER

**Father,
you have made the blood of the martyrs
the seed of Christians.
May the witness of St. Charles and his companions
and their loyalty to Christ in the face of torture
inspire countless men and women
to live the Christian faith.**

**We ask this through our Lord Jesus Christ, your Son,
who lives and reigns with you and the Holy Spirit,
one God, for ever and ever.**

See Lectionary for Mass, no. 576.

PRAYER OVER THE GIFTS

Pray, brethren . . .

**Lord,
accept the gifts we present at your altar.
As you gave your holy martyrs courage to die rather than sin,
help us to give ourselves completely to you.**

We ask this in the name of Jesus the Lord.

PRAYER AFTER COMMUNION

Let us pray.
Pause for silent prayer, if this has not preceded.
**Lord,
at this celebration of the triumph of your martyrs,
we have received the sacraments
which helped them endure their sufferings.
In the midst of our own hardships
may this eucharist keep us steadfast in faith and love.**

Grant this through Christ our Lord.

June 5

ST. BONIFACE, bishop and martyr
Memorial

Common of martyrs (p. 709 or 713); or Common of pastors: for missionaries (p. 726).

OPENING PRAYER

**Lord,
your martyr Boniface
spread the faith by his teaching
and witnessed to it with his blood.
By the help of his prayers
keep us loyal to our faith
and give us the courage to profess it in our lives.**

**Grant this through our Lord Jesus Christ, your Son,
who lives and reigns with you and the Holy Spirit,
one God, for ever and ever.**

June 6

ST. NORBERT, bishop

Common of pastors: for bishops (p. 719); or Common of holy men and women: for religious (p. 741).

OPENING PRAYER

**Father,
you made the bishop Norbert
an outstanding minister of your Church,
renowned for his preaching and pastoral zeal.
Always grant to your Church faithful shepherds
to lead your people to eternal salvation.**

**We ask this through our Lord Jesus Christ, your Son,
who lives and reigns with you and the Holy Spirit,
one God, for ever and ever.**

June 9

ST. EPHREM, deacon and doctor

Common of doctors of the Church (p. 729).

OPENING PRAYER

**Lord,
in your love fill our hearts with the Holy Spirit,
who inspired the deacon Ephrem to sing the praise
    of your mysteries
and gave him strength to serve you alone.**

**Grant this through our Lord Jesus Christ, your Son,
who lives and reigns with you and the Holy Spirit,
one God, for ever and ever.**

June 11

ST. BARNABAS, apostle
Memorial

Introductory Rites

Blessed are you, St. Barnabas: you were a man of faith filled with the Holy Spirit and counted among the apostles. (See Acts 11:24)

OPENING PRAYER

God our Father,
you filled St. Barnabas with faith and the Holy Spirit
and sent him to convert the nations.
Help us to proclaim the gospel by word and deed.

We ask this through our Lord Jesus Christ, your Son,
who lives and reigns with you and the Holy Spirit,
one God, for ever and ever.

See Lectionary for Mass, no. 580.

PRAYER OVER THE GIFTS

Pray, brethren . . .

Lord,
bless these gifts we present to you.
May they kindle in us the flame of love
by which St. Barnabas brought the light of the gospel
to the nations.

Grant this through Christ our Lord.

Preface of the Apostles I or II, pages 481–482.

Communion Rite

No longer shall I call you servants, for a servant knows not what his master does. Now I shall call you friends, for I have revealed to you all that I have heard from my Father. (John 15:15)

PRAYER AFTER COMMUNION

Let us pray.
Pause for silent prayer, if this has not preceded.
Lord,
hear the prayers of those who receive the pledge of
    eternal life
on the feast of St. Barnabas.
May we come to share the salvation
we celebrate in this sacrament.

We ask this in the name of Jesus the Lord.

June 13

ST. ANTHONY OF PADUA, priest and doctor
Memorial

Common of pastors (p. 721); or
Common of doctors of the Church (p.
729); or Common of holy men and
women: for religious (p. 741).

OPENING PRAYER

**Almighty God,
you have given St. Anthony to your people
as an outstanding preacher
and a ready helper in time of need.
With his assistance may we follow the gospel of Christ
and know the help of your grace in every difficulty.**

**Grant this through our Lord Jesus Christ, your Son,
who lives and reigns with you and the Holy Spirit,
one God, for ever and ever.**

June 19

ST. ROMUALD, abbot

Common of holy men and women: for
religious (p. 741).

OPENING PRAYER

**Father,
through St. Romuald
you renewed the life of solitude and prayer in your Church.
By our self-denial as we follow Christ
bring us the joy of heaven.**

**We ask this through our Lord Jesus Christ, your Son,
who lives and reigns with you and the Holy Spirit,
one God, for ever and ever.**

June 21

ST. ALOYSIUS GONZAGA, religious
Memorial

Introductory Rites

Who shall climb the mountain of the Lord and stand in
his holy place? The innocent man, the pure of heart! (See
Ps. 23:4, 3)

OPENING PRAYER

**Father of love,
giver of all good things,
in St. Aloysius you combined remarkable innocence
with the spirit of penance.
By the help of his prayers
may we who have not followed his innocence
follow his example of penance.**

**Grant this through our Lord Jesus Christ, your Son,
who lives and reigns with you and the Holy Spirit,
one God, for ever and ever.**

See Lectionary for Mass, no. 583.

PRAYER OVER THE GIFTS

Pray, brethren . . .

**Lord,
help us to follow the example of St. Aloysius
and always come to the eucharist
with hearts free from sin.
By our sharing in this mystery
make us rich in your blessings.**

We ask this in the name of Jesus the Lord.

Communion Rite

God gave them bread from heaven; men ate the bread of
angels. (Ps. 77:24-25)

PRAYER AFTER COMMUNION

Let us pray.
Pause for silent prayer, if this has not preceded.

**Lord,
you have nourished us with the bread of life.
Help us to serve you without sin.
By following the example of St. Aloysius
may we continue to spend our lives in thanksgiving.**

We ask this through Christ our Lord.

June 22

ST. PAULINUS OF NOLA, bishop

Common of pastors: for bishops (p. 719).

OPENING PRAYER

Lord,
you made St. Paulinus
renowned for his love of poverty
and concern for his people.
May we who celebrate his witness to the gospel
imitate his example of love for others.

We ask this through our Lord Jesus Christ, your Son,
who lives and reigns with you and the Holy Spirit,
one God, for ever and ever.

ST. JOHN FISHER, bishop and martyr,
AND ST. THOMAS MORE, martyr

Common of martyrs (p. 704).

OPENING PRAYER

Father,
you confirm the true faith
with the crown of martyrdom.
May the prayers of Saints John Fisher and Thomas More
give us the courage to proclaim our faith
by the witness of our lives.

Grant this through our Lord Jesus Christ, your Son,
who lives and reigns with you and the Holy Spirit,
one God, for ever and ever.

BIRTH OF ST. JOHN THE BAPTIST
Solemnity

VIGIL MASS

This Mass may be used on the evening of June 23, either before or after Evening Prayer I of the solemnity.

Introductory Rites

From his mother's womb, he will be filled with the Holy Spirit, he will be great in the sight of the Lord, and many will rejoice at his birth. (Luke 1:15, 14)

The Gloria is sung or said.

OPENING PRAYER

Let us pray
    [that we will follow the way of salvation]
Pause for silent prayer
All-powerful God,
help your people to walk the path to salvation.
By following the teaching of St. John the Baptist,
may we come to your Son, our Lord Jesus Christ,
who lives and reigns with you and the Holy Spirit,
one God, for ever and ever.

LITURGY OF THE WORD
See Lectionary for Mass, no. 586.
Profession of Faith

LITURGY OF THE EUCHARIST

PRAYER OVER THE GIFTS

Pray, brethren . . .

Lord,
look with favor on the gifts we bring
on this feast of St. John the Baptist.
Help us put into action
the mystery we celebrate in this sacrament.

We ask this in the name of Jesus the Lord.

Eucharistic Prayer:
Preface of John the Baptist, page **478**.

Communion Rite

Blessed be the Lord God of Israel, for he has visited and redeemed his people. (Luke 1:68)

PRAYER AFTER COMMUNION

Let us pray.
    Pause for silent prayer, if this has not preceded.
Father,
may the prayers of St. John the Baptist
lead us to the Lamb of God.
May this eucharist bring us the mercy of Christ,
who is Lord for ever and ever.

This formulary may also be used as a votive Mass.

MASS DURING THE DAY

Introductory Rites

> There was a man sent from God whose name was John.
> He came to bear witness to the light, to prepare an up-
> right people for the Lord. (John 1:6-7; Luke 1:17)

OPENING PRAYER

Let us pray

[that God will give us joy and peace]

Pause for silent prayer

**God our Father,
you raised up St. John the Baptist
to prepare a perfect people for Christ the
    Lord.
Give your Church joy in spirit
and guide those who believe in you
into the way of salvation and peace.**

**We ask this through our Lord Jesus Christ,
    your Son,
who lives and reigns with you and the Holy
    Spirit,
one God, for ever and ever.**

ALTERNATIVE OPENING PRAYER

Let us pray

[as we honor John the Baptist for the
    faith to recognize Christ in our midst]

Pause for silent prayer

**God our Father,
the voice of St. John the Baptist challenges us
    to repentance
and points the way to Christ the Lord.**

**Open our ears to his message, and free our
    hearts
to turn from our sins and receive the life
    of the gospel.**

We ask this through Christ our Lord.

LITURGY OF THE WORD

See Lectionary for Mass, no. 587.
Profession of Faith

LITURGY OF THE EUCHARIST

PRAYER OVER THE GIFTS

Pray, brethren . . .

**Father,
accept the gifts we bring to your altar
to celebrate the birth of St. John the Baptist,
who foretold the coming of our Savior
and made him known when he came.**

We ask this in the name of Jesus the Lord.

Eucharistic Prayer:
Preface of John the Baptist, page 478.

Communion Rite

> Through the tender compassion of our God, the dawn
> from on high shall break upon us. (Luke 1:78)

PRAYER AFTER COMMUNION

Let us pray.

Pause for silent prayer, if this has not preceded.

**Lord,
you have renewed us with this eucharist,
as we celebrate the feast of St. John the Baptist,
who foretold the coming of the Lamb of God.
May we welcome your Son as our Savior,
for he gives us new life,
and is Lord for ever and ever.**

June 27

ST. CYRIL OF ALEXANDRIA, bishop and doctor

Common of pastors: for bishops (p. 719); or Common of doctors of the Church (p. 729).

OPENING PRAYER

**Father,
the bishop Cyril courageously taught
that Mary was the Mother of God.
May we who cherish this belief
receive salvation through the incarnation of Christ your Son,
who lives and reigns with you and the Holy Spirit,
one God, for ever and ever.**

June 28

ST. IRENAEUS, bishop and martyr
Memorial

Common of martyrs (p. 709); or Common of pastors: for bishops (p. 719).

OPENING PRAYER

**Father,
you called St. Irenaeus to uphold your truth
and bring peace to your Church.
By his prayers renew us in faith and love
that we may always be intent
on fostering unity and peace.**

**Grant this through our Lord Jesus Christ, your Son,
who lives and reigns with you and the Holy Spirit,
one God, for ever and ever.**

See Lectionary for Mass, no. 589.

PRAYER OVER THE GIFTS

Pray, brethren . . .

**Lord,
as we celebrate the feast of St. Irenaeus
may this eucharist bring you glory,
increase our love of truth,
and help your Church to remain firm in faith and unity.**

We ask this in the name of Jesus the Lord.

PRAYER AFTER COMMUNION

Let us pray.
Pause for silent prayer, if this has not preceded.
**Lord,
by these holy mysteries increase our faith.
As the holy bishop Irenaeus reached eternal glory
by being faithful until death,
so may we be saved by living our faith.**

We ask this through Christ our Lord.

June 29

ST. PETER AND ST. PAUL, APOSTLES

Solemnity

VIGIL MASS

This Mass may be used on the evening of June 28, either before or after Evening Prayer I of the solemnity.

Introductory Rites

Peter the apostle and Paul the teacher of the Gentiles have brought us to know the law of the Lord.

The Gloria is sung or said.

OPENING PRAYER

Let us pray
  [that the prayers of the apostles will lead us to salvation]

Pause for silent prayer

Lord our God,
encourage us through the prayers of Saints Peter and Paul.
May the apostles who strengthened the faith of the infant Church
help us on our way of salvation.

We ask this through our Lord Jesus Christ, your Son,
who lives and reigns with you and the Holy Spirit,
one God, for ever and ever.

ALTERNATIVE OPENING PRAYER

Let us pray
  [to be true to the faith which has come to us through the apostles Peter and Paul]

Pause for silent prayer

Father in heaven,
the light of your revelation brought Saints Peter and Paul
the gift of faith in Jesus your Son.
Through their prayers
may we always give thanks for your life given us in Christ Jesus,
and for having been enriched by him in all knowledge and love.

We ask this through Christ our Lord.

LITURGY OF THE WORD

See Lectionary for Mass, no. 590.

Profession of Faith

LITURGY OF THE EUCHARIST

PRAYER OVER THE GIFTS

Pray, brethren . . .

Lord,
we present these gifts
on this feast of the apostles Peter and Paul.
Help us to know our own weakness
and to rejoice in your saving power.

Grant this through Christ our Lord.

Eucharistic Prayer:

Preface of Peter and Paul, Apostles, page 480.

Communion Rite

> Simon, son of John, do you love me more than these?
> Lord, you know all things; you know that I love you.
> (John 21:15, 17)

PRAYER AFTER COMMUNION

Let us pray.
Pause for silent prayer, if this has not preceded.
Father,
you give us light by the teaching of your apostles.
In this sacrament we have received
fill us with your strength.

We ask this in the name of Jesus the Lord.

MASS DURING THE DAY

Introductory Rites

> These men, conquering all human frailty, shed their
> blood and helped the Church to grow. By sharing the cup
> of the Lord's suffering, they became the friends of God.

OPENING PRAYER

Let us pray
[that we will remain true to the faith
of the apostles]
Pause for silent prayer
God our Father,
today you give us the joy
of celebrating the feast of the apostles
Peter and Paul.
Through them your Church first received
the faith.
Keep us true to their teaching.

Grant this through our Lord Jesus Christ, your
Son,
who lives and reigns with you and the Holy
Spirit,
one God, for ever and ever.

LITURGY OF THE WORD

See Lectionary for Mass, no. 591.

Profession of Faith

LITURGY OF THE EUCHARIST

ALTERNATIVE OPENING PRAYER

Let us pray
[one with Peter and Paul
in our faith in Christ
the Son of the living God]
Pause for silent prayer
Praise to you, the God and Father of our Lord
Jesus Christ,
who in your great mercy
have given us new birth and hope
through the power of Christ's resurrection.
Through the prayers of the apostles Peter and
Paul
may we who received this faith through their
preaching
share their joy in following the Lord
to the unfading inheritance
reserved for us in heaven.

We ask this in the name of Jesus the Lord.

PRAYER OVER THE GIFTS

Pray, brethren . . .

Lord,
may your apostles join their prayers to our offering
and help us to celebrate this sacrifice in love and unity.
We ask this through Christ our Lord.

Eucharistic Prayer:
Preface of Peter and Paul, Apostles,
page **480**.

Communion Rite

Peter said: You are the Christ, the Son of the living God.
Jesus answered: You are Peter, the rock on which I will
build my Church. (Matthew 16:16, 18)

PRAYER AFTER COMMUNION

Let us pray.
Pause for silent prayer, if this has not preceded.
Lord,
renew the life of your Church
with the power of this sacrament.
May the breaking of bread
and the teaching of the apostles
keep us united in your love.
We ask this in the name of Jesus the Lord.

SOLEMN BLESSING OR PRAYER OVER THE PEOPLE

The following may replace the simple blessing.

After the greeting, the deacon (or in his absence, the priest) gives the invitation in these or similar words:

Then the priest extends his hands over the people while he sings or says:

Bow your heads and pray for God's blessing.

The Lord has set you firm within his Church,
which he built upon the rock of Peter's faith.
May he bless you with a faith that never falters.
℟. Amen.

The Lord has given you knowledge of the faith
through the labors and preaching of St. Paul.
May his example inspire you to lead others to Christ
by the manner of your life.
℟. Amen.

May the keys of Peter, and the words of Paul,
their undying witness and their prayers,
lead you to the joy of that eternal home
which Peter gained by his cross, and Paul by the sword.
℟. Amen.

May almighty God bless you,
the Father, and the Son,⊹ and the Holy Spirit.

For a votive Mass of St. Peter or St. Paul, see pages **855–856**.

℟. Amen.

June 30

FIRST MARTYRS OF THE CHURCH OF ROME

Common of martyrs (p. 704).

OPENING PRAYER

**Father,
you sanctified the Church of Rome
with the blood of its first martyrs.
May we find strength from their courage
and rejoice in their triumph.**

**We ask this through our Lord Jesus Christ, your Son,
who lives and reigns with you and the Holy Spirit,
one God, for ever and ever.**

JULY

July 3

ST. THOMAS, apostle
Feast

Introductory Rites

You are my God: I will give you praise, O my God, I will
extol you, for you are my savior. (Ps. 117:28)

OPENING PRAYER

**Almighty Father,
as we honor Thomas the apostle,
let us always experience the help of his prayers.
May we have eternal life by believing in Jesus,
whom Thomas acknowledged as Lord,
who lives and reigns with you and the Holy Spirit,
one God, for ever and ever.**

See Lectionary for Mass, no. 593.

PRAYER OVER THE GIFTS

Pray, brethren . . .

**Lord,
we offer you our service and we pray:
protect the gifts you have given us
as we offer this sacrifice of praise
on the feast of your apostle Thomas.**

We ask this in the name of Jesus the Lord.

Preface of the Apostles I or II, pages
481–482.

Communion Rite

> Jesus spoke to Thomas: Put your hand here, and see the place
> of the nails. Doubt no longer, but believe. (See John 20:27)

PRAYER AFTER COMMUNION

Let us pray.

Pause for silent prayer, if this has not preceded.

Father,
in this sacrament we have received
the body and blood of Christ.
With St. Thomas we acknowledge him to be our Lord
**   and God.**
May we show by our lives that our faith is real.

We ask this through Christ our Lord.

July 4

ST. ELIZABETH OF PORTUGAL

Common of holy men and women: for those who worked for the under-privileged (p. 743).

OPENING PRAYER

Father of peace and love,
you gave St. Elizabeth the gift of reconciling enemies.
By the help of her prayers
give us the courage to work for peace among men,
that we may be called the sons of God.

We ask this through our Lord Jesus Christ, your Son,
who lives and reigns with you and the Holy Spirit,
one God, for ever and ever.

July 4

In the dioceses of the United States

INDEPENDENCE DAY
(and for Other Civic Observances)

OPENING PRAYER

Let us pray
[for peace and justice and truth here and in every land]
Pause for silent prayer

a   **God of love, Father of us all,**
    in wisdom and goodness you guide creation
    to fulfillment in Christ your Son.
    Open our hearts to the truth of his gospel,
    that your peace may rule in our hearts
    and your justice guide our lives.

    Grant this through our Lord Jesus Christ, your Son,
    who lives and reigns with you and the Holy Spirit,
    one God, for ever and ever.

b   **Father of the family of man,**
    open our hearts to greater love of your Son.
    Let national boundaries not set limits to our concern.
    Ward off the pride that comes with worldly
    **   wealth and power.**
    Give us the courage to open ourselves in love
    to the service of all your people.

    Grant this through our Lord Jesus Christ, your Son,
    who lives and reigns with you and the Holy Spirit,
    one God, for ever and ever.

c   **Father of the family of nations,**
    open our hearts to greater love of your Son.
    Grant that the boundaries of nations
    will not set limits to our love,
    and give us the courage to build a land
    that serves you in truth and justice.

    Grant this through our Lord Jesus Christ, your Son,
    who lives and reigns with you and the Holy Spirit,
    one God, for ever and ever.

See Lectionary for Mass, nos. 831-835.

PRAYER OVER THE GIFTS

a   **God our Father,**
you have given us in abundance
that we might give you praise
and serve all your people in love.
Accept these gifts we bring
for the salvation of all the world
and help us to live in love as you have commanded.
We ask this through Christ our Lord.

b   **Lord God,**
accept these gifts we bring to this altar
and teach us the wisdom of the gospel
which leads to true justice and lasting peace.
We ask this through Christ our Lord.

Preface of Independence Day and Other Civic Observances I or II, pages 499–500.

PRAYER AFTER COMMUNION

Let us pray.
Pause for silent prayer, if this has not preceded.

a   **Father,**
now that we have shared the body and blood of Christ,
teach us the proper use of your gifts
and true love for our brothers and sisters.
We ask this through Christ our Lord.

b   **God our Father,**
through the power of this eucharist
keep us constant in the love of your Son.
Help us to play our part in the life of this nation
that its thoughts may be directed
toward peace, justice,
and the loving service of all mankind.
We ask this through Christ our Lord.

c   **God our Father,**
through the food we have received
you bless and sanctify us and the fruit of our toil.
Help us to serve each other in justice and mercy
and share what we have
for the welfare of all men and women.
We ask this through Christ our Lord.

July 5

ST. ANTHONY ZACCARIA, priest

Common of pastors (p. 721); or Common of holy men and women: for teachers (p. 744) or for religious (p. 741).

OPENING PRAYER

**Lord,
enable us to grasp in the spirit of St. Paul
the sublime wisdom of Jesus Christ,
the wisdom which inspired St. Anthony Zaccaria
to preach the message of salvation in your Church.**

**Grant this through our Lord Jesus Christ, your Son,
who lives and reigns with you and the Holy Spirit,
one God, for ever and ever.**

July 6

ST. MARIA GORETTI, virgin and martyr

Common of martyrs (p. 709); or Common of virgins (p. 731).

OPENING PRAYER

**Father,
source of innocence and lover of chastity,
you gave St. Maria Goretti the privilege
of offering her life in witness to Christ.
As you gave her the crown of martyrdom,
let her prayers keep us faithful to your teaching.**

**We ask this through our Lord Jesus Christ, your Son,
who lives and reigns with you and the Holy Spirit,
one God, for ever and ever.**

July 11

ST. BENEDICT, abbot
Memorial

Common of holy men and women: for religious (p. 741).

OPENING PRAYER

**God our Father,
you made St. Benedict an outstanding guide
to teach men how to live in your service.
Grant that by preferring your love to everything else,
we may walk in the way of your commandments.**

**We ask this through our Lord Jesus Christ, your Son,
who lives and reigns with you and the Holy Spirit,
one God, for ever and ever.**

See Lectionary for Mass, no. 597.

PRAYER OVER THE GIFTS   **Pray, brethren . . .**

**Lord,
look kindly on these gifts we present
on the feast of St. Benedict.
By following his example in seeking you,
may we know unity and peace in your service.**

Grant this through Christ our Lord.

PRAYER AFTER COMMUNION   **Let us pray.**
Pause for silent prayer, if this has not preceded.
**Lord,
hear the prayers of all
who have received this pledge of eternal life.
By following the teaching of St. Benedict,
may we be faithful in doing your work
and in loving our brothers and sisters in true charity.**

We ask this in the name of Jesus the Lord.

July 13
ST. HENRY

Common of holy men and women
(p. 731).

OPENING PRAYER   **Lord,
you filled St. Henry with your love
and raised him from the cares of an earthly kingdom
to eternal happiness in heaven.
In the midst of the changes of this world,
may his prayers keep us free from sin
and help us on our way toward you.**

**Grant this through our Lord Jesus Christ, your Son,
who lives and reigns with you and the Holy Spirit,
one God, for ever and ever.**

July 14
ST. CAMILLUS DE LELLIS, priest

Common of holy men and women: for
those who worked for the underprivileged (p. 743).

OPENING PRAYER   **Father,
you gave St. Camillus a special love for the sick.
Through his prayers inspire us with your grace,
so that by serving you in our brothers and sisters
we may come safely to you at the end of our lives.**

**We ask this through our Lord Jesus Christ, your Son,
who lives and reigns with you and the Holy Spirit,
one God, for ever and ever.**

July 14

In the dioceses of the United States

BLESSED KATERI TEKAKWITHA, virgin

Memorial

Common of virgins (p. 731).

OPENING PRAYER

**Lord God,
you called the virgin, blessed Kateri Tekakwitha,
to shine among the Indian people
as an example of innocence of life.**

**Through her intercession,
may all peoples of every tribe, tongue, and nation,
having been gathered into your Church,
proclaim your greatness
in one song of praise.**

**We ask this through our Lord Jesus Christ, your Son,
who lives and reigns with you and the Holy Spirit,
one God, for ever and ever.**

July 15

ST. BONAVENTURE, bishop and doctor

Memorial

Common of pastors: for bishops (p. 719); or Common of doctors of the Church (p. 729).

OPENING PRAYER

**All-powerful Father,
may we who celebrate the feast of St. Bonaventure
always benefit from his wisdom
and follow the example of his love.**

**Grant this through our Lord Jesus Christ, your Son,
who lives and reigns with you and the Holy Spirit,
one God, for ever and ever.**

July 16

OUR LADY OF MOUNT CARMEL

Common of the Blessed Virgin Mary (p. 696).

OPENING PRAYER

**Father,
may the prayers of the Virgin Mary protect us
and help us to reach Christ her Son
who lives and reigns with you and the Holy Spirit,
one God, for ever and ever.**

July 21

ST. LAWRENCE OF BRINDISI, priest and doctor

Common of pastors (p. 721); or Common of doctors of the Church (p. 729).

OPENING PRAYER

Lord,
for the glory of your name and the salvation of souls
you gave St. Lawrence of Brindisi
courage and right judgment.
By his prayers,
help us to know what we should do
and give us the courage to do it.
We ask this through our Lord Jesus Christ, your Son,
who lives and reigns with you and the Holy Spirit,
one God, for ever and ever.

July 22

ST. MARY MAGDALENE
Memorial

Introductory Rites

The Lord said to Mary Magdalene: Go and tell my
brothers that I shall ascend to my Father and your Father,
to my God and to your God. (John 20:17)

OPENING PRAYER

Father,
your Son first entrusted to St. Mary Magdalene
the joyful news of his resurrection.
By her prayers and example
may we proclaim Christ as our living Lord
and one day see him in glory,
for he lives and reigns with you and the Holy Spirit,
one God, for ever and ever.

See Lectionary for Mass, no. 603.

PRAYER OVER THE GIFTS

Pray, brethren . . .

Lord,
accept the gifts we present in memory of St. Mary
    Magdalene;
her loving worship was accepted by your Son,
who is Lord for ever and ever.

Communion Rite

The love of Christ compels us to live not for ourselves but
for him who died and rose for us. (2 Cor. 5:14-15)

PRAYER AFTER COMMUNION

Let us pray.
Pause for silent prayer, if this has not preceded.
Father,
may the sacrament we have received
fill us with the same faithful love
that kept Mary Magdalene close to Christ,
who is Lord for ever and ever.

July 23

ST. BRIDGET, religious

Common of holy men and women (p. 745).

OPENING PRAYER

Lord our God,
you revealed the secrets of heaven to St. Bridget
as she meditated on the suffering and death of your Son.
May your people rejoice in the revelation of your glory.

Grant this through our Lord Jesus Christ, your Son,
who lives and reigns with you and the Holy Spirit,
one God, for ever and ever.

July 25

ST. JAMES, apostle
Feast

Introductory Rites

Walking by the Sea of Galilee, Jesus saw James and John,
the sons of Zebedee, mending their nets, and he called
them to follow him. (See Matthew 4:18, 21)

OPENING PRAYER

**Almighty Father,
by the martyrdom of St. James
you blessed the work of the early Church.
May his profession of faith give us courage
and his prayers bring us strength.**

**We ask this through our Lord Jesus Christ, your Son,
who lives and reigns with you and the Holy Spirit,
one God, for ever and ever.**

See Lectionary for Mass, no. 605.

PRAYER OVER THE GIFTS

Pray, brethren . . .

**Lord,
as we honor St. James,
the first apostle to share the cup of suffering and death,
wash away our sins
by the saving passion of your Son,
and make our sacrifice pleasing to you.**

We ask this through Christ our Lord.

Preface of the Apostles I or II, pages
481–482.
Communion Rite

By sharing the cup of the Lord's suffering, they became
the friends of God. (See Matthew 20:22-23)

PRAYER AFTER COMMUNION

Let us pray.
Pause for silent prayer, if this has not preceded.
**Father,
we have received this holy eucharist with joy
as we celebrate the feast of the apostle James.
Hear his prayers
and bring us your help.**

We ask this in the name of Jesus the Lord.

July 26

ST. JOACHIM AND ST. ANN, parents of Mary
Memorial

Introductory Rites

Praised be Joachim and Ann for the child they bore. The
Lord gave them the blessing of all the nations.

OPENING PRAYER

**God of our fathers,
you gave Saints Joachim and Ann
the privilege of being the parents of Mary,
the mother of your incarnate Son.
May their prayers help us to attain
the salvation you have promised to your people.**

**Grant this through our Lord Jesus Christ, your Son,
who lives and reigns with you and the Holy Spirit,
one God, for ever and ever.**

See Lectionary for Mass, no. 606.

PRAYER OVER THE GIFTS

Pray, brethren . . .

**Lord,
receive these gifts as signs of our love
and give us a share in the blessing you promised
to Abraham and his descendants.**

We ask this in the name of Jesus the Lord.

Communion Rite

They received a blessing from the Lord, and kindness
from God their Savior. (See Ps. 23:5)

PRAYER AFTER COMMUNION

Let us pray.
Pause for silent prayer, if this has not preceded.
**Father,
your Son was born as a man
so that men could be born again in you.
As you nourish us with the bread of life,
given only to your sons and daughters,
fill us with the Spirit who makes us your children.**

We ask this through Christ our Lord.

July 29

ST. MARTHA
Memorial

Introductory Rites

> As Jesus entered a certain village a woman called Martha
> welcomed him into her house. (Luke 10:38)

OPENING PRAYER

**Father,
your Son honored St. Martha
by coming to her home as a guest.
By her prayers
may we serve Christ in our brothers and sisters
and be welcomed by you into heaven, our true home.**

**We ask this through our Lord Jesus Christ, your Son,
who lives and reigns with you and the Holy Spirit,
one God, for ever and ever.**

See Lectionary for Mass, no. 607.

PRAYER OVER THE GIFTS

Pray, brethren . . .

**Father,
we praise you for your glory
on the feast of St. Martha.
Accept this service of our worship
as you accepted her love.**

Grant this through Christ our Lord.

Communion Rite

> Martha said to Jesus: You are the Christ, the Son of God,
> who was to come into this world. (John 11:27)

PRAYER AFTER COMMUNION

Let us pray.
Pause for silent prayer, if this has not preceded.
**Lord,
you have given us the body and blood of your Son
to free us from undue attachment to this passing life.
By following the example of St. Martha,
may we grow in love for you on earth
and rejoice for ever in the vision of your glory in heaven.**

We ask this in the name of Jesus the Lord.

July 30

ST. PETER CHRYSOLOGUS, bishop and doctor

Common of pastors: for bishops (p. 719); or Common of doctors of the Church (p. 729).

OPENING PRAYER

**Father,
you made St. Peter Chrysologus
an outstanding preacher of your incarnate Word.
May the prayers of St. Peter help us to cherish
the mystery of our salvation
and make its meaning clear in our love for others.**

**Grant this through our Lord Jesus Christ, your Son,
who lives and reigns with you and the Holy Spirit,
one God, for ever and ever.**

July 31

ST. IGNATIUS OF LOYOLA, priest
Memorial

Introductory Rites

At the name of Jesus every knee must bend, in heaven,
on earth, and under the earth; every tongue should proclaim to the glory of God the Father: Jesus Christ is Lord.
(Philemon 2:10-11)

OPENING PRAYER

**Father,
you gave St. Ignatius of Loyola to your Church
to bring greater glory to your name.
May we follow his example on earth
and share the crown of life in heaven.**

**We ask this through our Lord Jesus Christ, your Son,
who lives and reigns with you and the Holy Spirit,
one God, for ever and ever.**

See Lectionary for Mass, no. 609.

PRAYER OVER THE GIFTS

Pray, brethren . . .

**Lord God,
be pleased with the gifts we present to you
at this celebration in honor of St. Ignatius.
Make us truly holy by this eucharist
which you give us as the source of all holiness.**

We ask this in the name of Jesus the Lord.

Communion Rite

I have come to bring fire to the earth. How I wish it were
already blazing! (Luke 12:49)

PRAYER AFTER COMMUNION

Let us pray.
Pause for silent prayer, if this has not preceded.
Lord,
may the sacrifice of thanksgiving which we have offered
on the feast of St. Ignatius
lead us to the eternal praise of your glory.
Grant this through Christ our Lord.

AUGUST

August 1

ST. ALPHONSUS LIGUORI, bishop and doctor
Memorial

Common of pastors: for bishops (p. 719); or Common of doctors of the Church (p. 729).

OPENING PRAYER

Father,
you constantly build up your Church
by the lives of your saints.
Give us grace to follow St. Alphonsus
in his loving concern for the salvation of men,
and so come to share his reward in heaven.

Grant this through our Lord Jesus Christ, your Son,
who lives and reigns with you and the Holy Spirit,
one God, for ever and ever.

See Lectionary for Mass, no. 610.

PRAYER OVER THE GIFTS

Pray, brethren . . .

Father,
inflame our hearts with the Spirit of your love
as we present these gifts on the feast of St. Alphonsus,
who dedicated his life to you in the eucharist.

We ask this in the name of Jesus the Lord.

PRAYER AFTER COMMUNION

Let us pray.
Pause for silent prayer, if this has not preceded.
Lord,
you made St. Alphonsus
a faithful minister and preacher of this holy eucharist.
May all who believe in you receive it often
and give you never-ending praise.

We ask this through Christ our Lord.

August 2

ST. EUSEBIUS OF VERCELLI, bishop

Common of pastors: for bishops (p. 719).

OPENING PRAYER

Lord God,
St. Eusebius affirmed the divinity of your Son.
By keeping the faith he taught,
may we come to share the eternal life of Christ,
who lives and reigns with you and the Holy Spirit,
one God, for ever and ever.

August 4

ST. JOHN VIANNEY, priest

Memorial

Common of pastors (p. 721).

OPENING PRAYER

Father of mercy,
you made St. John Vianney outstanding
in his priestly zeal and concern for your people.
By his example and prayers,
enable us to win our brothers and sisters
to the love of Christ
and come with them to eternal glory.

We ask this through our Lord Jesus Christ, your Son,
who lives and reigns with you and the Holy Spirit,
one God, for ever and ever.

August 5

DEDICATION OF SAINT MARY MAJOR

Common of the Blessed Virgin Mary (p. 696).

OPENING PRAYER

Lord,
pardon the sins of your people.
May the prayers of Mary, the mother of your Son,
help to save us,
for by ourselves we cannot please you.

Grant this through our Lord Jesus Christ, your Son,
who lives and reigns with you and the Holy Spirit,
one God, for ever and ever.

August 6

TRANSFIGURATION
Feast

Introductory Rites

> In the shining cloud the Spirit is seen; from it the voice of
> the Father is heard: This is my Son, my beloved, in whom
> is all my delight. Listen to him. (See Matthew 17:5)

OPENING PRAYER

Let us pray
 **[that we may hear the Lord Jesus
   and share his everlasting life]**

Pause for silent prayer

**God our Father,
in the transfigured glory of Christ your Son,
you strengthen our faith
by confirming the witness of your prophets,
and show us the splendor of your beloved sons and daughters.
As we listen to the voice of your Son,
help us to become heirs to eternal life with him
who lives and reigns with you and the Holy Spirit,
one God, for ever and ever.**

LITURGY OF THE WORD

See Lectionary for Mass, no. 614.

LITURGY OF THE EUCHARIST

PRAYER OVER THE GIFTS

Pray, brethren . . .

**Lord,
by the transfiguration of your Son
make our gifts holy,
and by his radiant glory free us from our sins.**

We ask this in the name of Jesus the Lord.

Preface of the Transfiguration, page 467.

Communion Rite

> When Christ is revealed we shall be like him, for we shall
> see him as he is. (1 John 3:2)

PRAYER AFTER COMMUNION

Let us pray.

Pause for silent prayer, if this has not preceded.

**Lord,
you revealed the true radiance of Christ
in the glory of his transfiguration.
May the food we receive from heaven
change us into his image.**

We ask this in the name of Jesus the Lord.

August 7

ST. SIXTUS II, pope and martyr, AND COMPANIONS, martyrs

Common of martyrs (p. 704).

OPENING PRAYER

**Father,
by the power of the Holy Spirit
you enabled St. Sixtus and his companions to
   lay down their lives
for your word in witness to Jesus.
Give us the grace to believe in you
and the courage to profess our faith.**

**We ask this through our Lord Jesus Christ, your Son,
who lives and reigns with you and the Holy Spirit,
one God, for ever and ever.**

ST. CAJETAN, priest

Common of pastors (p. 721); or
Common of holy men and women: for
religious (p. 741).

OPENING PRAYER

**Lord,
you helped St. Cajetan
to imitate the apostolic way of life.
By his example and prayers
may we trust in you always
and be faithful in seeking your kingdom.**

**Grant this through our Lord Jesus Christ, your Son,
who lives and reigns with you and the Holy Spirit,
one God, for ever and ever.**

August 8

ST. DOMINIC, priest
Memorial

Common of pastors (p. 721); or
Common of holy men and women: for
religious (p. 741).

OPENING PRAYER

**Lord,
let the holiness and teaching of St. Dominic
come to the aid of your Church.
May he help us now with his prayers
as he once inspired people by his preaching.**

**We ask this through our Lord Jesus Christ, your Son,
who lives and reigns with you and the Holy Spirit,
one God, for ever and ever.**

See Lectionary for Mass, no. 617.

PRAYER OVER THE GIFTS   **Pray, brethren . . .**

Lord of mercy,
at the intercession of St. Dominic
hear our prayers,
and by the power of this sacrifice
give us the grace to preach and defend our faith.

Grant this through Christ our Lord.

PRAYER AFTER COMMUNION   **Let us pray.**
Pause for silent prayer, if this has not preceded.
Lord,
may your Church share with a living faith
the power of the sacrament we have received.
As the preaching of St. Dominic helped your Church to grow,
may his prayers help us to live for you.

We ask this in the name of Jesus the Lord.

August 10

ST. LAWRENCE, deacon and martyr

Feast

Introductory Rites
Today let us honor St. Lawrence, who spent himself for
the poor of the Church. Thus he merited to suffer martyrdom and to ascend in joy to Jesus Christ the Lord.

OPENING PRAYER   **Father,**
you called St. Lawrence to serve you by love
and crowned his life with glorious martyrdom.
Help us to be like him
in loving you and doing your work.

Grant this through our Lord Jesus Christ, your Son,
who lives and reigns with you and the Holy Spirit,
one God, for ever and ever.

See Lectionary for Mass, no. 618.

PRAYER OVER THE GIFTS   **Pray, brethren . . .**

Lord,
at this celebration in honor of St. Lawrence,
accept the gifts we offer
and let them become a help to our salvation.

We ask this in the name of Jesus the Lord.

Communion Rite

He who serves me, follows me, says the Lord; and where
I am, my servant will also be. (John 12:26)

PRAYER AFTER COMMUNION

Let us pray.

Pause for silent prayer, if this has not preceded.

**Lord,
we have received your gifts
on this feast of St. Lawrence.
As we offer you our worship in this eucharist,
may we experience the increase of your saving grace.**

We ask this through Christ our Lord.

August 11

ST. CLARE, virgin

Memorial

Common of virgins (p. 731); or
Common of holy men and women: for
religious (p. 741).

OPENING PRAYER

**God of mercy,
you inspired St. Clare with the love of poverty.
By the help of her prayers
may we follow Christ in poverty of spirit
and come to the joyful vision of your glory
in the kingdom of heaven.**

**We ask this through our Lord Jesus Christ, your Son,
who lives and reigns with you and the Holy Spirit,
one God, for ever and ever.**

August 13

ST. PONTIAN, pope and martyr,
AND ST. HIPPOLYTUS, priest and martyr

Common of martyrs (p. 704); or
Common of pastors (p. 721).

OPENING PRAYER

**Lord,
may the loyal suffering of your saints, Pontian and
    Hippolytus,
fill us with your love
and make our hearts steadfast in faith.**

**Grant this through our Lord Jesus Christ, your Son,
who lives and reigns with you and the Holy Spirit,
one God, for ever and ever.**

August 14

ST. MAXIMILIAN MARY KOLBE, priest and martyr

Memorial

Introductory Rites

Come, you whom my Father blessed, says the Lord: I tell you, whatever you did for one of the least of my brothers or sisters, you did for me. (Matthew 25:34, 40)

OPENING PRAYER

Gracious God,
you filled your priest and martyr,
St. Maximilian Kolbe,
with zeal for souls
and love for his neighbor.
Through the prayers of this devoted servant of
   Mary Immaculate,
grant that in our efforts to serve others for your glory
we too may become like Christ your Son,
who loved his own in the world even to the end,
and now lives and reigns with you and the Holy Spirit,
one God, for ever and ever.

First Reading: Wisdom 3:1-9 [Lectionary no. 713.5], or 1 John 3:13-18 [see Lectionary no. 740.15]
Responsorial Psalm: Psalm 116:10-11, 12-13, 16-17 [see Lectionary no. 363], with ℟. Precious in the eyes of the Lord is the death of his faithful ones.
Gospel: John 15:12-16 [Lectionary no. 778.9]

PRAYER OVER THE GIFTS

Pray brethren . . .

We offer these gifts to you, Lord God,
with the prayer that,
inspired by the example of St. Maximilian Kolbe,
we may learn to offer our very lives to you.

We ask this through Christ our Lord.

Communion Rite

There is no greater love than this: to lay down one's life for one's friends. (John 15:13)

PRAYER AFTER COMMUNION

Let us pray.

Pause for silent prayer, if this has not preceded.

Lord Jesus,
renewed by your body and blood,
we pray that the same fire of charity
which St. Maximilian Kolbe drew from this
   eucharistic banquet
may also inflame our hearts
with heroic love for others.

You live and reign for ever and ever.

August 15

ASSUMPTION
Solemnity

VIGIL MASS

This Mass may be used on the evening of August 14, either before or after Evening Prayer I of the solemnity.

Introductory Rites

> All honor to you, Mary! Today you were raised above the choirs of angels to lasting glory with Christ.

The Gloria is sung or said.

OPENING PRAYER

Let us pray
[that the Virgin Mary will help us
with her prayers]

Pause for silent prayer

Almighty God,
you gave a humble virgin
the privilege of being the mother of your Son,
and crowned her with the glory of heaven.
May the prayers of the Virgin Mary
bring us to the salvation of Christ
and raise us up to eternal life.

We ask this through our Lord Jesus Christ,
your Son,
who lives and reigns with you and the Holy
Spirit,
one God, for ever and ever.

ALTERNATIVE OPENING PRAYER

Let us pray
[with Mary to the Father, in whose
presence she now dwells]

Pause for silent prayer

Almighty Father of our Lord Jesus Christ,
you have revealed the beauty of your power
by exalting the lowly virgin of Nazareth
and making her the mother of our Savior.
May the prayers of this woman clothed with
the sun
bring Jesus to the waiting world
and fill the void of incompletion
with the presence of her child,
who lives and reigns with you and the Holy
Spirit,
one God, for ever and ever.

LITURGY OF THE WORD

See Lectionary for Mass, no. 621.

Profession of Faith

LITURGY OF THE EUCHARIST

PRAYER OVER THE GIFTS

Pray, brethren . . .

Lord,
receive this sacrifice of praise and peace
in honor of the assumption of the Mother of God.
May our offering bring us pardon
and make our lives a thanksgiving to you.

We ask this in the name of Jesus the Lord.

Eucharistic Prayer:
Preface of the Assumption, page 476.

Communion Rite

Blessed is the womb of the Virgin Mary; she carried the
Son of the eternal Father. (See Luke 11:27)

PRAYER AFTER COMMUNION

Let us pray.

Pause for silent prayer, if this has not preceded.

**God of mercy,
we rejoice because Mary, the mother of our Lord,
was taken into the glory of heaven.
May the holy food we receive at this table
free us from evil.**

We ask this through Christ our Lord.

MASS DURING THE DAY

Introductory Rites

A great sign appeared in heaven: a woman clothed with
the sun, the moon beneath her feet, and a crown of
twelve stars on her head. (Rev. 12:1)

or:

Let us rejoice in the Lord and celebrate this feast in honor
of the Virgin Mary, at whose assumption the angels rejoice, giving praise to the Son of God.

OPENING PRAYER

Let us pray

**[that we will join Mary, the mother
of the Lord, in the glory of heaven]**

Pause for silent prayer

**All-powerful and ever-living God,
you raised the sinless Virgin Mary, mother
of your Son,
body and soul to the glory of heaven.
May we see heaven as our final goal
and come to share her glory.**

**We ask this through our Lord Jesus Christ,
your Son,
who lives and reigns with you and the Holy
Spirit,
one God, for ever and ever.**

ALTERNATIVE OPENING PRAYER

Let us pray

**[that with the help of Mary's prayers
we too may reach our heavenly home]**

Pause for silent prayer

**Father in heaven,
all creation rightly gives you praise,
for all life and all holiness come from you.
In the plan of your wisdom
she who bore the Christ in her womb
was raised body and soul in glory to be with
him in heaven.
May we follow her example in reflecting your
holiness
and join in her hymn of endless life and
praise.**

We ask this through Christ our Lord.

LITURGY OF THE WORD

See Lectionary for Mass, no. 622.

LITURGY OF THE EUCHARIST

PRAYER OVER THE GIFTS   **Pray, brethren . . .**

Lord,
receive this offering of our service.
You raised the Virgin Mary to the glory of heaven.
By her prayers, help us to seek you
and to live in your love.

Grant this through Christ our Lord.

Eucharistic Prayer:
Preface of the Assumption, page **476**.

Communion Rite

> All generations will call me blessed, for the Almighty has
> done great things for me. (Luke 1:48-49)

PRAYER AFTER COMMUNION   **Let us pray.**
Pause for silent prayer, if this has not preceded.
Lord,
may we who receive this sacrament of salvation
be led to the glory of heaven
by the prayers of the Virgin Mary.

We ask this in the name of Jesus the Lord.

August 16

ST. STEPHEN OF HUNGARY

Common of holy men and women (p. 735).

OPENING PRAYER   **Almighty Father,**
grant that St. Stephen of Hungary,
who fostered the growth of your Church on earth,
may continue to be our powerful helper in heaven.

We ask this through our Lord Jesus Christ, your Son,
who lives and reigns with you and the Holy Spirit,
one God, for ever and ever.

August 19

ST. JOHN EUDES, priest

Common of pastors (p. 721); or
Common of holy men and women: for
religious (p. 741).

OPENING PRAYER

Father,
you chose the priest John Eudes
to preach the infinite riches of Christ.
By his teaching and example
help us to know you better
and live faithfully in the light of the gospel.

Grant this through our Lord Jesus Christ, your Son,
who lives and reigns with you and the Holy Spirit,
one God, for ever and ever.

August 20

ST. BERNARD, abbot and doctor
Memorial

Common of doctors of the Church (p.
729); or Common of holy men and
women: for religious (p. 741).

OPENING PRAYER

Heavenly Father,
St. Bernard was filled with zeal for your house
and was a radiant light in your Church.
By his prayers
may we be filled with this spirit of zeal
and walk always as children of light.

We ask this through our Lord Jesus Christ, your Son,
who lives and reigns with you and the Holy Spirit,
one God, for ever and ever.

See Lectionary for Mass, no. 625.

PRAYER OVER THE GIFTS

Pray, brethren . . .

Lord our God,
may the eucharist we offer
be a sign of unity and peace
as we celebrate the memory of St. Bernard,
who strove in word and deed
to bring harmony to your Church.

We ask this through Christ our Lord.

PRAYER AFTER COMMUNION

Let us pray.
Pause for silent prayer, if this has not preceded.
Father,
may the holy food we have received
at this celebration of the feast of St. Bernard
continue your work of salvation in us.
By his example, give us courage,
by his teachings, make us wise,
so that we too may burn with love for your Word, Jesus
** Christ,**
who is Lord for ever and ever.

August 21

ST. PIUS X, pope
Memorial

Common of pastors: for popes (p. 717).

OPENING PRAYER

Father,
to defend the Catholic faith
and to make all things new in Christ,
you filled St. Pius X
with heavenly wisdom and apostolic courage.
May his example and teaching
lead us to the reward of eternal life.

Grant this through our Lord Jesus Christ, your Son,
who lives and reigns with you and the Holy Spirit,
one God, for ever and ever.

See Lectionary for Mass, no. 626.

PRAYER OVER THE GIFTS

Pray, brethren . . .

Lord,
be pleased to accept our offerings.
May we follow the teaching of St. Pius X,
and so come to these mysteries with reverence
and receive them with faith.

We ask this through Christ our Lord.

PRAYER AFTER COMMUNION

Let us pray.
Pause for silent prayer, if this has not preceded.
Lord our God,
we honor the memory of St. Pius X
by sharing the bread of heaven.
May it strengthen our faith and unite us in your love.

We ask this in the name of Jesus the Lord.

August 22

QUEENSHIP OF MARY
Memorial

Introductory Rites
> The queen stands at your right hand arrayed in cloth of
> gold. (Ps. 44:10)

OPENING PRAYER

Father,
you have given us the mother of your Son
to be our queen and mother.
With the support of her prayers
may we come to share the glory of your children
in the kingdom of heaven.

We ask this through our Lord Jesus Christ, your Son,
who lives and reigns with you and the Holy Spirit,
one God, for ever and ever.

See Lectionary for Mass, no. 627.

PRAYER OVER THE GIFTS

Pray, brethren . . .

Lord,
celebrating the feast of the Virgin Mary,
we offer you our gifts and prayers:
may Christ, who offered himself as a perfect sacrifice,
bring mankind the peace and love of your kingdom,
where he lives and reigns for ever and ever.

Preface of the Blessed Virgin Mary I or
II, pages 473–474.

Communion Rite
> Blessed are you for your firm believing, that the promises
> of the Lord would be fulfilled. (Luke 1:45)

PRAYER AFTER COMMUNION

Let us pray.
Pause for silent prayer, if this has not preceded.
Lord,
we have eaten the bread of heaven.
May we who honor the memory of the Virgin Mary
share one day in your banquet of eternal life.

We ask this in the name of Jesus the Lord.

August 23

ST. ROSE OF LIMA, virgin

Common of virgins (p. 731); or
Common of holy men and women: for
religious (p. 741).

OPENING PRAYER

God our Father,
for love of you St. Rose gave up everything
to devote herself to a life of penance.
By the help of her prayers
may we imitate her selfless way of life on earth
and enjoy the fullness of your blessings in heaven.

Grant this through our Lord Jesus Christ, your Son,
who lives and reigns with you and the Holy Spirit,
one God, for ever and ever.

August 24

ST. BARTHOLOMEW, apostle

Feast

Introductory Rites

Day after day proclaim the salvation of the Lord. Proclaim
his glory to all nations. (Ps. 95:2-3)

OPENING PRAYER

Lord,
sustain within us the faith
which made St. Bartholomew ever loyal to Christ.
Let your Church be the sign of salvation
for all the nations of the world.

We ask this through our Lord Jesus Christ, your Son,
who lives and reigns with you and the Holy Spirit,
one God, for ever and ever.

See Lectionary for Mass, no. 629.

PRAYER OVER THE GIFTS

Pray, brethren . . .

Lord, we offer you this sacrifice of praise
on this feast of St. Bartholomew.
May his prayers win us your help.

We ask this in the name of Jesus the Lord.

Preface of the Apostles I or II, pages
481–482.

Communion Rite

I will give you the kingdom that my Father gave to me,
and in that kingdom you will eat and drink at my table. (Luke
22:29-30)

PRAYER AFTER COMMUNION

Let us pray.

Pause for silent prayer, if this has not preceded.

Lord, as we celebrate the feast of St. Bartholomew,
we receive the pledge of eternal salvation.
May it help us in this life and in the life to come.

Grant this through Christ our Lord.

August 25

ST. LOUIS

Common of holy men and women (p. 741).

OPENING PRAYER

**Father,
you raised St. Louis
from the cares of earthly rule
to the glory of your heavenly kingdom.
By the help of his prayers
may we come to your eternal kingdom
by our work here on earth.**

**Grant this through our Lord Jesus Christ, your Son,
who lives and reigns with you and the Holy Spirit,
one God, for ever and ever.**

ST. JOSEPH CALASANZ, priest

Common of holy men and women: for teachers (p. 744); or Common of pastors (p. 721).

OPENING PRAYER

**Lord,
you blessed St. Joseph Calasanz
with such charity and patience
that he dedicated himself
to the formation of Christian youth.
As we honor this teacher of wisdom
may we follow his example in working for truth.**

**We ask this through our Lord Jesus Christ, your Son,
who lives and reigns with you and the Holy Spirit,
one God, for ever and ever.**

August 27

ST. MONICA
Memorial

Common of holy men and women (p. 745).

OPENING PRAYER

**God of mercy,
comfort of those in sorrow,
the tears of St. Monica moved you
to convert her son St. Augustine to the faith of Christ.
By their prayers, help us to turn from our sins
and to find your loving forgiveness.**

**Grant this through our Lord Jesus Christ, your Son,
who lives and reigns with you and the Holy Spirit,
one God, for ever and ever.**

August 28

ST. AUGUSTINE, bishop and doctor
Memorial

Introductory Rites

The Lord opened his mouth in the assembly, and filled him with the spirit of wisdom and understanding, and clothed him in a robe of glory. (Sir. 15:5)

OPENING PRAYER

Lord,
renew in your Church
the spirit you gave St. Augustine.
Filled with this spirit,
may we thirst for you alone as the fountain of wisdom
and seek you as the source of eternal love.

We ask this through our Lord Jesus Christ, your Son,
who lives and reigns with you and the Holy Spirit,
one God, for ever and ever.

See Lectionary for Mass, no. 633.

PRAYER OVER THE GIFTS

Pray, brethren . . .

Lord,
as we celebrate the memorial of our salvation,
we pray that this sacrament may be for us
a sign of unity and a bond of love.

We ask this in the name of Jesus the Lord.

Communion Rite

Christ is your only teacher: and all of you are brothers.
(Matthew 23:10, 8)

PRAYER AFTER COMMUNION

Let us pray.
Pause for silent prayer, if this has not preceded.
Lord,
make us holy by our sharing at the table of Christ.
As members of his body,
help us to become what we have received.

Grant this through Christ our Lord.

August 29

BEHEADING OF ST. JOHN THE BAPTIST, martyr
Memorial

Introductory Rites

Lord, I shall expound your law before kings and not fear disgrace; I shall ponder your decrees, which I have always loved. (Ps. 118:46-47)

OPENING PRAYER

God our Father,
you called St. John the Baptist
to be the herald of your Son's birth and death.
As he gave his life in witness to truth and justice,
so may we strive to profess our faith in your gospel.

Grant this through our Lord Jesus Christ, your Son,
who lives and reigns with you and the Holy Spirit,
one God, for ever and ever.

See Lectionary for Mass, no. 634.

PRAYER OVER THE GIFTS

Pray, brethren . . .

Lord,
by these gifts we offer,
keep us faithful to your way of life,
which St. John the Baptist preached in the wilderness,
and to which he courageously witnessed
by shedding his blood.

We ask this through Christ our Lord.

Preface of John the Baptist, page 478.

Communion Rite

John's answer was: He must grow greater and I must grow less. (John 3:27, 30)

PRAYER AFTER COMMUNION

Let us pray.
Pause for silent prayer, if this has not preceded.
Lord,
may we who celebrate the martyrdom of St. John the Baptist
honor this sacrament of our salvation
and rejoice in the life it brings us.

We ask this in the name of Jesus the Lord.

SEPTEMBER

September 3

ST. GREGORY THE GREAT, pope and doctor
Memorial

Common of pastors: for popes (p. 717); or Common of doctors of the Church (p. 729).

OPENING PRAYER

**Father,
you guide your people with kindness
and govern us with love.
By the prayers of St. Gregory
give the spirit of wisdom
to those you have called to lead your Church.
May the growth of your people in holiness
be the eternal joy of our shepherds.**

**We ask this through our Lord Jesus Christ, your Son,
who lives and reigns with you and the Holy Spirit,
one God, for ever and ever.**

See Lectionary for Mass, no. 635.

PRAYER OVER THE GIFTS

Pray, brethren . . .

**Lord,
by this sacrifice you free the world from sin.
As we offer it in memory of St. Gregory,
may it bring us closer to eternal salvation.**

Grant this through Christ our Lord.

PRAYER AFTER COMMUNION

Let us pray.
Pause for silent prayer, if this has not preceded.

**Lord,
at this eucharist you give us Christ to be our living bread.
As we celebrate the feast of St. Gregory,
may we also come to know your truth
and live it in love for others.**

We ask this in the name of Jesus the Lord.

September 8

BIRTH OF MARY
Feast

Introductory Rites

Let us celebrate with joyful hearts the birth of the Virgin Mary, of whom was born the sun of justice, Christ our Lord.

OPENING PRAYER

**Father of mercy,
give your people help and strength from heaven.
The birth of the Virgin Mary's Son
was the dawn of our salvation.
May this celebration of her birthday
bring us closer to lasting peace.**

**Grant this through our Lord Jesus Christ, your Son,
who lives and reigns with you and the Holy Spirit,
one God, for ever and ever.**

See Lectionary for Mass, no. 636.

PRAYER OVER THE GIFTS

Pray, brethren . . .

**Father,
the birth of Christ your Son
increased the virgin mother's love for you.
May his sharing in our human nature
give us courage in our weakness,
free us from our sins,
and make our offering acceptable.**

We ask this in the name of Jesus the Lord.

Preface of the Blessed Virgin Mary I or II, pages **473–474**.

Communion Rite

The Virgin shall bear a son, who will save his people from their sins. (Is. 7:14; Matthew 1:21)

PRAYER AFTER COMMUNION

Let us pray.
Pause for silent prayer, if this has not preceded.
**Lord,
may your Church, renewed in this holy eucharist,
be filled with joy at the birth of the Virgin Mary,
who brought the dawn of hope and salvation to the world.**

We ask this through Christ our Lord.

September 9

In the dioceses of the United States: Memorial

ST. PETER CLAVER, priest

Common of pastors: for missionaries (p. 726).

OPENING PRAYER

God of mercy and love,
you offer all peoples
the dignity of sharing in your life.
By the example and prayers of St. Peter Claver,
strengthen us to overcome all racial hatreds
and to love each other as brothers and sisters.

We ask this through our Lord Jesus Christ, your Son,
who lives and reigns with you and the Holy Spirit,
one God, for ever and ever.

September 13

ST. JOHN CHRYSOSTOM, bishop and doctor
Memorial

Common of pastors: for bishops (p. 719); or Common of doctors of the Church (p. 729).

OPENING PRAYER

Father,
the strength of all who trust in you,
you made St. John Chrysostom renowned
for his eloquence and heroic in his sufferings.
May we learn from his teaching
and gain courage from his patient endurance.

We ask this through our Lord Jesus Christ, your Son,
who lives and reigns with you and the Holy Spirit,
one God, for ever and ever.

See Lectionary for Mass, no. 637.

PRAYER OVER THE GIFTS

Pray, brethren . . .

Lord, be pleased with this sacrifice we present
in honor of St. John Chrysostom,
for we gather to praise you as he taught us.

Grant this through Christ our Lord.

PRAYER AFTER COMMUNION

Let us pray.
Pause for silent prayer, if this has not preceded.
God of mercy,
may the sacrament we receive
in memory of St. John Chrysostom
make us strong in your love
and faithful in our witness to your truth.

We ask this in the name of Jesus the Lord.

September 14

TRIUMPH OF THE CROSS
Feast

Introductory Rites

We should glory in the cross of our Lord Jesus Christ, for he is our salvation, our life and our resurrection; through him we are saved and made free. (See Gal. 6:14)

OPENING PRAYER

Let us pray
[that the death of Christ on the cross
will bring us to the glory of the resurrection]

Pause for silent prayer

God our Father,
in obedience to you
your only Son accepted death on the cross
for the salvation of mankind.
We acknowledge the mystery of the cross on earth.
May we receive the gift of redemption in heaven.

We ask this through our Lord Jesus Christ, your Son,
who lives and reigns with you and the Holy Spirit,
one God, for ever and ever.

LITURGY OF THE WORD

See Lectionary for Mass, no. 638.

LITURGY OF THE EUCHARIST

PRAYER OVER THE GIFTS

Pray, brethren . . .

Lord,
may this sacrifice once offered on the cross
to take away the sins of the world
now free us from our sins.

We ask this through Christ our Lord.

Preface of the Triumph of the Cross, page **463**, or Preface of the Passion of the Lord I, page **434**.

Communion Rite

When I am lifted up from the earth, I will draw all men to myself, says the Lord. (John 12:32)

A period of silence may be observed after communion, or a psalm or song of praise may be sung.

PRAYER AFTER COMMUNION

Let us pray.
Pause for silent prayer, if this has not preceded.
**Lord Jesus Christ,
you are the holy bread of life.
Bring to the glory of the resurrection
the people you have redeemed by the wood of the cross.**

We ask this through Christ our Lord.

SOLEMN BLESSING OR PRAYER OVER THE PEOPLE

The following may replace the simple blessing.

After the greeting, the deacon (or in his absence, the priest) gives the invitation in these or similar words:

Bow your heads and pray for God's blessing.

Then the priest extends his hands over the people while he sings or says:

**May almighty God keep you from all harm
and bless you with every good gift.
℟. Amen.**

**May he set his Word in your heart
and fill you with lasting joy.
℟. Amen.**

**May you walk in his ways,
always knowing what is right and good,
until you enter your heavenly inheritance.
℟. Amen.**

**May almighty God bless you,
the Father, and the Son, ✛ and the Holy Spirit.
℟. Amen.**

For alternative texts, see pages 528–540.

September 15

OUR LADY OF SORROWS
Memorial

Introductory Rites

Simeon said to Mary: This child is destined to be a sign which men will reject; he is set for the fall and the rising of many in Israel; and your own soul a sword shall pierce. (Luke 2:34-35)

OPENING PRAYER

Father,
as your Son was raised on the cross,
his mother Mary stood by him, sharing his sufferings.
May your Church be united with Christ
in his suffering and death
and so come to share in his rising to new life,
where he lives and reigns with you and the Holy Spirit,
one God, for ever and ever.

See Lectionary for Mass, no. 639.

PRAYER OVER THE GIFTS

Pray, brethren . . .

God of mercy,
receive the prayers and gifts we offer
in praise of your name
on this feast of the Virgin Mary.
While she stood beside the cross of Jesus
you gave her to us as our loving mother.

Grant this through Christ our Lord.

Preface of the Blessed Virgin Mary I or II, pages **473–474**.

Communion Rite

Be glad to share in the sufferings of Christ! When he comes in glory, you will be filled with joy. (1 Peter 4:13)

PRAYER AFTER COMMUNION

Let us pray.
Pause for silent prayer, if this has not preceded.
Lord,
hear the prayers
of those who receive the sacraments of eternal salvation.
As we honor the compassionate love of the Virgin Mary,
may we make up in our own lives
whatever is lacking in the sufferings of Christ
for the good of the Church.

We ask this in the name of Jesus the Lord.

September 16

ST. CORNELIUS, pope and martyr,
AND ST. CYPRIAN, bishop and martyr
Memorial

Common of martyrs (p. 704); or
Common of pastors: for bishops (p.
719).

OPENING PRAYER

**God our Father,
in Saints Cornelius and Cyprian
you have given your people an inspiring example
of dedication to the pastoral ministry
and constant witness to Christ in their suffering.
May their prayers and faith give us courage
to work for the unity of your Church.**

**Grant this through our Lord Jesus Christ, your Son,
who lives and reigns with you and the Holy Spirit,
one God, for ever and ever.**

See Lectionary for Mass, no. 640.

PRAYER OVER THE GIFTS

Pray, brethren . . .

**Lord,
accept the gifts of your people
as we honor the suffering and death
of Saints Cornelius and Cyprian.
The eucharist gave them courage
to offer their lives for Christ.
May it keep us faithful in all our trials.**

We ask this through Christ our Lord.

PRAYER AFTER COMMUNION

Let us pray.
Pause for silent prayer, if this has not preceded.
**Lord,
by the example of your martyrs Cornelius and Cyprian
and by the sacrament we have received,
make us strong in the Spirit
so that we may offer faithful witness
to the truth of your gospel.**

We ask this in the name of Jesus the Lord.

September 17

ST. ROBERT BELLARMINE, bishop and doctor

Common of pastors: for bishops (p. 719; or Common of doctors of the Church (p. 729).

OPENING PRAYER

God our Father,
you gave St. Robert Bellarmine wisdom and goodness
to defend the faith of your Church.
By his prayers
may we always rejoice in the profession of our faith.

We ask this through our Lord Jesus Christ, your Son,
who lives and reigns with you and the Holy Spirit,
one God, for ever and ever.

September 19

ST. JANUARIUS, bishop and martyr

Common of martyrs (p. 709); or Common of pastors: for bishops (p. 719.

OPENING PRAYER

God our Father,
enable us who honor the memory of St. Januarius
to share with him the joy of eternal life.

Grant this through our Lord Jesus Christ, your Son,
who lives and reigns with you and the Holy Spirit,
one God, for ever and ever.

September 20

ST. ANDREW KIM TAEGON, priest and martyr,
ST. PAUL CHONG HASANG, AND COMPANIONS, martyrs*

Memorial

Introductory Rites

Let us all rejoice in the Lord, and keep a festival in honor of Andrew and Paul and their companions. Let us join with the angels in joyful praise to the Son of God.

OPENING PRAYER

**O God,
you have created all nations
and you are their salvation.
In the land of Korea your call to Catholic faith
formed a people of adoption,
whose growth you nurtured
by the blood of Andrew, Paul, and their companions.
Through their martyrdom and their intercession
grant us strength
that we too may remain faithful to your commandments
even until death.**

**We ask this through our Lord Jesus Christ, your Son,
who lives and reigns with you and the Holy Spirit,
one God, for ever and ever.**

First Reading: Wisdom 3:1-9c [Lectionary no. 713.5] or Romans 8:31b-39 [Lectionary 716.2]
Responsorial Psalm: Psalm 126:1-2, 2-3, 4-5, 6 [cf. Lectionary no. 715.4], with ℟. Those who sow in tears shall sing for joy when they reap.
Alleluia verse: 1 Peter 4:14 [Lectionary no. 717.4]
Gospel: Luke 9:23-26 [Lectionary no. 718.4]

PRAYER OVER THE GIFTS

Pray, brethren . . .

**All-powerful God,
in your goodness accept these gifts we offer
and through the intercession of your holy martyrs
grant that our own lives will become a sacrifice acceptable
   to you
for the salvation of all the world.**

We ask this in the name of Jesus the Lord.

Communion Rite

Whoever acknowledges me before the world, I will acknowledge before my Father in heaven. (Matthew 10:32)

PRAYER AFTER COMMUNION

**Lord, we have been nourished in this celebration of
   your holy martyrs
with the food that gave them strength.
Grant that we too will remain loyal to Christ
and labor in your Church for the salvation of all.**

We ask this in the name of Jesus the Lord.

* Provisional translation approved "ad interim" by the Executive Committee of the National Conference of Catholic Bishops, 30 June 1985.

September 21

ST. MATTHEW, apostle and evangelist

Feast

Introductory Rites

Go and preach to all nations: baptize them and teach them
to observe all that I have commanded you, says the Lord.
(Matthew 28:19-20)

OPENING PRAYER

**God of mercy,
you chose a tax collector, St. Matthew,
to share the dignity of the apostles.
By his example and prayers
help us to follow Christ
and remain faithful in your service.**

**We ask this through our Lord Jesus Christ, your Son,
who lives and reigns with you and the Holy Spirit,
one God, for ever and ever.**

See Lectionary for Mass, no. 643.

PRAYER OVER THE GIFTS

Pray, brethren . . .

**Lord,
accept the prayers and gifts we present
on this feast of St. Matthew.
Continue to guide us in your love
as you nourished the faith of your Church
by the preaching of the apostles.**

We ask this in the name of Jesus the Lord.

Preface of the Apostles I or II, pages
481–482.

Communion Rite

I did not come to call the virtuous, but sinners, says the
Lord. (Matthew 9:13)

PRAYER AFTER COMMUNION

Let us pray.
Pause for silent prayer, if this has not preceded.
**Father,
in this eucharist we have shared the joy of salvation
which St. Matthew knew when he welcomed your Son.
May this food renew us in Christ,
who came to call not the just
but sinners to salvation in his kingdom
where he is Lord for ever and ever.**

September 26

ST. COSMAS AND ST. DAMIAN, martyrs

Common of martyrs (p. 704).

OPENING PRAYER

**Lord,
we honor the memory of Saints Cosmas and Damian.
Accept our grateful praise
for raising them to eternal glory
and for giving us your fatherly care.**

**We ask this through our Lord Jesus Christ, your Son,
who lives and reigns with you and the Holy Spirit,
one God, for ever and ever.**

See Lectionary for Mass, no. 644.

PRAYER OVER THE GIFTS

Pray, brethren . . .

**Lord,
we who celebrate the death of your holy martyrs
offer you the sacrifice
which gives all martyrdom its meaning.
Be pleased with our praise.**

We ask this through Christ our Lord.

PRAYER AFTER COMMUNION

Let us pray.
Pause for silent prayer, if this has not preceded.
**Lord,
keep your gift ever strong within us.
May the eucharist we receive
in memory of Saints Cosmas and Damian
bring us salvation and peace.**

We ask this in the name of Jesus the Lord.

September 27

ST. VINCENT DE PAUL, priest

Memorial

Introductory Rites

The Spirit of God is upon me; he has anointed me. He sent
me to bring good news to the poor, and to heal the
broken-hearted. (Luke 4:18)

OPENING PRAYER

**God our Father,
you gave St. Vincent de Paul
the courage and holiness of an apostle
for the well-being of the poor
and the formation of the clergy.
Help us to be zealous in continuing his work.**

**Grant this through our Lord Jesus Christ, your Son,
who lives and reigns with you and the Holy Spirit,**

See Lectionary for Mass, no. 645.   **one God, for ever and ever.**

PRAYER OVER THE GIFTS

Pray, brethren . . .

Lord,
you helped St. Vincent
to imitate the love he celebrated in these mysteries.
By the power of this sacrifice
may we also become an acceptable gift to you.

We ask this in the name of Jesus the Lord.

Communion Rite

Give praise to the Lord for his kindness, for his wonderful
deeds toward men. He has filled the hungry with good
things, he has satisfied the thirsty. (Ps. 106:8-9)

PRAYER AFTER COMMUNION

Let us pray.
Pause for silent prayer, if this has not preceded.
Lord,
hear the prayers
of those you have renewed with your sacraments from
   heaven.
May the example and prayers of St. Vincent
help us to imitate your Son
in preaching the good news to the poor.

We ask this in the name of Jesus the Lord.

September 28

ST. WENCESLAUS, martyr

Common of martyrs (p. 709).

OPENING PRAYER

Lord,
you taught your martyr Wenceslaus
to prefer the kingdom of heaven
to all that the earth has to offer.
May his prayers free us from our self-seeking
and help us to serve you with all our hearts.

We ask this through our Lord Jesus Christ, your Son,
who lives and reigns with you and the Holy Spirit,
one God, for ever and ever.

September 29

ST. MICHAEL, ST. GABRIEL, AND ST. RAPHAEL, archangels

Feast

Introductory Rites

Bless the Lord, all you his angels, mighty in power, you obey his word and heed the sound of his voice. (Ps. 102:20)

OPENING PRAYER

God our Father,
in a wonderful way you guide the work of angels and men.
May those who serve you constantly in heaven
keep our lives safe from all harm on earth.

Grant this through our Lord Jesus Christ, your Son,
who lives and reigns with you and the Holy Spirit,
one God, for ever and ever.

See Lectionary for Mass, no. 647.

PRAYER OVER THE GIFTS

Pray, brethren . . .

Lord,
by the ministry of your angels
let our sacrifice of praise come before you.
May it be pleasing to you and helpful to our own salvation.

We ask this through Christ our Lord.

Preface of the Angels, page **477**.

Communion Rite

In the sight of the angels I will sing your praises, my God. (Ps. 137:1)

PRAYER AFTER COMMUNION

Let us pray.
Pause for silent prayer, if this has not preceded.

Lord,
hear the prayers of those you renew with the bread of life.
Made strong by the courage it gives,
and under the watchful care of the angels,
may we advance along the way of salvation.

We ask this in the name of Jesus the Lord.

September 30

ST. JEROME, priest and doctor

Memorial

Introductory Rites

The book of the law must be ever on your lips; reflect on it
night and day. Observe and do all that it commands: then
you will direct your life with understanding. (Josh. 1:8)

OPENING PRAYER

**Father,
you gave St. Jerome delight
in his study of holy scripture.
May your people find in your word
the food of salvation and the fountain of life.**

**We ask this through our Lord Jesus Christ, your Son,
who lives and reigns with you and the Holy Spirit,
one God, for ever and ever.**

See Lectionary for Mass, no. 648.

PRAYER OVER THE GIFTS

Pray, brethren . . .

**Lord,
help us to follow the example of St. Jerome.
In reflecting on your word
may we better prepare ourselves
to offer you this sacrifice of salvation.**

We ask this in the name of Jesus the Lord.

Communion Rite

When I discovered your teaching, I devoured it. Your
words brought me joy and gladness; you have called me
your own, O Lord my God. (Jer. 15:16)

PRAYER AFTER COMMUNION

Let us pray.

Pause for silent prayer, if this has not preceded.

**Lord,
let this holy eucharist we receive
on the feast of St. Jerome
stir up the hearts of all who believe in you.
By studying your sacred teachings,
may we understand the gospel we follow
and come to eternal life.**

Grant this through Christ our Lord.

OCTOBER

October 1

ST. THERESA OF THE CHILD JESUS, virgin
Memorial

Introductory Rites

The Lord nurtured and taught her; he guarded her as the apple of his eye. As the eagle spreads its wings to carry its young, he bore her on his shoulders. The Lord alone was her leader. (See Deut. 32:10-12)

OPENING PRAYER

God our Father,
you have promised your kingdom
to those who are willing to become like little children.
Help us to follow the way of St. Theresa with confidence
so that by her prayers
we may come to know your eternal glory.

Grant this through our Lord Jesus Christ, your Son,
who lives and reigns with you and the Holy Spirit,
one God, for ever and ever.

See Lectionary for Mass, no. 649.

PRAYER OVER THE GIFTS

Pray, brethren . . .

Lord,
we praise the wonder of your grace in St. Theresa.
As you were pleased with the witness she offered,
be pleased also to accept this service of ours.

We ask this through Christ our Lord.

Communion Rite

Unless you change and become like little children, says the Lord, you shall not enter the kingdom of heaven. (Matthew 18:3)

PRAYER AFTER COMMUNION

Let us pray.
Pause for silent prayer, if this has not preceded.
Lord,
by the power of your love
St. Theresa offered herself completely to you
and prayed for the salvation of all mankind.
May the sacraments we have received fill us with love
and bring us forgiveness.

We ask this in the name of Jesus the Lord.

October 2

GUARDIAN ANGELS
Memorial

Introductory Rites

Bless the Lord, all you angels of the Lord. Sing his glory
and praise for ever. (Dan. 3:58)

OPENING PRAYER

God our Father,
in your loving providence
you send your holy angels to watch over us.
Hear our prayers,
defend us always by their protection
and let us share your life with them for ever.

We ask this through our Lord Jesus Christ, your Son,
who lives and reigns with you and the Holy Spirit,
one God, for ever and ever.

See Lectionary for Mass, no. 650.

PRAYER OVER THE GIFTS

Pray, brethren . . .

Father,
accept the gifts we bring you
in honor of your holy angels.
Under their constant care,
keep us free from danger in this life
and bring us to the joy of eternal life,
where Jesus is Lord for ever and ever.

Preface of the Angels, page 477.

Communion Rite

In the sight of the angels I will sing your praises, my God.
(Ps. 137:1)

PRAYER AFTER COMMUNION

Let us pray.
Pause for silent prayer, if this has not preceded.
Lord,
you nourish us with the sacraments of eternal life.
By the ministry of your angels
lead us into the way of salvation and peace.

We ask this in the name of Jesus the Lord.

October 4

ST. FRANCIS OF ASSISI
Memorial

Introductory Rites

Francis, a man of God, left his home and gave away his wealth to become poor and in need. But the Lord cared for him.

OPENING PRAYER

**Father,
you helped St. Francis to reflect the image of Christ through a life of poverty and humility.
May we follow your Son
by walking in the footsteps of Francis of Assisi,
and by imitating his joyful love.**

Grant this through our Lord Jesus Christ, your Son, who lives and reigns with you and the Holy Spirit, one God, for ever and ever.

See Lectionary for Mass, no. 651.

PRAYER OVER THE GIFTS

Pray, brethren . . .

**Lord, as we bring you our gifts,
prepare us to celebrate the mystery of the cross, to which St. Francis adhered with such burning love.**

We ask this in the name of Jesus the Lord.

Communion Rite

Blessed are the poor in spirit; the kingdom of heaven is theirs! (Matthew 5:3)

PRAYER AFTER COMMUNION

Let us pray.
Pause for silent prayer, if this has not preceded.
**Lord, by the holy eucharist we have celebrated, help us to imitate
the apostolic love and zeal of St. Francis.
May we who receive your love
share it for the salvation of all mankind.**

We ask this through Christ our Lord.

October 6

ST. BRUNO, priest

Common of pastors (p. 721); or Common of holy men and women: for religious (p. 741).

OPENING PRAYER

> **Father, you called St. Bruno to serve you in solitude.**
> **In answer to his prayers help us to remain faithful to you amid the changes of this world.**
>
> **We ask this through our Lord Jesus Christ, your Son, who lives and reigns with you and the Holy Spirit, one God, for ever and ever.**

In the dioceses of the United States

BLESSED MARIE ROSE DUROCHER, virgin

Common of virgins (p. 731).

OPENING PRAYER

> **Lord,**
> **you enkindled in the heart of**
> **Blessed Marie Rose Durocher**
> **the flame of ardent charity**
> **and a great desire to collaborate,**
> **as teacher, in the mission of the Church.**
> **Grant us that same active love,**
> **so that, in responding to the needs**
> **of the world today,**
> **we may lead our brothers and sisters**
> **to eternal life.**
>
> **We ask this through our Lord Jesus Christ, your Son, who lives and reigns with you and the Holy Spirit, one God, for ever and ever.**

October 7

OUR LADY OF THE ROSARY
Memorial

Introductory Rites

Hail, Mary, full of grace, the Lord is with you; blessed are
you among women and blessed is the fruit of your womb.
(Luke 1:28, 42)

OPENING PRAYER

**Lord,
fill our hearts with your love,
and as you revealed to us by an angel
the coming of your Son as man,
so lead us through his suffering and death
to the glory of his resurrection,
who lives and reigns with you and the Holy Spirit,
one God, for ever and ever.**

See Lectionary for Mass, no. 653.

PRAYER OVER THE GIFTS

Pray, brethren . . .

**Lord,
may these gifts we offer in sacrifice transform our lives.
By celebrating the mysteries of your Son,
may we become worthy of the eternal life he promises,
for he is Lord for ever and ever.**

Preface of the Blessed Virgin Mary I or
II, pages **473–474**.

Communion Rite

You shall conceive and bear a Son, and you shall call his
name Jesus. (Luke 1:31)

PRAYER AFTER COMMUNION

Let us pray.
Pause for silent prayer, if this has not preceded.
**Lord our God,
in this eucharist we have proclaimed
the death and resurrection of Christ.
Make us partners in his suffering
and lead us to share his happiness
and the glory of eternal life,
where he is Lord for ever and ever.**

October 9

ST. DENIS, bishop and martyr, AND COMPANIONS, martyrs

Common of martyrs (p. 704).

OPENING PRAYER

> **Father,**
> **you sent St. Denis and his companions**
> **to preach your glory to the nations,**
> **and you gave them the strength**
> **to be steadfast in their sufferings for Christ.**
> **Grant that we may learn from their example**
> **to reject the power and wealth of this world**
> **and to brave all earthly trials.**
>
> **We ask this through our Lord Jesus Christ, your Son,**
> **who lives and reigns with you and the Holy Spirit,**
> **one God, for ever and ever.**

ST. JOHN LEONARDI, priest

Common of pastors: for missionaries (p. 726); or Common of holy men and women: for those who worked for the underprivileged (p. 743).

OPENING PRAYER

> **Father,**
> **giver of all good things,**
> **you proclaimed the good news to countless people**
> **through the ministry of St. John Leonardi.**
> **By the help of his prayers**
> **may the true faith continue to grow.**
>
> **Grant this through our Lord Jesus Christ, your Son,**
> **who lives and reigns with you and the Holy Spirit,**
> **one God, for ever and ever.**

October 14

ST. CALLISTUS I, pope and martyr

Common of martyrs (p. 709); or Common of pastors: for popes (p. 717).

OPENING PRAYER

> **God of mercy,**
> **hear the prayers of your people**
> **that we may be helped by St. Callistus,**
> **whose martyrdom we celebrate with joy.**
>
> **We ask this through our Lord Jesus Christ, your Son,**
> **who lives and reigns with you and the Holy Spirit,**
> **one God, for ever and ever.**

October 15

ST. TERESA OF JESUS, virgin and doctor
Memorial

Introductory Rites
Like a deer that longs for running streams, my soul longs
for you, my God. My soul is thirsting for the living God.
(Ps. 41:2-3)

OPENING PRAYER

**Father,
by your Spirit you raised up St. Teresa of Avila
to show your Church the way to perfection.
May her inspired teaching
awaken in us a longing for true holiness.**

**Grant this through our Lord Jesus Christ, your Son,
who lives and reigns with you and the Holy Spirit,
one God, for ever and ever.**

See Lectionary for Mass, no. 657
or nos. 725-730.

PRAYER OVER THE GIFTS

Pray, brethren . . .

**King of heaven,
accept the gifts we bring in your praise,
as you were pleased with St. Teresa's offering
of her life in your service.**

We ask this in the name of Jesus the Lord.

Communion Rite
For ever I will sing the goodness of the Lord; I will
proclaim your faithfulness to all generations. (Ps. 88:2)

PRAYER AFTER COMMUNION

Let us pray.

Pause for silent prayer, if this has not preceded.

**Lord our God,
watch over the family you nourish
with the bread from heaven.
Help us to follow St. Teresa's example
and sing your merciful love for ever.**

We ask this through Christ our Lord.

October 16

ST. HEDWIG, religious

Common of holy men and women: for
religious (p. 741).

OPENING PRAYER

**All-powerful God,
may the prayers of St. Hedwig bring us your help
and may her life of remarkable humility
be an example to us all.**

**We ask this through our Lord Jesus Christ, your Son,
who lives and reigns with you and the Holy Spirit,
one God, for ever and ever.**

ST. MARGARET MARY ALACOQUE, virgin

Common of virgins (p. 731); or
Common of holy men and women: for
religious (p. 741).

OPENING PRAYER

**Lord,
pour out on us the riches of the Spirit
which you bestowed on St. Margaret Mary.
May we come to know the love of Christ,
which surpasses all human understanding,
and be filled with the fullness of God.**

**Grant this through our Lord Jesus Christ, your Son,
who lives and reigns with you and the Holy Spirit,
one God, for ever and ever.**

October 17

ST. IGNATIUS OF ANTIOCH, bishop and martyr
Memorial

Introductory Rites

With Christ I am nailed to the cross. I live now not with my own life, but Christ lives within me. I live by faith in the Son of God, who loved me and sacrificed himself for me. (Gal. 2:19-20)

OPENING PRAYER

All-powerful and ever-living God,
you ennoble your Church
with the heroic witness of all
who give their lives for Christ.
Grant that the victory of St. Ignatius of Antioch
may bring us your constant help
as it brought him eternal glory.
We ask this through our Lord Jesus Christ, your Son,
who lives and reigns with you and the Holy Spirit,
one God, for ever and ever.

See Lectionary for Mass, no. 660.

PRAYER OVER THE GIFTS

Pray, brethren . . .

Lord,
receive our offering
as you accepted St. Ignatius
when he offered himself to you as the wheat of Christ,
formed into pure bread by his death for Christ,
who lives and reigns for ever and ever.

Communion Rite

I am the wheat of Christ, ground by the teeth of beasts to become pure bread.

PRAYER AFTER COMMUNION

Let us pray.
Pause for silent prayer, if this has not preceded.
Lord,
renew us by the bread of heaven
which we have received on the feast of St. Ignatius.
May it transform us into loyal and true Christians.

Grant this through Christ our Lord.

October 18

ST. LUKE, evangelist
Feast

Introductory Rites

> How beautiful on the mountains are the feet of the man
> who brings tidings of peace, joy and salvation. (Is. 52:7)

OPENING PRAYER

**Father,
you chose Luke the evangelist to reveal
by preaching and writing
the mystery of your love for the poor.
Unite in one heart and spirit
all who glory in your name,
and let all nations come to see your salvation.**

**Grant this through our Lord Jesus Christ, your Son,
who lives and reigns with you and the Holy Spirit,
one God, for ever and ever.**

See Lectionary for Mass, no. 481.

PRAYER OVER THE GIFTS   **Pray, brethren . . .**

**Father,
may your gifts from heaven free our hearts to serve you.
May the sacrifice we offer on the feast of St. Luke
bring us healing and lead us to eternal glory,
where Jesus is Lord for ever and ever.**

Preface of the Apostles II, page 482.

Communion Rite

> The Lord sent disciples to proclaim to all the towns: the
> kingdom of God is very near to you. (See Luke 10:1, 9)

PRAYER AFTER COMMUNION   **Let us pray.**
Pause for silent prayer, if this has not preceded.

**All-powerful God,
may the eucharist we have received at your altar
make us holy
and strengthen us in the faith of the gospel
preached by St. Luke.**

We ask this in the name of Jesus the Lord.

October 19
In the dioceses of the United States: Memorial

ST. ISAAC JOGUES AND ST. JOHN DE BRÉBEUF, priests and martyrs, AND COMPANIONS, martyrs

Common of martyrs (p. 704); or Common of pastors: for missionaries (p. 726).

OPENING PRAYER

**Father,
you consecrated the first beginnings
of the faith in North America
by the preaching and martyrdom
of Saints John and Isaac and their companions.
By the help of their prayers
may the Christian faith continue to grow
throughout the world.**

**We ask this through our Lord Jesus Christ, your Son,
who lives and reigns with you and the Holy Spirit,
one God, for ever and ever.**

ST. PAUL OF THE CROSS, priest

Introductory Rites

I resolved that while I was with you I would think of nothing but Jesus Christ and him crucified. (1 Cor. 2:2)

OPENING PRAYER

**Father,
you gave your priest St. Paul
a special love for the cross of Christ.
May his example inspire us
to embrace our own cross with courage.**

**Grant this through our Lord Jesus Christ, your Son,
who lives and reigns with you and the Holy Spirit,
one God, for ever and ever.**

See Lectionary for Mass, no. 663.

PRAYER OVER THE GIFTS

Pray, brethren . . .

**All-powerful God,
receive the gifts we offer
in memory of St. Paul of the Cross.
May we who celebrate the mystery
of the Lord's suffering and death
put into effect the self-sacrificing love
we proclaim in this eucharist.**

We ask this through Christ our Lord.

Communion Rite

We preach a Christ who was crucified; he is the power and
the wisdom of God. (1 Cor. 1:23-24)

PRAYER AFTER COMMUNION

Let us pray.

Pause for silent prayer, if this has not preceded.

**Lord,
in the life of St. Paul
you helped us to understand the mystery of the cross.
May the sacrifice we have offered strengthen us,
keep us faithful to Christ,
and help us to work in the Church
for the salvation of all mankind.**

We ask this in the name of Jesus the Lord.

October 23

ST. JOHN OF CAPISTRANO, priest

Common of pastors: for missionaries (p. 726).

OPENING PRAYER

**Lord,
you raised up St. John of Capistrano
to give your people comfort in their trials.
May your Church enjoy unending peace
and be secure in your protection.**

**We ask this through our Lord Jesus Christ, your Son,
who lives and reigns with you and the Holy Spirit,
one God, for ever and ever.**

October 24

ST. ANTHONY CLARET, bishop

Common of pastors: for missionaries (p. 726) or for bishops (p. 719).

OPENING PRAYER

**Father,
you endowed St. Anthony Claret
with the strength of love and patience
to preach the gospel to many nations.
By the help of his prayers
may we work generously for your kingdom
and gain our brothers and sisters for Christ,
who lives and reigns with you and the Holy Spirit,
one God, for ever and ever.**

October 28

ST. SIMON AND ST. JUDE, apostles
Feast

Introductory Rites

The Lord chose these holy men for their unfeigned love,
and gave them eternal glory.

OPENING PRAYER

**Father,
you revealed yourself to us
through the preaching of your apostles Simon and Jude.
By their prayers,
give your Church continued growth
and increase the number of those who believe in you.**

**Grant this through our Lord Jesus Christ, your Son,
who lives and reigns with you and the Holy Spirit,
one God, for ever and ever.**

See Lectionary for Mass, no. 666.

PRAYER OVER THE GIFTS

Pray, brethren . . .

**Lord,
each year we recall the glory
of your apostles Simon and Jude.
Accept our gifts
and prepare us to celebrate these holy mysteries.**

We ask this in the name of Jesus the Lord.

Preface of the Apostles I or II, pages
481–482.

Communion Rite

If anyone loves me, he will hold to my words, and my
Father will love him, and we will come to him, and make
our home with him. (John 14:23)

PRAYER AFTER COMMUNION

Let us pray.
Pause for silent prayer, if this has not preceded.
**Father,
in your Spirit we pray:
may the sacrament we receive today
keep us in your loving care
as we honor the death of Saints Simon and Jude.**

We ask this through Christ our Lord.

NOVEMBER

November 1

ALL SAINTS
Solemnity

Introductory Rites

Let us all rejoice in the Lord and keep a festival in honor of all the saints. Let us join with the angels in joyful praise to the Son of God.

OPENING PRAYER

Let us pray
 [that the prayers of all the saints
 will bring us forgiveness for our sins]
Pause for silent prayer
Father, all-powerful and ever-living God,
 today we rejoice in the holy men
 and women of every time and place.
May their prayers bring us your forgiveness
 and love.

We ask this through our Lord Jesus Christ,
 your Son,
who lives and reigns with you and the Holy
 Spirit,
one God, for ever and ever.

ALTERNATIVE OPENING PRAYER

Let us pray
 [as we rejoice and keep festival
 in honor of all the saints]
Pause for silent prayer
God our Father,
source of all holiness,
the work of your hands is manifest
 in your saints,
the beauty of your truth is reflected
 in their faith.
May we who aspire to have part in their joy
be filled with the Spirit that blessed their lives,
so that having shared their faith on earth
we may also know their peace in your
 kingdom.

Grant this through Christ our Lord.

LITURGY OF THE WORD

See Lectionary for Mass, no. 667.

Profession of Faith

LITURGY OF THE EUCHARIST

PRAYER OVER THE GIFTS

Pray, brethren . . .

Lord,
receive our gifts in honor of the holy men and women
who live with you in glory.
May we always be aware
of their concern to help and save us.
We ask this in the name of Jesus the Lord.

Eucharistic Prayer:
Preface of All Saints, page 488.

Communion Rite

> Happy are the pure of heart for they shall see God. Happy
> the peacemakers; they shall be called sons of God. Happy
> are they who suffer persecution for justice' sake; the kingdom
> of heaven is theirs. (Matthew 5:8-10)

A period of silence may be observed
after communion, or a psalm or
song of praise may be sung.

PRAYER AFTER COMMUNION

Let us pray.
Pause for silent prayer, if this has not preceded.
Father, holy one,
we praise your glory reflected in the saints.
May we who share at this table
be filled with your love
and prepared for the joy of your kingdom,
where Jesus is Lord for ever and ever.

**SOLEMN BLESSING OR PRAYER
OVER THE PEOPLE**

The following may replace the simple
blessing.

After the greeting, the deacon (or in
his absence, the priest) gives the
invitation in these or similar words:

Bow your heads and pray for God's blessing.

Then the priest extends his hands
over the people while he sings or
says:

God is the glory and joy of all his saints,
whose memory we celebrate today.
May his blessing be with you always.
℞. Amen.

May the prayers of the saints deliver you from present evil;
may their example of holy living
turn your thoughts to the service of God and neighbor.
℞. Amen.

God's holy Church rejoices that her children
are one with the saints in lasting peace.
May you come to share with them
in all the joys of our Father's house.
℞. Amen.

May almighty God bless you,
the Father, and the Son, ✝and the Holy Spirit.
℞. Amen.

For alternative texts, see page 540, no.
25.

For the votive Mass of All Saints, see
below, page 858.

ALL SOULS

1

Even when November 2 falls on a
Sunday, All Souls Day is celebrated,
with the following Masses.

Introductory Rites

> Just as Jesus died and rose again, so will the Father bring
> with him those who have died in Jesus. Just as in Adam all
> men die, so in Christ all will be made alive. (1 Thess. 4:14;
> 1 Cor. 15:22)

OPENING PRAYER

Let us pray

 [for all our departed brothers and sisters]

Pause for silent prayer

Merciful Father,
hear our prayers and console us.
As we renew our faith in your Son,
whom you raised from the dead,
strengthen our hope that all our departed brothers and sisters
will share in his resurrection,
who lives and reigns with you and the Holy Spirit,
one God, for ever and ever.

LITURGY OF THE WORD

Lectionary for Mass, no. 668.

LITURGY OF THE EUCHARIST

PRAYER OVER THE GIFTS

Pray, brethren . . .

Lord,
we are united in this sacrament
by the love of Jesus Christ.
Accept these gifts
and receive our brothers and sisters
into the glory of your Son,
who is Lord for ever and ever.

Eucharistic Prayer:
Preface of Christian Death I-V, pages
494–498.

Communion Rite

I am the resurrection and the life, says the Lord. If anyone believes in me, even though he dies, he will live. Anyone who lives and believes in me, will not die. (See John 11:25-26)

A period of silence may be observed after communion, or a psalm or song of praise may be sung.

PRAYER AFTER COMMUNION

Let us pray.
Pause for silent prayer, if this has not preceded.
Lord God,
may the death and resurrection of Christ
which we celebrate in this eucharist
bring the departed faithful to the peace of your eternal home.

We ask this in the name of Jesus the Lord.

SOLEMN BLESSING OR PRAYER OVER THE PEOPLE

The following may replace the simple blessing.

After the greeting, the deacon (or in his absence, the priest) gives the invitation in these or similar words:

Then the priest extends his hands over the people while he sings or says:

Bow your heads and pray for God's blessing.

In his great love,
the God of all consolation gave man the gift of life.
May he bless you with faith
in the resurrection of his Son,
and with the hope of rising to new life.
R. Amen.

To us who are alive
may he grant forgiveness,
and to all who have died
a place of light and peace.
R. Amen.

As you believe that Jesus rose from the dead,
so may you live with him for ever in joy.
R. Amen.

May almighty God bless you,
the Father, and the Son, ✝ and the Holy Spirit.
R. Amen.

For alternative texts, see page 536.

ALL SOULS

2

Introductory Rites

Give them eternal rest, O Lord, and may your light shine
on them for ever. (See 4 Esdras 2:34-35)

OPENING PRAYER

Let us pray
  [for all our departed brothers and sisters]

Pause for silent prayer

**Lord God,
you are the glory of believers
and the life of the just.
Your Son redeemed us
by dying and rising to life again.
Since our departed brothers and sisters believed in the
    mystery of our resurrection,
let them share the joys and blessings of the life to come.**

**We ask this through our Lord Jesus Christ, your Son,
who lives and reigns with you and the Holy Spirit,
one God, for ever and ever.**

LITURGY OF THE WORD

See Lectionary for Mass, no. 668.

LITURGY OF THE EUCHARIST

PRAYER OVER THE GIFTS

Pray, brethren . . .

**All-powerful Father,
may this sacrifice wash away
the sins of our departed brothers and sisters in the blood of
  Christ.
You cleansed them in the waters of baptism.
In your loving mercy grant them pardon and peace.**

We ask this in the name of Jesus the Lord.

Eucharistic Prayer:
Preface of Christian Death I-V, pages
494–498.

Communion Rite

> May eternal light shine on them, O Lord, with all your saints for ever, for you are rich in mercy. Give them eternal rest, O Lord, and may perpetual light shine on them for ever, for you are rich in mercy. (See 4 Esdras 2:35, 34)

A period of silence may be observed after communion, or a psalm or song of praise may be sung.

PRAYER AFTER COMMUNION

Let us pray.
Pause for silent prayer, if this has not preceded.

Lord,
in this sacrament you give us your crucified and risen Son.
Bring to the glory of the resurrection our departed brothers
and sisters
who have been purified by this holy mystery.

Grant this through Christ our Lord.

SOLEMN BLESSING OR PRAYER OVER THE PEOPLE

The following may replace the simple blessing.

After the greeting, the deacon (or in his absence, the priest) gives the invitation in these or similar words:

Bow your heads and pray for God's blessing.

Then the priest extends his hands over the people while he sings or says:

In his great love,
the God of all consolation gave man the gift of life.
May he bless you with faith
in the resurrection of his Son,
and with the hope of rising to new life.
℞. Amen.

To us who are alive
may he grant forgiveness,
and to all who have died
a place of light and peace.
℞. Amen.

As you believe that Jesus rose from the dead,
so may you live with him for ever in joy.
℞. Amen.

May almighty God bless you,
the Father, and the Son, ☩ and the Holy Spirit.
℞. Amen.

For alternative texts, see page 536.

ALL SOULS

3

Introductory Rites

> God, who raised Jesus from the dead, will give new life
> to our own mortal bodies through his Spirit living in us.
> (See Rom. 8:11)

OPENING PRAYER

Let us pray

[for all our departed brothers and sisters]

Pause for silent prayer

God, our creator and redeemer,
by your power Christ conquered death
and returned to you in glory.
May all your people who have gone before us in faith
share his victory
and enjoy the vision of your glory for ever.

We ask this through our Lord Jesus Christ, your Son,
who lives and reigns with you and the Holy Spirit,
one God, for ever and ever.

LITURGY OF THE WORD

See Lectionary for Mass, no. 668.

LITURGY OF THE EUCHARIST

PRAYER OVER THE GIFTS

Pray, brethren . . .

Lord,
in your kindness accept these gifts for our
   departed brothers and sisters
and for all who sleep in Christ.
May his perfect sacrifice
free them from the power of death
and give them eternal life.

We ask this in the name of Jesus the Lord.

Eucharistic Prayer:
Preface of Christian Death I-V, pages
494–498.

Communion Rite

> We are waiting for our Savior, the Lord Jesus Christ; he
> will transfigure our lowly bodies into copies of his own
> glorious body. (Phil. 3:20-21)

A period of silence may be observed
after communion, or a psalm or song
of praise may be sung.

PRAYER AFTER COMMUNION

Let us pray.
Pause for silent prayer, if this has not preceded.
Lord,
may our sacrifice bring peace and forgiveness
to our brothers and sisters who have died.
Bring the new life given to them in baptism
to the fullness of eternal joy.

We ask this through Christ our Lord.

SOLEMN BLESSING OR PRAYER
OVER THE PEOPLE

The following may replace the simple
blessing.
After the greeting, the deacon (or in
his absence, the priest) gives the
invitation in these or similar words:
Then the priest extends his hands
over the people while he sings or
says:

Bow your heads and pray for God's blessing.

In his great love,
the God of all consolation gave man the gift of life.
May he bless you with faith
in the resurrection of his Son,
and with the hope of rising to new life.
℞. Amen.

To us who are alive may he grant forgiveness
and to all who have died a place of light and peace.
℞. Amen.

As you believe that Jesus rose from the dead,
so may you live with him for ever in joy.
℞. Amen.

May almighty God bless you,
the Father, and the Son, ✝ and the Holy Spirit.
For alternative texts, see page 536.   **℞. Amen.**

November 3

ST. MARTIN DE PORRES, religious

Common of holy men and women: for
religious (p. 741).
OPENING PRAYER

Lord,
you led Martin de Porres by a life of humility
to eternal glory.
May we follow his example
and be exalted with him in the kingdom of heaven.

Grant this through our Lord Jesus Christ, your Son,
who lives and reigns with you and the Holy Spirit,
one God, for ever and ever.

November 4

ST. CHARLES BORROMEO, bishop

Memorial

Common of pastors: for bishops (p. 719).

OPENING PRAYER

**Father,
keep in your people the spirit
which filled Charles Borromeo.
Let your Church be continually renewed
and show the image of Christ to the world
by being conformed to his likeness,
who lives and reigns with you and the Holy Spirit,
one God, for ever and ever.**

See Lectionary for Mass, no. 670.

PRAYER OVER THE GIFTS

Pray, brethren . . .

**Lord,
look with kindness on the gifts we bring to your altar
on this feast of St. Charles.
You made him an example of virtue
and concern for the pastoral ministry.
Through the power of this sacrifice
may we abound in good works.**

We ask this through Christ our Lord.

PRAYER AFTER COMMUNION

Let us pray.

Pause for silent prayer, if this has not preceded.

**Lord,
may the holy mysteries we have received
give us that courage and strength
which made St. Charles faithful in his ministry
and constant in his love.**

We ask this in the name of Jesus the Lord.

November 9

DEDICATION OF ST. JOHN LATERAN

Feast

Common of the dedication of a church (p. 695).

November 10

ST. LEO THE GREAT, pope and doctor

Memorial

Common of pastors: for popes (p. 717); or Common of doctors of the Church (p. 729).

OPENING PRAYER

**God our Father,
you will never allow the power of hell
to prevail against your Church,
founded on the rock of the apostle Peter.
Let the prayers of Pope Leo the Great
keep us faithful to your truth
and secure in your peace.**

**We ask this through our Lord Jesus Christ, your Son,
who lives and reigns with you and the Holy Spirit,
one God, for ever and ever.**

See Lectionary for Mass, no. 672.

PRAYER OVER THE GIFTS

Pray, brethren . . .

**Lord,
by these gifts we bring,
fill your people with your light.
May your Church continue to grow everywhere under your
   guidance
and under the leadership of shepherds pleasing to you.**

Grant this through Christ our Lord.

PRAYER AFTER COMMUNION

Let us pray.
Pause for silent prayer, if this has not preceded.
**Lord,
as you nourish your Church with this holy banquet,
govern it always with your love.
Under your powerful guidance
may it grow in freedom
and continue in loyalty to the faith.**

We ask this in the name of Jesus the Lord.

November 11

ST. MARTIN OF TOURS, bishop
Memorial

Introductory Rites

I will raise up for myself a faithful priest; he will do what is
in my heart and in my mind, says the Lord. (1 Sam. 2:35)

OPENING PRAYER

Father,
by his life and death
St. Martin of Tours offered you worship and praise.
Renew in our hearts the power of your love,
so that neither death nor life may separate us from you.

Grant this through our Lord Jesus Christ, your Son,
who lives and reigns with you and the Holy Spirit,
one God, for ever and ever.

See Lectionary for Mass, no. 673.

PRAYER OVER THE GIFTS

Pray, brethren . . .

Lord God,
bless these gifts we present
on this feast of St. Martin.
May this eucharist help us
in joy and sorrow.

We ask this in the name of Jesus the Lord.

Communion Rite

I tell you, anything you did for the least of my brothers,
you did for me, says the Lord. (Matthew 25:40)

PRAYER AFTER COMMUNION

Let us pray.
Pause for silent prayer, if this has not preceded.
Lord,
you have renewed us with the sacrament of unity:
help us to follow your will in all that we do.
As St. Martin gave himself completely to your service,
may we rejoice in belonging to you.

We ask this through Christ our Lord.

November 12

ST. JOSAPHAT, bishop and martyr
Memorial

Common of martyrs (p. 709); or Common of pastors: for bishops (p. 719).

OPENING PRAYER

Lord,
fill your Church with the Spirit
that gave St. Josaphat courage
to lay down his life for his people.
By his prayers
may your Spirit make us strong
and willing to offer our lives
for our brothers and sisters.

We ask this through our Lord Jesus Christ, your Son,
who lives and reigns with you and the Holy Spirit,
one God, for ever and ever.

See Lectionary for Mass, no. 674.

PRAYER OVER THE GIFTS

Pray, brethren . . .

God of mercy,
pour out your blessing upon these gifts,
and make us strong in the faith
which St. Josaphat professed by shedding his blood.

We ask this in the name of Jesus the Lord.

PRAYER AFTER COMMUNION

Let us pray.
Pause for silent prayer, if this has not preceded.

Lord,
may this eucharist we have shared
fill us with your Spirit of courage and peace.
Let the example of St. Josaphat
inspire us to spend our lives
working for the honor and unity of your Church.

Grant this through Christ our Lord.

November 13

In the dioceses of the United States

ST. FRANCES XAVIER CABRINI, virgin

Memorial

Common of virgins (p. 731).

OPENING PRAYER

**God our Father,
you called St. Frances Xavier Cabrini from Italy
to serve the immigrants of America.
By her example teach us concern for the stranger,
the sick, and the frustrated.
By her prayers help us to see Christ
in all the men and women we meet.**

**Grant this through our Lord Jesus Christ, your Son,
who lives and reigns with you and the Holy Spirit,
one God, for ever and ever.**

November 15

ST. ALBERT THE GREAT, bishop and doctor

Common of pastors: for bishops (p. 719); or Common of doctors of the Church (p. 729).

OPENING PRAYER

**God our Father,
you endowed St. Albert with the talent
of combining human wisdom with divine faith.
Keep us true to his teachings
that the advance of human knowledge
may deepen our knowledge and love of you.**

**Grant this through our Lord Jesus Christ, your Son,
who lives and reigns with you and the Holy Spirit,
one God, for ever and ever.**

November 16

ST. MARGARET OF SCOTLAND

Common of holy men and women: for those who worked for the underprivileged (p. 743).

OPENING PRAYER

**Lord,
you gave St. Margaret of Scotland
a special love for the poor.
Let her example and prayers
help us to become a living sign of your goodness.**

**We ask this through our Lord Jesus Christ, your Son,
who lives and reigns with you and the Holy Spirit,
one God, for ever and ever.**

ST. GERTRUDE, virgin

Common of virgins (p. 731); or Common of holy men and women: for religious (p. 741).

OPENING PRAYER

**Father,
you filled the heart of St. Gertrude
with the presence of your love.
Bring light into our darkness
and let us experience the joy of your presence
and the power of your grace.**

**Grant this through our Lord Jesus Christ, your Son,
who lives and reigns with you and the Holy Spirit,
one God, for ever and ever.**

November 17

ST. ELIZABETH OF HUNGARY, religious
Memorial

Common of holy men and women: for those who worked for the underprivileged (p. 743).

OPENING PRAYER

**Father,
you helped St. Elizabeth of Hungary
to recognize and honor Christ
in the poor of this world.
Let her prayers help us to serve our brothers and sisters
in time of trouble and need.**

**We ask this through our Lord Jesus Christ, your Son,
who lives and reigns with you and the Holy Spirit,
one God, for ever and ever.**

November 18

DEDICATION OF THE CHURCHES
OF ST. PETER AND ST. PAUL, apostles

Introductory Rites

You have made them princes over all the earth; they
declared your fame to all generations; for ever will the
nations declare your praise. (Ps. 44:17-18)

OPENING PRAYER

Lord,
give your Church the protection of the apostles.
From them it first received the faith of Christ.
May they help your Church to grow in your grace
until the end of time.

Grant this through our Lord Jesus Christ, your Son,
who lives and reigns with you and the Holy Spirit,
one God, for ever and ever.

See Lectionary for Mass, no. 679.

PRAYER OVER THE GIFTS

Pray, brethren . . .

Lord,
accept the gift of our worship
and hear our prayers for mercy.
Keep alive in our hearts the truth you gave us
through the ministry of your apostles Peter and Paul.

We ask this through Christ our Lord.

Preface of the Apostles I or II, pages
481–482.

Communion Rite

Lord, you have the words of everlasting life, and we
believe that you are God's Holy One. (John 6:69-70)

PRAYER AFTER COMMUNION

Let us pray.
Pause for silent prayer, if this has not preceded.
Lord,
you have given us bread from heaven.
May this celebration
in memory of your apostles Peter and Paul
bring us the joy of their constant protection.

We ask this in the name of Jesus the Lord.

November 21

PRESENTATION OF MARY
Memorial

Common of the Blessed Virgin Mary (p. 696).

OPENING PRAYER

**Eternal Father,
we honor the holiness and glory of the Virgin Mary.
May her prayers bring us
the fullness of your life and love.**

**We ask this through our Lord Jesus Christ, your Son,
who lives and reigns with you and the Holy Spirit,
one God, for ever and ever.**

November 22

ST. CECILIA, virgin and martyr
Memorial

Common of martyrs (p. 709); or Common of virgins (p. 731).

OPENING PRAYER

**Lord of mercy,
be close to those who call upon you.
With St. Cecilia to help us
hear and answer our prayers.**

**Grant this through our Lord Jesus Christ, your Son,
who lives and reigns with you and the Holy Spirit,
one God, for ever and ever.**

November 23

ST. CLEMENT I, pope and martyr

Common of martyrs (p. 709); or
Common of pastors: for popes (p. 717).

OPENING PRAYER

**All-powerful and ever-living God,
we praise your power and glory
revealed to us in the lives of all your saints.
Give us joy on this feast of St. Clement,
the priest and martyr
who bore witness with his blood to the love he proclaimed
and the gospel he preached.**

**We ask this through our Lord Jesus Christ, your Son,
who lives and reigns with you and the Holy Spirit,
one God, for ever and ever.**

ST. COLUMBAN, abbot

Common of pastors: for missionaries (p.
726); or Common of holy men and
women: for religious (p. 741).

OPENING PRAYER

**Lord,
you called St. Columban to live the monastic life
and to preach the gospel with zeal.
May his prayers and example
help us to seek you above all things
and to work with all our hearts
for the spread of the faith.**

**Grant this through our Lord Jesus Christ, your Son,
who lives and reigns with you and the Holy Spirit,
one God, for ever and ever.**

Fourth Thursday of November

In the dioceses of the United States

THANKSGIVING DAY

OPENING PRAYER

Let us pray
[that our gratitude to God may bear fruit
in loving service to our fellow men and women]
Pause for silent prayer
Father all-powerful,
your gifts of love are countless
and your goodness infinite.
On Thanksgiving Day we come before you
with gratitude for your kindness:
open our hearts to concern for our fellow men and women,
so that we may share your gifts in loving service.

We ask this through our Lord Jesus Christ, your Son,
who lives and reigns with you and the Holy Spirit,
one God, for ever and ever.

See Lectionary for Mass, nos. 881-885.

PRAYER OVER THE GIFTS

Pray, brethren . . .

God our Father,
from your hand we have received generous gifts
so that we might learn to share your blessings in gratitude.
Accept these gifts of bread and wine,
and let the perfect sacrifice of Jesus
draw us closer to all our brothers and sisters in the family
  of man.

Grant this through Christ our Lord.

Preface of Thanksgiving Day, page 501.

PRAYER AFTER COMMUNION

Let us pray.
Pause for silent prayer, if this has not preceded.
Lord God,
in this celebration
we have seen the depths of your love for every man
  and woman
and been reminded of our negligence toward others.
Help us to reach out in love to all your people,
so that we may share with them
the goods of time and eternity.

Grant this through Christ our Lord.

November 30

ST. ANDREW, apostle
Feast

Introductory Rites

By the Sea of Galilee the Lord saw two brothers, Peter and
Andrew. He called them: come and follow me, and I will
make you fishers of men. (See Matthew 4:18-19)

OPENING PRAYER

**Lord,
in your kindness hear our petitions.
You called Andrew the apostle
to preach the gospel and guide your Church in faith.
May he always be our friend in your presence
to help us with his prayers.**

**We ask this through our Lord Jesus Christ, your Son,
who lives and reigns with you and the Holy Spirit,
one God, for ever and ever.**

See Lectionary for Mass, no. 684.

PRAYER OVER THE GIFTS   **Pray, brethren . . .**

**All-powerful God,
may these gifts we bring on the feast of St. Andrew
be pleasing to you
and give life to all who receive them.**

We ask this in the name of Jesus the Lord.

Preface of the Apostles I or II, pages
481–482.

Communion Rite

Andrew told his brother Simon: We have found the
Messiah, the Christ; and he brought him to Jesus. (John
1:41-42)

PRAYER AFTER COMMUNION   **Let us pray.**
Pause for silent prayer, if this has not preceded.
**Lord,
may the sacrament we have received give us courage
to follow the example of Andrew the apostle.
By sharing in Christ's suffering
may we live with him for ever in glory,
for he is Lord for ever and ever.**

DECEMBER

December 3

ST. FRANCIS XAVIER, priest
Memorial

Common of pastors: for missionaries (p. 726).

OPENING PRAYER

God our Father,
by the preaching of St. Francis Xavier
you brought many nations to yourself.
Give his zeal for the faith to all who believe in you,
that your Church may rejoice in continued growth
throughout the world.

Grant this through our Lord Jesus Christ, your Son,
who lives and reigns with you and the Holy Spirit,
one God, for ever and ever.

See Lectionary for Mass, no. 685.

PRAYER OVER THE GIFTS

Pray, brethren . . .

Lord,
receive the gifts we bring on the feast of St. Francis Xavier.
As his zeal for the salvation of mankind
led him to the ends of the earth,
may we be effective witnesses to the gospel
and come with our brothers and sisters
to be with you in the joy of your kingdom.

We ask this through Christ our Lord.

PRAYER AFTER COMMUNION

Let us pray.
Pause for silent prayer, if this has not preceded.
Lord God,
may this eucharist fill us with the same love
that inspired St. Francis Xavier
to work for the salvation of all.
Help us to live in a manner more worthy of our Christian
    calling
and so inherit the promise of eternal life.

We ask this in the name of Jesus the Lord.

December 4

ST. JOHN DAMASCENE, priest and doctor

Common of pastors (p. 721); or Common of doctors of the Church (p. 729).

OPENING PRAYER

**Lord,
may the prayers of St. John Damascene help us,
and may the true faith he taught so well
always be our light and our strength.**

**We ask this through our Lord Jesus Christ, your Son,
who lives and reigns with you and the Holy Spirit,
one God, for ever and ever.**

December 6

ST. NICHOLAS, bishop

Common of pastors: for bishops (p. 719).

OPENING PRAYER

**Father,
hear our prayers for mercy,
and by the help of St. Nicholas
keep us safe from all danger,
and guide us on the way of salvation.**

**Grant this through our Lord Jesus Christ, your Son,
who lives and reigns with you and the Holy Spirit,
one God, for ever and ever.**

December 7

ST. AMBROSE, bishop and doctor
Memorial

Common of pastors: for bishops (p. 719); or Common of doctors of the Church (p. 729).

OPENING PRAYER

Lord,
you made St. Ambrose
an outstanding teacher of the Catholic faith
and gave him the courage of an apostle.
Raise up in your Church more leaders after your own heart,
to guide us with courage and wisdom.

We ask this through our Lord Jesus Christ, your Son,
who lives and reigns with you and the Holy Spirit,
one God, for ever and ever.

See Lectionary for Mass, no. 688.

PRAYER OVER THE GIFTS

Pray, brethren . . .

Lord,
as we celebrate these holy rites,
send your Spirit to give us the light of faith
which guided St. Ambrose to make your glory known.

We ask this in the name of Jesus the Lord.

PRAYER AFTER COMMUNION

Let us pray.
Pause for silent prayer, if this has not preceded.
Father,
you have renewed us by the power of this sacrament.
Through the teachings of St. Ambrose,
may we follow your way with courage
and prepare ourselves for the feast of eternal life.

Grant this through Christ our Lord.

December 8

IMMACULATE CONCEPTION
Solemnity

Introductory Rites

I exult for joy in the Lord, my soul rejoices in my God; for he has clothed me in the garment of salvation and robed me in the cloak of justice, like a bride adorned with her jewels. (Is. 61:10)

OPENING PRAYER

Let us pray
[that through the prayers of the sinless
Virgin Mary, God will free us from our sins]
Pause for silent prayer
Father,
you prepared the Virgin Mary
to be the worthy mother of your Son.
You let her share beforehand
in the salvation Christ would bring by
his death,
and kept her sinless from the first moment of
her conception.
Help us by her prayers
to live in your presence without sin.

We ask this through our Lord Jesus Christ,
your Son,
who lives and reigns with you and the Holy
Spirit,
one God, for ever and ever.

ALTERNATIVE OPENING PRAYER

Let us pray
[on this feast of Mary who experienced
the perfection of God's saving power]
Pause for silent prayer
Father,
the image of the Virgin is found in the Church.
Mary had a faith that your Spirit prepared
and a love that never knew sin,
for you kept her sinless from the first moment
of her conception.

Trace in our actions the lines of her love,
in our hearts her readiness of faith.
Prepare once again a world for your Son
who lives and reigns with you and the Holy
Spirit,
one God, for ever and ever.

LITURGY OF THE WORD

See Lectionary for Mass, no. 689.

Profession of Faith

LITURGY OF THE EUCHARIST

PRAYER OVER THE GIFTS

Pray, brethren . . .

Lord,
accept this sacrifice
on the feast of the sinless Virgin Mary.
You kept her free from sin
from the first moment of her life.
Help us by her prayers,
and free us from our sins.

We ask this in the name of Jesus the Lord.

Eucharistic Prayer:
Preface of the Immaculate Conception,
page 475.

Communion Rite

All honor to you, Mary! From you arose the sun of justice,
Christ our God.

A period of silence may be observed
after communion, or a psalm or song
of praise may be sung.

PRAYER AFTER COMMUNION

Let us pray.
Pause for silent prayer, if this has not preceded.
**Lord our God,
in your love, you chose the Virgin Mary
and kept her free from sin.
May this sacrament of your love
free us from our sins.**

Grant this through Christ our Lord.

**SOLEMN BLESSING OR PRAYER
OVER THE PEOPLE**

The following may replace the simple
blessing.

After the greeting, the deacon (or in
his absence, the priest) gives the
invitation in these or similar words:

Then the priest extends his hands
over the people while he sings or
says:

Bow your heads and pray for God's blessing.

**Born of the Blessed Virgin Mary,
the Son of God redeemed mankind.
May he enrich you with his blessings.
℟. Amen.**

**You received the author of life through Mary.
May you always rejoice in her loving care.
℟. Amen.**

**You have come to rejoice at Mary's feast.
May you be filled with the joys of the Spirit
and the gifts of your eternal home.
℟. Amen.**

**May almighty God bless you,
the Father, and the Son, ☩ and the Holy Spirit.
℟. Amen.**

For alternative text, see page 540, no. 26.

December 11

ST. DAMASUS I, pope

Common of pastors: for popes (p. 717).

OPENING PRAYER

Father,
as St. Damasus loved and honored your martyrs,
so may we continue to celebrate their witness for Christ,
who lives and reigns with you and the Holy Spirit,
one God, for ever and ever.

December 12

In the dioceses of the United States

OUR LADY OF GUADALUPE
Memorial

Common of the Blessed Virgin Mary (p. 696).

OPENING PRAYER

God of power and mercy,
you blessed the Americas at Tepeyac
with the presence of the Virgin Mary of Guadalupe.
May her prayers help all men and women
to accept each other as brothers and sisters.
Through your justice present in our hearts
may your peace reign in the world.

We ask this through our Lord Jesus Christ, your Son,
who lives and reigns with you and the Holy Spirit,
one God, for ever and ever.

ST. JANE FRANCES DE CHANTAL, religious

Common of holy men and women: for religious (p. 741).

OPENING PRAYER

Lord,
you chose St. Jane Frances to serve you
both in marriage and in religious life.
By her prayers
help us to be faithful in our vocation
and always to be the light of the world.

We ask this through our Lord Jesus Christ, your Son,
who lives and reigns with you and the Holy Spirit,
one God, for ever and ever.

December 13

ST. LUCY, virgin and martyr
Memorial

Common of martyrs (p. 709); or
Common of virgins (p. 731).

OPENING PRAYER

**Lord,
give us courage through the prayers of St. Lucy.
As we celebrate her entrance into eternal glory,
we ask to share her happiness in the life to come.**

**Grant this through our Lord Jesus Christ, your Son,
who lives and reigns with you and the Holy Spirit,
one God, for ever and ever.**

December 14

ST. JOHN OF THE CROSS, priest and doctor
Memorial

Introductory Rites
I should boast of nothing but the cross of our Lord Jesus
Christ; through him the world is crucified to me, and I to
the world. (Gal. 6:14)

OPENING PRAYER

**Father,
you endowed St. John of the Cross with a spirit of
self-denial and a love of the cross.
By following his example,
may we come to the eternal vision of your glory.**

**We ask this through our Lord Jesus Christ, your Son,
who lives and reigns with you and the Holy Spirit,
one God, for ever and ever.**

See Lectionary for Mass, no. 693.

PRAYER OVER THE GIFTS

Pray, brethren . . .

**Almighty Lord,
look upon the gifts we offer
in memory of St. John of the Cross.
May we imitate the love we proclaim
as we celebrate the mystery
of the suffering and death of Christ,
who is Lord for ever and ever.**

Communion Rite
If anyone wishes to come after me, he must renounce
himself, take up his cross, and follow me, says the Lord.
(Matthew 16:24)

PRAYER AFTER COMMUNION

Let us pray.
Pause for silent prayer, if this has not preceded.
**God our Father,
you have shown us the mystery of the cross
in the life of St. John.
May this sacrifice make us strong,
keep us faithful to Christ
and help us to work in the Church
for the salvation of all mankind.**

We ask this in the name of Jesus the Lord.

December 21

ST. PETER CANISIUS, priest and doctor

Common of pastors (p. 721); or
Common of doctors of the Church (p. 729).

OPENING PRAYER

**Lord,
you gave St. Peter Canisius
wisdom and courage to defend the Catholic faith.
By the help of his prayers
may all who seek the truth rejoice in finding you,
and may all who believe in you
be loyal in professing their faith.**

**Grant this through our Lord Jesus Christ, your Son,
who lives and reigns with you and the Holy Spirit,
one God, for ever and ever.**

December 23

ST. JOHN OF KANTY, priest

Common of pastors (p. 721); or
Common of holy men and women: for
those who worked for the underprivileged (p. 743).

OPENING PRAYER

**Almighty Father,
through the example of St. John of Kanty
may we grow in the wisdom of the saints.
As we show understanding and kindness to others,
may we receive your forgiveness.**

**We ask this through our Lord Jesus Christ, your Son,
who lives and reigns with you and the Holy Spirit,
one God, for ever and ever.**

December 26

ST. STEPHEN, first martyr
Feast

Introductory Rites

The gates of heaven opened for Stephen, the first of the martyrs; in heaven he wears the crown of victory.

OPENING PRAYER

**Lord,
today we celebrate the entrance of St. Stephen
into eternal glory.
He died praying for those who killed him.
Help us to imitate his goodness
and to love our enemies.**

**We ask this through our Lord Jesus Christ, your Son,
who lives and reigns with you and the Holy Spirit,
one God, for ever and ever.**

See Lectionary for Mass, no. 696.

PRAYER OVER THE GIFTS

Pray, brethren . . .

**Father,
be pleased with the gifts we bring in your honor
as we celebrate the memory of St. Stephen.**

Grant this through Christ our Lord.

Preface of Christmas I-III, pages 420–422.

Communion Rite

As they stoned him, Stephen prayed aloud: Lord Jesus, receive my spirit. (Acts 7:58)

PRAYER AFTER COMMUNION

Let us pray.

Pause for silent prayer, if this has not preceded.

**Lord,
we thank you for the many signs of your love for us.
Save us by the birth of your Son
and give us joy in honoring St. Stephen the martyr.**

We ask this through Christ our Lord.

December 27

ST. JOHN, apostle and evangelist
Feast

Introductory Rites

The Lord opened his mouth in the assembly, and filled him with the spirit of wisdom and understanding, and clothed him in a robe of glory. (Sir. 15:5)

or:

At the last supper, John reclined close to the Lord. Blessed apostle, to you were revealed the heavenly secrets! Your lifegiving words have spread over all the earth!

OPENING PRAYER

God our Father,
you have revealed the mysteries of your Word
through John the apostle.
By prayer and reflection
may we come to understand the wisdom he taught.

Grant this through our Lord Jesus Christ, your Son,
who lives and reigns with you and the Holy Spirit,
one God, for ever and ever.

See Lectionary for Mass, no. 697.

PRAYER OVER THE GIFTS

Pray, brethren . . .

Lord,
bless these gifts we present to you.
With St. John may we share
in the hidden wisdom of your eternal Word
which you reveal at this eucharistic table.

We ask this in the name of Jesus the Lord.

Preface of Christmas I-III, pages 420–422.

Communion Rite

The Word of God became man, and lived among us. Of his riches we have all received. (John 1:14, 16)

PRAYER AFTER COMMUNION

Let us pray.
Pause for silent prayer, if this has not preceded.
Almighty God,
St. John proclaimed that your Word became flesh
for our salvation.
Through this eucharist may your Son always live in us,
for he is Lord for ever and ever.

December 28

HOLY INNOCENTS, martyrs
Feast

Introductory Rites

These innocent children were slain for Christ. They follow the spotless Lamb, and proclaim for ever: Glory to you, Lord.

OPENING PRAYER

**Father,
the Holy Innocents offered you praise
by the death they suffered for Christ.
May our lives bear witness
to the faith we profess with our lips.**

**We ask this through our Lord Jesus Christ, your Son,
who lives and reigns with you and the Holy Spirit,
one God, for ever and ever.**

See Lectionary for Mass, no. 698.

PRAYER OVER THE GIFTS

Pray, brethren . . .

**Lord,
you give us your life even before we understand.
Receive the offerings we bring in love,
and free us from sin.**

We ask this in the name of Jesus the Lord.

Preface of Christmas I-III, pages 420–422.

Communion Rite

These have been ransomed for God and the Lamb as the first-fruits of mankind; they follow the Lamb wherever he goes. (Rev. 14:4)

PRAYER AFTER COMMUNION

Let us pray.
Pause for silent prayer, if this has not preceded.
**Lord,
by a wordless profession of faith in your Son,
the innocents were crowned with life at his birth.
May all people who receive your holy gifts today
come to share in the fullness of salvation.**

We ask this through Christ our Lord.

December 29

ST. THOMAS BECKET, bishop and martyr

Common of martyrs (p. 709); or
Common of pastors: for bishops (p.
719).

OPENING PRAYER

**Almighty God,
you granted the martyr Thomas
the grace to give his life for the cause of justice.
By his prayers
make us willing to renounce for Christ
our life in this world
so that we may find it in heaven.**

**We ask this through our Lord Jesus Christ, your Son,
who lives and reigns with you and the Holy Spirit,
one God, for ever and ever.**

December 31

ST. SYLVESTER I, pope

Common of pastors: for popes (p. 717).

OPENING PRAYER

**Lord,
help and sustain your people
by the prayers of Pope Sylvester.
Guide us always in this present life
and bring us to the joy that never ends.**

**We ask this through our Lord Jesus Christ, your Son,
who lives and reigns with you and the Holy Spirit,
one God, for ever and ever.**

COMMONS

COMMONS

1. In the individual commons, several Mass formularies, with antiphons and prayers, are arranged for convenience.

The priest, however, may interchange antiphons and prayers of the same common choosing according to the circumstances those texts which seem pastorally appropriate.

In addition, for Masses of memorial, the prayer over the gifts and the prayer after communion may be taken from the weekdays of the current liturgical season as well as from the commons.

2. In the common of martyrs and in the common of holy men and women, all the prayers may be used for men or women with the necessary change of gender.

3. In the individual commons, texts in the singular may be changed to the plural and vice versa.

4. Certain Masses which are given for specific seasons and circumstances should be used for those seasons and circumstances.

5. During the Easter season an **alleluia** should be added at the end of the entrance and communion antiphons.

6. On solemnities and feasts, one of the optional antiphons on page 747 may be said.

COMMON OF THE DEDICATION OF A CHURCH

1. ON THE DAY OF DEDICATION

The texts for Masses for the dedication of a church on the day of dedication and also for the dedication of an altar on the day of dedication are included in Appendix VIII (pages 1156–1162). The following entrance and communion antiphons may be used with those Masses. See *Dedication of a Church and an Altar* for additional recommendations for song.

Introductory Rites

God in his holy dwelling, God who has gathered us together in his house: he will strengthen and console his people.

or:

Let us go rejoicing to the house of the Lord. (Ps. 122:1)

Communion Rite

My house shall be called a house of prayer, says the Lord: in it all who ask shall receive, all who seek shall find, and all who knock shall have the door opened to them (alleluia). (Matthew 21:13; Luke 11:10)

or:

May the children of the Church be like olive branches around the table of the Lord (alleluia). (See Ps. 128:3)

2. ANNIVERSARY OF DEDICATION
A. In the Dedicated Church

Introductory Rites

Greatly to be feared is God in his sanctuary; he, the God of
Israel, gives power and strength to his people. Blessed be
God! (Ps. 67:36)

OPENING PRAYER

Father,
each year we recall the dedication of this church
   to your service.
Let our worship always be sincere
and help us to find your saving love in this church.

Grant this through our Lord Jesus Christ, your Son,
who lives and reigns with you and the Holy Spirit,
one God, for ever and ever.

See Lectionary for Mass, nos. 701-706.

PRAYER OVER THE GIFTS

Pray, brethren . . .

Lord,
as we recall the day you filled this church
with your glory and holiness,
may our lives also become an acceptable
   offering to you.

Grant this in the name of Jesus the Lord.

Preface of the Dedication of a Church
I, page **469.**

Communion Rite

You are the temple of God, and God's Spirit dwells in you.
The temple of God is holy; you are that temple. (1 Cor.
3:16-17)

PRAYER AFTER COMMUNION

Let us pray.

Pause for silent prayer, if this has not preceded.
Lord,
we know the joy and power of your blessing in our lives.
As we celebrate the dedication of this church,
may we give ourselves once more to your service.

Grant this through Christ our Lord.

BLESSING AT THE END OF MASS

The text of the solemn blessing, number
19 on page **536,** may be said with the
words to recall the dedication of this
church.

D. Outside the Dedicated Church

Introductory Rites

> I saw the holy city, new Jerusalem, coming down from
> God out of heaven, like a bride adorned in readiness for
> her husband. (Rev. 21:2)

OPENING PRAYER   Or:

God our Father,
from living stones, your chosen people,
you built an eternal temple to your glory.
Increase the spiritual gifts you have given to
** your Church,**
so that your faithful people may continue to
** grow**
into the new and eternal Jerusalem.

We ask this through our Lord Jesus Christ,
** your Son,**
who lives and reigns with you and the Holy
** Spirit,**
one God, for ever and ever.

Father,
you called your people to be your Church.
As we gather together in your name,
may we love, honor, and follow you
to eternal life in the kingdom you promise.

Grant this through our Lord Jesus Christ, your
** Son,**
who lives and reigns with you and the Holy
** Spirit,**
one God, for ever and ever.

See Lectionary for Mass, nos. 701-706.

PRAYER OVER THE GIFTS   **Pray, brethren . . .**

Lord,
receive our gifts.
May we who share this sacrament
experience the life and power it promises,
and hear the answer to our prayers.

We ask this in the name of Jesus the Lord.

Preface of the Dedication of a Church
II, page 470.

Communion Rite

> Like living stones let yourselves be built on Christ as a
> spiritual house, a holy priesthood. (1 Peter 2:5)

PRAYER AFTER COMMUNION   **Let us pray.**
Pause for silent prayer, if this has not preceded.

Father,
you make your Church on earth
a sign of the new and eternal Jerusalem.
By sharing in this sacrament
may we become the temple of your presence
and the home of your glory.

Grant this in the name of Jesus the Lord.

COMMON OF THE BLESSED VIRGIN MARY

These Masses are also used for the Saturday celebrations of the Blessed Virgin Mary and for votive Masses of the Blessed Virgin Mary.

1

Introductory Rites

Hail, holy Mother! The child to whom you gave birth is the King of heaven and earth for ever. (Sedulius)

OPENING PRAYER

Lord God,
give to your people the joy
of continual health in mind and body.
With the prayers of the Virgin Mary to help us,
guide us through the sorrows of this life
to eternal happiness in the life to come.

Grant this through our Lord Jesus Christ, your Son,
who lives and reigns with you and the Holy Spirit,
one God, for ever and ever.

Or:

Lord,
take away the sins of your people.
May the prayers of Mary the mother of your Son help us,
for alone and unaided we cannot hope to please you.

We ask this through our Lord Jesus Christ, your Son,
who lives and reigns with you and the Holy Spirit,
one God, for ever and ever.

See Lectionary for Mass, nos. 707–712.

PRAYER OVER THE GIFTS

Pray, brethren . . .

Father,
the birth of Christ your Son
deepened the virgin mother's love for you,
and increased her holiness.
May the humanity of Christ
give us courage in our weakness;
may it free us from our sins,
and make our offering acceptable.

We ask this through Christ our Lord.

Preface of the Blessed Virgin Mary I (feasts or memorials) or II (votive Masses), pages 473–474.

Communion Rite

Blessed is the womb of the Virgin Mary; she carried the
Son of the eternal Father. (See Luke 11:27)

PRAYER AFTER COMMUNION

Let us pray.

Pause for silent prayer, if this has not preceded.

Lord,
we rejoice in your sacraments and ask your mercy
as we honor the memory of the Virgin Mary.
May her faith and love
inspire us to serve you more faithfully
in the work of salvation.

Grant this in the name of Jesus the Lord.

2

Introductory Rites

Blessed are you, Virgin Mary, who carried the creator of all things in your womb; you gave birth to your maker, and remain for ever a virgin.

OPENING PRAYER   Or:

God of mercy,
give us strength.
May we who honor the memory of the Mother of God
rise above our sins and failings with the help of her prayers.

Grant this through our Lord Jesus Christ, your Son,
who lives and reigns with you and the Holy Spirit,
one God, for ever and ever.

Lord,
may the prayers of the Virgin Mary
bring us protection from danger
and freedom from sin
that we may come to the joy of your peace.

We ask this through our Lord Jesus Christ, your Son,
who lives and reigns with you and the Holy Spirit,
one God, for ever and ever.

See Lectionary for Mass, nos. 707-712.

PRAYER OVER THE GIFTS   **Pray, brethren . . .**

Lord,
we honor the memory of the mother of your Son.
May the sacrifice we share
make of us an everlasting gift to you.

Grant this through Christ our Lord.

Preface of the Blessed Virgin Mary I (feasts or memorials) or II (votive Masses), pages **473–474.**

Communion Rite

The Almighty has done great things for me. Holy is his name. (Luke 1:49)

PRAYER AFTER COMMUNION   **Let us pray.**

Pause for silent prayer, if this has not preceded.
Lord,
you give us the sacraments of eternal redemption.
May we who honor the memory of the Mother of your Son
rejoice in the abundance of your grace
and experience your unfailing help.

We ask this through Christ our Lord.

3

Introductory Rites

> You have been blessed, O Virgin Mary, above all other women on earth by the Lord the most high God; he has so exalted your name that your praises shall never fade from the mouths of men. (See Judith 13:23, 25)

OPENING PRAYER   Or:

Lord,
as we honor the glorious memory of the Virgin Mary,
we ask that by the help of her prayers
we too may come to share the fullness of your grace.
Grant this through our Lord Jesus Christ, your Son,
who lives and reigns with you and the Holy Spirit,
one God, for ever and ever.

Lord Jesus Christ,
you chose the Virgin Mary to be your mother,
a worthy home in which to dwell.
By her prayers keep us from danger
and bring us to the joy of heaven,
where you live and reign with the Father and the Holy Spirit,
one God, for ever and ever.

See Lectionary for Mass, nos. 707-712.

PRAYER OVER THE GIFTS   **Pray, brethren . . .**

Lord,
we bring you our sacrifice of praise
at this celebration in honor of Mary,
**   the mother of your Son.**
May this holy exchange of gifts
help us on our way to eternal salvation.

We ask this in the name of Jesus the Lord.

Preface of the Blessed Virgin Mary I (feasts or memorials) or II (votive Masses), pages 473–474.

Communion Rite

> All generations will call me blessed, because God has looked upon his lowly handmaid. (See Luke 1:48)

PRAYER AFTER COMMUNION   **Let us pray.**
Pause for silent prayer, if this has not preceded.
Lord,
we eat the bread of heaven.
May we who honor the memory of the Virgin Mary
come one day to your banquet of eternal life.

Grant this through Christ our Lord.

4. ADVENT SEASON

Introductory Rites

Let the clouds rain down the Just One, and the earth bring forth a Savior. (Is. 45:8)

or:

The angel said to Mary: You have won God's favor. You will conceive and bear a Son, and he will be called Son of the Most High. (Luke 1:30-32)

OPENING PRAYER

Father,
in your plan for our salvation
your Word became man,
announced by an angel and born of the Virgin Mary.
May we who believe that she is the Mother of God
receive the help of her prayers.

We ask this through our Lord Jesus Christ, your Son,
who lives and reigns with you and the Holy Spirit,
one God, for ever and ever.

See Lectionary for Mass, nos. 707-712.

PRAYER OVER THE GIFTS

Pray, brethren . . .

Lord,
may the power of your Spirit,
which sanctified Mary the mother of your Son,
make holy the gifts we place upon this altar.

We ask this through Christ our Lord.

Preface of the Blessed Virgin Mary I (feasts or memorials) or II (votive Masses), pages **473–474**, or Preface of Advent II, page **419**.

Communion Rite

The Virgin is with child and shall bear a son, and she will call him Emmanuel. (Is. 7:14)

PRAYER AFTER COMMUNION

Let us pray.

Pause for silent prayer, if this has not preceded.
Lord our God,
may the sacraments we receive
show us your forgiveness and love.
May we who honor the mother of your Son
be saved by his coming among us as man,
for he is Lord for ever and ever.

5. CHRISTMAS SEASON

Introductory Rites

> Giving birth to the King whose reign is unending, Mary knows the joys of motherhood together with a virgin's honor; none like her before, and there shall be none hereafter.
>
> or:
>
> O virgin Mother of God, the universe cannot hold him, and yet, becoming man, he confined himself in your womb.

OPENING PRAYER

**Father,
you gave the human race eternal salvation
through the motherhood of the Virgin Mary.
May we experience the help of her prayers in our lives,
for through her we received the very source of life,
your Son, our Lord Jesus Christ,
who lives and reigns with you and the Holy Spirit,
one God, for ever and ever.**

See Lectionary for Mass, nos. 707-712.

PRAYER OVER THE GIFTS

Pray, brethren . . .

**Lord,
accept our gifts and prayers
and fill our hearts with the light of your Holy Spirit.
Help us to follow the example of the Virgin Mary:
to seek you in all things
and to do your will with gladness.**

We ask this in the name of Jesus the Lord.

Preface of the Blessed Virgin Mary I (feasts or memorials) or II (votive Masses), pages **473–474.**

Communion Rite

> The Word of God became man, and lived among us, full of grace and truth. (John 1:14)

PRAYER AFTER COMMUNION

Let us pray.
Pause for silent prayer, if this has not preceded.
**Lord,
as we celebrate this feast of the Blessed Virgin Mary,
you renew us with the body and blood of Christ your Son.
May this sacrament give us a share in his life,
for he is Lord for ever and ever.**

6. EASTER SEASON

Introductory Rites

> The disciples were constantly at prayer together, with Mary the mother of Jesus, alleluia. (See Acts 1:14)

OPENING PRAYER   Or:

God our Father,
you give joy to the world
by the resurrection of your Son, our Lord Jesus Christ.
Through the prayers of his mother, the Virgin Mary,
bring us to the happiness of eternal life.

We ask this through our Lord Jesus Christ, your Son,
who lives and reigns with you and the Holy Spirit,
one God, for ever and ever.

God our Father,
you gave the Holy Spirit to your apostles
as they joined in prayer with Mary, the mother of Jesus.
By the help of her prayers
keep us faithful in your service
and let our words and actions be so inspired
as to bring glory to your name.

Grant this through our Lord Jesus Christ, your Son,
who lives and reigns with you and the Holy Spirit,
one God, for ever and ever.

See Lectionary for Mass, nos. 707-712.

PRAYER OVER THE GIFTS   **Pray, brethren . . .**

Father,
as we celebrate the memory of the Virgin Mary,
we offer you our gifts and prayers.
Sustain us by the love of Christ,
who offered himself as a perfect sacrifice on the cross,
and is Lord for ever and ever.

Preface of the Blessed Virgin Mary I (feasts or memorials) or II (votive Masses), pages **473–474**.

Communion Rite

> Rejoice, virgin mother, for Christ has arisen from his grave, alleluia.

PRAYER AFTER COMMUNION   **Let us pray.**

Pause for silent prayer, if this has not preceded.

Lord,
may this sacrament strengthen the faith in our hearts.
May Mary's Son, Jesus Christ,
whom we proclaim to be God and man,
bring us to eternal life
by the saving power of his resurrection,
for he is Lord for ever and ever.

OTHER PRAYERS FOR MASSES
OF THE BLESSED VIRGIN MARY

OPENING PRAYER

**All-powerful God,
we rejoice in the protection of the holy Virgin Mary.
May her prayers help to free us from all evils here on earth
and lead us to eternal joy in heaven.**

**Grant this through our Lord Jesus Christ, your Son,
who lives and reigns with you and the Holy Spirit,
one God, for ever and ever.**

See Lectionary for Mass, nos. 707-712.

PRAYER OVER THE GIFTS

Pray, brethren . . .

**Lord,
accept the prayers and gifts we present today
as we honor Mary, the Mother of God.
May they please you
and bring us your forgiveness and help.**

We ask this in the name of Jesus the Lord.

PRAYER AFTER COMMUNION

Let us pray.
Pause for silent prayer, if this has not preceded.
**Lord,
we are renewed with the sacraments of salvation.
May we who celebrate the memory of the Mother of God
come to realize the eternal redemption you promise.**

We ask this through Christ our Lord.

COMMON OF MARTYRS

1. FOR SEVERAL MARTYRS, OUTSIDE THE EASTER SEASON

Introductory Rites

The saints are happy in heaven because they followed
Christ. They rejoice with him for ever because they shed
their blood for love of him.

OPENING PRAYER

**Father,
we celebrate the memory of Saints N. and N.
who died for their faithful witnessing to Christ.
Give us the strength to follow their example,
loyal and faithful to the end.**

**We ask this through our Lord Jesus Christ, your Son,
who lives and reigns with you and the Holy Spirit,
one God, for ever and ever.**

See Lectionary for Mass, nos. 713-718.

PRAYER OVER THE GIFTS

Pray, brethren . . .

**Father,
receive the gifts we bring
in memory of your holy martyrs.
Keep us strong in our faith
and in our witness to you.**

Grant this through Christ our Lord.

Communion Rite

You are the men who have stood by me faithfully in my
trials, and now I confer a kingdom on you, says the Lord.
You will eat and drink at my table in my kingdom. (Luke
22:28-30)

PRAYER AFTER COMMUNION

Let us pray.

Pause for silent prayer, if this has not preceded.

**God our Father,
in your holy martyrs you show us the glory of the cross.
Through this sacrifice, strengthen our resolution
to follow Christ faithfully
and to work in your Church for the salvation of all.**

We ask this through Christ our Lord.

2. FOR SEVERAL MARTYRS, OUTSIDE THE EASTER SEASON

Introductory Rites

Many are the sufferings of the just, and from them all the Lord has delivered them; the Lord preserves all their bones, not one of them shall be broken. (Ps. 33:20-21)

OPENING PRAYER

**All-powerful, ever-living God,
turn our weakness into strength.
As you gave your martyrs N. and N.
the courage to suffer death for Christ,
give us the courage to live in faithful witness to you.**

**Grant this through our Lord Jesus Christ, your Son,
who lives and reigns with you and the Holy Spirit,
one God, for ever and ever.**

See Lectionary for Mass, nos. 713-718.

PRAYER OVER THE GIFTS

Pray, brethren . . .

**Lord,
accept the gifts we bring
to celebrate the feast of your martyrs.
May this sacrifice free us from sin
and make our service pleasing to you.**

We ask this through Christ our Lord.

Communion Rite

No one has greater love, says the Lord, than the man who lays down his life for his friends. (John 15:13)

PRAYER AFTER COMMUNION

Let us pray.

Pause for silent prayer, if this has not preceded.

**Lord,
we eat the bread from heaven
and become one body in Christ.
Never let us be separated from his love
and help us to follow your martyrs N. and N.
by having the courage to overcome all things through Christ,
who loved us all,
and lives and reigns with you for ever and ever.**

3. FOR SEVERAL MARTYRS, OUTSIDE THE EASTER SEASON

Introductory Rites

The salvation of the just comes from the Lord. He is their strength in time of need. (Ps. 36:39)

OPENING PRAYER   Or:

Lord,
may the victory of your martyrs give us joy.
May their example strengthen our faith,
and their prayers give us renewed courage.
We ask this through our Lord Jesus Christ, your Son,
who lives and reigns with you and the Holy Spirit,
one God, for ever and ever.

Lord,
hear the prayers of the martyrs N. and N.
and give us courage to bear witness to your truth.
Grant this through our Lord Jesus Christ, your Son,
who lives and reigns with you and the Holy Spirit,
one God, for ever and ever.

See Lectionary for Mass, nos. 713-718.

PRAYER OVER THE GIFTS   **Pray, brethren . . .**

Lord,
accept the gifts of your people
as we honor the suffering and death
of your martyrs N. and N.
As the eucharist gave them strength in persecution
may it keep us faithful in every difficulty.

We ask this through Christ our Lord.

Communion Rite

Whoever loses his life for my sake and the gospel, says the Lord, will save it. (Mark 8:35)

PRAYER AFTER COMMUNION   **Let us pray.**

Pause for silent prayer, if this has not preceded.

Lord,
keep this eucharist effective within us.
May the gift we receive
on this feast of the martyrs N. and N.
bring us salvation and peace.

Grant this in the name of Jesus the Lord.

4. FOR SEVERAL MARTYRS, OUTSIDE THE EASTER SEASON

Introductory Rites

The Lord will hear the just when they cry out, from all their afflictions he will deliver them. (Ps. 33:18)

OPENING PRAYER

Or:

**God our Father,
every year you give us the joy
of celebrating this feast of Saints N. and N.
May we who recall their birth to eternal life
imitate their courage in suffering for you.**

**Grant this through our Lord Jesus Christ, your
Son,
who lives and reigns with you and the Holy
Spirit,
one God, for ever and ever.**

**God our Father,
your generous gift of love
brought Saints N. and N. to unending glory.
Through the prayers of your martyrs
forgive our sins and free us from every
danger.**

**We ask this through our Lord Jesus Christ,
your Son,
who lives and reigns with you and the Holy
Spirit,
one God, for ever and ever.**

See Lectionary for Mass, nos. 713-718.

PRAYER OVER THE GIFTS

Pray, brethren . . .

**Lord,
you gave Saints N. and N. the fulfillment of their faith
in the vision of your glory.
May the gifts we bring to honor their memory
gain us your pardon and peace.**

We ask this in the name of Jesus the Lord.

Communion Rite

We are given over to death for Jesus, that the life of Jesus may be revealed in our dying flesh. (2 Cor. 4:11)

PRAYER AFTER COMMUNION

Let us pray.
Pause for silent prayer, if this has not preceded.

**Lord,
may this food of heaven
bring us a share in the grace you gave the martyrs N. and N.
From their bitter sufferings may we learn to become strong
and by patient endurance earn the victory of rejoicing
in your holiness.**

Grant this through Christ our Lord.

5. FOR SEVERAL MARTYRS, OUTSIDE THE EASTER SEASON

Introductory Rites

The holy martyrs shed their blood on earth for Christ;
therefore they have received an everlasting reward.

OPENING PRAYER

Lord,
we honor your martyrs N. and N.
who were faithful to Christ
even to the point of shedding their blood for him.
Increase our own faith and free us from our sins,
and help us to follow their example of love.

We ask this through our Lord Jesus Christ, your Son,
who lives and reigns with you and the Holy Spirit,
one God, for ever and ever.

See Lectionary for Mass, nos. 713-718.

PRAYER OVER THE GIFTS

Pray, brethren . . .

Or:

Lord,
be pleased with the gifts we bring.
May we who celebrate the mystery of the
  passion of your Son
make this mystery part of our lives
by the inspiration of the martyrs N. and N.

Grant this through Christ our Lord.

Lord,
may these gifts which we bring you in sacrifice
to celebrate the victory of Saints N. and N.
fill our hearts with your love
and prepare us for the reward you promise
to those who are faithful.

We ask this in the name of Jesus the Lord.

Communion Rite

Neither death nor life nor anything in all creation can
come between us and Christ's love for us. (See Rom.
8:38-39)

PRAYER AFTER COMMUNION

Let us pray.
Pause for silent prayer, if this has not preceded.
Lord,
you give us the body and blood of Christ your only Son
on this feast of your martyrs N. and N.
By being faithful to your love
may we live in you,
receive life from you,
and always be true to your inspiration.

We ask this in the name of Jesus the Lord.

6. FOR ONE MARTYR, OUTSIDE THE EASTER SEASON

Introductory Rites

This holy man fought to the death for the law of his God, never cowed by the threats of the wicked; his house was built on solid rock.

OPENING PRAYER

**God of power and mercy,
you gave N., your martyr, victory over pain and suffering.
Strengthen us who celebrate this day of his triumph
and help us to be victorious over the evils that threaten us.**

**Grant this through our Lord Jesus Christ, your Son,
who lives and reigns with you and the Holy Spirit,
one God, for ever and ever.**

See Lectionary for Mass, nos. 713-718.

PRAYER OVER THE GIFTS

Pray, brethren . . .

Or:

**Lord,
bless our offerings and make them holy.
May these gifts fill our hearts
with the love which gave St. N. victory
over all his suffering.**

We ask this through Christ our Lord.

**Lord,
accept the gifts we offer in memory of the
martyr N.
May they be pleasing to you
as was the shedding of his blood for the faith.**

Grant this through Christ our Lord.

Communion Rite

If anyone wishes to come after me, he must renounce himself, take up his cross, and follow me, says the Lord. (Matthew 16:24)

PRAYER AFTER COMMUNION

Let us pray.
Pause for silent prayer, if this has not preceded.
**Lord,
may the mysteries we receive
give us the spiritual courage which made your martyr N.
faithful in your service and victorious in his suffering.**

Grant this in the name of Jesus the Lord.

7. FOR ONE MARTYR, OUTSIDE THE EASTER SEASON

Introductory Rites

Here is a true martyr who shed his blood for Christ; his judges could not shake him by their menaces, and so he won through to the kingdom of heaven.

OPENING PRAYER

All-powerful, ever-living God,
you gave St. N. the courage to witness to the gospel of Christ
even to the point of giving his life for it.
By his prayers help us to endure all suffering for love of you
and to seek you with all our hearts,
for you alone are the source of life.

Grant this through our Lord Jesus Christ, your Son,
who lives and reigns with you and the Holy Spirit,
one God, for ever and ever.

See Lectionary for Mass, nos. 713-718.

PRAYER OVER THE GIFTS   **Pray, brethren . . .**

                                             Or:

God of love,
pour out your blessing on our gifts
and make our faith strong,
the faith which St. N. professed by shedding
   his blood.
We ask this through Christ our Lord.
	Lord,
	accept these gifts we present in memory of St.
	   N.,
	for no temptation could turn him away from
	   you.
	We ask this through Christ our Lord.

Communion Rite

I am the vine and you are the branches, says the Lord; he who lives in me, and I in him, will bear much fruit. (John 15:5)

PRAYER AFTER COMMUNION

Let us pray.
Pause for silent prayer, if this has not preceded.
Lord,
we are renewed by the mystery of the eucharist.
By imitating the fidelity of St. N. and by your patience
may we come to share the eternal life you have promised.

We ask this in the name of Jesus the Lord.

8. FOR SEVERAL MARTYRS, IN THE EASTER SEASON

Introductory Rites

Come, you whom my Father has blessed; inherit the kingdom prepared for you since the foundation of the world, alleluia. (Matthew 25:34)

OPENING PRAYER

Father,
you gave your martyrs N. and N.
the courage to die in witness to Christ and the gospel.
By the power of your Holy Spirit,
give us the humility to believe
and the courage to profess
the faith for which they gave their lives.

We ask this through our Lord Jesus Christ, your Son,
who lives and reigns with you and the Holy Spirit,
one God, for ever and ever.

Or:

God our all-powerful Father,
you strengthen our faith
and take away our weakness.
Let the prayers and example of your martyrs N. and N. help us
to share in the passion and resurrection of Christ
and bring us to eternal joy with all your saints.

We ask this through our Lord Jesus Christ, your Son,
who lives and reigns with you and the Holy Spirit,
one God, for ever and ever.

See Lectionary for Mass, nos. 713-718.

PRAYER OVER THE GIFTS

Pray, brethren . . .

Lord,
we celebrate the death of your holy martyrs.
May we offer the sacrifice which gives all martyrdom its meaning.

Grant this through Christ our Lord.

Communion Rite

Those who are victorious I will feed from the tree of life, which grows in the paradise of my God, alleluia. (Rev. 2:7)

PRAYER AFTER COMMUNION

Let us pray.
Pause for silent prayer, if this has not preceded.
Lord,
at this holy meal
we celebrate the heavenly victory of your martyrs N. and N.
May this bread of life
give us the courage to conquer evil,
so that we may come to share the fruit of the tree of life in paradise.

We ask this through Christ our Lord.

9. FOR SEVERAL MARTYRS, IN THE EASTER SEASON

Introductory Rites

These are the saints who were victorious in the blood of
the Lamb, and in the face of death they did not cling to life;
therefore they are reigning with Christ for ever, alleluia.
(Rev. 12:11)

OPENING PRAYER

Lord,
you gave your martyrs N. and N.
the privilege of shedding their blood
in boldly proclaiming the death and resurrection of your Son.
May this celebration of their victory give them honor
    among your people.

We ask this through our Lord Jesus Christ, your Son,
who lives and reigns with you and the Holy Spirit,
one God, for ever and ever.

See Lectionary for Mass, nos. 713-718.

PRAYER OVER THE GIFTS   Pray, brethren . . .

Lord,
fill these gifts with the blessing of your Holy Spirit
and fill our hearts with the love
which gave victory to Saints N. and N.
in dying for the faith.

We ask this through Christ our Lord.

Communion Rite

If we die with Christ, we shall live with him, and if we are
faithful to the end, we shall reign with him, alleluia. (2 Tim.
2:11-12)

PRAYER AFTER COMMUNION   Let us pray.
Pause for silent prayer, if this has not preceded.
Lord,
we are renewed by the breaking of one bread
in honor of the martyrs N. and N.
Keep us in your love
and help us to live the new life Christ won for us.

Grant this in the name of Jesus the Lord.

10. FOR ONE MARTYR, IN THE EASTER SEASON

Introductory Rites

Light for ever will shine on your saints, O Lord, alleluia.
(See 4 Esdras 2:35)

OPENING PRAYER

God our Father,
you have honored the Church with the victorious witness of
    St. N.,
who died for his faith.
As he imitated the sufferings and death of the Lord,
may we follow in his footsteps and come to eternal joy.

We ask this through our Lord Jesus Christ, your Son,
who lives and reigns with you and the Holy Spirit,
one God, for ever and ever.

See Lectionary for Mass, nos. 713-718.

PRAYER OVER THE GIFTS

Pray, brethren . . .

Lord,
accept this offering of praise and peace
in memory of your martyr N.
May it bring us your forgiveness
and inspire us to give you thanks now and for ever.

Grant this in the name of Jesus the Lord.

Communion Rite

I tell you solemnly: Unless a grain of wheat falls on the
ground and dies, it remains a single grain; but if it dies, it
yields a rich harvest, alleluia. (John 12:24-25)

PRAYER AFTER COMMUNION

Let us pray.
Pause for silent prayer, if this has not preceded.
Lord,
we receive your gifts from heaven
at this joyful feast.
May we who proclaim at this holy table
the death and resurrection of your Son
come to share his glory with all your holy martyrs.

Grant this through Christ our Lord.

OTHER PRAYERS FOR MARTYRS

For Missionary Martyrs

OPENING PRAYER

God of mercy and love,
through the preaching of your martyrs N. and N.
you brought the good news of Christ
to people who had not known him.
May the prayers of Saints N. and N.
make our own faith grow stronger.

We ask this through our Lord Jesus Christ, your Son,
who lives and reigns with you and the Holy Spirit,
one God, for ever and ever.

See Lectionary for Mass, nos. 713-718.

PRAYER OVER THE GIFTS

Pray, brethren . . .

Lord,
at this celebration of the eucharist
we honor the suffering and death of your martyrs N. and N.
In offering this sacrifice
may we proclaim the death of your Son
who gave these martyrs courage not only by his words
but also by the example of his own passion,
for he is Lord for ever and ever.

PRAYER AFTER COMMUNION

Let us pray.
Pause for silent prayer, if this has not preceded.
Lord,
may we who eat at your holy table
be inspired by the example of Saints N. and N.
May we keep before us the loving sacrifice of your Son,
and come to the unending peace of your kingdom.

We ask this in the name of Jesus the Lord.

For a Virgin Martyr

OPENING PRAYER

**God our Father,
you give us joy each year
in honoring the memory of St. N.
May her prayers be a source of help for us,
and may her example of courage and chastity be
 our inspiration.**

**Grant this through our Lord Jesus Christ, your Son,
who lives and reigns with you and the Holy Spirit,
one God, for ever and ever.**

See Lectionary for Mass, nos. 713-718.

PRAYER OVER THE GIFTS

Pray, brethren . . .

**Lord,
receive our gifts
as you accepted the suffering and death of St. N.
in whose honor we celebrate this eucharist.**

We ask this through Christ our Lord.

PRAYER AFTER COMMUNION

Let us pray.
Pause for silent prayer, if this has not preceded.
**Lord God,
you gave St. N. the crown of eternal joy
because she gave her life
rather than renounce the virginity she had promised
in witness to Christ.
With the courage this eucharist brings
help us to rise out of the bondage of our earthly desires
and attain to the glory of your kingdom.**

Grant this through Christ our Lord.

For a Holy Woman Martyr

OPENING PRAYER

Father,
in our weakness your power reaches perfection.
You gave St. N. the strength
to defeat the power of sin and evil.
May we who celebrate her glory share in her triumph.

We ask this through our Lord Jesus Christ, your Son,
who lives and reigns with you and the Holy Spirit,
one God, for ever and ever.

See Lectionary for Mass, nos. 713-718.

PRAYER OVER THE GIFTS

Pray, brethren . . .

Lord,
today we offer this sacrifice in joy
as we recall the victory of St. N.
May we proclaim to others the great things
you have done for us
and rejoice in the constant help of your martyr's prayers.

Grant this through Christ our Lord.

PRAYER AFTER COMMUNION

Let us pray.
Pause for silent prayer, if this has not preceded.
Lord,
by this sacrament you give us eternal joys
as we recall the memory of St. N.
May we always embrace the gift of life
we celebrate at this eucharist.

We ask this in the name of Jesus the Lord.

COMMON OF PASTORS

1. FOR POPES OR BISHOPS

Introductory Rites

The Lord chose him to be his high priest; he opened his treasures and made him rich in all goodness.

OPENING PRAYER

(for popes)

All-powerful and ever-living God,
you called St. N. to guide your people
by his word and example.
With him we pray to you:
watch over the pastors of your Church
with the people entrusted to their care,
and lead them to salvation.

We ask this through our Lord Jesus Christ,
   your Son,
who lives and reigns with you and the Holy
   Spirit,
one God, for ever and ever.

Or (for bishops):

Father,
you gave St. N. to your Church
as an example of a good shepherd.
May his prayers
help us on our way to eternal life.

Grant this through our Lord Jesus Christ, your
   Son,
who lives and reigns with you and the Holy
   Spirit,
one God, for ever and ever.

See Lectionary for Mass, nos. 719-724.

PRAYER OVER THE GIFTS

Pray, brethren . . .

Lord,
we offer you this sacrifice of praise
in memory of your saints.
May their prayers keep us from evil
now and in the future.

Grant this through Christ our Lord.

Communion Rite

The good shepherd gives his life for his sheep. (See John 10:11)

PRAYER AFTER COMMUNION

Let us pray.

Pause for silent prayer, if this has not preceded.

Lord God,
St. N. loved you
and gave himself completely in the service of your Church.
May the eucharist awaken in us that same love.

We ask this in the name of Jesus the Lord.

717

2. FOR POPES OR BISHOPS

Introductory Rites

The Lord sealed a covenant of peace with him, and made him a prince, bestowing the priestly dignity upon him for ever. (See Sir. 45:30)

OPENING PRAYER

(for popes)

Father,
you made St. N. shepherd of the whole
   Church
and gave to us the witness of his virtue and
   teaching.
Today as we honor this outstanding bishop,
we ask that our light may shine before men
and that our love for you may be sincere.

Grant this through our Lord Jesus Christ, your
   Son,
who lives and reigns with you and the Holy
   Spirit,
one God, for ever and ever.

Or (for bishops):

All-powerful God,
you made St. N. a bishop and leader of the
   Church
to inspire your people with his teaching and
   example.
May we give fitting honor to his memory
and always have the assistance of his prayers.

We ask this through our Lord Jesus Christ,
   your Son,
who lives and reigns with you and the Holy
   Spirit,
one God, for ever and ever.

See Lectionary for Mass, nos. 719-724.

PRAYER OVER THE GIFTS   **Pray, brethren . . .**

Lord,
may the sacrifice which wipes away the sins
   of all the world
bring us your forgiveness.
Help us as we offer it
on this yearly feast in honor of St. N.

Grant this through Christ our Lord.

Communion Rite

Lord, you know all things: you know that I love you. (John 21:17)

PRAYER AFTER COMMUNION   **Let us pray.**

Pause for silent prayer, if this has not preceded.
Lord God,
let the power of the gifts we receive
on this feast of St. N.
take full effect within us.
May this eucharist bring us your help in this life
and lead us to happiness in the unending life to come.

We ask this through Christ our Lord.

3. FOR BISHOPS

Introductory Rites

I will look after my sheep, says the Lord, and I will raise up
one shepherd who will pasture them. I, the Lord, will be
their God. (Ezek. 34:11, 23-24)

OPENING PRAYER

**All-powerful, ever-living God,
you made St. N. bishop and leader of your people.
May his prayers help to bring us your forgiveness and love.**

**We ask this through our Lord Jesus Christ, your Son,
who lives and reigns with you and the Holy Spirit,
one God, for ever and ever.**

See Lectionary for Mass, nos. 719-724.

PRAYER OVER THE GIFTS

Pray, brethren . . .

**Lord,
accept the gifts we bring to your holy altar
on this feast of St. N.
May our offering bring honor to your name
and pardon to your people.**

We ask this through Christ our Lord.

Communion Rite

You have not chosen me; I have chosen you. Go and bear
fruit that will last. (John 15:16)

PRAYER AFTER COMMUNION

Let us pray.
Pause for silent prayer, if this has not preceded.
**Lord,
may we who receive this sacrament
be inspired by the example of St. N.
May we learn to proclaim what he believed
and put his teaching into action.**

We ask this in the name of Jesus the Lord.

4. FOR BISHOPS

Introductory Rites

I will raise up for myself a faithful priest; he will do what is
in my heart and in my mind, says the Lord. (1 Sam. 2:35)

OPENING PRAYER

**Lord God,
you counted St. N. among your holy pastors,
renowned for faith and love which conquered evil in this
      world.
By the help of his prayers
keep us strong in faith and love
and let us come to share his glory.**

**Grant this through our Lord Jesus Christ, your Son,
who lives and reigns with you and the Holy Spirit,
one God, for ever and ever.**

See Lectionary for Mass, nos. 719-724.

PRAYER OVER THE GIFTS

Pray, brethren . . .

**Lord,
accept the gifts your people offer you
on this feast of St. N.
May these gifts bring us
your help for which we long.**

We ask this through Christ our Lord.

Communion Rite

I came that men may have life, and have it to the full, says
the Lord. (John 10:10)

PRAYER AFTER COMMUNION

Let us pray.

Pause for silent prayer, if this has not preceded.

**Lord our God,
you give us the holy body and blood
of your Son.
May the salvation we celebrate
be our undying hope.**

Grant this through Christ our Lord.

5. FOR PASTORS

Introductory Rites

> The Spirit of God is upon me; he has anointed me. He sent me to bring good news to the poor, and to heal the broken-hearted. (Luke 4:18)

OPENING PRAYER

**God our Father,
in St. (bishop) N. you gave
a light to your faithful people.
You made him a pastor of the Church
to feed your sheep with his word
and to teach them by his example.
Help us by his prayers to keep the faith he taught
and follow the way of life he showed us.**

**Grant this through our Lord Jesus Christ, your Son,
who lives and reigns with you and the Holy Spirit,
one God, for ever and ever.**

See Lectionary for Mass, nos. 719-724.

PRAYER OVER THE GIFTS

Pray, brethren . . .

**Father of mercy,
we have these gifts to offer in honor of your saints
who bore witness to your mighty power.
May the power of the eucharist
bring us your salvation.**

Grant this through Christ our Lord.

Communion Rite

> I, the Lord, am with you always, until the end of the world. (Matthew 28:20)

PRAYER AFTER COMMUNION

Let us pray.

Pause for silent prayer, if this has not preceded.

**Lord,
may the mysteries we receive
prepare us for the eternal joys
St. N. won by his faithful ministry.**

We ask this in the name of Jesus the Lord.

Or:

**All-powerful God,
by our love and worship
may we who share this holy meal
always follow the example of St. N.**

Grant this in the name of Jesus the Lord.

6. FOR PASTORS

Introductory Rites

I will give you shepherds after my own heart, and they shall feed you on knowledge and sound teaching. (Jer. 3:15)

or:

Priests of God, bless the Lord; praise God, all you that are holy and humble of heart. (Dan. 3:84, 87)

OPENING PRAYER

Lord God,
you gave your Saints (bishops) N. and N.
the spirit of truth and love
to shepherd your people.
May we who honor them on this feast
learn from their example
and be helped by their prayers.

We ask this through our Lord Jesus Christ, your Son,
who lives and reigns with you and the Holy Spirit,
one God, for ever and ever.

See Lectionary for Mass, nos. 719-724.

PRAYER OVER THE GIFTS

Pray, brethren . . .

Lord,
accept these gifts from your people.
May the eucharist we offer to your glory
in honor of Saints N. and N.
help us on our way to salvation.

Grant this in the name of Jesus the Lord.

Communion Rite

The Son of Man did not come to be served, but to serve, and to give his life as a ransom for many. (Matthew 20:28)

PRAYER AFTER COMMUNION

Let us pray.

Pause for silent prayer, if this has not preceded.

Lord,
we receive the bread of heaven
as we honor the memory of your Saints N. and N.
May the eucharist we now celebrate
lead us to eternal joys.

Grant this in the name of Jesus the Lord.

7. FOR PASTORS

Introductory Rites
Lord, may your priests be clothed in justice, and your holy ones leap for joy. (Ps. 131:9)

OPENING PRAYER

**All-powerful God,
hear the prayers of Saints N. and N.
Increase your gifts within us
and give us peace in our days.**

**We ask this through our Lord Jesus Christ, your Son,
who lives and reigns with you and the Holy Spirit,
one God, for ever and ever.**

See Lectionary for Mass, nos. 719-724.

PRAYER OVER THE GIFTS

Pray, brethren . . .

**Lord,
accept the gifts we bring to your altar
in memory of your Saints N. and N.
As you led them to glory through these mysteries,
grant us also your pardon and love.**

We ask this in the name of Jesus the Lord.

Communion Rite
Blessed is the servant whom the Lord finds watching when he comes; truly I tell you, he will set him over all his possessions. (Matthew 24:46-47)

or:

The Lord has put his faithful servant in charge of his household, to give them their share of bread at the proper time. (Luke 12:42)

PRAYER AFTER COMMUNION

Let us pray.
Pause for silent prayer, if this has not preceded.
**All-powerful God,
by the eucharist we share at your holy table
on this feast of Saints N. and N.
increase our strength of character and love for you.
May we guard from every danger the faith you have given us
and walk always in the way that leads to salvation.**

Grant this in the name of Jesus the Lord.

8. FOR FOUNDERS OF CHURCHES

Introductory Rites

My words that I have put in your mouth, says the Lord, will never be absent from your lips, and your gifts will be accepted on my altar. (Is. 59:21; 56:7)

OPENING PRAYER   Or:

God of mercy,
you gave our fathers the light of faith
through the preaching of St. N.
May we who glory in the Christian name
show in our lives the faith we profess.

We ask this through our Lord Jesus Christ,
  your Son,
who lives and reigns with you and the Holy
  Spirit,
one God, for ever and ever.

Lord,
look upon the family whom your St. (bishop)
  N. brought to life
with the word of truth
and nourished with the sacrament of life.
By his ministry you gave us the faith;
by his prayers help us grow in love.

Grant this through our Lord Jesus Christ, your
  Son,
who lives and reigns with you and the Holy
  Spirit,
one God, for ever and ever.

See Lectionary for Mass, nos. 719-724.

PRAYER OVER THE GIFTS   **Pray, brethren . . .**

Lord,
may the gifts your people bring
in memory of St. N.
bring us your gifts from heaven.

We ask this in the name of Jesus the Lord.

Communion Rite

The Son of Man came to give his life as a ransom for many.
(Mark 10:45)

PRAYER AFTER COMMUNION   **Let us pray.**

Pause for silent prayer, if this has not preceded.

Lord,
may this pledge of our eternal salvation
which we receive on this feast of St. N.
be our help now and always.

Grant this through Christ our Lord.

9. FOR FOUNDERS OF CHURCHES

Introductory Rites

The Lord chose these holy men for their unfeigned love, and gave them eternal glory. The Church has light by their teaching.

OPENING PRAYER

Lord,
look with love on the church of N.
Through the apostolic zeal of Saints N. and N.
you gave us the beginnings of our faith:
through their prayers keep alive our Christian love.
We ask this through our Lord Jesus Christ, your Son,
who lives and reigns with you and the Holy Spirit,
one God, for ever and ever.

Or:

Lord,
you called our fathers to the light of the gospel
by the preaching of your bishop N.
By his prayers help us to grow in the love and knowledge
of your Son, our Lord Jesus Christ,
who lives and reigns with you and the Holy Spirit,
one God, for ever and ever.

See Lectionary for Mass, nos. 719-724.

PRAYER OVER THE GIFTS

Pray, brethren . . .

Lord,
accept the gifts your people bring
on this feast of Saints N. and N.
Give us purity of heart
and make us pleasing to you.

We ask this through Christ our Lord.

Communion Rite

No longer shall I call you servants, for a servant knows not what his master does. Now I shall call you friends, for I have revealed to you all that I have heard from my Father.
(John 15:15)

PRAYER AFTER COMMUNION

Let us pray.

Pause for silent prayer, if this has not preceded.

Lord,
as we share in your gifts,
we celebrate this feast of Saints N. and N.
We honor the beginnings of our faith
and proclaim your glory in the saints.
May the salvation we receive from your altar
be our unending joy.

Grant this through Christ our Lord.

10. FOR MISSIONARIES

Introductory Rites

These are holy men who became God's friends and glorious heralds of his truth.

OPENING PRAYER

Father,
through your St. (bishop) N.
you brought those who had no faith
out of darkness into the light of truth.
By the help of his prayers,
keep us strong in our faith
and firm in the hope of the gospel he
   preached.

Grant this through our Lord Jesus Christ, your
   Son,
who lives and reigns with you and the Holy
   Spirit,
one God, for ever and ever.

Or:

All-powerful and ever-living God,
you made this day holy
by welcoming St. N. into the glory of your
   kingdom.
Keep us true to the faith he professed with
   untiring zeal,
and help us to bring it to perfection by acting in
   love.

We ask this through our Lord Jesus Christ,
   your Son,
who lives and reigns with you and the Holy
   Spirit,
one God, for ever and ever.

See Lectionary for Mass, nos. 719-724.

PRAYER OVER THE GIFTS

Pray, brethren . . .

All-powerful God,
look upon the gifts we bring on this feast
in honor of St. N.
May we who celebrate the mystery of the death of the Lord
imitate the love we celebrate.

We ask this through Christ our Lord.

Communion Rite

I will feed my sheep, says the Lord, and give them repose.
(Ezek. 34:15)

PRAYER AFTER COMMUNION

Let us pray.
Pause for silent prayer, if this has not preceded.
Lord,
St. N. worked tirelessly for the faith,
spending his life in its service.
With the power this eucharist gives
make your people strong in the same true faith
and help us to proclaim it everywhere
by all we say and do.

Grant this in the name of Jesus the Lord.

11. FOR MISSIONARIES

Introductory Rites

How beautiful on the mountains are the feet of the man
who brings tidings of peace, joy and salvation. (Is. 52:7)

OPENING PRAYER

**Father,
you made your Church grow
through the Christian zeal and apostolic work of St. N.
By the help of his prayers
give your Church continued growth in holiness and faith.**

**Grant this through our Lord Jesus Christ, your Son,
who lives and reigns with you and the Holy Spirit,
one God, for ever and ever.**

See Lectionary for Mass, nos. 719-724.

PRAYER OVER THE GIFTS

Pray, brethren . . .

**Lord,
be pleased with our prayers
and free us from all guilt.
In your love, wash away our sins
that we may celebrate the mysteries which set us free.**

Grant this in the name of Jesus the Lord.

Communion Rite

Go out to all the world, and tell the good news: I am with
you always, says the Lord. (Mark 16:15; Matthew 28:20)
or:
Live in me and let me live in you, says the Lord; he who
lives in me, and I in him, will bear much fruit. (John 15:4-5)

PRAYER AFTER COMMUNION

Let us pray.
Pause for silent prayer, if this has not preceded.
**Lord our God,
by these mysteries help our faith grow to maturity
in the faith the apostles preached and taught,
and the faith which St. N. watched over with such care.**

We ask this through Christ our Lord.

12. FOR MISSIONARIES

Introductory Rites

Proclaim his glory among the nations, his marvelous deeds to all the peoples; great is the Lord and worthy of all praise. (Ps. 95:3-4)

OPENING PRAYER

Or (for martyrs):

**God of mercy,
you gave us St. N. to proclaim the riches of Christ.
By the help of his prayers
may we grow in knowledge of you,
be eager to do good,
and learn to walk before you
by living the truth of the gospel.**

**Grant this through our Lord Jesus Christ, your Son,
who lives and reigns with you and the Holy Spirit,
one God, for ever and ever.**

**All-powerful God,
help us to imitate with steadfast love
the faith of Saints N. and N.
who won the crown of martyrdom
by giving their lives in the service of the gospel.**

**We ask this through our Lord Jesus Christ, your Son,
who lives and reigns with you and the Holy Spirit,
one God, for ever and ever.**

See Lectionary for Mass, nos. 719-724.

PRAYER OVER THE GIFTS   **Pray, brethren . . .**

**Lord,
we who honor the memory of St. N.
ask you to send your blessing on these gifts.
By receiving them may we be freed from all guilt
and share in the food from the heavenly table.**

We ask this through Christ our Lord.

Communion Rite

The Lord sent disciples to proclaim to all the towns: the kingdom of God is very near to you. (See Luke 10:1, 9)

PRAYER AFTER COMMUNION   **Let us pray.**

Pause for silent prayer, if this has not preceded.

**Lord,
let the holy gifts we receive fill us with life
so that we who rejoice in honoring the memory of St. N.
may also benefit from his example of apostolic zeal.**

Grant this through Christ our Lord.

COMMON OF DOCTORS OF THE CHURCH

1

See Lectionary for Mass, nos. 725-730.

Introductory Rites

The Lord opened his mouth in the assembly, and filled him with the spirit of wisdom and understanding, and clothed him in a robe of glory. (Sir. 15:5)

or:

The mouth of the just man utters wisdom, and his tongue speaks what is right; the law of his God is in his heart. (Ps. 36:30-31)

OPENING PRAYER

God our Father,
you made your St. (bishop) N. a teacher in your Church.
By the power of the Holy Spirit
establish his teaching in our hearts.
As you give him to us as a patron,
may we have the protection of his prayers.

Grant this through our Lord Jesus Christ, your Son,
who lives and reigns with you and the Holy Spirit,
one God, for ever and ever.

See Lectionary for Mass, nos. 725-730.

PRAYER OVER THE GIFTS

Pray, brethren . . .

Lord,
accept our sacrifice on this feast of St. N.,
and following his example
may we give you our praise
and offer you all we have.

Grant this in the name of Jesus the Lord.

Communion Rite

The Lord has put his faithful servant in charge of his household, to give them their share of bread at the proper time. (Luke 12:42)

PRAYER AFTER COMMUNION

Let us pray.
Pause for silent prayer, if this has not preceded.
God our Father,
Christ the living bread renews us.
Let Christ our teacher instruct us
that on this feast of St. N.
we may learn your truth
and practice it in love.

We ask this through Christ our Lord.

2

Introductory Rites

> The learned will shine like the brilliance of the firmament, and those who train many in the ways of justice will sparkle like the stars for all eternity. (Dan. 12:3)
>
> or:
>
> Let the peoples declare the wisdom of the saints and the Church proclaim their praises; their names shall live for ever. (See Sir. 44:15, 14)

OPENING PRAYER

**Lord God,
you filled St. N. with heavenly wisdom.
By his (her) help may we remain true to his (her) teaching
and put it into practice.**

**We ask this through our Lord Jesus Christ, your Son,
who lives and reigns with you and the Holy Spirit,
one God, for ever and ever.**

See Lectionary for Mass, nos. 725-730.

PRAYER OVER THE GIFTS

Pray, brethren . . .

**Lord,
by this celebration,
may your Spirit fill us with the same light of faith
that shines in the teaching of St. N.**

We ask this through Christ our Lord.

Communion Rite

> We preach a Christ who was crucified; he is the power and the wisdom of God. (1 Cor. 1:23-24)

PRAYER AFTER COMMUNION

Let us pray.

Pause for silent prayer, if this has not preceded.

**Lord,
you renew us with the food of heaven.
May St. N. remain our teacher and example
and keep us thankful for all we have received.**

Grant this in the name of Jesus the Lord.

COMMON OF VIRGINS

1

Introductory Rites

Here is a wise and faithful virgin who went with lighted lamp to meet her Lord.

OPENING PRAYER

God our Savior,
as we celebrate with joy the memory of the virgin N.,
may we learn from her example of faithfulness and love.

We ask this through our Lord Jesus Christ, your Son,
who lives and reigns with you and the Holy Spirit,
one God, for ever and ever.

See Lectionary for Mass, nos. 731-736.

PRAYER OVER THE GIFTS

Pray, brethren . . .

Lord,
we see the wonder of your love
in the life of the virgin N.
and her witness to Christ.
Accept our gifts of praise
and make our offering pleasing to you.

Grant this through Christ our Lord.

Communion Rite

The bridegroom is here; let us go out to meet Christ the Lord. (Matthew 25:6)

PRAYER AFTER COMMUNION

Let us pray.
Pause for silent prayer, if this has not preceded.
Lord God,
may this eucharist renew our courage and strength.
May we remain close to you, like St. N.,
by accepting in our lives
a share in the suffering of Jesus Christ,
who lives and reigns with you for ever and ever.

2

Introductory Rites

Let us rejoice and shout for joy, because the Lord of all things has favored this holy and glorious virgin with his love.

OPENING PRAYER

Or (for a virgin foundress):

**Lord God,
you endowed the virgin N. with gifts from heaven.
By imitating her goodness here on earth
may we come to share her joy in eternal life.**

**We ask this through our Lord Jesus Christ, your Son,
who lives and reigns with you and the Holy Spirit,
one God, for ever and ever.**

**Lord our God,
may the witness of your faithful bride the virgin N.
awaken the fire of divine love in our hearts.
May it inspire other young women to give their lives
to the service of Christ and his Church.**

**Grant this through our Lord Jesus Christ, your Son,
who lives and reigns with you and the Holy Spirit,
one God, for ever and ever.**

See Lectionary for Mass, nos. 731-736.

PRAYER OVER THE GIFTS

Pray, brethren . . .

**Lord,
may the gifts we bring you
help us follow the example of St. N.
Cleanse us from our earthly way of life,
and teach us to live the new life of your kingdom.**

We ask this through Christ our Lord.

Communion Rite

The five sensible virgins took flasks of oil as well as their lamps. At midnight a cry was heard: the bridegroom is here; let us go out to meet Christ the Lord. (Matthew 25:4, 6)

PRAYER AFTER COMMUNION

Let us pray.

Pause for silent prayer, if this has not preceded.

**Lord,
may our reception of the body and blood of your Son
keep us from harmful things.
Help us by the example of St. N.
to grow in your love on earth
that we may rejoice for ever in heaven.**

We ask this in the name of Jesus the Lord.

3

Introductory Rites

Come, bride of Christ, and receive the crown, which the
Lord has prepared for you for ever.

OPENING PRAYER

Or:

Lord,
you have told us that you live for ever
in the hearts of the chaste.
By the prayers of the virgin N.,
help us to live by your grace
and remain a temple of your Spirit.

Grant this through our Lord Jesus Christ, your
Son,
who lives and reigns with you and the Holy
Spirit,
one God, for ever and ever.

Lord,
hear the prayers of those who recall the devoted life of the virgin N.
Guide us on our way and help us to grow
in love and devotion as long as we live.

We ask this through our Lord Jesus Christ,
your Son,
who lives and reigns with you and the Holy
Spirit,
one God, for ever and ever.

See Lectionary for Mass, nos. 731-736.

PRAYER OVER THE GIFTS

Pray, brethren . . .

Lord,
receive our worship in memory of N. the virgin.
By this perfect sacrifice
make us grow in unselfish love for you
and for our brothers.

We ask this through Christ our Lord.

Communion Rite

The wise virgin chose the better part for herself, and it
shall not be taken away from her. (See Luke 10:42)

PRAYER AFTER COMMUNION

Let us pray.
Pause for silent prayer, if this has not preceded.
God of mercy,
we rejoice that on this feast of St. N.
you give us the bread of heaven.
May it bring us pardon for our sins,
health of body,
your grace in this life,
and glory in heaven.

Grant this through Christ our Lord.

4

Introductory Rites

Let virgins praise the name of the Lord, for his name alone
is supreme; its majesty outshines both earth and heaven.
(Ps. 148:12-14)

OPENING PRAYER

**Lord,
increase in us your gifts of mercy and forgiveness.
May we who rejoice at this celebration
in honor of the virgins N. and N.
receive the joy of sharing eternal life with them.**

**We ask this through our Lord Jesus Christ, your Son,
who lives and reigns with you and the Holy Spirit,
one God, for ever and ever.**

See Lectionary for Mass, nos. 731-736.

PRAYER OVER THE GIFTS

Pray, brethren . . .

**Lord,
we bring you our gifts and prayers.
We praise your glory on this feast of the virgins N. and N.,
whose witness to Christ was pleasing to you.
Be pleased also with the eucharist we now offer.**

Grant this through Christ our Lord.

Communion Rite

The bridegroom has come, and the virgins who were
ready have gone in with him to the wedding. (Matthew
25:10)

or:

Whoever loves me will be loved by my Father. We shall
come to him and make our home with him. (John 14:21,
23)

PRAYER AFTER COMMUNION

Let us pray.
Pause for silent prayer, if this has not preceded.
**Lord,
may the mysteries we receive
on this feast of the virgins N. and N.
keep us alert and ready to welcome your Son at his return,
that he may welcome us to the feast of eternal life.**

Grant this through Christ our Lord.

COMMON OF HOLY MEN AND WOMEN

The following Masses, if indicated for
a particular rank of saints, are used
for saints of that rank. If no indication
is given, the Masses may be used for
saints of any rank.

1

Introductory Rites

> May all your works praise you, Lord, and your saints bless
> you; they will tell of the glory of your kingdom and pro-
> claim your power. (Ps. 144:10-11)

OPENING PRAYER

Ever-living God,
the signs of your love are manifest
in the honor you give your saints.
May their prayers and their example encourage us
to follow your Son more faithfully.

We ask this through our Lord Jesus Christ, your Son,
who lives and reigns with you and the Holy Spirit,
one God, for ever and ever.

See Lectionary for Mass, nos. 737-742.

PRAYER OVER THE GIFTS

Pray, brethren . . .

Lord,
in your kindness hear our prayers
and the prayers which the saints offer on our behalf.
Watch over us that we may offer fitting service at your altar.

Grant this in the name of Jesus the Lord.

Communion Rite

> May the just rejoice as they feast in God's presence, and
> delight in gladness of heart. (Ps. 67:4)
> or:
> Blessed are those servants whom the Lord finds watching
> when he comes; truly I tell you, he will seat them at his
> table and wait on them. (Luke 12:37)

PRAYER AFTER COMMUNION

Let us pray.
Pause for silent prayer, if this has not preceded.
Father, our comfort and peace,
we have gathered as your family
to praise your name and honor your saints.
Let the sacrament we have received
be the sign and pledge of our salvation.

We ask this through Christ our Lord.

2

Introductory Rites

> The just man will rejoice in the Lord and hope in him, and
> all the upright of heart will be praised. (Ps. 63:11)

OPENING PRAYER

**God our Father,
you alone are holy;
without you nothing is good.
Trusting in the prayers of St. N.
we ask you to help us
to become the holy people you call us to be.
Never let us be found undeserving
of the glory you have prepared for us.**

**We ask this through our Lord Jesus Christ, your Son,
who lives and reigns with you and the Holy Spirit,
one God, for ever and ever.**

See Lectionary for Mass, nos. 737-742.

PRAYER OVER THE GIFTS

Pray, brethren . . .

**All-powerful God,
may the gifts we present
bring honor to your saints,
and free us from sin in mind and body.**

We ask this in the name of Jesus the Lord.

Communion Rite

> He who serves me, follows me, says the Lord; and where I
> am, my servant will also be. (John 12:26)

PRAYER AFTER COMMUNION

Let us pray.

Pause for silent prayer, if this has not preceded.

**Lord,
your sacramental gifts renew us
at this celebration of the birth of your saints to glory.
May the good things you give us
lead us to the joy of your kingdom.**

We ask this through Christ our Lord.

3

Introductory Rites

Lord, your strength gives joy to the just; they greatly delight in your saving help. You have granted them their heart's desire. (Ps. 20:2-3)

OPENING PRAYER

Father,
your saints guide us when in our weakness we tend to stray.
Help us who celebrate the birth of St. N. to glory
grow closer to you by following his (her) example.

We ask this through our Lord Jesus Christ, your Son,
who lives and reigns with you and the Holy Spirit,
one God, for ever and ever.

See Lectionary for Mass, nos. 737-742.

PRAYER OVER THE GIFTS

Pray, brethren . . .

Lord,
let the sacrifice we offer
in memory of St. N.
bring to your people the gifts of unity and peace.

Grant this in the name of Jesus the Lord.

Communion Rite

If anyone wishes to come after me, he must renounce himself, take up his cross, and follow me, says the Lord. (Matthew 16:24)

PRAYER AFTER COMMUNION

Let us pray.
Pause for silent prayer, if this has not preceded.
Lord,
may the sacraments we receive
on this feast in honor of St. N.
give us holiness of mind and body
and bring us into your divine life.

We ask this through Christ our Lord.

4

Introductory Rites

The teaching of truth was in his mouth, and no wrong was found on his lips; he walked with me in peace and justice, and turned many away from wickedness. (Mal. 2:6)

OPENING PRAYER

**Merciful Father,
we fail because of our weakness.
Restore us to your love
through the example of your saints.**

**We ask this through our Lord Jesus Christ, your Son,
who lives and reigns with you and the Holy Spirit,
one God, for ever and ever.**

See Lectionary for Mass, nos. 737-742.

PRAYER OVER THE GIFTS

Pray, brethren . . .

**Lord,
may this sacrifice we share
on the feast of St. N.
give you praise
and help us on our way to salvation.**

Grant this in the name of Jesus the Lord.

Communion Rite

Happy are the pure of heart, for they shall see God. Happy the peacemakers; they shall be called sons of God. Happy are they who suffer persecution for justice' sake; the kingdom of heaven is theirs. (Matthew 5:8-10)

PRAYER AFTER COMMUNION

Let us pray.
Pause for silent prayer, if this has not preceded.
**Lord,
our hunger is satisfied by your holy gift.
May we who have celebrated this eucharist
experience in our lives the salvation which it brings.**

We ask this in the name of Jesus the Lord.

5

Introductory Rites

The just man will flourish like the palm tree. Planted in the
courts of God's house, he will grow great like the cedars of
Lebanon. (Ps. 91:13-14)

OPENING PRAYER

Lord,
may the prayers of the saints
bring help to your people.
Give to us who celebrate the memory of your saints
a share in their eternal joy.

Grant this through our Lord Jesus Christ, your Son,
who lives and reigns with you and the Holy Spirit,
one God, for ever and ever.

See Lectionary for Mass, nos. 737-742.

PRAYER OVER THE GIFTS

Pray, brethren . . .

Lord,
give to us who offer these gifts at your altar
the same spirit of love that filled St. N.
By celebrating this sacred eucharist with pure minds
and loving hearts
may we offer a sacrifice that pleases you,
and brings salvation to us.

Grant this through Christ our Lord.

Communion Rite

Come to me, all you that labor and are burdened, and I will
give you rest, says the Lord. (Matthew 11:28)

PRAYER AFTER COMMUNION

Let us pray.
Pause for silent prayer, if this has not preceded.
Lord,
may the sacrament of holy communion which we receive
bring us health and strengthen us
in the light of your truth.

We ask this in the name of Jesus the Lord.

6

Introductory Rites

Blessed is the man who puts his trust in the Lord; he will be like a tree planted by the waters, sinking its roots into the moist earth; he will have nothing to fear in time of drought. (Jer. 17:7-8)

OPENING PRAYER

**All-powerful God,
help us who celebrate the memory of St. N.
to imitate his (her) way of life.
May the example of your saints
be our challenge to live holier lives.**

**Grant this through our Lord Jesus Christ, your Son,
who lives and reigns with you and the Holy Spirit,
one God, for ever and ever.**

See Lectionary for Mass, nos. 737-742.

PRAYER OVER THE GIFTS

Pray, brethren . . .

**Lord,
we bring our gifts to your holy altar
on this feast of your saints.
In your mercy let this eucharist
give you glory
and bring us to the fullness of your love.**

Grant this through Christ our Lord.

Communion Rite

As the Father has loved me, so have I loved you; remain in my love. (John 15:9)

PRAYER AFTER COMMUNION

Let us pray.
Pause for silent prayer, if this has not preceded.
**Lord our God,
may the divine mysteries we celebrate
in memory of your saint
fill us with eternal peace and salvation.**

We ask this in the name of Jesus the Lord.

7. FOR RELIGIOUS

Introductory Rites

The Lord is my inheritance and my cup; he alone will give me my reward. The measuring line has marked a lovely place for me; my inheritance is my great delight. (Ps. 15:5-6)

OPENING PRAYER

Lord God,
you kept St. N. faithful to Christ's pattern of poverty and humility.
May his (her) prayers help us to live in fidelity to our calling
and bring us to the perfection you have shown us in your Son,
who lives and reigns with you and the Holy Spirit,
one God, for ever and ever.

Or (for an abbot):

Lord,
in your abbot N.
you give an example of the gospel lived to perfection.
Help us to follow him
by keeping before us the things of heaven amid all the changes of this world.
Grant this through our Lord Jesus Christ, your Son,
who lives and reigns with you and the Holy Spirit,
one God, for ever and ever.

See Lectionary for Mass, nos. 737-742.

PRAYER OVER THE GIFTS

Pray, brethren . . .

God of all mercy,
you transformed St. N.
and made him (her) a new creature in your image.
Renew us in the same way
by making our gifts of peace acceptable to you.

We ask this in the name of Jesus the Lord.

Communion Rite

I solemnly tell you: those who have left everything and followed me will be repaid a hundredfold and will gain eternal life. (See Matthew 19:27-29)

PRAYER AFTER COMMUNION

Let us pray.

Pause for silent prayer, if this has not preceded.

All-powerful God,
may we who are strengthened by the power of this sacrament learn from the example of St. N.
to seek you above all things
and to live in this world as your new creation.

We ask this through Christ our Lord.

8. FOR RELIGIOUS

Introductory Rites

These are the saints who received blessings from the Lord,
a prize from God their Savior. They are the people that
long to see his face. (See Ps. 23:5-6)

OPENING PRAYER

God our Father,
you called St. N. to seek your kingdom in this world
by striving to live in perfect charity.
With his (her) prayers to give us courage,
help us to move forward with joyful hearts in the way of love.

We ask this through our Lord Jesus Christ, your Son,
who lives and reigns with you and the Holy Spirit,
one God, for ever and ever.

See Lectionary for Mass, nos. 737-742.

PRAYER OVER THE GIFTS

Pray, brethren . . .

Lord,
may the gifts we bring to your altar
in memory of St. N.
be acceptable to you.
Free us from the things that keep us from you
and teach us to seek you as our only good.

We ask this through Christ our Lord.

Communion Rite

Taste and see the goodness of the Lord; blessed is he who
hopes in God. (Ps. 33:9)

PRAYER AFTER COMMUNION

Let us pray.
Pause for silent prayer, if this has not preceded.
Lord,
by the power of this sacrament and the example of St. N.
guide us always in your love.
May the good work you have begun in us
reach perfection in the day of Christ Jesus
who is Lord for ever and ever.

9. FOR THOSE WHO WORKED FOR THE UNDERPRIVILEGED

Introductory Rites

Come, you whom my Father has blessed, says the Lord: I was ill and you comforted me. I tell you, anything you did for one of my brothers, you did for me. (Matthew 25:34, 36, 40)

OPENING PRAYER

Lord God,
you teach us that the commandments of heaven
are summarized in love of you and love of our neighbor.
By following the example of St. N.
in practicing works of charity
may we be counted among the blessed in your kingdom.

Grant this through our Lord Jesus Christ, your Son,
who lives and reigns with you and the Holy Spirit,
one God, for ever and ever.

See Lectionary for Mass, nos. 737-742.

PRAYER OVER THE GIFTS

Pray, brethren . . .

Lord,
accept the gifts of your people.
May we who celebrate the love of your Son
also follow the example of your saints
and grow in love for you and for one another.

We ask this through Christ our Lord.

Communion Rite

No one has greater love, says the Lord, than the man who lays down his life for his friends. (John 15:13)

or:

By the love you have for one another, says the Lord, everyone will know that you are my disciples. (John 13:35)

PRAYER AFTER COMMUNION

Let us pray.

Pause for silent prayer, if this has not preceded.

Lord,
may we who are renewed by these mysteries
follow the example of St. N.
who worshiped you with love
and served your people with generosity.

We ask this through Christ our Lord.

Or:

Lord,
we who receive the sacrament of salvation ask
your mercy.
Help us to imitate the love of St. N.
and give to us a share in his (her) glory.

Grant this through Christ our Lord.

10. FOR TEACHERS

Introductory Rites

Let the children come to me, and do not stop them, says the Lord; to such belongs the kingdom of God. (Mark 10:14)

or:

The man that keeps these commandments and teaches them, he is the one who will be called great in the kingdom of heaven, says the Lord. (Matthew 5:19)

OPENING PRAYER

**Lord God,
you called St. N. to serve you in the Church
by teaching his (her) fellow man the way of salvation.
Inspire us by his (her) example:
help us to follow Christ our teacher,
and lead us to our brothers and sisters in heaven.**

**We ask this through our Lord Jesus Christ, your Son,
who lives and reigns with you and the Holy Spirit,
one God, for ever and ever.**

See Lectionary for Mass, nos. 737-742.

PRAYER OVER THE GIFTS

Pray, brethren . . .

**Lord,
accept the gifts your people bring
in memory of your saints.
May our sharing in this mystery
help us to live the example of love you give us.**

Grant this in the name of Jesus the Lord.

Communion Rite

Unless you change, and become like little children, says the Lord, you shall not enter the kingdom of heaven. (Matthew 18:3)

or:

I am the light of the world, says the Lord; the man who follows me will have the light of life. (John 8:12)

PRAYER AFTER COMMUNION

Let us pray.

Pause for silent prayer, if this has not preceded.

**All-powerful God,
may this holy meal help us
to follow the example of your saints
by showing in our lives
the light of truth and love for our brothers.**

We ask this in the name of Jesus the Lord.

11. FOR HOLY WOMEN

Introductory Rites

Honor the woman who fears the Lord. Her sons will bless
her, and her husband praise her. (See Prov. 31:30, 28)

OPENING PRAYER

God our Father,
every year you give us joy on this feast of St. N.
As we honor her memory by this celebration,
may we follow the example of her holy life.

We ask this through our Lord Jesus Christ,
   your Son,
who lives and reigns with you and the Holy
   Spirit,
one God, for ever and ever.

Or (for several):

All-powerful God,
may the prayers of Saints N. and N. bring us
   help from heaven
as their lives have already given us
an example of holiness.

We ask this through our Lord Jesus Christ,
   your Son,
who lives and reigns with you and the Holy
   Spirit,
one God, for ever and ever.

See Lectionary for Mass, nos. 737-742.

PRAYER OVER THE GIFTS

Pray, brethren . . .

Lord,
may the gifts we present in memory of St. N.
bring us your forgiveness and salvation.

We ask this in the name of Jesus the Lord.

Communion Rite

The kingdom of heaven is like a merchant in search of fine
pearls; on finding one rare pearl he sells everything he has
and buys it. (Matthew 13:45-46)

PRAYER AFTER COMMUNION

Let us pray.
Pause for silent prayer, if this has not preceded.
All-powerful God,
fill us with your light and love
by the sacrament we receive on the feast of St. N.
May we burn with love for your kingdom
and let our light shine before men.

We ask this through Christ our Lord.

12. FOR HOLY WOMEN

Introductory Rites

> Praise to the holy woman whose home is built on faithful
> love and whose pathway leads to God. (See Prov. 14:1-2)

OPENING PRAYER   Or:

Father,
rewarder of the humble,
you blessed St. N. with charity and patience.
May her prayers help us, and her example in-
** spire us**
to carry our cross and to love you always.
We ask this through our Lord Jesus Christ,
** your Son,**
who lives and reigns with you and the Holy
** Spirit,**
one God, for ever and ever.

Lord,
pour upon us the spirit of wisdom and love
with which you filled your servant St. N.
By serving you as she did,
may we please you with our faith and our ac-
** tions.**
Grant this through our Lord Jesus Christ, your
** Son,**
who lives and reigns with you and the Holy
** Spirit,**
one God, for ever and ever.

See Lectionary for Mass, nos. 737-742.

PRAYER OVER THE GIFTS   **Pray, brethren . . .**

Lord,
receive the gifts your people bring to you
in honor of your saints.
By the eucharist we celebrate
may we progress toward salvation.

Grant this in the name of Jesus the Lord.

Communion Rite

> Whoever does the will of my Father in heaven is my
> brother and sister and mother, says the Lord. (Matthew
> 12:50)

PRAYER AFTER COMMUNION   **Let us pray.**

Pause for silent prayer, if this has not preceded.

Lord,
we receive your gifts
at this celebration in honor of St. N.
May they free us from sin
and strengthen us by your grace.

We ask this in the name of Jesus the Lord.

OPTIONAL ANTIPHONS FOR SOLEMNITIES AND FEASTS

Introductory Rites

1. Let us all rejoice in the Lord, and keep a festival in honor of the holy (martyr, pastor) N. Let us join with the angels in joyful praise to the Son of God.

2. Let us all rejoice in the Lord as we honor St. N., our protector. On this day this faithful friend of God entered heaven to reign with Christ for ever.

3. Let us rejoice in celebrating the victory of our patron saint. On earth he proclaimed Christ's love for us. Now Christ leads him to a place of honor before his Father in heaven.

4. Let us rejoice in celebrating the feast of the blessed martyr N. He fought for the law of God on earth; now Christ has granted him an everlasting crown of glory.

5. All his saints and all who fear the Lord, sing your praises to our God; for the Lord our almighty God is King of all creation. Let us rejoice and give him glory.

6. We celebrate the day when blessed N. received his reward; with all the saints he is seated at the heavenly banquet in glory.

RITUAL MASSES

RITUAL MASSES

I. CHRISTIAN INITIATION

A

Election or Enrollment of Names

Introductory Rites

Let hearts rejoice who search for the Lord. Seek the Lord and his strength, seek always the face of the Lord. (Ps. 104:3-4)

OPENING PRAYER

**God our Father,
you always work to save us,
and now we rejoice in the great love
you give to your chosen people.
Protect all who are about to become your children,
and continue to bless those who are already baptized.**

**Grant this through our Lord Jesus Christ, your Son,
who lives and reigns with you and the Holy Spirit,
one God, for ever and ever.**

PRAYER OVER THE GIFTS

Pray, brethren . . .

**Ever-living God,
in baptism, the sacrament of our faith,
you restore us to life.
Accept the prayers and gifts of your people;
forgive our sins and fulfill our hopes and desires.**

The preface proper to the particular Sunday of Lent, or, if the celebration occurs on a day other than Sunday, one of the prefaces for the season of Lent is said.

We ask this in the name of Jesus the Lord.

Communion Rite

I will put my law within them, I will write it on their hearts; then I shall be their God, and they will be my people. (Jer. 31:33)

PRAYER AFTER COMMUNION

Let us pray.
Pause for silent prayer, if this has not preceded.
**Lord,
may the sacraments we receive
cleanse us of sin and free us from guilt,
for our sins bring us sorrow
but your promise of salvation brings us joy.**

We ask this through Christ our Lord.

The Mass of Friday of the Fourth Week of Lent, page 184, may be used.

B

The Scrutinies

This Mass is celebrated when the scrutinies are used: either on the Sundays designated for them (the Third, Fourth and Fifth Sundays of Lent) or at other times.

Introductory Rites

I will prove my holiness through you. I will gather you from the ends of the earth; I will pour clean water on you and wash away all your sins. I will give you a new spirit within you, says the Lord. (Ezek. 36:23-26)

OPENING PRAYER

First Scrutiny

**Lord,
you call these chosen ones
to the glory of a new birth in Christ, the second Adam.
Help them grow in wisdom and love
as they prepare to profess their faith in you.**

**Grant this through our Lord Jesus Christ, your Son,
who lives and reigns with you and the Holy Spirit,
one God, for ever and ever.**

See Lectionary for Mass, no. 745.

Second Scrutiny

**Almighty and eternal God,
may your Church increase in true joy.
May these candidates for baptism,
and all the family of man,
be reborn into the life of your kingdom.**

**We ask this through our Lord Jesus Christ, your Son,
who lives and reigns with you and the Holy Spirit,
one God, for ever and ever.**

See Lectionary for Mass, no. 746.

Third Scrutiny

**Lord,
enlighten your chosen ones with the word of life.
Give them a new birth
in the waters of baptism
and make them living members of the Church.**

**Grant this through our Lord Jesus Christ, your Son,
who lives and reigns with you and the Holy Spirit,
one God, for ever and ever.**

See Lectionary for Mass, no. 747.

PRAYER OVER THE GIFTS

First Scrutiny

Pray, brethren . . .

**Lord God,
give faith and love to your children
and lead them safely to the supper
you have prepared for them.
We ask this in the name of Jesus the Lord.**

Second Scrutiny

Pray, brethren . . .

**Lord,
we offer these gifts
in joy and thanksgiving for our salvation.
May the example of our faith and love
help your chosen ones on their way to salvation.
Grant this through Christ our Lord.**

Third Scrutiny

Pray, brethren . . .

**Almighty God,
hear our prayers for these men and women
who have begun to learn the Christian faith,
and by this sacrifice prepare them for baptism.
We ask this through Christ our Lord.**

The preface proper to the particular Sunday of Lent, or, if the celebration occurs on a day other than Sunday, one of the prefaces for the season of Lent is said.

When Eucharistic Prayer I is used, the special forms of **Remember, Lord, your people** and **Father, accept this offering** are said:

**Remember, Lord, these godparents
who will present your chosen men and women for baptism**
(the names of the godparents are mentioned).
Lord, remember all of us . . .

**Father,
accept this offering
from your whole family.
We offer it especially for the men and women
you call to share your life
through the living waters of baptism.**

[Through Christ our Lord. Amen.]

Communion Rite

When the gospel of the Samaritan woman is read:

Whoever drinks the water that I shall give him, says the Lord, will have a spring inside him, welling up for eternal life. (John 4:13-14)

When the gospel of the man born blind is read:

The Lord rubbed my eyes: I went away and washed; then I could see, and I believed in God. (See John 9:11)

When the gospel of Lazarus is read:

He who lives and believes in me will not die for ever, says the Lord. (John 11:26)

PRAYER AFTER COMMUNION

First Scrutiny

Let us pray.
Pause for silent prayer, if this has not preceded.

**Lord,
be present in our lives
with your gifts of salvation.
Prepare these men and women for your sacraments
and protect them in your love.**

We ask this in the name of Jesus the Lord.

Second Scrutiny

Let us pray.
Pause for silent prayer, if this has not preceded.

**Lord,
be close to your family.
Rule and guide us on our way to your kingdom
and bring us to the joy of salvation.**

Grant this through Christ our Lord.

Third Scrutiny

Let us pray.
Pause for silent prayer, if this has not preceded.

**Lord,
may your people be one in spirit
and serve you with all their heart.
Free them from all fear.
Give them joy in your gifts
and love for those
who are to be reborn as your children.**

We ask this through Christ our Lord.

C

Baptism

This Mass is celebrated for the baptism of adults, especially when confirmation is given in the same service. It may also be celebrated for the baptism of children, and may be said on any day except the Sundays of Advent, Lent, and Easter, solemnities, Ash Wednesday, and the weekdays of Holy Week.

1

Introductory Rites

Put on the new man, created in the image of God, in justice and in the holiness of truth. (Eph. 4:24)

OPENING PRAYER

**Lord God,
in baptism we die with Christ
to rise again in him.
Strengthen us by your Spirit
to walk in the newness of life
as your adopted children.**

**We ask this through our Lord Jesus Christ, your Son,
who lives and reigns with you and the Holy Spirit,
one God, for ever and ever.**

See Lectionary for Mass, nos. 752-762.

PRAYER OVER THE GIFTS

Pray, brethren . . .

**Lord,
you have renewed these men and women
in the likeness of Christ your Son
(have sealed them with your Spirit)
and united them to your priestly people.
Accept them with the sacrifice offered by your Church.**

Grant this through Christ our Lord.

When Eucharistic Prayer I is used, the special forms of Remember, Lord, your people and Father, accept this offering are said:

**Remember, Lord, these godparents
who have presented your chosen men and women
for baptism**
(the names of the godparents are mentioned).
Lord, remember all of us . . .

**Father, accept this offering
from your whole family
and from those born into new life
by water and the Holy Spirit
with all their sins forgiven.
Keep them one in Christ Jesus the Lord,
and may their names be written in the book of life.
[Through Christ our Lord. Amen.]**

In other eucharistic prayers, the following are included:

Eucharistic Prayer II

**. . . and all the clergy.
Remember also those who have been baptized (and confirmed) today as members of your family.
Help them to follow Christ your Son with loving hearts.**

Eucharistic Prayer III

**. . . gathered here before you.
Strengthen those who have now become your people
by the waters of rebirth
(and the gift of the Holy Spirit).
Help them to walk in newness of life.**

Eucharistic Prayer IV

**. . . who take part in this offering,
those here present,
those born again today
by water and the Holy Spirit,
and all your people . . .**

Communion Rite

Think of how God loves you! He calls you his own children, and that is what you are. (1 John 3:1)

PRAYER AFTER COMMUNION

Let us pray.
Pause for silent prayer, if this has not preceded.
**Lord,
by this sacrament
you make us one family in Christ your Son,
one in the sharing of his body and blood,
one in the communion of his Spirit.
Help us grow in love for one another
and come to the full maturity of the body of Christ,
who is Lord for ever and ever.**

2

Introductory Rites

God has saved us by living water which gives our lives a
fresh beginning, and he put his Spirit in us, so that healed
by his grace, we may share his life and hope to live for
ever. (Titus 3:5, 7)

OPENING PRAYER

Lord God,
your word of life gives us a new birth.
May we receive it with open hearts,
live it with joy,
and express it in love.

We ask this through our Lord Jesus Christ, your Son,
who lives and reigns with you and the Holy Spirit,
one God, for ever and ever.

See Lectionary for Mass, nos. 752-762.

PRAYER OVER THE GIFTS

Pray, brethren . . .

Lord,
you welcome us to your table
where bread and wine are prepared for us.
May we who celebrate this eucharistic feast
be counted as fellow-citizens of the saints
and members of your household.

Grant this through Christ our Lord.

Special petitions in the eucharistic
prayer, as in the preceding Mass.

Communion Rite

My dearest friends, we are now God's children. What we
shall be in his glory has not yet been revealed. (1 John 3:2)

PRAYER AFTER COMMUNION

Let us pray.
Pause for silent prayer, if this has not preceded.
Lord,
in this eucharist
we proclaim the death and resurrection of your Son.
May the power of this sacrament
give us courage to proclaim it also in our lives.

Grant this through Christ our Lord.

D

Confirmation

One of the following Masses is celebrated when confirmation is given within Mass or immediately before or after it, except on the Sundays of Advent, Lent, and Easter, solemnities, Ash Wednesday, and the weekdays of Holy Week. Red or white vestments are worn.

1

Introductory Rites

I will pour clean water on you and I will give you a new heart, a new spirit within you, says the Lord. (Ezek. 36:25-26)

OPENING PRAYER

God of power and mercy,
send your Holy Spirit to live in our hearts
and make us temples of his glory.
We ask this through our Lord Jesus Christ,
  your Son,
who lives and reigns with you and the Holy
  Spirit,
one God, for ever and ever.

See Lectionary for Mass, nos. 763-767.

Or:

Lord,
fulfill your promise.
Send your Holy Spirit to make us witnesses
  before the world
to the good news proclaimed by Jesus Christ
  our Lord,
who lives and reigns with you and the Holy
  Spirit,
one God, for ever and ever.

PRAYER OVER THE GIFTS

Pray, brethren . . .

Lord,
we celebrate the memorial of our redemption
by which your Son won for us the gift of the Holy Spirit.
Accept our offerings,
and send us your Spirit
to make us more like Christ
in bearing witness to the world.

We ask this through Christ our Lord.

When Eucharistic Prayer I is used, the special form of **Father, accept this offering** is said:

Father, accept this offering
from your whole family
and from those reborn in baptism
and confirmed by the coming of the Holy Spirit.
Protect them with your love and keep them close to you.

[Through Christ our Lord. Amen.]

Communion Rite

All you who have been enlightened, who have experienced the gift of heaven and who have received your share of the Holy Spirit: rejoice in the Lord. (See Heb. 6:4)

PRAYER AFTER COMMUNION

Let us pray.
Pause for silent prayer, if this has not preceded.
Lord,
help those you have anointed by your Spirit
and fed with the body and blood of your Son.
Support them through every trial
and by their works of love
build up the Church in holiness and joy.

Grant this through Christ our Lord.

SOLEMN BLESSING

God our Father
made you his children by water and the Holy Spirit:
may he bless you
and watch over you with his fatherly love.

℟. Amen.

Jesus Christ the Son of God
promised that the Spirit of truth
would be with his Church for ever:
may he bless you and give you courage
in professing the true faith.

℟. Amen.

The Holy Spirit
came down upon the disciples
and set their hearts on fire with love:
may he bless you,
keep you one in faith and love
and bring you to the joy of God's kingdom.

℟. Amen.

May almighty God bless you,
the Father, and the Son, ✟ and the Holy Spirit.

℟. Amen.

Or:
PRAYER OVER THE PEOPLE
The deacon or celebrant gives the invitation in these or similar words:

Bow your heads and pray for God's blessing.

God our Father,
complete the work you have begun
and keep the gifts of your Holy Spirit
active in the hearts of your people.
Make them ready to live his gospel
and eager to do his will.
May they never be ashamed
to proclaim to all the world Christ crucified
living and reigning for ever and ever.

℟. Amen.

May almighty God bless you,
the Father, and the Son, ✟ and the Holy Spirit.
℟. Amen.

2

Introductory Rites

The love of God has been poured into our hearts by his
Spirit living in us. (See Rom. 5:5; 8:11)

OPENING PRAYER

**Lord,
send us your Holy Spirit
to help us walk in unity of faith
and grow in the strength of his love
to the full stature of Christ,
who lives and reigns with you and the Holy Spirit,
one God, for ever and ever.**

See Lectionary for Mass, nos. 763-767.

PRAYER OVER THE GIFTS

Pray, brethren . . .

**Lord,
you have signed our brothers and sisters
with the cross of your Son
and anointed them with the oil of salvation.
As they offer themselves with Christ,
continue to fill their hearts with your Spirit.**

We ask this through Christ our Lord.

When Eucharistic Prayer I is used, the
special form of **Father, accept this offering** is said, page **757.**

Communion Rite

Look up at him with gladness and smile; taste and see the
goodness of the Lord. (Ps. 33:6, 9)

PRAYER AFTER COMMUNION

Let us pray.
Pause for silent prayer, if this has not preceded.
**Lord,
you give your Son as food
to those you anoint with your Spirit.
Help them to fulfill your law
by living in freedom as your children.
May they live in holiness
and be your witnesses to the world.**

We ask this through Christ our Lord.

3

OTHER PRAYERS

OPENING PRAYER

Lord,
fulfill the promise given by your Son
and send the Holy Spirit
to enlighten our minds
and lead us to all truth.

Grant this through our Lord Jesus Christ, your Son,
who lives and reigns with you and the Holy Spirit,
one God, for ever and ever.

See Lectionary for Mass, nos. 763-767.

PRAYER OVER THE GIFTS

Pray, brethren . . .

Lord,
accept the offering of your family
and help those who receive the gift of your Spirit
to keep him in their hearts
and come to the reward of eternal life.

We ask this through Christ our Lord.

When Eucharistic Prayer I is used, the special form of **Father, accept this offering** is said, page 757.

PRAYER AFTER COMMUNION

Let us pray.
Pause for silent prayer, if this has not preceded.
Lord,
we have shared the one bread of life.
Send the Spirit of your love
to keep us one in faith and peace.

We ask this in the name of Jesus the Lord.

II. HOLY ORDERS

Except on the Sundays of Advent, Lent, and Easter, solemnities, and the feasts of the Apostles, the Mass for the conferring of holy orders may be arranged as follows:

(a) the entrance and communion antiphons given below are used;

(b) the appropriate prayers should be chosen from those given below for a bishop (pp. 793 or 794), for priests (p. 797), or for the ministers of the Church (p. 801);

(c) the readings should be taken from those indicated for ordinations; these readings may also be used, at least in part, on days when the ritual Mass for the conferring of holy orders is prohibited;

(d) unless there is a more proper preface, the preface of the priesthood (p. 436) may be used at the ordination of a priest.

Introductory Rites

He who serves me, follows me, says the Lord; and where I am, my servant will also be. (John 12:26)

or (for the ordination of priests):

The Spirit of God is upon me; he has anointed me. He sent me to bring good news to the poor, and to heal the broken-hearted. (Luke 4:18)

When Eucharistic Prayer I is used, the special form of Father, accept this offering is said.

**Father, accept this offering
from your whole family
and from those you have chosen for the order of
 deacons, presbyters or bishops.
Protect the gifts you have given them,
and let them yield a harvest worthy of you.**

[Through Christ our Lord. Amen.]

Communion Rite

Father, make them holy in the truth. As you sent me into the world, I have sent them into the world. (John 17:17-18)

III. VIATICUM

Except on the Sundays of Advent, Lent, and Easter, solemnities, Ash Wednesday, and the weekdays of Holy Week, either the Mass of the Holy Eucharist (p. 844) or, according to circumstances, the Mass for the sick (p. 828) may be celebrated, with the following prayers.

OPENING PRAYER

Father,
your Son, Jesus Christ, is our way, our truth, and our life.

Our brother (sister) N. entrusts himself (herself) to you
with full confidence in all your promises.
Refresh him (her) with the body and blood of your Son
and lead him (her) to your kingdom in peace.

We ask this through our Lord Jesus Christ, your Son,
who lives and reigns with you and the Holy Spirit,
one God, for ever and ever.

PRAYER OVER THE GIFTS

Pray, brethren . . .

Father,
the suffering, death, and resurrection of Jesus,
the true paschal lamb,
has opened heaven for us.
May our offering become his sacrifice
and lead our brother (sister) N. to eternal life.

We ask this through Christ our Lord.

PRAYER AFTER COMMUNION

Let us pray.
Pause for silent prayer, if this has not preceded.
Lord,
you are the source of eternal health
for those who believe in you.
May our brother (sister) N.,
who has been refreshed with food and drink from heaven,
safely reach your kingdom of light and life.

We ask this through Christ our Lord.

IV. WEDDING MASS

1. For the Celebration of Marriage

When marriage is celebrated during Mass, white vestments are worn and the wedding Mass is used. If the marriage is celebrated on a Sunday or solemnity, the Mass of the day is used with the nuptial blessing and, where appropriate, the special final blessing.

The liturgy of the word relating to the marriage celebration is extremely helpful in emphasizing the meaning of the sacrament and the obligations of marriage. When the wedding Mass may not be used (during the Easter triduum or on Christmas, Epiphany, Ascension, Pentecost, The Body and Blood of Christ, or solemnities which are holy days of obligation) one of the readings for marriage may be chosen. On the Sundays of the Christmas season and on Sundays in ordinary time, in Masses which are not parish Masses, the wedding Mass may be said without change.

When a marriage is celebrated during Advent, Lent or other days of penance, the parish priest should advise the couple to take into consideration the special nature of these times.

A

Introductory Rites

May the Lord send you help from his holy place and from Zion may he watch over you. May he grant you your heart's desire and lend his aid to all your plans. (Ps. 19:3, 5)

OPENING PRAYER

Or:

Father,
you have made the bond of marriage
a holy mystery,
a symbol of Christ's love for his Church.
Hear our prayers for N. and N.
With faith in you and in each other
they pledge their love today.
May their lives always bear witness
to the reality of that love.

We ask this through our Lord Jesus Christ,
your Son,
who lives and reigns with you and the Holy
Spirit,
one God, for ever and ever.

Father,
when you created mankind
you willed that man and wife should be one.
Bind N. and N.
in the loving union of marriage
and make their love fruitful
so that they may be living witnesses
to your divine love in the world.

We ask this through our Lord Jesus Christ,
your Son,
who lives and reigns with you and the Holy
Spirit,
one God, for ever and ever.

See Lectionary for Mass, nos. 774-778.

PRAYER OVER THE GIFTS   **Pray, brethren . . .**

Lord,
accept our offering
for this newly-married couple, N. and N.
By your love and providence you have brought
** them together;**
now bless them all the days of their married life.

We ask this through Christ our Lord.

Preface of Marriage I, page 489.

When Eucharistic Prayer I is used, the special form of **Father, accept this offering** is said. The words in brackets and parentheses may be omitted if desired.

Father, accept this offering
from your whole family
and from N. and N., for whom we now pray.
You have brought them to their wedding day:
grant them (the gift and joy of children and)
a long and happy life together.

[**Through Christ our Lord. Amen.**]

NUPTIAL BLESSING

After the Lord's Prayer, the prayer **Deliver us** is omitted. The priest faces the bride and bridegroom and says the following blessing over them.

If one or both of the parties will not be receiving communion, the words in the introduction to the nuptial blessing, **through the sacrament of the body and blood of Christ,** may be omitted.

If desired, in the prayer **Father, by your power,** two of the first three paragraphs may be omitted, keeping only the paragraph which corresponds to the reading of the Mass.

In the last paragraph of this prayer, the words in parentheses may be omitted whenever circumstances suggest it, for example, if the couple is advanced in years.

With hands joined, the priest says:

My dear friends, let us turn to the Lord and pray
that he will bless with his grace this woman (or N.)
now married in Christ to this man (or N.)
and that (through the sacrament of the body and blood
   of Christ,)
he will unite in love the couple he has joined in this holy bond.

All pray silently for a short while. Then the priest extends his hands and continues:

Father,
by your power you have made everything out of nothing.
In the beginning you created the universe
and made mankind in your own likeness.

You gave man the constant help of woman
so that man and woman should no longer be two, but
   one flesh,
and you teach us that what you have united
may never be divided.

Father,
by your plan man and woman are united,
and married life has been established
as the one blessing that was not forfeited by original sin
or washed away in the flood.

Look with love upon this woman, your daughter,
now joined to her husband in marriage.
She asks your blessing.
Give her the grace of love and peace.
May she always follow the example of the holy women
whose praises are sung in the scriptures.

May her husband put his trust in her
and recognize that she is his equal
and the heir with him to the life of grace.
May he always honor her and love her
as Christ loves his bride, the Church.

Father,
keep them always true to your commandments.
Keep them faithful in marriage
and let them be living examples of Christian life.

Give them the strength which comes from the gospel
so that they may be witnesses of Christ to others.
(Bless them with children
and help them to be good parents.
May they live to see their children's children.)
And, after a happy old age,
grant them fullness of life with the saints
in the kingdom of heaven.

The Mass continues in the usual way.   **We ask this through Christ our Lord.**

Communion Rite

Christ loves his Church, and he sacrificed himself for her
so that she could become like a holy and untouched bride.
(See Eph. 5:25-27)

PRAYER AFTER COMMUNION   **Let us pray.**

Pause for silent prayer, if this has not preceded.
**Lord,
in your love
you have given us this eucharist
to unite us with one another and with you.
As you have made N. and N.
one in this sacrament of marriage
(and in the sharing of the one bread and the one cup),
so now make them one in love for each other.**

We ask this through Christ our Lord.

SOLEMN BLESSING   **God the eternal Father keep you in love with each other,
so that the peace of Christ may stay with you
and be always in your home. ℟. Amen.**

**May (your children bless you,)
your friends console you
and all men live in peace with you. ℟. Amen.**

**May you always bear witness to the love of God in this world
so that the afflicted and the needy
will find in you generous friends
and welcome you into the joys of heaven. ℟. Amen.**

**May almighty God bless you,
the Father, and the Son, ✠ and the Holy Spirit. ℟. Amen.**

B

Introductory Rites

Fill us with your love, O Lord, and we will sing for joy all
our days. May the goodness of the Lord be upon us, and
give success to the work of our hands. (Ps. 89:14, 17)

OPENING PRAYER

**Father,
hear our prayers for N. and N.,
who today are united in marriage before your altar.
Give them your blessing,
and strengthen their love for each other.**

**We ask this through our Lord Jesus Christ, your Son,
who lives and reigns with you and the Holy Spirit,
one God, for ever and ever.**

See Lectionary for Mass, nos. 774-778.

PRAYER OVER THE GIFTS

Pray, brethren . . .

**Lord,
accept the gifts we offer you
on this happy day.
In your fatherly love
watch over and protect N. and N.,
whom you have united in marriage.**

We ask this through Christ our Lord.

Preface of Marriage II, page **490**.

When Eucharistic Prayer I is used, the
special form of **Father, accept this offering** is said. The words in brackets
and parentheses may be omitted if desired.

**Father, accept this offering
from your whole family
and from N. and N., for whom we now pray.
You have brought them to their wedding day:
grant them (the gift and joy of children and)
a long and happy life together.**

[Through Christ our Lord. Amen.]

NUPTIAL BLESSING

After the Lord's Prayer, the prayer Deliver us is omitted. The priest faces the bride and bridegroom and says the following blessing over them.

In the prayer Holy Father, either the paragraph, Holy Father, you created mankind, or the paragraph, Father, to reveal the plan of your love, may be omitted, keeping only the paragraph which corresponds to the reading of the Mass.

With hands joined, the priest says:

**Let us pray to the Lord for N. and N.
who come to God's altar at the beginning of their married life
so that they may always be united in love for each other
(as now they share in the body and blood of Christ).**

All pray silently for a short while. Then the priest extends his hands and continues:

**Holy Father, you created mankind in your own image
and made man and woman to be joined as husband and wife
in union of body and heart
and so fulfill their mission in this world.**

**Father,
to reveal the plan of your love,
you made the union of husband and wife
an image of the covenant between you and your people.
In the fulfillment of this sacrament,
the marriage of Christian man and woman
is a sign of the marriage between Christ and the Church.
Father, stretch out your hand, and bless N. and N.**

**Lord,
grant that as they begin to live this sacrament
they may share with each other the gifts of your love
and become one in heart and mind
as witnesses to your presence in their marriage.
Help them to create a home together
(and give them children to be formed by the gospel
and to have a place in your family).**

**Give your blessings to N., your daughter,
so that she may be a good wife (and mother),
caring for the home,
faithful in love for her husband,
generous and kind.
Give your blessings to N., your son,
so that he may be a faithful husband
(and a good father).**

**Father,
grant that as they come together to your table on earth,
so they may one day have the joy of sharing your feast
in heaven.**

We ask this through Christ our Lord.

The Mass continues in the usual way.

Communion Rite
> I give you a new commandment: love one another as I
> have loved you, says the Lord. (John 13:34)

PRAYER AFTER COMMUNION

Let us pray.

Pause for silent prayer, if this has not preceded.
**Lord,
we who have shared the food of your table
pray for our friends N. and N.,
whom you have joined together in marriage.
Keep them close to you always.
May their love for each other
proclaim to all the world
their faith in you.**

We ask this through Christ our Lord.

SOLEMN BLESSING

**May God, the almighty Father,
give you his joy
and bless you (in your children).**

℟. **Amen.**

**May the only Son of God have mercy on you
and help you in good times and in bad.**

℟. **Amen.**

**May the Holy Spirit of God
always fill your hearts with his love.**

℟. **Amen.**

**May almighty God bless you,
the Father, and the Son, ✠ and the Holy Spirit.**

℟. **Amen.**

C

Introductory Rites

Lord, I will bless you day after day, and praise your name for ever; for you are kind to all, and compassionate to all your creatures. (Ps. 144:2, 9)

OPENING PRAYER

**Almighty God,
hear our prayers for N. and N.,
who have come here today
to be united in the sacrament of marriage.
Increase their faith in you and in each other,
and through them bless your Church
   (with Christian children).**

**We ask this through our Lord Jesus Christ, your Son,
who lives and reigns with you and the Holy Spirit,
one God, for ever and ever.**

See Lectionary for Mass, nos. 774-778.

PRAYER OVER THE GIFTS

Pray, brethren . . .

**Lord,
hear our prayers
and accept the gifts we offer for N. and N.
Today you have made them one in the sacrament
   of marriage.
May the mystery of Christ's unselfish love,
which we celebrate in this eucharist,
increase their love for you and for each other.**

We ask this through Christ our Lord.

Preface of Marriage III, page **491**.

When Eucharistic Prayer I is used, the special form of **Father, accept this offering** is said. The words in brackets and parentheses may be omitted if desired.

**Father, accept this offering
from your whole family
and from N. and N., for whom we now pray.
You have brought them to their wedding day:
grant them (the gift and joy of children and)
a long and happy life together.**

[Through Christ our Lord. Amen.]

NUPTIAL BLESSING

After the Lord's Prayer, the prayer
Deliver us is omitted. The priest faces
the bride and bridegroom and says the
following blessing over them:

My dear friends, let us ask God
for his continued blessings upon this bridegroom and
his bride (or N. and N.).

All pray silently for a short while.
Then the priest extends his hands
and continues:

Holy Father,
creator of the universe,
maker of man and woman in your own likeness,
source of blessing for married life,
we humbly pray to you for this woman
who today is united with her husband in this sacrament
  of marriage.

May your fullest blessing come upon her and her husband
so that they may together rejoice in your gift of married love
(and enrich your Church with their children).

Lord,
may they both praise you when they are happy
and turn to you in their sorrows.
May they be glad that you help them in their work
and know that you are with them in their need.
May they pray to you in the community of the Church,
and be your witnesses in the world.
May they reach old age in the company of their friends,
and come at last to the kingdom of heaven.

We ask this through Christ our Lord.

The Mass continues in the usual way.

Communion Rite

> I will bless the Lord at all times, his praise shall be ever on
> my lips. Taste and see the goodness of the Lord; blessed is
> he who hopes in God. (Ps. 33:1, 9)

PRAYER AFTER COMMUNION

Let us pray.
Pause for silent prayer, if this has not preceded.
Almighty God,
may the sacrifice we have offered
and the eucharist we have shared
strengthen the love of N. and N.,
and give us all your fatherly aid.

We ask this through Christ our Lord.

SOLEMN BLESSING

May the Lord Jesus, who was a guest at the wedding
  in Cana,
bless you and your families and friends.

℟. Amen.

May Jesus, who loved his Church to the end,
always fill your hearts with his love.

℟. Amen.

May he grant that, as you believe in his resurrection,
so you may wait for him in joy and hope.

℟. Amen.

May almighty God bless you,
the Father, and the Son, ✝ and the Holy Spirit.

℟. Amen.

2. The Anniversaries of Marriage

On marriage anniversaries, especially the twenty-fifth and fiftieth anniversaries, the Mass of thanksgiving (p. 833) may be celebrated with the following prayers, if a votive Mass is permitted.

These prayers may also be used if desired at weekday Masses in ordinary time.

A. The Anniversary

OPENING PRAYER

God our Father,
you created man and woman
to love each other
in the bond of marriage.
Bless and strengthen N. and N.
May their marriage become an increasingly more
    perfect sign
of the union between Christ and his Church.

We ask this through our Lord Jesus Christ, your Son,
who lives and reigns with you and the Holy Spirit,
one God, for ever and ever.

PRAYER OVER THE GIFTS

Pray, brethren . . .

Father,
the blood and water that flowed
from the wounded heart of Christ your Son
was a sign of the mystery of our rebirth:
accept these gifts we offer in thanksgiving.
Continue to bless the marriage of N. and N.
with all your gifts.

Grant this in the name of Jesus the Lord.

PRAYER AFTER COMMUNION

Let us pray.
Pause for silent prayer, if this has not preceded.
Lord,
you give us food and drink from heaven.
Bless N. and N. on their anniversary.
Let their love grow stronger
that they may find within themselves
a greater peace and joy.
Bless their home
that all who come to it in need
may find in it an example of goodness
and a source of comfort.

We ask this through Christ our Lord.

B. The Twenty-fifth Anniversary of Marriage

OPENING PRAYER

Father,
you have blessed and sustained N. **and** N.
in the bond of marriage.
Continue to increase their love
throughout the joys and sorrows of life,
and help them to grow in holiness all their days.

Grant this through our Lord Jesus Christ, your Son,
who lives and reigns with you and the Holy Spirit,
one God, for ever and ever.

PRAYER OVER THE GIFTS

Pray, brethren . . .

Father,
accept these gifts which we offer in thanksgiving
 for N. **and** N.
May they bring them continued peace and happiness.

We ask this through Christ our Lord.

PRAYER AFTER COMMUNION

Let us pray.
Pause for silent prayer, if this has not preceded.
Father,
you bring N. **and** N. **(and their children and friends) together**
at the table of your family.
Help them grow in love and unity,
that they may rejoice together
in the wedding feast of heaven.

Grant this through Christ our Lord.

C. The Fiftieth Anniversary of Marriage

OPENING PRAYER

God, our Father,
bless N. and N.
We thank you for their long and happy marriage
(for the children they have brought into the world)
and for all the good they have done.
As you blessed the love of their youth,
continue to bless their life together
with gifts of peace and joy.

We ask this through our Lord Jesus Christ, your Son,
who lives and reigns with you and the Holy Spirit,
one God, for ever and ever.

PRAYER OVER THE GIFTS

Pray, brethren . . .

Lord,
accept the gifts we offer in thanksgiving for N. and N.
With trust in you and in each other
they have shared life together.
Hear their prayers,
and keep them in your peace.

We ask this through Christ our Lord.

PRAYER AFTER COMMUNION

Let us pray.
Pause for silent prayer, if this has not preceded.
Lord,
as we gather at the table of your Son,
bless N. and N. on their wedding anniversary.
Watch over them in the coming years,
and after a long and happy life together
bring them to the feast of eternal life.

Grant this through Christ our Lord.

V. CONSECRATION TO A LIFE OF VIRGINITY

This Mass may be celebrated with white
vestments, except on the Sundays of
Advent, Lent, and Easter, solemnities,
Ash Wednesday, and the weekdays of
Holy Week.

Introductory Rites

**Seek the Lord and his strength, seek the face of the Lord.
Remember the marvels he has done.** (Ps. 104:4-5)

OPENING PRAYER

**Lord,
you have given your servants
the desire to serve you in chastity.
Complete the work you have begun.
Make their gift of self whole-hearted
and bring this first beginning to its perfect end.**

**We ask this through our Lord Jesus Christ, your Son,
who lives and reigns with you and the Holy Spirit,
one God, for ever and ever.**

See Lectionary for Mass, nos. 784-788.

PRAYER OVER THE GIFTS

Pray, brethren . . .

**Father,
through this sacrifice
give your servants perseverance
in what they have begun.
When your Son comes in glory
may he welcome them
into the joy of his kingdom,
where he is Lord for ever and ever.**

When Eucharistic Prayer I is used, the
special form of **Father, accept this offering** is said:

**Father, accept and sanctify this offering
from your whole family and from these your servants,
which we make to you on the day of their consecration.
By your grace
they join themselves more closely to your Son today.
May they joyfully meet him
when he comes in glory at the end of time.**

[Through Christ our Lord. Amen.]

In the other eucharistic prayers the
consecration to a life of virginity may
be suitably commemorated as follows:

a) In the intercessions of Eucharistic
Prayer II, after the words **and all the
clergy,** there is added:

**Remember also these sisters of ours
whom you have consecrated this day
by anointing them with the Holy Spirit.
May they keep the lamp of love and faith burning brightly
as they serve you and your people unceasingly,
watching for the coming of Christ, the Bridegroom.**

b) In the intercessions of Eucharistic Prayer III, after the words your Son has gained for you, there is added:

Lord, strengthen these servants of yours in their holy purpose, as they strive to follow Christ your Son in consecrated holiness by giving witness to his love in their religious life.

c) In the intercessions of Eucharistic Prayer IV, those consecrated may be commemorated in this way:

. . . bishops and clergy everywhere.
Remember also our sisters
whom you have consecrated this day
by a perpetual dedication
to your worship and the service of mankind.
Remember those who take part in this offering . . .

Communion Rite

Like a deer that longs for running streams, my soul longs for you, my God. (Ps. 41:2)

PRAYER AFTER COMMUNION

Let us pray.
Pause for silent prayer, if this has not preceded.
Lord,
you have strengthened us by your sacred gifts.
We pray now for your servants N. and N.
May their daily lives enrich the world
and bear fruit in the Church.
We ask this through Christ our Lord.

SOLEMN BLESSING

The almighty Father
has poured into your hearts
the desire to live a life of holy virginity.
May he keep you safe under his protection.
R̸. Amen.

May the Lord Jesus Christ,
with whose sacred heart
the hearts of virgins are united,
fill you with his divine love.
R̸. Amen.

May the Holy Spirit,
by whom the Virgin Mary conceived her Son,
today consecrate your hearts
and fill you with a burning desire
to serve God and his Church.
R̸. Amen.

May almighty God,
the Father, and the Son, ✛ and the Holy Spirit.
bless all of you who have taken part in this celebration.
R̸. Amen.

VI. RELIGIOUS PROFESSION

These Masses may be celebrated with white vestments, except on the Sundays of Advent, Lent, and Easter, solemnities, Ash Wednesday, and the weekdays of Holy Week.

A
First Religious Profession

Introductory Rites

Here am I, Lord; I come to do your will. Your law is written on my heart. (Ps. 39:8-9)

OPENING PRAYER

Lord,
you have inspired our brothers (sisters)
with the resolve to follow Christ more closely.
Grant a blessed ending to the journey
on which they have set out,
so that they may be able to offer you
the perfect gift of their loving service.

We ask this through our Lord Jesus Christ, your Son,
who lives and reigns with you and the Holy Spirit,
one God, for ever and ever.

See Lectionary for Mass, nos. 784-788.

PRAYER OVER THE GIFTS

Pray, brethren . . .

Lord,
receive the gifts and prayers which we offer to you
as we celebrate the beginning of this religious profession.
Grant that these first fruits of your servants
may be nourished by your grace
and be the promise of a richer harvest.

We ask this through Christ our Lord.

Preface of Religious Profession, page 492; intercessions of the eucharistic prayers, as in the following Mass.

Communion Rite

He who has done the will of God is my brother, my sister, and my mother. (Mark 3:35)

PRAYER AFTER COMMUNION

Let us pray.
Pause for silent prayer, if this has not preceded.
Lord,
may the sacred mysteries we have shared bring us joy.
By their power grant that your servants
may constantly fulfill the religious duties they now take up
and freely give their service to you.

We ask this through Christ our Lord.

B

Perpetual Profession

1

Introductory Rites

> I rejoiced when I heard them say: Let us go to the house of
> the Lord. Jerusalem, we stand as pilgrims in your courts!
> (Ps. 121:1-2)

OPENING PRAYER

God our Father,
you have caused the grace of baptism
to bear such fruit in your servants,
that they now strive to follow your Son more closely.
Let them rightly aim at truly evangelical perfection
and increase the holiness and apostolic zeal of your Church.

We ask this through our Lord Jesus Christ, your Son,
who lives and reigns with you and the Holy Spirit,
one God, for ever and ever.

See Lectionary for Mass, nos. 784-788.

PRAYER OVER THE GIFTS

Pray, brethren . . .

Lord,
accept the gifts and the vows of your servants.
Strengthen them by your love
as they profess the evangelical counsels.

We ask this through Christ our Lord.

Preface of Religious Profession, page
492.

In the eucharistic prayers, the offering of the professed may be mentioned according to the texts below:

I. For men
a) In Eucharistic Prayer I, the special
form of **Father, accept this offering** is
said:

Father, accept and sanctify this offering
from your whole family and from these your servants,
which we make to you on the day of their profession.
By your grace
they have dedicated their lives to you today.
When your Son returns in glory,
may they share the joy of the unending Paschal feast.

[Through Christ our Lord. Amen.]

b) In the intercessions of Eucharistic
Prayer II, after the words **and all the
clergy**, there is added:

Lord, remember also these our brothers
who have today dedicated themselves to serve you always.
Grant that they may always raise their minds and hearts to you
and glorify your name.

c) In the intercessions of Eucharistic Prayer III, after the words **your Son has gained for you**, there is added:

**Strengthen also these servants of yours in their holy purpose,
for they have dedicated themselves
by the bonds of religious consecration to serve you always.
Grant that they may give witness in your Church
to the new and eternal life won by Christ's redemption.**

d) In the intercessions of Eucharistic Prayer IV, the professed may be mentioned in this way:

**. . . bishop, and bishops and clergy everywhere.
Remember these our brothers
who unite themselves more closely to you today
by their perpetual profession.
Remember those who take part in this offering . . .**

II. For women
a) In Eucharistic Prayer I, the special form of **Father, accept this offering** is said:

**Father, accept and sanctify this offering
from your whole family and from these your servants,
which we make to you on the day of their consecration.
By your grace
they join themselves more closely to your Son today.
When he comes in glory at the end of time,
may they joyfully meet him.**

[Through Christ our Lord. Amen.]

b) In the intercessions of Eucharistic Prayer II, after the words **and all the clergy**, there is added:

**Remember all these sisters of ours
who have left all things for your sake,
so that they might find you in all things
and by forgetting self serve the needs of all.**

c) In the intercessions of Eucharistic Prayer III, after the words **your Son has gained for you**, there is added:

**Lord, strengthen these servants of yours in their holy purpose,
as they strive to follow Christ your Son in consecrated holiness
by giving witness to his love in their religious life.**

d) In the intercessions of Eucharistic Prayer IV, the professed may be mentioned in this way:

**. . . bishop, and bishops and clergy everywhere.
Remember our sisters who have consecrated themselves to
   you today
by the bond of religious profession.
Remember those who take part in this offering . . .**

Communion Rite

I am nailed with Christ to the cross; I am alive, not by my
own life but by Christ's life within me. (Gal. 2:19-20)

PRAYER AFTER COMMUNION

Let us pray.
Pause for silent prayer, if this has not preceded.
Lord,
as we share these sacred mysteries,
we pray for these your servants
who are bound to you by their holy offering.
Increase in them the fire of your Holy Spirit
and unite them in eternal fellowship with your Son,
who is Lord for ever and ever.

SOLEMN BLESSING

May God who is the source of all good intentions
enlighten your minds and strengthen your hearts.
May he help you to fulfill with steadfast faith all you have
promised.
℟. **Amen.**

May the Lord enable you to travel in the joy of Christ
as you follow along his way,
and may you gladly share each other's burdens.
℟. **Amen.**

May the love of God unite you, and make you a true family
praising his name and showing forth Christ's love.
℟. **Amen.**

May almighty God,
the Father, and the Son, ☩ and the Holy Spirit,
bless all of you who have taken part in these sacred
celebrations.
℟. **Amen.**

2

Introductory Rites

I will offer sacrifice in your temple; I will fulfill the vows my
lips have promised. (Ps. 65:13-14)

OPENING PRAYER

**Lord, holy Father,
confirm the resolve of your servants (N. and N.).
Grant that the grace of baptism,
which they wish to strengthen with new bonds,
may work its full effect in them,
so that they may offer you their praise
and spread Christ's kingdom with apostolic zeal.**

**We ask this through our Lord Jesus Christ, your Son,
who lives and reigns with you and the Holy Spirit,
one God, for ever and ever.**

See Lectionary for Mass, nos. 784-788.

PRAYER OVER THE GIFTS

Pray, brethren . . .

**Lord,
accept the offerings of your servants
and make them a sign of salvation.
Fill with the gifts of your Holy Spirit
those whom you have called by your fatherly providence
to follow your Son more closely.**

We ask this through Christ our Lord.

Preface of Religious Profession, page
492; intercessions of the eucharistic
prayers, as in the preceding Mass.

Communion Rite

Taste and see the goodness of the Lord; blessed is he who
hopes in God. (Ps. 33:9)

PRAYER AFTER COMMUNION

Let us pray.
Pause for silent prayer, if this has not preceded.
Lord,
may the reception of this sacrament
and the solemnizing of this profession bring us joy.
Let this twofold act of devotion
help your servants to serve the Church and mankind
in the spirit of your love.

We ask this through Christ our Lord.

SOLEMN BLESSING

God inspires all holy desires and brings them to fulfillment.
May he protect you always by his grace,
so that you may fulfill the duties of your vocation with a
     faithful heart.

℟. Amen.

May he make each of you a witness
and sign of his love for all people.

℟. Amen.

May he make those bonds
with which he has bound you to Christ on earth
endure for ever in heavenly love.

℟. Amen.

May almighty God,
the Father, and the Son, ✝ and the Holy Spirit,
bless all of you who have taken part in this celebration.

℟. Amen.

C
Renewal of Vows

The entrance and communion antiphons, if used, may be taken from one of the three preceding Masses.

OPENING PRAYER

God our Father,
guide of mankind and ruler of creation,
look upon these your servants,
who wish to confirm their offering of themselves to you.
As the years pass by,
help them to enter more deeply into the mystery of the Church
and to dedicate themselves more generously
to the good of mankind.

We ask this through our Lord Jesus Christ, your Son,
who lives and reigns with you and the Holy Spirit,
one God, for ever and ever.

See Lectionary for Mass, nos. 784-788.

PRAYER OVER THE GIFTS

Pray, brethren . . .

Lord,
look mercifully upon the gifts of your people,
and upon the renewed offering by our brothers (sisters)
of their chastity, poverty, and obedience.
Change these temporal gifts into a sign of eternal life
and conform the minds of those who offer them
to the likeness of your Son
who is Lord for ever and ever.

Preface of Religious Profession, page 492: intercessions of the eucharistic prayers, as in the preceding Masses.

PRAYER AFTER COMMUNION

Let us pray.
Pause for silent prayer, if this has not preceded.
Lord,
now that we have received these heavenly sacraments,
we pray that your servants will trust only in your grace,
be strengthened by the power of Christ
and protected with the help of the Holy Spirit.

We ask this through Christ our Lord.

MASSES AND PRAYERS
FOR
VARIOUS NEEDS AND OCCASIONS

MASSES AND PRAYERS

FOR

VARIOUS NEEDS AND OCCASIONS

1. This section gives Masses and prayers which may be used for various needs and occasions.

The texts in the first three parts of this section may be used either in Masses with a congregation or in Masses without a congregation. The texts in the fourth part must generally be used in Masses without a congregation, unless at certain times there is a persuasive pastoral reason for using them in a Mass with a congregation.

2. The Lectionary gives proper readings for the Masses which have a complete formulary of antiphons and prayers.

3. In weekday Masses in Ordinary Time, the priest may always use the three prayers of this series or only the opening prayer; he should observe the norm of no. 1 above.

4. Masses for various needs and occasions are celebrated in the color proper to the day or the season or in violet if they bear a penitential character, for example, Masses nos. 23, 28, and 40.

MASSES AND PRAYERS
FOR
VARIOUS NEEDS AND OCCASIONS

I. FOR THE CHURCH

1. FOR THE UNIVERSAL CHURCH

A

OPENING PRAYER

**God our Father,
in your care and wisdom
you extend the kingdom of Christ to embrace the world
to give all men redemption.**

**May the Catholic Church be the sign of our salvation,
may it reveal for us the mystery of your love,
and may that love become effective in our lives.**

**Grant this through our Lord Jesus Christ, your Son,
who lives and reigns with you and the Holy Spirit,
one God, for ever and ever.**

PRAYER OVER THE GIFTS

Pray, brethren . . .

**God of mercy,
look on our offering,
and by the power of this sacrament
help all who believe in you
to become the holy people you have called to be your own.**

We ask this in the name of Jesus the Lord.

PRAYER AFTER COMMUNION

Let us pray.
Pause for silent prayer, if this has not preceded.
**God our Father,
we are sustained by your sacraments;
we are renewed by this pledge of love at your altar.**

**May we live by the promises of your love which we receive,
and become a leaven in the world
to bring salvation to mankind.**

Grant this through Christ our Lord.

B

OPENING PRAYER

God our Father,
by the promise you made
in the life, death, and resurrection of Christ your Son,
you bring together in your Spirit, from all the nations,
a people to be your own.
Keep the Church faithful to its mission:
may it be a leaven in the world
renewing us in Christ,
and transforming us into your family.

We ask this through our Lord Jesus Christ, your Son,
who lives and reigns with you and the Holy Spirit,
one God, for ever and ever.

PRAYER OVER THE GIFTS

Pray, brethren . . .

Lord,
receive our gifts.
May the Church, born from the side of Christ crucified,
continue to grow in holiness
through the sacrifice which gave it life.

We ask this through Christ our Lord.

PRAYER AFTER COMMUNION

Let us pray.
Pause for silent prayer, if this has not preceded.
Lord,
hear the prayers of those you renew
by the sacrament of Christ your Son.
May the work of your Church continue
to make known the mystery of salvation to the poor,
whom you have promised the chief place in your kingdom.

Grant this in the name of Jesus the Lord.

C

OPENING PRAYER

God our Father,
may your Church always be your holy people,
united as you are one with the Son and the Holy Spirit.
May it be for all the world a sign of your unity and holiness,
as it grows to perfection in your love.

We ask this through our Lord Jesus Christ, your Son,
who lives and reigns with you and the Holy Spirit,
one God, for ever and ever.

PRAYER OVER THE GIFTS

Pray, brethren . . .

**Lord,
we celebrate this memorial of the love of your Son.
May his saving work bring salvation to the world
through the ministry of your Church.**

We ask this through Christ our Lord.

PRAYER AFTER COMMUNION

Let us pray.
Pause for silent prayer, if this has not preceded.

**God our Father,
you comfort and encourage your Church in this sacrament;
keep us faithful to Christ
that our work on earth
may build your eternal kingdom in freedom.**

We ask this through Christ our Lord.

D

OPENING PRAYER

**Almighty and eternal God,
in Christ your Son
you have shown your glory to the world.
Guide the work of your Church:
help it to proclaim your name,
to persevere in faith
and to bring your salvation to people everywhere.**

**We ask this through our Lord Jesus Christ, your Son,
who lives and reigns with you and the Holy Spirit,
one God, for ever and ever.**

PRAYER OVER THE GIFTS

Pray, brethren . . .

**God our Father,
by the sacrifice of Christ
you freed your Church from sin
and made it holy.
May we, who are one with Christ, the head of the Church,
be one with his offering;
may we be united in serving you with all our hearts.**

Grant this in the name of Jesus the Lord.

PRAYER AFTER COMMUNION

Let us pray.

Pause for silent prayer, if this has not preceded.

Lord,
may we grow in freedom
under your guidance and love;
may we persevere in faithful service
of the Church you nourish at this altar.

Grant this in the name of Jesus the Lord.

E

(For the local Church)

OPENING PRAYER

God our Father,
in all the churches scattered throughout the world
you show forth the one, holy, catholic and apostolic Church.
Through the gospel and the eucharist
bring your people together in the Holy Spirit
and guide us in your love.
Make us a sign of your love for all people,
and help us to show forth
the living presence of Christ in the world,
who lives and reigns with you and the Holy Spirit,
one God, for ever and ever.

PRAYER OVER THE GIFTS

Pray, brethren . . .

Lord,
we celebrate the memorial of the love of your Son.
May his saving work bring salvation to all the world
through the ministry of your Church.

We ask this in the name of Jesus the Lord.

PRAYER AFTER COMMUNION

Let us pray.

Pause for silent prayer, if this has not preceded.

Father,
you sustain us with the word and body of your Son.
Watch over us with loving care;
help this Church to grow in faith,
holiness, charity, and loving service.

Grant this in the name of Jesus the Lord.

The prayers over the gifts and prayers after communion which are given in the preceding Masses may also be used.

2. FOR THE POPE
(especially on the anniversary of election)

A

This Mass is celebrated on the anniversary of the election of the pope in places where special celebrations are held, except on the Sundays of Advent, Lent, and Easter, solemnities, Ash Wednesday, and the weekdays of Holy Week.

Introductory Rites

You are Peter, the rock on which I will build my Church. The gates of hell will not hold out against it. To you I will give the keys of the kingdom of heaven. (Matthew 16:18-19)

OPENING PRAYER

Father of providence,
look with love on N. our Pope,
your appointed successor to St. Peter
on whom you built your Church.
May he be the visible center and foundation
of our unity in faith and love.

Grant this through our Lord Jesus Christ, your Son,
who lives and reigns with you and the Holy Spirit,
one God, for ever and ever.

Or:

God our Father, shepherd and guide,
look with love on N. your servant,
the pastor of your Church.
May his word and example inspire and guide the Church,
and may he, and all those entrusted to his care,
come to the joy of everlasting life.

Grant this through our Lord Jesus Christ, your Son,
who lives and reigns with you and the Holy Spirit,
one God, for ever and ever.

See Lectionary for Mass, no. 805.

PRAYER OVER THE GIFTS **Pray, brethren . . .**

Lord,
be pleased with our gifts
and give guidance to your holy Church
together with N. our Pope,
to whom you have entrusted the care of your flock.

We ask this in the name of Jesus the Lord.

Communion Rite

> Simon, son of John, do you love me more than these?
> Lord, you know all things; you know that I love you. (John
> 21:15, 17)

PRAYER AFTER COMMUNION

Let us pray.

Pause for silent prayer, if this has not preceded.

God our Father,
we have eaten at your holy table.
By the power of this sacrament,
make your Church firm in unity and love,
and grant strength and salvation
to your servant N.,
together with the flock you have entrusted
    to his care.

Grant this through Christ our Lord.

B

Another prayer for the pope

OPENING PRAYER

Lord,
source of eternal life and truth,
give to your shepherd N.
a spirit of courage and right judgment,
a spirit of knowledge and love.
By governing with fidelity those entrusted to his care
may he, as successor to the apostle Peter
    and vicar of Christ,
build your Church into a sacrament of unity, love, and peace
    for all the world.

We ask this through our Lord Jesus Christ, your Son,
who lives and reigns with you and the Holy Spirit,
one God, for ever and ever.

3. FOR THE BISHOP

(especially on the anniversary of ordination)

A

This Mass is celebrated on the anniversary of the election of the bishop in places where special celebrations are held, except on the Sundays of Advent, Lent, and Easter, solemnities, Ash Wednesday, and the weekdays of Holy Week.

Introductory Rites

I will look after my sheep, says the Lord, and I will raise up one shepherd who will pasture them. I, the Lord, will be their God. (Ezek. 34:11, 23-24)

OPENING PRAYER

God, eternal shepherd,
you tend your Church in many ways,
and rule us with love.
Help your chosen servant N.
as pastor for Christ,
to watch over your flock.
Help him to be a faithful teacher,
a wise administrator, and a holy priest.

We ask this through our Lord Jesus Christ,
   your Son,
who lives and reigns with you and the Holy
   Spirit,
one God, for ever and ever.

Or:

God our Father, our shepherd and guide,
look with love on N. your servant,
your appointed pastor of the Church.
May his word and example inspire and guide
   the Church;
may he, and all those in his care,
come to the joy of everlasting life.

Grant this through our Lord Jesus Christ, your
   Son,
who lives and reigns with you and the Holy
   Spirit,
one God, for ever and ever.

See Lectionary for Mass, no. 805.

PRAYER OVER THE GIFTS   **Pray, brethren . . .**

Lord,
accept these gifts which we offer for your servant N.,
   your chosen priest.
Enrich him with the gifts and virtues of a true apostle
for the good of your people.

We ask this through Christ our Lord.

Communion Rite
    The Son of Man did not come to be served, but to serve,
    and to give his life as a ransom for many. (Matthew 20:28)

PRAYER AFTER COMMUNION

Let us pray.
Pause for silent prayer, if this has not preceded.
**Lord,
by the power of these holy mysteries
increase in our bishop N. your gifts of wisdom and love.
May he fulfill his pastoral ministry
and receive the eternal rewards
you promise to your faithful servants.**

Grant this through Christ our Lord.

B

Another prayer for the bishop

OPENING PRAYER

**Lord our God,
you have chosen your servant N.
to be a shepherd of your flock
in the tradition of the apostles.
Give him a spirit of courage and right judgment,
a spirit of knowledge and love.
By governing with fidelity those entrusted to his care
may he build your Church as a sign of salvation for the world.**

**We ask this through our Lord Jesus Christ, your Son,
who lives and reigns with you and the Holy Spirit,
one God, for ever and ever.**

4. FOR THE ELECTION OF A POPE OR BISHOP

Introductory Rites

I will raise up for myself a faithful priest; he will do what is
in my heart and in my mind, says the Lord. (1 Sam. 2:35)

OPENING PRAYER

**Lord God,
you are our eternal shepherd and guide.
In your mercy grant your Church a shepherd
who will walk in your ways
and whose watchful care will bring us your blessing.**

**We ask this through our Lord Jesus Christ, your Son,
who lives and reigns with you and the Holy Spirit,
one God, for ever and ever.**

See Lectionary for Mass, nos. 800-804.

PRAYER OVER THE GIFTS

Pray, brethren . . .

**Lord,
bless us with the fullness of your love.
By these gifts we offer you,
give us the joy of having a shepherd to lead your Church
who will be pleasing and acceptable to you.**

We ask this through Christ our Lord.

Communion Rite

The Lord says, I have chosen you from the world, to go and
to bear fruit that will last. (John 15:16)

PRAYER AFTER COMMUNION

Let us pray.
Pause for silent prayer, if this has not preceded.
**Lord,
you renew us with the saving sacrament
of the body and blood of your Son.
In your love for us
give us the joy of receiving a shepherd
who will be an example of goodness to your people
and will fill our hearts and minds with the trust of the gospel.**

We ask this in the name of Jesus the Lord.

5. FOR A COUNCIL OR SYNOD

Introductory Rites

To crown all things there must be love, to bind them together and bring them to completion; and may the peace of Christ rule in your hearts. (Col. 3:14-15)

OPENING PRAYER

Or:

Lord,
protector and ruler of your Church,
fill your servants with a spirit of understanding,
   truth and peace.
Help them to strive with all their hearts
to learn what is pleasing to you,
and to follow it with all their strength.

We ask this through our Lord Jesus Christ,
   your Son,
who lives and reigns with you and the Holy
   Spirit,
one God, for ever and ever.

God our Father,
you judge your people with kindness
and rule us with love.
Give a spirit of wisdom
to those you have entrusted with authority
in your Church
that your people may come to know the truth
   more fully
and grow in holiness.

Grant this through our Lord Jesus Christ, your
   Son,
who lives and reigns with you and the Holy
   Spirit,
one God, for ever and ever.

See Lectionary for Mass, nos. 826-830.

PRAYER OVER THE GIFTS

Pray, brethren . . .

God of love,
look upon the gifts of your servants,
and give us light to know your way,
to understand it clearly,
and to follow it in confidence.

We ask this through Christ our Lord.

Communion Rite

Where charity and love are found, God is there. The love of Christ has gathered us together.

PRAYER AFTER COMMUNION

Let us pray.

Pause for silent prayer, if this has not preceded.

God of mercy,
may the holy gifts we receive
strengthen your servants in the truth
and inspire them to seek the honor of your name.

Grant this in the name of Jesus the Lord.

6. FOR PRIESTS

Introductory Rites
> The Spirit of God is upon me; he has anointed me. He sent me to bring good news to the poor, and to heal the broken-hearted. (Luke 4:18)

OPENING PRAYER

Father,
you have appointed your Son Jesus Christ
**   eternal High Priest.**
Guide those he has chosen to be ministers of
**   word and sacrament**
and help them to be faithful
in fulfilling the ministry they have received.

Grant this through our Lord Jesus Christ, your
**   Son,**
who lives and reigns with you and the Holy
**   Spirit,**
one God, for ever and ever.

Or:

Lord our God,
you guide your people by the ministry of
**   priests.**
Keep them faithful in obedient service to you
that by their life and ministry
they may bring you glory in Christ.

We ask this through our Lord Jesus Christ,
**   your Son,**
who lives and reigns with you and the Holy
**   Spirit,**
one God, for ever and ever.

See Lectionary for Mass, nos. 719-724.

PRAYER OVER THE GIFTS   **Pray, brethren . . .**

Father,
in your plan for salvation you have appointed priests
to minister to your people at your holy altars.
By the power of this sacrament
may their priestly service always be pleasing to you
and bring lasting good to your Church.

We ask this through Christ our Lord.

Communion Rite
> Father, make them holy in the truth. As you sent me into the world, I have sent them into the world. (John 17:17-18)

PRAYER AFTER COMMUNION   **Let us pray.**
Pause for silent prayer, if this has not preceded.
Lord,
may the sacrifice we offer and receive
give life to your priests and all your people.
Keep them joined to you by a love that will never end,
and make them worthy members of your household.

We ask this in the name of Jesus the Lord.

7. FOR THE PRIEST HIMSELF

A

Especially for a priest who has been given pastoral responsibilities

OPENING PRAYER

Father,
you have given me charge of your family
not because I am worthy
but because of your infinite love.
Help me to fulfill my priestly ministry
under your loving rule
by guiding the people entrusted to my care.

Grant this through our Lord Jesus Christ, your Son,
who lives and reigns with you and the Holy Spirit,
one God, for ever and ever.

PRAYER OVER THE GIFTS

Pray, brethren . . .

Father,
with your power and love
you guide us through the changes of time and season.
Help me to use properly the gifts you have given me.
By the power of this sacrifice
fill the hearts of your priest and people with love,
that the shepherd may have a faithful people
and the people a loving shepherd.

Grant this through Christ our Lord.

PRAYER AFTER COMMUNION

Let us pray.

Pause for silent prayer, if this has not preceded.

All-powerful and ever-living God,
every virtue has its source in you
and reaches perfection under your guidance.
By sharing in the mystery of this eucharist
help me to do what is right
and to preach what is true,
that by my teaching and living
I may help your faithful people
grow in the knowledge of your love.

Grant this through Christ our Lord.

B

OPENING PRAYER

**God of mercy,
hear my prayers
and fill my heart with the light of your Holy Spirit.
May I worthily minister your mysteries,
faithfully serve your Church,
and come to love you with a never-ending love.**

**Grant this through our Lord Jesus Christ, your Son,
who lives and reigns with you and the Holy Spirit,
one God, for ever and ever.**

PRAYER OVER THE GIFTS

Pray, brethren . . .

**All-powerful God,
accept these gifts we offer you
and see in them your Son Jesus Christ,
who is both priest and sacrifice.
May I who share in his priesthood
always be a spiritual offering pleasing to you.**

Grant this through Christ our Lord.

PRAYER AFTER COMMUNION

Let us pray.
Pause for silent prayer, if this has not preceded.
**Father,
you strengthen me with bread from heaven
and give me the joy of sharing the cup of the new covenant.
Keep me faithful in your service
and let me spend my entire life working with courage and love
for the salvation of mankind.**

Grant this through Christ our Lord.

C
On the anniversary of ordination

OPENING PRAYER

**Father,
unworthy as I am, you have chosen me
to share in the eternal priesthood of Christ
and the ministry of your Church.
May I be an ardent but gentle servant
of your gospel and your sacraments.**

**Grant this through our Lord Jesus Christ, your Son,
who lives and reigns with you and the Holy Spirit,
one God, for ever and ever.**

PRAYER OVER THE GIFTS

Pray, brethren . . .

**Lord,
in your mercy, accept our offering
and help me to fulfill the ministry you have given me
in spite of my unworthiness.**

Grant this through Christ our Lord.

PRAYER AFTER COMMUNION

Let us pray.
Pause for silent prayer, if this has not preceded.
**Lord,
on this anniversary of my ordination
I have celebrated the mystery of faith
to the glory of your name.
May I always live in truth
the mysteries I handle at your altar.**

Grant this in the name of Jesus the Lord.

8. FOR THE MINISTERS OF THE CHURCH

OPENING PRAYER

Father,
you have taught the ministers of your Church
not to desire that they be served but to serve their brothers
    and sisters.
May they be effective in their work
and persevering in their prayer,
performing their ministry with gentleness and concern
    for others.
We ask this through our Lord Jesus Christ, your Son,
who lives and reigns with you and the Holy Spirit,
one God, for ever and ever.

PRAYER OVER THE GIFTS

Pray, brethren . . .

Father,
your Son washed the feet of his disciples
as an example for us.
Accept our gifts and our worship;
by offering ourselves as a spiritual sacrifice
may we be filled with the spirit of humility and love.

We ask this through Christ our Lord.

PRAYER AFTER COMMUNION

Let us pray.
Pause for silent prayer, if this has not preceded.

Lord,
you renew your servants with food and drink from heaven.
Keep them faithful as ministers of word and sacrament,
working for your glory
and for the salvation of those who believe in you.

Grant this in the name of Jesus the Lord.

9. FOR PRIESTLY VOCATIONS

Introductory Rites

Jesus says to his disciples: ask the Lord to send workers
into his harvest. (Matthew 9:38)

OPENING PRAYER

Father,
in your plan for our salvation you provide shepherds for your
   people.
Fill your Church with the spirit of courage and love.
Raise up worthy ministers for your altars
and ardent but gentle servants of the gospel.

Grant this through our Lord Jesus Christ, your Son,
who lives and reigns with you and the Holy Spirit,
one God, for ever and ever.

See Lectionary for Mass, nos. 806-810.

PRAYER OVER THE GIFTS

Pray, brethren . . .

Lord,
accept our prayers and gifts.
Give the Church more priests
and keep them faithful in their love and service.

Grant this in the name of Jesus the Lord.

Communion Rite

This is how we know what love is: Christ gave up his life for
us; and we too must give up our lives for our brothers.
(1 John 3:16)

PRAYER AFTER COMMUNION

Let us pray.
Pause for silent prayer, if this has not preceded.
Lord,
hear the prayers of those who are renewed
with the bread of life at your holy table.
By this sacrament of love
bring to maturity
the seeds you have sown
in the field of your Church;
may many of your people choose to serve you
by devoting themselves to the service of their brothers and
   sisters.

We ask this through Christ our Lord.

10. FOR RELIGIOUS

OPENING PRAYER

**Father,
you inspire and bring to fulfillment every good intention.
Guide your people in the way of salvation
and watch over those who have left all things
to give themselves entirely to you.
By following Christ and renouncing worldly power and profit,
may they serve you and their brothers faithfully
in the spirit of poverty and humility.**

**We ask this through our Lord Jesus Christ, your Son,
who lives and reigns with you and the Holy Spirit,
one God, for ever and ever.**

PRAYER OVER THE GIFTS

Pray, brethren . . .

**Lord,
by these holy gifts we offer
make holy those you gather together in your name.
May they be faithful in keeping their vows
and may they serve you with undivided hearts.**

We ask this in the name of Jesus the Lord.

PRAYER AFTER COMMUNION

Let us pray.
Pause for silent prayer, if this has not preceded.
**Lord,
you have gathered your servants together in your love
to share the one bread of life.
Make them one in their concern for each other
and in their common dedication to the works of charity.
By their holy way of life
may they be true witnesses of Christ to all the world.**

We ask this in the name of Jesus the Lord.

11. FOR RELIGIOUS VOCATIONS

Introductory Rites

If you wish to be perfect, go, sell what you own, give it all to the poor, then come, and follow me. (Matthew 19:21)

OPENING PRAYER

Father,
you call all who believe in you to grow perfect in love
by following in the footsteps of Christ your Son.
May those whom you have chosen to serve you as religious
provide by their way of life
a convincing sign of your kingdom
for the Church and the whole world.

We ask this through our Lord Jesus Christ, your Son,
who lives and reigns with you and the Holy Spirit,
one God, for ever and ever.

See Lectionary for Mass, nos. 806-810.

Or (to be said by the religious themselves):

Lord,
look with love on your family.
May it increase in numbers,
lead its members to perfect love,
and work effectively for the salvation of all men.

Grant this through our Lord Jesus Christ, your Son,
who lives and reigns with you and the Holy Spirit,
one God, for ever and ever.

PRAYER OVER THE GIFTS

Pray, brethren . . .

Father,
in your love accept the gifts we offer you,
and watch over those who wish to follow your Son
more closely, and to serve you joyfully in religious life.
Give them spiritual freedom
and love for their brothers and sisters.

We ask this through Christ our Lord.

Communion Rite

I solemnly tell you: those who have left everything and followed me will be repaid a hundredfold and will gain eternal life. (Matthew 19:27-29)

PRAYER AFTER COMMUNION

Let us pray.
Pause for silent prayer, if this has not preceded.

Father,
make your people grow strong
by sharing this spiritual food and drink.
Keep them faithful to the call of the gospel
that the world may see in them
the living image of your Son, Jesus Christ,
who is Lord for ever and ever.

Or (to be said by the religious themselves):

Lord,
by the power of this sacrament
keep us faithful in your service.
May we be witnesses of your love to the world
and strive with courage for good things
which alone last for ever.

We ask this in the name of Jesus the Lord.

12. FOR THE LAITY

OPENING PRAYER

God our Father,
you send the power of the gospel into the world
as a life-giving leaven.
Fill with the Spirit of Christ
those whom you call to live in the midst of the world
and its concerns;
help them by their work on earth
to build up your eternal kingdom.

We ask this through our Lord Jesus Christ, your Son,
who lives and reigns with you and the Holy Spirit,
one God, for ever and ever.

PRAYER OVER THE GIFTS

Pray, brethren . . .

Father,
you have given your Son
to save the whole world by his sacrifice.
By the power of this offering,
help all your people
to fill the world with the Spirit of Christ.

Grant this through Christ our Lord.

PRAYER AFTER COMMUNION

Let us pray.
Pause for silent prayer, if this has not preceded.
Lord,
you share with us the fullness of your love,
and give us new courage at this eucharistic feast.
May the people you call to work in the world
be effective witnesses to the truth of the gospel
and make your Church a living presence
in the midst of that world.

We ask this through Christ our Lord.

13. FOR UNITY OF CHRISTIANS

A

Introductory Rites

I am the Good Shepherd. I know my sheep, and mine know me, says the Lord, just as the Father knows me and I know the Father. I give my life for my sheep. (John 10:14-15)

OPENING PRAYER

Almighty and eternal God,
you keep together those you have united.
Look kindly on all who follow Jesus your Son.
We are all consecrated to you by our common baptism;
make us one in the fullness of faith
and keep us one in the fellowship of love.

We ask this through our Lord Jesus Christ,
   your Son,
who lives and reigns with you and the Holy Spirit,
one God, for ever and ever.

Or:

Lord,
lover of mankind,
fill us with the love your Spirit gives.
May we live in a manner worthy of our calling;
make us witnesses of your truth to all men
and help us work to bring all believers together
in the unity of faith and the fellowship of peace.

Grant this through our Lord Jesus Christ, your Son,
who lives and reigns with you and the Holy Spirit,
one God, for ever and ever.

See Lectionary for Mass, nos. 811-815.

PRAYER OVER THE GIFTS

Pray, brethren . . .

Lord,
by one perfect sacrifice
you gained us as your people.
Bless us and all your Church
with gifts of unity and peace.

We ask this in the name of Jesus the Lord.

Preface of Christian Unity, page 493.

Communion Rite

Because there is one bread, we, though many, are one body, for we all share in the one loaf and in the one cup. (See 1 Cor. 10:17)

PRAYER AFTER COMMUNION

Let us pray.
Pause for silent prayer, if this has not preceded.
Lord,
may this holy communion,
the sign and promise of our unity in you,
make that unity a reality in your Church.

We ask this through Christ our Lord.

B

Save us, Lord our God, and gather us together from the nations, that we may proclaim your holy name and glory in your praise. (Ps. 105:47)

OPENING PRAYER

Or:

**God our Father,
you bring many nations together
to unite in praising your name.
Make us able and willing to do what you ask.
May the people you call to your kingdom
be one in faith and love.**

**We ask this through our Lord Jesus Christ,
your Son,
who lives and reigns with you and the Holy
Spirit,
one God, for ever and ever.**

**Lord,
hear the prayers of your people
and bring the hearts of believers together in
your praise
and in common sorrow for their sins.
Heal all divisions among Christians
that we may rejoice in the perfect unity of your
Church
and move together as one
to eternal life in your kingdom.**

**Grant this through our Lord Jesus Christ, your
Son,
who lives and reigns with you and the Holy
Spirit,
one God, for ever and ever.**

See Lectionary for Mass, nos. 811-815.

PRAYER OVER THE GIFTS

Pray, brethren . . .

**Lord,
hear our prayer for your mercy
as we celebrate this memorial of our salvation.
May this sacrament of your love
be our sign of unity and our bond of charity.**

We ask this through Christ our Lord.

Preface of Christian Unity, page 493.

Communion Rite

To crown all things there must be love, to bind them together and bring them to completion; and may the peace of Christ rule in your hearts, that peace to which all of you are called as one body. (Col. 3:14-15)

PRAYER AFTER COMMUNION

Let us pray.
Pause for silent prayer, if this has not preceded.

**Lord,
fill us with the Spirit of love;
by the power of this sacrifice
bring together in love and peace
all who believe in you.**

Grant this in the name of Jesus the Lord.

C

Introductory Rites

There is one body and one spirit as there is one hope held
out to you by your call; there is one Lord, one faith, one
baptism; one God, the Father of all, and through all; he
lives in all of us. (Eph. 4:4-6)

OPENING PRAYER   Or:

Father,
look with love on your people
and pour out upon them the gifts of your
  Spirit.
May they constantly grow in the love of truth.
May they study and work together
for perfect unity among Christians.

We ask this through our Lord Jesus Christ,
  your Son,
who lives and reigns with you and the Holy
  Spirit,
one God, for ever and ever.

Lord,
pour out upon us the fullness of your mercy
and by the power of your Spirit
remove divisions among Christians.
Let your Church rise more clearly as a sign for
  all the nations
that the world may be filled with the light of
  your Spirit
and believe in Jesus Christ whom you have
  sent,
who lives and reigns with you and the Holy
  Spirit,
one God, for ever and ever.

See Lectionary for Mass, nos. 811-815.

PRAYER OVER THE GIFTS   **Pray, brethren . . .**

Father,
may the sacrifice we offer you
free us from our sins
and bring together all who are joined by one baptism
to share this mystery of the eucharist.

Grant this through Christ our Lord.

Preface of Christian Unity, page 493.

Communion Rite

May all be one as you are, Father, in me, and I in you; may
they be one in us: I in them and you in me, may they be
completely one. (John 17:21, 23)

PRAYER AFTER COMMUNION   **Let us pray.**
Pause for silent prayer, if this has not preceded.
Lord,
we who share in the sacraments of Christ
ask you to renew the gift of holiness
  in your Church.
May all who glory in the name of Christian
come to serve you in the unity of faith.

We ask this through Christ our Lord.

14. FOR THE SPREAD OF THE GOSPEL

This Mass may be celebrated whenever there are special celebrations for the missions, even on Sundays of Ordinary Time, but not on a Sunday of Advent, Lent, or the Easter season or on a solemnity.

A

Introductory Rites

May God bless us in his mercy; may he make his face shine on us, that we might know his ways on earth and his saving power among all the nations. (Ps. 66:2-3)

OPENING PRAYER

Or:

God our Father,
you will all men to be saved
and come to the knowledge of your truth.
Send workers into your great harvest
that the gospel may be preached to every creature
and your people, gathered together by the word of life
and strengthened by the power of the sacraments,
may advance in the way of salvation and love.

We ask this through our Lord Jesus Christ, your Son,
who lives and reigns with you and the Holy Spirit,
one God, for ever and ever.

God our Father,
you sent your Son into the world to be its true light.
Pour out the Spirit he promised us
to sow the truth in men's hearts
and awaken in them obedience to the faith.
May all men be born again to new life in baptism
and enter the fellowship of your one holy people.

Grant this through our Lord Jesus Christ, your Son,
who lives and reigns with you and the Holy Spirit,
one God, for ever and ever.

See Lectionary for Mass, nos. 816-820.

PRAYER OVER THE GIFTS **Pray, brethren . . .**

Lord,
look upon the face of Christ your Son
who gave up his life to set all men free.
Through him may your name be praised
among all peoples from East to West,
and everywhere may one sacrifice be offered to give you glory.

We ask this through Christ our Lord.

Communion Rite

Teach all nations to carry out everything I have commanded you. I am with you always, until the end of the world. (Matthew 28:20)

PRAYER AFTER COMMUNION **Let us pray.**

Pause for silent prayer, if this has not preceded.
Lord, you renew our life with this gift of redemption.
Through this help to eternal salvation
may the true faith continue to grow throughout the world.

We ask this in the name of Jesus the Lord.

B

Introductory Rites

Proclaim his glory among the nations, his marvelous deeds
to all the peoples; great is the Lord and worthy of all praise.
(Ps. 95:3-4)

OPENING PRAYER

**Father,
you will your Church to be the sacrament of salvation for all
    peoples.
Make us feel more urgently
the call to work for the salvation of all men,
until you have made us all one people.
Inspire the hearts of all your people
to continue the saving work of Christ everywhere
until the end of the world.**

**Grant this through our Lord Jesus Christ, your Son,
who lives and reigns with you and the Holy Spirit,
one God, for ever and ever.**

See Lectionary for Mass, nos. 816-820.

PRAYER OVER THE GIFTS

Pray, brethren . . .

**Lord,
the suffering and death of Christ your Son
won your salvation for all the world.
May the prayers and gifts of your Church
come before you and be pleasing in your sight.**

We ask this through Christ our Lord.

Communion Rite

All you nations, praise the Lord, proclaim him, all you
peoples! For steadfast is his kindly mercy to us, and everlasting his fidelity. (Ps. 116:1-2)

or:

Go out to the whole world, and preach the gospel to all
creation, says the Lord. (Mark 16:15)

PRAYER AFTER COMMUNION

Let us pray.

Pause for silent prayer, if this has not preceded.

**Lord,
make us holy by the eucharist we share at your table.
Through the sacrament of your Church
may all peoples receive the salvation your Son brought us
through his suffering and death on the cross,
for he is Lord for ever and ever.**

15. FOR PERSECUTED CHRISTIANS

Introductory Rites

Lord, be true to your covenant, forget not the life of your poor ones for ever. Rise up, O God, and defend your cause; do not ignore the shouts of your enemies. (See Ps. 73:20, 19, 22, 23)

OPENING PRAYER

**Father,
in your mysterious providence,
your Church must share in the sufferings of Christ your Son.
Give the spirit of patience and love
to those who are persecuted for their faith in you
that they may always be true and faithful witnesses
to your promise of eternal life.**

**We ask this through our Lord Jesus Christ, your Son,
who lives and reigns with you and the Holy Spirit,
one God, for ever and ever.**

See Lectionary for Mass, nos. 821-825.

PRAYER OVER THE GIFTS

Pray, brethren . . .

**Lord,
accept the prayers and gifts we offer.
May those who suffer persecution
because of their faithful service to you
rejoice in uniting their sacrifice to that of Christ your Son
and realize that their names are written in heaven
among your chosen people.**

We ask this through Christ our Lord.

Communion Rite

Happy are you when they curse you, and persecute you for my sake, says the Lord; rejoice and leap for joy, because there is a great reward for you in heaven. (Matthew 5:11-12)

PRAYER AFTER COMMUNION

Let us pray.
Pause for silent prayer, if this has not preceded.
**Lord,
by the power of this sacrament
make your people strong in the truth.
Help your faithful people who suffer persecution
to carry their cross in the footsteps of Christ your Son
and in the midst of their sufferings
rejoice to be called Christians.**

We ask this through Christ our Lord.

16. FOR PASTORAL OR SPIRITUAL MEETINGS

Introductory Rites

Where two or three are gathered together in my name, says the Lord, I am there among them. (Matthew 18:20)

or:

To crown all things there must be love, to bind them together and bring them to completion; and may the peace of Christ rule in your hearts. (Col. 3:14-15)

OPENING PRAYER

Or:

**Lord,
pour out on us the spirit of understanding, truth, and peace.
Help us to strive with all our hearts
to know what is pleasing to you,
and when we know your will
make us determined to do it.**

**We ask this through our Lord Jesus Christ, your Son,
who lives and reigns with you and the Holy Spirit,
one God, for ever and ever.**

**God our Father,
your Son promised to be with all who gather in his name.
Make us aware of his presence among us
and fill us with his grace, mercy, and peace,
so that we may live in truth and love.**

**Grant this through our Lord Jesus Christ, your Son,
who lives and reigns with you and the Holy Spirit,
one God, for ever and ever.**

See Lectionary for Mass, nos. 826-830.

PRAYER OVER THE GIFTS

Pray, brethren . . .

**God our Father,
look with love on the gifts of your people.
Help us to understand what is right and good in your sight
and to proclaim it faithfully to our brothers and sisters.**

We ask this through Christ our Lord.

Communion Rite

Where charity and love are found, God is there. The love of Christ has gathered us together.

PRAYER AFTER COMMUNION

Let us pray.
Pause for silent prayer, if this has not preceded.
**God of mercy,
may the holy gifts we receive
give us strength in doing your will,
and make us effective witnesses of your truth
to all whose lives we touch.**

We ask this in the name of Jesus the Lord.

II. FOR CIVIL NEEDS

17. FOR THE NATION, (STATE,) OR CITY

OPENING PRAYER

God our Father,
you guide everything in wisdom and love.
Accept the prayers we offer for our nation;
by the wisdom of our leaders and integrity of our citizens,
may harmony and justice be secured
and may there be lasting prosperity and peace.

We ask this through our Lord Jesus Christ, your Son,
who lives and reigns with you and the Holy Spirit,
one God, for ever and ever.

18. FOR THOSE WHO SERVE IN PUBLIC OFFICE

OPENING PRAYER

Almighty and eternal God,
you know the longings of men's hearts
and you protect their rights.
In your goodness,
watch over those in authority,
so that people everywhere may enjoy
freedom, security, and peace.

We ask this through our Lord Jesus Christ, your Son,
who lives and reigns with you and the Holy Spirit,
one God, for ever and ever.

19. FOR THE CONGRESS

OPENING PRAYER

Father,
you guide and govern everything with order and love.
Look upon the members of Congress
and fill them with the spirit of your wisdom.
May they always act in accordance with your will
and their decisions be for the peace and well-being of all.

We ask this through our Lord Jesus Christ, your Son,
who lives and reigns with you and the Holy Spirit,
one God, for ever and ever.

20. FOR THE PRESIDENT

OPENING PRAYER

God our Father,
all earthly powers must serve you.
Help our President N.
to fulfill his responsibilities worthily and well.
By honoring and striving to please you at all times,
may he secure peace and freedom
for the people entrusted to him.

We ask this through our Lord Jesus Christ, your Son,
who lives and reigns with you and the Holy Spirit,
one God, for ever and ever.

21. FOR THE PROGRESS OF PEOPLES

OPENING PRAYER

Father,
you have given all peoples one common origin,
and your will is to gather them as one family in yourself.
Fill the hearts of all men with the fire of your love
and the desire to ensure justice for all their brothers and
    sisters.
By sharing the good things you give us
may we secure justice and equality for every human being,
an end to all division,
and a human society built on love and peace.

We ask this through our Lord Jesus Christ, your Son,
who lives and reigns with you and the Holy Spirit,
one God, for ever and ever.

PRAYER OVER THE GIFTS

Pray, brethren . . .

Lord,
hear the prayers of those who call on you,
and accept the offering of your Church.
Fill all men with the spirit of the sons of God,
until all injustice is conquered by love
and there is one family of man
established in your peace.

We ask this through Christ our Lord.

PRAYER AFTER COMMUNION

Let us pray.
Pause for silent prayer, if this has not preceded.
Lord,
you renew us with the one bread
that restores the human family to life.
By our sharing in the sacrament of unity,
fill us with a strong and unselfish love
that we may work for the progress of all peoples
and lovingly bring the work of justice to perfection.

We ask this through Christ our Lord.

22. FOR PEACE AND JUSTICE

A

Introductory Rites

Give peace, Lord, to those who wait for you; listen to the
prayers of your servants, and guide us in the way of justice.

(See Sir. 36:18-19)

OPENING PRAYER   Or:

God our Father,
you reveal that those who work for peace
will be called your sons.
Help us to work without ceasing
for that justice
which brings true and lasting peace.
We ask this through our Lord Jesus Christ,
    your Son,
who lives and reigns with you and the Holy
    Spirit,
one God, for ever and ever.

Lord,
you guide all creation with fatherly care.
As you have given all men one common origin,
bring them together peacefully into one family
and keep them united in brotherly love.

We ask this through our Lord Jesus Christ,
    your Son,
who lives and reigns with you and the Holy
    Spirit,
one God, for ever and ever.

See Lectionary for Mass, nos. 831-835.

PRAYER OVER THE GIFTS   **Pray, brethren . . .**

Lord,
may the saving sacrifice of your Son, our King and
    peacemaker,
which we offer through these sacramental signs of unity and
    peace,
bring harmony and concord to all your children.

We ask this through Christ our Lord.

Communion Rite

Happy the peacemakers; they shall be called sons of God.

(Matthew 5:9)

or:

Peace I leave with you, my own peace I give you, says the
Lord. (John 14:27)

PRAYER AFTER COMMUNION   **Let us pray.**

Pause for silent prayer, if this has not preceded.

Lord,
you give us the body and blood of your Son
and renew our strength.
Fill us with the spirit of love
that we may work effectively to establish among men
Christ's farewell gift of peace.

We ask this through Christ our Lord.

B

Other prayers for peace

1

OPENING PRAYER

God our Father,
creator of the world,
you establish the order which governs all the ages.
Hear our prayer and give us peace in our time
that we may rejoice in your mercy
and praise you without end.

We ask this through our Lord Jesus Christ, your Son,
who lives and reigns with you and the Holy Spirit,
one God, for ever and ever.

2

OPENING PRAYER

God of perfect peace,
violence and cruelty can have no part with you.
May those who are at peace with one another
hold fast to the good will that unites them;
may those who are enemies forget their hatred
and be healed.

We ask this through our Lord Jesus Christ, your Son,
who lives and reigns with you and the Holy Spirit,
one God, for ever and ever.

23. IN TIME OF WAR OR CIVIL DISTURBANCE

Introductory Rites

The Lord says: my plans for you are peace and not disaster; when you call to me, I will listen to you, and I will bring you back to the place from which I exiled you. (Jer. 29:11, 12, 14)

or:

The snares of death overtook me, the ropes of hell tightened around me; in my distress I called upon the Lord, and he heard my voice. (Ps. 17:5-7)

OPENING PRAYER

God of power and mercy,
you destroy war and put down earthly pride.
Banish violence from our midst and wipe away
  our tears
that we may all deserve to be called your
  sons and daughters.

We ask this through our Lord Jesus Christ,
  your Son,
who lives and reigns with you and the Holy
  Spirit,
one God, for ever and ever.

Or:

God our Father,
maker and lover of peace,
to know you is to live,
and to serve you is to reign.
All our faith is in your saving help;
protect us from men of violence
and keep us safe from weapons of hate.

We ask this through our Lord Jesus Christ,
  your Son,
who lives and reigns with you and the Holy
  Spirit,
one God, for ever and ever.

See Lectionary for Mass, nos. 836-840.

PRAYER OVER THE GIFTS

Pray, brethren . . .

Lord,
remember Christ your Son who is peace itself
and who has washed away our hatred with his blood.
Because you love all men,
look with mercy on us.
Banish the violence and evil within us,
and by this offering restore tranquility and peace.

We ask this through Christ our Lord.

Communion Rite

The Lord says, peace I leave with you, my own peace I give you; not as the world gave do I give. Do not let your heart be troubled or afraid. (John 14:27)

PRAYER AFTER COMMUNION

Let us pray.
Pause for silent prayer, if this has not preceded.

Father,
you satisfy our hunger with the one bread
that gives strength to mankind.
Help us to overcome war and violence,
and to establish your law of love and justice.

We ask this through Christ our Lord.

III. FOR VARIOUS PUBLIC NEEDS

24. BEGINNING OF THE CIVIL YEAR

This Mass may not be celebrated on
January 1, the solemnity of Mary the
Mother of God.

Introductory Rites

Lord, you will crown the year with your goodness; to you
we give thanks and praise. (Ps. 64:12)

OPENING PRAYER

**Almighty God,
with you there is no beginning and no end
for you are the origin and goal of all creation.
May this new year which we dedicate to you
bring us abundant prosperity and growth in holy living.**

**We ask this through our Lord Jesus Christ, your Son,
who lives and reigns with you and the Holy Spirit,
one God, for ever and ever.**

See Lectionary for Mass, nos. 841-845.

PRAYER OVER THE GIFTS

Pray, brethren . . .

**Lord,
let this sacrifice we offer
be pleasing in your sight;
may all who celebrate this new year with joy
live the entire year in your love.**

We ask this through Christ our Lord.

Communion Rite

Jesus Christ is the same yesterday, today, and for ever.
(Heb. 13:8)

PRAYER AFTER COMMUNION

Let us pray.
Pause for silent prayer, if this has not preceded.
**Lord,
be close to your people who receive these holy mysteries;
as we place all our trust in your protection,
keep us safe from danger throughout this year.**

Grant this through Christ our Lord.

25. FOR THE BLESSING OF HUMAN LABOR

A

Introductory Rites

May the goodness of the Lord be upon us, and give success to the work of our hands. (Ps. 89:17)

OPENING PRAYER

God our Creator,
it is your will that man accept the duty of work.
In your kindness may the work we begin
bring us growth in this life
and help to extend the kingdom of Christ.

We ask this through our Lord Jesus Christ,
    your Son,
who lives and reigns with you and the Holy
    Spirit,
one God, for ever and ever.

Or:

God our Father,
by the labor of man you govern and guide to
    perfection
the work of creation.
Hear the prayers of your people
and give all men work that enhances their
    human dignity
and draws them closer to each other
in the service of their brothers.

We ask this through our Lord Jesus Christ,
    your Son,
who lives and reigns with you and the Holy
    Spirit,
one God, for ever and ever.

See Lectionary for Mass, nos. 846-850.

PRAYER OVER THE GIFTS

Pray, brethren . . .

God our Father,
you provide the human race with food for strength
and with the eucharist for its renewal;
may these gifts which we offer
always bring us health of mind and body.

Grant this through Christ our Lord.

Communion Rite

Let everything you do or say be in the name of the Lord
with thanksgiving to God. (Col. 3:17)

PRAYER AFTER COMMUNION

Let us pray.
Pause for silent prayer, if this has not preceded.
Lord,
hear the prayers
of those who gather at your table of unity and love.
By doing the work you have entrusted to us
may we sustain our life on earth
and build up your kingdom in faith.

Grant this through Christ our Lord.

B

Other prayers

OPENING PRAYER

God our Father,
you have placed all the powers of nature
under the control of man and his work.
May we bring the spirit of Christ to all our efforts
and work with our brothers and sisters at our common task,
establishing true love and guiding your creation to perfect
    fulfillment.

We ask this through our Lord Jesus Christ, your Son,
who lives and reigns with you and the Holy Spirit,
one God, for ever and ever.

See Lectionary for Mass, nos. 846-850.

PRAYER OVER THE GIFTS

Pray, brethren . . .

Lord,
receive the gifts of your Church,
and by the human labor we offer you
join us to the saving work of Christ,
who is Lord for ever and ever.

PRAYER AFTER COMMUNION

Let us pray.
Pause for silent prayer, if this has not preceded.
Lord,
guide and govern us by your help in this life
as you have renewed us by the mysteries of eternal life.

We ask this through Christ our Lord.

26. FOR PRODUCTIVE LAND

A

Introductory Rites

May the goodness of the Lord be upon us, and give success to the work of our hands. (Ps. 89:17)

OPENING PRAYER

God our Father,
we acknowledge you as the only source of growth and
  abundance.
With your help we plant our crops
and by your power they produce our harvest.
In your kindness and love
make up for what is lacking in our efforts.

We ask this through our Lord Jesus Christ, your Son,
who lives and reigns with you and the Holy Spirit,
one God, for ever and ever.

See Lectionary for Mass, nos. 851-855.

PRAYER OVER THE GIFTS

Pray, brethren . . .

Lord God,
you are indeed the loving Father
who provides us with food for body and spirit.
Make our work fruitful and give us a rich harvest.
Help us bring you glory
by using well the good things we receive from you.

We ask this through Christ our Lord.

Preface of Ordinary Time V, page 450.

Communion Rite

The Lord will shower his gifts, and our land will yield its
fruits. (Ps. 84:13)

PRAYER AFTER COMMUNION

Let us pray.
Pause for silent prayer, if this has not preceded.
Lord,
you renew us with your sacraments.
Guide the work of our hands,
for in you we live and move and have our being.
Bless the crops we plant
and let them yield a rich harvest.

We ask this through Christ our Lord.

B

Other prayers

OPENING PRAYER

Lord God,
pour out your blessing upon your people
and make our land productive
that we may enjoy its harvest with grateful hearts
and give honor to your holy name.

Grant this through our Lord Jesus Christ, your Son,
who lives and reigns with you and the Holy Spirit,
one God, for ever and ever.

See Lectionary for Mass, nos. 851-855.

PRAYER OVER THE GIFTS

Pray, brethren . . .

Lord,
accept our gifts.
We offer you bread, made from grains of wheat,
to be changed into the body of your Son.
By the power of your blessing
change the seeds we have planted
into a rich harvest for your people.

We ask this in the name of Jesus the Lord.

PRAYER AFTER COMMUNION

Let us pray.
Pause for silent prayer, if this has not preceded.
All-powerful God,
bless your faithful people with a rich harvest
for bodily nourishment and spiritual growth.
May we come to share for ever in the good things
promised by the eucharist we have received.

We ask this through Christ our Lord.

27. AFTER THE HARVEST

Introductory Rites

The earth has yielded its fruit, the Lord our God has blessed us. (Ps. 66:7-8)

OPENING PRAYER   Or:

**Father, God of goodness,
you give man the land to provide him with food.
May the produce we harvest sustain our lives,
and may we always use it for your glory and the good of all.
We ask this through our Lord Jesus Christ, your Son,
who lives and reigns with you and the Holy Spirit,
one God, for ever and ever.**

**Lord,
we thank you for the harvest earth has produced
for the good of man.
These gifts witness to your infinite love;
may the seeds of charity and justice also bear fruit in our hearts.
Grant this through our Lord Jesus Christ, your Son,
who lives and reigns with you and the Holy Spirit,
one God, for ever and ever.**

See Lectionary for Mass, nos. 856-860.

PRAYER OVER THE GIFTS   **Pray, brethren . . .**

**Lord,
make holy the gifts we offer with gratitude
from the produce of the earth.
As you have made our land bear a rich harvest,
make our hearts fruitful with your life and love.**

We ask this through Christ our Lord.

Preface of Ordinary Time V, page 450.

Communion Rite

Lord, the earth is filled with your gift from heaven; man grows bread from earth, and wine to cheer his heart. (Ps. 103:13-15)

PRAYER AFTER COMMUNION   **Let us pray.**
Pause for silent prayer, if this has not preceded.

**Lord,
we thank you for the fruits of the earth.
May the power of this saving mystery
bring us even greater gifts.**

We ask this through Christ our Lord.

28. IN TIME OF FAMINE
OR FOR THOSE WHO SUFFER FROM FAMINE

A

Introductory Rites

Lord, be true to your covenant, forget not the life of your
poor ones for ever. (Ps. 73:20, 19)

OPENING PRAYER

All-powerful Father,
God of goodness,
you provide for all your creation.
Give us an effective love for our brothers and sisters
who suffer from lack of food.
Help us do all we can to relieve their hunger,
that they may serve you with carefree hearts.

We ask this through our Lord Jesus Christ, your Son,
who lives and reigns with you and the Holy Spirit,
one God, for ever and ever.

See Lectionary for Mass, nos. 861-865.

PRAYER OVER THE GIFTS

Pray, brethren . . .

Lord,
look upon this offering which we make to you
from the many good things you have given us.
This eucharist is the sign of your abundant life
and the unity of all men in your love.
May it keep us aware of our Christian duty
to give our brothers a just share in what is ours.

We ask this through Christ our Lord.

Communion Rite

Come to me, all you that labor and are burdened, and I will
give you rest, says the Lord. (Matthew 11:28)

PRAYER AFTER COMMUNION

Let us pray.
Pause for silent prayer, if this has not preceded.
God, all-powerful Father,
may the living bread from heaven
give us the courage and strength
to go to the aid of our hungry brothers and sisters.

We ask this through Christ our Lord.

B

Other prayers, to be said by those suffering from hunger

OPENING PRAYER

**God our Father,
maker not of death, but of life,
you provide all men with food.
Mercifully take away hunger and starvation from our midst
that we may serve you with joyful, carefree hearts.**

**We ask this through our Lord Jesus Christ, your Son,
who lives and reigns with you and the Holy Spirit,
one God, for ever and ever.**

See Lectionary for Mass, nos. 861-865

PRAYER OVER THE GIFTS

Pray, brethren . . .

**Merciful Lord,
in our need we offer you these gifts.
Grant that they may bring us new health and salvation.**

We ask this through Christ our Lord.

PRAYER AFTER COMMUNION

Let us pray.
Pause for silent prayer, if this has not preceded.
**Lord,
may the food we receive from heaven
give us hope and strength
to work for our own needs
and those of our brothers and sisters.**

We ask this in the name of Jesus the Lord.

29. FOR REFUGEES AND EXILES

Introductory Rites

He has put his angels in charge of you, to guard you in all your ways. (Ps. 90:11)

or:

The Lord says: my plans for you are peace and not disaster; when you call to me, I will listen to you, and I will bring you back to the place from which I exiled you. (Jer. 29:11, 12, 14)

OPENING PRAYER

Lord,
no one is a stranger to you
and no one is ever far from your loving care.
In your kindness watch over refugees and exiles,
those separated from their loved ones,
young people who are lost,
and those who have left or run away from home.
Bring them back safely to the place where they long to be
and help us always to show your kindness
to strangers and to those in need.

We ask this through our Lord Jesus Christ, your Son,
who lives and reigns with you and the Holy Spirit,
one God, for ever and ever.

See Lectionary for Mass, nos. 866-870.

PRAYER OVER THE GIFTS

Pray, brethren . . .

Lord,
your Son gave his life to gather your scattered children
   into one family.
May this sacrifice unite the hearts of all men in peace
and help us to grow in brotherly love.

We ask this through Christ our Lord.

Communion Rite

You are my stronghold and my refuge, O my God. (Ps. 90:2)

PRAYER AFTER COMMUNION

Let us pray.

Pause for silent prayer, if this has not preceded.

Lord,
you have refreshed us with the one bread
   and the one cup.
Help us to offer our love and friendship
to strangers and to all those in need,
that we may be united one day with all your people
in the land of the living.

We ask this through Christ our Lord.

30. FOR THOSE UNJUSTLY DEPRIVED OF LIBERTY

OPENING PRAYER

**Father,
your Son came among us as a slave
to free the human race from the bondage of sin.
Rescue those unjustly deprived of liberty
and restore them to the freedom you wish for all men
   as your sons.**

**We ask this through our Lord Jesus Christ, your Son,
who lives and reigns with you and the Holy Spirit,
one God, for ever and ever.**

PRAYER OVER THE GIFTS

Pray, brethren . . .

**Lord,
we offer you the sacrament
which saves the human race.
May it release those unjustly deprived of liberty
and give them freedom of mind and heart for ever.**

We ask this through Christ our Lord.

PRAYER AFTER COMMUNION

Let us pray.
Pause for silent prayer, if this has not preceded.
**Lord,
mindful of the value of our own liberty
we ask your mercy for our brothers and sisters.
Restore their freedom
that they may work for your justice.**

We ask this in the name of Jesus the Lord.

31. FOR PRISONERS

OPENING PRAYER

**Father of mercy,
the secrets of all hearts are known to you alone.
You know who is just and you forgive the unjust.
Hear our prayers for those in prison.
Give them patience and hope in their sufferings,
and bring them home again soon.**

**We ask this through our Lord Jesus Christ, your Son,
who lives and reigns with you and the Holy Spirit,
one God, for ever and ever.**

Or, for those held in prison for the
Gospel, see prayers for persecuted
Christians, number 15, page 811.

32. FOR THE SICK

Introductory Rites

Have mercy on me, God, for I am sick; heal me, Lord, my bones are racked with pain. (Ps. 6:3)

or:

The Lord has truly borne our sufferings; he has carried all our sorrows. (See Is. 53:4)

OPENING PRAYER   Or:

Father,
your Son accepted our sufferings
to teach us the virtue of patience in human illness.
Hear the prayers we offer for our sick brothers and sisters.
May all who suffer pain, illness or disease
realize that they are chosen to be saints,
and know that they are joined to Christ
in his suffering for the salvation of the world,
who lives and reigns with you and the Holy Spirit,
one God, for ever and ever.

All-powerful and ever-living God,
the lasting health of all who believe in you,
hear us as we ask your loving help for the sick;
restore their health,
that they may again offer joyful thanks in your Church.

Grant this through our Lord Jesus Christ, your Son,
who lives and reigns with you and the Holy Spirit,
one God, for ever and ever.

See Lectionary for Mass, nos. 871-875.

PRAYER OVER THE GIFTS   **Pray, brethren . . .**

God our Father,
your love guides every moment of our lives.
Accept the prayers and gifts we offer
for our sick brothers and sisters;
restore them to health
and turn our anxiety for them into joy.

We ask this in the name of Jesus the Lord.

Communion Rite

I will make up in my own body what is lacking in the suffering of Christ, for the sake of his body, the Church. (Col. 1:24)

PRAYER AFTER COMMUNION   **Let us pray.**

Pause for silent prayer, if this has not preceded.

God our Father,
our help in human weakness,
show our sick brothers and sisters
the power of your loving care.
In your kindness make them well
and restore them to your Church.

We ask this through Christ our Lord.

33. FOR THE DYING

The Mass for the sick (p. 828) is celebrated, with the following prayers:

OPENING PRAYER

God of power and mercy,
you have made death itself
the gateway to eternal life.
Look with love on our dying brother (sister),
and make him (her) one with your Son in his suffering
    and death,
that, sealed with the blood of Christ,
he (she) may come before you free from sin.

We ask this through our Lord Jesus Christ, your Son,
who lives and reigns with you and the Holy Spirit,
one God, for ever and ever.

PRAYER OVER THE GIFTS

Pray, brethren . . .

Father,
accept this sacrifice we offer
for our dying brother (sister),
and by it free him (her) from all his (her) sins.
As he (she) accepted the sufferings you asked him (her)
    to bear in this life,
may he (she) enjoy happiness and peace for ever
    in the life to come.

We ask this through Christ our Lord.

PRAYER AFTER COMMUNION

Let us pray.
Pause for silent prayer, if this has not preceded.
Lord,
by the power of this sacrament,
keep your servant safe in your love.
Do not let evil conquer him (her) at the hour of death,
but let him (her) go in the company of your angels
to the joy of eternal life.

We ask this through Christ our Lord.

34. IN TIME OF EARTHQUAKE

OPENING PRAYER

God our Father,
you set the earth on its foundation.
Keep us safe from the danger of earthquakes
and let us always feel the presence of your love.
May we be secure in your protection
and serve you with grateful hearts.

We ask this through our Lord Jesus Christ, your Son,
who lives and reigns with you and the Holy Spirit,
one God, for ever and ever.

35. FOR RAIN

OPENING PRAYER

Lord God,
in you we live and move and have our being.
Help us in our present time of trouble,
send us the rain we need,
and teach us to seek your lasting help
on the way to eternal life.

We ask this through our Lord Jesus Christ, your Son,
who lives and reigns with you and the Holy Spirit,
one God, for ever and ever.

36. FOR FINE WEATHER

OPENING PRAYER

All-powerful and ever-living God,
we find security in your forgiveness.
Give us the fine weather we pray for
so that we may rejoice in your gifts of kindness
and use them always for your glory and our good.

We ask this through our Lord Jesus Christ, your Son,
who lives and reigns with you and the Holy Spirit,
one God, for ever and ever.

37. TO AVERT STORMS

OPENING PRAYER

Father,
all the elements of nature obey your command.
Calm the storms that threaten us
and turn our fear of your power
into praise of your goodness.

Grant this through our Lord Jesus Christ, your Son,
who lives and reigns with you and the Holy Spirit,
one God, for ever and ever.

38. FOR ANY NEED

A

Introductory Rites

I am the Savior of all people, says the Lord. Whatever their troubles, I will answer their cry, and I will always be their Lord.

OPENING PRAYER

**God our Father,
our strength in adversity,
our health in weakness,
our comfort in sorrow,
be merciful to your people.
As you have given us the punishment we deserve,
give us also new life and hope as we rest in your kindness.**

**We ask this through our Lord Jesus Christ, your Son,
who lives and reigns with you and the Holy Spirit,
one God, for ever and ever.**

See Lectionary for Mass, nos. 876-880.

PRAYER OVER THE GIFTS

Pray, brethren . . .

**Lord,
receive the prayers and gifts we offer:
may your merciful love set us free from the punishment
we receive for our sins.**

We ask this in the name of Jesus the Lord.

Communion Rite

Come to me, all you that labor and are burdened, and I will give you rest, says the Lord. (Matthew 11:28)

PRAYER AFTER COMMUNION

Let us pray.

Pause for silent prayer, if this has not preceded.

**Lord,
look kindly on us in our sufferings,
and by the death your Son endured for us
turn away from us your anger
and the punishment our sins deserve.**

We ask this through Christ our Lord.

B

Introductory Rites

Awake, Lord, why are you slumbering? Awake, do not reject us for ever. Why do you turn away your face, and ignore our sufferings? We are flung face down in the dust; awake, Lord, help us and deliver us. (Ps. 43:23-26)

OPENING PRAYER

**All-powerful Father,
God of mercy,
look kindly on us in our suffering.
Ease our burden and make our faith strong
that we may always have confidence and trust
in your fatherly care.**

**Grant this through our Lord Jesus Christ, your Son,
who lives and reigns with you and the Holy Spirit,
one God, for ever and ever.**

See Lectionary for Mass, nos. 876-880.

PRAYER OVER THE GIFTS

Pray, brethren . . .

**Lord,
accept the gifts we offer you in faith
and let the sufferings we bear with love
become a sacrifice of praise to your glory.**

We ask this through Christ our Lord.

Communion Rite

If you ask my Father for anything in my name, he will give it to you. Ask and you shall receive, that your joy may be full. (John 16:23-24)

PRAYER AFTER COMMUNION

Let us pray.
Pause for silent prayer, if this has not preceded.
**Lord,
as you have renewed and strengthened us with your holy
gifts,
help us to face the difficulties of the future with courage
and to give greater encouragement to our brothers in their
present need.**

We ask this in the name of Jesus the Lord.

39. IN THANKSGIVING

A

Introductory Rites

Sing and play music in your hearts to the Lord, always
giving thanks for everything to God the Father in the name
of our Lord Jesus Christ. (Eph. 5:19-20)

OPENING PRAYER

**Father of mercy,
you always answer your people in their sufferings.
We thank you for your kindness
and ask you to free us from all evil,
that we may serve you in happiness all our days.**

**We ask this through our Lord Jesus Christ, your Son,
who lives and reigns with you and the Holy Spirit,
one God, for ever and ever.**

See Lectionary for Mass, nos. 881-885.

PRAYER OVER THE GIFTS

Pray, brethren . . .

**Lord,
you gave us your only Son
to free us from death and from every evil.
Mercifully accept this sacrifice
in gratitude for saving us from our distress.**

We ask this through Christ our Lord.

Preface of Weekdays IV, page **457.**

Communion Rite

I will give thanks to you with all my heart, O Lord, for you
have answered me. (Ps. 137:1)

or:

What return can I make to the Lord for all that he gives to
me? I will take the cup of salvation, and call on the name of
the Lord. (Ps. 115:12-13)

PRAYER AFTER COMMUNION

Let us pray.
Pause for silent prayer, if this has not preceded.
**All-powerful God,
by this bread of life
you free your people from the power of sin
and in your love renew their strength.
Help us grow constantly in the hope of eternal glory.**

Grant this through Christ our Lord.

B

Other prayers

OPENING PRAYER

**God and Father of all gifts,
we praise you, the source of all we have and are.
Teach us to acknowledge always
the many good things your infinite love has given us.
Help us to love you with all our heart and all our strength.**

**We ask this through our Lord Jesus Christ, your Son,
who lives and reigns with you and the Holy Spirit,
one God, for ever and ever.**

See Lectionary for Mass, nos. 881-885.

PRAYER OVER THE GIFTS

Pray, brethren . . .

**Lord,
we offer you this sacrifice of praise
for all you have given us
even though we are unworthy of your love.
May we always use your many gifts
to bring glory to your name.**

We ask this through Christ our Lord.

PRAYER AFTER COMMUNION

Let us pray.
Pause for silent prayer, if this has not preceded.

**God our Father,
in this spiritual food
you have given back to us the sacrifice we offered you in
     thanksgiving,
the saving sacrament of Christ your Son.
By these gifts of strength and joy sustain us in your service
and bring us to your gift of eternal life.**

Grant this through Christ our Lord.

IV. FOR PARTICULAR NEEDS

40. FOR FORGIVENESS OF SINS

Introductory Rites

Lord, you are merciful to all, and hate nothing you have created. You overlook the sins of men to bring them to repentance. You are the Lord our God. (See Wis. 11:24-25, 27)

OPENING PRAYER

Lord,
hear the prayers of those who call on you,
forgive the sins of those who confess to you,
and in your merciful love
give us your pardon and your peace.

We ask this through our Lord Jesus Christ,
your Son,
who lives and reigns with you and the Holy
Spirit,
one God, for ever and ever.

Or:

Lord,
be merciful to your people
and free us from our sins.
May your loving forgiveness keep us safe
from the punishment we deserve.

We ask this through our Lord Jesus Christ,
your Son,
who lives and reigns with you and the Holy
Spirit,
one God, for ever and ever.

See Lectionary for Mass, nos. 886-890.

PRAYER OVER THE GIFTS   **Pray, brethren . . .**

Lord,
by this sacrifice of peace and praise,
mercifully cleanse us from our sins
and guide the desires of our hearts.

We ask this through Christ our Lord.

Preface of Ordinary Time IV, page **449.**

Communion Rite

There will be rejoicing among the angels of God, says the Lord, over one sinner who repents. (Luke 15:10)

PRAYER AFTER COMMUNION   **Let us pray.**

Pause for silent prayer, if this has not preceded.
God of mercy,
by the gifts we have shared
forgive us our sins.
Help us to avoid them in the future
and let us serve you with all our hearts.

Grant this through Christ our Lord.

41. FOR CHARITY

OPENING PRAYER

Lord,
fill our hearts with the spirit of your charity,
that we may please you by our thoughts,
and love you in our brothers and sisters.

We ask this through our Lord Jesus Christ, your Son,
who lives and reigns with you and the Holy Spirit,
one God, for ever and ever.

PRAYER OVER THE GIFTS

Pray, brethren . . .

Lord,
in your kindness make these gifts holy.
Accept our spiritual sacrifice
and help us show your love to all men.

We ask this in the name of Jesus the Lord.

PRAYER AFTER COMMUNION

Let us pray.
Pause for silent prayer, if this has not preceded.
Father,
you give us the one bread of life.
Fill us with the power of your Holy Spirit
and renew within us your gift of perfect love for others.

We ask this through Christ our Lord.

42. FOR PROMOTING HARMONY

OPENING PRAYER

God our Father,
source of unity and love,
make your faithful people one in heart and mind
that your Church may live in harmony,
be steadfast in its profession of faith,
and secure in unity.

We ask this through our Lord Jesus Christ, your Son,
who lives and reigns with you and the Holy Spirit,
one God, for ever and ever.

PRAYER OVER THE GIFTS

Pray, brethren . . .

Father,
you teach us by your sacraments
and help us grow to be like you.
You have made us desire your gift of charity.
By this sacrifice help us to obtain it
and remain faithful to your way.

We ask this through Christ our Lord.

PRAYER AFTER COMMUNION

Let us pray.
Pause for silent prayer, if this has not preceded.
Lord,
as we receive the sacrament of unity,
help us live together in your household
united in mind and heart.
May we experience the peace we preach to others
and cling to the peace we receive in the eucharist.

We ask this in the name of Jesus the Lord.

43. FOR THE FAMILY

OPENING PRAYER

Father,
we look to your loving guidance and order
as the pattern of all family life.
By following the example of the holy family of your Son,
   in mutual love and respect,
may we come to the joy of our home in heaven.

We ask this through our Lord Jesus Christ, your Son,
who lives and reigns with you and the Holy Spirit,
one God, for ever and ever.

PRAYER OVER THE GIFTS

Pray, brethren . . .

Lord,
accept our gifts
and through the prayers of Mary, the virgin Mother of God,
   and of her husband Joseph,
bring security and understanding to our families.

We ask this in the name of Jesus the Lord.

PRAYER AFTER COMMUNION

Let us pray.
Pause for silent prayer, if this has not preceded.
Father,
we want to live as Jesus, Mary, and Joseph,
in peace with you and one another.
May this communion strengthen us
to face the troubles of life.

Grant this through Christ our Lord.

44. FOR RELATIVES AND FRIENDS

OPENING PRAYER

**Father,
by the power of your Spirit
you have filled the hearts of your faithful people
with gifts of love for one another.
Hear the prayers we offer for our relatives and friends.
Give them health of mind and body
that they may do your will with perfect love.**

**We ask this through our Lord Jesus Christ, your Son,
who lives and reigns with you and the Holy Spirit,
one God, for ever and ever.**

PRAYER OVER THE GIFTS

Pray, brethren . . .

**Lord,
have mercy on our relatives and friends
for whom we offer this sacrifice of praise.
May these holy gifts gain them the help of your blessing
and bring them to the joy of eternal glory.**

We ask this through Christ our Lord.

PRAYER AFTER COMMUNION

Let us pray.
Pause for silent prayer, if this has not preceded.
**Lord,
we who receive these holy mysteries
pray for the relatives and friends you have given us in love.
Pardon their sins.
Give them your constant encouragement
and guide them throughout their lives,
until the day when we, with all who have served you,
will rejoice in your presence for ever.**

Grant this through Christ our Lord.

45. FOR OUR OPPRESSORS

OPENING PRAYER

Father,
according to your law of love
we wish to love sincerely all who oppress us.
Help us to follow the commandments of your new covenant,
that by returning good for the evil done to us,
we may learn to bear the ill-will of others out of love for you.

Grant this through our Lord Jesus Christ, your Son,
who lives and reigns with you and the Holy Spirit,
one God, for ever and ever.

PRAYER OVER THE GIFTS

Pray, brethren . . .

Father,
because we desire to be at peace with all men,
we offer you this sacrifice for those who oppress us.
We celebrate the memory of the death of your Son,
who reconciled us to you when we were enemies.

We ask this through Christ our Lord.

PRAYER AFTER COMMUNION

Let us pray.
Pause for silent prayer, if this has not preceded.
Lord God,
by the sacrament of peace
help us to be at peace with all men;
make those who oppress us pleasing to you
and reconciled with us.

We ask this through Christ our Lord.

46. FOR A HAPPY DEATH

Introductory Rites

Though I walk in the valley of darkness, I fear no evil, for
you are with me, Lord, my God. (Ps. 22:4)

OPENING PRAYER

**Father,
you made us in your own image
and your Son accepted death for our salvation.
Help us to keep watch in prayer at all times.
May we be free from sin when we leave this world
and rejoice in peace with you for ever.**

**We ask this through our Lord Jesus Christ, your Son,
who lives and reigns with you and the Holy Spirit,
one God, for ever and ever.**

See Lectionary for Mass, nos. 891-895.

PRAYER OVER THE GIFTS

Pray, brethren . . .

**Lord,
by the death of your Son,
you have destroyed our death.
By the power of this sacrament
keep us obedient to your will until death.
May we leave this world with confidence and peace
and come to share in the gift of his resurrection.**

We ask this through Christ our Lord.

Communion Rite

None of us lives for himself, none dies for himself; so
whether we live or die, we belong to the Lord. (Rom.
14:7-8)

or:

Be watchful, pray constantly, that you may be worthy to
stand before the Son of Man (Luke 21:36)

PRAYER AFTER COMMUNION

Let us pray.

Pause for silent prayer, if this has not preceded.

**Lord,
in receiving these sacred mysteries,
the pledge of unending life,
we pray for your loving help at the hour of our death.
Give us the victory over our enemy
and bring us to eternal peace in the glory of your kingdom.**

We ask this through Christ our Lord.

VOTIVE MASSES

VOTIVE MASSES

1. HOLY TRINITY

The Mass of the solemnity of the Holy Trinity (p. 392) is celebrated. White vestments are worn.

2. HOLY CROSS

The Mass of the feast of the Triumph of the Cross, September 14 (p. 636) is celebrated. Red vestments are worn.

3. HOLY EUCHARIST

The Mass of the solemnity of the Body and Blood of Christ (p. 394) is celebrated. White vestments are worn. The following texts may also be used.

A

Introductory Rites

The Lord opened the gates of heaven and rained down manna for them to eat. He gave them bread from heaven; men ate the bread of angels. (Ps. 77:23-25)

OPENING PRAYER

Father,
you have brought to fulfillment the work of our redemption
through the Easter mystery of Christ your Son.
May we who faithfully proclaim his death and resurrection
  in these sacramental signs
experience the constant growth of your salvation in our lives.

We ask this through our Lord Jesus Christ, your Son,
who lives and reigns with you and the Holy Spirit,
one God, for ever and ever.

See Lectionary for Mass, nos. 904-909.

PRAYER OVER THE GIFTS

Pray, brethren . . .

Lord,
hear our prayer for your mercy
as we celebrate this memorial of our salvation.
May this sacrament of love be for us
the sign of unity and the bond of charity.

We ask this through Christ our Lord.

Preface of the Holy Eucharist I or II, pages 464-465.

Communion Rite

I am the living bread from heaven, says the Lord. If anyone eats this bread he will live for ever; the bread I shall give is my flesh for the life of the world. (John 6:51-52)

PRAYER AFTER COMMUNION

Let us pray.

Pause for silent prayer, if this has not preceded.

**Lord,
may our sharing at this holy table make us holy.
By the body and blood of Christ
join all your people in brotherly love.**

Grant this through Christ our Lord.

B

This Mass may also be celebrated as a votive Mass of Jesus Christ the High Priest.

Introductory Rites

The Lord has sworn an oath and he will not retract: you are a priest for ever, in the line of Melchisedech. (Ps. 109:4)

OPENING PRAYER

**Father,
for your glory and our salvation
you appointed Jesus Christ eternal High Priest.
May the people he gained for you by his blood
come to share in the power of his cross and resurrection
by celebrating his memorial in this eucharist,
for he lives and reigns with you and the Holy Spirit,
one God, for ever and ever.**

See Lectionary for Mass, nos. 904-909.

PRAYER OVER THE GIFTS

Pray, brethren . . .

**Lord,
may we offer these mysteries worthily and often,
for whenever this memorial sacrifice is celebrated
the work of our redemption is renewed.**

We ask this through Christ our Lord.

Preface of the Holy Eucharist I or II, pages 464–465.

Communion Rite

This body will be given for you. This is the cup of the new covenant in my blood; whenever you receive them, do so in remembrance of me. (1 Cor. 11:24-25)

PRAYER AFTER COMMUNION

Let us pray.

Pause for silent prayer, if this has not preceded.

**Lord,
by sharing in this sacrifice
which your Son commanded us to offer as his memorial,
may we become, with him, an everlasting gift to you.**

We ask this through Christ our Lord.

4. HOLY NAME

White vestments are worn.

Introductory Rites

> At the name of Jesus every knee must bend, in heaven, on earth, and under the earth; every tongue should proclaim to the glory of God the Father: Jesus Christ is Lord. (Phil. 2:10-11)

OPENING PRAYER

**Lord,
may we who honor the holy name of Jesus
enjoy his friendship in this life
and be filled with eternal joy in his kingdom,
where he lives and reigns with you and the Holy Spirit,
one God, for ever and ever.**

See Lectionary for Mass, nos. 922-927.

PRAYER OVER THE GIFTS

Pray, brethren . . .

**All-powerful Father,
accept our gifts in the name of Jesus Christ your Son.
We have faith that we will receive
whatever we ask for in his name
for this is what he promised.**

We ask this through Christ our Lord.

Communion Rite

> No other name under heaven has been given to men by which we can be saved. (Acts 4:12)

PRAYER AFTER COMMUNION

Let us pray.
Pause for silent prayer, if this has not preceded.

**God of mercy,
may we honor our Lord Jesus Christ by these holy mysteries,
for you wish all men to worship him
and find salvation in his name.**

We ask this through Christ our Lord.

5. PRECIOUS BLOOD

Red vestments are worn.

Introductory Rites

By your blood, O Lord, you have redeemed us from every tribe and tongue, from every nation and people: you have made us into the kingdom of God. (Rev. 5:9-10)

OPENING PRAYER

**Father,
by the blood of your own Son
you have set all men free and saved us from death.
Continue your work of love within us,
that by constantly celebrating the mystery of our salvation
we may reach the eternal life it promises.**

**We ask this through our Lord Jesus Christ, your Son,
who lives and reigns with you and the Holy Spirit,
one God, for ever and ever.**

See Lectionary for Mass, nos. 916-921.

PRAYER OVER THE GIFTS

Pray, brethren . . .

**Lord,
by offering these gifts in this eucharist
may we come to Jesus, the mediator of the new covenant,
find salvation in the sprinkling of his blood
and draw closer to the kingdom
where he is Lord for ever and ever.**

Preface of the Passion of the Lord I, page 434.

Communion Rite

The cup that we bless is a communion with the blood of Christ; and the bread that we break is a communion with the body of the Lord. (See 1 Cor. 10:16)

PRAYER AFTER COMMUNION

Let us pray.

Pause for silent prayer, if this has not preceded.

**Lord,
you renew us with the food and drink of salvation.
May the blood of our Savior
be for us a fountain of water
springing up to eternal life.
We ask this through Christ our Lord.**

Or:

**Lord,
you renew us with food and drink from heaven.
Defend us from those who threaten us with evil
for you have set us free and saved us from death
by the blood of your Son Jesus Christ,
who is Lord for ever and ever.**

6. SACRED HEART

White vestments are worn. Either the
Mass of the solemnity of the Sacred
Heart (p. 396) or the following Mass
is celebrated:

Introductory Rites
>The thoughts of his heart last through every generation,
>that he will rescue them from death and feed them in
>time of famine. (Ps. 32:11, 19)

OPENING PRAYER

**Lord God,
give us the strength and love of the heart of your Son
that, by becoming one with him,
we may have eternal salvation.**

**We ask this through our Lord Jesus Christ, your Son,
who lives and reigns with you and the Holy Spirit,
one God, for ever and ever.**

See Lectionary for Mass, nos. 910-915.

PRAYER OVER THE GIFTS

Pray, brethren . . .

**Father of mercy,
in your great love for us
you have given us your only Son.
May he take us up into his own perfect sacrifice,
that we may offer you fitting worship.**

We ask this through Christ our Lord.

Preface of the Sacred Heart, page 462.

Communion Rite
>The Lord says: If anyone is thirsty, let him come to me;
>whoever believes in me, let him drink. Streams of living
>water shall flow out from within him. (John 7:37-38)
>or:
>One of the soldiers pierced Jesus' side with a lance, and at
>once there flowed out blood and water. (John 19:34)

PRAYER AFTER COMMUNION

Let us pray.
Pause for silent prayer, if this has not preceded.
**Lord,
we have received your sacrament of love.
By becoming more like Christ on earth
may we share his glory in heaven,
where he lives and reigns for ever and ever.**

7. HOLY SPIRIT

Red vestments are worn.

A

Introductory Rites

> The love of God has been poured into our hearts by his Spirit
> living in us. (See Rom. 5:5; 8:11)

OPENING PRAYER

**Father,
you taught the hearts of your faithful people
by sending them the light of your Holy Spirit.
In that Spirit give us right judgment
and the joy of his comfort and guidance.**

**We ask this through our Lord Jesus Christ, your Son,
who lives and reigns with you and the Holy Spirit,
one God, for ever and ever.**

See Lectionary for Mass, no. 928.

PRAYER OVER THE GIFTS

Pray, brethren . . .

**Lord,
make this offering holy
and cleanse our hearts from sin.
Send the light of your Holy Spirit.**

We ask this through Christ our Lord.

Preface of the Holy Spirit I, page **471**.

Communion Rite

> Confirm, O God, what you have done in us, from your
> holy temple in Jerusalem. (Ps. 67:29)

PRAYER AFTER COMMUNION

Let us pray.
Pause for silent prayer, if this has not preceded.
**Lord,
fill our hearts with your Holy Spirit
to free us from our sins
and make us rich in love for you and one another.**

We ask this through Christ our Lord.

B

Introductory Rites

When the Spirit of truth comes, says the Lord, he will
lead you to the whole truth. (John 16:13)

OPENING PRAYER   Or:

Lord,
may the Helper, the Spirit who comes from
you,
fill our hearts with light
and lead us to all truth
as your Son promised,
for he lives and reigns with you and the Holy
Spirit,
one God, for ever and ever.

God our Father,
no secret is hidden from you,
for every heart is open to you
and every wish is known.
Fill our hearts with the light of your Holy Spirit
to free our thoughts from sin,
that we may perfectly love you and fittingly
praise you.
Grant this through our Lord Jesus Christ, your
Son,
who lives and reigns with you and the Holy
Spirit,
one God, for ever and ever.

See Lectionary for Mass, no. 928.

PRAYER OVER THE GIFTS   **Pray, brethren . . .**

Father,
look with kindness
on the gifts we bring to your altar.
May we worship you in spirit and truth:
give us the humility and faith
to make our offering pleasing to you.

We ask this through Christ our Lord.

Preface of the Holy Spirit II, page 472.

Communion Rite

The Lord says, the Spirit who comes from the Father will
glorify me. (John 15:26; 16:14)

PRAYER AFTER COMMUNION   **Let us pray.**

Pause for silent prayer, if this has not preceded.

Lord our God,
you renew us with food from heaven;
fill our hearts with the gentle love of your Spirit.
May the gifts we have received in this life
lead us to the gift of eternal joy.

We ask this through Christ our Lord.

C

Introductory Rites

The Spirit of God is upon me; he sent me to bring good
news to the poor, says the Lord. (Luke 4:18)

OPENING PRAYER   Or:

God our Father,
pour out the gifts of your Holy Spirit on the
** world.**
You sent the Spirit on your Church
to begin the teaching of the gospel:
now let the Spirit continue to work in the world
through the hearts of all who believe.

We ask this through our Lord Jesus Christ,
** your Son,**
who lives and reigns with you and the Holy
** Spirit,**
one God, for ever and ever.

Father,
as your Spirit guides us and your loving care
** keeps us safe,**
be close to us in your mercy and listen to those
** who call on you.**
Strengthen and protect by your kindness
the faith of all who believe in you.

We ask this through our Lord Jesus Christ,
** your Son,**
who lives and reigns with you and the Holy
** Spirit,**
one God, for ever and ever.

See Lectionary for Mass, no. 928.

PRAYER OVER THE GIFTS   **Pray, brethren . . .**

Lord,
may the fire of your Spirit,
which filled the hearts of the disciples of Jesus
with courage and love,
make holy the sacrifice we offer in your sight.

We ask this in the name of Jesus the Lord.

Preface of the Holy Spirit I or II, pages
471–472.

Communion Rite

Lord, you send out your Spirit, and things are created: you
renew the face of the earth. (Ps. 103:30)

PRAYER AFTER COMMUNION   **Let us pray.**
Pause for silent prayer, if this has not preceded.

Lord,
through this eucharist,
send the Holy Spirit of Pentecost into our hearts
to keep us always in your love.

We ask this through Christ our Lord.

8. BLESSED VIRGIN MARY

A Mass from the common of the Blessed
Virgin Mary (p. 696) is used, in accord
with the liturgical season.

9. ANGELS

White vestments are worn.

Introductory Rites

> Bless the Lord, all you his angels, mighty in power, you
> obey his word and heed the sound of his voice. (Ps.
> 102:20)

OPENING PRAYER

**God our Father,
in a wonderful way you guide and govern the work
  of angels and men.
May those who serve you constantly in heaven
keep our lives safe and sure on earth.**

**We ask this through our Lord Jesus Christ, your Son,
who lives and reigns with you and the Holy Spirit,
one God, for ever and ever.**

PRAYER OVER THE GIFTS

Pray, brethren . . .

**Lord,
by the ministry of your angels
let this sacrifice of praise we offer come before you.
May it be pleasing to you
and helpful to our salvation.**

We ask this through Christ our Lord.

Preface of the Angels, page 477.

Communion Rite

> In the sight of the angels I will sing your praises, my God.
> (Ps. 137:1)

PRAYER AFTER COMMUNION

Let us pray.
Pause for silent prayer, if this has not preceded.
**Lord,
hear the prayers of those you renew with bread from heaven.
Strengthened by this food,
may we, with the care of the angels,
make progress in the way of salvation.**

We ask this through Christ our Lord.

The Mass of the Guardian Angels, October 2 (p. 648), may also be celebrated.

10. ST. JOSEPH

White vestments are worn.

Introductory Rites

The Lord has put his faithful servant in charge of his household. (Luke 12:42)

OPENING PRAYER

**God,
in your infinite wisdom and love
you chose Joseph to be the husband of Mary,
    the mother of your Son.
May we have the help of his prayers in heaven
and enjoy his protection on earth.**

**We ask this through our Lord Jesus Christ, your Son,
who lives and reigns with you and the Holy Spirit,
one God, for ever and ever.**

PRAYER OVER THE GIFTS

Pray, brethren . . .

**Lord,
may we who are about to offer this sacrifice of praise
have the prayers of Joseph
to encourage us in our work,
for you entrusted your only Son to his fatherly care on earth.**

We ask this through Christ our Lord.

Preface of St. Joseph, husband of Mary, page **479**.

Communion Rite

Come, good and faithful servant! Share the joy of your Lord! (Matthew 25:21)

PRAYER AFTER COMMUNION

Let us pray.
Pause for silent prayer, if this has not preceded.
**Lord,
you renew us with these life-giving sacraments:
may we always live in holiness and justice.
Let our constant help be the prayers and example of Joseph,
the just and obedient man,
who helped to carry out the great mysteries of our salvation.**

We ask this through Christ our Lord.

The Mass of the solemnity of Saint Joseph, March 19 (p. **570**), or of Saint Joseph the Worker, May 1 (p. **580**), may also be celebrated.

11. APOSTLES

Red vestments are worn.

Introductory Rites

You have not chosen me; I have chosen you. Go and bear
fruit that will last. (John 15:16)

OPENING PRAYER

Lord,
give your Church the constant joy of honoring the holy
apostles.
May we continue to be guided and governed by those leaders
whose teaching and example have been our inspiration.

We ask this through our Lord Jesus Christ, your Son,
who lives and reigns with you and the Holy Spirit,
one God, for ever and ever.

See Lectionary for Mass, no. 929.

PRAYER OVER THE GIFTS

Pray, brethren . . .

Lord,
pour out on us the Holy Spirit
who filled your apostles,
that we may acknowledge the gifts we have received through
them
and offer this sacrifice of praise to your glory.

We ask this through Christ our Lord.

Preface of the Apostles I or II, pages
481–482.

Communion Rite

You who have followed me will sit on thrones, and judge
the twelve tribes of Israel, says the Lord. (Matthew 19:28)

PRAYER AFTER COMMUNION

Let us pray.
Pause for silent prayer, if this has not preceded.
God our Father,
keep us faithful to the teaching of the apostles,
united in prayer and in the breaking of bread,
and one in joy and simplicity of heart.

We ask this in the name of Jesus the Lord.

12. ST. PETER, apostle

Red vestments are worn.

Introductory Rites

The Lord said to Simon Peter: I have prayed that your faith
may not fail; and you in your turn must strengthen your
brothers. (Luke 22:32)

OPENING PRAYER

**Lord,
you gave your apostle Peter the keys of the kingdom of
   heaven,
entrusting him with supreme power to bind and to loose.
By the help of his prayers
free us from the bonds of our sins.**

**We ask this through our Lord Jesus Christ, your Son,
who lives and reigns with you and the Holy Spirit,
one God, for ever and ever.**

PRAYER OVER THE GIFTS

Pray, brethren . . .

**Lord,
accept our gifts in honor of Peter your apostle,
for by a secret revelation you taught him to acknowledge you
as the living God and Christ as your Son,
and you gave him the further privilege of witnessing to his
   Lord
by his victorious suffering and death.**

We ask this through Christ our Lord.

Preface of the Apostles I, page **481**.

Communion Rite

Peter said: You are the Christ, the Son of the living God.
Jesus answered: You are Peter, the rock on which I will
build my Church. (Matthew 16:16, 18)

PRAYER AFTER COMMUNION

Let us pray.
Pause for silent prayer, if this has not preceded.

**Lord,
hear the prayer of those you have called to this table of
   salvation
in honor of Peter your apostle.
Keep us faithful to your Son,
who alone has the word of eternal life,
that he may lead us as the loyal sheep of his flock
to the eternal joys of your kingdom.**

We ask this through Christ our Lord.

13. ST. PAUL, apostle

Red vestments are worn.

Introductory Rites

> I know whom I have believed. I am sure that he, the just
> judge, will guard my pledge until the day of judgment.
> (2 Tim. 1:12; 4:8)

OPENING PRAYER

**Lord God,
you appointed Paul your apostle to preach the good news
  of salvation.
Fill the entire world with the faith
he carried to so many peoples and nations,
that your Church may continue to grow.**

**We ask this through our Lord Jesus Christ, your Son,
who lives and reigns with you and the Holy Spirit,
one God, for ever and ever.**

PRAYER OVER THE GIFTS

Pray, brethren . . .

**Lord,
as we celebrate this holy eucharist
may your Spirit fill us with the light
which led Paul the apostle
to make your glory known.**

We ask this through Christ our Lord.

Preface of the Apostles I, page **481**.

Communion Rite

> I live by faith in the Son of God, who loved me and
> sacrificed himself for me. (Gal. 2:20)

PRAYER AFTER COMMUNION

Let us pray.
Pause for silent prayer, if this has not preceded.
**Lord,
you renew us with the communion of the body and blood
  of your Son.
May Christ be our life
and nothing separate us from his love.
Following the teachings of St. Paul, may we live in love
for our brothers and sisters.**

We ask this through Christ our Lord.

14. ONE APOSTLE

The votive Mass of an apostle is celebrated as on his feast. But if two apostles are honored together on the feast day and the festal Mass is not appropriate for a votive Mass of one of them alone, the following Mass is used. Red vestments are worn.

Introductory Rites

Day after day proclaim the salvation of the Lord. Proclaim his glory to all nations. (Ps. 95:2-3)

OPENING PRAYER

**Lord,
strengthen us in the faith
which made the apostle N. so loyal to Christ your Son,
and by the help of his prayers
let your Church become the sign of salvation for all people.**

**We ask this through our Lord Jesus Christ, your Son,
who lives and reigns with you and the Holy Spirit,
one God, for ever and ever.**

See Lectionary for Mass, no. 929.

PRAYER OVER THE GIFTS

Pray, brethren . . .

**Lord,
accept our gifts in memory of N., the apostle.
By the help of his example
may we live the gospel of Christ
and work together for the faith.**

We ask this through Christ our Lord.

Preface of the Apostles II, page 482.

Communion Rite

I will give you the kingdom that my Father gave to me, and in that kingdom you will eat and drink at my table. (Luke 22:29-30)

PRAYER AFTER COMMUNION

Let us pray.
Pause for silent prayer, if this has not preceded.
**Lord,
may the pledge of salvation we receive
as we honor the memory of your apostle N.
bring us help in this life
and lead us to your kingdom.**

We ask this through Christ our Lord.

15. ALL SAINTS

White vestments are worn.

Introductory Rites

> The saints are happy in heaven because they followed
> Christ. They rejoice with him for ever.

OPENING PRAYER

> **God of all holiness,**
> **you gave your saints**
> **different gifts on earth**
> **but one reward in heaven.**
> **May their prayers be our constant encouragement**
> **for each of us to walk worthily in our vocation.**
>
> **We ask this through our Lord Jesus Christ, your Son,**
> **who lives and reigns with you and the Holy Spirit,**
> **one God, for ever and ever.**

PRAYER OVER THE GIFTS

> **Pray, brethren . . .**
>
> **Lord,**
> **receive our gifts in honor of the holy men and women**
> **who live with you in glory.**
> **May we always be aware of their concern**
> **to help and save us.**
>
> **Grant this through Christ our Lord.**

Preface of Holy Men and Women I or
II, pages **486–487**.

Communion Rite

> Happy are the pure of heart for they shall see God. Happy
> the peacemakers; they shall be called sons of God. Happy
> are they who suffer persecution for justice' sake; the kingdom
> of heaven is theirs. (Matthew 5:8-10)

PRAYER AFTER COMMUNION

> **Let us pray.**
> Pause for silent prayer, if this has not preceded.
> **God,**
> **you feed us with one bread**
> **and sustain us with one hope.**
> **By your love make our faith strong**
> **that with all your saints**
> **we may become one body, one spirit in Christ,**
> **and rise to eternal glory with him,**
> **who is Lord for ever and ever.**

MASSES FOR THE DEAD

MASSES FOR THE DEAD

1. Although for convenience complete Masses with antiphons and prayers are given, all the texts are interchangeable. This is true especially of the prayers, but the appropriate changes in gender and number should be made.

Similarly, if prayers for funerals or anniversaries are used in other circumstances, the inappropriate words should be omitted.

2. In the Easter season the **alleluia** at the end of the antiphons may be omitted if desired.

MASSES FOR THE DEAD

1. FUNERAL MASS

A. Outside the Easter Season

Introductory Rites

Give them eternal rest, O Lord, and may perpetual light
shine on them for ever. (See 4 Esdras 2:34-35)

OPENING PRAYER   Or:

Almighty God, our Father,
we firmly believe that your Son died and rose
  to life.
We pray for our brother (sister) N.
who has died in Christ.
Raise him (her) at the last day
to share the glory of the risen Christ,
who lives and reigns with you and the Holy
  Spirit,
one God, for ever and ever.

God,
you have called your son (daughter) N. from
  this life.
Father of all mercy,
fulfill his (her) faith and hope in you,
and lead him (her) safely home to heaven,
to be happy with you for ever.

We ask this through our Lord Jesus Christ,
  your Son,
who lives and reigns with you and the Holy
  Spirit,
one God, for ever and ever.

See Lectionary for Mass, nos. 789-793.

PRAYER OVER THE GIFTS   **Pray, brethren . . .**

Lord,
receive the gifts we offer for the salvation of N.
May Christ be merciful in judging our brother (sister) N.
for he (she) believed in Christ
as his (her) Lord and Savior.

Preface of Christian Death I-V, pages   **We ask this through Christ our Lord.**
494–498.

Communion Rite

May eternal light shine on them, O Lord, with all your
saints for ever, for you are rich in mercy. Give them eternal
rest, O Lord, and may perpetual light shine on them for
ever, for you are rich in mercy. (See 4 Esdras 2:35, 34)

PRAYER AFTER COMMUNION   **Let us pray.**

Pause for silent prayer, if this has not preceded.

Lord God,
your Son Jesus Christ gave us
the sacrament of his body and blood
to guide us on our pilgrim way to your kingdom.
May our brother (sister) N., who shared in the eucharist,
come to the banquet of life Christ has prepared for us.

We ask this through Christ our Lord.

B. Outside the Easter Season

Introductory Rites

The Lord will open to them the gate of paradise, and they will return to that homeland where there is no death, but only lasting joy.

OPENING PRAYER

**God of mercy,
you are the hope of sinners
and the joy of saints.
We pray for our brother (sister) N.,
whose body we honor with Christian burial.
Give him (her) happiness with your saints,
and raise up his (her) body in glory at the last day
to be in your presence for ever.**

**Grant this through our Lord Jesus Christ, your Son,
who lives and reigns with you and the Holy Spirit,
one God, for ever and ever.**

See Lectionary for Mass, nos. 789-793.

PRAYER OVER THE GIFTS

Pray, brethren . . .

**Lord,
accept this sacrifice we offer for our brother (sister) N.
on the day of his (her) burial.
May your love cleanse him (her)
from his (her) human weakness
and forgive any sins he (she) may have committed.**

We ask this through Christ our Lord.

Preface of Christian Death I-V, pages 494–498.

Communion Rite

We are waiting for our Savior, the Lord Jesus Christ; he will transfigure our lowly bodies into copies of his own glorious body. (Phil. 3:20-21)

PRAYER AFTER COMMUNION

Let us pray.

Pause for silent prayer, if this has not preceded.

**Father, all-powerful God,
we pray for our brother (sister) N.
whom you have called (today) from this world.
May this eucharist cleanse him (her),
forgive his (her) sins,
and raise him (her) up to eternal joy in your presence.**

We ask this through Christ our Lord.

C. During the Easter Season

Introductory Rites

Just as Jesus died and rose again, so will the Father bring with him those who have died in Jesus. Just as in Adam all men die, so in Christ all will be made alive, alleluia. (1 Thess. 4:14; 1 Cor. 15:22)

OPENING PRAYER

**Lord, hear our prayers.
By raising your Son from the dead, you have given us faith.
Strengthen our hope that N., our brother (sister),
will share in his resurrection.**

**We ask this through our Lord Jesus Christ, your Son,
who lives and reigns with you and the Holy Spirit,
one God, for ever and ever.**

See Lectionary for Mass, nos. 789-793.

PRAYER OVER THE GIFTS   **Pray, brethren . . .**

**Lord,
we are united in this sacrament
by the love of Jesus Christ.
Accept these gifts
and receive our brother (sister) N.
into the glory of your Son,
who is Lord for ever and ever.**

Preface of Christian Death I-V, pages 494–498.

Communion Rite

I am the resurrection and the life, says the Lord. If anyone believes in me, even though he dies, he will live. Anyone who lives and believes in me, will not die, alleluia. (See John 11:25-26)

PRAYER AFTER COMMUNION   **Let us pray.**
Pause for silent prayer, if this has not preceded.
**Lord God,
may the death and resurrection of Christ
which we celebrate in this eucharist
bring our brother (sister) N. the peace of your eternal home.**

We ask this in the name of Jesus the Lord.

D. Other Prayers for a Funeral Mass

OPENING PRAYER

**Father, almighty God,
our brother (sister) N. believed that Christ is the risen Lord.
Release him (her) from sin and grant to him (her) the freedom
of your perfect peace.
May our brother (sister) N. be with you
in the glory of your kingdom on the last day.**

**We ask this through our Lord Jesus Christ, your Son,
who lives and reigns with you and the Holy Spirit,
one God, for ever and ever.**

See Lectionary for Mass, nos. 789-793.

PRAYER OVER THE GIFTS

Pray, brethren . . .

**All-powerful Father,
may this sacrifice wash away
the sins of our brother (sister) N. in the blood of Christ.
You cleansed him (her) in the waters of baptism.
In your loving mercy grant him (her) pardon and peace.**

We ask this in the name of Jesus the Lord.

PRAYER AFTER COMMUNION

Let us pray.

Pause for silent prayer, if this has not preceded.

**Lord,
in this sacrament you give us your crucified and risen Son.
Bring to the glory of the resurrection our brother (sister) N.
who has been purified by this holy mystery.**

Grant this through Christ our Lord.

2. ANNIVERSARY MASS

A. Outside the Easter Season

Introductory Rites

God will wipe every tear from their eyes; there will be no
more death, no more weeping or pain, for the old order
has passed away. (Rev. 21:4)

OPENING PRAYER

**Lord God,
you are the glory of believers
and the life of the just.
Your Son redeemed us
by dying and rising to life again.
Our brother (sister) N. was faithful
and believed in our own resurrection.
Give to him (her) the joys and blessings
of the life to come.**

**We ask this through our Lord Jesus Christ, your Son,
who lives and reigns with you and the Holy Spirit,
one God, for ever and ever.**

See Lectionary for Mass, nos. 789-793.

PRAYER OVER THE GIFTS

Pray, brethren . . .

**Lord,
accept these gifts we offer
for N. our brother (sister).
May they free him (her) from sin
and bring him (her) to the happiness of life in your presence.**

We ask this through Christ our Lord.

Preface of Christian Death I-V, pages
494–498.

Communion Rite

I am the resurrection and the life, says the Lord. Anyone
who believes in me will have eternal life; he will not be
condemned but pass from death to life. (John 11:25; 3:36;
5:24)

PRAYER AFTER COMMUNION

Let us pray.
Pause for silent prayer, if this has not preceded.
**Lord,
you renew our lives by this holy eucharist;
free N. our brother (sister) from sin
and raise him (her) to eternal life.**

We ask this in the name of Jesus the Lord.

B. Outside the Easter Season

Introductory Rites

Lord Jesus, you shed your precious blood for them, so
grant them eternal rest.

OPENING PRAYER

**Lord,
we keep the anniversary
of the death (burial) of our brother (sister) N.
Give him (her) the unending joy of your love
in the company of all your saints.**

**We ask this through our Lord Jesus Christ, your Son,
who lives and reigns with you and the Holy Spirit,
one God, for ever and ever.**

See Lectionary for Mass, nos. 789-793.

PRAYER OVER THE GIFTS

Pray, brethren . . .

**Lord,
as we make this sacrifice of praise
we celebrate the memory of our brother (sister) N.
May this offering of peace
win for him (her) a place with your saints.**

We ask this in the name of Jesus the Lord.

Preface of Christian Death I-V, pages
494–498.

Communion Rite

Lord, you are our rest after toil, our life after death; grant
them eternal rest.

PRAYER AFTER COMMUNION

Let us pray.

Pause for silent prayer, if this has not preceded.

**Lord,
accept the prayers and gifts
we offer for our brother (sister) N.
May your love and forgiveness free him (her)
from every trace of sin.**

We ask this in the name of Jesus the Lord.

C. During the Easter Season

Introductory Rites

God, who raised Jesus from the dead, will give new life to
our own mortal bodies through his Spirit living in us,
alleluia. (See Rom. 8:11)

OPENING PRAYER

**Almighty and merciful God,
may our brother (sister) N. share the victory of Christ
who loved us so much that he died and rose again
to bring us new life.**

**We ask this through our Lord Jesus Christ, your Son,
who lives and reigns with you and the Holy Spirit,
one God, for ever and ever.**

See Lectionary for Mass, nos. 789-793.

PRAYER OVER THE GIFTS

Pray, brethren . . .

**God of love,
by this sacrifice
wash away the sins of our brother (sister) N.
in the blood of Jesus Christ.
In your love complete what you began
in the waters of baptism.**

Grant this through Christ our Lord.

Preface of Christian Death I-V, pages
494–498.

Communion Rite

I am the living bread from heaven, says the Lord. If anyone
eats this bread he will live for ever; the bread I shall give is
my flesh for the life of the world, alleluia. (John 6:51-52)

PRAYER AFTER COMMUNION

Let us pray.

Pause for silent prayer, if this has not preceded.

**Lord,
we celebrate your Son's death for us
and his rising to eternal glory.
May these Easter mysteries free our brother (sister) N.
and bring him (her) to share in the joyful resurrection to come.**

We ask this through Christ our Lord.

D. Other Prayers on an Anniversary

OPENING PRAYER

Lord,
may the death of your Son
bring forgiveness to our brother (sister) N.
who prayed for this grace.
May he (she) come into your presence
and rejoice in your glory for ever.

We ask this through our Lord Jesus Christ, your Son,
who lives and reigns with you and the Holy Spirit,
one God, for ever and ever.

See Lectionary for Mass, nos. 789-793.

PRAYER OVER THE GIFTS

Pray, brethren . . .

Lord,
may the sacrifice we offer
bring everlasting joy to our brother (sister) N.
who knew you by the light of faith.

We ask this in the name of Jesus the Lord.

PRAYER AFTER COMMUNION

Let us pray.
Pause for silent prayer, if this has not preceded.
Lord,
the eucharist we share joins us to your Son
and brings us his life.
May this eucharist free our brother (sister) N. from his (her)
    sins
and lead him (her) to your presence in heaven.

Grant this through Christ our Lord.

E. Other Prayers on an Anniversary

OPENING PRAYER

**God of mercy,
we keep this anniversary
of the death (burial) of N. our brother (sister).
Give him (her) light, happiness and peace.**

**We ask this through our Lord Jesus Christ, your Son,
who lives and reigns with you and the Holy Spirit,
one God, for ever and ever.**

See Lectionary for Mass, nos. 789-793.

PRAYER OVER THE GIFTS

Pray, brethren . . .

**Lord,
accept our prayers and offerings.
Make your son (daughter) N. one with you
in peace and happiness.**

We ask this in the name of Jesus the Lord.

PRAYER AFTER COMMUNION

Let us pray.
Pause for silent prayer, if this has not preceded.
**Lord,
in your mercy
may this sacrifice we offer
for our brother (sister) N.
free him (her) from his (her) sins
and bring him (her) to the light and happiness
of your kingdom.**

We ask this in the name of Jesus the Lord.

3. VARIOUS COMMEMORATIONS

A. For One Person

Introductory Rites

The Lord will open to them the gate of paradise, and they will return to that homeland where there is no death, but only lasting joy.

OPENING PRAYER

Or:

Lord God, almighty Father,
you have made the cross for us a sign of strength
and marked us as yours in the sacrament of the resurrection.
Now that you have freed our brother (sister) N. from this mortal life
make him (her) one with your saints in heaven.

We ask this through our Lord Jesus Christ, your Son,
who lives and reigns with you and the Holy Spirit,
one God, for ever and ever.

Lord of mercy,
hear our prayer.
May our brother (sister) N.,
whom you called your son (daughter) on earth,
enter the kingdom of peace and light,
where your saints live in glory.

We ask this through our Lord Jesus Christ, your Son,
who lives and reigns with you and the Holy Spirit,
one God, for ever and ever.

See Lectionary for Mass, nos. 789–793.

PRAYER OVER THE GIFTS

Pray, brethren . . .

Lord,
in your mercy
may this sacrifice of praise,
this offering of peace,
bring our brother (sister) N.
to the fullness of risen life.

We ask this through Christ our Lord.

Preface of Christian Death I–V, pages 494–498.

Communion Rite

All that the Father gives to me will come to me; the man who comes to me, I shall never turn away. (John 6:37)

PRAYER AFTER COMMUNION

Let us pray.
Pause for silent prayer, if this has not preceded.
Lord,
you give us life in this sacrament.
May our brother (sister) N. who received life at your table
enter into the everlasting peace and joy of Christ your Son,
who is Lord for ever and ever.

B. For One Person

Introductory Rites

I know that my Redeemer lives, and on the last day I shall
rise again; in my body I shall look on God, my Savior (Job
19:25-26)

OPENING PRAYER

**Lord,
in your mercy
free our brother (sister) N. from his (her) sins.
As you made him (her) one with Christ here on earth,
raise him (her) to join your saints
in the glory of the resurrection.**

**We ask this through our Lord Jesus Christ, your Son,
who lives and reigns with you and the Holy Spirit,
one God, for ever and ever.**

See Lectionary for Mass, nos. 789-793.

PRAYER OVER THE GIFTS

Pray, brethren . . .

**Lord,
may this offering help our brother (sister) N.,
for by this sacrifice
you take away the sins of the world.**

Grant this in the name of Jesus the Lord.

Preface of Christian Death I-V, pages
494–498.

Communion Rite

This is the bread come down from heaven, says the Lord.
He who eats this bread will live for ever. (See John 6:50)

PRAYER AFTER COMMUNION

Let us pray.

Pause for silent prayer, if this has not preceded.

**Lord,
may the sacrifice of your Church
help our brother (sister) N.;
may he (she) who received this sacrament of your mercy
join the saints who are united to Christ,
who is Lord for ever and ever.**

C. For More than One Person or for All the Dead

Introductory Rites

> Give them eternal rest, O Lord, and let them share your
> glory.

OPENING PRAYER   Or:

God, our creator and redeemer,
by your power Christ conquered death
and returned to you in glory
May all your people who have gone before us
**   in faith**
share his victory
and enjoy the vision of your glory for ever,
where Christ lives and reigns with you and the
**   Holy Spirit,**
one God, for ever and ever.

God, our maker and redeemer,
in your mercy hear our prayer.
Grant forgiveness and peace
to our brothers (sisters) N. and N.
who longed for your mercy.

We ask this through our Lord Jesus Christ,
**   your Son,**
who lives and reigns with you and the Holy
**   Spirit,**
one God, for ever and ever.

See Lectionary for Mass, nos. 789-793.

PRAYER OVER THE GIFTS   **Pray, brethren . . .**

> **Lord,**
> **receive this sacrifice**
> **for our brothers and sisters.**
> **On earth you gave them the privilege of believing in Christ:**
> **grant them the eternal life promised by that faith.**
>
> **We ask this through Christ our Lord.**

Preface of Christian Death I-V, pages
494–498.

Communion Rite

> God sent his only Son into the world so that we could have
> life through him. (1 John 4:9)

PRAYER AFTER COMMUNION

Let us pray.   Or:

Pause for silent prayer, if this has not preceded.

Lord,
may our sacrifice bring peace and forgiveness
to our brothers and sisters who have died.
Bring the new life given to them in baptism
to the fullness of eternal joy.

We ask this through Christ our Lord.

Lord of mercy,
may our prayer and sacrifice
free our brothers and sisters
and bring them to eternal salvation.

We ask this through Christ our Lord.

D. For More than One Person or for All the Dead

Introductory Rites

God loved the world so much, he gave his only Son,
that all who believe in him might not perish, but might
have eternal life. (John 3:16)

OPENING PRAYER

Or:

All-powerful and ever-living God,
you give new life to mankind
and perfect joy to your saints in heaven.
Give our brothers (sisters) N. and N. the fullness of freedom
in the kingdom of your glory.
We ask this through our Lord Jesus Christ,
your Son,
who lives and reigns with you and the Holy
Spirit,
one God, for ever and ever.

Merciful Lord of the living and the dead,
forgive the sins of our brothers (sisters) N. and
N.
for whom we pray.
May they praise you for ever
in the joy of your presence.
Grant this through our Lord Jesus Christ, your
Son,
who lives and reigns with you and the Holy
Spirit,
one God, for ever and ever.

See Lectionary for Mass, nos. 789-793.

PRAYER OVER THE GIFTS

Pray, brethren . . .

Lord,
in your kindness accept these gifts we offer for N. and N.
and for all who sleep in Christ.
May his perfect sacrifice
free them from the power of death
and give them everlasting life.
We ask this through Christ our Lord.

Preface of Christian Death I-V, pages
494–498.

Communion Rite

We are waiting for our Savior, the Lord Jesus Christ; he
will transfigure our lowly bodies into copies of his own
glorious body. (Phil. 3:20-21)

PRAYER AFTER COMMUNION

Let us pray.
Pause for silent prayer, if this has not preceded.
All-powerful God,
have mercy upon our brothers and sisters
who have gone before us in faith;
may this eucharist be for us the way to salvation
and for them the means of forgiveness.
We ask this through Christ our Lord.

E. For More than One Person or for All the Dead

Introductory Rites

> Happy are those who have died in the Lord; let them rest
> from their labors for their good deeds go with them. (Rev.
> 14:13)

OPENING PRAYER   Or:

God of love,
the peace of heaven is your gift.
Forgive our brothers (sisters) N. and N.
and all who die in Christ
and free them from their sins.
Make them one with Christ
in the glory of his resurrection,
for he lives and reigns with you and the Holy
** Spirit,**
one God, for ever and ever.

Lord,
have mercy on our brothers (sisters) who have
** died.**
May their faith and hope in you be rewarded
** by eternal life.**

We ask this through our Lord Jesus Christ,
** your Son,**
who lives and reigns with you and the Holy
** Spirit,**
one God, for ever and ever.

See Lectionary for Mass, nos. 789-793.

PRAYER OVER THE GIFTS   **Pray, brethren . . .**

Lord,
receive the gifts we offer
to win peace and rest for our brothers and sisters.
By this eucharist, which brings man salvation,
count them among those whom you have freed from death.

We ask this through Christ our Lord.

Preface of Christian Death I-V, pages
494–498.

Communion Rite

> Grant eternal rest, O Lord, to those in whose memory we
> receive the body and blood of Christ.

PRAYER AFTER COMMUNION

Let us pray.   Or:

Pause for silent prayer, if this has not preceded.

Lord,
we receive the sacrament of salvation;
may this eucharist be the sign of your loving
** care**
for your people on earth
and a source of eternal forgiveness
for our departed brothers and sisters.

We ask this in the name of Jesus the Lord.

Lord,
may our brothers and sisters,
and all who sleep in Christ,
share in the light of eternal life,
the life they came to know
by sharing in this sacrament.

We ask this through Christ our Lord.

VARIOUS PRAYERS FOR THE DEAD

1. FOR A POPE

A

OPENING PRAYER

God our Father,
you reward all who believe in you.
May your servant, N. our Pope, vicar of Peter
    and shepherd of your Church,
who faithfully administered the mysteries of your
    forgiveness and love on earth,
rejoice with you for ever in heaven.

We ask this through our Lord Jesus Christ, your Son,
who lives and reigns with you and the Holy Spirit,
one God, for ever and ever.

See Lectionary for Mass, nos. 789-793.

PRAYER OVER THE GIFTS

Pray, brethren . . .

Lord,
by this sacrifice which brings us peace,
give your servant, N. our Pope,
the reward of eternal happiness
and let your mercy win for us
the gift of your life and love.

We ask this through Christ our Lord.

PRAYER AFTER COMMUNION

Let us pray.
Pause for silent prayer, if this has not preceded.
Lord,
you renew us with the sacraments of your divine life.
Hear our prayers for your servant, N. our Pope.
You made him the center of the unity of your Church on earth,
count him now among the flock of the blessed in your king-
    dom.

Grant this through Christ our Lord.

B

OPENING PRAYER

**Father,
in your wise and loving care
you made your servant, N., Pope and teacher of all
    your Church.
He did the work of Christ on earth.
May your Son welcome him to eternal glory,
where he lives and reigns with you and the Holy Spirit,
one God, for ever and ever.**

See Lectionary for Mass, nos. 789-793.

PRAYER OVER THE GIFTS

Pray, brethren . . .

**Lord,
look with kindness on the prayers and gifts of your Church.
By the power of this sacrifice
may your servant N.
whom you appointed high priest of your flock,
be counted now among your priests in the life of your king-
    dom.**

We ask this through Christ our Lord.

PRAYER AFTER COMMUNION

Let us pray.
Pause for silent prayer, if this has not preceded.
**Lord,
hear the prayers of the people you feed
with the gifts of your protection and love.
May your servant N.
who was a faithful minister of your mysteries on earth
praise your goodness for ever in the glory of your saints.**

We ask this through Christ our Lord.

C

OPENING PRAYER

Father,
eternal shepherd,
hear the prayers of your people
for your servant N.
who governed your Church with love.
In your mercy bring him with the flock entrusted to his care
to the reward you have promised your faithful servants.

We ask this through our Lord Jesus Christ, your Son,
who lives and reigns with you and the Holy Spirit,
one God, for ever and ever.

See Lectionary for Mass, nos. 789-793.

PRAYER OVER THE GIFTS

Pray, brethren . . .

Lord,
in your love receive this sacrifice of peace your people offer.
We entrust your servant N. to your mercy
      with faith and confidence.
In the human family he was an instrument of your peace and
      love.
May he rejoice in those gifts for ever with your saints.

We ask this through Christ our Lord.

PRAYER AFTER COMMUNION

Let us pray.
Pause for silent prayer, if this has not preceded.
Lord,
at this meal of eternal life
we ask your mercy for your servant N.
May he rejoice for ever in the possession of that truth
in which he made your people strong by his faith.

We ask this through Christ our Lord.

2. FOR A BISHOP

A. For the Diocesan Bishop

OPENING PRAYER

**All-powerful God,
you made N., your servant,
the guide of your family.
May he enjoy the reward of all his work
and share the eternal joy of his Lord.**

**We ask this through our Lord Jesus Christ, your Son,
who lives and reigns with you and the Holy Spirit,
one God, for ever and ever.**

See Lectionary for Mass, nos. 789-793.

PRAYER OVER THE GIFTS

Pray, brethren . . .

**Merciful God,
may this sacrifice,
which N. your servant offered during his life
for the salvation of the faithful,
help him now to find pardon and peace.**

We ask this through Christ our Lord.

PRAYER AFTER COMMUNION

Let us pray.
Pause for silent prayer, if this has not preceded.
**Lord,
give your mercy and love to N. your servant.
He hoped in Christ and preached Christ.
By this sacrifice may he share with Christ
the joy of eternal life.**

We ask this through Christ our Lord.

B. For Another Bishop

OPENING PRAYER

God our Father,
may your servant N., who was our bishop,
rejoice in the fellowship of the successors of the apostles
whose office he shared in this life.

We ask this through our Lord Jesus Christ, your Son,
who lives and reigns with you and the Holy Spirit,
one God, for ever and ever.

See Lectionary for Mass, nos. 789-793.

PRAYER OVER THE GIFTS

Pray, brethren . . .

Lord,
accept our offering for N. your servant.
You gave him the dignity of high priesthood in this world.
Let him now share the joy of your saints in the kingdom
  of heaven.

We ask this through Christ our Lord.

PRAYER AFTER COMMUNION

Let us pray.
Pause for silent prayer, if this has not preceded.
All-powerful Father, God of mercy,
you gave N. your servant
the privilege of doing the work of Christ on earth.
By this sacrifice free him from sin
and bring him to eternal life with Christ in heaven,
who is Lord for ever and ever.

3. FOR A PRIEST

A

OPENING PRAYER

**Lord,
you gave N. your servant and priest
the privilege of a holy ministry in this world.
May he rejoice for ever in the glory of your kingdom.**

**We ask this through our Lord Jesus Christ, your Son,
who lives and reigns with you and the Holy Spirit,
one God, for ever and ever.**

See Lectionary for Mass, nos. 789-793.

PRAYER OVER THE GIFTS

Pray, brethren . . .

**All-powerful God,
by this eucharist may N. your servant and priest
rejoice for ever in the vision of the mysteries
which he faithfully ministered here on earth.**

We ask this through Christ our Lord.

PRAYER AFTER COMMUNION

Let us pray.
Pause for silent prayer, if this has not preceded.
**God of mercy,
we who receive the sacraments of salvation
pray for N. your servant and priest.
You made him a minister of your mysteries on earth.
May he rejoice in the full knowledge of your truth in heaven.**

We ask this through Christ our Lord.

B

OPENING PRAYER

Lord,
hear the prayers we offer for N. your servant and priest.
He faithfully fulfilled his ministry to your name.
May he rejoice for ever in the fellowship of your saints.

We ask this through our Lord Jesus Christ, your Son,
who lives and reigns with you and the Holy Spirit,
one God, for ever and ever.

See Lectionary for Mass, nos. 789-793.

PRAYER OVER THE GIFTS

Pray, brethren . . .

Lord God of mercy,
may the sacrifice we offer for N. your servant and priest
bring him forgiveness and life
as once he offered sacrifice to you
in his wholehearted service to your Church.

We ask this through Christ our Lord.

PRAYER AFTER COMMUNION

Let us pray.
Pause for silent prayer, if this has not preceded.
Lord,
hear the prayers of those you renew
with the food of life at your holy table.
By the power of this sacrifice
may N. your servant and priest
rejoice in your presence for ever
as he served you faithfully in the Church.

We ask this through Christ our Lord.

4. FOR A DEACON

OPENING PRAYER

God of mercy,
you gave N. your servant
the privilege of serving your Church.
Bring him now to the joy of eternal life.

We ask this through our Lord Jesus Christ, your Son,
who lives and reigns with you and the Holy Spirit,
one God, for ever and ever.

See Lectionary for Mass, nos. 789-793.

PRAYER OVER THE GIFTS

Pray, brethren . . .

Lord,
be merciful to N. your servant
for whose salvation we offer you this sacrifice.
He ministered during his life to Christ your Son.
May he rise with all your faithful servants to eternal glory.

We ask this through Christ our Lord.

PRAYER AFTER COMMUNION

Let us pray.
Pause for silent prayer, if this has not preceded.
Lord,
you fill us with holy gifts.
Hear our prayers for N. your deacon
whom you counted among the servants of your Church.
By this sacrifice free him from the power of death
and give him a share in the reward you have promised
to all who serve you faithfully.

We ask this through Christ our Lord.

5. FOR A RELIGIOUS

OPENING PRAYER

All-powerful God,
out of love for Christ and his Church,
N. served you faithfully in the religious life.
May he (she) rejoice at the coming of your glory
and enjoy eternal happiness
with his (her) brothers (sisters) in your kingdom.

We ask this through our Lord Jesus Christ, your Son,
who lives and reigns with you and the Holy Spirit,
one God, for ever and ever.

6. FOR ONE PERSON

A

OPENING PRAYER

Lord,
those who die still live in your presence
and your saints rejoice in complete happiness.
Listen to our prayers for N. your son (daughter)
who has passed from the light of this world,
and bring him (her) to the joy of eternal radiance.

We ask this through our Lord Jesus Christ, your Son,
who lives and reigns with you and the Holy Spirit,
one God, for ever and ever.

See Lectionary for Mass, nos. 789-793.

PRAYER OVER THE GIFTS

Pray, brethren . . .

Lord,
be pleased with this sacrifice we offer for N. your servant.
May he (she) find in your presence
the forgiveness he (she) always longed for
and come to praise your glory for ever
in the joyful fellowship of your saints.

We ask this through Christ our Lord.

PRAYER AFTER COMMUNION

Let us pray.
Pause for silent prayer, if this has not preceded.

Lord,
we thank you for the holy gifts we receive
and pray for N. our brother (sister).
By the suffering and death of your Son
free him (her) from the bonds of his (her) sins
and bring him (her) to endless joy in your presence.

We ask this through Christ our Lord.

B

OPENING PRAYER

Lord,
may our prayers come before you
and lead N. your servant to eternal joy.
You created him (her) in your image
and made him (her) your son (daughter).
In your mercy now welcome him (her) to a place in your
    kingdom.

We ask this through our Lord Jesus Christ, your Son,
who lives and reigns with you and the Holy Spirit,
one God, for ever and ever.

See Lectionary for Mass, nos. 789-793.

PRAYER OVER THE GIFTS

Pray, brethren . . .

Lord,
in your love accept the gifts
we offer in faith for N. your son (daughter).
May the sacrifice you have chosen to be the one source
**   of healing for mankind**
bring him (her) eternal salvation.

We ask this through Christ our Lord.

PRAYER AFTER COMMUNION

Let us pray.
Pause for silent prayer, if this has not preceded.
Lord,
as you renew us by this sacred food,
free N. our brother (sister) from the power of death
and give him (her) a share in the joyful resurrection of Christ,
who is Lord for ever and ever.

C

OPENING PRAYER

Lord of mercy,
hear our prayers and forgive our brother (sister) N.
**   all his (her) sins.**
Give him (her) life on the day of resurrection
and peaceful rest in the light of your love.

We ask this through our Lord Jesus Christ, your Son,
who lives and reigns with you and the Holy Spirit,
one God, for ever and ever.

See Lectionary for Mass, nos. 789-793.

PRAYER OVER THE GIFTS

Pray, brethren . . .

All-powerful and ever-living God,
your Son offered himself to be our bread of life
and poured out his blood to be our cup of salvation.
Have mercy on your servant N.,
and let the eucharist we offer be for him (her) a help
**   to salvation.**

We ask this through Christ our Lord.

PRAYER AFTER COMMUNION

Let us pray.
Pause for silent prayer, if this has not preceded.
Lord, we have received the pledge of eternal life.
Hear the prayers we offer for your son (daughter) N.
Freed from the limitations of this life,
may he (she) be one with all the redeemed
in the joy of eternal life.

We ask this through Christ our Lord.

7. FOR A YOUNG PERSON

OPENING PRAYER

Lord God,
the days allotted to each of us are in your fatherly care.
Though we are saddened
that our brother (sister) N. was with us for so short a time,
we entrust him (her) to you with confidence.
May he (she) live, radiant and for ever young,
in the happiness of your kingdom.

We ask this through our Lord Jesus Christ, your Son,
who lives and reigns with you and the Holy Spirit,
one God, for ever and ever.

8. FOR ONE WHO WORKED IN THE SERVICE OF THE GOSPEL

OPENING PRAYER

Lord,
hear our prayers for your son (daughter) N.,
who labored so generously
to bring your gospel to the world.
May he (she) be the more worthy
to share the rewards of your kingdom.

We ask this through our Lord Jesus Christ, your Son,
who lives and reigns with you and the Holy Spirit,
one God, for ever and ever.

9. FOR ONE WHO SUFFERED A LONG ILLNESS

OPENING PRAYER

Lord God,
in his (her) suffering and long illness
our brother (sister) N. served you faithfully
by imitating the patience of your Son, Jesus Christ.
May he (she) also share in the reward of his glory
where he lives and reigns with you and the Holy Spirit,
one God, for ever and ever.

10. FOR ONE WHO DIED SUDDENLY

OPENING PRAYER

Lord,
as we mourn the sudden death of our brother (sister) N.,
comfort us with the great power of your love
and strengthen us in our faith
that he (she) is with you for ever.

We ask this through our Lord Jesus Christ, your Son,
who lives and reigns with you and the Holy Spirit,
one God, for ever and ever.

11. FOR SEVERAL PERSONS

A

OPENING PRAYER

Lord,
be merciful to your servants N. and N.
You cleansed them from sin in the fountain of new birth.
Bring them now to the happiness of life in your kingdom.

We ask this through our Lord Jesus Christ, your Son,
who lives and reigns with you and the Holy Spirit,
one God, for ever and ever.

See Lectionary for Mass, nos. 789-793.

PRAYER OVER THE GIFTS

Pray, brethren . . .

Lord,
we offer you this sacrifice.
Hear our prayers for N. and N.,
and through this offering
grant our brothers (sisters) your everlasting forgiveness.

We ask this through Christ our Lord.

PRAYER AFTER COMMUNION

Let us pray.
Pause for silent prayer, if this has not preceded.
Lord,
we who receive your sacraments
ask your mercy and love.
By sharing in the power of this eucharist
may our brothers (sisters) win forgiveness of their sins,
enter your kingdom,
and praise you for all eternity.

We ask this through Christ our Lord.

B

OPENING PRAYER

Lord,
we entrust to you our brothers (sisters) N. and N.
that they may live with you for ever.
By your merciful love
wash away whatever sins they may have committed in human
  weakness
while they lived on earth.

We ask this through our Lord Jesus Christ, your Son,
who lives and reigns with you and the Holy Spirit,
one God, for ever and ever.

See Lectionary for Mass, nos. 789-793.

PRAYER OVER THE GIFTS

Pray, brethren . . .

Lord,
be merciful to your servants N. and N.
for whom we offer you this sacrifice of peace.
They were faithful to you in this life;
reward them with life for ever in your presence.

We ask this through Christ our Lord.

PRAYER AFTER COMMUNION

Let us pray.
Pause for silent prayer, if this has not preceded.
All-powerful God,
by the power of this sacrament
give our brothers (sisters) eternal happiness
in the fellowship of the just.

We ask this through Christ our Lord.

C

OPENING PRAYER

All-powerful and ever-living God,
you never refuse mercy to those who call upon you with faith.
Be merciful to your servants N. and N.
They left this life believing in your name;
may they be counted among your saints for ever.

We ask this through our Lord Jesus Christ, your Son,
who lives and reigns with you and the Holy Spirit,
one God, for ever and ever.

See Lectionary for Mass, nos. 789-793.

PRAYER OVER THE GIFTS

Pray, brethren . . .

Lord God,
as your Son offered himself to you as a living sacrifice,
accept the sacrifice of your Church.
Free your servants N. and N. from all their sins
and lead them to the reward of life without end.

We ask this through Christ our Lord.

PRAYER AFTER COMMUNION

Let us pray.
Pause for silent prayer, if this has not preceded.
Father all-powerful, God of mercy,
may the sacraments we receive free us from our sins.
May this sacrifice be our prayer for pardon,
our strength in weakness,
our support in all we do,
and may it be for the living and the dead
the forgiveness of all their sins
and the pledge of eternal redemption.

We ask this through Christ our Lord.

12. FOR A MARRIED COUPLE

OPENING PRAYER

Lord,
pardon the sins of your servants N. and N.
In this life they were joined in true married
  love.
Now let the fullness of your own love
unite them for life eternal.

We ask this through our Lord Jesus Christ,
  your Son,
who lives and reigns with you and the Holy
  Spirit,
one God, for ever and ever.

Or (for one deceased spouse only):

Lord,
pardon the sins of your servant N.
and watch over him (her) with constant
  kindness.
In this life true married love ever united them;
May the fullness of your own love unite them
  for life eternal.

We ask this through our Lord Jesus Christ,
  your Son,
who lives and reigns with you and the Holy
  Spirit,
one God, for ever and ever.

13. FOR PARENTS

OPENING PRAYER

Almighty God,
you command us to honor father and mother.
In your mercy forgive the sins of my (our) parents
and let me (us) one day see them again
in the radiance of eternal joy.

We ask this through our Lord Jesus Christ, your Son,
who lives and reigns with you and the Holy Spirit,
one God, for ever and ever.

See Lectionary for Mass, nos. 789-793.

PRAYER OVER THE GIFTS

Pray, brethren . . .

Lord,
receive the sacrifice we offer for my (our) parents.
Give them eternal joy in the land of the living,
and let me (us) join them one day in the happiness of the
  saints.

We ask this through Christ our Lord.

PRAYER AFTER COMMUNION

Let us pray.
Pause for silent prayer, if this has not preceded.
Lord,
may this sharing in the sacrament of heaven
win eternal rest and light for my (our) parents
and prepare me (us) to share eternal glory with them.

We ask this through Christ our Lord.

14. FOR RELATIVES, FRIENDS, AND BENEFACTORS

OPENING PRAYER

**Father,
source of forgiveness and salvation for all mankind,
hear our prayer.
By the prayers of the ever-virgin Mary,
may our friends, relatives, and benefactors
who have gone from this world
come to share eternal happiness with all your saints.**

**We ask this through our Lord Jesus Christ, your Son,
who lives and reigns with you and the Holy Spirit,
one God, for ever and ever.**

See Lectionary for Mass, nos. 789-793.

PRAYER OVER THE GIFTS

Pray, brethren . . .

**God of infinite mercy,
hear our prayers
and by this sacrament of our salvation
forgive all the sins of our relatives, friends, and benefactors.**

We ask this through Christ our Lord.

PRAYER AFTER COMMUNION

Let us pray.
Pause for silent prayer, if this has not preceded.
**Father all-powerful, God of mercy,
we have offered you this sacrifice of praise
for our relatives, friends, and benefactors.
By the power of this sacrament
free them from all their sins
and give them the joy of eternal light.**

We ask this through Christ our Lord.

FUNERAL MASS OF A BAPTIZED CHILD

A

Introductory Rites

Come, you whom my Father has blessed; inherit the kingdom prepared for you since the foundation of the world (E.S. alleluia). (Matthew 25:34)

OPENING PRAYER

God of mercy and love,
you called this child to yourself
at the dawn of his (her) life.
By baptism you made him (her) your child
and we believe that he (she) is already in your kingdom.
Hear our prayers
and let us one day share eternal life with him (her).

We ask this through our Lord Jesus Christ, your Son,
who lives and reigns with you and the Holy Spirit,
one God, for ever and ever.

See Lectionary for Mass, nos. 794-798.

PRAYER OVER THE GIFTS

Pray, brethren . . .

Lord,
make holy these gifts we offer you.
These parents return to you the child you gave them.
May they have fullness of joy with him (her) in your kingdom.

We ask this through Christ our Lord.

Preface of Christian Death I–V, pages 494–498.

Communion Rite

We were baptized with Christ and buried with him in death; we believe that we shall also come to life with Christ (E.S. alleluia). (See Rom. 6:4, 8)

PRAYER AFTER COMMUNION

Let us pray.
Pause for silent prayer, if this has not preceded.
Lord,
hear the prayers of those who share in the body and
    blood of your Son.
Comfort those who mourn for this child
and sustain them with the hope of eternal life.

We ask this through Christ our Lord.

B. Other Prayers

OPENING PRAYER

**God our Father,
you know how much our hearts are saddened
by the death of this child.
As we who live mourn his (her) death
strengthen us in our faith
that he (she) is already at peace in your eternal kingdom.**

**We ask this through our Lord Jesus Christ, your Son,
who lives and reigns with you and the Holy Spirit,
one God, for ever and ever.**

See Lectionary for Mass, nos. 794-798.

PRAYER OVER THE GIFTS

Pray, brethren . . .

**Father,
receive this sacrifice we offer
as a sign of our love for you,
and comfort us by your merciful love.
We accept what you have asked of us,
for we trust in your wisdom and goodness.**

We ask this through Christ our Lord.

PRAYER AFTER COMMUNION

Let us pray.
Pause for silent prayer, if this has not preceded.
**Lord,
you feed us with the gift of your eucharist.
May we rejoice with this child
at the feast of eternal life in your kingdom.**

We ask this through Christ our Lord.

FUNERAL MASS OF A CHILD WHO DIED BEFORE BAPTISM

If a child whom the parents wished to be baptized should die before baptism, the local ordinary, taking into consideration pastoral circumstances, may permit the funeral to be celebrated either in the home of the child or even according to the plan of funeral rites customarily used in the region.

In funerals of this kind there should ordinarily be a liturgy of the word, as described in the ritual. If at times the celebration of Mass is considered opportune, the following texts should be used.

The doctrine of the necessity of baptism should not be weakened in the catechesis of the faithful.

Introductory Rites

God will wipe every tear from their eyes; there will be no more death, no more weeping or pain, for the old order has passed away. (Rev. 21:4)

OPENING PRAYER

Lord,
listen to the prayers of this family
that has faith in you.
In their sorrow at the death of this child,
may they find hope in your infinite mercy.

We ask this through our Lord Jesus Christ,
your Son,
who lives and reigns with you and the Holy
Spirit,
one God, for ever and ever.

Or:

Father of all consolation,
from whom nothing is hidden,
you know the faith of these parents
who mourn the death of their child.
May they find comfort in knowing
that he (she) is entrusted to your loving care.

We ask this through our Lord Jesus Christ,
your Son,
who lives and reigns with you and the Holy
Spirit,
one God, for ever and ever.

See Lectionary for Mass, no. 799.

PRAYER OVER THE GIFTS

Pray, brethren . . .

Father,
receive this sacrifice we offer
as a sign of our love for you,
and comfort us by your merciful love.
We accept what you have asked of us,
for we trust in your wisdom and goodness.

We ask this through Christ our Lord.

Preface of Christian Death I–V, pages 494–498.

Communion Rite

The Lord has destroyed death for ever; God has wiped away the tears from every face. (Is. 25:8)

PRAYER AFTER COMMUNION

Let us pray.
Pause for silent prayer, if this has not preceded.
Lord,
hear the prayers of those who share in the body and
blood of your Son.
By these sacred mysteries
you have filled them with the hope of eternal life.
May they be comforted in the sorrows of this present life.

We ask this through Christ our Lord.

RITE OF BLESSING AND SPRINKLING HOLY WATER

SAMPLE FORMULAS FOR THE GENERAL INTERCESSIONS

PREPARATION FOR MASS

THANKSGIVING AFTER MASS

RITE OF BLESSING AND SPRINKLING HOLY WATER

1. The rite of blessing and sprinkling of holy water may be celebrated in all churches and chapels at all Sunday Masses celebrated on Sunday or on Saturday evening.

When this rite is celebrated it takes the place of the penitential rite at the beginning of Mass. The *Kyrie* is also omitted.

2. After greeting the people the priest remains standing at his chair. A vessel containing the water to be blessed is placed before him. Facing the people, he invites them to pray, using these or similar words:

Dear friends,
this water will be used
to remind us of our baptism.
Ask God to bless it,
and to keep us faithful
to the Spirit he has given us.

After a brief silence, he joins his hands and continues:

God our Father,
your gift of water
brings life and freshness to the earth;
it washes away our sins and brings us eternal life.

We ask you now to bless ✝ this water,
and to give us your protection on this day
which you have made your own.
Renew the living spring of your life within us
and protect us in spirit and body,
that we may be free from sin
and come into your presence
to receive your gift of salvation.
We ask this through Christ our Lord.

Or:

Lord God almighty,
creator of all life,
of body and soul,
we ask you to bless ✝ this water:
as we use it in faith
forgive our sins
and save us from all illness
and the power of evil.

Lord,
in your mercy
give us living water,
always springing up as a fountain of salvation:
free us, body and soul, from every danger,
and admit us to your presence
in purity of heart.

Grant this through Christ our Lord.

Or (during the Easter season):

Lord God almighty,
hear the prayers of your people:
we celebrate our creation and redemption.
Hear our prayers and bless ✝ this water
which gives fruitfulness to the fields,
and refreshment and cleansing to man.
You chose water to show your goodness
when you led your people to freedom
through the Red Sea
and satisfied their thirst in the desert
with water from the rock.
Water was the symbol used by the prophets
to foretell your new covenant with man.
You made the water of baptism holy
by Christ's baptism in the Jordan:
by it you give us a new birth
and renew us in holiness.
May this water remind us of our baptism
and let us share the joy
of all who have been baptized at Easter.

We ask this through Christ our Lord.

3. Where it is customary, salt may be mixed with the holy water. The priest blesses the salt, saying:

Almighty God,
we ask you to bless ✠ this salt
as once you blessed the salt scattered over the water
by the prophet Elisha.
Wherever this salt and water is sprinkled,
drive away the power of evil,
and protect us always
by the presence of your Holy Spirit.

Grant this through Christ our Lord.

Then he pours the salt into the water in silence.

4. Taking the sprinkler, the priest sprinkles himself and his ministers, then the rest of the clergy and people. He may move through the church for the sprinkling of the people. Meanwhile, an antiphon or another appropriate song is sung.

Outside the Easter Season

Cleanse us, Lord, from all our sins; wash us, and we shall be whiter than snow. (Ps. 50:9)

I will pour clean water over you and wash away all your defilement. A new heart will I give you, says the Lord. (Ezek. 36:25-26)

Praised be the Father of our Lord Jesus Christ: a God so merciful and kind. He has given us a new birth, a living hope, by raising Jesus his Son from death. Salvation is our undying inheritance, preserved for us in heaven, salvation at the end of time. (See 1 Peter 1:3-5)

In the Easter Season

I saw water flowing from the right side of the temple, alleluia. It brought God's life and his salvation, and the people sang in joyful praise: alleluia, alleluia. (See Ezek. 47:1-2, 9)

You are a people God claims as his own to praise him who called you out of darkness into his marvelous light, alleluia. (See 1 Peter 2:9)

Lord Jesus, from your wounded side flowed streams of cleansing water: the world was washed of all its sin, all life made new again, alleluia.

5. When he returns to his place and the song is finished, the priest faces the people and, with joined hands, says (unless the opening prayer of Mass follows immediately):

May almighty God cleanse us of our sins,
and through the eucharist we celebrate
make us worthy to sit at his table
in his heavenly kingdom.
Amen.

The people answer:

6. When it is prescribed, the *Gloria* is then sung or said.

SAMPLE FORMULAS FOR THE GENERAL INTERCESSIONS

1. GENERAL FORMULA I

Introduction

My brothers and sisters,
God our Father
wants all mankind to be saved
and calls us to the knowledge of the truth.
Let us pray to him with all our hearts.

Intercessions led by the deacon or
other minister

A.   For the holy Church of God:
        that the Lord guide and protect it,
        we pray to the Lord:

        ℟. Lord, hear our prayer.

B.   For all the peoples of the world:
        that the Lord unite them in peace and harmony,
        we pray to the Lord:

        ℟. Lord, hear our prayer.

C.   For all our brothers and sisters in need:
        that the Lord assist them,
        we pray to the Lord:

        ℟. Lord, hear our prayer.

D.   For ourselves and our community:
        that we offer an acceptable sacrifice,
        we pray to the Lord:

        ℟. Lord, hear our prayer.

Concluding prayer by the priest

God of love,
our refuge and our strength,
hear the prayers of your Church,
and grant us today
what we ask of you in faith.
We ask this through Christ our Lord.

℟. Amen.

2. GENERAL FORMULA II

Introduction

My brothers and sisters,
through this common prayer,
let us pray to our Lord Jesus Christ
not only for ourselves and our own needs,
but for all mankind.

Intercessions led by the deacon or
other minister

A.

1. For all Christian people,
we pray to the giver of all good things,
Christ the Lord:

℟. **Christ, hear us.**

2. For those who do not yet believe,
we pray to the giver of spiritual gifts,
Christ the Lord:

℟. **Christ, hear us.**

B.

1. For those who hold public office,
we pray to the ruler of mankind,
Christ the Lord:

℟. **Christ, hear us.**

2. For fine weather and the fruits of the earth,
we pray to the king of the universe,
Christ the Lord:

℟. **Christ, hear us.**

C.

1. For those who cannot be present here,
we pray to him who knows our hearts,
Christ the Lord:

℟. **Christ, hear us.**

2. For all who have gone before us in faith,
we pray to the judge of all mankind,
Christ the Lord:

℟. **Christ, hear us.**

D.

1. For all who call upon him in faith,
we pray for the mercy of our Savior,
Christ the Lord.

℟. **Christ, hear us.**

2. Let us implore the mercy of Christ the Lord
and trust in his goodness to help us in our needs.
We pray to the Lord:

℟. **Christ, hear us.**

Concluding prayer by the priest

Father,
we come before you with faith and love
to praise your goodness
and to acknowledge our need.
We ask you to hear the prayers we make
in the name of Jesus the Lord.   ℟. **Amen.**

3. ADVENT

My brothers and sisters,
as we prepare for the coming of our Lord Jesus Christ,
let us earnestly ask his mercy.
He came into the world
to preach the good news to the poor
and to heal the repentant sinner.
Let us ask him to come again to our world today,
bringing salvation to all who stand in need.

Intercessions led by the deacon or
other minister

A.   1. That the Lord Jesus may be with his Church
and guide it always,
we pray to the Lord:

℟. Lord, have mercy.

2. That the Lord Jesus may enrich with spiritual gifts
our Pope, our bishop, and all bishops,
we pray to the Lord:

℟. Lord, have mercy.

B.   1. That the Lord Jesus may bless the world with his peace
and the protection of his love,
we pray to the Lord:

℟. Lord, have mercy.

2. That the Lord Jesus may guide those in authority
to follow his will
and to seek the good of all mankind,
we pray to the Lord:

℟. Lord, have mercy.

C.   1. That the Lord Jesus may heal the sick,
rid the world of hunger,
and protect us from all disasters,
we pray to the Lord:

℟. Lord, have mercy.

2. That the Lord Jesus may rescue those deprived of freedom
and all who are oppressed
because of what they believe or what they are,
we pray to the Lord:

℟. Lord, have mercy.

D.   1. That the Lord Jesus may keep us true
to our faith in Christ,
and help us to witness to his love before all men,
we pray to the Lord:

℟. Lord, have mercy.

**2. That the Lord Jesus may find us
watching and ready at his coming,
we pray to the Lord:**

℟. **Lord, have mercy.**

Concluding prayer by the priest

**Almighty, ever-living God,
your will for mankind
is that none should be lost
and all should be saved.
Hear the prayers of your people,
guide the course of the world in your peace
and let your Church serve you in tranquility and joy.
We ask this through Christ our Lord.**

℟. **Amen.**

4. CHRISTMAS SEASON

Introduction

My brothers and sisters,
today (tonight, at this season),
the kindness and love of God our Savior
has appeared among us.
Let us offer our prayers to God,
not trusting in our own good deeds,
but in his love for all mankind.

Intercessions led by the deacon or other minister

A. For the Church of God:
that we will joyfully proclaim and live our faith
in Christ the Word
who was born for us of the sinless Virgin Mary,
we pray to the Lord:

℟. Lord, have mercy.

B. For the peace and well-being of the whole world:
that God's gifts to us in this life
will lead us to salvation in the life to come,
we pray to the Lord:

℟. Lord, have mercy.

C. For those who suffer from hunger, sickness, or loneliness:
that the mystery of Christ's birth (manifestation)
will bring them health and peace,
we pray to the Lord:

℟. Lord, have mercy.

D. For our community and our families,
who welcome Christ into their lives:
that they learn to receive him
in the poor and suffering people of this world,
we pray to the Lord:

℟. Lord, have mercy.

Concluding prayer by the priest

Lord God,
Mary gave birth to your Son Jesus Christ, our Lord,
in purity and love.
May she bring our prayers before you,
for we make them in the name of Jesus the Lord.

℟. Amen.

5. LENT I

**My brothers and sisters,
we should pray at all times,
but especially during this season of Lent:
we should faithfully keep watch with Christ
and pray to our Father.**

Intercessions led by the deacon or
other minister

A.   **That Christians everywhere
may be responsive to the word of God
during this holy season,
we pray to the Lord:**

℟.   **Lord, have mercy.**

B.   **That people everywhere may work for peace
to make these days the acceptable time
of God's help and salvation,
we pray to the Lord:**

℟.   **Lord, have mercy.**

C.   **That all who have sinned or grown lukewarm
may turn to God again
during this time of reconciliation,
we pray to the Lord:**

℟.   **Lord, have mercy.**

D.   **That we ourselves may learn to repent
and turn from sin
with all our hearts,
we pray to the Lord:**

℟.   **Lord, have mercy.**

Concluding prayer by the priest

**Lord,
may your people turn again to you
and serve you with all their hearts.
With confidence we have asked your help:
may we now know your mercy and love in our lives.
We ask this through Christ our Lord.**

℟.   **Amen.**

6. LENT II

My brothers and sisters,
as Easter draws near,
let us earnestly pray to the Lord,
that we who are baptized, and the entire world,
may come to share more fully in the life Christ brings us
through his suffering, death, and resurrection.

A.   That those who will be baptized at Easter
        may grow in faith and understanding,
        we pray to the Lord:

        ℟. Lord, hear our prayer.

B.   That those who are helpless and abandoned
        may be given the blessings of peace and security,
        we pray to the Lord:

        ℟. Lord, hear our prayer.

C.   That those who are afflicted and tempted
        may be strengthened by God's grace,
        we pray to the Lord:

        ℟. Lord, hear our prayer.

D.   That we may all learn to set our own interests aside,
        and reach out in love to our brothers and sisters,
        we pray to the Lord:

        ℟. Lord, hear our prayer.

Father,
have mercy on your Church in its need,
hear the prayers we offer with all our hearts,
and never abandon the people who share your life.
We ask this through Christ our Lord.

℟. Amen.

7. MONDAY, TUESDAY, WEDNESDAY OF HOLY WEEK

Introduction

On these days when Christ prayed and entreated his Father
in the anguish of his passion,
let us pray to the Lord
with humility and sorrow for our sins.
May our Father hear and answer our prayers
out of love for his Son, Jesus Christ.

Intercessions led by the deacon or
other minister

A.   For God's Church, the Bride of Christ,
that she may be purified by his blood,
we pray to the Lord:

℟. Lord, hear our prayer.

B.   For the world in which we live,
that God may give us health and peace through the blood of Christ,
we pray to the Lord:

℟. Lord, hear our prayer.

C.   For the sick and suffering,
that God may give them courage and strength
to share the suffering of Christ,
we pray to the Lord:

℟. Lord, hear our prayer.

D.   For believers and unbelievers everywhere,
for all our brothers and sisters around the world,
that the suffering and death of our Lord Jesus Christ
may lead us to the glory of rising again,
we pray to the Lord:

℟. Lord, hear our prayer.

Concluding prayer by the priest

Father,
be near to your people
and hear our prayers.
We have many needs that we cannot express,
but you know them, and we ask you to help us
through the suffering and death of your Son Jesus Christ,
who is Lord for ever and ever.

℟. Amen.

8. EASTER SEASON

Introduction

My brothers and sisters,
with joy at Christ's rising from the dead,
let us turn to God our Father in prayer.
He heard and answered the prayers
of the Son he loved so much:
let us trust that he will hear our petitions.

Intercessions led by the deacon or
other minister

A. That pastors may lead in faith and serve in love
the flock entrusted to their care
by Christ the Good Shepherd,
we pray to the Lord:

℞. Lord, hear our prayer.

B. That the whole world may rejoice in the blessing of true peace,
the peace Christ himself gives us,
we pray to the Lord:

℞. Lord, hear our prayer.

C. That our suffering brothers and sisters
may have their sorrow turned into lasting joy,
we pray to the Lord:

℞. Lord, hear our prayer.

D. That our community may have the faith and strength
to bear witness to Christ's resurrection,
we pray to the Lord:

℞. Lord, hear our prayer.

Concluding prayer by the priest

Father,
you know the many different needs
your people have in this life.
Hear us and answer the prayers
of all who believe in you.
We ask this through Christ our Lord.

℞. Amen.

9. ORDINARY TIME I

Introduction

**Gathered together in Christ
as brothers and sisters,
let us call to mind God's many blessings
and ask him to hear the prayers
which he himself inspires us to ask.**

Intercessions led by the deacon or
other minister

A.   **For our Pope N., our Bishop N., all the Church's ministers
and the people they have been called to lead and serve,
we pray to the Lord:**

     ℞. **Lord, hear our prayer.**

B.   **For those who serve us in public office
and for all those entrusted with the common good,
we pray to the Lord:**

     ℞. **Lord, hear our prayer.**

C.   **For all travelers, by land, air, or sea;
for prisoners; and for those unjustly deprived of freedom,
we pray to the Lord:**

     ℞. **Lord, hear our prayer.**

D.   **For all of us gathered in this holy place
in faith, reverence, and love of God,
we pray to the Lord:**

     ℞. **Lord, hear our prayer.**

Concluding prayer by the priest

**Father,
hear the prayers of your Church.
In your love,
make up for what is lacking in our faith.
We ask this through Christ our Lord.**

℞. **Amen.**

10. ORDINARY TIME II

Introduction

My brothers and sisters,
we are gathered to celebrate the mystery
of our salvation in Jesus Christ.
Let us ask God our Father
to open for all the world this fountain of life and blessing.

Intercessions led by the deacon or
other minister

A.   For all who have dedicated themselves to God,
that he will help them to be faithful to their promise,
we pray to the Lord:

℞. Lord, hear our prayer.

B.   For peace among nations,
that God may rid the world of violence,
and let us serve him in freedom,
we pray to the Lord:

℞. Lord, hear our prayer.

C.   For the aged who suffer from loneliness and infirmity,
that we will sustain them by our love,
we pray to the Lord:

℞. Lord, hear our prayer.

D.   For all of us gathered here,
that God will teach us to use wisely
the good things he has given us,
that they will lead us closer to him
and to the eternal blessings he promises,
we pray to the Lord:

℞. Lord, hear our prayer.

Concluding prayer by the priest

Father,
hear the prayers of your people.
Give us what you have inspired us
to ask you for in faith.
We ask this through Christ our Lord.

℞. Amen.

General Formula I or II may also be
used during Ordinary Time.

11. MASSES FOR THE DEAD

Introduction

Let us pray with faith and confidence to God our Father
who lives for ever and who can do all things.
He raised his Son, Jesus Christ, from death.
May he give peace and salvation to the living and the dead.

Intercessions led by the deacon or
other minister

A. That God may bring all Christians together
in unity and faith,
we pray to the Lord:

℟. Lord, hear our prayer.

B. That God may take the evil of war away from our world,
we pray to the Lord:

℟. Lord, hear our prayer.

C. That God may show himself a Father
to those who lack food, work, and shelter,
we pray to the Lord:

℟. Lord, hear our prayer.

D. 1. That N., who once began eternal life in baptism,
may join the company of the saints for ever,
we pray to the Lord:

℟. Lord, hear our prayer.

2. That on the last day
God may raise up N.,
who received the body of Christ,
the bread of eternal life,
we pray to the Lord:

℟. Lord, hear our prayer.

(for a priest)

That N., who served the Church as a priest,
may worship God for ever in the liturgy of heaven,
we pray to the Lord:

℟. Lord, hear our prayer.

3. That our relatives and friends
who have gone before us in faith
may receive the reward of eternal life,
we pray to the Lord:

℟. Lord, hear our prayer.

4. **That all who have gone to their rest
   in the hope of rising again
   may come into the light of God's presence,
   we pray to the Lord:**

   ℟. **Lord, hear our prayer.**

5. **That all who suffer from mental or physical illness
   may receive help and comfort,
   we pray to the Lord:**

   ℟. **Lord, hear our prayer.**

6. **That all gathered here to show their faith and love
   may be reunited in the glory of God's kingdom,
   we pray to the Lord:**

   ℟. **Lord, hear our prayer.**

Concluding prayer by the priest

**Lord Jesus Christ,
hear our prayers for our brother (sister) N.
and for all who have gone before us in faith to eternal life.
Free them from all their sins
and let them share in the fullness of salvation
in the kingdom where you are Lord for ever and ever.**

℟. **Amen.**

PREPARATION FOR MASS

Prayer of St. Ambrose

Lord Jesus Christ,
I approach your banquet table
in fear and trembling,
for I am a sinner,
and dare not rely on my own worth
but only on your goodness and mercy.
I am defiled by many sins in body and soul,
and by my unguarded thoughts and words.
Gracious God of majesty and awe,
I seek your protection,
I look for your healing.
Poor troubled sinner that I am,
I appeal to you, the fountain of all mercy.
I cannot bear your judgment,
but I trust in your salvation.
Lord, I show my wounds to you
and uncover my shame before you.
I know my sins are many and great,
and they fill me with fear,
but I hope in your mercies, for they cannot be numbered.
Lord Jesus Christ, eternal king, God and man,
crucified for mankind,
look upon me with mercy and hear my prayer,
for I trust in you.
Have mercy on me,
full of sorrow and sin,
for the depth of your compassion never ends.
Praise to you, saving sacrifice,
offered on the wood of the cross for me and for all mankind.
Praise to the noble and precious blood,
flowing from the wounds of my crucified Lord Jesus Christ
and washing away the sins of the whole world.
Remember, Lord, your creature,
whom you have redeemed with your blood.
I repent my sins,
and I long to put right what I have done.
Merciful Father, take away all my offenses and sins;
purify me in body and soul,
and make me worthy to taste the holy of holies.
May your body and blood,
which I intend to receive, although I am unworthy,
be for me the remission of my sins,
the washing away of my guilt, the end of my evil thoughts,
and the rebirth of my better instincts.
May it incite me to do the works pleasing to you
and profitable to my health in body and soul,
and be a firm defense
against the wiles of my enemies. Amen.

Prayer of St. Thomas Aquinas

Almighty and ever-living God,
I approach the sacrament of your only-begotten Son,
    our Lord Jesus Christ.
I come sick to the doctor of life,
unclean to the fountain of mercy,
blind to the radiance of eternal light,
and poor and needy to the Lord of heaven and earth.
Lord, in your great generosity,
heal my sickness, wash away my defilement,
enlighten my blindness, enrich my poverty,
and clothe my nakedness.
May I receive the bread of angels,
the King of kings and Lord of lords,
with humble reverence,
with the purity and faith,
the repentance and love, and the determined purpose
that will help to bring me to salvation.
May I receive the sacrament of the Lord's body and blood,
and its reality and power.
Kind God,
may I receive the body of your only-begotten Son,
    our Lord Jesus Christ,
born from the womb of the Virgin Mary,
and so be received into his mystical body
and numbered among his members.
Loving Father,
as on my earthly pilgrimage
I now receive your beloved Son
under the veil of a sacrament,
may I one day see him face to face in glory,
who lives and reigns with you for ever. Amen.

Prayer to the Virgin Mary

Mother of mercy and love,
blessed Virgin Mary,
I am a poor and unworthy sinner,
and I turn to you in confidence and love.
You stood by your Son
as he hung dying on the cross.
Stand also by me, a poor sinner,
and by all the priests
who are offering Mass today
here and throughout the entire Church.
Help us to offer a perfect and acceptable sacrifice
in the sight of the holy and undivided Trinity,
our most high God. Amen.

Statement of Intention

My purpose is to celebrate Mass
and to make present the body and blood of our Lord Jesus Christ
according to the rite of the holy Roman Church
to the praise of our all-powerful God
and all his assembly in the glory of heaven,
for my good and the good of all his pilgrim Church on earth,
and for all who have asked me to pray for them
in general and in particular,
and for the good of the holy Roman Church.

May the almighty and merciful Lord
grant us joy and peace,
amendment of life, room for true repentance,
the grace and comfort of the Holy Spirit,
and perseverance in good works. Amen.

THANKSGIVING AFTER MASS

Prayer of St. Thomas Aquinas

Lord, Father all-powerful and ever-living God,
I thank you,
for even though I am a sinner, your unprofitable servant,
not because of my worth but in the kindness of your mercy,
you have fed me
with the precious body and blood of your Son, our Lord
    Jesus Christ.
I pray that this holy communion
may not bring me condemnation and punishment
but forgiveness and salvation.
May it be a helmet of faith
and a shield of good will.
May it purify me from evil ways
and put an end to my evil passions.
May it bring me charity and patience,
humility and obedience,
and growth in the power to do good.
May it be my strong defense
against all my enemies, visible and invisible,
and the perfect calming of all my evil impulses,
bodily and spiritual.
May it unite me more closely to you, the one true God,
and lead me safely through death
to everlasting happiness with you.
And I pray that you will lead me, a sinner,
to the banquet where you, with your Son and Holy Spirit,
are true and perfect light,
total fulfillment, everlasting joy, gladness without end,
and perfect happiness to your saints.
Grant this through Christ our Lord. Amen.

Prayer to Our Redeemer

Soul of Christ, make me holy.
Body of Christ, be my salvation.
Blood of Christ, let me drink your wine.
Water flowing from the side of Christ, wash me clean.
Passion of Christ, strengthen me.
Kind Jesus, hear my prayer;
hide me within your wounds
and keep me close to you.
Defend me from the evil enemy.
Call me at my death
to the fellowship of your saints,
that I may sing your praise with them
through all eternity. Amen.

Prayer of Self-dedication to Jesus Christ

Lord Jesus Christ,
take all my freedom,
my memory, my understanding, and my will.
All that I have and cherish
you have given me.
I surrender it all to be guided by your will.
Your grace and your love
are wealth enough for me.
Give me these, Lord Jesus,
and I ask for nothing more.

Prayer to Jesus Christ Crucified

My good and dear Jesus,
I kneel before you,
asking you most earnestly
to engrave upon my heart
a deep and lively faith, hope, and charity,
with true repentance for my sins,
and a firm resolve to make amends.
As I reflect upon your five wounds,
and dwell upon them with deep compassion and grief,
I recall, good Jesus, the words the prophet David spoke
long ago concerning yourself:
they have pierced my hands and my feet,
they have counted all my bones!

The Universal Prayer
(attributed to Pope Clement XI)

Lord, I believe in you: increase my faith.
I trust in you: strengthen my trust.
I love you: let me love you more and more.
I am sorry for my sins: deepen my sorrow.

I worship you as my first beginning,
I long for you as my last end,
I praise you as my constant helper,
and call on you as my loving protector.

Guide me by your wisdom,
correct me with your justice,
comfort me with your mercy,
protect me with your power.

I offer you, Lord, my thoughts: to be fixed on you;
my words: to have you for their theme;
my actions: to reflect my love for you;
my sufferings: to be endured for your greater glory.

I want to do what you ask of me:
in the way you ask,
for as long as you ask,
because you ask it.

Lord, enlighten my understanding,
strengthen my will,
purify my heart,
and make me holy.

Help me to repent of my past sins
and to resist temptation in the future.
Help me to rise above my human weaknesses
and to grow stronger as a Christian.

Let me love you, my Lord and my God,
and see myself as I really am:
a pilgrim in this world,
a Christian called to respect and love
all whose lives I touch,
those in authority over me
or those under my authority,
my friends and my enemies.

Help me to conquer anger with gentleness,
greed by generosity,
apathy by fervor.
Help me to forget myself
and reach out toward others.

Make me prudent in planning,
courageous in taking risks.
Make me patient in suffering, unassuming in prosperity.

Keep me, Lord, attentive at prayer,
temperate in food and drink,
diligent in my work,
firm in my good intentions.

Let my conscience be clear,
my conduct without fault,
my speech blameless,
my life well-ordered.

Put me on guard against my human weaknesses.
Let me cherish your love for me,
keep your law,
and come at last to your salvation.

Teach me to realize that this world is passing,
that my true future is the happiness of heaven,
that life on earth is short,
and the life to come eternal.

Help me to prepare for death
with a proper fear of judgment,
but a greater trust in your goodness.
Lead me safely through death
to the endless joy of heaven.

Grant this through Christ our Lord. Amen.

Prayer to the Virgin Mary

Mary, holy virgin mother,
I have received your Son, Jesus Christ.
With love you became his mother,
gave birth to him, nursed him,
and helped him grow to manhood.
With love I return him to you,
to hold once more,
to love with all your heart,
and to offer to the Holy Trinity
as our supreme act of worship
for your honor and for the good
of all your pilgrim brothers and sisters.

Mother, ask God to forgive my sins
and to help me serve him more faithfully.
Keep me true to Christ until death,
and let me come to praise him with you
for ever and ever. Amen.

Appendix II

RITES OF
THE BLESSING OF OILS
AND
CONSECRATING THE CHRISM

RITES OF
THE BLESSING OF OILS
AND
CONSECRATING THE CHRISM

INTRODUCTION

1. The bishop is to be looked on as the high priest of his flock. The life in Christ of his faithful is in some way derived from and dependent upon the bishop.[1]

He concelebrates the chrism Mass with priests from the different parts of his diocese and during it consecrates the chrism and blesses the other holy oils. This Mass is therefore one of the chief expressions of the fullness of the bishop's priesthood and is looked on as a symbol of the close bond between the bishop and his priests. For the chrism the bishop consecrates is used to anoint the newly baptized and to trace the sign of Christ on those to be confirmed; the oil of catechumens is used to prepare and dispose them for baptism; the oil of the sick, to strengthen them amid their infirmities.

2. The Christian liturgy has adopted the Old Testament usage of anointing kings, priests, and prophets with consecratory oil because they prefigured Christ, whose name means "the anointed of the Lord."

Similarly, the chrism is a sign that Christians, incorporated by baptism into the paschal mystery of Christ, dying, buried, and rising with him,[2] are sharers in his kingly and prophetic priesthood and that by confirmation they receive the spiritual anointing of the Spirit who is given to them.

The oil of catechumens extends the effects of the baptismal exorcism: it strengthens the candidates with the power to renounce the devil and sin before they go to the font of life for rebirth.

The oil of the sick, for the use of which James is the witness,[3] provides the sick with a remedy for both spiritual and bodily illness, so that they may have strength to bear up under evil and obtain pardon for their sins.

I. THE OILS

3. The matter suitable for a sacrament is olive oil or, according to local conditions, another oil extracted from plants.

4. The chrism is made of oil and some aromatic substance.

5. The chrism may be mixed either in private prior to the consecration or by the bishop during the liturgical rite itself.

II. THE MINISTER

6. Consecration of the chrism belongs exclusively to a bishop.

7. If the conference of bishops decides to retain its use, the oil of catechumens is blessed by the bishop together with the other oils at the chrism Mass.

However, in the case of the baptism of adults, priests have the faculty to bless the oil of catechumens before the anointing at the designated stage in the catechumenate.

8. The oil to be used in the anointing of the sick must be blessed for this purpose by the bishop or by a priest who has the faculty in virtue of the law itself or of its special concession to him by the Holy See.

In virtue of the law itself the following may bless the oil for use in the anointing of the sick:

a) those who are the equivalents in law to a diocesan bishop;

b) in the case of necessity, any priest, but only within the celebration of the sacrament.

III. TIME OF THE BLESSING

9. The blessing of the oil of the sick and of catechumens and the consecration of the chrism are carried out by the bishop as a rule on Holy Thursday at the proper Mass to be celebrated in the morning.

10. If it is difficult for the clergy and people to gather on that day, the blessing may be advanced to an earlier day, but still close to Easter. The proper chrism Mass is always used.

IV. PLACE OF THE BLESSING WITHIN THE MASS

11. In keeping with longstanding practice in the Latin liturgy, the blessing of the oil of the sick takes place before the end of the eucharistic prayer; the blessing of the oil of catechumens and the consecration of the chrism, after communion.

12. For pastoral reasons, however, it is permissible for the entire rite of blessing to take place after the liturgy of the word, according to the rite described below.

[1] See II Vatican Council, Constitution on the Sacred Liturgy, *Sacrosanctum Concilium*, no. 42.
[2] Ibid., no. 6.
[3] James 5:14.

RITES OF THE BLESSING OF OILS AND CONSECRATING THE CHRISM

Preparations

13. For the blessing of oils the following preparations are made in addition to what is needed for Mass:

In the sacristy or other appropriate place:

—vessels of oils;

—balsam or perfume for the preparation of the chrism if the bishop wishes to mix the chrism during the liturgical service;

—bread, wine, and water for Mass, which are carried with the oils before the preparation of the gifts.

In the sanctuary:

—table for the vessels of oil, placed so that the people may see the entire rite easily and take part in it;

—chair for the bishop, if the blessing takes place in front of the altar.

Rite of Blessing

14. The chrism Mass is always concelebrated. It is desirable that there be some priests from the various sections of the diocese among the priests who concelebrate with the bishop and are his witnesses and the co-workers in the ministry of the holy chrism.

15. The preparation of the bishop, the concelebrants, and other ministers, their entrance into the church, and everything from the beginning of Mass until the end of the liturgy of the word take place as indicated in the rite of concelebration. The deacons who take part in the blessing of oils walk ahead of the concelebrating priests to the altar.

16. After the renewal of commitment to priestly service the deacons and ministers appointed to carry the oils or, in their absence, some priests and ministers together with the faithful who will carry the bread, wine, and water, go in procession to the sacristy or other place where the oils and other offerings have been prepared.

Returning to the altar, they follow this order: first the minister carrying the vessel of balsam, if the bishop wishes to prepare the chrism, then the minister with the vessel for the oil of the catechumens, if it is to be blessed, the minister with the vessel for the oil of the sick, lastly a deacon or priest carrying the oil for the chrism. The ministers who carry the bread, wine, and water for the celebration of the eucharist follow them.

17. During the procession through the church, the choir leads the singing of the hymn "O Redeemer" or some other appropriate song, in place of the offertory song.

18. When the procession comes to the altar or the chair, the bishop receives the gifts. The deacon who carries the vessel of oil for the chrism shows it to the bishop, saying in a loud voice: **The oil for the holy chrism.** The bishop takes the vessel and gives it to one of the assisting deacons to place on the table. The same is done by those who carry the vessels for the oil of the sick and the oil of the catechumens. The first says: **The oil of the sick;** the second says: **The oil of catechumens.** The bishop takes the vessels in the same way, and the ministers place them on the table.

19. Then the Mass continues, as in the rite of concelebration, until the end of the eucharistic prayer, unless the entire rite of blessing takes place immediately (see no. 12). In this case everything is done as described below (no. 26).

Blessing of the Oil of the Sick

20. Before the bishop says **Through Christ our Lord/you give us all these gifts** in Eucharistic Prayer I, or the doxology **Through him** in the other eucharistic prayers, the one who carried the vessel for oil of the sick brings it to the altar and holds it in front of the bishop while he blesses the oil.

The bishop says or sings this prayer:

**God of all consolation,
you chose and sent your Son to heal the world.
Graciously listen to our prayer of faith:
send the power of your Holy Spirit, the Consoler,
into this precious oil, this soothing ointment,
this rich gift, this fruit of the earth.**

Bless this oil ✛ and sanctify it for our use.

**Make this oil a remedy for all who are anointed with it;
heal them in body, in soul, and in spirit,
and deliver them from every affliction.**

**We ask this through our Lord Jesus Christ, your Son,
who lives and reigns with you and the Holy Spirit,
one God, for ever and ever.
℟. Amen.**

The conclusion **Who lives and reigns with you** is said only when this blessing takes place outside the eucharistic prayer.

When Eucharistic Prayer I is used, the beginning of the prayer **Through Christ our Lord/you give us all these** gifts is changed to: **Through whom you give us all these gifts.**

After the blessing, the vessel with the oil of the sick is returned to its place, and the Mass continues until the communion rite is completed.

Blessing of the Oil of Catechumens

21. After the prayer after communion, the ministers place the oils to be blessed on a table suitably located in the center of the sanctuary. The concelebrating priests stand around the bishop on either side, in a semicircle, and the other ministers stand behind him. The bishop then blesses the oil of catechumens, if it is to be blessed, and consecrates the chrism.

22. When everything is ready, the bishop faces the people and, with his hands extended, sings or says the following prayer:

Lord God,
protector of all who believe in you,
bless ✠ this oil
and give wisdom and strength
to all who are anointed with it
in preparation for their baptism.
Bring them to a deeper understanding of the gospel,
help them to accept the challenge of Christian living,
and lead them to the joy of new birth
in the family of your Church.
We ask this through Christ our Lord.
℟. Amen.

Consecration of the Chrism

23. Then the bishop pours the balsam or prefume in the oil and mixes the chrism in silence, unless this was done beforehand.

24. After this he sings or says the invitation:

Let us pray
that God our almighty Father
will bless this oil
so that all who are anointed with it
may be inwardly transformed
and come to share in eternal salvation.

25. Then the bishop may breathe over the opening of the vessel of chrism. With his hands extended, he sings one of the following consecratory prayers.

Consecratory Prayer

a   God our maker,
        source of all growth in holiness,
        accept the joyful thanks and praise
        we offer in the name of your Church.

    In the beginning, at your command,
        the earth produced fruit-bearing trees.
    From the fruit of the olive tree
        you have provided us with oil for holy chrism.
    The prophet David sang of the life and joy
        that the oil would bring us in the sacraments of your love.

    After the avenging flood,
        the dove returning to Noah with an olive branch
        announced your gift of peace.
    This was a sign of a greater gift to come.

a   **Now the waters of baptism wash away the sins of men,
and by the anointing with olive oil
you make us radiant with your joy.**

**At your command,
Aaron was washed with water,
and your servant Moses, his brother,
anointed him priest.
This too foreshadowed greater things to come.
After your Son, Jesus Christ our Lord,
asked John for baptism in the waters of Jordan,
you sent the Spirit upon him
in the form of a dove
and by the witness of your own voice
you declared him to be your only, well-beloved Son.
In this you clearly fulfilled the prophecy of David,
that Christ would be anointed with the oil of gladness
beyond his fellow men.**

All the concelebrants extend their right hands toward the chrism, without saying anything, until the end of the prayer.

**And so, Father, we ask you to bless ☩ this oil
   you have created.
Fill it with the power of your Holy Spirit
through Christ your Son.
It is from him that chrism takes its name
and with chrism you have anointed
for yourself priests and kings,
prophets and martyrs.**

**Make this chrism a sign of life and salvation
for those who are to be born again in the waters
   of baptism.
Wash away the evil they have inherited from sinful Adam,
and when they are anointed with this holy oil
make them temples of your glory,
radiant with the goodness of life
that has its source in you.**

**Through this sign of chrism
grant them royal, priestly, and prophetic honor,
and clothe them with incorruption.
Let this be indeed the chrism of salvation
for those who will be born again of water
   and the Holy Spirit.
May they come to share eternal life
in the glory of your kingdom.
We ask this through Christ our Lord.**

℞   **Amen.**

Consecratory Prayer

b   **Father,**
     we thank you for the gifts
     you have given us in your love:
     we thank you for life itself and for the sacraments
     that strengthen it and give it fuller meaning.

     In the Old Covenant you gave your people
     a glimpse of the power of this holy oil
     and when the fullness of time had come
     you brought that mystery to perfection
     in the life of our Lord Jesus Christ, your Son.

     By his suffering, dying, and rising to life
     he saved the human race.
     He sent your Spirit to fill the Church
     with every gift needed to complete your saving work.

     From that time forward, through the sign of holy chrism,
     you dispense your life and love to men.
     By anointing them with the Spirit,
     you strengthen all who have been reborn in baptism.
     Through that anointing
     you transform them into the likeness of Christ your Son
     and give them a share
     in his royal, priestly, and prophetic work.

All the concelebrants extend their
right hands toward the chrism without saying anything, until the end of
the prayer.

     And so, Father, by the power of your love,
     make this mixture of oil and perfume
     a sign and source ✛ of your blessing.
     Pour out the gifts of your Holy Spirit
     on our brothers and sisters who will be anointed with it.
     Let the splendor of holiness shine on the world
     from every place and thing signed with this oil.

     Above all, Father, we pray
     that through this sign of your anointing
     you will grant increase to your Church
     until it reaches the eternal glory
     where you, Father, will be the all in all,
     together with Christ your Son, in the unity of the Holy Spirit,
     for ever and ever. ℟. Amen.

26. When the entire rite of blessing of oils is to be celebrated after the liturgy of the word, at the end of the renewal of commitment to priestly service the bishop goes with the concelebrants to the table where the blessing of the oil of the sick and of the oil of the chrism are to take place, and everything is done as described above (nos. 20-25).

27. After the final blessing of the Mass, the bishop puts incense in the censer, and the procession to the sacristy is arranged.

The blessed oils are carried by the ministers immediately after the cross, and the choir and people sing some verses of the hymn "O Redeemer" or some other appropriate song.

28. In the sacristy the bishop may instruct the priests about the reverent use and safe custody of the holy oils.

THE ORDER OF MASS

(MUSICAL SETTING A)

THE ORDER OF MASS
(Musical Setting A)

GREETING

In the name of the Father, and of the Son, and of the Ho - ly Spir - it. ℞. A - men.

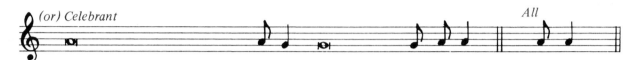

In the name of the Father, and of the Son, and of the Ho - ly Spir - it. ℞. A - men.

a)

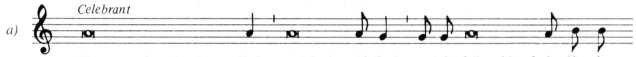

The grace of our Lord Jesus Christ and the love of God and the fellowship of the Ho - ly

Spir - it be with you all. ℞. And al - so with you.

b)

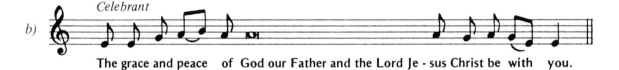

The grace and peace of God our Father and the Lord Je - sus Christ be with you.

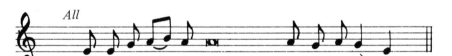

℞. Bless-ed be God, the Father of our Lord Je - sus Christ.

℞. And al - so with you.

c)

The Lord be with you. ℞. And al - so with you.

Peace be with you. ℞. And al - so with you.

PENITENTIAL RITE

My brothers and sis-ters, to prepare ourselves to celebrate the sacred mys-ter-ies, let us call

to mind our sins.

a)

I confess to almighty God,
and to you, my brothers and sisters,
that I have sinned through my own fault
in my thoughts and in my words,
in what I have done,
and in what I have failed to do;
and I ask blessed Mary, ever virgin,
all the angels and saints,
and you, my brothers and sisters,
to pray for me to the Lord our God.

b)

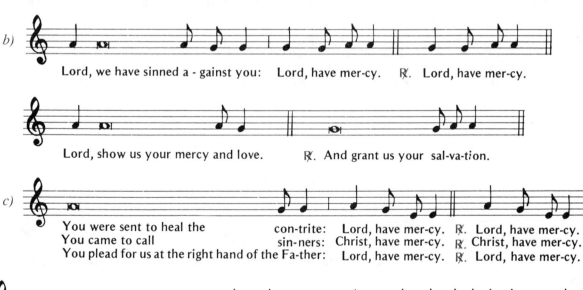

Lord, we have sinned a - gainst you: Lord, have mer-cy. ℟. Lord, have mer-cy.

Lord, show us your mercy and love. ℟. And grant us your sal-va-tion.

c)

You were sent to heal the con-trite: Lord, have mer-cy. ℟. Lord, have mer-cy.
You came to call sin-ners: Christ, have mer-cy. ℟. Christ, have mer-cy.
You plead for us at the right hand of the Fa-ther: Lord, have mer-cy. ℟. Lord, have mer-cy.

May almighty God have mercy on us, for-give us our sins, and bring us to ev - er - last - ing

life. ℟. A - men.

OPENING PRAYER

Let us pray.   *Long form:* Let us pray that. . . . .

Sample opening prayer with three members and long form conclusion

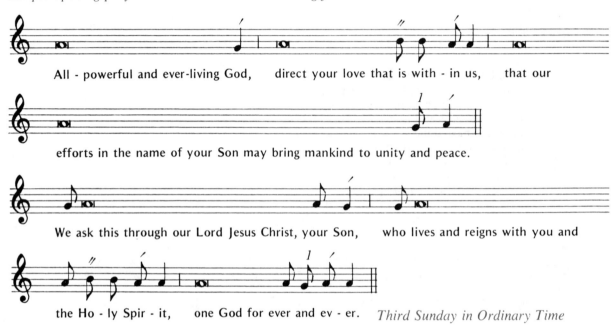

All - powerful and ever-living God,   direct your love that is with - in us,   that our

efforts in the name of your Son may bring mankind to unity and peace.

We ask this through our Lord Jesus Christ, your Son,   who lives and reigns with you and

the Ho - ly Spir - it,   one God for ever and ev - er.   *Third Sunday in Ordinary Time*

Sample opening prayer with two members and long form conclusion

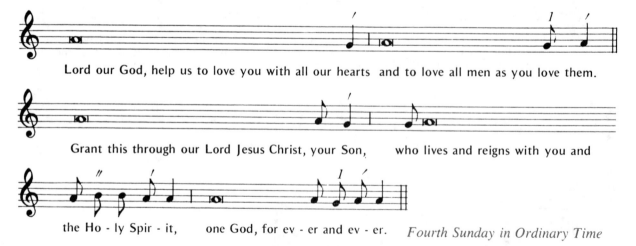

Lord our God, help us to love you with all our hearts and to love all men as you love them.

Grant this through our Lord Jesus Christ, your Son,   who lives and reigns with you and

the Ho - ly Spir - it,   one God, for ev - er and ev - er.   *Fourth Sunday in Ordinary Time*

OPTIONAL INTRODUCTION

Let us pray for unity and peace:

Let us pray for a greater love of God and of our fel - low man:

For Prayer over the Gifts and Prayer after Communion

Three members

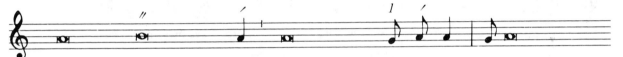

Lord, you give us the body and blood of your Son;   lead us by your Spirit to honor you not

only with our lips but with our lives   that we may enter your king-dom.   We ask this through

Christ our Lord.   A - men.

Two members

Lord, may your forgiving love turn us from sin,   and keep us on the way that leads to you.

We ask this through Christ our Lord.   A - men.

GENERAL INTERCESSIONS

a) Let us pray to the Lord. ℟. Lord, hear our prayer.

b) Let us pray to the Lord. ℟. Lord, hear us, hear our prayer.

c) We pray to the Lord. ℟. Lord, hear our prayer.

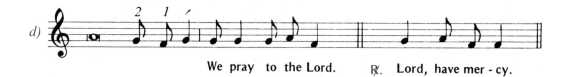

d) We pray to the Lord. ℟. Lord, have mer-cy.

e) Let us pray to the Lord. ℟. Lord, have mer-cy.

EUCHARISTIC PRAYER

℣. The Lord be with you. ℟. And al - so with you.

℣. Lift up your hearts. ℟. We lift them up to the Lord.

℣. Let us give thanks to the Lord our God. ℟. It is right to give him thanks and praise.

Or:

℣. The Lord be with you. ℟. And also with you.

℣. Lift up your hearts. ℟. We lift them up to the Lord.

℣. Let us give thanks to the Lord our God. ℟. It is right to give him thanks and praise.

ACCLAMATION

Ho - ly, ho - ly, ho - ly Lord, God of power and might, heav - en and earth

are full of your glo - ry. Ho - san - na in the high-est. Bless-ed is he who

comes in the name of the Lord. Ho - san - na in the high - est.

ADVENT I

The two comings of Christ

℣. The Lord be with you. ℟. And al-so with you.

℣. Lift up your hearts. ℟. We lift them up to the Lord.

℣. Let us give thanks to the Lord our God. ℟. It is right to give him thanks and praise.

Father, all-powerful and ev-er-liv-ing God, we do well always and everywhere to

give you thanks through Je-sus Christ our Lord. When he humbled himself

to come among us as a man, he ful-filled the plan you formed long a-go and

o-pened for us the way to sal-va-tion. Now we watch for the day, hop-

ing that the salvation promised us will be ours when Christ our Lord will come a-

gain in his glo-ry. And so, with all the choirs of an-gels in heav-en

we proclaim your glo-ry and join in their unend-ing hymn of praise:

ADVENT II

Waiting for the two comings of Christ

℣. The Lord be with you.   ℟. And al-so with you.

℣. Lift up your hearts.   ℟. We lift them up to the Lord.

℣. Let us give thanks to the Lord our God.   ℟. It is right to give him thanks and praise.

Father, all-powerful and ev-er-liv-ing God, we do well always and everywhere to give you thanks through Je-sus Christ our Lord. His future coming was pro-claimed by all the proph-ets. The virgin mother bore him in her womb with love be-yond all tell-ing. John the Baptist was his her-ald and made him known when at last he came. In his love Christ has filled us with joy as we prepare to cel-e-brate his birth, so that when he comes he may find us watch-ing in prayer, our hearts filled with won-der and praise. And so, with all the choirs of an-gels in heav-en we proclaim your glo-ry and join in their unend-ing hymn of praise:

CHRISTMAS I

Christ the light

℣. The Lord be with you. ℟. And al - so with you.

℣. Lift up your hearts. ℟. We lift them up to the Lord.

℣. Let us give thanks to the Lord our God. ℟. It is right to give him thanks and praise.

Father, all-powerful and ev - er - liv - ing God, we do well always and everywhere to

give you thanks through Je - sus Christ our Lord. In the wonder of the in - car -

na - tion your eternal Word has brought to the eyes of faith a new and ra - diant vi -

sion of your glo - ry. In him we see our God made vis - i - ble and so are caught

up in love of the God we can-not see. And so, with all the choirs of an -

gels in heav - en we proclaim your glo - ry and join in their unend -

ing hymn of praise:

CHRISTMAS II

Christ restores unity to all creation

CHRISTMAS III

Divine and human exchange in the Incarnation of the Word

℣. The Lord be with you.   ℟. And al - so with you.

℣. Lift up your hearts.   ℟. We lift them up to the Lord.

℣. Let us give thanks to the Lord our God.   ℟. It is right to give him thanks and praise.

Father, all-powerful and ev - er - liv - ing God, we do well always and everywhere to

give you thanks through Je - sus Christ our Lord. To - day in him a new

light has dawned up - on the world: God has be - come one with man, and man

has be - come one a - gain with God. Your e - ternal Word has taken upon him -

self our hu - man weak - ness, giving our mortal nature im - mor - tal val - ue.

So marvelous is this oneness be - tween God and man that in Christ man re - stores

to man the gift of ev - er - last - ing life. In our joy we sing to your

glo - ry with all the choirs of an - gels:

EPIPHANY

Christ the light of the nations

℣. The Lord be with you. ℟. And al - so with you.

℣. Lift up your hearts. ℟. We lift them up to the Lord.

℣. Let us give thanks to the Lord our God. ℟. It is right to give him thanks and praise.

Father, all-powerful and ev - er - liv - ing God, we do well al - ways and eve - ry - where

to give you thanks. To - day you revealed in Christ your eternal plan of sal -

va - tion and showed him as the light of all peo - ples. Now that his glory

has shone a - mong us you have renewed hu - man - i - ty in his im - mor - tal im -

age. Now, with an - gels and arch - an - gels, and the whole com - pa - ny

of heav - en, we sing the unend - ing hymn of your praise:

BAPTISM OF THE LORD

Consecration and mission of Christ

℣. The Lord be with you. ℟. And al-so with you.

℣. Lift up your hearts. ℟. We lift them up to the Lord.

℣. Let us give thanks to the Lord our God. ℟. It is right to give him thanks and praise.

Father, all-powerful and ev-er-liv-ing God, we do well al-ways and eve-ry-where to give you thanks. You celebrated your new gift of bap-tism by signs and won-ders at the Jor-dan. Your voice was heard from heav-en to awaken faith in the presence among us of the Word made man. Your Spirit was seen as a dove, revealing Je-sus as your serv-ant, and a-nointing him with joy as the Christ, sent to bring to the poor the good news of sal-va-tion. In our un-ending joy we echo on earth the song of the an-gels in heav-en as they praise your glo-ry for ev-er:

LENT I

The spiritual meaning of Lent

℣. The Lord be with you.   ℟. And al - so with you.

℣. Lift up your hearts.   ℟. We lift them up to the Lord.

℣. Let us give thanks to the Lord our God.   ℟. It is right to give him thanks and praise.

Father, all-powerful and ev - er - liv - ing God,   we do well always and everywhere to

give you thanks   through Je - sus Christ   our Lord.   Each year you give us this

joyful season when we prepare to celebrate the pas - chal mys - ter - y   with mind and

heart re - newed.   You give us a spirit of loving reverence for you,   our Fa - ther,

and of will - ing serv - ice to our neigh - bor.   As we recall the great events that

gave us new life in Christ,   you bring the image of your Son to per - fec - tion with - in

us.   Now, with an - gels and arch - an - gels,   and the whole com - pa - ny of

heav - en,   we sing the unend - ing hymn of your praise:

LENT II

The spirit of penance

℣. The Lord be with you. ℟. And al-so with you.

℣. Lift up your hearts. ℟. We lift them up to the Lord.

℣. Let us give thanks to the Lord our God. ℟. It is right to give him thanks and praise.

Father, all-powerful and ev-er-liv-ing God, we do well al-ways and eve-ry-where to give you thanks. This great season of grace is your gift to your fam-i-ly to re-new us in spir-it. You give us strength to pu-ri-fy our hearts, to con-trol our de-sires, and so to serve you in free-dom. You teach us how to live in this pass-ing world with our heart set on the world that will nev-er end.

Now, with all the saints and an-gels, we praise you for ev-er:

LENT III

The fruits of self-denial

℣. The Lord be with you.   ℟. And al - so with you.

℣. Lift up your hearts.   ℟. We lift them up to the Lord.

℣. Let us give thanks to the Lord our God.   ℟. It is right to give him thanks and praise.

Father, all-powerful and ev - er - liv - ing God,   we do well al - ways and eve - ry - where

to give you thanks.   You ask us to ex - press our thanks by self - de - ni - al.

We are to master our sinfulness and con - quer our pride.   We are to show to those

in need your good - ness to our - selves.   Now, with all the saints and

an - gels,   we praise you for ev - er:

LENT IV

The reward of fasting

℣. The Lord be with you. ℟. And al-so with you.

℣. Lift up your hearts. ℟. We lift them up to the Lord.

℣. Let us give thanks to the Lord our God. ℟. It is right to give him thanks and praise.

Father, all-powerful and ev-er-liv-ing God, we do well al-ways and eve-ry-where to give you thanks. Through our observance of Lent you correct our faults and raise our minds to you, you help us grow in ho-li-ness, and offer us the reward of ev-er-last-ing life through Je-sus Christ our Lord. Through him the angels and all the choirs of heav-en worship in awe be-fore your pres-ence. May our voic-es be one with theirs as they sing with joy the hymn of your glo-ry:

FIRST SUNDAY OF LENT

The temptation of the Lord

℣. The Lord be with you. ℟. And al - so with you.

℣. Lift up your hearts. ℟. We lift them up to the Lord.

℣. Let us give thanks to the Lord our God. ℟. It is right to give him thanks and praise.

Father, all-powerful and ev - er - liv - ing God, we do well always and everywhere to

give you thanks through Je - sus Christ our Lord. His fast of for - ty days

makes this a ho - ly sea - son of self - de - ni - al. By re - jecting the devil's

temp-ta - tions he has taught us to rid ourselves of the hidden cor - rup - tion of e - vil, and

so to share his paschal meal in pu - ri - ty of heart, until we come to its ful - fill -

ment in the prom - ised land of heav - en. Now we join the an - gels and the

saints as they sing their unend - ing hymn of praise:

SECOND SUNDAY OF LENT

Transfiguration

℣. The Lord be with you. ℟. And al - so with you.

℣. Lift up your hearts. ℟. We lift them up to the Lord.

℣. Let us give thanks to the Lord our God. ℟. It is right to give him thanks and praise.

Father, all-powerful and ev - er - liv - ing God, we do well always and everywhere to give

you thanks through Je - sus Christ our Lord. On your holy mountain he re -

vealed him - self in glo - ry in the presence of his dis - ci - ples. He had al -

read -y pre - pared them for his ap - proach - ing death. He wanted to teach

them through the Law and the Proph - ets that the promised Christ had first to suf - fer

and so come to the glo - ry of his res - ur - rec - tion. In our unending joy we echo

on earth the song of the an - gels in heav-en as they praise your glo - ry for ev - er:

THIRD SUNDAY OF LENT
The woman of Samaria

℣. The Lord be with you.   ℟. And al - so with you.

℣. Lift up your hearts.   ℟. We lift them up to the Lord.

℣. Let us give thanks to the Lord our God.   ℟. It is right to give him thanks and praise.

Father, all-powerful and ev - er - liv - ing God, we do well always and everywhere to give

you thanks through Je - sus Christ our Lord.   When he asked the woman of Samaria

for wa - ter to drink, Christ had already pre-pared for her the gift of faith.   In his

thirst to re-ceive her faith he awakened in her heart the fire of your love.   With thank-

ful praise, in compa-ny with the an - gels, we glo - ri - fy the won-ders of your power:

FOURTH SUNDAY OF LENT

The man born blind

℣. The Lord be with you.   ℟. And al-so with you.

℣. Lift up your hearts.   ℟. We lift them up to the Lord.

℣. Let us give thanks to the Lord our God.   ℟. It is right to give him thanks and praise.

Father, all-powerful and ev-er-liv-ing God, we do well always and everywhere to give

you thanks through Je-sus Christ our Lord. He came among us as a man,

to lead mankind from dark-ness in-to the light of faith. Through Adam's fall

we were born as slaves of sin, but now through bap-tism in Christ we are re-born

as your a-dopt-ed chil-dren. Earth u-nites with heav-en to sing the new

song of cre-a-tion, as we adore and praise you for ev-er:

FIFTH SUNDAY OF LENT

Lazarus

℣. The Lord be with you. ℟. And al - so with you.

℣. Lift up your hearts. ℟. We lift them up to the Lord.

℣. Let us give thanks to the Lord our God. ℟. It is right to give him thanks and praise.

Father, all-powerful and ev - er - liv - ing God, we do well always and everywhere to give you thanks through Je - sus Christ our Lord. As a man like us, Jesus wept for Laz - a - rus his friend. As the e-ter-nal God, he raised Laz - a - rus from the dead. In his love for us all, Christ gives us the sac - ra - ments to lift us up to ev - er - last - ing life. Through him the angels of heaven offer their prayer of ad - o-ra-tion as they re - joice in your pres-ence for ev - er. May our voices be one with theirs in their tri-um-phant hymn of praise:

PASSION OF THE LORD I
The power of the cross

℣. The Lord be with you.   ℟. And al - so with you.

℣. Lift up your hearts.   ℟. We lift them up to the Lord.

℣. Let us give thanks to the Lord our God.   ℟. It is right to give him thanks and praise.

Father, all-powerful and ev - er - liv - ing God, we do well al - ways and eve - ry - where to

give you thanks. The suffering and death of your Son brought life to the whole

world, moving our hearts to praise your glo - ry. The power of the cross reveals

your judg-ment on this world and the kingship of Christ cru - ci - fied. We

praise you, Lord, with all the an - gels and saints in their song of joy:

PASSION OF THE LORD II

The victory of the passion

℣. The Lord be with you.   ℟. And al - so with you.

℣. Lift up your hearts.   ℟. We lift them up to the Lord.

℣. Let us give thanks to the Lord our God.   ℟. It is right to give him thanks and praise.

Father, all-powerful and ev - er - liv - ing God, we do well always and everywhere to give

you thanks through Je - sus Christ our Lord. The days of his life-giving death

and glorious resurrec-tion are ap - proach-ing. This is the hour when he triumphed o - ver

Sa - tan's pride, the time when we cel-e - brate the great e - vent of our re-demp-tion.

Through Christ the angels of heaven offer their prayer of ad - o - ra -tion as they re -

joice in your pres-ence for ev - er. May our voices be one with theirs in their

tri-um-phant hymn of praise:

PASSION SUNDAY (PALM SUNDAY)

The redeeming work of Christ

℣. The Lord be with you. ℟. And al - so with you.

℣. Lift up your hearts. ℟. We lift them up to the Lord.

℣. Let us give thanks to the Lord our God. ℟. It is right to give him thanks and praise.

Father, all-powerful and ev - er - liv - ing God, we do well always and everywhere to give

you thanks through Je - sus Christ our Lord. Though he was sin-less, he

suffered will-ing-ly for sin-ners. Though in - no - cent, he accepted death to save the

guil-ty. By his dying he has de - stroyed our sins. By his ris-ing he has raised us up

to ho - li - ness of life. We praise you, Lord, with all the an-gels in their song of joy:

PRIESTHOOD (CHRISM MASS)

The priesthood of Christ and the ministry of priests

℣. The Lord be with you.   ℟. And al - so with you.

℣. Lift up your hearts.   ℟. We lift them up to the Lord.

℣. Let us give thanks to the Lord our God.   ℟. It is right to give him thanks and praise.

Father, all-powerful and ev - er - liv-ing God, we do well al - ways and eve-ry-where to give

you thanks. By your Ho - ly Spir-it you anointed your on-ly Son High Priest of the

new and e - ter - nal cov - e - nant. With wis - dom and love you have planned

that this one priest-hood should con-tin-ue in the Church. Christ gives the dignity of

a roy-al priest-hood to the peo-ple he has made his own. From these, with a broth-

er's love, he chooses men to share his sa - cred min-is-try by the lay-ing on of hands.

He ap-points them to renew in his name the sacrifice of our re-demp-tion as they set before

your family his pas - chal meal.   He calls them to lead your holy peo-ple in love, nour -

ish them by your word,   and strength-en them through the sac-ra - ments.   Fa-ther,

they are to give their lives in your serv-ice   and for the salva-tion of your peo-ple   as they

strive to grow in the likeness of Christ   and honor you by their courageous witness of faith

and love.   We praise you, Lord, with all the an-gels and saints   in their song of joy:

EASTER I

The paschal mystery

℣. The Lord be with you. ℟. And al-so with you.

℣. Lift up your hearts. ℟. We lift them up to the Lord.

℣. Let us give thanks to the Lord our God. ℟. It is right to give him thanks and praise.

Father, all-powerful and ev-er-liv-ing God, we do well always and everywhere to give

you thanks through Je-sus Christ our Lord. We praise you with greater joy than

ever on this East-er day, night, when Christ be-came our pas-chal sac-ri-fice. He is the

true Lamb who took away the sins of the world. By dying he de-stroyed our death;

by ris-ing he re-stored our life. And so, with all the choirs of an-gels in heav-en

we proclaim your glo-ry and join in their unend-ing hymn of praise:

EASTER II

New life in Christ

℣. The Lord be with you. ℟. And al-so with you.

℣. Lift up your hearts. ℟. We lift them up to the Lord.

℣. Let us give thanks to the Lord our God. ℟. It is right to give him thanks and praise.

Father, all-powerful and ev-er-liv-ing God, we do well always and everywhere to give

you thanks through Je-sus Christ our Lord. We praise you with greater joy than

ever in this East-er sea-son, when Christ be-came our pas-chal sac-ri-fice. He

has made us chil-dren of the light, ris-ing to new and ev-er-last-ing life. He has

o-pened the gates of heav-en to re-ceive his faith-ful peo-ple. His death is our

ran-som from death; his res-ur-rec-tion is our ris-ing to life. The joy of the resurrection

re-news the whole world, while the choirs of heav-en sing for ev-er to your glo-ry:

EASTER III

Christ lives and intercedes for us for ever

℣. The Lord be with you. ℟. And al-so with you.

℣. Lift up your hearts. ℟. We lift them up to the Lord.

℣. Let us give thanks to the Lord our God. ℟. It is right to give him thanks and praise.

Father, all-powerful and ev-er-liv-ing God, we do well always and everywhere to give you thanks through Je-sus Christ our Lord. We praise you with greater joy than ever in this East-er sea-son, when Christ be-came our pas-chal sac-ri-fice. He is still our priest, our ad-vo-cate who al-ways pleads our cause. Christ is the victim who dies no more, the Lamb, once slain, who lives for ev-er. The joy of the resurrection re-news the whole world, while the choirs of heav-en sing for ev-er to your glo-ry:

EASTER IV

The restoration of the universe through the paschal mystery

℣. The Lord be with you. ℟. And al-so with you.

℣. Lift up your hearts. ℟. We lift them up to the Lord.

℣. Let us give thanks to the Lord our God. ℟. It is right to give him thanks and praise.

Father, all-powerful and ev-er-liv-ing God, we do well always and everywhere to give

you thanks through Je-sus Christ our Lord. We praise you with greater joy

than ever in this East-er sea-son, when Christ be-came our pas-chal sac-ri-fice. In him

a new age has dawned, the long reign of sin is end-ed, a broken world has been re-

newed, and man is once a-gain made whole. The joy of the resurrection re-news

the whole world, while the choirs of heav-en sing for ev-er to your glo-ry:

EASTER V

Christ is priest and victim

℣. The Lord be with you. ℟. And al-so with you.

℣. Lift up your hearts. ℟. We lift them up to the Lord.

℣. Let us give thanks to the Lord our God. ℟. It is right to give him thanks and praise.

Father, all-powerful and ev-er-liv-ing God, we do well always and everywhere to give

you thanks through Je-sus Christ our Lord. We praise you with greater joy than

ever in this East-er sea-son, when Christ be-came our pas-chal sac-ri-fice. As he

offered his bod-y on the cross, his per-fect sac-ri-fice ful-filled all oth-ers. As he

gave himself into your hands for our sal-va-tion, he showed himself to be the priest,

the al-tar, and the lamb of sac-ri-fice. The joy of the resurrection re-news the whole

world, while the choirs of heav-en sing for ev-er to your glo-ry:

ASCENSION I

The mystery of the ascension

℣. The Lord be with you. ℟. And al-so with you.

℣. Lift up your hearts. ℟. We lift them up to the Lord.

℣. Let us give thanks to the Lord our God. ℟. It is right to give him thanks and praise.

Father, all-powerful and ev-er-liv-ing God, we do well al-ways and eve-ry-where to

give you thanks. [To-day] the Lord Jesus, the king of glo-ry, the conqueror

of sin and death, ascended to heav-en while the an-gels sang his prais-es. Christ, the

mediator be-tween God and man, judge of the world and Lord of all, has passed beyond

our sight, not to a-ban-don us but to be our hope. Christ is the beginning, the

head of the Church; where he has gone, we hope to fol-low. The joy of the

resurrection and ascension re-news the whole world, while the choirs of heav-en sing for

ev-er to your glo-ry:

ASCENSION II

The mystery of the ascension

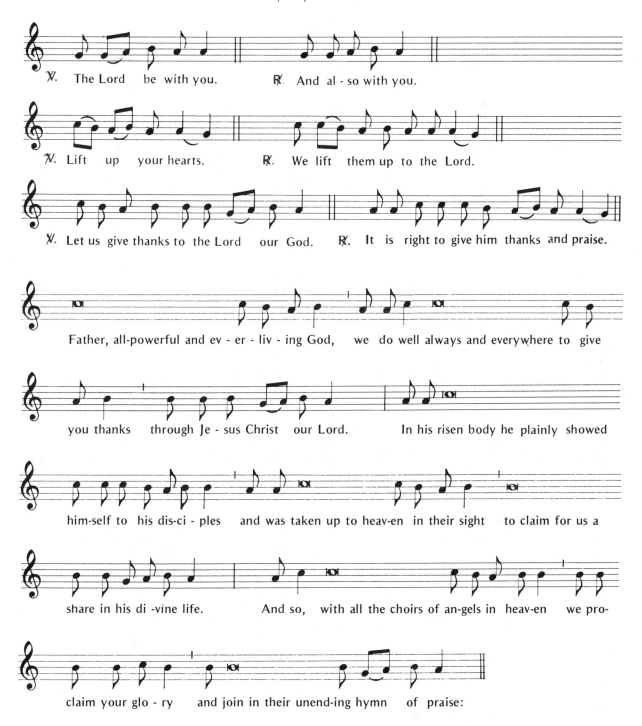

℣. The Lord be with you. ℟. And al - so with you.

℣. Lift up your hearts. ℟. We lift them up to the Lord.

℣. Let us give thanks to the Lord our God. ℟. It is right to give him thanks and praise.

Father, all-powerful and ev - er - liv - ing God, we do well always and everywhere to give

you thanks through Je - sus Christ our Lord. In his risen body he plainly showed

him-self to his dis-ci - ples and was taken up to heav-en in their sight to claim for us a

share in his di -vine life. And so, with all the choirs of an-gels in heav-en we pro-

claim your glo - ry and join in their unend-ing hymn of praise:

PENTECOST

The mystery of Pentecost

℣. The Lord be with you.   ℟. And al - so with you.

℣. Lift up your hearts.   ℟. We lift them up to the Lord.

℣. Let us give thanks to the Lord our God.   ℟. It is right to give him thanks and praise.

Father, all-powerful and ev - er - liv - ing God,   we do well al-ways and eve-ry-where to give

you thanks.   To - day you sent the Holy Spir-it on those marked out to be your

children by sharing the life of your on - ly Son,   and so you brought the pas-chal mys-ter-y

to its com-ple-tion.   To - day we celebrate the great begin-ning of your Church

when the Holy Spirit   made known to all peoples the one true God,   and created from the

many languages of man   one voice to pro-fess one faith.   The joy of the resurrection

re-news the whole world,   while the choirs of heav-en sing for ev - er to your glo - ry:

SUNDAYS IN ORDINARY TIME I

The paschal mystery and the people of God

℣. The Lord be with you.   ℟. And al-so with you.

℣. Lift up your hearts.   ℟. We lift them up to the Lord.

℣. Let us give thanks to the Lord our God.   ℟. It is right to give him thanks and praise.

Father, all-powerful and ev-er-liv-ing God, we do well always and everywhere to give

you thanks through Je-sus Christ our Lord. Through his cross and resurrection

he freed us from sin and death and called us to the glory that has made us a cho-sen race,

a roy-al priest-hood, a holy nation, a peo-ple set a-part. Everywhere we proclaim your

might-y works for you have called us out of dark-ness into your own won-der-ful light.

And so, with all the choirs of an-gels in heav-en we proclaim your glo-ry and join in

their unend-ing hymn of praise:

SUNDAYS IN ORDINARY TIME II
The mystery of salvation

℣. The Lord be with you.   ℟. And al-so with you.

℣. Lift up your hearts.   ℟. We lift them up to the Lord.

℣. Let us give thanks to the Lord our God.   ℟. It is right to give him thanks and praise.

Father, all-powerful and ev-er-liv-ing God, we do well always and everywhere to give

you thanks through Je-sus Christ our Lord. Out of love for sin-ful man, he

hum-bled himself to be born of the Vir-gin. By suffering on the cross he freed us from

un-end-ing death, and by ris-ing from the dead he gave us e-ter-nal life. And so,

with all the choirs of an-gels in heav-en we proclaim your glo-ry and join in their un-

end-ing hymn of praise:

SUNDAYS IN ORDINARY TIME III

The salvation of man by a man

℣. The Lord be with you.

℟. And al - so with you.

℣. Lift up your hearts.

℟. We lift them up to the Lord.

℣. Let us give thanks to the Lord our God.

℟. It is right to give him thanks and praise.

Father, all-powerful and ev - er-liv - ing God, we do well al-ways and eve-ry -where to give

you thanks. We see your in - fi - nite power in your lov-ing plan of sal-va-tion.

You came to our rescue by your power as God, but you wanted us to be saved by

one like us. Man re-fused your friend-ship, but man himself was to re-store it

through Je - sus Christ our Lord. Through him the angels of heaven offer their prayer

of ad - o - ra - tion as they re-joice in your pres-ence for ev - er. May our voic-es

be one with theirs in their tri-um-phant hymn of praise:

SUNDAYS IN ORDINARY TIME IV

The history of salvation

℣. The Lord be with you.   ℟. And al-so with you.

℣. Lift up your hearts.   ℟. We lift them up to the Lord.

℣. Let us give thanks to the Lord our God.   ℟. It is right to give him thanks and praise.

Father, all-powerful and ev-er-liv-ing God, we do well always and everywhere to give

you thanks through Je-sus Christ our Lord.   By his birth we are re-born.   In

his suf-fer-ing we are freed from sin.   By his rising from the dead we rise to ev-er-

last-ing life.   In his return to you in glo-ry   we enter into your heav-en-ly king-dom.

And so, we join the an-gels and the saints   as they sing their un-end-ing hymn of praise:

SUNDAYS IN ORDINARY TIME V

Creation

℣. The Lord be with you.   ℟. And al - so with you.

℣. Lift up your hearts.   ℟. We lift them up to the Lord.

℣. Let us give thanks to the Lord our God.   ℟. It is right to give him thanks and praise.

Father, all-powerful and ev - er - liv - ing God, we do well al-ways and eve-ry-where to give

you thanks. All things are of your mak-ing, all times and seasons o - bey your laws,

but you chose to create man in your own im - age, setting him over the whole world in

all its won-der. You made man the stew-ard of cre - a - tion, to praise you day

by day for the marvels of your wis-dom and power, through Je - sus Christ our Lord.

We praise you, Lord, with all the an-gels in their song of joy:

SUNDAYS IN ORDINARY TIME VI

The pledge of an eternal Easter

℣. The Lord be with you. ℟. And al-so with you.

℣. Lift up your hearts. ℟. We lift them up to the Lord.

℣. Let us give thanks to the Lord our God. ℟. It is right to give him thanks and praise.

Father, all-powerful and ev-er-liv-ing God, we do well al-ways and eve-ry-where to give

you thanks. In you we live and move and have our be-ing. Each day you show

us a Fa-ther's love; your Holy Spirit, dwelling with-in us, gives us on earth the hope of

un-end-ing joy. Your gift of the Spir-it, who raised Je-sus from the dead, is the

fore-taste and prom-ise of the pas-chal feast of heav-en. With thankful praise,

in compa-ny with the an-gels, we glo-ri-fy the won-ders of your power:

SUNDAYS IN ORDINARY TIME VII

Salvation through the obedience of Christ

℣. The Lord be with you. ℟. And al - so with you.

℣. Lift up your hearts. ℟. We lift them up to the Lord.

℣. Let us give thanks to the Lord our God. ℟. It is right to give him thanks and praise.

Father, all-powerful and ev - er - liv - ing God, we do well al-ways and eve-ry -where to

give you thanks. So great was your love that you gave us your Son as our re -

deem-er. You sent him as one like our-selves, though free from sin, that you might

see and love in us what you see and love in Christ. Your gifts of grace, lost

by dis - o - be - di - ence, are now re-stored by the o - be - di - ence of your Son. We

praise you, Lord, with all the an-gels and saints in their song of joy:

SUNDAYS IN ORDINARY TIME VIII

The Church united in the mystery of the Trinity

℣. The Lord be with you. ℟. And al-so with you.

℣. Lift up your hearts. ℟. We lift them up to the Lord.

℣. Let us give thanks to the Lord our God. ℟. It is right to give him thanks and praise.

Father, all-powerful and ev-er-liv-ing God, we do well al-ways and eve-ry-where to give you thanks. When your children sinned and wandered far from your friend-ship, you reunited them with yourself through the blood of your Son and the power of the Ho-ly Spir-it. You gather them into your Church, to be one as you, Father, are one with your Son and the Ho-ly Spir-it. You call them to be your peo-ple, to praise your wis-dom in all your works. You make them the bod-y of Christ and the dwell-ing-place of the Ho-ly Spir-it. In our joy we sing to your glo-ry with all the choirs of an-gels:

WEEKDAYS I

All things made one in Christ

℣. The Lord be with you.   ℟. And al-so with you.

℣. Lift up your hearts.   ℟. We lift them up to the Lord.

℣. Let us give thanks to the Lord our God.   ℟. It is right to give him thanks and praise.

Father, all-powerful and ev-er-liv-ing God, we do well always and everywhere to give you thanks through Je-sus Christ our Lord. In him you have re-newed all things and you have given us all a share in his rich-es. Though his nature was di-vine, he stripped him-self of glo-ry and by shedding his blood on the cross he brought his peace to the world. There-fore he was exalted a-bove all cre-a-tion and became the source of e-ter-nal life to all who serve him. And so, with all the choirs of an-gels in heav-en we proclaim your glo-ry and join in their unend-ing hymn of praise:

WEEKDAYS II

Salvation through Christ

℣. The Lord be with you. ℟. And al-so with you.

℣. Lift up your hearts. ℟. We lift them up to the Lord.

℣. Let us give thanks to the Lord our God. ℟. It is right to give him thanks and praise.

Father, all-powerful and ev-er-liv-ing God, we do well al-ways and eve-ry-where to give

you thanks. In love you created man, in jus-tice you con-demned him, but in mercy

you re-deemed him, through Je-sus Christ our Lord. Through him the angels and

all the choirs of heav-en worship in awe be-fore your pres-ence. May our voic-es

be one with theirs as they sing with joy the hymn of your glo-ry:

WEEKDAYS III

The praise of God in creation and through the conversion of man

℣. The Lord be with you. ℟. And al - so with you.

℣. Lift up your hearts. ℟. We lift them up to the Lord.

℣. Let us give thanks to the Lord our God. ℟. It is right to give him thanks and praise.

Father, all-powerful and ev - er - liv - ing God, we do well al-ways and eve- ry-where to give

you thanks. Through your beloved Son you created our hu-man fam- i - ly. Through

him you re-stored us to your like-ness. Therefore it is your right to receive the

obedience of all cre - a -tion, the praise of the Church on earth, the thanksgiving of your

saints in heav-en. We too re-joice with the an-gels as we proclaim your glo-ry for ev -er:

WEEKDAYS IV

Praise of God is his gift

℣. The Lord be with you.   ℟. And al-so with you.

℣. Lift up your hearts.   ℟. We lift them up to the Lord.

℣. Let us give thanks to the Lord our God.   ℟. It is right to give him thanks and praise.

Father, all-powerful and ev-er-liv-ing God, we do well al-ways and eve-ry-where to give

you thanks. You have no need of our praise, yet our desire to thank you is it-self

your gift. Our prayer of thanksgiving adds noth-ing to your great-ness, but makes us

grow in your grace, through Je-sus Christ our Lord. In our joy we sing to your

glo-ry with all the choirs of an-gels:

WEEKDAYS V

The mystery of Christ is proclaimed

℣. The Lord be with you. ℟. And al - so with you.

℣. Lift up your hearts. ℟. We lift them up to the Lord.

℣. Let us give thanks to the Lord our God. ℟. It is right to give him thanks and praise.

Father, all-powerful and ev - er - liv - ing God, we do well always and everywhere to give

you thanks through Je - sus Christ our Lord. With love we cel - e - brate his death.

With living faith we proclaim his res - ur - rec - tion. With unwaver-ing hope we await his

re-turn in glo - ry. Now, with the saints and all the an-gels we praise you for ev - er:

WEEKDAYS VI

Salvation in Christ

℣. The Lord be with you. ℟. And al-so with you.

℣. Lift up your hearts. ℟. We lift them up to the Lord.

℣. Let us give thanks to the Lord our God. ℟. It is right to give him thanks and praise.

Father, it is our duty and our sal-va-tion, always and everywhere to give you thanks

through your be-lov-ed Son, Je-sus Christ. He is the Word through whom you

made the u-ni-verse, the Sav-ior you sent to re-deem us. By the power of the Ho-ly

Spir-it he took flesh and was born of the Vir-gin Mar-y. For our sake he opened

his arms on the cross; he put an end to death and revealed the res-ur-rec-tion. In

this he ful-filled your will and won for you a ho-ly peo-ple. And so we join the

an-gels and the saints in pro-claim-ing your glo-ry:

HOLY TRINITY

The mystery of the Holy Trinity

ANNUNCIATION

March 25

The mystery of the Incarnation

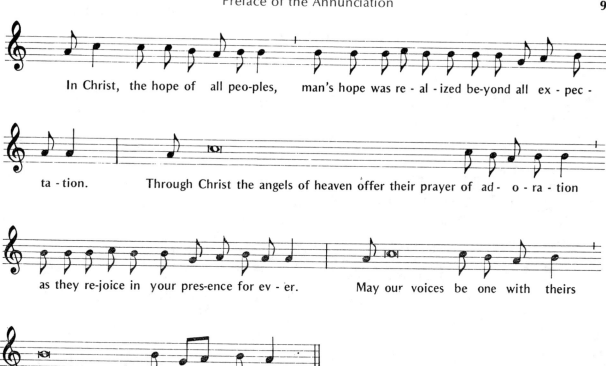

In Christ, the hope of all peo-ples, man's hope was re - al -ized be-yond all ex - pec -ta - tion. Through Christ the angels of heaven offer their prayer of ad - o - ra - tion as they re-joice in your pres-ence for ev - er. May our voices be one with theirs in their trium-phant hymn of praise:

SACRED HEART

The boundless love of Christ

℣. The Lord be with you. ℟. And al-so with you.

℣. Lift up your hearts. ℟. We lift them up to the Lord.

℣. Let us give thanks to the Lord our God. ℟. It is right to give him thanks and praise.

Father, all-powerful and ev-er-liv-ing God, we do well always and everywhere to give you thanks through Je-sus Christ our Lord. Lifted high on the cross, Christ gave his life for us, so much did he love us. From his wounded side flowed blood and wa-ter, the foun-tain of sacramen-tal life in the Church. To his o-pen heart the Savior in-vites all men, to draw water in joy from the springs of sal-va-tion. Now, with all the saints and an-gels, we praise you for ev-er:

TRIUMPH OF THE CROSS

The triumph of the glorious cross

℣. The Lord be with you. ℞. And al-so with you.

℣. Lift up your hearts. ℞. We lift them up to the Lord.

℣. Let us give thanks to the Lord our God. ℞. It is right to give him thanks and praise.

Father, all-powerful and ev-er-liv-ing God, we do well al-ways and eve-ry-where to give

you thanks. You de-creed that man should be saved through the wood of the cross.

The tree of man's defeat became his tree of vic-to-ry; where life was lost, there life

has been re-stored through Christ our Lord. Through him the choirs of angels

and all the pow-ers of heav-en praise and wor-ship your glo-ry. May our voices

blend with theirs as we join in their un-end-ing hymn:

HOLY EUCHARIST I

The sacrifice and sacrament of Christ

℣. The Lord be with you. ℟. And al-so with you.

℣. Lift up your hearts. ℟. We lift them up to the Lord.

℣. Let us give thanks to the Lord our God. ℟. It is right to give him thanks and praise.

Father, all-powerful and ev-er-liv-ing God, we do well always and everywhere to give

you thanks through Je-sus Christ our Lord. He is the true and e-ter-nal priest

who es-tab-lished this un-end-ing sac-ri-fice. He offered himself as a victim

for our de-liv-er-ance and taught us to make this of-fer-ing in his mem-o-ry.

As we eat his bod-y which he gave for us, we grow in strength. As we drink his

blood which he poured out for us, we are washed clean. Now, with an-gels and arch-

an-gels, and the whole com-pa-ny of heav-en, we sing the unend-ing hymn of your praise:

HOLY EUCHARIST II

The effects of the holy eucharist

℣. The Lord be with you.   ℞. And al - so with you.

℣. Lift up your hearts.   ℞. We lift them up to the Lord.

℣. Let us give thanks to the Lord our God.   ℞. It is right to give him thanks and praise.

Father, all-powerful and ev - er - liv - ing God, we do well always and everywhere to give

you thanks through Je - sus Christ our Lord.   At the last supper, as he sat at

ta - ble with his a - pos - tles, he offered himself to you as the spot-less lamb, the ac -

cept - a - ble gift that gives you per - fect praise. Christ has giv - en us this memorial of his

pas - sion to bring us its sav - ing power until the end of time. In this great sacrament you

feed your people and strength - en them in ho - li - ness, so that the family of mankind may

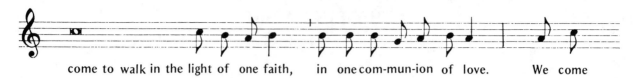

come to walk in the light of one faith,   in one com-mun-ion of love.   We come

then to this wonderful sacrament to be fed at your ta - ble   and grow into the like-ness of

the ris - en Christ.   Earth u -nites with heav-en   to sing the new song of cre -

a - tion   as we adore   and praise you for ev - er:

PRESENTATION OF THE LORD

February 2

The mystery of the Presentation of the Lord

℣. The Lord be with you.   ℟. And al-so with you.

℣. Lift up your hearts.   ℟. We lift them up to the Lord.

℣. Let us give thanks to the Lord our God.   ℟. It is right to give him thanks and praise.

Father, all-powerful and ev-er-liv-ing God, we do well always and everywhere to give

you thanks through Je-sus Christ our Lord. To-day your Son, who shares your

eternal splendor, was present-ed in the tem-ple, and re-vealed by the Spirit as the glo-ry

of Is-ra-el and the light of all peo-ples. Our hearts are joyful, for we have

seen your sal-va-tion, and now with the an-gels and saints we praise you for ev-er:

TRANSFIGURATION

August 6

The mystery of the transfiguration

℣. The Lord be with you. ℟. And al-so with you.

℣. Lift up your hearts. ℟. We lift them up to the Lord.

℣. Let us give thanks to the Lord our God. ℟. It is right to give him thanks and praise.

Father, all-powerful and ev-er-liv-ing God, we do well always and everywhere to give you thanks through Je-sus Christ our Lord. He re-vealed his glory to the dis-ci-ples to strength-en them for the scan-dal of the cross. His glory shone from a bod-y like our own, to show that the Church, which is the body of Christ, would one day share his glo-ry. In our unending joy we echo on earth the song of the an-gels in heav-en as they praise your glo-ry for ev-er:

CHRIST THE KING

Christ, the King of the universe

℣. The Lord be with you. ℟. And al-so with you.

℣. Lift up your hearts. ℟. We lift them up to the Lord.

℣. Let us give thanks to the Lord our God. ℟. It is right to give him thanks and praise.

Father, all-powerful and ev-er-liv-ing God, we do well al-ways and eve-ry-where to give you thanks. You a-nointed Jesus Christ, your only Son, with the oil of glad-ness, as the eternal priest and u-ni-ver-sal king. As priest he offered his life on the al-tar of the cross and redeemed the human race by this one per-fect sac-ri-fice of peace. As king he claims dominion o-ver all cre-a-tion, that he may

present to you, his almight-y Fa-ther,   an eternal and u - ni - ver - sal king-dom:

a king-dom of truth and life,   a kingdom of ho - li - ness and grace,   a kingdom of

jus-tice, love,   and peace.   And so, with all the choirs of an-gels in heav-en

we proclaim your glo - ry   and join in their unend-ing hymn   of praise:

DEDICATION OF A CHURCH I

Anniversary of the Dedication

A. Celebration in the Dedicated Church

The mystery of God's temple, which is the Church

℣. The Lord be with you.   ℟. And al-so with you.

℣. Lift up your hearts.   ℟. We lift them up to the Lord.

℣. Let us give thanks to the Lord our God.   ℟. It is right to give him thanks and praise.

Father, all-powerful and ev-er-liv-ing God, we do well al-ways and eve-ry-where to give you thanks. We thank you now for this house of prayer in which you bless your fam-i-ly as we come to you on pil-grim-age. Here you reveal your presence by sac-ra-men-tal signs, and make us one with you through the un-seen bond of grace. Here you build your temple of liv-ing stones, and bring the Church to its

full stature as the body of Christ through-out the world,　　to reach its perfection at last in

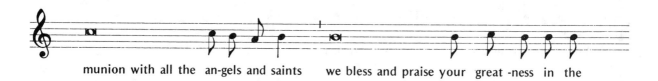

the heavenly city of Je- ru - sa - lem,　　which is the vi-sion of your peace.　　In com-

munion with all the an-gels and saints　　we bless and praise your great -ness in the

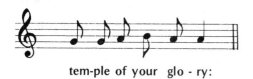

tem-ple of your glo - ry:

DEDICATION OF A CHURCH II

Anniversary of the Dedication

B. Celebration in Other Churches

The mystery of the Church, the bride of Christ and the
temple of the Spirit

℣. The Lord be with you. ℟. And al-so with you.

℣. Lift up your hearts. ℟. We lift them up to the Lord.

℣. Let us give thanks to the Lord our God. ℟. It is right to give him thanks and praise.

Father, all-powerful and ev-er-liv-ing God, we do well al-ways and eve-ry-where to

give you thanks. Your house is a house of prayer, and your pres-ence makes it

a place of bless-ing. You give us grace upon grace to build the tem-ple of your

Spir-it, creating its beau-ty from the ho-li-ness of our lives. Your house of prayer

is also the prom-ise of the Church in heav-en. Here your love is al-ways at work,

pre-paring the Church on earth for its heavenly glory as the sin-less bride of Christ, the joy-

ful moth-er of a great com-pa-ny of saints. Now, with the saints and all the an-gels

we praise you for ev-er:

HOLY SPIRIT I

The Spirit sent by the Lord upon his Church

℣. The Lord be with you.   ℟. And al-so with you.

℣. Lift up your hearts.   ℟. We lift them up to the Lord.

℣. Let us give thanks to the Lord our God.   ℟. It is right to give him thanks and praise.

Father, all-powerful and ev-er-liv-ing God, we do well always and everywhere to give

you thanks through Je-sus Christ our Lord. He as-cend-ed a-bove all the

heav-ens, and from his throne at your right hand poured into the hearts of your adopt-

ed chil-dren the Ho-ly Spir-it of your prom-ise. With steadfast love we sing

your un-end-ing praise; we join with the hosts of heav-en in their tri-um-phant song:

HOLY SPIRIT II

The working of the Spirit in the Church

℣. The Lord be with you. ℟. And al-so with you.

℣. Lift up your hearts. ℟. We lift them up to the Lord.

℣. Let us give thanks to the Lord our God. ℟. It is right to give him thanks and praise.

Father, all-powerful and ev-er-liv-ing God, we do well al-ways and eve-ry-where to give you thanks. You give your gifts of grace for eve-ry time and sea-son as you guide the Church in the mar-vel-ous ways of your prov-i-dence. You give us your Holy Spirit to help us al-ways by his power, so that with loving trust we may turn to you in all our trou-bles, and give you thanks in all our joys, through Je-sus Christ our Lord. In our joy we sing to your glo-ry with all the choirs of an-gels:

BLESSED VIRGIN MARY I

Motherhood of Mary

℣. The Lord be with you.   ℟. And al - so with you.

℣. Lift up your hearts.   ℟. We lift them up to the Lord.

℣. Let us give thanks to the Lord our God.   ℟. It is right to give him thanks and praise.

Father, all-powerful and ev - er - liv - ing God, we do well always and everywhere to give

you thanks
as we celebrate ... of   the Bless-ed Vir - gin Mar - y.   Through the
as we honor

power of the Ho - ly Spir-it, she be-came the virgin mother of your only Son, our Lord

Je - sus Christ, who is for ev - er the light of the world.   Through him the choirs

of angels and all the powers of heav-en praise and wor-ship your glo -ry.   May

our voic-es blend with theirs as we join in their un-end - ing hymn:

BLESSED VIRGIN MARY II

The Church echoes Mary's song of praise

℣. The Lord be with you.   ℟. And al - so with you.

℣. Lift up your hearts.   ℟. We lift them up to the Lord.

℣. Let us give thanks to the Lord our God.   ℟. It is right to give him thanks and praise.

Father, all-powerful and ev - er - liv - ing God, we do well always and everywhere to give

you thanks, and to praise you for your gifts as we contemplate your saints in glo - ry.

In celebrating the memory of the Bless-ed Vir-gin Mar-y, it is our spe-cial joy to ech - o

her song of thanks-giv-ing. What wonders you have worked through-out the world.

All gen - er - a - tions have shared the great-ness of your love. When you looked on

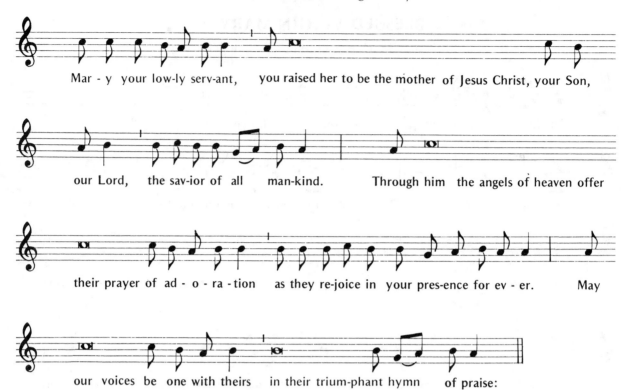

Mar - y your low-ly serv-ant, you raised her to be the mother of Jesus Christ, your Son,

our Lord, the sav-ior of all man-kind. Through him the angels of heaven offer

their prayer of ad - o - ra - tion as they re-joice in your pres-ence for ev - er. May

our voices be one with theirs in their trium-phant hymn of praise:

IMMACULATE CONCEPTION

December 8

The mystery of Mary and the Church

℣. The Lord be with you.   ℟. And al - so with you.

℣. Lift up your hearts.   ℟. We lift them up to the Lord.

℣. Let us give thanks to the Lord our God.   ℟. It is right to give him thanks and praise.

Father, all-powerful and ev - er - liv - ing God, we do well al-ways and eve-ry-where to give you thanks. You al-lowed no stain of Ad - am's sin to touch the Vir - gin Mar - y. Full of grace, she was to be a worthy moth-er of your Son, your sign of favor to the Church at its be-gin-ning, and the promise of its perfection as the bride of Christ, ra-diant in beau-ty. Purest of virgins, she was to bring forth your Son, the inno-cent lamb who takes a - way our sins. You chose her from all women to be our ad - vo - cate with you and our pat-tern of ho - li - ness. In our joy we sing to your glo - ry with all the choirs of an - gels:

ASSUMPTION

August 15

Mary assumed into glory

℣. The Lord be with you. ℟. And al - so with you.

℣. Lift up your hearts. ℟. We lift them up to the Lord.

℣. Let us give thanks to the Lord our God. ℟. It is right to give him thanks and praise.

Father, all-powerful and ev - er - liv - ing God, we do well always and everywhere to give

you thanks through Je - sus Christ our Lord. To - day the virgin Mother of God was taken

up into heaven to be the beginning and the pattern of the Church in its per-fec-tion, and a

sign of hope and comfort for your peo-ple on their pil - grim way. You would

not allow decay to touch her bod-y, for she had given birth to your Son, the Lord of

all life, in the glory of the in - car - na - tion. In our joy we sing to your

glo - ry with all the choirs of an - gels:

ANGELS

The glory of God in the angels

℣. The Lord be with you.   ℟. And al - so with you.

℣. Lift up your hearts.   ℟. We lift them up to the Lord.

℣. Let us give thanks to the Lord our God.   ℟. It is right to give him thanks and praise.

Father, all-powerful and ev - er - liv - ing God, we do well al-ways and eve-ry-where to

give you thanks. In praising your faithful angels and archangels, we al-so praise your

glo - ry, for in honor-ing them, we hon-or you, their cre - a - tor. Their splen-dor

shows us your great-ness, which surpasses in good-ness the whole of cre - a - tion.

Through Christ our Lord the great army of angels rejoic-es in your glo - ry. In adoration

and joy we make their hymn of praise our own:

ST. JOHN THE BAPTIST

The mission of John the Baptist

℣. The Lord be with you. ℟. And al-so with you.

℣. Lift up your hearts. ℟. We lift them up to the Lord.

℣. Let us give thanks to the Lord our God. ℟. It is right to give him thanks and praise.

Father, all-powerful and ev-er-liv-ing God, we do well always and everywhere to give you thanks through Je-sus Christ our Lord. We praise your greatness as we hon-or the proph-et who pre-pared the way be-fore your Son. You set John the Baptist apart from oth-er men, marking him out with spe-cial fa-vor. His birth brought great re-joic-ing: even in the womb he leapt for joy, so near was man's sal-va-tion. You chose John the Baptist from all the proph-ets to show the

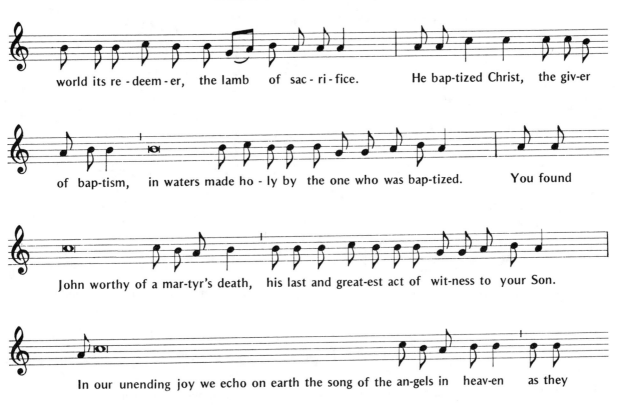

world its re-deem-er, the lamb of sac-ri-fice. He bap-tized Christ, the giv-er

of bap-tism, in waters made ho-ly by the one who was bap-tized. You found

John worthy of a mar-tyr's death, his last and great-est act of wit-ness to your Son.

In our unending joy we echo on earth the song of the an-gels in heav-en as they

praise your glo-ry for ev-er:

ST. JOSEPH, HUSBAND OF MARY

The mission of Saint Joseph

℣. The Lord be with you. ℟. And al-so with you.

℣. Lift up your hearts. ℟. We lift them up to the Lord.

℣. Let us give thanks to the Lord our God. ℟. It is right to give him thanks and praise.

Father, all-powerful and ev-er-liv-ing God, we do well always and everywhere to give you thanks as we hon-or Saint Jo-seph. He is that just man, that wise and loy-al serv-ant, whom you placed at the head of your fam-i-ly. With a husband's love he cher-ished Mar-y, the vir-gin Moth-er of God. With fatherly care he watched over Je-sus Christ your Son, con-ceived by the power of the Ho-ly Spir-it. Through Christ the choirs of angels and all the powers of heav-en praise and wor-ship your glo-ry. May our voic-es blend with theirs as we join in their un-end-ing hymn:

ST. PETER AND ST. PAUL, APOSTLES

The twofold mission of Peter and Paul in the Church

℣. The Lord be with you. ℟. And al - so with you.

℣. Lift up your hearts. ℟. We lift them up to the Lord.

℣. Let us give thanks to the Lord our God. ℟. It is right to give him thanks and praise.

Father, all-powerful and ev - er - liv - ing God, we do well al - ways and eve - ry - where to

give you thanks. You fill our hearts with joy as we honor your great a - pos - tles:

Peter, our leader in the faith, and Paul, its fear - less preach-er. Peter raised up the

Church from the faith-ful flock of Is - ra - el. Paul brought your call to the na-tions, and

be-came the teach-er of the world. Each in his chosen way gathered into unity the one

fam- i -ly of Christ. Both shared a mar-tyr's death and are praised through-out the world.

Now, with the apostles and all the an-gels and saints, we praise you for ev - er:

APOSTLES I

The apostles are shepherds of God's people

℣. The Lord be with you. ℞. And al - so with you.

℣. Lift up your hearts. ℞. We lift them up to the Lord.

℣. Let us give thanks to the Lord our God. ℞. It is right to give him thanks and praise.

Father, all-powerful and ev - er - liv - ing God, we do well al-ways and eve-ry-where to

give you thanks. You are the e - ter - nal Shep-herd who nev-er leaves his flock

un - tend - ed. Through the a - pos - tles you watch over us and pro-tect us al-ways.

You made them shepherds of the flock to share in the work of your Son, and from their

place in heav-en they guide us still. And so, with all the choirs of an-gels in heav-

en we proclaim your glo - ry and join in their unend-ing hymn of praise:

APOSTLES II

Apostolic foundation and witness

℣. The Lord be with you.　℟. And al-so with you.

℣. Lift up your hearts.　℟. We lift them up to the Lord.

℣. Let us give thanks to the Lord our God.　℟. It is right to give him thanks and praise.

Father, all-powerful and ev-er-liv-ing God, we do well al-ways and eve-ry-where to

give you thanks. You founded your Church on the apostles to stand firm for ev-er

as the sign on earth of your infi-nite ho-li-ness and as the living gospel for all men to

hear. With stead-fast love we sing your un-end-ing praise; we join with the hosts of

heav-en in their tri-um-phant song:

MARTYRS

The sign and example of martyrdom

℣. The Lord be with you. ℟. And al-so with you.

℣. Lift up your hearts. ℟. We lift them up to the Lord.

℣. Let us give thanks to the Lord our God. ℟. It is right to give him thanks and praise.

Father, all-powerful and ev-er-liv-ing God, we do well al-ways and eve-ry-where to give you thanks. Your holy martyr N. followed the ex-am-ple of Christ, and gave his/her life for the glo-ry of your name. His/Her death re-veals your power shin-ing through our hu-man weak-ness. You choose the weak and make them strong in bearing wit-ness to you, through Je-sus Christ our Lord. In our unending joy we echo on earth the song of the an-gels in heav-en as they praise your glo-ry for ev-er:

PASTORS

The presence of shepherds in the Church

℣. The Lord be with you. ℟. And al-so with you.

℣. Lift up your hearts. ℟. We lift them up to the Lord.

℣. Let us give thanks to the Lord our God. ℟. It is right to give him thanks and praise.

Father, all-powerful and ev-er-liv-ing God, we do well al-ways and eve-ry-where to give

you thanks. You give the Church this feast in hon-or of Saint N.; you in-spire

us by his ho-ly life, in-struct us by his preach-ing, and give us your pro-tec-tion in an-

swer to his prayers. We join the an-gels and the saints as they sing their un-end-ing

hymn of praise:

** The above cadence is based on a saint's name with the accent on the
first syllable.* For names with a different accent-structure:
    the accent coincides with the note b (ti);
    the preceding two syllables are sung on b (ti) and a (la) respectively;

example:

in hon-or of Saint Al-phon-sus;

VIRGINS AND RELIGIOUS

The sign of a life consecrated to God

℣. The Lord be with you. ℟. And al-so with you.

℣. Lift up your hearts. ℟. We lift them up to the Lord.

℣. Let us give thanks to the Lord our God. ℟. It is right to give him thanks and praise.

Father, all-powerful and ev-er-liv-ing God, we do well al-ways and eve-ry-where to give you thanks. To-day we honor your saints who consecrated their lives to Christ for the sake of the king-dom of heav-en. What love you show us as you recall mankind to its first in-no-cence, and invite us to taste on earth the gifts of the world to come!

Now, with the saints and all the an-gels we praise you for ev-er:

HOLY MEN AND WOMEN I

The glory of the saints

℣. The Lord be with you. ℟. And al - so with you.

℣. Lift up your hearts. ℟. We lift them up to the Lord.

℣. Let us give thanks to the Lord our God. ℟. It is right to give him thanks and praise.

Father, all-powerful and ev - er - liv - ing God, we do well al-ways and eve - ry - where to

give you thanks. You are glo-ri-fied in your saints, for their glo - ry is the crown-

ing of your gifts. In their lives on earth you give us an ex-am-ple. In our com-mun-ion

with them you give us their friend-ship. In their prayer for the Church you give us strength

and pro-tec-tion. This great company of witnesses spurs us on to vic-to-ry, to share

their prize of everlast-ing glo - ry, through Je - sus Christ our Lord. With angels and

archangels and the whole com-pa-ny of saints we sing our un-end-ing hymn of praise:

HOLY MEN AND WOMEN II

The activity of the saints

℣. The Lord be with you. ℟. And al-so with you.

℣. Lift up your hearts. ℟. We lift them up to the Lord.

℣. Let us give thanks to the Lord our God. ℟. It is right to give him thanks and praise.

Father, all-powerful and ev-er-liv-ing God, we do well al-ways and eve-ry-where to

give you thanks. You re-new the Church in every age by raising up men and women

out-stand-ing in ho-li-ness, liv-ing wit-ness-es of your un-chang-ing love. They

in-spire us by their he-ro-ic lives, and help us by their con-stant prayers to be the

liv-ing sign of your sav-ing power. We praise you, Lord, with all the an-gels

and saints in their song of joy:

ALL SAINTS

November 1

Jerusalem, our mother

℣. The Lord be with you. ℟. And al - so with you.

℣. Lift up your hearts. ℟. We lift them up to the Lord.

℣. Let us give thanks to the Lord our God. ℟. It is right to give him thanks and praise.

Father, all-powerful and ev - er - liv - ing God, we do well al-ways and eve - ry - where to

give you thanks. To-day we keep the festival of your ho - ly cit-y, the heavenly

Je-ru-sa-lem, our moth-er. A-round your throne the saints, our broth-ers and sis-ters,

sing your praise for ev - er. Their glo - ry fills us with joy, and their com-mun-ion

with us in your Church gives us inspi-ra -tion and strength as we hasten on our pilgrimage of

faith, ea-ger to meet them. With their great company and all the an-gels we

praise your glo - ry as we cry out with one voice:

MARRIAGE I

The dignity of the marriage bond

℣. The Lord be with you. ℞. And al - so with you.

℣. Lift up your hearts. ℞. We lift them up to the Lord.

℣. Let us give thanks to the Lord our God. ℞. It is right to give him thanks and praise.

Father, all-powerful and ev - er - liv - ing God, we do well al-ways and eve-ry-where to give

you thanks. By this sacrament your grace u - nites man and wom-an in an un-break -

a - ble bond of love and peace. You have designed the chaste love of hus-band and

wife for the increase both of the hu-man fam - i - ly and of your own fam - i - ly born in bap-tism.

You are the loving Father of the world of na-ture; you are the lov-ing Fa-ther of the new

cre - a - tion of grace.   In Christian marriage you bring together the two or-ders of cre - a -

tion: nature's gift of children en-rich-es the world   and your grace en-rich-es al -so your

Church.   Through Christ the choirs of angels and all the saints   praise and wor-ship your

glo - ry.   May our voic-es blend with theirs   as we join in their un-end - ing hymn:

MARRIAGE II

The great sacrament of marriage

℣. The Lord be with you. ℟. And al-so with you.

℣. Lift up your hearts. ℟. We lift them up to the Lord.

℣. Let us give thanks to the Lord our God. ℟. It is right to give him thanks and praise.

Father, all-powerful and ev-er-liv-ing God, we do well always and everywhere to give you thanks through Je-sus Christ our Lord. Through him you entered into a new cov-e-nant with your peo-ple. You restored man to grace in the sav-ing mys-ter-y of re-demp-tion. You gave him a share in the divine life through his un-ion with Christ. You made him an heir of Christ's e-ter-nal glo-ry. This outpouring of love in the new cov-e-nant of grace is symbolized in the marriage covenant that seals the love of hus-band and wife and re-flects your di-vine plan of love. And so, with the angels and all the saints in heav-en we proclaim your glo-ry and join in their unend-ing hymn of praise:

MARRIAGE III

Marriage, a sign of God's love

℣. The Lord be with you. ℟. And al-so with you.

℣. Lift up your hearts. ℟. We lift them up to the Lord.

℣. Let us give thanks to the Lord our God. ℟. It is right to give him thanks and praise.

Father, all-powerful and ev-er-liv-ing God, we do well al-ways and eve-ry-where to give you thanks. You cre-a-ted man in love to share your di-vine life. We see his high destiny in the love of hus-band and wife, which bears the im-print of your own di-vine love. Love is man's or-i-gin, love is his con-stant call-ing, love is his ful-fill-ment in heav-en. The love of man and woman is made holy in the sac-ra-ment of mar-riage, and be-comes the mir-ror of your ev-er-last-ing love. Through Christ the choirs of angels and all the saints praise and wor-ship your glo-ry. May our voic-es blend with theirs as we join in their un-end-ing hymn:

RELIGIOUS PROFESSION

The religious life, serving God by imitating Christ

℣. The Lord be with you. ℟. And al-so with you.

℣. Lift up your hearts. ℟. We lift them up to the Lord.

℣. Let us give thanks to the Lord our God. ℟. It is right to give him thanks and praise.

Father, all-powerful and ev - er - liv - ing God, we do well always and everywhere to give you thanks through Je - sus Christ our Lord. He came, the son of a vir-gin moth-er, named those blessed who were pure of heart, and taught by his whole life the per-fec-tion of chas-ti-ty. He chose always to fulfill your ho - ly will, and be-came obedient even to dy-ing for us, offering him-self to you as a per-fect ob - la - tion. He consecrated more closely to your service those who leave all things for your sake, and prom-ised that they would find a heav-en-ly treas-ure. And so, we join the an-gels and the saints as they sing their un-end-ing hymn of praise:

CHRISTIAN UNITY

The unity of Christ's body, which is the Church

℣. The Lord be with you.   ℟. And al - so with you.

℣. Lift up your hearts.   ℟. We lift them up to the Lord.

℣. Let us give thanks to the Lord our God.   ℟. It is right to give him thanks and praise.

Father, all-powerful and ev - er - liv - ing God, we do well always and everywhere to give

you thanks through Je - sus Christ our Lord. Through Christ you bring us to the knowl -

edge of your truth, that we may be united by one faith and one bap-tism to be - come

his bod - y. Through Christ you have giv-en the Ho - ly Spir-it to all peo - ples. How

wonderful are the works of the Spir-it, re-vealed in so man - y gifts! Yet how mar -

velous is the unity the Spirit creates from their diversi-ty, as he dwells in the hearts of your chil -

dren, filling the whole Church with his pres-ence and guid-ing it with his wis-dom! In

our joy we sing to your glo - ry with all the choirs of an-gels:

CHRISTIAN DEATH I

The hope of rising in Christ

℣. The Lord be with you. ℟. And al-so with you.

℣. Lift up your hearts. ℟. We lift them up to the Lord.

℣. Let us give thanks to the Lord our God. ℟. It is right to give him thanks and praise.

Father, all-powerful and ev-er-liv-ing God, we do well always and everywhere to give

you thanks through Je-sus Christ our Lord. In him, who rose from the dead, our

hope of res-ur-rec-tion dawned. The sad-ness of death gives way to the bright prom-ise

of im-mor-tal-i-ty. Lord, for your faithful people life is changed, not end-ed. When

the body of our earthly dwell-ing lies in death we gain an everlast-ing dwell-ing place in heav-

en. And so, with all the choirs of an-gels in heav-en we proclaim your glo-ry

and join in their unend-ing hymn of praise:

CHRISTIAN DEATH II

Christ's death, our life

℣. The Lord be with you. ℟. And al - so with you.

℣. Lift up your hearts. ℟. We lift them up to the Lord.

℣. Let us give thanks to the Lord our God. ℟. It is right to give him thanks and praise.

Father, all-powerful and ev - er - liv - ing God, we do well always and everywhere to give

you thanks through Je - sus Christ our Lord. He chose to die that he might free

all men from dy - ing. He gave his life that we might live to you a - lone for ev - er.

In our joy we sing to your glo - ry with all the choirs of an-gels:

CHRISTIAN DEATH III

Christ, salvation and life

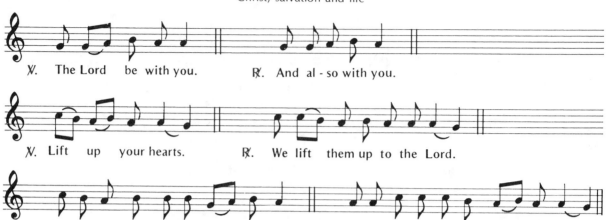

℣. The Lord be with you.   ℟. And al-so with you.

℣. Lift up your hearts.   ℟. We lift them up to the Lord.

℣. Let us give thanks to the Lord our God.   ℟. It is right to give him thanks and praise.

Father, all-powerful and ev-er-liv-ing God, we do well always and everywhere to give

you thanks through Je-sus Christ our Lord. In him the world is saved, man is re-

born, and the dead rise a-gain to life. Through Christ the angels of heaven offer their

prayer of ad-o-ra-tion as they re-joice in your pres-ence for ev-er. May our voic-es

be one with theirs in their trium-phant hymn of praise:

CHRISTIAN DEATH IV

From earthly life to heaven's glory

℣. The Lord be with you. ℟. And al - so with you.

℣. Lift up your hearts. ℟. We lift them up to the Lord.

℣. Let us give thanks to the Lord our God. ℟. It is right to give him thanks and praise.

Father, all-powerful and ev - er - liv - ing God, we do well al-ways and eve-ry-where to give

you thanks. By your power you bring us to birth. By your prov- i -dence you rule our

lives. By your com-mand you free us at last from sin as we re-turn to the dust from

which we came. Through the sav-ing death of your Son we rise at your word to the glo -

ry of the res - ur - rec - tion. Now we join the an-gels and the saints as they sing their

un - end - ing hymn of praise :

CHRISTIAN DEATH V

Our resurrection through Christ's victory

℣. The Lord be with you. ℟. And al-so with you.

℣. Lift up your hearts. ℟. We lift them up to the Lord.

℣. Let us give thanks to the Lord our God. ℟. It is right to give him thanks and praise.

Father, all-powerful and ev-er-liv-ing God, we do well always and everywhere to give

you thanks through Je-sus Christ our Lord. Death is the just re-ward for our sins,

yet, when at last we die, your loving kindness calls us back to life in com-pa-ny with Christ,

whose vic-to-ry is our re-demp-tion. Our hearts are joyful, for we have seen your

sal-va-tion, and now with the an-gels and saints we praise you for ev-er:

INDEPENDENCE DAY AND OTHER CIVIC OBSERVANCES I

In the dioceses of the United States

℣. The Lord be with you. ℟. And al-so with you.

℣. Lift up your hearts. ℟. We lift them up to the Lord.

℣. Let us give thanks to the Lord our God. ℟. It is right to give him thanks and praise.

Father, all-powerful and ev-er-liv-ing God, we do well to sing your praise for

ev-er, and to give you thanks in all we do through Je-sus Christ our Lord.

He spoke to men a mes-sage of peace and taught us to live as broth-ers.

His message took form in the vi-sion of our fa-thers as they fashioned a na-tion

where men might live as one. This message lives on in our midst as a task

for men to-day and a prom-ise for to-mor-row. We thank you, Father, for

your bless - ings in the past   and for all that, with your help, we must yet   a - chieve.

And so, with hearts full of love,   we join the angels, today and every day of our lives,

to sing your glo - ry   in a hymn of end - less praise:

INDEPENDENCE DAY AND OTHER CIVIC OBSERVANCES II

In the dioceses of the United States

℣. The Lord be with you. ℟. And al-so with you.

℣. Lift up your hearts. ℟. We lift them up to the Lord.

℣. Let us give thanks to the Lord our God. ℟. It is right to give him thanks and praise.

Father, all-powerful and ev-er-liv-ing God, we praise your one-ness and truth.

We praise you as the God of cre-a-tion, as the Father of Je-sus, the

Sav-ior of man-kind, in whose image we seek to live. He loved the

children of the lands he walked and en-riched them with his witness of jus-tice and

truth. He lived and died that we might be re-born in the Spir-it and filled with

love of all men. And so, with hearts full of love, we join the angels, today and

every day of our lives, to sing your glo-ry in a hymn of end-less praise:

THANKSGIVING DAY

In the dioceses of the United States

℣. The Lord be with you. ℟. And al-so with you.

℣. Lift up your hearts. ℟. We lift them up to the Lord.

℣. Let us give thanks to the Lord our God. ℟. It is right to give him thanks and praise.

Father, we do well to join all creation, in heav-en and on earth, in praising you, our might-y God, through Je-sus Christ our Lord. You made man to your own im-age and set him o-ver all cre-a-tion. Once you chose a people and gave them a des-ti-ny and, when you brought them out of bond-age to free-dom they carried with them the promise that all men would be blessed and all men could be free. What the prophets pledged was fulfilled in Je-sus Christ, your Son and our sav-ing Lord.

It has come to pass in every generation for all men who have believed that Jesus, by his

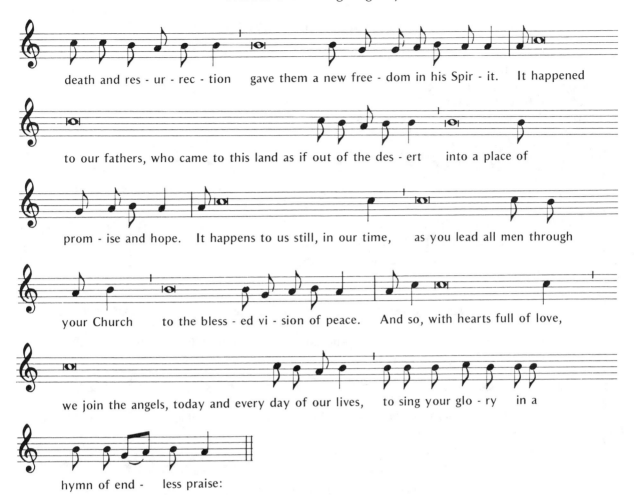

death and res - ur - rec - tion   gave them a new free - dom in his Spir - it.   It happened

to our fathers, who came to this land as if out of the des - ert   into a place of

prom - ise and hope.   It happens to us still, in our time,   as you lead all men through

your Church   to the bless - ed vi - sion of peace.   And so, with hearts full of love,

we join the angels, today and every day of our lives,   to sing your glo - ry   in a

hymn of end - less praise:

EUCHARISTIC PRAYER I

Father, accept this offering
from your whole family.
Grant us your peace in this life,
save us from final damnation,
and count us among those you have chosen.

Bless and approve our of - fer - ing;   make it acceptable to you,   an of - fer - ing in

spir - it and in truth.   Let it become for us the body and blood of Je - sus Christ,   your

on - ly Son, our Lord.   The day before he suf - fered   he took bread in his sa - cred

hands   and looking up to heaven, to you, his al - might - y Fa - ther,   he gave you thanks

and praise.   He broke the bread, gave it to his disci - ples, and said: Take this, all of you, and

eat it: this is my bod - y which will be giv - en up for you. When supper was ended, he took

the cup.   A - gain he gave you thanks and praise,   gave the cup to his disci - ples, and

said: Take this, all of you, and drink from it: this is the cup of my blood,   the blood

of the new and ev - er - last - ing cov - e - nant.   It will be shed for you and for all

so that sins may be for - giv - en.   Do this in mem - o - ry of me.

Let us pro - claim the mys - ter - y of faith:

(Acclamations, see Eucharistic Prayer II)

Father, we celebrate the memory of Christ, your Son. We, your people and your ministers,

recall his passion, his resurrection from the dead, and his as - cen - sion in - to glo - ry;

and from the many gifts you have given us we offer to you, God of glory and

maj - es - ty, this ho - ly and per - fect sac - ri - fice: the bread of life and the cup

of e - ter - nal sal - va - tion. Look with favor on these offer - ings and accept them

as once you accepted the gifts of your serv - ant A - bel, the sacrifice of Abraham,

our father in faith, and the bread and wine offered by your priest Mel - chis - e - dech.

Al - might - y God, we pray that your angel may take this sacrifice to your al - tar in heav - en.

Then, as we receive from this altar the sacred body and blood of your Son, let us be

filled with eve - ry grace and bless - ing.

Through him
you give us all these gifts.
You fill them with life and goodness,
you bless them and make them holy.

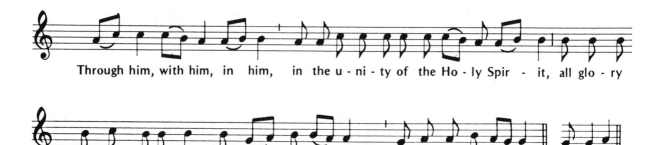

Through him, with him, in him, in the u - ni - ty of the Ho - ly Spir - it, all glo - ry

and hon - or is yours, al - might - y Fa - ther, for ev - er and ev - er. ℟. A - men.

EUCHARISTIC PRAYER II

Lord, you are holy in - deed, the foun-tain of all ho - li - ness. Let your Spir-it come upon

these gifts to make them ho - ly, so that they may become for us the body ✠ and blood of our

Lord, Je - sus Christ. Be - fore he was given up to death, a death he freely ac - cept - ed,

he took bread and gave you thanks. He broke the bread, gave it to his disci - ples, and said:

Take this, all of you, and eat it: this is my bod-y which will be giv-en up for you. When

supper was ended, he took the cup. A - gain he gave you thanks and praise, gave the cup

to his disci - ples, and said: Take this, all of you, and drink from it: this is the cup of my

blood, the blood of the new and ev-er - last - ing cov - e - nant. It will be shed for you and

for all so that sins may be for-giv-en. Do this in mem - o - ry of me.

Let us pro-claim the mys-ter-y of faith:

ACCLAMATIONS

a)

Christ has died,   Christ is ris - en,   Christ will come   a - gain.

b)

Dy - ing you de - stroyed our death,   ris-ing you re - stored our life. Lord Je - sus,   come

in glo - ry.

c)

When we eat   this bread and drink this cup,   we pro-claim your death,   Lord Je - sus,

un - til   you come in glo - ry.

d)

Lord, by your cross   and res - ur - rec - tion   you have set us free.   You are the

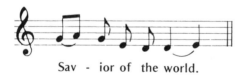

Sav - ior of the world.

In memory of his death and resur-rec-tion, we offer you, Father, this life-giving bread, this sav-ing cup. We thank you for counting us worthy to stand in your pres-ence and serve you. May all of us who share in the body and blood of Christ be brought together in unity by the Ho-ly Spir-it. Lord, remember your Church throughout the world; make us grow in love, together with N. our Pope, N. our bish-op, and all the cler-gy.

[In Masses for the dead the following may be added:]

Re-member N., whom you have called from this life. In baptism he/she died with Christ: may he/she also share his res-ur-rec-tion.

Re-member our brothers and sisters who have gone to their rest in the hope of rising a-gain; bring them and all the departed into the light of your pres-ence. Have mer-cy on us all;

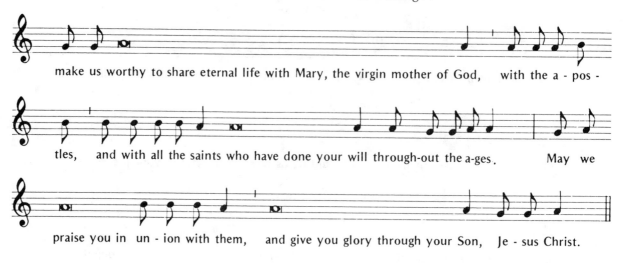

make us worthy to share eternal life with Mary, the virgin mother of God,   with the a - pos -

tles,   and with all the saints who have done your will through-out the a-ges.   May we

praise you in un - ion with them,   and give you glory through your Son,   Je - sus Christ.

Through him, with him, in   him,   in the u - ni - ty of the Ho - ly Spir - it,   all glo - ry

and hon - or is yours, al - might - y Fa - ther,   for ev - er and ev - er.

℟. A - men.

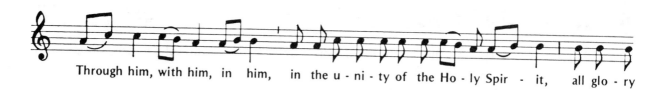

EUCHARISTIC PRAYER III

Fa-ther,   you are holy in-deed,   and all creation rightly gives you praise.   All life,

all holiness comes from you through your Son, Jesus Christ our Lord,   by the working of the

Ho - ly Spir-it.   From age to age you gather a people to your-self,   so that from

east to west a perfect offering may be made to the glo - ry of your name.   And so,

Fa - ther,   we bring you these gifts.   We ask you to make them holy by the power of

your Spir-it,   that they may become the body ☩ and blood of your Son,   our Lord Je - sus

Christ,   at whose command we cel - e - brate this eu-cha-rist.   On the night he   was

be-trayed,   he took bread and gave you thanks and praise.   He broke the bread,   gave it

to his dis- ci - ples, and said: Take this, all of you, and eat it: this is my bod-y   which

will be giv-en up for you.   When supper was ended, he took the cup.   A - gain he

gave you thanks and praise, gave the cup to his disci-ples, and said: Take this, all of you,

and drink from it: this is the cup of my blood, the blood of the new and ev - er - last -

ing cov - e - nant. It will be shed for you and for all so that sins may be for-giv-en.

Do this in mem - o - ry of me. Let us pro-claim the mys - ter - y of faith:

(Acclamations, see Eucharistic Prayer II)

Fa - ther, calling to mind the death your Son endured for our salva-tion, his glorious resurrec -

tion and ascension into heav-en, and ready to greet him when he comes a - gain, we

offer you in thanksgiving this holy and liv-ing sac - ri - fice. Look with favor on your

Church's of - fer - ing, and see the Victim whose death has reconciled us to your-self.

Grant that we, who are nourished by his body and blood, may be filled with his Ho - ly

Spir-it, and become one bod-y, one spir-it in Christ. May he make us an everlasting

gift to you and enable us to share in the inheritance of your saints, with Mary, the virgin

mother of God;   with the a-postles, the martyrs, (Saint N.) and all your saints,   on whose

constant intercession we re - ly for help.   Lord, may this sacrifice, which has made our

peace with you,   ad - vance the peace and salvation of all the world.   Strengthen in faith

and love your pilgrim Church on earth;   your serv-ant, Pope N., our bishop N., and all the

bish-ops,   with the clergy and the entire people your Son has gained for you.   Fa - ther,

hear the prayers of the family you have gathered here be - fore you.   In mercy and love

u - nite all your chil-dren wher - ev - er they may be.   Welcome into your kingdom   our

departed brothers and sis-ters,   and all who have left this world in your friend-ship.   We

hope to enjoy for ever the vision of your glo - ry,   through Christ our Lord, from whom

all good things come.

Re-mem-ber N.   In baptism he/she died with Christ: may he/she also share his resurrec-tion,

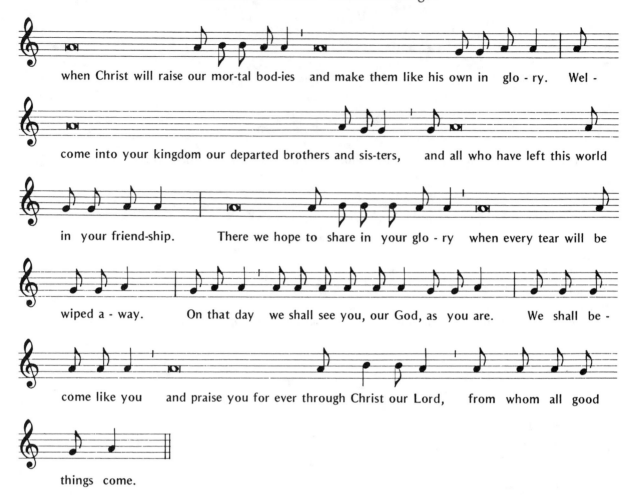

when Christ will raise our mor-tal bod-ies and make them like his own in glo - ry. Wel -

come into your kingdom our departed brothers and sis-ters, and all who have left this world

in your friend-ship. There we hope to share in your glo - ry when every tear will be

wiped a - way. On that day we shall see you, our God, as you are. We shall be -

come like you and praise you for ever through Christ our Lord, from whom all good

things come.

DOXOLOGY

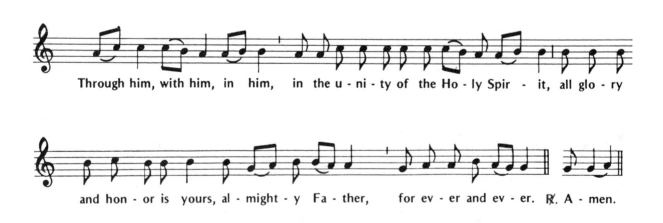

Through him, with him, in him, in the u - ni - ty of the Ho - ly Spir - it, all glo - ry

and hon - or is yours, al - might - y Fa - ther, for ev - er and ev - er. ℟. A - men.

EUCHARISTIC PRAYER IV

Father in heav-en, it is right that we should give you thanks and glo - ry; you are the

one God, liv-ing and true. Through all e - ter - ni - ty you live in un-ap-proach -

a - ble light. Source of life and goodness, you have created all things, to fill your

creatures with eve-ry bless-ing and lead all men to the joy-ful vi-sion of your light.

Countless hosts of angels stand before you to do your will; they look upon your splen -

dor and praise you, night and day. U - nit - ed with them, and in the name of

every crea-ture un - der heav-en, we too praise your glo - ry as we sing: Holy. . . . .

Fa-ther, we acknowledge your great-ness: all your actions show your wis-dom and love.

You formed man in your own like-ness and set him over the whole world to serve you, his

cre-a - tor, and to rule o - ver all crea-tures. Even when he disobeyed you and lost

your friend-ship you did not abandon him to the power of death, but helped all men to

seek and find you.   A - gain and again you offered a covenant to man, and through the

prophets taught him to hope for sal-va-tion.   Fa-ther, you so loved the world that in the

full-ness of time you sent your only Son to be our Sav-ior.   He was conceived through the

power of the Ho - ly Spir-it, and born of the Vir-gin Mar- y, a man like us in all things

but sin.   To the poor he proclaimed the good news of sal-va-tion, to pris-on-ers, free-dom,

and to those in sor-row, joy.   In ful-fillment of your will he gave himself up to death;

but by rising from the dead, he de-stroyed death and re-stored life.   And that we might live

no longer for our-selves but for him, he sent the Holy Spirit from you, Fa-ther, as his first

gift to those who be-lieve, to complete his work on earth and bring us the full-ness of grace.

Fa-ther, may this Holy Spirit sancti-fy these of-fer-ings.   Let them become the body ✠ and

blood of Je - sus Christ our Lord   as we celebrate the great mystery which he left us as an

ev-er-last-ing cov - e - nant.   He always loved those who were his own in the world.   When

the time came for him to be glorified by you, his heav-en-ly Fa-ther,   he showed the depth of

his love.   While they were at supper, he took bread,   said the bless-ing, broke the bread

and gave it to his dis-ci-ples, say-ing: Take this, all of you, and eat it: this is my bod-y

which will be giv-en up for you.   In the same way, he took the cup, filled with wine.

He gave you thanks,   and giving the cup to his dis-ci-ples, said: Take this, all of you, and

drink from it: this is the cup of my blood,   the blood of the new and ev-er-last-ing cov - e -

nant.   It will be shed for you and for all so that sins may be for-giv-en.   Do this

in mem- o-ry of me.   Let us pro-claim the mys - ter - y of faith:

(Acclamations, see Eucharistic Prayer II)

Fa-ther, we now celebrate this memorial of our re-demp-tion. We re-call Christ's death,

his descent among the dead, his resurrection, and his ascension to your right hand; and,

look-ing forward to his coming in glo - ry, we offer you his bod-y and blood, the acceptable

sacrifice which brings sal-va-tion to the whole world. Lord, look upon this sacrifice which

you have given to your Church; and by your Holy Spirit, gather all who share this one bread

and one cup in - to the one bod - y of Christ, a living sac-ri-fice of praise.

Lord, remember those for whom we offer this sac-ri-fice, es - pecially N. our Pope, N. our

bish-op, and bishops and cler-gy eve-ry-where. Re-member those who take part in this

of-fer-ing, those here present and all your peo-ple, and all those who seek you with a

sin-cere heart. Re-member those who have died in the peace of Christ and all the dead whose

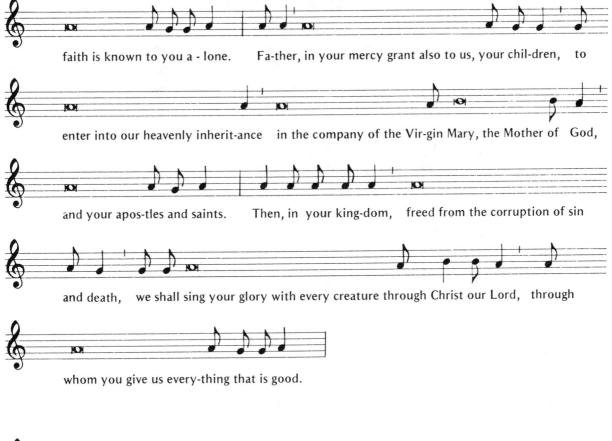

faith is known to you a - lone. Fa-ther, in your mercy grant also to us, your chil-dren, to

enter into our heavenly inherit-ance in the company of the Vir-gin Mary, the Mother of God,

and your apos-tles and saints. Then, in your king-dom, freed from the corruption of sin

and death, we shall sing your glory with every creature through Christ our Lord, through

whom you give us every-thing that is good.

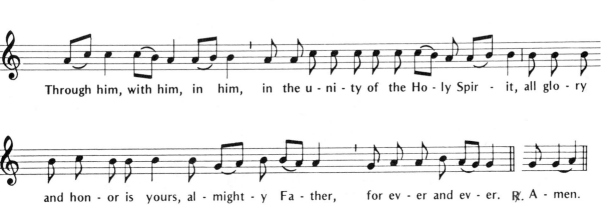

Through him, with him, in him, in the u - ni - ty of the Ho - ly Spir - it, all glo - ry

and hon - or is yours, al - might - y Fa - ther, for ev - er and ev - er. ℟. A - men.

THE LORD'S PRAYER

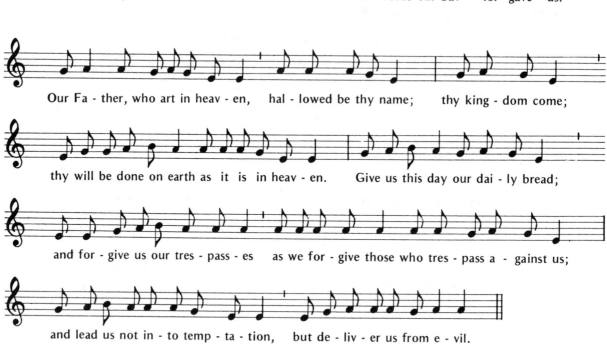

Let us pray with confidence to the Fa - ther in the words our Sav - ior gave us.

Our Fa - ther, who art in heav - en, hal - lowed be thy name; thy king - dom come;

thy will be done on earth as it is in heav - en. Give us this day our dai - ly bread;

and for - give us our tres - pass - es as we for - give those who tres - pass a - gainst us;

and lead us not in - to temp - ta - tion, but de - liv - er us from e - vil.

De - liver us, Lord, from every evil, and grant us peace in our day. In your mer-cy

keep us free from sin and protect us from all anx - i - e - ty as we wait in joy-ful hope

for the coming of our Sav-ior, Je - sus Christ.

For the king - dom, the power and the glo - ry are yours, now and for ev - er.

RITE OF PEACE

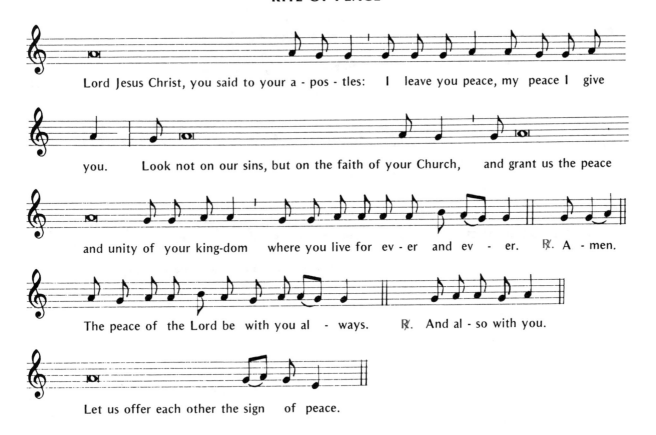

Lord Jesus Christ, you said to your a - pos - tles: I leave you peace, my peace I give you. Look not on our sins, but on the faith of your Church, and grant us the peace and unity of your king-dom where you live for ev - er and ev - er. ℟. A - men.

The peace of the Lord be with you al - ways. ℟. And al - so with you.

Let us offer each other the sign of peace.

CONCLUDING RITE

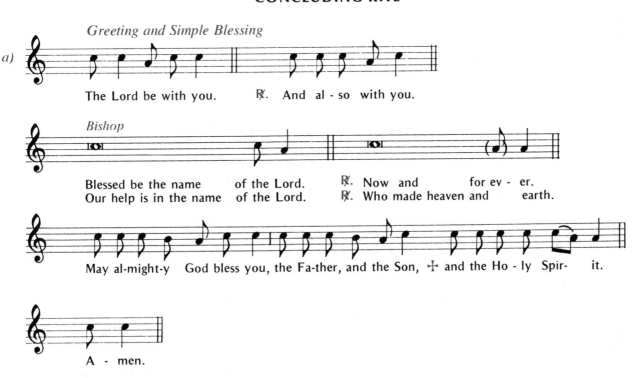

Greeting and Simple Blessing

a)

The Lord be with you. ℟. And al - so with you.

Bishop

Blessed be the name of the Lord. ℟. Now and for ev - er.
Our help is in the name of the Lord. ℟. Who made heaven and earth.

May al-might-y God bless you, the Fa-ther, and the Son, ☩ and the Ho - ly Spir- it.

A - men.

Greeting and Simple Blessing

b)

The Lord be with you.   ℟. And al - so with you.

Bishop

Blessed be the name   of the Lord.   ℟. Now and   for ev - er.
Our help is in the name   of the Lord.   ℟. Who made heaven and   earth.

May al-might-y   God bless you, the Fa-ther, and the Son,✝ and the Ho - ly Spir - it.

A - men.

SOLEMN BLESSING

One-phrase texts: *Two-phrase texts:*

a)

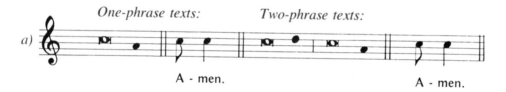

A - men.   A - men.

Three-phrase texts:

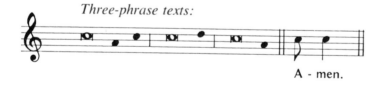

A - men.

Example: Greeting and Solemn Blessing

a)

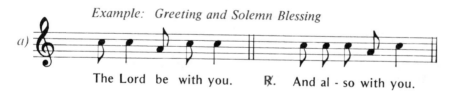

The Lord be with you.   ℟. And al - so with you.

Deacon

Bow your heads and pray for God's   bless-ing.

You believe that the Son of God once came to us;   you look for him to come a - gain.

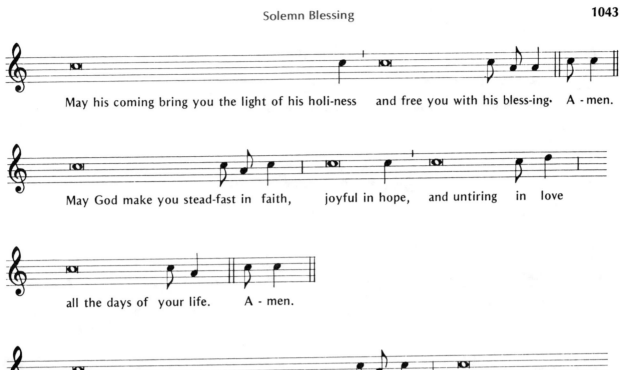

May his coming bring you the light of his holi-ness and free you with his bless-ing. A - men.

May God make you stead-fast in faith, joyful in hope, and untiring in love

all the days of your life. A - men.

You rejoice that our Redeemer came to live with us as man. When he comes again

in glo - ry, may he reward you with end-less life. A - men. May al-might - y

God bless you, the Fa-ther, and the Son, ✝ and the Ho - ly Spir - it. A - men.

SOLEMN BLESSING

One-phrase texts: *Two-phrase texts:*

A - men.   A - men.

Three-phrase texts:

A - men.

Example: Greeting and Solemn Blessing

b)

The Lord be with you.   ℟. And al - so with you.

Deacon

Bow your heads   and pray for God's bless - ing.

You believe that the Son of God once came to us;   you look for him to   come a - gain.

May his coming bring you the light of his holi-ness   and free you with his bless - ing.

A - men.   May God make you steadfast in faith,   joyful in hope,   and untiring

in love   all the days of your life.   A - men.   You rejoice that our Redeemer

came to live with us as man.   When he comes again in glo - ry,   may he reward you

with end-less life.   A - men.   May al-might-y God bless you,   the Fa - ther,

and the Son, ✝ and the Ho - ly Spir - it.   A - men.

PRAYER OVER THE PEOPLE

Greeting, Prayer over the People and Blessing

a) The Lord be with you. ℟. And al - so with you.

Deacon

Bow your heads and pray for God's bless-ing.

Lord, have mercy on your peo-ple. Grant us in this life the good things that lead to the

everlasting life you pre-pare for us. We ask this through Christ our Lord. A - men.

May al-might-y God bless you, the Fa-ther, and the Son, ☩ and the Ho - ly Spir- it.

A - men.

b) The Lord be with you. ℟. And al - so with you.

Deacon

Bow your heads and pray for God's bless - ing.

Lord, have mercy on your peo-ple. Grant us in this life the good things that lead

to the everlasting life you pre-pare for us.   We ask this through Christ our Lord.

A - men.   May al-might-y God bless you,   the Fa - ther,   and the Son, ☩

and the Ho - ly Spir - it.   A - men.

DISMISSAL

a)

Go in the peace of Christ.   ℟. Thanks be to God.

b)

The Mass is end-ed, go in peace.   ℟. Thanks be to God.

c)

Go in peace to love and serve the Lord.   ℟. Thanks be to God.

Let us bless the Lord.   ℟. Thanks be to God.

EUCHARISTIC PRAYER: TONE I

Introductory dialogue

℣. The Lord be with you. ℟. And al - so with you.

℣. Lift up your hearts. ℟. We lift them up to the Lord.

℣. Let us give thanks to the Lord our God. ℟. It is right to give him thanks and praise.

PREFACE I of ADVENT

Fa - ther, all - powerful and ev - er - liv - ing God, we do well always and everywhere

to give you thanks through Je - sus Christ our Lord. When he humbled himself to come

a - mong us as a man, he ful - filled the plan you formed long a - go and

o - pened for us the way to sal - va - tion. Now we watch for the day hoping

that the salvation promised us will be ours when Christ our Lord will come a - gain in

his glo - ry. And so, with all the choirs of an - gels in heav - en we proclaim your

glo - ry and join in their un - end - ing hymn of praise:

Final Doxology:

Through him, with him, in him, in the unity of the Ho - ly Spir - it, all

glory and honor is yours al - might - y Fa - ther, for - ev - er and ev - er. A - men.

EUCHARISTIC PRAYER: TONE II

Introductory dialogue

℣. The Lord be with you.   ℟. And also with you.

℣. Lift up your hearts.   ℟. We lift them up to the Lord.

℣. Let us give thanks to the Lord our God.   ℟. It is right to give him thanks and praise.

PREFACE I of ADVENT

Fa - ther, all powerful and ever - liv - ing God, we do well always and everywhere to

give you thanks through Je - sus Christ our Lord. When he humbled himself to come

among us as a man, he fulfilled the plan you formed long a - go and opened for

us the way to sal - va - tion. Now we watch for the day hoping that the salvation

promised us will be ours when Christ our Lord will come a-gain in his glo-ry.

And so, with all the choirs of angels in heav-en we proclaim your glory and join in

their unending hymn of praise:

FINAL DOXOLOGY

Through him, with him, in him, in the unity of the Ho-ly Spir-it, all glory and

honor is yours, almight-y Fa-ther, for ever and ev-er. ℟. A-men.

INVITATION TO THE LORD'S PRAYER

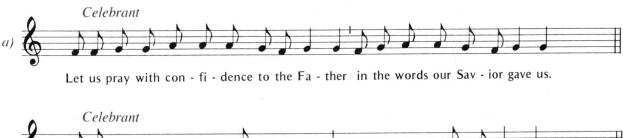

Celebrant

a) Let us pray with con-fi-dence to the Fa-ther in the words our Sav-ior gave us.

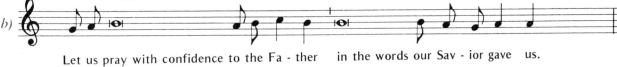

Celebrant

b) Let us pray with confidence to the Fa-ther in the words our Sav-ior gave us.

Celebrant

c) Let us pray with confidence to the Fa-ther in the words our Sav-ior gave us.

THE RITE OF PEACE

℣. The peace of the Lord be with you al - ways.   ℟. And al - so with you.

CONCLUDING RITE

Priest:

℣. The Lord be with you.   ℟. And also with you.

℣. May al - might - y God bless you,   the Fa - ther,   and the Son,

and the Ho - ly Spir - it.   ℟. A - men.

Deacon (or Priest)

℣. Go in the peace of Christ.   ℟. Thanks   be to God.

(or)

℣. The Mass is end - ed, go in peace.

(or)

℣. Go in peace to love and serve the Lord.

Verses before the Blessing by a Bishop

℣. Bless - ed be the name of the Lord.   ℟. Now and for - ev - er.

℣. Our help is in the name of the Lord.   ℟. Who made heav - en and earth.

LORD'S PRAYER

Our Fa - ther, who art in heav - en, hal - lowed be thy name; thy king - dom come;

thy will be done on earth as it is in heav - en. Give us this day our dai - ly bread;

and for - give us our tres - pass - es as we forgive those who tres - pass a - gainst us;

and lead us not in - to temp - ta - tion, but de - liv - er us from e - vil.

Appendix IV

ORDO MISSAE

ORDO MISSAE CUM POPULO

RITUS INITIALES

1. Populo congregato, sacerdos cum ministris ad altare accedit, dum cantus ad introitum peragitur.

2. Cum ad altare pervenerit, facta cum ministris debita reverentia, osculo altare veneratur et, pro opportunitate, illud incensat. Postea cum ministris sedem petit.

Cantu ad introitum absoluto, sacerdos et fideles, stantes, signant se, dum sacerdos, ad populum conversus, dicit:

Populus respondet:

In nómine Patris, et Fílii, et Spíritus Sancti. Amen.

Deinde sacerdos, manus extendens, populum salutat, dicens:

Grátia Dómini nostri Iesu Christi, et cáritas Dei, et communicátio Sancti Spíritus sit cum ómnibus vobis.
vel:
Dóminus vobíscum.
Et cum spíritu tuo.

Populus respondet:

Episcopus, loco Dóminus vobíscum, in hac prima salutatione dicit: Pax vobis.

3. Sacerdos, vel diaconus vel alius minister idoneus, potest brevissimis verbis introducere fideles in Missam illius diei.

Deinde sequitur actus paenitentialis. Sacerdos fideles invitat ad paenitentiam:

Fratres, agnoscámus peccáta nostra, ut apti simus ad sacra mystéria celebránda.

Fit brevis pausa silentii. Postea omnes simul faciunt confessionem:

Confíteor Deo omnipoténti et vobis, fratres,
quia peccávi nimis
cogitatióne, verbo, ópere et omissióne:
mea culpa, mea culpa, mea máxima culpa.

Et, percutientes sibi pectus, dicunt:
Deinde prosequuntur:

Ideo precor beátam Maríam semper Vírginem,
omnes Angelos et Sanctos,
et vos, fratres, oráre pro me
ad Dóminum Deum nostrum.

Sequitur absolutio sacerdotis:

Misereátur nostri omnípotens Deus
et, dimíssis peccátis nostris,
perdúcat nos ad vitam aetérnam.
Amen.

Populus respondet:

Aliae formulae salutationis et actus paenitentialis ad libitum inveniuntur in Appendice, p. 1088.

4. Sequuntur invocationes Kýrie, eléison, nisi iam praecesserint in aliqua formula actus paenitentialis.

℣. Kýrie, eléison.
℟. Kýrie, eléison.

℣. Christe, eléison.
℟. Christe, eléison.

℣. Kýrie, eléison.
℟. Kýrie, eléison.

5. Deinde, quando praescribitur, cantatur vel dicitur hymnus:

Glória in excélsis Deo
et in terra pax homínibus bonae voluntátis.
Laudámus te,
benedícimus te,
adorámus te,
glorificámus te,
grátias ágimus tibi propter magnam glóriam tuam,
Dómine Deus, Rex caeléstis,
Deus Pater omnípotens.
Dómine Fili unigénite, Iesu Christe,
Dómine Deus, Agnus Dei, Fílius Patris,
qui tollis peccáta mundi, miserére nobis;
qui tollis peccáta mundi, súscipe deprecatiónem nostram.
Qui sedes ad déxteram Patris, miserére nobis.
Quóniam tu solus Sanctus, tu solus Dóminus,
tu solus Altíssimus,
Iesu Christe, cum Sancto Spíritu: in glória Dei Patris. Amen.

6. Quo hymno finito, sacerdos, manibus iunctis, dicit:

Orémus.

Et omnes una cum sacerdote per aliquod temporis spatium in silentio orant.

Tunc sacerdos, manibus extensis, dicit orationem; qua finita, populus acclamat:

Amen.

LITURGIA VERBI

7. Deinde lector ad ambonem pergit, et legit primam lectionem, quam omnes sedentes auscultant.

Ad finem lectionis significandam, lector subdit:

Omnes acclamant:

Verbum Dómini.
Deo grátias.

8. Psalmista, seu cantor, psalmum dicit, populo responsum proferente.

9. Postea, si habenda sit secunda lectio, lector eam in ambone legit, ut supra.

Ad finem lectionis significandam, lector subdit:

Omnes acclamant:

Verbum Dómini.
Deo grátias.

10. Sequitur Allelúia, vel alter cantus.

11. Interim sacerdos incensum, si adhibetur, imponit. Postea diaconus, Evangelium prolaturus, ante sacerdotem inclinatus, benedictionem petit, submissa voce dicens:

Sacerdos submissa voce dicit:

Iube, domne, benedícere.

Dóminus sit in corde tuo et in lábiis tuis:
ut digne et competénter annúnties Evangélium suum:
in nómine Patris, et Fílii, ☩ et Spíritus Sancti.

Diaconus respondet:

Amen.

Si vero non adest diaconus, sacerdos ante altare inclinatus secreto dicit:

Munda cor meum ac lábia mea, omnípotens Deus,
ut sanctum Evangélium tuum digne váleam nuntiáre.

12. Postea diaconus, vel sacerdos, ad ambonem pergit, ministris pro opportunitate cum incenso et cereis eum comitantibus, et dicit:

Populus respondet:

Dóminus vobíscum.
Et cum spíritu tuo.

Diaconus, vel sacerdos:

et interim signat librum et seipsum in fronte, ore et pectore.

Léctio sancti Evangélii secúndum N. ,

Populus acclamat:

Glória tibi, Dómine.

Deinde diaconus, vel sacerdos, librum, si incensum adhibetur, thurificat, et Evangelium proclamat.

13. Finito Evangelio, diaconus, vel sacerdos dicit:

Verbum Dómini,

omnibus acclamantibus:

Laus tibi, Christe.

Deinde librum osculatur dicens secreto:

Per evangélica dicta deleántur nostra delícta.

14. Deinde fit homilia, quae habenda est omnibus diebus dominicis et festis de praecepto; aliis diebus commendatur.

15. Homilia expleta, fit, quando praescribitur, professio fidei:

Credo in unum Deum,
Patrem omnipoténtem, factórem caeli et terrae,
visibílium ómnium et invisibílium.
Et in unum Dóminum Iesum Christum,
Fílium Dei unigénitum,
et ex Patre natum ante ómnia sáecula.
Deum de Deo, lumen de lúmine, Deum verum de Deo vero,
génitum, non factum, consubstantiálem Patri:
per quem ómnia facta sunt.

Qui propter nos hómines et propter nostram salútem
descéndit de caelis.

Ad verba quae sequuntur, usque ad
factus est, omnes se inclinant.

**Et incarnátus est de Spíritu Sancto
ex María Vírgine, et homo factus est.
Crucifíxus étiam pro nobis sub Póntio Piláto;
passus et sepúltus est,
et resurréxit tértia die, secúndum Scriptúras,
et ascéndit in caelum, sedet ad déxteram Patris.
Et íterum ventúrus est cum glória, iudicáre vivos et mórtuos,
cuius regni non erit finis.
Et in Spíritum Sanctum, Dóminum et vivificántem:
qui ex Patre Filióque procédit.
Qui cum Patre et Fílio simul adorátur et conglorificátur:
qui locútus est per prophétas.
Et unam, sanctam, cathólicam et apostólicam Ecclésiam.
Confíteor unum baptísma in remissiónem peccatórum.
Et exspécto resurrectiónem mortuórum,
et vitam ventúri sáeculi. Amen.**

16. Deinde fit oratio universalis, seu
oratio fidelium (cf. in Appendice,
p. 1117).

LITURGIA EUCHARISTICA

17. His absolutis, incipit cantus ad
offertorium. Interim ministri corporale, purificatorium, calicem et
missale in altari collocant.

18. Expedit ut fideles participationem
suam oblatione manifestent, af-
ferendo sive panem et vinum ad
Eucharistiae celebrationem, sive
alia dona, quibus necessitatibus
Ecclesiae et pauperum subveniatur.

19. Sacerdos, stans ad altare, accipit
patenam cum pane, eamque aliquantulum elevatam super altare
tenet, secreto dicens:

**Benedíctus es, Dómine, Deus univérsi,
quia de tua largitáte accépimus panem,
quem tibi offérimus,
fructum terrae et óperis mánuum hóminum:
ex quo nobis fiet panis vitae.**

Deinde deponit patenam cum pane
super corporale.

Si vero cantus ad offertorium non
peragitur, sacerdoti licet haec verba
elata voce proferre; in fine populus
acclamare potest:

Benedíctus Deus in sáecula.

20. Diaconus, vel sacerdos, infundit vinum et parum aquae in calicem, dicens secreto:

**Per huius aquae et vini mystérium
eius efficiámur divinitátis consórtes,
qui humanitátis nostrae fíeri dignátus est párticeps.**

21. Postea sacerdos accipit calicem, eumque aliquantulum elevatum super altare tenet, secreto dicens:

**Benedíctus es, Dómine, Deus univérsi,
quia de tua largitáte accépimus vinum,
quod tibi offérimus,
fructum vitis et óperis mánuum hóminum,
ex quo nobis fiet potus spiritális.**

Deinde calicem super corporale deponit.

Si vero cantus ad offertorium non peragitur, sacerdoti licet haec verba elata voce proferre; in fine populus acclamare potest:

Benedíctus Deus in sáecula.

22. Postea sacerdos, inclinatus, dicit secreto:

**In spíritu humilitátis et in ánimo contríto
suscipiámur a te, Dómine;
et sic fiat sacrifícium nostrum in conspéctu tuo hódie,
ut pláceat tibi, Dómine Deus.**

23. Et, pro opportunitate, incensat oblata et altare. Postea vero diaconus vel minister incensat sacerdotem et populum.

24. Deinde sacerdos, stans ad latus altaris, lavat manus, dicens secreto:

**Lava me, Dómine, ab iniquitáte mea,
et a peccáto meo munda me.**

25. Stans postea in medio altaris, versus ad populum, extendens et iungens manus, dicit:

**Oráte, fratres:
ut meum ac vestrum sacrifícium
acceptábile fiat apud Deum Patrem omnipoténtem.**

Populus respondet:

**Suscípiat Dóminus sacrifícium de mánibus tuis
ad laudem et glóriam nóminis sui,
ad utilitátem quoque nostram
totiúsque Ecclésiae suae sanctae.**

26. Deinde, manibus extensis, sacerdos dicit orationem super oblata; qua finita, populus acclamat: Amen.

PREX EUCHARISTICA

27. Tunc sacerdos incipit Precem eucharisticam.

Manus extendens, dicit:

Dóminus vobíscum.

Populus respondet:

Et cum spíritu tuo.

Sacerdos, manus elevans, prosequitur:

Sursum corda.

Populus:

Habémus ad Dóminum.

Sacerdos, manibus extensis, subdit:

Grátias agámus Dómino Deo nostro.

Populus:

Dignum et iustum est.

Sacerdos prosequitur praefationem manibus extensis.

In fine autem praefationis iungit manus et, una cum populo, ipsam praefationem concludit, cantans vel clara voce dicens:

Sanctus, Sanctus, Sanctus Dóminus Deus Sábaoth.
Pleni sunt caeli et terra glória tua.
Hosánna in excélsis.
Benedíctus qui venit in nómine Dómini.
Hosánna in excélsis.

28. In omnibus Missis licet sacerdoti celebranti illas partes Precis eucharisticae cantare, quae in Missis concelebratis cantari possunt.

In Prece eucharistica prima, seu Canone Romano, ea quae inter parentheses includuntur omitti possunt.

PRAEFATIONES

I

De mysterio paschali et de populo Dei

℣. Dóminus vobíscum.
℟. Et cum spíritu tuo.

℣. Sursum corda.
℟. Habémus ad Dóminum.

℣. Grátias agámus Dómino Deo nostro.
℟. Dignum et iustum est.

Vere dignum et iustum est, aequum et salutáre,
nos tibi semper et ubíque grátias ágere:
Dómine, sancte Pater, omnípotens aetérne Deus:
per Christum Dóminum nostrum.

Cuius hoc miríficum fuit opus per paschále mystérium,
ut de peccáto et mortis iugo ad hanc glóriam vocarémur,
qua nunc genus eléctum, regále sacerdótium,
gens sancta et acquisitiónis pópulus dicerémur,
et tuas annuntiarémus ubíque virtútes,
qui nos de ténebris ad tuum admirábile lumen vocásti.

Et ídeo cum Angelis et Archángelis,
cum Thronis et Dominatiónibus,
cumque omni milítia caeléstis exéstis exércitus,
hymnum glóriae tuae cánimus,
sine fine dicéntes:

Sanctus, Sanctus, Sanctus Dóminus Deus Sábaoth.
Pleni sunt caeli et terra glória tua.
Hosánna in excélsis.
Benedíctus qui venit in nómine Dómini.
Hosánna in excélsis.

II

De mysterio salutis

℣. **Dóminus vobíscum.**
℟. **Et cum spíritu tuo.**

℣. **Sursum corda.**
℟. **Habémus ad Dóminum.**

℣. **Grátias agámus Dómino Deo nostro.**
℟. **Dignum et iustum est.**

Vere dignum et iustum est, aequum et salutáre,
nos tibi semper et ubíque grátias ágere:
Dómine, sancte Pater, omnípotens aetérne Deus:
per Christum Dóminum nostrum.

Qui, humánis miserátus erróribus,
de Vírgine nasci dignátus est.
Qui, crucem passus, a perpétua morte nos liberávit
et, a mórtuis resúrgens, vitam nobis donávit aetérnam.

Et ídeo cum Angelis et Archángelis,
cum Thronis et Dominatiónibus,
cumque omni milítia caeléstis exércitus,
hymnum glóriae tuae cánimus,
sine fine dicéntes:

Sanctus, Sanctus, Sanctus Dóminus Deus Sábaoth.
Pleni sunt caeli et terra glória tua.
Hosánna in excélsis.
Benedíctus qui venit in nómine Dómini.
Hosánna in excélsis.

III

De universali restauratione in Christo

℣. Dóminus vobíscum.
℟. Et cum spíritu tuo.

℣. Sursum corda.
℟. Habémus ad Dóminum.

℣. Grátias agámus Dómino Deo nostro.
℟. Dignum et iustum est.

Vere dignum et iustum est, aequum et salutáre,
nos tibi semper et ubíque grátias ágere:
Dómine, sancte Pater, omnípotens aetérne Deus:
per Christum Dóminum nostrum.

In quo ómnia instauráre tibi complácuit,
et de plenitúdine eius nos omnes accípere tribuísti.
Cum enim in forma Dei esset, exinanívit semetípsum,
ac per sánguinem crucis suae pacificávit univérsa;
unde exaltátus est super ómnia
et ómnibus obtemperántibus sibi
factus est causa salútis aetérnae.

Et ídeo cum Angelis et Archángelis,
cum Thronis et Dominatiónibus,
cumque omni milítia caeléstis exércitus,
hymnum glóriae tuae cánimus,
sine fine dicéntes:

Sanctus, Sanctus, Sanctus Dóminus Deus Sábaoth.
Pleni sunt caeli et terra glória tua.
Hosánna in excélsis.
Benedíctus qui venit in nómine Dómini.
Hosánna in excélsis.

IV

De salute per Christum

℣. Dóminus vobíscum.
℟. Et cum spíritu tuo.

℣. Sursum corda.
℟. Habémus ad Dóminum.

℣. Grátias agámus Dómino Deo nostro.
℟. Dignum et iustum est.

Vere dignum et iustum est, aequum et salutáre,
nos tibi semper et ubíque grátias ágere:
Dómine, sancte Pater, omnípotens aetérne Deus:

Qui bonitáte hóminem condidísti,
ac iustítia damnátum misericórdia redemísti:
per Christum Dóminum nostrum.

Per quem maiestátem tuam laudant Angeli,
adórant Dominatiónes, tremunt Potestátes.
Caeli caelorúmque Virtútes, ac beáta Séraphim,
sócia exsultatióne concélebrant.
Cum quibus et nostras voces ut admítti iúbeas, deprecámur,
súpplici confessióne dicéntes:

Sanctus, Sanctus, Sanctus Dóminus Deus Sábaoth.
Pleni sunt caeli et terra glória tua.
Hosánna in excélsis.
Benedíctus qui venit in nómine Dómini.
Hosánna in excélsis.

PRECES EUCHARISTICAE

PREX EUCHARISTICA I (SEU CANON ROMANUS)

80. Sacerdos, manibus extensis, dicit:

Te ígitur, clementíssime Pater,
per Iesum Christum, Fílium tuum, Dóminum nostrum,
súpplices rogámus ac pétimus,

Iungit manus et dicit:

uti accépta hábeas

Signat semel super panem et calicem simul, dicens:

et benedícas ✛ haec dona, haec múnera,
haec sancta sacrifícia illibáta,

Extensis manibus prosequitur:

in primis, quae tibi offérimus
pro Ecclésia tua sancta cathólica:
quam pacificáre, custodíre, adunáre
et régere dignéris toto orbe terrárum:
una cum fámulo tuo Papa nostro N.
et Antístite nostro N.
et ómnibus orthodóxis atque cathólicae
et apostólicae fídei cultóribus.

81. Commemoratio pro vivis.
Iungit manus et orat aliquantulum pro quibus orare intendit.

Meménto, Dómine, famulórum famularúmque tuárum
N. et N.

Deinde, manibus extensis, prosequitur:

et ómnium circumstántium,
quorum tibi fides cógnita est et nota devótio,
pro quibus tibi offérimus:
vel qui tibi ófferunt hoc sacrifícium laudis,
pro se suísque ómnibus:
pro redemptióne animárum suárum,
pro spe salútis et incolumitátis suae:
tibíque reddunt vota sua aetérno Deo, vivo et vero.

82. Infra Actionem.

Communicántes,
et memóriam venerántes,
in primis gloriósae semper Vírginis Maríae,
Genetrícis Dei et Dómini nostri Iesu Christi:
† sed et beáti Ioseph, eiúsdem Vírginis Sponsi,
et beatórum Apostolórum ac Mártyrum tuórum,
Petri et Pauli, Andréae,
(Iacóbi, Ioánnis, Thomae, Iacóbi, Philíppi,
Bartholomáei, Mattháei, Simónis et Thaddáei:
Lini, Cleti, Cleméntis, Xysti,
Cornélii, Cypriáni, Lauréntii, Chrysógoni,
Ioánnis et Pauli, Cosmae et Damiáni)
et ómnium Sanctórum tuórum;
quorum méritis precibúsque concédas,
ut in ómnibus protectiónis tuae muniámur auxílio.
(Per Christum Dóminum nostrum. Amen.)

COMMUNICANTES PROPRIA

In Nativitate Domini et per octavam

83. Communicántes,
et (noctem sacratíssimam) diem sacratíssimum celebrántes,
(qua) quo beátae Maríae intemeráta virgínitas
huic mundo édidit Salvatórem:
sed et memóriam venerántes,
in primis eiúsdem gloriósae semper Vírginis Maríae,
Genetrícis eiúsdem Dei et Dómini nostri Iesu Christi: †

In Epiphania Domini

84. Communicántes,
et diem sacratíssimum celebrántes,
quo Unigénitus tuus,
in tua tecum glória coaetérnus,
in veritáte carnis nostrae visibíliter corporális appáruit:
sed et memóriam venerántes,
in primis gloriósae semper Vírginis Maríae,
Genetrícis eiúsdem Dei et Dómini nostri Iesu Christi: †

A Missa Vigiliae paschalis usque ad
dominicam II Paschae

85. Communicántes,
et (noctem sacratíssimam) diem sacratíssimum celebrántes
Resurrectiónis Dómini nostri Iesu Christi secúndum carnem:
sed et memóriam venerántes,
in primis gloriósae semper Vírginis Maríae,
Genetrícis eiúsdem Dei et Dómini nostri Iesu Christi: †

In Ascensione Domini

86. Communicántes,
et diem sacratíssimum celebrántes,
quo Dóminus noster,
unigénitus Fílius tuus,
unítam sibi fragilitátis nostrae substántiam
in glóriae tuae déxtera collocávit:
sed et memóriam venerántes,
in primis gloriósae semper Vírginis Maríae,
Genetrícis eiúsdem Dei et Dómini nostri Iesu Christi: †

In dominica Pentecostes

87. Communicántes,
et diem sacratíssimum Pentecóstes celebrántes,
quo Spíritus Sanctus
Apóstolis in ígneis linguis appáruit:
sed et memóriam venerántes,
in primis gloriósae semper Vírginis Maríae,
Genetrícis Dei et Dómini nostri Iesu Christi: †

88. Manibus extensis, prosequitur:

Hanc ígitur oblatiónem servitútis nostrae,
sed et cunctae famíliae tuae,
quáesumus, Dómine, ut placátus accípias:
diésque nostros in tua pace dispónas,
atque ab aetérna damnatióne nos éripi
et in electórum tuórum iúbeas grege numerári.

Iungit manus.

(Per Christum Dóminum nostrum. Amen.)

A Missa Vigiliae paschalis usque ad
dominicam II Paschae

89. Hanc ígitur oblatiónem servitútis nostrae,
sed et cunctae famíliae tuae,
quam tibi offérimus
pro his quoque, quos regeneráre dignátus es ex aqua et
    Spíritu Sancto,
tríbuens eis remissiónem ómnium peccatórum,
quáesumus, Dómine, ut placátus accípias:
diésque nostros in tua pace dispónas,
atque ab aetérna damnatióne nos éripi
et in electórum tuórum iúbeas grege numerári.

Iungit manus.

(Per Christum Dóminum nostrum. Amen.)

---

90. Tenens manus expansas super oblata, dicit:

Quam oblatiónem tu, Deus, in ómnibus, quáesumus, benedíctam, adscríptam, ratam, rationábilem, acceptabilémque fácere dignéris: ut nobis Corpus et Sanguis fiat dilectíssimi Fílii tui, Dómini nostri Iesu Christi.

Iungit manus.

91. In formulis quae sequuntur, verba Domini proferantur distincte et aperte, prouti natura eorundem verborum requirit.

Qui, prídie quam paterétur,

Accipit panem, eumque parum elevatum super altare tenens, prosequitur:

accépit panem in sanctas ac venerábiles manus suas,

Elevat oculos.

et elevátis óculis in caelum ad te Deum Patrem suum omnipoténtem, tibi grátias agens benedíxit, fregit, dedítque discípulis suis, dicens:

Parum se inclinat.

ACCÍPITE ET MANDUCÁTE EX HOC OMNES: HOC EST ENIM CORPUS MEUM, QUOD PRO VOBIS TRADÉTUR.

Hostiam consecratam ostendit populo, reponit super patenam, et genuflexus adorat.

92. Postea prosequitur:

Símili modo, postquam cenátum est,

Accipit calicem, eumque parum elevatum super altare tenens, prosequitur:

accípiens et hunc praeclárum cálicem in sanctas ac venerábiles manus suas, item tibi grátias agens benedíxit, dedítque discípulis suis, dicens:

Parum se inclinat.

ACCÍPITE ET BÍBITE EX EO OMNES: HIC EST ENIM CALIX SÁNGUINIS MEI NOVI ET AETÉRNI TESTAMÉNTI, QUI PRO VOBIS ET PRO MULTIS EFFUNDÉTUR IN REMISSIÓNEM PECCATÓRUM. HOC FÁCITE IN MEAM COMMEMORATIÓNEM.

Calicem ostendit populo, deponit super corporale, et genuflexus adorat.

93. Deinde dicit:

Mystérium fídei.

Et populus prosequitur, acclamans:

Mortem tuam annuntiámus, Dómine, et tuam resurrectiónem confitémur, donec vénias.

Aliae acclamationes, p. 1089.

94. Postea, extensis manibus, sacerdos dicit:

Unde et mémores, Dómine,
nos servi tui,
sed et plebs tua sancta,
eiúsdem Christi, Fílii tui, Dómini nostri,
tam beátae passiónis,
necnon et ab ínferis resurrectiónis,
sed et in caelos gloriósae ascensiónis:
offérimus praeclárae maiestáti tuae
de tuis donis ac datis
hóstiam puram,
hóstiam sanctam,
hóstiam immaculátam,
Panem sanctum vitae aetérnae
et Cálicem salútis perpétuae.

95. Supra quae propítio ac seréno vultu
respícere dignéris:
et accépta habére,
sícuti accépta habére dignátus es
múnera púeri tui iusti Abel,
et sacrifícium Patriárchae nostri Abrahae,
et quod tibi óbtulit summus sacérdos tuus
Melchísedech,
sanctum sacrifícium, immaculátam hóstiam.

96. Inclinatus, iunctis manibus, prosequitur:

Súpplices te rogámus, omnípotens Deus:
iube haec perférri per manus sancti Angeli tui
in sublíme altáre tuum,
in conspéctu divínae maiestátis tuae;
ut, quotquot ex hac altáris participatióne
sacrosánctum Fílii tui Corpus et Sánguinem
sumpsérimus,

Erigit se atque seipsum signat, dicens: **omni benedictióne caelésti et grátia repleámur.**

Iungit manus.   **(Per Christum Dóminum nostrum. Amen.)**

97. Commemoratio pro defunctis.

Manibus extensis, dicit:

Meménto étiam, Dómine, famulórum famularúmque
tuárum N. et N.,
qui nos praecessérunt cum signo fídei,
et dórmiunt in somno pacis.

Iungit manus et orat aliquantulum pro iis defunctis, pro quibus orare intendit.

Deinde, extensis manibus, prosequitur:

Ipsis, Dómine, et ómnibus in Christo quiescéntibus,
locum refrigérii, lucis et pacis,
ut indúlgeas, deprecámur.

Iungit manus.   **(Per Christum Dóminum nostrum. Amen.)**

98. Manu dextera percutit sibi pectus, dicens:

Et extensis manibus prosequitur:

Nobis quoque peccatóribus fámulis tuis,

de multitúdine miseratiónum tuárum sperántibus,
partem áliquam et societátem donáre dignéris
cum tuis sanctis Apóstolis et Martýribus:
cum Ioánne, Stéphano,
Matthía, Bárnaba,
(Ignátio, Alexándro,
Marcellíno, Petro,
Felicitáte, Perpétua,
Agatha, Lúcia,
Agnéte, Caecília, Anastásia)
et ómnibus Sanctis tuis:
intra quorum nos consórtium,
non aestimátor mériti, sed véniae,
quáesumus, largítor admítte.
Per Christum Dominum nostrum.

Iungit manus:

99. Et prosequitur:

Per quem haec omnia, Domine,
semper bona creas, sanctíficas, vivíficas, benedícis,
et praestas nobis.

100. Accipit patenam cum hostia et calicem, et utrumque elevans, dicit:

Per ipsum, et cum ipso, et in ipso,
est tibi Deo Patri omnipoténti,
in unitáte Spíritus Sancti,
omnis honor et glória
per ómnia sáecula saeculórum.
Amen.

Populus acclamat:

Deinde sequitur ritus communionis, p. 1080.

PREX EUCHARISTICA II

101. ℣. Dóminus vobíscum.
      ℟. Et cum spíritu tuo.

      ℣. Sursum corda.
      ℟. Habémus ad Dóminum.

      ℣. Grátias agámus Dómino Deo nostro.
      ℟. Dignum et iustum est.

Vere dignum et iustum est, aequum et salutáre,
nos tibi, sancte Pater, semper et ubíque grátias ágere
per Fílium dilectiónis tuae Iesum Christum,
Verbum tuum per quod cuncta fecísti:
quem misísti nobis Salvatórem et Redemptórem,
incarnátum de Spíritu Sancto et ex Vírgine natum.

Qui voluntátem tuam adímplens
et pópulum tibi sanctum acquírens
exténdit manus cum paterétur,
ut mortem sólveret et resurrectiónem manifestáret.
Et ídeo cum Angelis et ómnibus Sanctis
glóriam tuam praedicámus, una voce dicéntes:

Sanctus, Sanctus, Sanctus Dóminus Deus Sábaoth.
Pleni sunt caeli et terra glória tua.
Hosánna in excélsis.
Benedíctus qui venit in nómine Dómini.
Hosánna in excélsis.

102. Sacerdos, manibus extensis, dicit:

Vere Sanctus es, Dómine, fons omnis sanctitátis.

103. Iungit manus, easque expansas super oblata tenens, dicit:

Haec ergo dona, quáesumus,
Spíritus tui rore sanctífica,

Iungit manus et signat semel super panem et calicem simul, dicens:

ut nobis Corpus et ✠ Sanguis fiant
Dómini nostri Iesu Christi.

Iungit manus.

104. In formulis quae sequuntur, verba Domini proferantur distincte et aperte, prouti natura eorundem verborum requirit.
Accipit panem, eumque parum elevatum super altare tenens, prosequitur:

Qui cum Passióni voluntárie traderétur,

accépit panem et grátias agens fregit,
dedítque discípulis suis, dicens:

Parum se inclinat.

ACCÍPITE ET MANDUCÁTE EX HOC OMNES:
HOC EST ENIM CORPUS MEUM,
QUOD PRO VOBIS TRADÉTUR.

Hostiam consecratam ostendit populo, reponit super patenam, et genuflexus adorat.

105. Postea prosequitur:

Símili modo, postquam cenátum est,

Accipit calicem, eumque parum elevatum super altare tenens, prosequitur:

accípiens et cálicem,
íterum grátias agens dedit discípulis suis, dicens:

Parum se inclinat.

ACCÍPITE ET BÍBITE EX EO OMNES:
HIC EST ENIM CALIX SÁNGUINIS MEI
NOVI ET AETÉRNI TESTAMÉNTI,
QUI PRO VOBIS ET PRO MULTIS EFFUNDÉTUR
IN REMISSIÓNEM PECCATÓRUM.
HOC FÁCITE IN MEAM COMMEMORATIÓNEM.

Calicem ostendit populo, deponit super corporale, et genuflexus adorat.

106. Deinde dicit:

Mystérium fídei.

Et populus prosequitur, acclamans:

Mortem tuam annuntiámus, Dómine,
et tuam resurrectiónem confitémur, donec vénias.

Aliae acclamationes, p. 1089.

107. Deinde sacerdos, extensis manibus, dicit:

Mémores ígitur mortis et resurrectiónis eius,
tibi, Dómine, panem vitae et cálicem salútis offérimus,
grátias agéntes, quia nos dignos habuísti
astáre coram te et tibi ministráre.

Et súpplices deprecámur,
ut Córporis et Sánguinis Christi partícipes
a Spíritu Sancto congregémur in unum.
Recordáre, Dómine, Ecclésiae tuae toto orbe diffúsae,
ut eam in caritáte perfícias
una cum Papa nostro N. et Epíscopo nostro N.
et univérso clero.

In Missis pro defunctis addi potest:

Meménto fámuli tui (fámulae tuae) N.,
quem (quam) (hódie) ad te ex hoc mundo vocásti.
Concéde, ut, qui (quae) complantátus (complantáta)
   fuit similitúdini mortis Fílii tui,
simul fiat et resurrectiónis ipsíus.

Meménto étiam fratrum nostrórum,
qui in spe resurrectiónis dormiérunt,
omniúmque in tua miseratióne defunctórum,
et eos in lumen vultus tui admítte.
Omnium nostrum, quáesumus, miserére,
ut cum beáta Dei Genetríce Vírgine María,
beátis Apóstolis et ómnibus Sanctis,
qui tibi a sáeculo placuérunt,
aetérnae vitae mereámur esse consórtes,
et te laudémus et glorificémus

Iungit manus.

per Fílium tuum Iesum Christum.

108. Accipit patenam cum hostia et calicem, et utrumque elevans, dicit:

Per ipsum, et cum ipso, et in ipso,
est tibi Deo Patri omnipoténti,
in unitáte Spíritus Sancti,
omnis honor et glória
per ómnia sáecula saeculórum.

Populus acclamat:

Amen.

Deinde sequitur ritus communionis, p. 1080.

PREX EUCHARISTICA III

109. Sacerdos, manibus extensis, dicit:

Vere Sanctus es, Dómine,
et mérito te laudat omnis a te cóndita creatúra,
quia per Fílium tuum,
Dóminum nostrum Iesum Christum,
Spíritus Sancti operánte virtúte,
vivíficas et sanctíficas univérsa,
et pópulum tibi congregáre non désinis,
ut a solis ortu usque ad occásum
oblátio munda offerátur nómini tuo.

110. Iungit manus, easque expansas super oblata tenens, dicit:

Súpplices ergo te, Dómine, deprecámur,
ut haec múnera, quae tibi sacránda detúlimus,
eódem Spíritu sanctificáre dignéris,

Iungit manus et signat semel super panem et calicem simul, dicens:

ut Corpus et ✝ Sanguis fiant
Fílii tui Dómini nostri Iesu Christi,
cuius mandáto haec mystéria celebrámus.

Iungit manus.

111. In formulis quae sequuntur, verba Domini proferantur distincte et aperte, prouti natura eorundem verborum requirit:

Accipit panem eumque parum elevatum super altare tenens, prosequitur:

Ipse enim in qua nocte tradebátur

accépit panem
et tibi grátias agens benedíxit,
fregit, dedítque discípulis suis, dicens:

Parum se inclinat.

ACCÍPITE ET MANDUCÁTE EX HOC OMNES:
HOC EST ENIM CORPUS MEUM,
QUOD PRO VOBIS TRADÉTUR.

Hostiam consecratam ostendit populo, deponit super patenam, et genuflexus adorat.

112. Postea prosequitur:

Símili modo, postquam cenátum est,

Accipit calicem, eumque parum elevatum super altare tenens, prosequitur:

accípiens cálicem,
et tibi grátias agens benedíxit,
dedítque discípulis suis, dicens:

Parum se inclinat.

ACCÍPITE ET BÍBITE EX EO OMNES:
HIC EST ENIM CALIX SÁNGUINIS MEI
NOVI ET AETÉRNI TESTAMÉNTI,
QUI PRO VOBIS ET PRO MULTIS EFFUNDÉTUR
IN REMISSIÓNEM PECCATÓRUM.
HOC FÁCITE IN MEAM COMMEMORATIÓNEM.

Calicem ostendit populo, deponit super corporale, et genuflexus adorat.

113. Deinde dicit:

Mystérium fídei.

Et populus prosequitur, acclamans:

Mortem tuam annuntiámus, Dómine,
et tuam resurrectiónem confitémur, donec vénias.

Aliae acclamationes, p. 1089.

114. Deinde sacerdos, extensis manibus, dicit:

Mémores ígitur, Dómine,
eiúsdem Fílii tui salutíferae passiónis
necnon mirábilis resurrectiónis
et ascensiónis in caelum,
sed et praestolántes álterum eius advéntum,
offérimus tibi, grátias reteréntes,
hoc sacrifícium vivum et sanctum.

Réspice, quáesumus, in oblatiónem Ecclésiae tuae
et, agnóscens Hóstiam,
cuius voluísti immolatióne placári,
concéde, ut qui Córpore et Sánguine Fílii tui refícimur,
Spíritu eius Sancto repléti,
unum corpus et unus spíritus inveniámur in Christo.

Ipse nos tibi perfíciat munus aetérnum,
ut cum eléctis tuis hereditátem cónsequi valeámus,
in primis cum beatíssima Vírgine, Dei Genetríce, María,
cum beátis Apóstolis tuis et gloriósis Martýribus
(cum Sancto N.: Sancto diei vel patrono)
et ómnibus Sanctis,
quorum intercessióne
perpétuo apud te confídimus adiuvári.

Haec Hóstia nostrae reconciliatiónis profíciat,
quáesumus, Dómine,
ad totíus mundi pacem atque salútem.
Ecclésiam tuam, peregrinántem in terra,
in fide et caritáte firmáre dignéris
cum fámulo tuo Papa nostro N. et Epíscopo nostro N.,
cum episcopáli órdine et univérso clero
et omni pópulo acquisitiónis tuae.
Votis huius famíliae, quam tibi astáre voluísti,
adésto propítius.
Omnes fílios tuos ubíque dispérsos
tibi, clemens Pater, miserátus coniúnge.

† Fratres nostros defúnctos
et omnes qui, tibi placéntes, ex hoc sáeculo transiérunt,
in regnum tuum benígnus admítte,
ubi fore sperámus,
ut simul glória tua perénniter satiémur,

Iungit manus.

per Christum Dóminum nostrum,
per quem mundo bona cuncta largíris. †

115. Accipit patenam cum hostia et calicem, et utrumque elevans, dicit:

Per ipsum, et cum ipso, et in ipso,
est tibi Deo Patri omnipoténti,
in unitáte Spíritus Sancti,
omnis honor et glória
per ómnia sáecula saeculórum.
Amen.

Populus acclamat:

Deinde sequitur ritus communionis, p. 1080.

---

116. Quando haec prex eucharistica in Missis pro defunctis adhibetur, dici potest:

†Meménto fámuli tui (fámulae tuae) N.,
quem (quam) (hódie) ad te ex hoc mundo vocásti.
Concéde, ut, qui (quae) complantátus (complantáta)
**   fuit similitúdini mortis Fílii tui,**
simul fiat et resurrectiónis ipsíus,
quando mórtuos suscitábit in carne de terra
et corpus humilitátis nostrae
configurábit córpori claritátis suae.
Sed et fratres nostros defúnctos,
et omnes qui, tibi placéntes, ex hoc sáeculo transiérunt,
in regnum tuum benígnus admítte,
ubi fore sperámus,
ut simul glória tua perénniter satiémur,
quando omnem lácrimam abstérges ab óculis nostris,
quia te, sícuti es, Deum nostrum vidéntes,
tibi símiles érimus cuncta per sáecula,
et te sine fine laudábimus,

Iungit manus.

per Christum Dóminum nostrum,
per quem mundo bona cuncta largíris. †

Accipit patenam cum hostia et calicem, et utrumque elevans, dicit:

Per ipsum, et cum ipso, et in ipso,
est tibi Deo Patri omnipoténti,
in unitáte Spíritus Sancti,
omnis honor et glória
per ómnia sáecula saeculórum.
Amen.

Populus acclamat:

Deinde sequitur ritus communionis, p. 1080.

117. ℣. Dóminus vobíscum.
℞. Et cum spíritu tuo.

℣. Sursum corda.
℞. Habémus ad Dóminum.

℣. Grátias agámus Dómino Deo nostro.
℞. Dignum et iustum est.

Vere dignum est tibi grátias ágere,
vere iustum est te glorificáre, Pater sancte,
quia unus es Deus vivus et verus,
qui es ante sáecula et pérmanes in aetérnum,
inaccessíbilem lucem inhábitans;
sed et qui unus bonus atque fons vitae cuncta fecísti,
ut creatúras tuas benedictiónibus adimpléres
multásque laetificáres tui lúminis claritáte.

Et ídeo coram te innúmerae astant turbae angelórum,
qui die ac nocte sérviunt tibi
et, vultus tui glóriam contemplántes,
te incessánter gloríficant.
Cum quibus et nos et, per nostram vocem,
omnis quae sub caelo est creatúra
nomen tuum in exsultatióne confitémur, canéntes:

Sanctus, Sanctus, Sanctus Dóminus Deus Sábaoth.
Pleni sunt caeli et terra glória tua.
Hosánna in excélsis.
Benedíctus qui venit in nómine Dómini.
Hosánna in excélsis.

118. Sacerdos, manibus extensis, dicit:

Confitémur tibi, Pater sancte,
quia magnus es et ómnia ópera tua
in sapiéntia et caritáte fecísti.
Hóminem ad tuam imáginem condidísti,
eíque commisísti mundi curam univérsi,
ut, tibi soli Creatóri sérviens,
creatúris ómnibus imperáret.
Et cum amicítiam tuam, non obóediens, amisísset,
non eum dereliquísti in mortis império.

Omnibus enim misericórditer subvenísti,
ut te quaeréntes invenírent.
Sed et fóedera plúries homínibus obtulísti
eósque per prophétas erudísti in exspectatióne salútis.

Et sic, Pater sancte, mundum dilexísti,
ut, compléta plenitúdine témporum,
Unigénitum tuum nobis mítteres Salvatórem.
Qui, incarnátus de Spíritu Sancto
et natus ex María Vírgine,
in nostra condiciónis forma est conversátus
per ómnia absque peccáto;
salútem evangelizávit paupéribus,
redemptiónem captívis,
maestis corde laetítiam.

Ut tuam vero dispensatiónem impléret,
in mortem trádidit semetípsum
ac, resúrgens a mórtuis,
mortem destrúxit vitámque renovávit.
Et, ut non ámplius nobismetípsis viverémus,
sed sibi, qui pro nobis mórtuus est atque surréxit,
a te, Pater, misit Spíritum Sanctum
primítias credéntibus,
qui, opus suum in mundo perfíciens,
omnem sanctificatiónem compléret.

119. Iungit manus, easque expansas super oblata tenens, dicit:

Quáesumus ígitur, Dómine,
ut idem Spíritus Sanctus
haec múnera sanctificáre dignétur,

Iungit manus et signat semel super panem et calicem simul, dicens:

ut Corpus et ✝ Sanguis fiant
Dómini nostri Iesu Christi

Iungit manus.

ad hoc magnum mystérium celebrándum,
quod ipse nobis relíquit in foedus aetérnum.

120. In formulis quae sequuntur, verba Domini proferantur distincte et aperte, prouti natura eorundem verborum requirit.

Ipse enim, cum hora venísset
ut glorificarétur a te, Pater sancte,
ac dilexísset suos qui erant in mundo,
in finem diléxit eos:
et cenántibus illis

Accipit panem, eumque parum elevatum super altare tenens, prosequitur:

accépit panem, benedíxit ac fregit,
dedítque discípulis suis, dicens:

Parum se inclinat.

ACCÍPITE ET MANDUCÁTE EX HOC OMNES:
HOC EST ENIM CORPUS MEUM,
QUOD PRO VOBIS TRADÉTUR.

Hostiam consecratam ostendit populo, deponit super patenam, et genuflexus adorat.

121. Postea prosequitur:
Accipit calicem, eumque parum elevatum super altare tenens, prosequitur:

Símili modo

accípiens cálicem, ex genímine vitis replétum,
grátias egit, dedítque discípulis suis, dicens:

Parum se inclinat.

ACCÍPITE ET BÍBITE EX EO OMNES:
HIC EST ENIM CALIX SÁNGUINIS MEI
NOVI ET AETÉRNI TESTAMÉNTI,
QUI PRO VOBIS ET PRO MULTIS EFFUNDÉTUR
IN REMISSIÓNEM PECCATÓRUM.
HOC FÁCITE IN MEAM COMMEMORATIÓNEM.

Calicem ostendit populo, deponit super corporale, et genuflexus adorat.

122. Deinde dicit:

Mystérium fídei.

Et populus prosequitur, acclamans:

Mortem tuam annuntiámus, Dómine,
et tuam resurrectiónem confitémur, donec vénias.

Aliae acclamationes, p. 1089.

123. Deinde sacerdos, extensis manibus, dicit:

Unde et nos, Dómine, redemptiónis nostrae memoriále
nunc celebrántes,
mortem Christi
eiúsque descénsum ad ínferos recólimus,
eius resurrectiónem
et ascensiónem ad tuam déxteram profitémur,
et, exspectántes ipsíus advéntum in glória,
offérimus tibi eius Corpus et Sánguinem,
sacrifícium tibi acceptábile et toti mundo salutáre.

Réspice, Dómine, in Hóstiam,
quam Ecclésiae tuae ipse parásti,
et concéde benígnus ómnibus,
qui ex hoc uno pane participábunt et cálice,
ut, in unum corpus a Sancto Spíritu congregáti,
in Christo hóstia viva perficiántur,
ad laudem glóriae tuae.

Nunc ergo, Dómine, ómnium recordáre,
pro quibus tibi hanc oblatiónem offérimus:
in primis fámuli tui, Papae nostri N.,
Epíscopi nostri N., et Episcopórum órdinis univérsi,
sed et totíus cleri, et offeréntium,
et circumstántium,
et cuncti pópuli tui,
et ómnium, qui te quaerunt corde sincéro.

Meménto étiam illórum,
qui obiérunt in pace Christi tui,
et ómnium defunctórum,
quorum fidem tu solus cognovísti.

Nobis ómnibus, fíliis tuis, clemens Pater, concéde,
ut caeléstem hereditátem cónsequi valeámus
cum beáta Vírgine, Dei Genetríce, María,
cum Apóstolis et Sanctis tuis
in regno tuo, ubi cum univérsa creatúra,
a corruptióne peccáti et mortis liberáta,
te glorificémus per Christum Dóminum nostrum,

Iungit manus.

per quem mundo bona cuncta largíris.

124. *Accipit patenam cum hostia et calicem, et utrumque elevans, dicit:*

Per ipsum, et cum ipso, et in ipso,
est tibi Deo Patri omnipoténti,
in unitáte Spíritus Sancti,
omnis honor et glória
per ómnia sáecula saeculórum.

Populus acclamat:

Amen.

RITUS COMMUNIONIS

125. Calice et patena depositis, sacerdos, iunctis manibus, dicit:

**Praecéptis salutáribus móniti,
et divína institutióne formáti,
audémus dícere:**

Extendit manus et, una cum populo, pergit:

**Pater noster, qui es in caelis:
sanctificétur nomen tuum;
advéniat regnum tuum;
fiat volúntas tua, sicut in caelo, et in terra.
Panem nostrum cotidiánum da nobis hódie;
et dimítte nobis débita nostra,
sicut et nos dimíttimus debitóribus nostris;
et ne nos indúcas in tentatiónem;
sed líbera nos a malo.**

126. Manibus extensis, sacerdos solus prosequitur, dicens:

**Líbera nos, quáesumus, Dómine, ab ómnibus malis,
da propítius pacem in diébus nostris,
ut, ope misericórdiae tuae adiúti,
et a peccáto simus semper líberi
et ab omni perturbatióne secúri:
exspectántes beátam spem
et advéntum Salvatóris nostri Iesu Christi.**

Iungit manus.

Populus orationem concludit, acclamans:

**Quia tuum est regnum,
et potéstas, et glória
in sáecula.**

127. Deinde sacerdos, manibus extensis, clara voce dicit:

**Dómine Iesu Christe, qui dixísti Apóstolis tuis:
Pacem relínquo vobis, pacem meam do vobis:
ne respícias peccáta nostra,
sed fidem Ecclésiae tuae;
eámque secúndum voluntátem tuam
pacificáre et coadunáre dignéris.**

Iungit manus.
           Populus respondet:

**Qui vivis et regnas in sáecula saeculórum.
Amen.**

128. Sacerdos, ad populum conversus, extendens et iungens manus, subdit:
           Populus respondet:

**Pax Dómini sit semper vobíscum.
Et cum spíritu tuo.**

129. Deinde, pro opportunitate, diaconus, vel sacerdos, subiungit:

Offérte vobis pacem.

Et omnes, iuxta locorum consuetudines, pacem et caritatem sibi invicem significant; sacerdos pacem dat diacono vel ministro.

130. Deinde accipit hostiam eamque super patenam frangit, et particulam immittit in calicem, dicens secreto:

Haec commíxtio Córporis et Sánguinis Dómini nostri Iesu Christi fiat accipiéntibus nobis in vitam aetérnam.

131. Interim cantatur vel dicitur:

Quod etiam pluries repeti potest, si fractio panis protrahitur. Ultima tamen vice dicitur: dona nobis pacem.

Agnus Dei, qui tollis peccáta mundi: miserére nobis.
Agnus Dei, qui tollis peccáta mundi: miserére nobis.
Agnus Dei, qui tollis peccáta mundi: dona nobis pacem.

132. Sacerdos deinde, manibus iunctis, dicit secreto:

a

Dómine Iesu Christe, Fili Dei vivi,
qui ex voluntáte Patris,
cooperánte Spíritu Sancto,
per mortem tuam mundum vivificásti:
libera me per hoc sacrosánctum Corpus et Sánguinem tuum
ab ómnibus iniquitátibus meis et univérsis malis:
et fac me tuis semper inhaerére mandátis,
et a te numquam separári permíttas.

Vel:

b

Percéptio Córporis et Sánguinis tui, Dómine Iesu Christe,
non mihi provéniat in iudícium et condemnatiónem:
sed pro tua pietáte prosit mihi ad tutaméntum
mentis et córporis,
et ad medélam percipiéndam.

133. Sacerdos genuflectit, accipit hostiam, eamque aliquantulum elevatam super patenam tenens, ad populum versus, clara voce dicit:

Ecce Agnus Dei, ecce qui tollit peccáta mundi.
Beáti qui ad cenam Agni vocáti sunt.

Et una cum populo semel subdit:

Dómine, non sum dignus, ut intres sub tectum meum,
sed tantum dic verbo
et sanábitur ánima mea.

134. Et sacerdos, ad altare versus, secreto dicit:

Et reverenter sumit Corpus Christi.

Corpus Christi custódiat me in vitam aetérnam.

Deinde accipit calicem et secreto dicit:

Et reverenter sumit Sanguinem Christi.

Sanguis Christi custódiat me in vitam aetérnam.

135. Postea accipit patenam vel pyxidem, accedit ad communicandos, et hostiam parum elevatam unicuique eorum ostendit, dicens:

Communicandus respondet:

Et communicatur.

Eo modo agit et diaconus, si sacram Communionem distribuit.

Corpus Christi.

Amen.

136. Si adsint sub utraque specie communicandi, servetur ritus suo loco descriptus.

137. Dum sacerdos sumit Corpus Christi, incipit cantus ad Communionem.

138. Distributione Communionis expleta, sacerdos vel diaconus purificat patenam super calicem et ipsum calicem.

Dum purificationem peragit, sacerdos dicit secreto:

Quod ore súmpsimus, Dómine, pura mente capiámus, et de múnere temporáli fiat nobis remédium sempitérnum.

139. Tunc sacerdos ad sedem redire potest. Pro opportunitate sacrum silentium, per aliquod temporis spatium, servari, vel psalmus aut canticum laudis proferri potest.

140. Deinde, stans ad sedem vel ad altare, sacerdos dicit:

Orémus.

Et omnes una cum sacerdote per aliquod temporis spatium in silentio orant, nisi silentium iam praecesserit. Deinde sacerdos, manibus extensis, dicit orationem post Communionem. Populus in fine acclamat:

Amen.

RITUS CONCLUSIONIS

141. Sequuntur, si habendae sint, breves annuntiationes ad populum.

142. Deinde fit dimissio. Sacerdos, versus ad populum, extendens manus, dicit:

Dóminus vobíscum.

Populus respondet:

Et cum spíritu tuo.

Sacerdos benedicit populum, dicens:

Benedícat vos omnípotens Deus, Pater, et Fílius,⨯ et Spíritus Sanctus. Amen.

Populus respondet:

143. Deinde diaconus, vel ipse sacerdos, manibus iunctis, ad populum versus dicit:

Populus respondet:

Ite, missa est. Deo grátias.

144. Deinde sacerdos altare osculo de more veneratur, ut initio. Facta denique debita reverentia cum ministris, recedit.

145. Si qua actio liturgica immediate sequatur, ritus dimissionis omittuntur.

ORDO MISSAE SINE POPULO

RITUS INITIALES

1. Sacerdos, facta cum ministro debita reverentia, signat se, dicens:

> Minister respondet:

In nómine Patris, et Fílii, et Spíritus Sancti.
Amen.

2. Tunc sacerdos, ad ministrum conversus et manus extendens, eum salutat, dicens:

> Minister respondet:

Dóminus vobíscum.
Et cum spíritu tuo.

Adhiberi possunt etiam aliae formulae salutationis, quae in Appendice inveniuntur, p. 1088.

3. Postea sacerdos et minister faciunt confessionem:

Confíteor Deo omnipoténti et tibi, frater,
quia peccávi nimis
cogitatióne, verbo, ópere et omissióne:

Et, percutientes sibi pectus, dicunt:

mea culpa, mea culpa, mea máxima culpa.

Deinde prosequuntur:

Ideo precor beátam Maríam semper Vírginem,
omnes Angelos et Sanctos, et te, frater,
oráre pro me ad Dóminum Deum nostrum.

Sequitur absolutio sacerdotis:

Misereátur nostri omnípotens Deus
et, dimíssis peccátis nostris,
perdúcat nos ad vitam aetérnam.
Amen.

> Minister respondet:

4. Tunc sacerdos ascendit ad altare, illud veneratur osculo, et accedit ad missale in sinistro latere altaris collocato, et legit antiphonam ad introitum.

5. Sequuntur invocationes Kýrie, eléison, quas sacerdos dicit alternatim cum ministro.

Sac.: Kýrie, eléison.
Min.: Kýrie, eléison.

Sac.: Christe, eléison.
Min.: Christe, eléison.

Sac.: Kýrie, eléison.
Min.: Kýrie, eléison.

6. Deinde, quando praescribitur, sacerdos et minister simul dicunt hymnum Glória in excélsis Deo, p. 1055.

7. Quo finito, sacerdos, manibus iunctis, dicit:

Orémus.

Et, facta aliqua pausa silentii, extendit manus et dicit orationem; qua expleta, minister acclamat:

Amen.

LITURGIA VERBI

8. Tunc minister vel ipse sacerdos legit primam lectionem, psalmum et, si habenda est, secundam lectionem necnon alterum cantum.

9. Deinde sacerdos, inclinatus, secreto dicit:

Munda cor meum ac lábia mea, omnípotens Deus, ut sanctum Evangélium tuum digne váleam nuntiáre.

10. Postea, iunctis manibus, dicit:

Dóminus vobíscum.

Minister respondet:

Et cum spíritu tuo.

Sacerdos:

Léctio sancti Evangélii secúndum N.,

Et interim signat librum et seipsum in fronte, ore et pectore.

Minister acclamat:

Glória tibi, Dómine.

Deinde sacerdos Evangelium legit. Quo finito, librum osculatur, dicens secreto: **Per evangélica dicta deleantur nostra delícta.**

Minister autem acclamat:

Laus tibi, Christe.

11. Quando dicendum est, sacerdos et minister simul dicunt symbolum, p. 1056.

12. Postea fieri potest oratio universalis seu oratio fidelium, in qua ipse sacerdos etiam intentiones profert, ministro respondente. Cf. in Appendice, p. 1117.

LITURGIA EUCHARISTICA

13. Minister corporale, purificatorium et calicem super altare deponit, nisi iam initio Missae ibidem sint posita. Sacerdos ad medium altaris accedit.

14. Tunc minister affert patenam cum pane, quam sacerdos accipit et aliquantulum elevatam super altare tenet, dicens:

**Benedíctus es, Dómine, Deus univérsi,
quia de tua largitáte accépimus panem,
quem tibi offérimus,
fructum terrae et óperis mánuum hóminum,
ex quo nobis fiet panis vitae.**

Deponit deinde patenam cum pane super corporale.

15. Postea sacerdos infundit vinum et parum aquae in calicem, dicens secreto:

Per huius aquae et vini mystérium
eius efficiámur divinitátis consórtes,
qui humanitátis nostrae fíeri dignátus est párticeps.

16. Postea accipit calicem, eumque aliquantulum elevatum super altare tenet, dicens:

Benedíctus es, Dómine, Deus univérsi,
quia de tua largitáte accépimus vinum,
quod tibi offérimus,
fructum vitis et óperis mánuum hóminum,
ex quo nobis fiet potus spiritális.

Deinde calicem super corporale deponit.

17. Postea, inclinatus, dicit secreto:

In spíritu humilitátis et in ánimo contríto
suscipiámur a te, Dómine,
et sic fiat sacrifícium nostrum in conspéctu tuo hódie,
ut pláceat tibi, Dómine Deus.

18. Deinde, stans ad latus altaris, lavat manus, dicens secreto:

Lava me, Dómine, ab iniquitáte mea,
et a peccáto meo munda me.

19. Stans postea in medio altaris, versus ad ministrum, extendens et iungens manus, dicit:

Oráte, fratres,
ut meum ac vestrum sacrifícium
acceptábile fiat apud Deum Patrem omnipoténtem.

Minister respondet:

Suscípiat Dóminus sacrifícium de mánibus tuis
ad laudem et glóriam nóminis sui,
ad utilitátem quoque nostram
totiúsque Ecclésiae suae sanctae.

Deinde, manibus extensis, sacerdos dicit orationem super oblata; qua finita, minister acclamat: Amen.

20. Tunc sacerdos dicit Precem eucharisticam, iuxta normas, quae in singulis Precibus eucharisticis continentur.

21. Post doxologiam in fine Precis eucharisticae, iunctis manibus, sacerdos dicit:

Praecéptis salutáribus móniti,
et divína institutióne formáti, audémus dícere:

Extendit manus et, una cum ministro, pergit:

Pater noster, qui es in caelis:
sanctificétur nomen tuum; advéniat regnum tuum;
fiat volúntas tua, sicut in caelo, et in terra.
Panem nostrum cotidiánum da nobis hódie;
et dimítte nobis débita nostra,
sicut et nos dimíttimus debitóribus nostris;
et ne nos indúcas in tentatiónem; sed líbera nos a malo.

22. Manibus extensis, sacerdos solus
prosequitur, dicens:

Líbera nos, quáesumus, Dómine, ab ómnibus malis,
da propítius pacem in diébus nostris,
ut, ope misericórdiae tuae adiúti,
et a peccáto simus semper líberi
et ab omni perturbatióne secúri:
exspectántes beátam spem
et advéntum Salvatóris nostri Iesu Christi.

Iungit manus. Minister orationem
concludit, acclamans:

Quia tuum est regnum,
et potéstas, et glória
in sáecula.

23. Tunc sacerdos, manibus extensis,
clara voce dicit:

Dómine Iesu Christe, qui dixísti Apóstolis tuis:
Pacem relínquo vobis, pacem meam do vobis:
ne respícias peccáta nostra,
sed fidem Ecclésiae tuae;
eámque secúndum voluntátem tuam
pacificáre et coadunáre dignéris.

Iungit manus.

       Minister respondet:

Qui vivis et regnas in sáecula saeculórum.
Amen.

24. Sacerdos, ad ministrum conversus, extendens et iungens manus,
subdit:

       Minister respondet:

Pax Dómini sit semper vobíscum.
Et cum spíritu tuo.

Et sacerdos, pro opportunitate,
pacem dat ministro.

25. Postea accipit hostiam, eamque
super patenam frangit, interim cum
ministro dicens:

Agnus Dei, qui tollis peccáta mundi: miserére nobis.
Agnus Dei, qui tollis peccáta mundi: miserére nobis.
Agnus Dei, qui tollis peccáta mundi: dona nobis pacem.

His dictis, particulam immittit in
calicem, dicens secreto:

Haec commíxtio Córporis et Sánguinis Dómini nostri Iesu
Christi fiat accipiéntibus nobis in vitam aetérnam.

26. Sacerdos deinde, manibus iunctis, dicit secreto: a

Dómine Iesu Christe, Fili Dei vivi,
qui ex voluntáte Patris, cooperánte Spíritu Sancto,
per mortem tuam mundum vivificásti:
líbera me per hoc sacrosánctum Corpus et Sánguinem tuum
ab ómnibus iniquitátibus meis et univérsis malis:
et fac me tuis semper inhaerére mandátis,
et a te numquam separári permíttas.

       Vel:

b

Percéptio Córporis et Sánguinis tui, Dómine Iesu Christe,
non mihi provéniat in iudícium et condemnatiónem:
sed pro tua pietáte prosit mihi ad tutaméntum
   mentis et córporis, et ad medélam percipiéndam.

27. Sacerdos genuflectit, accipit hostiam, eamque aliquantulum elevatam super patenam tenens, ad ministrum versus, clara voce dicit:

Ecce Agnus Dei, ecce qui tollit peccáta mundi.
Beáti qui ad cenam Agni vocáti sunt.

Et una cum ministro semel subdit:

Dómine, non sum dignus, ut intres sub tectum meum,
sed tantum dic verbo
et sanábitur ánima mea.

Si minister non est communicandus, sacerdos, accepta hostia, et stans ad altare conversus, statim dicit: Dómine, non sum dignus, etc.

28. Et deinde, ad altare versus, secreto dicit:
Et reverenter sumit Corpus Christi.

Corpus Christi custódiat me in vitam aetérnam.

Deinde accipit calicem et secreto dicit:
Et reverenter sumit Sanguinem Christi.

Sanguis Christi custódiat me in vitam aetérnam.

29. Quo facto, sacerdos dicit antiphonam ad Communionem.

30. Postea accipit patenam, accedit ad ministrum, si communicandus est, et hostiam parum elevatam ei ostendit, dicens:
          Minister respondet:
Et communicatur.

Corpus Christi.
Amen.

31. Deinde sacerdos purificat patenam super calicem et ipsum calicem. Calix, patena, corporale et purificatorium a ministro ad abacum deferuntur, vel super altare relinquuntur.

Dum purificationem peragit, sacerdos dicit secreto:

Quod ore súmpsimus, Dómine, pura mente capiámus,
et de múnere temporáli fiat nobis remédium sempitérnum.

32. Sacrum silentium per aliquod temporis spatium servari potest.

33. Postea sacerdos, manibus iunctis, dicit:

Orémus.

Et facta aliqua pausa silentii, nisi iam praecesserit, extendit manus et dicit orationem post Communionem. Minister in fine acclamat:

Amen.

RITUS CONCLUSIONIS

34. Deinde sacerdos, versus ad ministrum, extendens manus, dicit:
          Minister respondet:

Dóminus vobíscum.
Et cum spíritu tuo.

Et sacerdos benedicit ministrum, dicens:
          Minister respondet:

Benedícat vos omnípotens Deus,
Pater, et Fílius, ✠ et Spíritus Sanctus.
Amen.

35. Denique sacerdos altare osculo veneratur et, facta cum ministro debita reverentia, recedit.

APPENDIX

Formulae salutationis initio Missae

a ℣. **Grátia Dómini nostri Iesu Christi, et cáritas Dei, et communicátio Sancti Spíritus sit cum ómnibus vobis.**
℟. **Et cum spíritu tuo.**

b ℣. **Grátia vobis et pax a Deo Patre nostro et Dómino Iesu Christo.**
℟. **Benedíctus Deus et Pater Dómini nostri Iesu Christi.**

Vel:

℟. **Et cum spíritu tuo.**

c ℣. **Dóminus vobíscum.**
℟. **Et cum spíritu tuo.**

Formulae actus paenitentialis

Loco actus paenitentialis, qui in Ordine Missae invenitur, unus e sequentibus adhiberi potest:

1. Sacerdos fideles invitat ad paenitentiam:

Fratres, agnoscámus peccáta nostra, ut apti simus ad sacra mystéria celebránda.

Fit brevis pausa silentii.

Postea sacerdos dicit: **Miserére nostri, Dómine.**
Populus respondet: **Quia peccávimus tibi.**

Sacerdos: **Osténde nobis, Dómine, misericórdiam tuam.**
Populus: **Et salutáre tuum da nobis.**

Sequitur absolutio sacerdotis: **Misereátur nostri omnípotens Deus et, dimíssis peccátis nostris, perdúcat nos ad vitam aetérnam.**

Populus respondet: **Amen.**

2. Sacerdos fideles invitat ad paenitentiam:

Fratres, agnoscámus peccáta nostra, ut apti simus ad sacra mystéria celebránda.

Fit brevis pausa silentii.

Deinde sacerdos, vel alius minister idoneus, sequentes, vel alias, invocationes cum Kýrie, eléison profert:

Qui missus es sanáre contrítos corde: Kýrie, eléison.
Populus respondet: **Kýrie, eléison.**

Sacerdos:	**Qui peccatóres vocáre venísti: Christe, eléison.**
Populus:	**Christe, eléison.**
Sacerdos:	**Qui ad déxteram Patris sedes, ad interpellándum pro nobis: Kýrie, eléison.**
Populus:	**Kýrie, eléison.**
Sequitur absolutio sacerdotis:	**Misereátur nostri omnípotens Deus et, dimíssis peccátis nostris, perdúcat nos ad vitam aetérnam.**
Populus respondet:	**Amen.**

Acclamationes post Consecrationem

ad libitum seligendae

Mortem tuam annuntiámus, Dómine, et tuam resurrectiónem confitémur, donec vénias.

Quotiescúmque manducámus panem hunc et cálicem bíbimus, mortem tuam annuntiámus, Dómine, donec vénias.

Salvátor mundi, salva nos, qui per crucem et resurrectiónem tuam liberásti nos.

I. MISSAE DE TEMPORE

1

IN ADVENTU

Ant. ad introitum   Cf. Zac. 14:5, 7

Ecce Dóminus véniet, et omnes Sancti eius cum eo;
et erit in die illa lux magna.

Collecta

Deus, qui salutáre tuum cunctis terrae fínibus declarásti,
tríbue, quáesumus,
ut nativitátis eius glóriam laetánter praestolémur.
Per Dóminum.

Lectio prima   Is. 35:1-10

Deus ipse veniet et salvabit vos

Léctio libri Isaíae prophétae

Laetábitur desérta et ínvia,
et exsultábit solitúdo et florébit quasi lílium.
Gérminans germinábit
et exsultábit laetabúnda et laudans.
Glória Líbani data est ei, decor Carméli et Saron;
ipsi vidébunt glóriam Dómini et decórem Dei nostri.
Confortáte manus dissolútas et génua debília roboráte;
dícite pusillánimis:
"Confortámini et nolíte timére;
ecce Deus vester ultiónem addúcet retributiónis:
Deus ipse véniet et salvábit vos".
Tunc aperiéntur óculi caecórum,
et aures surdórum patébunt;
tunc sáliet sicut cervus claudus,
et apérta erit lingua mutórum;
quia scissae sunt in desérto aquae,
et torréntes in solitúdine.
Et quae erat árida erit in stagnum, et sítiens in fontes aquárum.
In cubílibus, in quibus prius dracónes habitábant,
oriétur viror cálami et iunci.
Et erit ibi sémita et via, et via sancta vocábitur;
non transíbit per eam pollútus;
et haec erit vobis dirécta via,
ita ut stulti non errent per eam.

1090

Non erit ibi leo,
et mala béstia non ascéndet per eam nec inveniétur ibi;
et ambulábunt qui liberáti fúerint, et redémpti a Dómino converténtur
et vénient in Sion cum laude,
et laetítia sempitérna super caput eórum;
gáudium et laetítiam obtinébunt,
et fúgiet dolor et gémitus.

    Verbum Dómini.

Psalmus responsorius   Ps. 84:9ab-10, 11-12, 13-14

℞. (Is. 35:4d) Ecce Deus noster et salvábit nos.

Audiam quid loquátur Dóminus Deus,
quóniam loquétur pacem ad plebem suam et sanctos suos.
Verúmtamen prope timéntes eum salutáre ipsíus,
ut inhábitet glória in terra nostra.

℞. Ecce Deus noster et salvábit nos.

Misericórdia et véritas obviavérunt sibi,
iustítia et pax osculátae sunt.
Véritas de terra orta est, et iustítia de caelo prospéxit.

℞. Ecce Deus noster et salvábit nos.

Etenim Dóminus dabit benignitátem,
et terra nostra dabit fructum suum.
Iustítia ante eum ambulábit, et ponet in via gressus suos.

℞. Ecce Deus noster et salvábit nos.

℣. Allelúia.   ℞. Allelúia.

℣. Ecce véniet Dóminus ut salvet pópulum suum;
    beáti qui paráti sunt occúrrere illi.   ℞. Allelúia.

Evangelium   Mc. 1:1-8

Rectas facite semitas Domini

✠ Inítium sancti Evangélii secúndum Marcum

Inítium Evangélii Iesu Christi Fílii Dei. Sicut scriptum est in Isaía prophéta: "Ecce ego mitto ángelum meum ante fáciem tuam, qui praeparábit viam tuam ante te. Vox clamántis in desérto: 'Paráte viam Dómini, rectas fácite sémitas eius'".

Fuit Ioánnes in desérto baptízans et práedicans baptísmum paeniténtiae in remissiónem peccatórum. Et egrediebátur ad eum omnis Iudáeae régio et Ierosolymítae univérsi et baptizabántur ab illo in Iordánis flúmine confiténtes peccáta sua.

Et erat Ioánnes vestítus pilis caméli, et zona pellícea circa lumbos eius, et locústas et mel silvéstre edébat et praedicábat dicens: "Venit fórtior me post me, cuius non sum dignus procúmbens sólvere corrígiam calceamentórum eius. Ego baptizávi vos aqua, ille vero baptizábit vos Spíritu Sancto".

    Verbum Dómini.

Super oblata

Placáre, Dómine, quáesumus,
nostrae précibus humilitátis et hóstiis,
et ubi nulla súppetunt suffrágia meritórum,
tuae nobis indulgéntiae succúrre praesídiis.
Per Christum.

Ant. ad communionem   2 Tim. 4:8

Corónam iustítiae reddet iustus iudex
iis qui díligunt advéntum eius.

Post communionem

Repléti cibo spiritális alimóniae,
súpplices te, Dómine, deprecámur,
ut, huius participatióne mystérii,
dóceas nos terréna sapiénter perpéndere,
et per illa caeléstibus inhaerére.
Per Christum.

2

TEMPORE NATIVITATIS

Ant. ad introitum   Cf. Ioan. 1:1

In princípio et ante sáecula Deus erat Verbum,
et ipse nasci dignátus est Salvátor mundi.

Collecta

Ante sollemnitatem Epiphaniae

Deus, qui pópulo tuo, Unigéniti tui nativitáte,
redemptiónis efféctum mirabíliter inchoásti,
ita, quáesumus, fídei fámulis tuis tríbue firmitátem,
ut usque ad promíssum glóriae práemium,
ipso gubernánte, pervéniant.
Per Dóminum.

Post sollemnitatem Epiphaniae

Deus, qui per Fílium tuum
aeternitátis tuae lumen cunctis géntibus suscitásti,
da plebi tuae fulgórem plenum sui Redemptóris agnóscere,
ut ad perpétuam claritátem per eius increménta pervéniat.
Per Dóminum.

Lectio prima Tit. 3:4-7

Secundum misericordiam suam salvos nos fecit

Léctio Epístolae beáti Pauli apóstoli ad Titum

Cum appáruit benígnitas et humánitas Salvatóris nostri Dei, non ex opéribus iustítiae, quae fécimus nos, sed secúndum suam misericórdiam salvos nos fecit per lavácrum regeneratiónis et renovatiónis Spíritus Sancti, quem effúdit in nos abúnde per Iesum Christum Salvatórem nostrum; ut iustificáti grátia ipsíus, herédes simus secúndum spem vitae aetérnae.

Verbum Dómini.

Psalmus responsorius Ps. 97:1, 2-3ab, 3cd-4, 5-6

℟. (3c) Vidérunt omnes términi terrae salutáre Dei nostri.

Cantáte Dómino cánticum novum,
quia mirabília fecit.
Salvávit sibi déxtera eius,
et brácchium sanctum eius.

℟. Vidérunt omnes términi terrae salutáre Dei nostri.

Notum fecit Dóminus salutáre suum,
in conspéctu géntium revelávit iustítiam suam.
Recordátus est misericórdiae suae
et veritátis suae dómui Israel.

℟. Vidérunt omnes términi terrae salutáre Dei nostri.

Vidérunt omnes términi terrae
salutáre Dei nostri.
Iubiláte Deo, omnis terra,
erúmpite, exsultáte et psállite.

℟. Vidérunt omnes términi terrae salutáre Dei nostri.

Psállite Dómino in cíthara,
in cíthara et voce psalmi;
in tubis ductílibus et voce tubae córneae,
iubiláte in conspéctu regis Dómini.

℟. Vidérunt omnes términi terrae salutáre Dei nostri.

℣. **Allelúia.** ℟. **Allelúia.** Hebr. 1:1-2

℣. **Multifárie olim Deus loquens pátribus in prophétis,**
novíssime diébus istis locútus est nobis in Fílio. ℟. **Allelúia.**

Evangelium   Lc. 2:15-20

Invenerunt pastores Mariam et Ioseph et infantem

✠ Léctio sancti Evangélii secúndum Lucam

Factum est, ut discessérunt ab eis ángeli in caelum, pastóres loquebántur ad ínvicem: "Transeámus usque Béthlehem et videámus hoc verbum, quod factum est, quod Dóminus osténdit nobis". Et venérunt festinántes et invenérunt Maríam et Ioseph et infántem pósitum in praesépio.

Vidéntes autem cognovérunt de verbo, quod dictum erat illis de púero hoc. Et omnes qui audiérunt miráti sunt, et de his quae dicta erant a pastóribus ad ipsos.

María autem conservábat ómnia verba haec, cónferens in corde suo. Et revérsi sunt pastóres glorificántes et laudántes Deum, in ómnibus quae audíerant et víderant, sicut dictum est ad illos.

Verbum Dómini.

Super oblata

Súscipe, Dómine, múnera nostra,
quibus exercéntur commércia gloriósa,
ut, offeréntes quae dedísti,
teípsum mereámur accípere.
Per Christum.

Ant. ad communionem   Ioan. 3:16

Sic Deus diléxit mundum, ut Fílium suum unigénitum daret,
ut omnis, qui credit in eum, non péreat,
sed hábeat vitam aetérnam.

Post communionem

Deus, qui nos sacraménti tui participatióne contíngis,
virtútis eius efféctus in nostris córdibus operáre,
ut suscipiéndo múneri tuo per ipsum munus aptémur.
Per Christum.

3
IN QUADRAGESIMA

Ant. ad introitum   Ps. 68:17

Exáudi nos, Dómine, quóniam benígna est misericórdia tua;
secúndum multitúdinem miseratiónum tuárum réspice nos,
Dómine.

Collecta

Concéde nobis, omnípotens Deus,
ut per ánnua quadragesimális exercítia saraménti,
et ad intellegéndum Christi proficiámus arcánum,
et efféctus eius digna conversatióne sectémur.
Per Dóminum.

Lectio prior   Ez. 18:21-28

Numquid voluntatis meae est mors impii,
et non ut convertatur a viis suis et vivat?

Léctio libri Ezechiélis prophétae

Haec dicit Dóminus Deus:
"Si ímpius égerit paeniténtiam ab ómnibus peccátis suis, quae
operátus est, et custodíerit ómnia praecépta mea et fécerit
iudícium et iustítiam, vita vivet et non moriétur; ómnium
iniquitátum eius, quas operátus est, non recordábor; in iustítia
sua, quam operátus est, vivet. Numquid voluntátis meae est mors
ímpii? dicit Dóminus Deus, et non ut convertátur a viis suis et
vivat?

Si autem avérterit se iustus a iustítia sua et fécerit iniquitátem
secúndum omnes abominatiónes, quas operári solet ímpius,
numquid vivet? Omnes iustítiae eius, quas fécerat, non recorda-
búntur; in praevaricatióne, qua praevaricátus est, et in peccáto
suo, quod peccávit, in ipsis moriétur.

Et dixístis: 'Non est aequa via Dómini'. Audíte ergo, domus
Israel: Numquid via mea non est aequa, et non magis viae vestrae
pravae sunt? Cum enim avérterit se iustus a iustítia sua et fécerit
iniquitátem, moriétur in eis, in iniustítia quam operátus est
moriétur.

Et, cum avérterit se ímpius ab impietáte sua, quam operátus
est, et fécerit iudícium et iustítiam, ipse ánimam suam vivificábit;
consíderans enim et avértens se ab ómnibus iniquitátibus suis,
quas operátus est, vita vivet et non moriétur".

Verbum Dómini.

Psalmus responsorius   Ps. 129:1-2, 3-4a, 4b-6, 7-8

℟. (7bc) Apud Dóminum misericórdia,
et copiósa apud eum redémptio.

De profúndis clamávi ad te, Dómine;
Dómine, exáudi vocem meam.

Fiant aures tuae intendéntes
in vocem deprecatiónis meae.

℟. Apud Dóminum misericórdia, et copiósa apud eum redémptio.

Si iniquitátes observáveris, Dómine,
Dómine, quis sustinébit?
Quia apud te propitiátio est,
et timébimus te.

℟. Apud Dóminum misericórdia, et copiósa apud eum redémptio.

Sustínui te, Dómine;
sustínuit ánima mea in verbo eius,
sperávit ánima mea in Dómino.
Magis quam custódes auróram,
speret Israel in Dómino.

℟. Apud Dóminum misericórdia, et copiósa apud eum redémptio.

Quia apud Dóminum misericórdia,
et copiósa apud eum redémptio.
Et ipse rédimet Israel
ex ómnibus iniquitátibus eius.

℟. Apud Dóminum misericórdia, et copiósa apud eum redémptio.

In Quadragesima, ante et post Versum ante Evangelium, pro opportunitate
adhiberi potest una ex his acclamationibus, aut alia his similis: Laus tibi,
Christe, rex aeternae gloriae; Laus et honor tibi, Domine Iesu; Gloria et laus
tibi, Christe; Gloria tibi, Christe, Verbo Dei.

Versus ante Evangelium   2 Cor. 6:2b

Ecce nunc tempus acceptábile,
ecce nunc dies salútis.

Evangelium   Mt. 5:43-48

Estote perfecti sicut Pater vester caelestis

✠ Léctio sancti Evangélii secúndum Mattháeum

In illo témpore: Dixit Iesus discípulis suis:

"Audístis quia dictum est: 'Díliges próximum tuum et ódio
habébis inimícum tuum'. Ego autem dico vobis: Dilígite inimícos
vestros, benefácite his qui odérunt vos et oráte pro persequén-
tibus et calumniántibus vos, ut sitis fílii Patris vestri qui in caelis
est, qui solem suum oríri facit super bonos et malos et pluit super
iustos et iniústos.

Si enim dilígitis eos qui vos díligunt, quam mercédem habébitis? nonne et publicáni hoc fáciunt? Et si salutavéritis fratres vestros tantum, quid ámplius fácitis? nonne et éthnici hoc fáciunt?

Estóte ergo vos perfécti, sicut et Pater vester caeléstis perféctus
est".

Verbum Dómini.

Super oblata

Haec hóstia, Dómine, quáesumus, emúndet nostra delícta,
et, ad celebránda festa paschália,
fidélium tuórum córpora mentésque santíficet.
Per Christum.

Ant. ad communionem   Ps. 50:12

Cor mundum crea in me, Deus,
et spíritum rectum ínnova in viscéribus meis.

Post communionem

Accépto, Dómine, pígnore salútis aetérnae,
fac nos, quáesumus, sic téndere congruénter,
ut ad eam perveníre possímus.
Per Christum.

4

TEMPORE PASCHALI

Ant. ad introitum   Apoc. 19:6-7

Gaudeámus et exsultémus et demus glóriam Deo,
quóniam regnávit Dóminus Deus noster omnípotens, allelúia.

Collecta

Ante sollemnitatem Ascensionis

Semper exsúltet pópulus tuus, Deus,
renováta ánimae iuventúte,
ut, qui nunc laetátur in adoptiónis se glóriam restitútum,
resurrectiónis diem spe certae gratulatiónis exspéctet.
Per Dóminum.

Post sollemnitatem Ascensionis

Supplicatiónibus nostris, Dómine, adésto propítius,
ut, sicut humáni géneris Salvatórem
tecum in tua crédimus maiestáte,
ita usque ad consummatiónem sáeculi manére nobíscum,
sicut ipse promísit, sentiámus.
Per Dóminum.

Lectio prima   Act. 13:26-33

Repromissionem adimplevit Deus resuscitans Iesum

Léctio Actuum Apostolórum

In diébus illis: Cum venísset Paulus Antiochíam Pisídiae, dicébat in synagóga:

"Viri fratres, fílii géneris Abraham et qui in vobis timent Deum, vobis verbum salútis huius missum est.

Qui enim habitábant Ierúsalem et príncipes eius hunc ignorántes et voces prophetárum, quae per omne sábbatum legúntur, iudicántes implevérunt et nullam causam mortis inveniéntes in eo petiérunt a Piláto, ut interfícerent eum. Cumque consummássent ómnia quae de eo scripta erant, deponéntes eum de ligno posuérunt eum in monuménto.

Deus vero suscitávit eum a mórtuis tértia die, qui visus est per dies multos his qui simul ascénderant cum eo de Galiláea in Ierúsalem, qui usque nunc sunt testes eius ad plebem.

Et nos vobis annuntiámus eam, quae ad patres nostros repromíssio facta est; quóniam hanc Deus adimplévit fíliis nostris resúscitans Iesum, sicut et in psalmo secúndo scriptum est: 'Fílius meus es tu; ego hódie génui te'".

Verbum Dómini.

Psalmus responsorius   Ps. 2:6-7, 8-9, 10-11

℞. (7) Fílius meus es tu; ego hódie génui te. vel Allelúia.

"Ego autem constítui regem meum
super Sion, montem sanctum meum!".
Praedicábo decrétum eius:
Dóminus dixit ad me: "Fílius meus es tu;
ego hódie génui te.

℞. Fílius meus es tu; ego hódie génui te. vel Allelúia.

Póstula a me, et dabo tibi gentes hereditátem tuam,
et possessiónem tuam términos terrae.
Reges eos in virga férrea,
et tamquam vas fíguli confrínges eos".

℞. Fílius meus es tu; ego hódie génui te. vel Allelúia.

Et nunc, reges, intellégite,
erudímini, qui iudicátis terram.
Servíte Dómino in timóre,
et exsultáte ei cum tremóre.

℞. Fílius meus es tu; ego hódie génui te. vel Allelúia.

℣. Allelúia.   ℞. Allelúia.   Apoc. 1:5ab

℣. Iesu Christe, testis fidélis, primogénite mortuórum,
    dilexísti nos et lavísti peccáta nostra in sánguine tuo.
℞. Allelúia.

Evangelium   Lc. 24:35-48

Sic oportebat Christum pati et resurgere a mortuis tertia die

✝ **Léctio sancti Evangélii secúndum Lucam**

In illo témpore: Narrábant discípuli quae gesta erant in via, et quómodo cognovérunt eum in fractióne panis.

Dum autem haec loquúntur, stetit Iesus in médio eórum et dicit eis: "Pax vobis: ego sum, nolite timére". Conturbáti vero et contérriti existimábant se spíritum vidére. Et dixit eis: "Quid turbáti estis, et cogitatiónes ascéndunt in corda vestra? Vidéte manus meas et pedes, quia ego ipse sum; palpáte et vidéte quia spíritus carnem et ossa non habet, sicut me vidétis habére".

Et, cum hoc dixísset, osténdit eis manus et pedes. Adhuc autem illis non credéntibus et mirántibus prae gáudio, dixit: "Habétis hic áliquid quod manducétur?" At illi obtulérunt ei partem piscis assi et favum mellis. Et, cum manducásset coram eis, sumens relíquias dedit eis.

Et dixit ad eos: "Haec sunt verba quae locútus sum ad vos, cum adhuc essem vobíscum, quóniam necésse est impléri ómnia quae scripta sunt in lege Móysi et Prophétis et psalmis de me". Tunc apéruit illis sensum, ut intellégerent Scriptúras.

Et dixit eis: "Quóniam sic scriptum est, et sic oportébat Christum pati et resúrgere a mórtuis tértia die et praedicári in nómine eius paeniténtiam et remissiónem peccatórum in omnes gentes, incipiéntibus ab Ierosólyma. Vos autem testes estis horum".

Verbum Dómini.

Super oblata

Concéde, quáesumus, Dómine,
semper nos per haec mystéria paschália gratulári,
ut contínua nostrae reparatiónis operátio
perpétuae nobis fiat causa laetítiae.
Per Christum.

Ant. ad communionem   Cf. Lc. 24:46, 26

Opórtuit pati Christum, et resúrgere a mórtuis,
et ita intráre in glóriam suam, allelúia.

Post communionem

Exáudi, Dómine, preces nostras,
ut redemptiónis nostrae sacrosáncta commércia
et vitae nobis cónferant praeséntis auxílium
et gáudia sempitérna concílient.
Per Christum.

Dominica Pentecostes dicitur Missa de Spiritu Sancto, p. 1113.

5
PER ANNUM, I

Ant. ad introitum
Ps. 94:6-7

Veníte, adorémus Deum, et procidámus ante Dóminum,
qui fecit nos; quia ipse est Dóminus Deus noster.

Collecta

Omnípotens sempitérne Deus,
quem patérno nómine invocáre praesúmimus,
pérfice in córdibus nostris spíritum adoptiónis filiórum,
ut promíssam hereditátem íngredi mereámur.
Per Dóminum.

Lectio prima
Eph. 4:1-6

Unum corpus, unus Dominus, una fides, unum baptisma

Léctio Epístolae beáti Pauli apóstoli ad Ephésios

Fratres: Obsecro vos ego vinctus in Dómino, ut digne ambulétis
vocatióne qua vocáti estis cum omni humilitáte et mansuetúdine,
cum patiéntia supportántes ínvicem in caritáte; sollíciti serváre
unitátem spíritus in vínculo pacis: unum corpus et unus spíritus,
sicut vocáti estis in una spe vocatiónis vestrae; unus Dóminus, una
fides, unum baptísma; unus Deus et Pater ómnium, qui est super
omnes et per ómnia et in ómnibus nobis.

Verbum Dómini.

Psalmus responsorius
Cf. Dan. 3:52-53, 58-59

Benedíctus es, Dómine, Deus patrum nostrórum.

℟. Et laudábilis et gloriósus in sáecula.

Et benedíctum nomen glóriae tuae quod est sanctum.

℟. Et laudábile et gloriósum in sáecula.

Benedíctus es in templo sancto glóriae tuae.

℟. Et laudábilis et gloriósus in sáecula.

Benedícant te omnes Angeli et Sancti tui.

℟. Et laudent te, et gloríficent in sáecula.

Benedícant te caeli, terra, mare,
et ómnia quae in eis sunt.

℟. Et laudent te, et gloríficent in sáecula.

℣. Allelúia.   ℟. Allelúia.

℣. Tu Rex glóriae, Christe,
    tu Patris sempitérnus es Fílius.   ℟. Allelúia.

Evangelium   Mt. 5:1-12a

Gaudete et exsultate, quoniam merces vestra copiosa est in caelis

✠ **Léctio sancti Evangélii secúndum Matthǽum**

In illo témpore: Videns Iesus turbas ascéndit in montem, et,
cum sedísset, accessérunt ad eum discípuli eius, et apériens os
suum docébat eos dicens:

"Beáti páuperes spíritu, quóniam ipsórum est regnum
caelórum.

Beáti mites, quóniam ipsi possidébunt terram.

Beáti qui lugent, quóniam ipsi consolabúntur.

Beáti qui esúriunt et sítiunt iustítiam, quóniam ipsi satura-
búntur.

Beáti misericórdes, quóniam ipsi misericórdiam consequéntur.

Beáti mundo corde, quóniam ipsi Deum vidébunt.

Beáti pacífici, quóniam fílii Dei vocabúntur.

Beáti qui persecutiónem patiúntur propter iustítiam, quóniam
ipsórum est regnum caelórum.

Beáti estis, cum maledíxerint vobis et persecúti vos fúerint et
díxerint omne malum advérsum vos, mentiéntes, propter me:
gaudéte et exsultáte, quóniam merces vestra copiósa est in caelis".

Verbum Dómini.

Super oblata

Concéde nobis, quáesumus, Dómine,
haec digne frequentáre mystéria,
quia, quóties huius hóstiae commemorátio celebrátur,
opus nostrae redemptiónis exercétur.
Per Christum.

Ant. ad communionem   Ps. 33:9

Gustáte et vidéte, quóniam suávis est Dóminus;
beátus vir, qui sperat in eo.

Post communionem

Spíritum nobis, Dómine, tuae caritátis infúnde,
ut, quos uno caelésti pane satiásti,
una fácias pietáte concórdes.
Per Christum.

6

PER ANNUM, II

Ant. ad introitum   Ps. 65:4

Omnis terra adóret te, Deus, et psallat tibi;
psalmum dicat nómini tuo, Altíssime.

Collecta

Sancti nóminis tui, Dómine,
timórem páriter et amórem fac nos habére perpétuum,
quia numquam tua gubernatióne destítuis,
quos in soliditáte tuae dilectiónis instítuis.
Per Dóminum.

Lectio prima   Deut. 6:2-6

Audi, Israel: Diliges Dominum ex toto corde tuo

Léctio libri Deuteronómii

Locútus est Móyses pópulo dicens:
  "Time Dóminum Deum tuum et custódi ómnia mandáta et
praecépta eius, quae ego praecípio tibi et fíliis ac nepótibus tuis
cunctis diébus vitae tuae, ut prolongéntur dies tui.
  Audi, Israel, et obsérva, ut fácias quae praecépit tibi Dóminus, et
bene sit tibi, et multiplicéris ámplius, sicut pollícitus est Dóminus
Deus patrum tuórum tibi terram lacte et melle manántem.
  Audi, Israel: Dóminus Deus noster Dóminus unus est. Díliges
Dóminum Deum tuum ex toto corde tuo et ex tota ánima tua et ex
tota fortitúdine tua. Erúntque verba haec, quae ego praecípio tibi
hódie, in corde tuo".
  Verbum Dómini.

Psalmus responsorius   Ps. 17:2-3a, 3bc-4, 47 et 51ab

℟. (2) Díligam te, Dómine, fortitúdo mea.

Díligam te, Dómine, fortitúdo mea.
Dómine, firmaméntum meum
et refúgium meum et liberátor meus;

℟. Díligam te, Dómine, fortitúdo mea.

Deus meus, adiútor meus, et sperábo in eum:
protéctor meus, et cornu salútis meae, et suscéptor meus.
Laudábilem invocábo Dóminum,
et ab inimícis meis salvus ero.

℟. Díligam te, Dómine, fortitúdo mea.

Vivat Dóminus, et benedíctus Adiútor meus,
et exaltétur Deus salútis meae.
Magníficans salútes regis sui,
et fáciens misericórdiam Christo suo.

℟. Díligam te, Dómine, fortitúdo mea.

℣. Allelúia. ℟. Allelúia.   1 Ioan. 2:5

℣. Qui servat verbum Christi,
    vere in hoc cáritas Dei perfécta est. ℟. Allelúia.

Evangelium   Lc. 4:14-21

Hodie impleta est haec Scriptura

☩ Léctio sancti Evangélii secúndum Lucam

In illo témpore: Regréssus est Iesus in virtúte Spíritus in
Galiláeam, et fama éxiit per univérsam regiónem de illo. Et ipse
docébat in synagógis eórum et magnificabátur ab ómnibus.

Et venit Názareth, ubi erat nutrítus, et intrávit secúndum
consuetúdinem suam die sábbati in synagógam et surréxit légere.
Et tráditus est illi liber Isaíae prophétae. Et, ut revólvit librum,
invénit locum, ubi scriptum erat:

"Spíritus Dómini super me; propter quod unxit me, evange-
lizáre paupéribus misit me, sanáre contrítos corde, praedicáre captívis remissiónem et caecis visum, dimíttere con-
fráctos in remissiónem, praedicáre annum Dómini accéptum
et diem retributiónis".

Et, cum plicuísset librum, réddidit minístro et sedit. Et ómnium
in synagóga óculi erant intendéntes in eum.

Coepit autem dícere ad illos: "Quia hódie impléta est haec
Scriptúra in áuribus vestris".

Verbum Dómini.

Super oblata

Concéde nobis, miséricors Deus,
ut haec nostra tibi oblátio sit accépta,
et per eam nobis fons omnis benedictiónis aperiátur.
Per Christum.

Ant. ad communionem   Ioan. 6:52

Panis, quem ego dédero, caro mea est pro sáeculi vita, dicit
Dóminus.

Post communionem

Pane mensae caeléstis refécti, te, Dómine, deprecámur,
ut hoc nutriméntum caritátis corda nostra confírmet,
quátenus ad tibi ministrándum in frátribus excitémur.
Per Christum.

Ant. ad communionem   Ioan. 15:26; 6:11

**Spíritus qui a Patre procédit,
ille me clarificábit, dicit Dóminus.**

Post communionem

**Dómine Deus noster,
qui nos vegetáre dignátus es caeléstibus aliméntis,
suavitátem Spíritus tui penetrálibus nostri cordis infúnde,
ut, quae temporáli devotióne percépimus,
sempitérno múnere capiámus.
Per Christum.**

II. MISSAE PRO CELEBRATIONIBUS SANCTORUM

Missae quae in hac serie inveniuntur adhiberi possunt etiam tamquam
Missae votivae in honorem Sanctorum.

7

DE BEATA MARIA VIRGINE

Ant. ad introitum   Sedulius

**Salve, sancta parens, eníxa puérpera Regem,
qui caelum terramque regit in sáecula saeculórum.**

Collecta

**Famulórum tuórum, quáesumus, Dómine, delíctis ignósce,
ut, qui tibi placére de áctibus nostris non valémus,
Genetrícis Fílii tui Dómini nostri intercessióne salvémur.
Per Dóminum.**

Lectio prima   Gal. 4:4-7
Misit Deus Filium suum, factum ex muliere

Léctio Epístolae beáti Pauli apóstoli ad Gálatas

Fratres: Ubi venit plenitúdo témporis, misit Deus Fílium suum, factum ex mulíere, factum sub lege, ut eos qui sub lege erant redímeret, ut adoptiónem filiórum reciperémus. Quóniam autem estis fílii, misit Deus Spíritum Fílii sui in corda vestra clamántem: "Abba, Pater". Itaque iam non est servus, sed fílius. Quod si fílius, et heres per Deum.

Verbum Dómini.

Psalmus responsorius   Lc. 1:46-47, 48-49, 50-51, 52-53, 54-55
℟. (49) **Fecit mihi magna qui potens est, et sanctum nomen eius.**
**Magníficat ánima mea Dominum:
et exsultávit spíritus meus in Deo salutári meo.**
℟. **Fecit mihi magna qui potens est, et sanctum nomen eius.**

Quia respéxit humilitátem ancillae suae:
ecce enim ex hoc beátam me dicent omnes generatiónes.
Quia fecit mihi magna qui potens est,
et sanctum nomen eius.

℟. Fecit mihi magna qui potens est, et sanctum nomen eius.

Et misericórdia eius a progénie in progénies timéntibus eum.
Fecit poténtiam in brácchio suo: dispérsit supérbos mente cordis sui.

℟. Fecit mihi magna qui potens est, et sanctum nomen eius.

Depósuit poténtes de sede, et exaltávit húmiles.
Esuriéntes implévit bonis, et dívites dimísit inánes.

℟. Fecit mihi magna qui potens est, et sanctum nomen eius.

Suscépit Israel púerum suum, recordátus misericórdiae suae.
Sicut locútus est ad patres nostros, Abraham, et sémini eius in saecula.

℟. Fecit mihi magna qui potens est, et sanctum nomen eius.

℣. Allelúia. ℟. Allelúia.

℣. Felix es, sacra Virgo María, et omni laude digníssima;
quia ex te ortus est sol iustítiae, Christus Deus noster.
℟. Allelúia.

Evangelium Lc. 11:27-28

Beatus venter qui te portavit

✠ Léctio sancti Evangélii secúndum Lucam

In illo témpore: Loquénte Iesu ad turbas, extóllens vocem quaedam múlier de turba dixit illi: "Beátus venter qui te portávit, et úbera quae suxísti". At ille dixit: "Quinímmo beáti qui áudiunt verbum Dei et custódiunt illud".
Verbum Dómini.

Super oblata

Unigéniti tui, Dómine, nobis succúrrat humánitas,
ut, qui natus de Vírgine
Matris integritátem non mínuit, sed sacrávit,
a nostris nos piáculis éxuens,
oblatiónem nostram tibi reddat accéptam. Per Christum.

Ant. ad communionem Cf. Lc. 11:27

Beáta víscera Maríae Vírginis,
quae portavérunt aetérni Patris Fílium.

Post communionem

Quos caelésti, Dómine, mystério recreásti,
poténti semper virtúte defénde, et ad aetérnam pátriam,
beáta Vírgine María adiuvánte, perveníre concéde.
Per Christum.

8
DE SANCTIS APOSTOLIS ET MARTYRIBUS

Ant. ad introitum

Gaudent in caelis ánimae Sanctórum,
qui Christi vestígia sunt secúti;
et quia pro eius amóre sánguinem suum fudérunt,
ídeo cum Christo exsúltant sine fine.

Collecta

Pro Apostolis
Deus, qui nos per beatos Apostolos
intercedentibus sanctis N. N., concede propitius,
ut semper augeatur Ecclesia incrementis
in te credentium populorum.
Per Dominum.

Vel pro Martyribus
Praesta, Dómine, précibus nostris cum exsultatióne provéntum,
ut sanctorum martyrum N. et N.,
quorum diem passiónis ánnua devotióne recólimus,
étiam fídei constántiam subsequámur.
Per Dóminum.

Lectio prima   Sap. 3:1-9
Quasi holocausti hostiam accepit illos
Léctio libri Sapiéntiae
Iustórum ánimae in manu Dei sunt,
et non tanget illos torméntum mortis.
Visi sunt óculis insipiéntium mori,
et aestimáta est afflíctio éxitus illórum,
et, quod a nobis est iter, extermínium; illi autem sunt in pace.
Et si coram homínibus torménta passi sunt,
spes illórum immortalitáte plena est.
In paucis vexáti, in multis bene disponéntur,
quóniam Deus tentávit eos et invénit illos dignos se.
Tamquam aurum in fornáce probávit illos,
et quasi holocáusti hóstiam accépit illos
et in témpore erit respéctus illórum.
Fulgébunt iusti et tamquam scintíllae in arundinéto discúrrent;
iudicábunt natiónes et dominabúntur pópulis,
et regnábit Dóminus illórum in perpétuum.
Qui confídunt in illo intéllegent veritátem,
et fidéles in dilectióne acquiéscent illi,
quóniam donum et pax est eléctis eius.
    Verbum Dómini.

Psalmus responsorius   Ps. 125:1-2ab, 2cd-3, 4-5, 6

℟. (5) Qui séminant in lácrimis, in exsultatióne metent.

In converténdo Dóminus captivitátem Sion,
facti sumus quasi somniántes.
Tunc replétum est gáudio os nostrum,
et lingua nostra exsultatióne.

℟. Qui séminant in lácrimis, in exsultatióne metent.

Tunc dicébant inter gentes:
"Magnificávit Dóminus fácere cum eis".
Magnificávit Dóminus fácere nobíscum;
facti sumus laetántes.

℟. Qui séminant in lácrimis, in exsultatióne metent.

Convérte, Dómine, captivitátem nostram,
sicut torréntes in Austro.
Qui séminant in lácrimis,
in exsultatióne metent.

℟. Qui séminant in lácrimis, in exsultatióne metent.

Eúntes ibant et flebant,
semen spargéndum portántes;
veniéntes autem vénient in exsultatióne
portántes manípulos suos.

℟. Qui séminant in lácrimis, in exsultatióne metent.

℣. Allelúia. ℟. Allelúia.

℣. Te Deum laudámus, te Dóminum confitémur;
   te mártyrum candidátus laudat exércitus. ℟. Allelúia.

Evangelium   Ioan. 15:18-21

Si me persecuti sunt, et vos persequentur

✝ **Léctio sancti Evangélii secúndum Ioánnem**

In illo témpore: Dixit Iesus discípulis suis:

"Si mundus vos odit, scitóte quia me priórem vobis ódio hábuit.
Si de mundo fuissétis, mundus quod suum erat dilígeret; quia
vero de mundo non estis, sed ego elégi vos de mundo, proptérea
odit vos mundus.

Mementóte sermónis mei, quem ego dixi vobis: Non est servus
maior dómino suo. Si me persecúti sunt, et vos persequéntur; si
sermónem meum servavérunt, et vestrum servábunt. Sed haec
ómnia fácient vobis propter nomen meum, quia nésciunt eum qui
misit me".

Verbum Dómini.

Super oblata

Pro Apostolis

**Gloria, Domine, sanctorum Apostolorum N. N.,
perpetuam venerantes,
quaesumus, ut vota nostra suscipias
et ad sacra mysteria celebranda nos digne perducas.
Per Christum.**

Pro Martyribus

**Súscipe, sancte Pater, múnera,
quae in sanctórum mártyrum
commemoratióne deférimus,
et nobis, fámulis tuis, concéde,
ut in confessióne tui nóminis inveníri stábiles mereámur.
Per Christum.**

Ant. ad communionem   Lc. 22:28-30

**Vos estis qui permansístis mecum in tentatiónibus meis,
et ego dispóno vobis regnum, dicit Dóminus,
ut edátis et bibátis super mensam meam in regno meo.**

Post communionem

Pro Apostolis

**Perceptis, Domine, sacramentis,   .
supplices in Spiritu Sancto deprecamur,
ut quae pro Apostolorum N. N.
veneranda gerimus passione, nos in tua dilectione conservent.
Per Christum.**

Pro Martyribus

**Deus, qui crucis mystérium
in sanctis martýribus tuis mirabíliter illustrásti,
concéde propítius, ut, ex hoc sacrifício roboráti,
Christo fidéliter haereámus,
et in Ecclésia ad salútem ómnium operémur.
Per Christum.**

9

DE SANCTIS

Ant. ad introitum   Ps. 144:10-11

**Confiteántur tibi, Dómine, ómnia ópera tua,
et sancti tui benedícent tibi:
glóriam regni tui dicent, et poténtiam tuam loquéntur.**

Collecta

**Omnípotens aetérne Deus,
qui per glorificatiónem Sanctórum
novíssima dilectiónis tuae nobis arguménta largíris,
concéde propítius,
ut, ad Unigénitum tuum fidéliter imitándum,
et ipsórum intercessióne commendémur,
et incitémur exémplo. Per Dóminum.**

Lectio prima   Eph. 3:14-19

Scire supereminentem scientiae caritatem Christi

Léctio Epístolae beáti Pauli apóstoli ad Ephésios

Fratres: Flecto génua mea ad Patrem Dómini nostri Iesu Christi, ex quo omnis patérnitas in caelis et in terra nominátur; ut det vobis secúndum divítias glóriae suae virtúte corroborári per Spíritum eius in interiórem hóminem; Christum habitáre per fidem in córdibus vestris; in caritáte radicáti et fundáti, ut possítis comprehéndere cum ómnibus sanctis quae sit latitúdo et longitúdo et sublímitas et profúndum; scire étiam supereminéntem sciéntiae caritátem Christi, ut impleámini in omnem plenitúdinem Dei.

Verbum Dómini.

Psalmus responsorius   Ps. 1:1-2, 3, 4 et 6

℟. (Ps. 39:5a) **Beátus vir qui pósuit Dóminum spem suam.**

**Beátus vir qui non ábiit in consílio impiórum,
et in via peccatórum non stetit,
et in convéntu derisórum non sedit;
sed in lege Dómini volúntas eius,
et in lege eius meditátur die ac nocte.**

℟. **Beátus vir qui pósuit Dóminum spem suam.**

**Et erit tamquam lignum plantátum secus decúrsus aquarum,
quod fructum suum dabit in témpore suo;
et fólium eius non défluet,
et ómnia quaecúmque fáciet prosperabúntur.**

℟. **Beátus vir qui pósuit Dóminum spem suam.**

**Non sic ímpii, non sic, sed tamquam pulvis quem próicit ventus.
Quóniam novit Dóminus viam iustórum,
et iter impiórum períbit.**

℟. **Beátus vir qui pósuit Dóminum spem suam.**

℣. Allelúia. ℟. Allelúia.   Ioan. 15:4 et 5b

℣. Manéte in me, et ego in vobis, dicit Dóminus:
   qui manet in me fert fructum multum. ℟. Allelúia.

Evangelium   Ioan. 15:1-8

Qui manet in me, et ego in eo, hic fert fructum multum

✛ Léctio sancti Evangélii secúndum Ioánnem

In illo témpore: Dixit Iesus discípulis suis:

"Ego sum vitis vera, et Pater meus agrícola est. Omnem pálmitem in me non feréntem fructum tollet eum, et omnem qui fert fructum purgábit eum, ut fructum plus áfferat.

Iam vos mundi estis propter sermónem quem locútus sum vobis. Manéte in me, et ego in vobis. Sicut palmes non potest ferre fructum a semetípso, nisi mánserit in vite, sic nec vos, nisi in me manséritis.

Ego sum vitis, vos pálmites; qui manet in me, et ego in eo, hic fert fructum multum, quia sine me nihil potéstis fácere. Si quis in me non mánserit, mittétur foras sicut palmes et aréscet, et cólligent eum et in ignem mittent, et ardet. Si manséritis in me, et verba mea in vobis mánserint, quodcúmque voluéritis petétis, et fiet vobis.

In hoc clarificátus est Pater meus, ut fructum plúrimum afferátis et efficiámini mei discípuli".

Verbum Dómini.

Super oblata

Preces nostras, Dómine, quáesumus, propitiátus admítte,
et, ut digne tuis famulémur altáribus,
Sanctórum tuórum nos intercessióne custódi.
Per Christum.

Ant. ad communionem   Ps. 67:4

Iusti epuléntur, et exsúltent in conspéctu Dei,
et delecténtur in laetítia.

Post communionem

Omnípotens sempitérne Deus,
Pater totíus consolatiónis et pacis,
praesta famíliae tuae, in celebritáte Sanctórum
ad laudem tui nóminis congregátae,
ut, per Unigéniti tui sumpta mystéria,
pignus accípiat redemptiónis aetérnae.
Per Christum.

III. MISSAE VOTIVAE

Hae Missae votivae sumuntur etiam ad celebrandum mysterium vel sanctum, die quo in calendario inscribuntur.
Pro Missa votiva B. M. V. dicitur Missa, quae invenitur p. 1104.

10

DE SANCTISSIMA EUCHARISTIA

Ant. ad introitum   Ps. 80:17

Cibávit eos ex ádipe fruménti, et de petra melle saturávit eos.

Collecta

Deus, qui nobis sub Sacraménto mirábili
passiónis tuae memóriam reliquísti,
tríbue, quáesumus,
ita nos Córporis et Sánguinis tui sacra mystéria venerári,
ut redemptiónis tuae fructum in nobis iúgiter sentiámus.
Qui vivis et regnas.

Lectio prima   1 Cor. 10:16-17

Unus panis, unum corpus multi sumus

Léctio Epístolae primae beáti Pauli apóstoli ad Corínthios

Fratres: Calix benedictiónis, cui benedícimus, nonne communicátio Sánguinis Christi est? et panis, quem frángimus, nonne participátio Córporis Dómini est?
Quóniam unus panis, unum corpus multi sumus, omnes qui de uno pane participámus.

Verbum Dómini.

Psalmus responsorius   Ps. 22:1-3a, 3b-4, 5, 6

℟. (1) **Dóminus pascit me, et nihil mihi déerit.**

Dóminus pascit me, et nihil mihi déerit:
in páscuis viréntibus me collocávit,
super aquas quiétis edúxit me, ánimam meam refécit.

℟. **Dóminus pascit me, et nihil mihi déerit.**

Dedúxit me super sémitas iustítiae propter nomen suum.
Nam et si ambulávero in valle umbrae mortis,
non timébo mala, quóniam tu mecum es.
Virga tua et báculus tuus ipsa me consoláta sunt.

℟. **Dóminus pascit me, et nihil mihi déerit.**

Parásti in conspéctu meo mensam
advérsus eos qui tríbulant me;
impinguásti in óleo caput meum,
et calix meus redúndat.

℟. Dóminus pascit me, et nihil mihi déerit.

Etenim benígnitas et misericórdia subsequéntur me
ómnibus diébus vitae meae,
et inhabitábo in domo Dómini
in longitúdinem diérum.

℟. Dóminus pascit me, et nihil mihi déerit.

℣. Allelúia. ℟. Allelúia.   Ioan. 6:51-52

℣. Ego sum panis vivus, qui de caelo descéndi, dicit Dóminus;
    si quis manducáverit ex hoc pane, vivet in aetérnum.
℟. Allelúia.

Evangelium   Ioan. 6:51-59

Caro mea vere est cibus, et sanguis meus vere est potus

✠ Léctio sancti Evangélii secúndum Ioánnem

In illo témpore: Dixit Iesus turbis Iudaeórum:

"Ego sum panis vivus qui de caelo descéndi. Si quis
manducáverit ex hoc pane vivet in aetérnum, et panis, quem ego
dabo, caro mea est pro mundi vita".

Litigábant ergo Iudáei ad ínvicem dicéntes: "Quómodo potest
hic nobis carnem suam dare ad manducándum?"

Dixit ergo eis Iesus: "Amen, amen dico vobis, nisi
manducavéritis carnem Fílii hóminis et bibéritis eius sánguinem,
non habébitis vitam in vobis.

Qui mandúcat meam carnem et bibit meum sánguinem habet
vitam aetérnam, et ego resuscitábo eum in novíssimo die. Caro
enim mea vere est cibus, et sanguis meus vere est potus.

Qui mandúcat meam carnem et bibit meum sánguinem in me
manet, et ego in illo. Sicut misit me vivens Pater, et ego vivo
propter Patrem, et qui mandúcat me, et ipse vivet propter me.

Hic est panis qui de caelo descéndit. Non sicut manducavérunt
patres vestri manna et mórtui sunt. Qui mandúcat hunc panem
vivet in aetérnum".

Verbum Dómini.

Super oblata

Ecclésiae tuae, quáesumus, Dómine,
unitátis et pacis propítius dona concéde,
quae sub oblátis munéribus mýstice designántur.
Per Christum.

Ant. ad communionem

Qui mandúcat meam carnem et bibit meum sánguinem,
in me manet et ego in eo, dicit Dóminus.

Post communionem

Fac nos, quáesumus, Dómine,
divinitátis tuae sempitérna fruitióne repléri,
quam pretiósi Córporis et Sánguinis tui
temporális percéptio praefigúrat.
Qui vivis.

11

DE SPIRITU SANCTO

Ant. ad introitum

Cáritas Dei diffúsa est in córdibus nostris,
per inhabitántem Spíritum eius in nobis.

Collecta

Mentes nostras, quáesumus, Dómine,
Paráclitus qui a te procédit illúminet,
et indúcat in omnem, sicut tuus promísit Fílius, veritátem.
Per Dóminum.

Lectio prima

Caritas Dei diffusa est in cordibus nostris per Spiritum Sanctum,
qui datus est nobis

Léctio Epístolae beáti Pauli apóstoli ad Romános

Fratres: Iustificáti ex fide pacem habeámus ad Deum per Dóminum nostrum Iesum Christum, per quem et habémus accéssum per fidem in grátiam istam, in qua stamus et gloriámur in spe glóriae filiórum Dei.

Spes autem non confúndit, quia cáritas Dei diffúsa est in córdibus nostris per Spíritum Sanctum, qui datus est nobis.

Ut quid enim Christus, cum adhuc infírmi essémus, secúndum tempus pro ímpiis mórtuus est? Vix enim pro iusto quis móritur; nam pro bono fórsitan quis áudeat mori? Comméndat autem caritátem suam Deus in nobis, quóniam, cum adhuc peccatóres essémus, secúndum tempus Christus pro nobis mórtuus est.

Verbum Dómini.

Psalmus responsorius   Ps. 95:1-2a, 2b-3, 9-10a, 11-12

℟. (3) Annuntiáte in ómnibus pópulis mirabília Dei.

Cantáte Dómino cánticum novum,
cantáte Dómino, omnis terra.
Cantáte Dómino, benedícite nómini eius,

℟. Annuntiáte in ómnibus pópulis mirabília Dei.

annuntiáte de die in diem salutáre eius.
Annuntiáte inter gentes glóriam eius,
in ómnibus pópulis mirabília eius.

℟. Annuntiáte in ómnibus pópulis mirabília Dei.

Adoráte Dóminum in splendóre sancto.
Contremíscite a fácie eius, univérsa terra,
dícite in géntibus: "Dóminus regnávit".

℟. Annuntiáte in ómnibus pópulis mirabília Dei.

Laeténtur caeli et exsúltet terra,
sonet mare et plenitúdo eius;
gaudébunt campi et ómnia quae in eis sunt.
Tunc exsultábunt ómnia ligna silvárum.

℟. Annuntiáte in ómnibus pópulis mirabília Dei.

℣. Allelúia.   ℟. Allelúia.

℣. Veni, Sancte Spíritus,
     reple tuórum corda fidélium,
     et tui amóris in eis ignem accénde.   ℟. Allelúia.

Evangelium   Ioan. 14:23-26
Spiritus Sanctus docebit vos omnia

✠ Léctio sancti Evangélii secúndum Ioánnem

In illo témpore: Dixit Iesus discípulis suis:
   "Si quis díligit me, sermónem meum servábit, et Pater meus
díliget eum, et ad eum veniémus et mansiónem apud eum
faciémus. Qui non díligit me, sermónes meos non servat. Et
sermónem quem audístis non est meus, sed eius, qui misit me,
Patris.
   Haec locútus sum vobis apud vos manens. Paráclitus autem
Spíritus Sanctus, quem mittet Pater in nómine meo, ille vos
docébit ómnia et súggeret vobis ómnia quaecúmque díxero
vobis".
   Verbum Dómini.

Super oblata

Haec oblátio, quáesumus, Dómine,
cordis nostri máculas emúndet,
ut Sancti Spíritus digna efficiátur habitátio.
Per Christum.

12
PRO DEFUNCTIS

Ant. ad introitum

Dona eis, Dómine, réquiem sempitérnam
et imple splendóribus ánimas eórum.

Collecta

Deus, qui Unigénitum tuum, devícta morte,
ad caeléstia transíre fecísti,
concéde fámulis tuis N. et N.,
ut, huius vitae mortalitáte destrúcta,
te conditórem et redemptórem possint perpétuo contemplári.
Per Dóminum.

Lectio prima   2 Cor. 5:1, 6-10

Habemus domum aeternam in caelis

Léctio Epístolae secúndae beáti Pauli apóstoli ad Corínthios

Fratres: Scimus quóniam, si terréstris domus nostra huius
habitatiónis dissolvátur, quod aedificatiónem ex Deo habémus
domum non manufáctam, aetérnam in caelis.

Audéntes ígitur, semper sciéntes quóniam, dum sumus in
córpore, peregrinámur a Dómino (per fidem enim ambulámus et
non per spéciem), audémus autem et bonam voluntátem
habémus magis peregrinári a córpore et praeséntes esse ad
Dóminum. Et ídeo conténdimus sive abséntes sive praeséntes
placére illi.

Omnes enim nos manifestári opórtet ante tribúnal Christi, ut
réferat unusquísque própria córporis, prout gessit, sive bonum
sive malum.

Verbum Dómini.

Psalmus responsorius   Ps. 26:1, 4, 7 et 8b et 9a, 13-14

℟. (13) Credo vidére bona Dómini in terra vivéntium.

Dóminus illuminátio mea et salus mea, quem timébo?
Dóminus protéctor vitae meae, a quo trepidábo?

℟. Credo vidére bona Dómini in terra vivéntium.

Unum pétii a Dómino, hoc requíram:
ut hábitem in domo Dómini ómnibus diébus vitae meae,
ut vídeam voluptátem Dómini,
et vísitem templum eius.

℟. Credo vidére bona Dómini in terra vivéntium.

Exáudi, Dómine, vocem meam qua clamávi,
miserére mei et exáudi me.
Fáciem tuam, Dómine, requíram.
Ne avértas fáciem tuam a me.

℟. Credo vidére bona Dómini in terra vivéntium.

Credo vidére bona Dómini in terra vivéntium.
Exspécta Dóminum, viríliter age,
et confortétur cor tuum, et sústine Dóminum.

℟. Credo vidére bona Dómini in terra vivéntium.

℟. Allelúia vel Versus ante Evangelium (p. 1096)   Apoc. 14:13

Beáti mórtui qui in Dómino moriúntur;
requiéscant a labóribus suis;
ópera enim illórum sequúntur illos.

Evangelium   Ioan. 6:37-40

Qui credit in Filium habet vitam aeternam, et ego resuscitabo eum
in novissimo die

✠ Léctio sancti Evangélii secúndum Ioánnem

In illo témpore: Dixit Iesus turbis:
   "Omne, quod dat mihi Pater, ad me véniet; et eum, qui venit ad
me, non eíciam foras. Quia descéndi de caelo non ut fáciam
voluntátem meam, sed voluntátem eius, qui misit me.
   Haec est autem volúntas eius, qui misit me, Patris, ut omne,
quod dedit mihi, non perdam ex eo, sed resúscitem illud in
novíssimo die.
   Haec est autem volúntas Patris mei, qui misit me, ut omnis qui
videt Fílium et credit in eum hábeat vitam aetérnam; et ego
resuscitábo eum in novíssimo die".
   Verbum Dómini.

Super oblata
Hóstias, quáesumus, Dómine,
quas tibi pro fámulis tuis offérimus,
propitiátus inténde,
ut, quibus fídei christiánae méritum contulísti,
dones et práemium.
Per Christum.

Ant. ad communionem
Pro quorum memória Corpus et Sanguis Christi súmitur:
dona eis, Dómine, réquiem sempitérnam.

Post communionem

Multíplica, Dómine, his sacrifíciis suscéptis,
super fámulos tuos defúnctos misericórdiam tuam,
et, quibus donásti baptísmi grátiam,
da eis aeternórum plenitúdinem gaudiórum.
Per Christum.

APPENDIX

FORMULA GENERALIS ORATIONIS FIDELIUM

Ad Deum Patrem omnipoténtem,
qui vult omnes hómines salvos fíeri
et ad agnitiónem veritátis veníre,
tota mentis nostrae, fratres caríssimi, dirigátur orátio.

1. Pro Ecclésia sancta Dei:
ut eam Dóminus custodíre et fovére dignétur,
Dóminum deprecémur.

℞. Praesta, aetérne omnípotens Deus.

2. Pro totíus orbis pópulis:
ut inter eos Dóminus concórdiam serváre dignétur,
Dóminum deprecémur.

℞. Praesta, aetérne omnípotens Deus.

3. Pro ómnibus qui váriis premúntur necessitátibus:
ut omnes Dóminus subleváre dignétur,
Dóminum deprecémur.

℞. Praesta, aetérne omnípotens Deus.

4. Pro nobismetípsis ac pro nostra communitáte:
ut nos omnes Dóminus hóstiam sibi acceptábilem
admíttere dignétur,
Dóminum deprecémur.

℞. Praesta, aetérne omnípotens Deus.

Omnípotens sempitérne Deus,
qui salvas omnes et néminem vis períre,
exáudi preces pópuli tui, et praesta;
ut et mundi cursus pacífico nobis tuo órdine dirigátur,
et Ecclésia tua tranquílla devotióne laetétur.
Per Christum Dóminum nostrum.

℞. Amen.

RITE OF COMMISSIONING
A SPECIAL MINISTER
TO DISTRIBUTE HOLY COMMUNION
ON A SINGLE OCCASION

RITE OF COMMISSIONING
A SPECIAL MINISTER
TO DISTRIBUTE HOLY COMMUNION
ON A SINGLE OCCASION

A person who, in a case of real necessity, is authorized to distribute holy communion on a single occasion* should normally be commissioned according to the following rite.

During the breaking of the bread and the commingling, the person who is to distribute holy communion comes to the altar and stands before the celebrant. After the **Lamb of God** the priest blesses him/her with these words:

**Today you are to distribute
the body and blood of Christ
to your brothers and sisters.
May the Lord bless ✢ you, N.**

℞. **Amen.**

When the priest has himself received communion in the usual way, he gives communion to the minister of the eucharist. Then he gives him/her the paten or other vessel with the hosts. They then go to give communion to the people.

*See instruction *Immensae caritatis* I, nos. 2, 6.

Appendix VI

ADDITIONAL EUCHARISTIC PRAYERS

EUCHARISTIC PRAYERS FOR MASSES WITH CHILDREN AND MASSES OF RECONCILIATION

FOREWORD

On 1 November 1974 the Sacred Congregation for Divine Worship approved the draft Latin texts of five new eucharistic prayers which Pope Paul VI had asked it to prepare: three eucharistic prayers for Masses with children and two for Masses of reconciliation.

These prayers were composed in response to requests made by several conferences of bishops and by individual bishops from various regions subsequent to the 27 April 1973 circular letter of the Congregation for Divine Worship concerning eucharistic prayers, *Eucharistiae participationem*.

The Directory for Masses with Children (1 November 1973) previously had indicated that the Apostolic See was considering the approval of special eucharistic prayers for Masses with children. It included a directive stating that the presidential prayers of the Sacramentary should be adapted in Masses with children in such a way that the children consider them to be expressions of their own religious life (see Directory for Masses with Children, no. 51). However, with regard to the eucharistic prayer, the same document decreed that only Eucharistic Prayers I–IV were to be used with children "until the Apostolic See makes other provision for Masses with children" (no. 52). This, in fact, was to occur one year later with the publication of the three eucharistic prayers for Masses with children.

The two eucharistic prayers for Masses of reconciliation originally were intended for use during the Holy Year of 1975. However, in its decree of approval, *Postquam de precibus*, the Congregation for Divine Worship stated that these eucharistic prayers could also be used to great advantage for other special celebrations with the theme of reconciliation and penance, especially during Lent and on the occasion of pilgrimages or spiritual meetings.

The use of the eucharistic prayers for Masses with children is restricted to Masses which are celebrated for children only or Masses at which the majority of the participants are children. The Congregation for Divine Worship further stated that an assembly of children is to be understood in accordance with the Directory for Masses with Children, that is, one consisting of children who have not yet reached the age of preadolescence.

The English translations of the five eucharistic prayers were approved for use in the dioceses of the United States of America by the Bishops' Committee on the Liturgy and by the Executive Committee of the National Conference of Catholic Bishops. Confirmation of that decision was decreed by the Sacred Congregation for Divine Worship on 5 June 1975 (Prot. CD 738/75). The decree noted that all three eucharistic prayers for Masses with children and the two eucharistic prayers for Masses of reconciliation may be used in the dioceses of the United States *ad experimentum* for three years. That faculty was extended for another three years on 10 December 1977 (Prot. CD 2250/77). And finally on 15 December 1980 (Prot. CD 2210/80) the Sacred Congregation for the Sacraments and Divine Worship extended the faculty for the use of these prayers indefinitely, until further notice.

Eucharistic Prayers for Masses with Children

INTRODUCTION

1. The texts of the eucharistic prayer adapted for children must contribute toward their taking part more fruitfully in Masses for adults.

Thus the Directory for Masses with Children establishes that some texts of the Mass are never to be altered for children "lest the difference between Masses with children and Masses with adults become too great." Among such texts are the "acclamations and responses of the people to the priest's greetings."[1] The dialogue for the preface of these eucharistic prayers is therefore always the same as in Masses for adults and the same holds for the *Sanctus,* apart from what is stated in nos. 18 and 23.

2. In keeping with the apostolic constitution *Missale Romanum,* the words of the Lord in every formulary of the canon are also exactly the same.[2]

3. Before the words Do this in memory of me a sentence has been introduced, Then he said to them, in order to make clearer for children the distinction between what is said over the bread and wine and what refers to the celebration's being repeated.

4. Each of the three eucharistic prayers for Masses with children contains, with a very few exceptions, all those elements that, according to the General Instruction of the Roman Missal no. 55, make up the eucharistic prayer.

5. Not only do they contain the required elements, but they also express those elements that, following tradition, have always been expressed, for example, in the anamnesis or the epiclesis, but in a simpler style of language, suited to the understanding of children.

6. Although a simpler style of language was adopted, the authors always had in mind the importance of avoiding the danger of childish language, which would jeopardize the dignity of the eucharistic celebration, especially if it affected the words to be said by the celebrant himself.

7. Because the principles of active participation are in some respects even more significant for children, the number of acclamations in the eucharistic prayers for Masses with children has been increased, in order to enlarge this kind of participation and make it more effective.[3] This has been done without obscuring the nature of the eucharistic prayer as a presidential prayer.

8. Because it is very difficult for only one eucharistic prayer to be used throughout the world in Masses with children, in view of cultural differences and the mentality of various peoples, it seemed appropriate to propose at least three texts differing in character (explained in nos. 23–25).

TRANSLATION OF THESE PRAYERS INTO VARIOUS LANGUAGES

9. It is for the conference of bishops to choose one of the drafts proposed here and to see that the text is translated into the vernacular so that it corresponds fully to pastoral, pedagogical, and liturgical needs. This text must be approved by the conference of bishops and sent to the Apostolic See for confirmation.

10. It is strongly recommended that this work of translation be given to a group of men and women with competences not only in the area of liturgy, but also of pedagogy, catechetics, language, and music.

11. The committee of translators should always remember that in this case the Latin text is not intended for liturgical use. Therefore it is not to be merely translated.

The Latin text does determine the purpose, substance, and general form of these prayers and these elements should be the same in the translations into the various languages. Features proper to Latin (which never developed a special style of speaking with children) are never to be carried over into the vernacular texts intended for liturgical use: specifically, the Latin preference for compound sentences, the somewhat ornate and repetitious style, and the so-called cursus. The style of the vernacular text is in every aspect to be adapted to the spirit of the respective language as well as to the manner of speaking with children in each language concerning matters of great importance. These principles are all the more pertinent in the case of languages that are far removed from Latin, especially non-Western languages. An example of translation for each eucharistic prayer in one of the Western languages is provided as a possible aid to the translator.

12. In translating these texts careful distinction should be made between the several literary genres that occur in the eucharistic prayer, namely, the preface, the intercessions, acclamations, etc., in keeping with the sound principles laid down in the instruction of 25 January 1969 for the translation of liturgical texts.[4]

13. In addition, the conferences of bishops should see that new *musical settings* in keeping with the culture of the region are prepared for the parts of the prayers to be sung by the children.

LITURGICAL USE OF THESE PRAYERS

14. Use of these prayers is strictly limited to Masses celebrated with children. But the right of the bishop as determined in the Directory for Masses with Children[5] remains intact.

---

1. See Directory for Masses with Children, no. 39: *AAS* 66 (1974) 41–42.
2. *AAS* 61 (1969) 219.
3. See Directory for Masses with Children, no. 22: *AAS* 66 (1974) 36.

4. See Consilium for the Implementation of the Constitution on the Liturgy, *Instruction on Translation of Liturgical Texts,* 25 January 1969: *Notitiae* 5 (1969) 3–12.
5. See Directory for Masses with Children, no. 19: *AAS* 66 (1974) 35.

15. From the three texts of the eucharistic prayer the one that seems best suited to the circumstances of the children should be chosen: either the first for its greater simplicity, the second for its greater participation, or the third for the variations it affords.

16. Introducing new acclamations into liturgical use is made easier if a cantor or one of the children leads and then all repeat the acclamations in song or recitation. Care should be taken in the preparation of texts in the vernacular, however, that acclamations have a simple introduction, for example, use of a cue word to invite the acclamation.

17. In place of the new acclamations found in these eucharistic prayers, the conferences of bishops may introduce others, provided these convey the same spirit.

18. It is necessary that children too learn to sing or recite the *Sanctus*, but the rule remains in effect that sometimes it is permissible to use "with the melodies appropriate translations accepted by competent authority, even if these do not agree completely with the liturgical texts, in order to facilitate the participation of the children."[6] Wherever, among the various peoples, responsorial singing is the custom, the conference of bishops may also allow responsorial singing of the *Sanctus*.

19. The place for the acclamation by the faithful at the end of the consecration has been slightly changed. This is done for pedagogical reasons. In order that the children may clearly understand the connection between the words of the Lord, Do this in memory of me, and the anamnesis by the priest celebrant, the acclamation, whether of memorial or of praise, is not made until after the anamnesis has been recited.

20. To encourage participation by the children, it is permissible, in keeping with the Directory for Masses with Children, to insert special reasons for giving thanks before the dialogue for the preface.[7] The regulations of the Directory no. 33 also apply for participation by means of gestures and postures. Above all, great stress should be placed on inner participation, and what is said in no. 23 about the celebration as festive, familial, and meditative is especially true of the eucharistic prayer.

21. To encourage this inner participation, which should be a matter of deepest concern for pastors of children, careful catechetical instruction must precede and follow the celebration. Among the texts that this catechesis will rightly clarify for the children, a preeminent place belongs to the eucharistic prayers, which will be used at the high point in the celebration.[8]

22. The rubrics for the individual eucharistic prayers appearing in the Latin text are all to be incorporated into the vernacular text.

Special rubrics for concelebration as are found in the four eucharistic prayers already in use are lacking in these prayers. In view of the psychology of children it seems better to refrain from concelebration when Mass is celebrated with them.

A. EUCHARISTIC PRAYER I

23. In order to accustom the children more easily to the *Sanctus*, Eucharistic Prayer I divides it into the two parts concluded by the acclamation, Hosanna in the highest. In keeping with no. 16, these acclamations may be sung or recited by repeating them after a cantor or one of the children. The third time the entire *Sanctus* may be sung by all. After the anamnesis of Prayer I, one of the acclamations approved for the four eucharistic prayers may be used in place of the simpler acclamation given in the text.

B. EUCHARISTIC PRAYER II

24. In Eucharistic Prayer II, except for the *Sanctus* and the acclamation after the anamnesis, other optional acclamations may be substituted. The acclamations that have been inserted after the words of the Lord spoken over the bread and the wine must be regarded as a shared meditation on the eucharistic mystery and sung as such.

C. EUCHARISTIC PRAYER III

25. In Eucharistic Prayer III variable parts are indicated for only one occasion, namely, for the Easter season. It is intended, however, that similar variable parts be approved by the conference of bishops for other seasons and occasions and, after the requisite confirmation by the Apostolic See, put into use in keeping with the circular letter on eucharistic prayers no. 10.[9] In preparing these texts care should be taken to ensure the due correlation of their three parts (preface, part after the *Sanctus*, epiclesis).

After the consecration, the same acclamation occurs three times in the same way in order that the character of praise and thanksgiving belonging to the entire eucharistic prayer may be conveyed to the children.

---

6. See *ibid.*, no. 31: *AAS* 66 (1974) 39.

7. See *ibid.*, no. 22: *AAS* 66 (1974) 37.

8. See *ibid.*, no. 12: *AAS* 66 (1974) 33.

9. *AAS* 65 (1973) 344.

EUCHARISTIC PRAYER FOR MASSES WITH CHILDREN

I

The priest begins the eucharistic prayer.
With hands extended he sings or says:

Priest: **The Lord be with you.**

People: **And also with you.**

Priest: **Lift up your hearts.**

People: **We lift them up to the Lord.**

Priest: **Let us give thanks to the Lord our God.**

People: **It is right to give him thanks and praise.**

Celebrant alone

The priest, with hands extended, continues:

God our Father,
you have brought us here together
so that we can give you thanks and praise
for all the wonderful things you have done.

We thank you for all that is beautiful in the world
and for the happiness you have given us.
We praise you for daylight
and for your word which lights up our minds.
We praise you for the earth,
and all the people who live on it,
and for our life which comes from you.

We know that you are good.
You love us and do great things for us.
[So we all sing (say) together:

Holy, holy, holy Lord, God of power and might,
heaven and earth are full of your glory.
    Hosanna in the highest.]

Celebrant alone

The priest, with hands extended, says:

Father,
you are always thinking about your people;
you never forget us.
You sent us your Son Jesus,
who gave his life for us
and who came to save us.

He cured sick people;
he cared for those who were poor
and wept with those who were sad.
He forgave sinners
and taught us to forgive each other.
He loved everyone
and showed us how to be kind.
He took children in his arms and blessed them.
[So we are glad to sing (say):

Blessed is he who comes in the name of the Lord.
    Hosanna in the highest.]

Celebrant alone

The priest, with hands extended, continues:

God our Father,
all over the world your people praise you.
So now we pray with the whole Church:
with N., our pope, and N., our bishop.
In heaven the blessed Virgin Mary,
the apostles and all the saints
always sing your praise.
Now we join with them and with the angels
to adore you as we sing (say):

All say:

Holy, holy, holy Lord, God of power and might,
heaven and earth are full of your glory.
    Hosanna in the highest.
Blessed is he who comes in the name of the Lord.
    Hosanna in the highest.

Celebrant alone

The priest, with hands extended, says:

God our Father,
you are most holy
and we want to show you that we are grateful.

Celebrant with concelebrants

We bring you bread and wine

He joins his hands and, holding them outstretched over the offerings, says:

and ask you to send your Holy Spirit to make these gifts

He joins his hands and, making the sign of the cross once over both bread and chalice, says:

the body ✝ and blood of Jesus your Son.

With hands joined, he continues:

Then we can offer to you
what you have given to us.

On the night before he died,
Jesus was having supper with his apostles.

He takes the bread and, raising it a little above the altar, continues:

He took bread from the table.
He gave you thanks and praise.
Then he broke the bread, gave it to his friends, and said:

He bows slightly.

Take this, all of you, and eat it:
this is my body which will be given up for you.

He shows the consecrated host to the people, places it on the paten, and genuflects in adoration.

Then he continues:

When supper was ended,

He takes the chalice and, raising it a little above the altar, continues:

Jesus took the cup that was filled with wine.
He thanked you, gave it to his friends, and said:

He bows slightly.

Take this, all of you, and drink from it:
this is the cup of my blood,
the blood of the new and everlasting covenant.
It will be shed for you and for all
so that sins may be forgiven.
Then he said to them:
do this in memory of me.

Celebrant with concelebrants

He shows the chalice to the people, places it on the corporal, and genuflects in adoration. Then, with hands extended, the priest says:

We do now what Jesus told us to do.
We remember his death and his resurrection
and we offer you, Father, the bread that gives us
** life,**
and the cup that saves us.
Jesus brings us to you;
welcome us as you welcome him.

Celebrant alone

Let us proclaim our faith:

All say: **a   Christ has died,
Christ is risen,
Christ will come again.**

**b   Dying you destroyed our death,
rising you restored our life.
Lord Jesus, come in glory.**

**c   When we eat this bread and drink this cup,
we proclaim your death, Lord Jesus,
until you come in glory.**

**d   Lord, by your cross and resurrection
you have set us free.
You are the Savior of the world.**

Celebrant with concelebrants

*Then, with hands extended, the priest
continues:*

**Father,
because you love us,
you invite us to come to your table.
Fill us with the joy of the Holy Spirit
as we receive the body and blood of your Son.**

Celebrant or one concelebrant

**Lord,
you never forget any of your children.
We ask you to take care of those we love,
especially of N. and N.,
and we pray for those who have died.**

**Remember everyone who is suffering from pain or
sorrow.
Remember Christians everywhere
and all other people in the world.**

**We are filled with wonder and praise
when we see what you do for us
through Jesus your Son,
and so we sing:**

Celebrant alone or with concelebrants

He joins his hands, takes the chalice
and the paten with the host and, lifting
them up, he sings or says:

**Through him,
with him,
in him,
in the unity of the Holy Spirit,
all glory and honor is yours,
almighty Father,
for ever and ever.**

The people respond: **Amen.**

EUCHARISTIC PRAYER FOR MASSES WITH CHILDREN

II

The priest begins the eucharistic prayer.
With hands extended he sings or says:

Priest:	**The Lord be with you.**
People:	**And also with you.**
Priest:	**Lift up your hearts.**
People:	**We lift them up to the Lord.**
Priest:	**Let us give thanks to the Lord our God.**
People:	**It is right to give him thanks and praise.**

Celebrant alone

The priest, with hands extended,
continues:

**God, our loving Father,
we are glad to give you thanks and praise
because you love us.
With Jesus we sing your praise:**

All say:

Glory to God in the highest.

or

Hosanna in the highest.

The priest says:

**Because you love us,
you gave us this great and beautiful world.
With Jesus we sing your praise:**

All say:

Glory to God in the highest.

or

Hosanna in the highest.

The priest says:

**Because you love us,
you sent Jesus your Son
to bring us to you
and to gather us around him
as the children of one family.
With Jesus we sing your praise:**

All say: **Glory to God in the highest.**

or

Hosanna in the highest.

The priest says: **For such great love**
we thank you with the angels and saints
as they praise you and sing (say):

All say: **Holy, holy, holy Lord, God of power and might,**
heaven and earth are full of your glory.
Hosanna in the highest.
Blessed is he who comes in the name of the Lord.
Hosanna in the highest.

Celebrant alone
The priest, with hands extended, says: **Blessed be Jesus, whom you sent**
to be the friend of children and of the poor.

He came to show us
how we can love you, Father,
by loving one another.
He came to take away sin,
which keeps us from being friends,
and hate, which makes us all unhappy.

He promised to send the Holy Spirit,
to be with us always
so that we can live as your children.

All say: **Blessed is he who comes in the name of the Lord.**
Hosanna in the highest.

Celebrant with concelebrants
He joins his hands and, holding them
outstretched over the offerings, says: **God our Father,**
we now ask you
to send your Holy Spirit
to change these gifts of bread and wine

He joins his hands and, making the sign
of the cross once over both bread and
chalice, says: **into the body ☩ and blood**
of Jesus Christ, our Lord.

The night before he died,
Jesus your Son showed us how much you love us.
When he was at supper with his disciples,

He takes the bread and, raising it a little above the altar, continues:

he took bread,
and gave you thanks and praise.
Then he broke the bread,
gave it to his friends, and said:

He bows slightly.

Take this, all of you, and eat it:
this is my body which will be given up for you.

He shows the consecrated host to the people while all say:

Jesus has given his life for us.

He places the consecrated host on the paten, and genuflects in adoration. Then he continues:

When supper was ended,

He takes the chalice and, raising it a little above the altar, continues:

Jesus took the cup that was filled with wine.
He thanked you, gave it to his friends, and said:

He bows slightly.

Take this, all of you, and drink from it:
this is the cup of my blood,
the blood of the new and everlasting covenant.
It will be shed for you and for all
so that sins may be forgiven.

He shows the chalice to the people while all say:

Jesus has given his life for us.

The priest continues:

Then he said to them:
do this in memory of me.

Celebrant with concelebrants

He places the chalice on the corporal and genuflects in adoration. Then, with hands extended, the priest says:

And so, loving Father,
we remember that Jesus died and rose again
to save the world.
He put himself into our hands
to be the sacrifice we offer you.

All say:

We praise you, we bless you, we thank you.

Celebrant with concelebrants
The priest says:

**Lord our God,
listen to our prayer.
Send the Holy Spirit
to all of us who share in this meal.
May this Spirit bring us closer together
in the family of the Church,
with N., our pope,
N., our bishop,
all other bishops,
and all who serve your people.**

All say:

We praise you, we bless you, we thank you.

Celebrant or one concelebrant
The priest says:

**Remember, Father, our families and friends (. . .),
and all those we do not love as we should.
Remember those who have died (. . .).
Bring them home to you
to be with you for ever.**

All say:

We praise you, we bless you, we thank you.

Celebrant or one concelebrant
The priest says:

**Gather us all together into your kingdom.
There we shall be happy for ever
with the Virgin Mary, Mother of God and our mother.
There all the friends
of Jesus the Lord
will sing a song of joy.**

All say:

We praise you, we bless you, we thank you.

Celebrant alone or with concelebrants
He joins his hands, takes the chalice
and the paten with the host and, lifting
them up, he sings or says:

**Through him,
with him
in him,
in the unity of the Holy Spirit,
all glory and honor is yours,
almighty Father,
for ever and ever.**

The people respond:

Amen.

EUCHARISTIC PRAYER FOR MASSES WITH CHILDREN

III

The priest begins the eucharistic prayer.
With hands extended he sings or says:

Priest: **The Lord be with you.**

People: **And also with you.**

Priest: **Lift up your hearts.**

People: **We lift them up to the Lord.**

Priest: **Let us give thanks to the Lord our God.**

People: **It is right to give him thanks and praise.**

Celebrant alone

The priest, with hands extended, continues:

We thank you,
God our Father.

† You made us to live for you and for each other.
We can see and speak to one another,
and become friends
and share our joys and sorrows.

And so, Father, we gladly thank you
with every one who believes in you;
with the saints and the angels,
we rejoice and praise you, saying:

---

† During the Easter season this section
may be replaced by the following:

You are the living God;
you have called us to share in your life,
and to be happy with you for ever.
You raised up Jesus, your Son,
the first among us to rise from the dead,
and gave him new life.
You have promised to give us new life also,
a life that will never end,
a life with no more anxiety and suffering.

All say:

Holy, holy, holy Lord, God of power and might,
heaven and earth are full of your glory.
    Hosanna in the highest.
Blessed is he who comes in the name of the Lord.
    Hosanna in the highest.

Celebrant alone
The priest, with hands extended, says:

Yes, Lord, you are holy;
you are kind to us and to all.
For this we thank you.
We thank you above all for your Son, Jesus Christ.

† You sent him into this world
because people had turned away from you
and no longer loved each other.
He opened our eyes and our hearts
to understand that we are brothers and sisters
and that you are Father of us all.

He now brings us together to one table
and asks us to do what he did.

Celebrant with concelebrants

He joins his hands and, holding them
outstretched over the offerings, says:

Father,
we ask you to bless these gifts of bread and wine
and make them holy.

He joins his hands and, making the sign
of the cross once over both bread and
chalice, says:

Change them for us into the body ✢ and blood
    of Jesus Christ, your Son.

---

† During the Easter season this section
may be replaced by the following:

He brought us the good news
of life to be lived with you for ever in heaven.
He showed us the way to that life,
the way of love.
He himself has gone that way before us.

He now brings . . .

With hands joined, he continues:

He takes the bread and, raising it a little above the altar, continues:

**On the night before he died for us,
he had supper for the last time with his disciples.**

**He took bread
and gave you thanks.
He broke the bread
and gave it to his friends, saying:**

He bows slightly.

**Take this, all of you, and eat it:
this is my body which will be given up for you.**

He shows the consecrated host to the people, places it on the paten, and genuflects in adoration.

He takes the chalice and, raising it a little above the altar, continues:

**In the same way he took a cup of wine.
He gave you thanks
and handed the cup to his disciples, saying:**

He bows slightly.

**Take this, all of you, and drink from it:
this is the cup of my blood,
the blood of the new and everlasting covenant.
It will be shed for you and for all
so that sins may be forgiven.
Then he said to them:
do this in memory of me.**

Celebrant with concelebrants

He shows the chalice to the people, places it on the corporal and genuflects in adoration. Then, with hands extended, the priest says:

**God our Father,
we remember with joy
all that Jesus did to save us.
In this holy sacrifice,
which he gave as a gift to his Church,
we remember his death and resurrection.**

Celebrant or one concelebrant

**Father in heaven,
accept us together with your beloved Son.
He willingly died for us,
but you raised him to life again.
We thank you and say:**

All say:

Glory to God in the highest
(or some other suitable acclamation of praise).

The priest says: **Jesus now lives with you in glory,**
but he is also here on earth, among us.
We thank you and say:

All say: **Glory to God in the highest**
(or some other suitable acclamation of praise).

The priest says: **One day he will come in glory**
and in his kingdom
there will be no more suffering,
no more tears, no more sadness.
We thank you and say:

All say: **Glory to God in the highest**
(or some other suitable acclamation of praise).

Celebrant or one concelebrant

The priest says: **Father in heaven,**
you have called us
to receive the body and blood of Christ at this table
and to be filled with the joy of the Holy Spirit.
Through this sacred meal
give us strength to please you more and more.

Celebrant or one concelebrant **Lord, our God,**
remember N., our pope,
N., our bishop, and all other bishops.

† Help all who follow Jesus
to work for peace
and to bring happiness to others.

---

† During the Easter season this section
may be replaced by the following: **Fill all Christians with the gladness of Easter.**
Help us to bring this joy
to all who are sorrowful.

**Bring us all at last
together with Mary, the Mother of God,
and all the saints,
to live with you
and to be one with Christ in heaven.**

Celebrant alone or with concelebrants

He joins his hands, takes the chalice
and the paten with the host and, lifting
them up, he sings or says:

**Through him,
with him,
in him,
in the unity of the Holy Spirit,
all glory and honor is yours,
almighty Father,
for ever and ever.**

The people respond: **Amen.**

Eucharistic Prayers for Masses of Reconciliation

INTRODUCTION

1. The intentions for the celebration of the Holy Year have been proposed on many occasions by Pope Paul VI and it seems appropriate for these intentions to resound repeatedly in liturgical celebrations, especially in the sacrifice of the Mass, including the eucharistic prayer. For this reason two texts of the eucharistic prayer have been prepared to shed light on aspects of reconciliation, insofar as they may be the object of thanksgiving.

2. The conference of bishops may choose one text to be used in its territory during the Holy Year for Masses when celebrations express the intentions of the year. The texts may also be used after the Holy Year in Masses when the mystery of reconciliation is the special theme set before the faithful.

3. These proposed texts contain all the elements that make up a eucharistic prayer in accordance with the General Instruction of the Roman Missal no. 55. The order of these elements is the same as in Eucharistic Prayers II-IV of the Roman Missal.

4. The rubrics are given in the Latin texts. To assist those who are to prepare translations, a version in a Western language is added for each prayer. When a eucharistic prayer is published in a vernacular language, the rubrics are also to be printed.

In the text of the prayers the parts to be recited by concelebrants are indicated and the rubrics given for concelebration.

EUCHARISTIC PRAYER
FOR MASSES OF RECONCILIATION

I

*The priest begins the eucharistic prayer.
With hands extended he sings or says:*

Priest: **The Lord be with you.**

People: **And also with you.**

Priest: **Lift up your hearts.**

People: **We lift them up to the Lord.**

Priest: **Let us give thanks to the Lord our God.**

People: **It is right to give him thanks and praise.**

Celebrant alone

The priest, with hands extended, continues:

**Father, all-powerful and ever-living God,
we do well always and everywhere to give you
    thanks and praise.
You never cease to call us
to a new and more abundant life.**

**God of love and mercy,
you are always ready to forgive;
we are sinners,
and you invite us
to trust in your mercy.**

**Time and time again
we broke your covenant,
but you did not abandon us.
Instead, through your Son, Jesus our Lord,
you bound yourself even more closely to the
    human family
by a bond that can never be broken.**

**Now is the time
for your people to turn back to you
and to be renewed in Christ your Son,
a time of grace and reconciliation.**

**You invite us
to serve the family of mankind
by opening our hearts
to the fullness of your Holy Spirit.**

**In wonder and gratitude,
we join our voices with the choirs of heaven
to proclaim the power of your love
and to sing of our salvation in Christ:**

All say: **Holy, holy, holy Lord, God of power and might,
heaven and earth are full of your glory.
Hosanna in the highest.
Blessed is he who comes in the name of the Lord.
Hosanna in the highest.**

Celebrant alone

The priest, with hands extended, says:

**Father,
from the beginning of time
you have always done what is good for man
so that we may be holy as you are holy.**

Celebrant with concelebrants

He joins his hands and, holding them
outstretched over the offerings, says:

**Look with kindness on your people
gathered here before you:
send forth the power of your Spirit
so that these gifts may become for us**

He joins his hands and, making the sign
of the cross over both bread and
chalice, says:

**the body ✝ and blood of your beloved Son,
Jesus the Christ,
in whom we have become your sons and
daughters.**

With hands joined, he continues:

**When we were lost
and could not find the way to you,
you loved us more than ever:
Jesus, your Son, innocent and without sin,
gave himself into our hands
and was nailed to a cross.
Yet before he stretched out his arms
between heaven and earth
in the everlasting sign of your covenant,
he desired to celebrate the Paschal feast
in the company of his disciples.**

He takes the bread and, raising it a little
above the altar, continues:

**While they were at supper,
he took bread and gave you thanks and praise.
He broke the bread, gave it to his disciples,
and said:**

He bows slightly.

**Take this, all of you, and eat it:
this is my body which will be given
   up for you.**

He shows the consecrated host to the people, places it on the paten, and genuflects in adoration. Then he continues:

**At the end of the meal,
knowing that he was to reconcile all things in
   himself
by the blood of his cross,**

He takes the chalice and, raising it a little above the altar, continues:

**he took the cup, filled with wine.
Again he gave you thanks, handed the cup to
   his friends, and said:**

He bows slightly.

**Take this, all of you, and drink from it:
this is the cup of my blood,
the blood of the new and everlasting
   covenant.
It will be shed for you and for all
so that sins may be forgiven.
Do this in memory of me.**

Celebrant alone

He shows the chalice to the people, places it on the corporal and genuflects in adoration. He sings or says:

Then the people take up the acclamation in these words:

Let us proclaim the mystery of faith:

a   **Christ has died,
Christ is risen,
Christ will come again.**

b   **Dying you destroyed our death,
rising you restored our life.
Lord Jesus, come in glory.**

c   **When we eat this bread and drink this cup,
we proclaim your death, Lord Jesus,
until you come in glory.**

d   **Lord, by your cross and resurrection
you have set us free.
You are the Savior of the world.**

Celebrant with concelebrants
Then, with hands extended, the priest says:

**We do this in memory of Jesus Christ,
our Passover and our lasting peace.
We celebrate his death and resurrection
and look for the coming of that day
when he will return to give us the fullness of joy.
Therefore we offer you, God ever faithful and true,
the sacrifice which restores man to your friendship.**

**Father,
look with love
on those you have called
to share in the one sacrifice of Christ.
By the power of your Holy Spirit
make them one body,
healed of all division.**

Celebrant or one concelebrant

**Keep us all
in communion of mind and heart
with N., our pope, and N., our bishop.*
Help us to work together
for the coming of your kingdom,
until at last we stand in your presence
to share the life of the saints,
in the company of the Virgin Mary and the
     apostles,
and of our departed brothers and sisters
whom we commend to your mercy.**

**Then, freed from every shadow of death,
we shall take our place in the new creation
and give you thanks
with Christ, our risen Lord.**

Celebrant alone or with concelebrants
He joins his hands, takes the chalice and the paten with the host and, lifting them up, he sings or says:

**Through him,
with him,
in him,
in the unity of the Holy Spirit,
all glory and honor is yours,
almighty Father,
for ever and ever.**

The people respond: **Amen.**

---

*When several are to be named, a general form is used: for N., our bishop, and his assistant bishops, as in no. 172 of the General Instruction.

EUCHARISTIC PRAYER
FOR MASSES OF RECONCILIATION

II

The priest begins the eucharistic prayer. With hands extended he sings or says:

Priest:	**The Lord be with you.**
People:	**And also with you.**
Priest:	**Lift up your hearts.**
People:	**We lift them up to the Lord.**
Priest:	**Let us give thanks to the Lord our God.**
People:	**It is right to give him thanks and praise.**

Celebrant alone

The priest, with hands extended, continues:

Father, all-powerful and ever-living God,
we praise and thank you through Jesus Christ
   our Lord
for your presence and action in the world.

In the midst of conflict and division,
we know it is you
who turn our minds to thoughts of peace.
Your Spirit changes our hearts:
enemies begin to speak to one another,
those who were estranged join hands in friendship,
and nations seek the way of peace together.

Your Spirit is at work
when understanding puts an end to strife,
when hatred is quenched by mercy,
and vengeance gives way to forgiveness.

For this we should never cease
to thank and praise you.
We join with all the choirs of heaven
as they sing for ever to your glory:

All say:

Holy, holy, holy Lord, God of power and might.
Heaven and earth are full of your glory.
   Hosanna in the highest.
Blessed is he who comes in the name of the Lord.
   Hosanna in the highest.

The priest, with hands extended, says:

**God of power and might,
we praise you through your Son, Jesus Christ,
who comes in your name.
He is the Word that brings salvation.
He is the hand you stretch out to sinners.
He is the way that leads to your peace.**

**God our Father,
we had wandered far from you,
but through your Son you have brought us back.
You gave him up to death
so that we might turn again to you
and find our way to one another.**

**Therefore we celebrate the reconciliation
Christ has gained for us.**

Celebrant with concelebrants

He joins his hands and, holding them
outstretched over the offerings, says:

**We ask you to sanctify these gifts
by the power of your Spirit,**

He joins his hands and, making the sign
of the cross once over both bread and
chalice, says:

as we now fulfill your Son's ☩ command.

With hands joined, he continues:

**While he was at supper
on the night before he died for us,**

He takes the bread and, raising it a little
above the altar, continues:

**he took bread in his hands,
and gave you thanks and praise.
He broke the bread,
gave it to his disciples, and said:**

He bows slightly.

**Take this, all of you, and eat it:
this is my body which will be given up
for you.**

He shows the consecrated host to the
people, places it on the paten, and
genuflects in adoration. Then he
continues:

At the end of the meal he took the cup.

He takes the chalice and, raising it a
little above the altar, continues:

**Again he praised you for your goodness,
gave the cup to his disciples, and said:**

He bows slightly.

**Take this, all of you, and drink from it:
this is the cup of my blood,
the blood of the new and everlasting
  covenant.
It will be shed for you and for all
so that sins may be forgiven.
Do this in memory of me.**

Celebrant alone

He shows the chalice to the people,
places it on the corporal and genuflects
in adoration. He sings or says:

Let us proclaim the mystery of faith:

Then the people take up the acclamation in these words:

a **Christ has died,
Christ is risen,
Christ will come again.**

b **Dying you destroyed our death,
rising you restored our life.
Lord Jesus, come in glory.**

c **When we eat this bread and drink this cup,
we proclaim your death, Lord Jesus,
until you come in glory.**

d **Lord, by your cross and resurrection
you have set us free.
You are the Savior of the world.**

Celebrant with concelebrants

Then, with hands extended, the priest
says:

**Lord our God,
your Son has entrusted to us
this pledge of his love.
We celebrate the memory of his death and
  resurrection
and bring you the gift you have given us,
the sacrifice of reconciliation.
Therefore, we ask you, Father,
to accept us, together with your Son.**

**Fill us with his Spirit
through our sharing in this meal.
May he take away all that divides us.**

Celebrant or one concelebrant

**May this Spirit keep us always in communion
with N., our pope, N., our bishop,***
**with all the bishops and all your people.
Father, make your Church throughout the world
a sign of unity and an instrument of your peace.**

**You have gathered us here
around the table of your Son,
in fellowship with the Virgin Mary, Mother of God,
and all the saints.**

**In that new world where the fullness of your peace
will be revealed,
gather people of every race, language, and
way of life
to share in the one eternal banquet**

He joins his hands.

with Jesus Christ the Lord.

Celebrant alone or with concelebrants

*He takes the chalice and the paten with
the host and, lifting them up, he sings
or says:*

**Through him,
with him,
in him,
in the unity of the Holy Spirit,
all glory and honor is yours,
almighty Father,
for ever and ever.**

The people respond: **Amen.**

---

*When several are to be named, a general form is used: for N., our bishop, and his assistant bishops, as in
no. 172 of the General Instruction.

ANOINTING OF THE SICK

DURING MASS

ANOINTING OF THE SICK DURING MASS

These Mass texts are taken from *Pastoral Care of the Sick: Rites of Anointing and Viaticum* (1983 edition), nos. 131–148. Other prayers and rites are given there.

OPENING PRAYER

Father,
you raised your Son's cross
as the sign of victory and life.

May all who share in his suffering
find in these sacraments
a source of fresh courage and healing.

We ask this through our Lord
Jesus Christ, your Son,
who lives and reigns with you and the
Holy Spirit,
one God, for ever and ever.

ALTERNATIVE OPENING PRAYER

God of compassion
you take every family under your care
and know our physical and spiritual needs.

Transform our weakness by the
strength of your grace
and confirm us in your covenant
so that we may grow in faith and love.

We ask this through our Lord
Jesus Christ, your Son,
who lives and reigns with you and the
Holy Spirit,
one God, for ever and ever.

The liturgy of anointing follows the homily.

PRAYER OVER THE GIFTS

Merciful God,
as these simple gifts of bread and wine
will be transformed into the risen Lord,
so may he unite our sufferings with his
and cause us to rise to new life.

We ask this through Christ our Lord.

or:

Lord,
we bring you these gifts,
to become the health-giving body and blood of your Son.
In his name
heal the ills which afflict us
and restore to us the joy of life renewed.

We ask this through Christ our Lord.

PREFACE

℣. The Lord be with you.
℟. And also with you.

℣. Lift up your hearts.
℟. We lift them up to the Lord.

℣. Let us give thanks to the Lord our God.
℟. It is right to give him thanks and praise.

Father, all-powerful and ever-living God,
we do well always and everywhere to give you thanks,
for you have revealed to us
in Christ the healer
your unfailing power and steadfast compassion.

In the splendor of his rising
your Son conquered suffering and death
and bequeathed to us his promise
of a new and glorious world,
where no bodily pain will afflict us
and no anguish of spirit.

Through your gift of the Spirit
you bless us, even now,
with comfort and healing,
strength and hope,
forgiveness and peace.

In this supreme sacrament of your love
you give us the risen body of your Son:
a pattern of what we shall become
when he returns again at the end of time.

In gladness and joy
we unite with the angels and saints
in the great canticle of creation,
as we say (sing):

Holy, holy, holy Lord, God of power and might,
heaven and earth are full of your glory.
    Hosanna in the highest.
Blessed is he who comes in the name of the Lord.
    Hosanna in the highest.

Special intercessions: The following texts may be used in the first three eucharistic prayers:

When Eucharistic Prayer I is used, the special form of **Father, accept this offering,** is said:

**Father, accept this offering
from your whole family,
and especially from those who ask for healing
of body, mind, and spirit.
Grant us your peace in this life,
save us from final damnation,
and count us among those you have chosen.**

When Eucharistic Prayer II is used, after the words **and all the clergy,** there is added:

**Remember also those who ask for healing
in the name of your Son,
that they may never cease to praise you
for the wonders of your power.**

When Eucharistic Prayer III is used, after the words **the family you have gathered here,** there is added:

**Hear especially the prayers of those who ask for healing
in the name of your Son,
that they may never cease to praise you
for the wonders of your power.**

PRAYER AFTER COMMUNION

**Merciful God,
in celebrating these mysteries
your people have received the gifts of unity and peace.**

**Heal the afflicted
and make them whole
in the name of your only Son,
who lives and reigns for ever and ever.**

or:

**Lord,
through these sacraments
you offer us the gift of healing.**

**May this grace bear fruit among us
and make us strong in your service.**

We ask this through Christ our Lord.

SOLEMN BLESSING

Then the priest blesses the sick persons and others present, using one of the following:

May the God of all consolation
bless you in every way
and grant you hope all the days of your life.
℞. **Amen.**

May God restore you to health
and grant you salvation.
℞. **Amen.**

May God fill your heart with peace
and lead you to eternal life.
℞. **Amen.**

May almighty God bless you,
the Father, and the Son, ☩ and the Holy Spirit.
℞. **Amen.**

or:

May the Lord be with you to protect you.
℞. **Amen.**

May he guide you and give you strength.
℞. **Amen.**

May he watch over you, keep you in his care,
and bless you with his peace.
℞. **Amen.**

May almighty God bless you,
the Father, and the Son, ☩ and the Holy Spirit.
℞. **Amen.**

or:

May the blessing of almighty God,
the Father, and the Son, ☩ and the Holy Spirit
come upon you and remain with you for ever.
℞. **Amen.**

DISMISSAL

The deacon (or the priest) then dismisses the people and commends the sick to their care.

He may use these or similar words:

Go in the peace of Christ,
to serve him in the sick
and in all who need your love.

Appendix VIII

DEDICATION OF A CHURCH
AND AN ALTAR

DEDICATION OF A CHURCH

The texts for the rites are contained in
The Roman Pontifical and in *Dedication
of a Church and an Altar.*

OPENING PRAYER

Lord,
fill this place with your presence,
and extend your hand
to all those who call upon you.

May your word here proclaimed
and your sacraments here celebrated
strengthen the hearts of all the faithful.

We ask this through our Lord Jesus Christ, your Son,
who lives and reigns with you and the Holy Spirit,
one God, for ever and ever.

LITURGY OF THE WORD

First Reading: Nehemiah 8:1-4a, 5-6,
8-10 [Lectionary no. 70]
Responsorial Psalm: Psalm 19B: 8-9,
10, 15 [see Lectionary no. 70] with ℟.
Your words, Lord, are spirit and life.
Second Reading: Lectionary nos. 702,
704
Gospel verse: Lectionary no. 705
Gospel: Lectionary no. 706

PRAYER OVER THE GIFTS

Lord,
accept the gifts of a rejoicing Church.

May your people,
who are gathered in this sacred place,
arrive at eternal salvation
through the mysteries in which they share.

Grant this through Christ our Lord.

EUCHARISTIC PRAYER

Eucharistic Prayer I or III is said, with the
following preface, which is an integral
part of the rite of the dedication of a
church. With hands extended the
bishop sings or says:

PREFACE

The mystery of God's temple

℣. The Lord be with you.
℟. And also with you.

℣. Lift up your hearts.
℟. We lift them up to the Lord.

℣. Let us give thanks to the Lord our God.
℟. It is right to give him thanks and praise.

Father, all-powerful and ever-living God,
we do well always and everywhere to give you thanks.

The whole world is your temple,
shaped to resound with your name.
Yet you also allow us to dedicate to your service
places designed for your worship.

With hearts full of joy
we consecrate to your glory
this work of our hands, this house of prayer.

Here is foreshadowed the mystery of your true temple;
this church is the image on earth of your heavenly city:

For you made the body of your Son
born of the Virgin,
a temple consecrated to your glory,
the dwelling place of your godhead in all its fullness.

You have established the Church as your holy city,
founded on the apostles,
with Jesus Christ its cornerstone.

You continue to build your Church with chosen stones,
enlivened by the Spirit,
and cemented together by love.

In that holy city you will be all in all for endless ages,
and Christ will be its light for ever.

Through Christ we praise you, Lord,
with all the angels and saints in their song of joy:

Holy, holy, holy Lord, God of power and might,
heaven and earth are full of your glory.
    Hosanna in the highest.
Blessed is he who comes in the name of the Lord.
    Hosanna in the highest.

Special intercessions: The following texts may be used in Eucharistic Prayers I and III:

In Eucharistic Prayer I the special form of **Father, accept this offering** is said:

Father,
accept this offering
from your whole family,
and from your servants
who with heart and hand
have given and built this church
as an offering to you (in honor of N.).
Grant us your peace in this life,
save us from final damnation,
and count us among those you have chosen.

In the intercessions of Eucharistic Prayer III, after the words, with . . . the entire people your Son has gained for you, the following is said:

Father,
accept the prayers of those who dedicate this church to you.

May it be a place of salvation and sacrament
where your Gospel of peace is proclaimed
and your holy mysteries celebrated.

Guided by your word and secure in your peace
may your chosen people now journeying through life
arrive safely at their eternal home.

There may all your children
now scattered abroad
be settled at last in your city of peace.

PRAYER AFTER COMMUNION

Lord,
through these gifts
increase the vision of your truth in our minds.
May we always worship you in your holy temple,
and rejoice in your presence with all your saints.
Grant this through Christ our Lord.

SOLEMN BLESSING

The Lord of earth and heaven
has assembled you before him this day
to dedicate this house of prayer.
May he fill you with the blessings of heaven.   ℟. Amen.

God the Father wills that all his children
scattered through the world
become one family in his Son.
May he make you his temple,
the dwelling place of his Holy Spirit.   ℟. Amen.

May God free you from every bond of sin,
dwell within you and give you joy.
May you live with him for ever
in the company of all his saints.   ℟. Amen.

May almighty God bless you,
the Father, and the Son, ✝ and the Holy Spirit.   ℟. Amen.

DEDICATION OF A CHURCH ALREADY IN USE

The texts for the rites are contained in *The Roman Pontifical* and in *Dedication of a Church and an Altar.*

The opening prayer, prayer over the gifts, prayer after communion, and blessing are taken from the Mass for the Dedication of a Church, page 1156.

Lectionary: nos. 701-706.

EUCHARISTIC PRAYER

Eucharistic Prayer I or III is said, with the following preface. With hands extended the bishop sings or says:

PREFACE

The edifice and the Church of God

℣. **The Lord be with you.**
℟. **And also with you.**

℣. **Lift up your hearts.**
℟. **We lift them up to the Lord.**

℣. **Let us give thanks to the Lord our God.**
℟. **It is right to give him thanks and praise.**

Father of holiness and power,
we give you thanks and praise
through Jesus Christ, your Son.

For you have blessed this work of our hands
and your presence makes it a house of prayer;
nor do you ever refuse us welcome
when we come in before you as your pilgrim people.

In this house
  you realize the mystery of your dwelling among us:
for in shaping us here as your holy temple
you enrich your whole Church,
which is the very body of Christ,
and thus bring closer to fulfillment
the vision of your peace,
the heavenly city of Jerusalem.

And so, with all your angels and saints,
who stand in your temple of glory,
we praise you and give you thanks, as we sing:

Holy, holy, holy Lord, God of power and might,
heaven and earth are full of your glory.
  Hosanna in the highest.
Blessed is he who comes in the name of the Lord.
  Hosanna in the highest.

SOLEMN BLESSING: see page 1158.

DEDICATION OF AN ALTAR

The texts for the rites are contained in *The Roman Pontifical* and in *Dedication of a Church and an Altar*.

OPENING PRAYER

Lord,
you willed that all things be drawn to your Son,
mounted on the altar of the cross.
Bless those who dedicate this altar to your service.

May it be the table of our unity,
a banquet of plenty,
and a source of the Spirit,
in whom we grow daily as your faithful people.

We ask this through our Lord Jesus Christ, your Son,
who lives and reigns with you and the Holy Spirit,
one God, for ever and ever.

Lectionary: nos. 701-706, or from the Mass of the day.

PRAYER OVER THE GIFTS

Lord,
send your Spirit upon this altar
to sanctify these gifts;
may he prepare our hearts
to receive them worthily.

Grant this through Christ our Lord.

EUCHARISTIC PRAYER

Eucharistic Prayer I or III is said, with the following preface, which is an integral part of the rite of the dedication of an altar:

PREFACE

The altar, a symbol of Christ

℣. The Lord be with you.
℟. And also with you.

℣. Lift up your hearts.
℟. We lift them up to the Lord.

℣. Let us give thanks to the Lord our God.
℟. It is right to give him thanks and praise.

Father, all-powerful and ever-living God,
we do well always and everywhere to give you thanks
through Jesus Christ our Lord.

True priest and true victim,
he offered himself to you
on the altar of the cross
and commanded us to celebrate
that same sacrifice,
until he comes again.

Therefore your people have built this altar
and have dedicated it to your name
with grateful hearts.

This is a truly sacred place.

Here the sacrifice of Christ is offered in mystery,
perfect praise is given to you,
and our redemption is made continually present.

Here is prepared the Lord's table,
at which your children,
nourished by the body of Christ,
are gathered into a Church, one and holy.

Here your people drink of the Spirit,
the stream of living water,
flowing from the rock of Christ.
They will become, in him,
a worthy offering and a living altar.

We praise you, Lord,
with all the angels and saints in their song of joy:

Holy, holy, holy Lord, God of power and might,
heaven and earth are full of your glory.
  Hosanna in the highest.
Blessed is he who comes in the name of the Lord.
  Hosanna in the highest.

PRAYER AFTER COMMUNION

Lord,
may we always be drawn
to this altar of sacrifice.

United in faith and love,
may we be nourished by the body of Christ
and transformed into his likeness,
who lives and reigns with you and the Holy Spirit,
one God, for ever and ever.

SOLEMN BLESSING

May God, who has given you the dignity
of a royal priesthood,
strengthen you in your holy service
and make you worthy to share in his sacrifice.   ℞. Amen.

May he, who invites you to the one table
and feeds you with the one bread,
make you one in heart and mind.   ℞. Amen.

May all to whom you proclaim Christ
be drawn to him
by the example of your love.   ℞. Amen.

May almighty God bless you,
the Father, and the Son, ✝ and the Holy Spirit.   ℞. Amen.

BLESSING OF A CHURCH

The texts for the rites are contained in *The Roman Pontifical* and in *Dedication of a Church and an Altar.*

On the days listed in the Table of Liturgical Days, nos. 1–4 (page 62, above), the prayer of the day is used. On other days, the following prayer is said:

Lord,
bless this church,
which we have been privileged to build with your help.
May all who gather here in faith
to listen to your word
and celebrate your sacraments,
experience the presence of Christ,
who promised to be with those
gathered in his name,
for he lives and reigns with you and the Holy Spirit,
one God, for ever and ever.

Lectionary: nos. 701-706, or from the Mass of the day.

SOLEMN BLESSING: see page 1158.

BLESSING OF A
CHALICE AND PATEN

BLESSING OF A CHALICE AND PATEN

Introduction

1.   The chalice and paten in which wine and bread are offered, consecrated, and received,[1] since they are intended solely and permanently for the celebration of the eucharist, become "sacred vessels."

2.   The intention, however, of devoting these vessels entirely to the celebration of the eucharist is made manifest before the community by a special blessing which is preferably imparted during Mass.

3.   Any bishop or priest may bless a chalice and paten, provided these have been made according to the norms laid down in the General Instruction of the Roman Missal, nos. 290–295.

4.   If it is a chalice or paten alone that is to be blessed, the text should be suitably adapted.

Rite of Blessing within Mass

5.   In the liturgy of the word, apart from the days listed in the Table of Liturgical Days, nos. 1–9 (p. 62), one or two readings may be taken from those given below in nos. 6–8.

Liturgy of the Word

Readings from Sacred Scripture

6.   1.   1 Corinthians 10:14-22a [Lectionary no. 442] Our blessing-cup is a communion with the blood of Christ.
      2.   1 Corinthians 11:23-26 [Lectionary no. 40] This cup is the new covenant in my blood.

Responsorial Psalm

7.   1.   Psalm 16:5 and 8, 9-10, 11 [Lectionary no. 159]
            R. (5a) The Lord is my inheritance and my cup.
      2.   Psalm 23:1-3a, 3b-4, 5, 6 [Lectionary no. 493]
            R. (5a, d) You prepared a banquet before me; my cup overflows.

[1]See the General Instruction of the Roman Missal, no. 289.

Gospels

8. 1. Matthew 20:20-28 [Lectionary no. 605] You shall indeed drink my cup.
    2. Mark 14:12-16, 22-26 [Lectionary, nos. 909, 921] This is my body. This is my blood.

■ 9. After the reading of the word of God the homily is given in which the celebrant explains the biblical readings and the meaning of the blessing of a chalice and paten that are used in the celebration of the Lord's Supper.

Liturgy of the Eucharist

■ 10. When the general intercessions are finished, ministers or representatives of the community that are presenting the chalice and paten place them on the altar. Meanwhile the following antiphon is sung.

I will take the cup of salvation and call on the name of the Lord.

Another appropriate song may be sung.

■ 11. When the singing is finished, the celebrant says:

Let us pray.

All pray in silence for a brief period. The celebrant then continues:

■ **Lord,
with joy we place on your altar
this cup and this paten,
vessels with which we will celebrate
the sacrifice of Christ's new covenant.**

**May they be sanctified,
for in them the body and blood of Christ
will be offered, consecrated and received.**

**Lord, when we celebrate Christ's
    faultless sacrifice on earth,
may we be renewed in strength
and filled with your Spirit,
until we join with your saints
at your table in heaven.**

Glory and honor be yours for ever and ever.

℟. **Blessed be God for ever.**

12. Afterward the ministers place a corporal on the altar. Some of the congregation bring bread, wine, and water for the celebration of the Lord's sacrifice. The celebrant puts the gifts in the newly blessed paten and chalice and offers them in the usual way. Meanwhile the following antiphon may be sung with Psalm 116:10-19.

I will take the cup of salvation and offer a sacrifice of praise (alleluia).

Another appropriate song may be sung.

■ 13. When he has said the prayer Lord God, we ask you to receive us, the celebrant may incense the gifts and the altar.

14. If circumstances of the celebration permit, it is appropriate that the congregation should receive the blood of Christ from the newly blessed chalice.

Appendix X

ADDITIONAL PRESIDENTIAL PRAYERS

ADDITIONAL PRESIDENTIAL PRAYERS

INTRODUCTION

The presidential prayers[1] contained in this Appendix are provisional translations of new liturgical texts added to the second typical edition of the *Missale Romanum* by decree of the Congregation for the Sacraments and Divine Worship, 25 March 1975 (Prot. N. 1970/74). Upon the recommendation of the Bishops' Committee on the Liturgy, this provisional translation was approved by the Administrative Committee of the National Conference of Catholic Bishops on 24 September 1980 and the prayers are included in this edition of the Sacramentary for provisional use *ad interim* in the dioceses of the United States of America. They may be used at the discretion of the priest celebrant.

Also included in this Appendix are the presidential prayers originally approved for use during the Bicentennial celebration of American independence in 1976.[2] These texts may be used on July 4, Independence Day, or, when permitted by the norms for the liturgical year and Roman Calendar, on other civic observances.

1. English translation of *Sacramentary: Additional Presidential Prayers* © 1980, International Committee on English in the Liturgy, Inc. All rights reserved.

2. The Bicentennial Mass was approved by the National Conference of Catholic Bishops and confirmed by the Congregation for the Sacraments and Divine Worship (Prot. CD 45/75).

1. BLESSING OF AN ABBOT OR ABBESS

(Ritual Mass)

This Mass may be said on any day except the Sundays of Advent, Lent, and Easter, solemnities, Ash Wednesday, and during Holy Week. White vestments are used.

OPENING PRAYER

For an abbot:

**Lord and shepherd of your people,
you have chosen N., your servant,
to be abbot of this community.
By his teaching and example
may he guide his brothers along right paths
and receive with them
an everlasting reward in heaven.**

**We ask this through our Lord Jesus Christ, your Son,
who lives and reigns with you and the Holy Spirit,
one God, for ever and ever.**

For an abbess:

**Lord and shepherd of your people,
you have chosen N., your servant,
to be abbess of this community.
By her teaching and example
may she guide her sisters along right paths
and receive with them
an everlasting reward in heaven.**

**We ask this through our Lord Jesus Christ, your Son,
who lives and reigns with you and the Holy Spirit,
one God, for ever and ever.**

PRAYER OVER THE GIFTS

Pray, brethren . . .

**All-powerful God,
accept these gifts from the hands of your servants
who offer themselves as a spiritual sacrifice.
Fill them with humility, obedience, and peace.**

We ask this through Christ our Lord.

PRAYER AFTER COMMUNION

Let us pray.
Pause for silent prayer, if this has not preceded.

**God of everlasting love,
we have celebrated the mystery of faith.
Grant that we may run eagerly in the paths of the Gospel
and give you glory in all that we do.**

We ask this in the name of Jesus the Lord.

2. TWENTY-FIFTH OR FIFTIETH ANNIVERSARY
OF RELIGIOUS PROFESSION

(Ritual Mass)

The entrance and communion antiphons, if used, may be taken from one of the Masses for religious profession, pages 777–782.

OPENING PRAYER

God of faithfulness,
enable us to give you thanks
for your goodness to N., our brother/sister.
Today he/she comes to rededicate that gift
which he/she first received from you.
Intensify within him/her your spirit of perfect love,
that he/she may devote himself/herself more fervently
to the service of your glory
and the work of salvation.
We ask this through our Lord Jesus Christ, your Son,
who lives and reigns with you and the Holy Spirit,
one God, for ever and ever.

PRAYER OVER THE GIFTS

Pray, brethren . . .

All-powerful God,
together with these gifts
accept the offering of self
which N., our brother/sister, wishes to reaffirm today.

By the power of your Spirit
conform him/her more truly
to the likeness of your beloved Son.

We ask this through Christ our Lord.

PRAYER AFTER COMMUNION

Let us pray.

Pause for silent prayer, if this has not preceded.

God of love,
in this joyful anniversary celebration
you have fed us
with the body and blood of your Son.
Refreshed by heavenly food and drink
may our brother/sister, N., advance happily on that journey
which began in you and leads to you.
Grant this through Christ our Lord.

3. FOR THOSE WHO WILL DIE TODAY

(Masses and Prayers for Various Needs and Occasions)

OPENING PRAYER

**God of mercy,
always and everywhere
you reveal your love for all creation.**

**Hear our prayers for those who will die today
that, redeemed by the blood of your Son
and freed from the taint of sin,
they may go forth from this world
and rest for ever in the embrace of your mercy.**

**We ask this through our Lord Jesus Christ, your Son,
who lives and reigns with you and the Holy Spirit,
one God, for ever and ever.**

4. MARY, MOTHER OF THE CHURCH

(Votive Mass)

OPENING PRAYER

**God of mercies,
your only Son, while hanging on the cross,
appointed Mary, his mother,
to be our mother also.**

**Like her,
and under her loving care,
may your Church grow day by day,
rejoice in the holiness of its children,
and so attract to itself all the peoples of the earth.**

**We ask this through our Lord Jesus Christ, your Son,
who lives and reigns with you and the Holy Spirit,
one God, for ever and ever.**

PRAYER OVER THE GIFTS

Pray, brethren . . .

**Lord,
accept our gifts
and make them the sacrament of our salvation.**

**By its power
warm our hearts with the love of Mary,
Mother of the Church,
and join us more closely with her
in sharing the redeeming work of her Son.**

We ask this through Christ our Lord.

EUCHARISTIC PRAYER   PREFACE

Mary as model and mother of the Church

℣. The Lord be with you.
℟. And also with you.

℣. Lift up your hearts.
℟. We lift them up to the Lord.

℣. Let us give thanks to the Lord our God.
℟. It is right to give him thanks and praise.

Father, all-powerful and ever-living God,
we do well always and everywhere to give you thanks;
we especially praise you and proclaim your glory
as we honor the Blessed Virgin Mary.

She received your Word in the purity of her heart,
and, conceiving in her virgin womb,
gave birth to our Savior
and so nurtured the Church at its very beginning.

She accepted God's parting gift of love
as she stood beneath the cross
and so became the mother of all those
who were brought to life
through the death of her only Son.

She joined her prayers with those of the apostles,
as together they awaited the coming of your Spirit,
and so became the perfect pattern of the Church at prayer.

Raised to the glory of heaven,
she cares for the pilgrim Church with a mother's love,
following its progress homeward
until the day of the Lord dawns in splendor.

Now, with all the angels and saints,
we proclaim your glory
and join in their unending hymn of praise:

Holy, holy, holy Lord, God of power and might,
heaven and earth are full of your glory.
    Hosanna in the highest.
Blessed is he who comes in the name of the Lord.
    Hosanna in the highest.

PRAYER AFTER COMMUNION

Let us pray.

Pause for silent prayer, if this has not preceded.

**Lord,
we have received the foretaste and promise
of the fullness of redemption.
We pray that your Church,
through the intercession of the Virgin Mother,
may proclaim the Gospel to all nations
and by the power of the Spirit
reach to the ends of the earth.
We ask this through Christ our Lord.**

5. HOLY NAME OF MARY

(Votive Mass)

A Mass from the Common of the Blessed Virgin Mary is used, in accord with the liturgical season, substituting the following opening prayer.

OPENING PRAYER

**God of heaven and earth,
your Son, Jesus the Lord,
while dying on the altar of the cross
chose Mary, his mother, to be our mother also.
Grant that we
who entrust ourselves to her maternal care
may always be protected
when we call upon her name.**

**We ask this through our Lord Jesus Christ, your Son,
who lives and reigns with you and the Holy Spirit,
one God, for ever and ever.**

6. INDEPENDENCE DAY AND OTHER CIVIC OBSERVANCES

(Masses and Prayers for Various Needs and Occasions)

Introductory Rites

> Give peace, Lord, to those who wait for you; listen to the prayers of your servants, and guide us in the way of justice.
> (See Sir. 36:18-19)

The Gloria may be said.

OPENING PRAYER

Let us pray
  [in gratitude for the many blessings bestowed upon our nation]
Pause for silent prayer

All-powerful Father,
today we rededicate ourselves to your service,
and to the works of justice and freedom for all.

As you have called us from many peoples to be one nation,
help us to give witness in our lives
and in our life as a nation
to the rich diversity of your gifts.

We ask this through our Lord Jesus Christ, your Son,
who lives and reigns with you and the Holy Spirit,
one God, for ever and ever.

ALTERNATIVE OPENING PRAYER

Let us pray
  [for God's blessing on our country]
Pause for silent prayer

Father of all nations and ages,
we recall the day when our country claimed its place among the family of nations.
For what has been achieved we give you thanks;
for the work that still remains we ask your help.
Grant that under your providence
our country may share your blessings
with all the peoples of the earth.

We ask this through Christ our Lord.

LITURGY OF THE WORD

The following scriptural readings are suggested for the eucharistic celebration of Independence Day. Other readings may be selected from the Lectionary for Mass.

First Reading: Isaiah 32:15-20 [Lectionary 831.2] The effect of justice will be peace.
Responsorial Psalm: Psalm 72:1-2, 3-4, 7-8, 12-13, 17 [Lectionary 833.1] with ℟.(7): Justice shall flourish in his time, and fullness of peace for ever.
Second Reading: 1 Peter 1:3-9 [Lectionary 347] In his great mercy he gave us new birth.
Alleluia: John 14:27 [Lectionary 834.2] Peace I leave with you, says the Lord, my own peace I give you.
Gospel: John 14:23-29 [Lectionary 835.3] Peace is what I give to you.

LITURGY OF THE EUCHARIST

PRAYER OVER THE GIFTS

God of mercy,
as we present this bread and wine
make all of us a leaven for good,
to make the good news of Christ
    present everywhere.
Draw the hearts of all to yourself,
and make our country one nation
dedicated to your service.
We ask this through Christ our Lord.

ALTERNATIVE PRAYER OVER THE GIFTS

Father,
through the coming together of many
    peoples
our nation has been molded into one.
As the grains of wheat became this one
    bread
and the many grapes this one cup,
so may we remain united in peace with you
and be a source of peace to others.
We ask this in the name of Jesus the Lord.

Eucharistic Prayer:
Preface for Independence Day and
Other Civic Observances I, II, pages
499, 500.

Communion Rite
> Lord, you are the source of life, and in the light of your glory
> we find happiness. (Ps. 36:10)

A period of silence may be observed
after communion, or a psalm or song of
praise may be sung.

PRAYER AFTER COMMUNION

Lord,
in this eucharist
you show us here on earth
an image and foretaste of the unity and joy
of your people in heaven.
Deepen our unity and increase our joy
that all who believe in you
may work together to build the city of lasting
    peace.
We ask this through Christ our Lord.

ALTERNATIVE PRAYER AFTER COMMUNION

Father,
may the love we share in this eucharist
flow in rich blessing throughout our land.
With your grace may we as a nation
place our trust in you
and seek to do your will.
We ask this through Christ our Lord.

SOLEMN BLESSING

The following may replace the simple
blessing.

After the greeting, the deacon (or in his
absence, the priest) gives the invitation
in these or similar words:

Bow your heads and pray for
God's blessing.

Then the priest extends his hands over the people while he sings or says:

**God the Father has called us
to be one family of peoples.
May he fill your hearts with a deep longing
for peace and harmony.
℟. Amen.**

**The Son of God came to share our lives
and make us children of the one Father.
May he enable you to grow in wisdom and grace
before God and the human family.
℟. Amen.**

**The Holy Spirit is the bond of love
between Father and Son.
May he be the bond of love among you,
in our nation, and among all peoples.
℟. Amen.**

**May almighty God bless you,
the Father, and the Son, ✠ and the Holy Spirit.
℟. Amen.**

ALPHABETICAL INDEX OF CELEBRATIONS

INDEX OF PREFACES

SACRAMENTARY SUPPLEMENT

NEW MEMORIALS AND FEASTS
FOR THE ROMAN CALENDAR
AND FOR THE PARTICULAR CALENDAR OF THE
DIOCESES OF THE UNITED STATES OF AMERICA

THE PROCLAMATION OF THE BIRTH OF CHRIST

THE PROCLAMATION OF THE DATE OF EASTER
ON EPIPHANY

THE RECEPTION OF THE HOLY OILS

THE LITURGICAL PRESS

Collegeville   Minnesota

Concordat cum originali:

Reverend Monsignor Alan F. Detscher
Executive Director
Secretariat for the Liturgy
National Conference of Catholic Bishops

ACKNOWLEDGMENTS

Liturgical texts for the memorials of Blessed Katharine Drexel, Blessed Junipero Serra, Blessed Juan Diego and Our Lady of Guadalupe © 1987 and 1990, United States Catholic Conference (USCC), 3211 Fourth Street, NE, Washington, DC 20017-1194 USA. All rights reserved.

Liturgical texts for the memorials of Saint Lawrence Ruiz and Companions and Saint Andrew Dung-Lac, and Companions © 1988 and 1989, International Committee on English in the Liturgy, Inc. (ICEL), 1275 K Street, NW, Suite 1202, Washington DC 20005-4097 USA. All rights reserved.

The Proclamation of the Birth of Christ, The Proclamation of the Date of Easter on Epiphany, The Reception of the Holy Oils © 1994, United States Catholic Conference (USCC), 3211 Fourth Street, NE, Washington, DC 20017-1194 USA. All rights reserved.

The Proclamation of the Birth of Christ, The Proclamation of the Date of Easter on Epiphany, and *The Reception of the Holy Oils* were confirmed by the Congregation for Divine Worship: Prot. N. 699/88 of 27 January 1989 and Prot. N. 230/89 of 12 December 1989.

The other liturgical texts contained in this Supplement were at various times approved by the National Conference of Catholic Bishops and confirmed by the Apostolic See by decrees of the Congregation for Divine Worship.

Published by authority of the Committee on the Liturgy, National Conference of Catholic Bishops, Washington, D.C.

ISBN 0-8146-2344-1

CONTENTS

NEW MEMORIALS AND FEASTS
FOR THE ROMAN CALENDAR
AND FOR THE PARTICULAR CALENDAR OF THE
DIOCESES OF THE UNITED STATES OF AMERICA

March 3

[In the dioceses of the United States]

BLESSED KATHARINE DREXEL, virgin

Common of virgins (p. 731).

OPENING PRAYER

**Ever-loving God,
you called Blessed Katharine Drexel
to teach the message of the Gospel
and to bring the life of the Eucharist
to the African American and Native American peoples.**

**By her prayers and example,
enable us to work for justice
among the poor and the oppressed,
and keep us undivided in love
in the eucharistic community of your Church.**

**Grant this through our Lord Jesus Christ, your Son,
who lives and reigns with you and the Holy Spirit,
one God, for ever and ever.**

July 1

[In the dioceses of the United States]

BLESSED JUNIPERO SERRA, priest

Common of pastors: for pastors (p. 721)
or for missionaries (p. 726).

OPENING PRAYER

**God most high,
your servant Junipero Serra
brought the gospel of Christ
to the peoples of Mexico and California
and firmly established the Church among them.
By his intercession,
and through the example of his evangelical zeal,
inspire us to be faithful witnesses of Jesus Christ,
who lives and reigns with you and the Holy Spirit,
one God, for ever and ever.**

August 18

[In the dioceses of the United States]

ST. JANE FRANCES DE CHANTAL, religious

Common of holy men and women: for religious (p. 741).

OPENING PRAYER

**Lord,
you chose St. Jane Frances to serve you
both in marriage and in religious life.
By her prayers
help us to be faithful in our vocation
and always to be the light of the world.**

**We ask this through our Lord Jesus Christ, your Son,
who lives and reigns with you and the Holy Spirit,
one God, for ever and ever.**

September 28

ST. LAWRENCE RUIZ AND COMPANIONS, martyrs

Common of martyrs (p. 704).

OPENING PRAYER

**Lord God,
in our service to you and to our neighbor
give us the patience of the holy martyrs,
Lawrence and his companions;
for those who suffer persecution for justice' sake
are blessed in the Kingdom of heaven.**

**We ask this through our Lord Jesus Christ, your Son,
who lives and reigns with you and the Holy Spirit,
one God, for ever and ever.**

October 20

[In the dioceses of the United States]

ST. PAUL OF THE CROSS, priest

Introductory Rites

> I resolved that while I was with you I would think of nothing
> but Jesus Christ and him crucified. (1 Corinthians 2:2)

OPENING PRAYER

**Father,
you gave your priest St. Paul
a special love for the cross of Christ.
May his example inspire us
to embrace our own cross with courage.**

**Grant this through our Lord Jesus Christ, your Son,
who lives and reigns with you and the Holy Spirit,
one God, for ever and ever.**

See Lectionary for Mass, no. 663.

PRAYER OVER THE GIFTS

Pray, brethren . . .

**All-powerful God,
receive the gifts we offer
in memory of St. Paul of the Cross.
May we who celebrate the mystery
of the Lord's suffering and death
put into effect the self-sacrificing love
we proclaim in this eucharist.**

We ask this through Christ our Lord.

Communion Rite

> We preach a Christ who was crucified; he is the power and
> the wisdom of God. (1 Corinthians 1:23-24)

PRAYER AFTER COMMUNION

Let us pray.
Pause for silent prayer, if this has not preceded.
**Lord,
in the life of St. Paul
you helped us to understand the mystery of the cross.
May the sacrifice we have offered strengthen us,
keep us faithful to Christ,
and help us to work in the Church
for the salvation of all mankind.**

We ask this in the name of Jesus the Lord.

November 18

[In the dioceses of the United States]

ST. ROSE PHILIPPINE DUCHESNE, virgin

Common of virgins (p. 731).

OPENING PRAYER

**Gracious God,
you filled the heart of Philippine Duchesne
with charity and missionary zeal,
and gave her the desire
to make you known among all peoples.**

**Fill us, who honor her memory today,
with that same love and zeal
to extend your kingdom to the ends of the earth.**

**We ask this through our Lord Jesus Christ, your Son,
who lives and reigns with you and the Holy Spirit,
one God, for ever and ever.**

November 23

[In the dioceses of the United States]

BLESSED MIGUEL AGUSTÍN PRO, priest and martyr

Common of martyrs (p. 709) or
Common of pastors: for pastors (p. 721).

OPENING PRAYER

**God our Father,
you gave your servant Miguel Agustín
the grace to seek ardently your greater glory
and the salvation of your people.
Grant that, through his intercession
and following his example,
we may serve you and glorify you
by performing our daily duties with fidelity and joy
and effectively helping our neighbor.**

**We ask this through our Lord Jesus Christ, your Son,
who lives and reigns with you and the Holy Spirit,
one God, for ever and ever.**

November 24

ST. ANDREW DUNG-LAC, priest, AND COMPANIONS, martyrs
Memorial

Introductory Rites

We should boast of nothing but the cross of our Lord Jesus
Christ. For to us who are saved the word of the cross is the
power of God. (Galatians 6:14a; 1 Corinthians 1:18)

OPENING PRAYER

**O God,
the source and origin of all fatherhood,
you kept the blessed martyrs Andrew and his companions
faithful to the cross of your Son
even to the shedding of their blood.
Through their intercession
enable us to spread your love among our brothers and
    sisters,
that we may be called and may truly be your children.**

**We ask this through our Lord Jesus Christ, your Son,
who lives and reigns with you and the Holy Spirit,
one God, for ever and ever.**

PRAYER OVER THE GIFTS

Pray, brethren . . .

**Father most holy,
accept the gifts we bring
as we honor the sufferings of the Vietnamese martyrs.
Amid the trials of life
help us to remain faithful to you
and to present our lives
as an offering that is pleasing in your sight.**

We ask this through Christ our Lord.

Preface of Martyrs (P 66), p. 483.

Communion Rite

Blessed are those who suffer persecution for the sake of justice;
the kingdom of heaven is theirs. (Matthew 5:10)

PRAYER AFTER COMMUNION

Let us pray.

Pause for silent prayer, if this has not preceded.

**Nourished by the one bread that we have received
on this feast of the holy martyrs,
we beg you, Lord,
that we may remain in your love,
and through patience inherit your promised reward.**

We make this prayer through Christ our Lord.

December 9

[In the dioceses of the United States]

BLESSED JUAN DIEGO

Common of holy men and women (p. 735).

OPENING PRAYER

**Lord God,
through blessed Juan Diego
you made known the love of Our Lady of Guadalupe
toward your people.**

**Grant by his intercession
that we who follow the counsel of Mary, our Mother,
may strive continually to do your will.**

**We ask this through our Lord Jesus Christ, your Son,
who lives and reigns with you and the Holy Spirit,
one God, for ever and ever.**

December 12

[In the dioceses of the United States]

OUR LADY OF GUADALUPE
Feast

Introductory Rites

A great sign appeared in the sky, a woman clothed with the sun, with the moon under her feet, and on her head a crown of twelve stars. (Revelation 12:1)

OPENING PRAYER

**God of power and mercy,
you blessed the Americas at Tepeyac
with the presence of the Virgin Mary of Guadalupe.
May her prayers help all men and women
to accept each other as brothers and sisters.
Through your justice present in our hearts
may your peace reign in the world.**

**We ask this through our Lord Jesus Christ, your Son,
who lives and reigns with you and the Holy Spirit,
one God, for ever and ever.**

See *Lectionary for Mass,* nos. 707–712.

PRAYER OVER THE GIFTS   **Pray, brethren . . .**

Lord,
accept the gifts we present to you
on this feast of Our Lady of Guadalupe,
and grant that this sacrifice
will strengthen us to fulfill your commandments
as true sons and daughters of the Virgin Mary.

We ask this through Christ our Lord.

Preface of the Blessed Virgin Mary I
or II (P 56 or P 57), pages **473–474.**

Communion Rite

The Lord has cast down the mighty from their thrones, and
has lifted up the lowly. (Luke 1:52)

or:

God has not acted thus for any other nation; to no other people has he shown his love so clearly. (See Psalm 147:20)

PRAYER AFTER COMMUNION   **Let us pray.**
Pause for silent prayer, if this has not preceded.
Lord,
may the Body and Blood of your Son,
which we receive in this sacrament,
reconcile us always in your love.
May we who rejoice in the holy Mother of Guadalupe
live united and at peace in this world
until the day of the Lord dawns in glory.

We ask this through Christ our Lord.

THE PROCLAMATION OF THE BIRTH OF CHRIST

THE PROCLAMATION OF THE DATE OF EASTER ON EPIPHANY

THE RECEPTION OF THE HOLY OILS

THE PROCLAMATION OF THE BIRTH OF CHRIST

THE PROCLAMATION OF THE BIRTH OF CHRIST

Introduction

1. The *Roman Martyrology* for Christmas day contains a formal announcement of the birth of Christ in the style of a proclamation. It begins with creation and relates the birth of the Lord to the major events and personages of sacred and secular history. The particular events contained in the proclamation help to situate the birth of Jesus in the context of salvation history.

2. *The Proclamation of the Birth of Christ* may be sung or proclaimed after the greeting and introduction of the Christmas Midnight Mass. The Gloria and opening prayer immediately follow the proclamation.

3. The proclamation may also be sung or proclaimed at the Liturgy of the Hours. If it is used at Morning or Evening Prayer, it follows the introduction of the hour and precedes the hymn. When it is proclaimed during the Office of Readings, it precedes the *Te Deum*.

4. According to circumstances, the proclamation may be sung or recited at the ambo by a deacon, cantor, or reader.

5. After the greeting of the Mass, the celebrant or another minister may briefly introduce the Mass and *The Proclamation of the Birth of Christ* which follows, using these or similar words.

Throughout the season of Advent, the Church has reflected on God's promises, so often spoken by the prophets, to send a savior to the people of Israel who would be Emmanuel, that is, God with us. In the fullness of time those promises were fulfilled. With hearts full of joy let us listen to the proclamation of our Savior's birth.

6. The deacon (or other minister) then proclaims the birth of our Lord Jesus Christ:

The Proclamation of the Birth of Christ

To - day, the twenty - fifth day of De - cem - ber,

unknown ages from the time when God created the heavens and the earth

and then formed man and woman in his own im - age.

Several thousand years after the flood, when God made the rainbow shine forth as

a sign of the cov - e - nant. Twenty-one centuries from the time of Abra - ham and Sarah;

thirteen centuries after Moses led the people of Israel out of E - gypt.

Eleven hundred years from the time of Ruth and the judges;

one thousand years from the anointing of David as king;

in the sixty - fifth week according to the prophecy of Dan - iel.

In the one hundred and ninety - fourth O - lympiad;

the seven hundred and fifty-second year from the foundation of the city of Rome.

The forty - second year of the reign of Octavian Augustus;

the whole world be-ing at peace, Jesus Christ, eternal God and Son of the eternal Father,

desiring to sanctify the world by his most merciful coming,

being conceived by the Ho-ly Spirit, and nine months having passed since his conception,

was born in Bethlehem of Judea of the Virgin Ma - ry.

Today is the nativity of our Lord Je - sus Christ according to the flesh.

THE PROCLAMATION OF THE BIRTH OF CHRIST

Today, the twenty-fifth day of December,
unknown ages from the time when God created the heavens and the earth
  and then formed man and woman in his own image.

Several thousand years after the flood,
when God made the rainbow shine forth as a sign of the covenant.

Twenty-one centuries from the time of Abraham and Sarah;
thirteen centuries after Moses led the people of Israel out of Egypt.

Eleven hundred years from the time of Ruth and the Judges;
one thousand years from the anointing of David as king;
in the sixty-fifth week according to the prophecy of Daniel.

In the one hundred and ninety-fourth Olympiad;
the seven hundred and fifty-second year from the foundation of the city of Rome.

The forty-second year of the reign of Octavian Augustus;
the whole world being at peace,
Jesus Christ, eternal God and Son of the eternal Father,
desiring to sanctify the world by his most merciful coming,
being conceived by the Holy Spirit,
and nine months having passed since his conception,
was born in Bethlehem of Judea of the Virgin Mary.

Today is the nativity of our Lord Jesus Christ according to the flesh.

7. The Gloria and opening prayer then follow.

THE PROCLAMATION OF THE DATE
OF EASTER ON EPIPHANY

THE PROCLAMATION OF THE DATE
OF EASTER ON EPIPHANY

Introduction

1. *The Proclamation of the Date of Easter on Epiphany* dates from a time when calendars were not readily available. It was necessary to make known the date of Easter in advance, since many celebrations of the liturgical year depend on its date. The number of Sundays that follow Epiphany, the date of Ash Wednesday, and the number of Sundays that follow Pentecost are all computed in relation to Easter.

2. Although calendars now give the date of Easter and the other feasts in the liturgical year for many years in advance, the Epiphany proclamation still has value. It is a reminder of the centrality of the resurrection of the Lord in the liturgical year and the importance of the great mysteries of faith which are celebrated each year.

3. The proclamation may be sung or proclaimed at the ambo by a deacon, cantor, or reader either after the gospel or after the prayer after communion.

4. Each year the proper dates for Holy Thursday, Easter, Ash Wednesday, Ascension, Pentecost, and the First Sunday of Advent must be inserted into the text. These dates are found in the table which is included with the introductory documents of the *Sacramentary*. The form to be used for announcing each date is: the *date* of *month*, e.g., ''the seventh of April.''

5. On the solemnity of the Epiphany, after the homily or after the prayer after communion, the deacon or, in his absence, another minister announces the date of Easter and the other feasts of the liturgical year according to the following text.

The Proclamation of the Date of Easter

Dear broth- ers and sis- ters,   the glory of the Lord has shone up - on— us,

and shall ever be manifest among us,   until the day of his re- turn.

Through the rhythms of times and sea- sons   let us celebrate the mys- ter- ies of

sal - va - tion.   Let us recall the year's cul - mi - na- tion,

the Easter Tri- du - um of the Lord: his last supper,   his cruci- fix- ion,

his burial, and his rising,   celebrated be - tween   the eve - ning of the

(date)   of *(month)*   and the eve- ning of the *(date)*   of *(month)*.

(Date of Holy Thursday)   *(Date of Easter)*

Each Eas - ter — as on each Sun- day — the Holy Church makes present the great and

sav- ing deed   by which Christ has for ev - er con - quered sin— and death.

From Eas - ter are reckoned all the days we keep ho - ly.

Ash Wednesday, the beginning of Lent, will occur on the *(date)* of *(month)*.

The As-cension of the Lord will be commemorated on the *(date)* of *(month)*.

Pente-cost, the joyful conclusion of the sea-son of Easter, will be celebrated on the

(date) of *(month)*. And this year the First Sunday of Advent will be on the

(date) of *(month.)* Like - wise the pilgrim Church proclaims the
(No-vember)
(De-cember)

passover of Christ in the feasts of the holy Mother of God, in the feasts of the A -

pos- tles and Saints, and in the commemoration of the faith- ful de - part - ed.

To Je- sus Christ, who was, who is, and who is to come, Lord of time and history,

be endless praise, for ev - er and ev - er. A - men._____

Alternate Amen

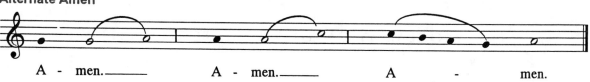

A - men._____ A - men._____ A - men.

THE PROCLAMATION OF THE DATE OF EASTER

Dear brothers and sisters, the glory of the Lord has shone upon us,
and shall ever be manifest among us, until the day of his return.
Through the rhythms of times and seasons
　let us celebrate the mysteries of salvation.

Let us recall the year's culmination, the Easter Triduum of the Lord:
his last supper, his crucifixion, his burial, and his rising celebrated
　　between the evening of the (date) of (month)
　　　　　　　　　(date of Holy Thursday)
　　and the evening of the (date) of (month).
　　　　　　　(date of Easter Sunday)

Each Easter—as on each Sunday—
the Holy Church makes present the great and saving deed
　by which Christ has for ever conquered sin and death.

From Easter are reckoned all the days we keep holy.
Ash Wednesday, the beginning of Lent, will occur on the date of month.
The Ascension of the Lord will be commemorated on the date of month.
Pentecost, the joyful conclusion of the season of Easter,
　will be celebrated on the date of month.
And this year the First Sunday of Advent will be on the date of month.

Likewise the pilgrim Church proclaims the passover of Christ
in the feasts of the holy Mother of God, in the feasts of the Apostles and Saints,
and in the commemoration of the faithful departed.

To Jesus Christ, who was, who is, and who is to come, Lord of time and history,
be endless praise, for ever and ever.

℞. Amen. [Amen. Amen.]

THE RECEPTION OF THE HOLY OILS
BLESSED AT THE CHRISM MASS

THE RECEPTION OF THE HOLY OILS
BLESSED AT THE CHRISM MASS

Introduction

1. It is appropriate that the oil of the sick, the oil of catechumens, and the holy chrism, which are blessed by the bishop during the Chrism Mass, be presented to and received by the local parish community.

2. The reception of the holy oils may take place at the Mass of the Lord's Supper on Holy Thursday or on another suitable day after the celebration of the Chrism Mass.

3. The oils should be reserved in a suitable repository in the sanctuary or near the baptismal font.

4. The oils, in suitable vessels, are carried in the procession of the gifts, before the bread and wine, by members of the assembly.

5. The oils are received by the priest and are then placed on a suitably prepared table in the sanctuary or in the repository where they will be reserved.

6. As each of the oils is presented, the following or other words may be used to explain the significance of the particular oil.

7. The people's response my be sung.

THE RECEPTION OF THE HOLY OILS
BLESSED AT THE CHRISM MASS

Presenter of the Oil of the Sick:

The oil of the sick.

Priest:

May the sick who are anointed with this oil experience the compassion of Christ and his saving love, in body, mind, and soul.

The people may respond:

Blessed be God for ever.

Presenter of the Oil of Catechumens:

The oil of catechumens.

Priest:

Through anointing with this oil may our catechumens who are preparing to receive the saving waters of baptism be strengthened by Christ to resist the power of Satan and reject evil in all its forms.

The people may respond:

Blessed be God for ever.

Presenter of the Holy Chrism:

The holy Chrism.

Priest:

Through anointing with this perfumed Chrism may children and adults, who are baptized and confirmed, and presbyters, who are ordained, experience the gracious gift of the Holy Spirit.

The people may respond:

Blessed be God for ever.

The bread and wine for the eucharist are then received and the Mass continues in the usual way.